Standing Up with G̲a’ax̲sta’las

Women and Indigenous Studies Series

The series publishes works establishing a new understanding of Indigenous women's perspectives and experiences, by researchers in a range of fields. By bringing women's issues to the forefront, this series invites and encourages innovative scholarship that offers new insights on Indigenous questions past, present, and future. Books in this series will appeal to readers seeking stimulating explorations and in-depth analysis of the roles, relationships, and representations of Indigenous women in history, politics, culture, ways of knowing, health, and community well-being.

Other books in the series:

Indigenous Encounters with Neoliberalism: Place, Women, and the Environment in Canada and Mexico, by Isabel Altamirano-Jiménez

Being Again of One Mind: Oneida Women and the Struggle for Decolonization, by Lina Sunseri

Indigenous Women and Feminism: Politics, Activism, Culture, edited by Cheryl Suzack, Shari M. Huhndorf, Jeanne Perreault, and Jean Barman

Taking Medicine: Women's Healing Work and Colonial Contact in Southern Alberta, 1880-1930, by Kristin Burnett

Standing Up with G̱a’ax̱sta’las

Jane Constance Cook and the Politics of Memory, Church, and Custom

LESLIE A. ROBERTSON

and the

KWAGU’Ł GIX̱SA̱M CLAN

UBC Press • Vancouver • Toronto

21 20 19 18 17 16 15 14 13 5 4 3 2

Printed in Canada on FSC-certified ancient-forest-free paper (100% post-consumer recycled) that is processed chlorine- and acid-free.

Women and Indigenous Studies Series, ISSN 1924-1410
ISBN 978-0-7748-2384-5 (bound); ISBN 978-0-7748-2385-2 (pbk.)

Cataloguing-in-publication data for this book is available from Library and Archives Canada.

Canada

UBC Press gratefully acknowledges the financial support for our publishing program of the Government of Canada (through the Canada Book Fund), the Canada Council for the Arts, and the British Columbia Arts Council.

This book has been published with the help of a grant from the Canadian Federation for the Humanities and Social Sciences, through the Awards to Scholarly Publications Program, using funds provided by the Social Sciences and Humanities Research Council of Canada, and with the help of the K.D. Srivastava Fund.

Printed and bound in Canada by Friesens
Set in Garamond and Charis by Artegraphica Design Co. Ltd.
Copy editor: Lesley Erickson
Proofreader: Helen Godolphin

UBC Press
The University of British Columbia
2029 West Mall
Vancouver, BC V6T 1Z2
www.ubcpress.ca

For G̲wa̲yułalas, Emily

Contents

xi List of Illustrations

xv Foreword
Nella Nelson

xix Acknowledgments

1 Prologue

10 Introduction: "Having Oneness on Your Face"

Researching the Story of G̲a'ax̲sta'las
Writing the "Granny Cook Book"
On Hope

23 Part I – The Living Text: Traces of Jane Cook

Anthropology and the Peoples Formerly Known as the Kwakiutl
Forging the Authentic: "Kwakiutlness"
Agency in the Archives: Making Northwest Coast History
Narrating from the Villages: Word Memorials
Memory in Practice

53 PART II – *DUK̲WA̲'ESA̲LA* (LOOKING AROUND ON THE BEACH): ANCESTORS

Hutłilala (Pay Attention): Genealogies
The House of 'Nulis (Grandfather)
K̲wak̲'waballas and Na̲ge (Stephen Cook)
'Lul p̓a̲da̲x'ida̲n's 'nalx̲ (When Our World Became Dark)
G̲wa̲yuła̲las (Emily Whonnock) and Captain Gilbert
Around 1865: Tsax̲is
William H. Gilbert (Jane Cook's Father)
Pax Brittanica: The Bombardment of Fort Rupert
T̓samas: Victoria
A̲wi'nak̓wa (Rocky Place): G̲wa̲yuła̲las (Emily)

103 PART III – STRANGER THAN FICTION: SURVIVING THE MISSIONARY

Arrival: Alfred James Hall
Tsax̲is, 1878-80
The "Gospel Plough": Conversion
"Good Marriage Prospects": Hygiene, Domestication, and Women
"The Burden of Souls"
"Extra Sight": Christian Capitalism
"Spirits Broken": Schooling in 'Ya̲lis

154 PART IV – "CHILDREN OF THE POTLATCH SYSTEM," 1888-1912

X̲wâ'x̲was: Tradition of the Gĭlgilgam, a Clan of the Nimkish
"We Are of the People, We Know the Custom": Marriage
"What He Wants to Inform You Of": Witchcraft and the Potlatch
The Anglican Women's Auxiliary
The Cook Big House
Edward Curtis: Translations

192 PART V – "WE AS THE SUPPRESSED PEOPLE," 1913-18

"We Are Agitating": Land
"Never Be Intimidated": On Activism
"Is This Justice?": Law, Liquor, and Power
"In This My Country": The McKenna-McBride Royal Commission
"We Who Wish to Uplift Our People": On Marriage

232 Part vi – "We Are the Aboriginee, Which Is Not a Citizen," 1918-27

"We Whose Ancestors Made This System"
"Informations": The Potlatch Trials
"Something Like an Equal Footing": The Allied Indian Tribes of BC
"When the Tide Is Out, Our Table Is Set": Fishing Rights
T̓sa̱ka̱'atsi (Hospital) – "For Indians Only"
"After Consultation": Representing Potlatchers
"There Was Eight of Us": G̱a'ax̱sta'las as Grandmother

285 Part vii – "With the Potlatch Custom in My Blood," 1930-39

Franz Boas and the "Official Lady Interpreter"
Meeting G̱a'ax̱sta'las, 1930
"What Is a Parson to Do?": Church and Custom
"A System That Works Right Around in a Circle": The *Christian Science Monitor*
On Giving, in 2008
G̱a'ax̱sta'las's 135th Birthday: The Cook Fishing Fleet
R v Stephen Cook et al.: Taxing Fishers
Up against a Stone Wall: Potlatching in 'Ya̱lis
"We Are All Indians Here": Special Meetings on the Potlatch, 1936
"Unlovely Things": Christianity versus the Custom
"A Glory Rather Than a Sin"
"Better to Prevent Than to Cure": The TB Preventorium

343 Part viii – One Voice from Many: Citizenship, 1940-48

"The Dead and Their Debts": Revisiting the Potlatch Ban
"We'll Knock at the Doors": The Native Brotherhood of BC
Life with Granny Cook in the 1940s
Unnatural Circumstances: Schooling
"A Shining Quality": The *Native Voice*
"Let Us Go Forward, to Survive the Times": The BC Indian Arts and Welfare Society

390 Part ix – A Tower of Strength: Word Memorials, 1951

Word Memorials

403 PART X – DŁA<u>X</u>W'IT̓SINE' (FOR YOUR STANDING), FEASTING

Gi<u>x</u>s<u>a</u>m Ancestor Legend
Wa<u>xa</u>widi, Wasden T̓se<u>k</u>a (Winter Ceremonial), November 2005
Yakudłasdzi, Speck Memorial Potlatch, October 2006
Kwagu'ł Gi<u>x</u>s<u>a</u>m Feast, May 2007

471 Notes

542 Bibliography

556 Index

Illustrations

Descent Charts

G̲a'ax̲sta'las, Jane Constance Gilbert / xxi

Na̲ge, Stephen Cook / xxii

Jane and Stephen Cook / xxiii

Map

Kwakwa̲ka̲'wakw tribes and villages in British Columbia / xxiv

Photographs

1 Jane Constance Cook, 1914 / 24
2 Frame of house erected in Dzawadi (Knight Inlet) by Wanukw / 58
3 Chief 'Nulis and G̲a'ax̲sta'las / 62
4 Edwin Newman with 'Nulis ancestor mask / 64
5 'Nulis mask (closed) / 65
6 'Nulis mask (open) / 65
7 Wedłidi Speck, Nella Nelson, and Billy Wasden / 68
8 William Wasden Jr.'s family emblem / 72
9 Stephen Cook, G̲ag̲a, and Bert Cook / 73
10 Captain William H. Gilbert, 1877 / 88
11 Elizabeth Hall and Reverend Alfred Hall, ca. 1870s / 106

12 Sample of letter from Reverend Hall, ca. 1880s / 112
13 Tsaxis village, 1894 / 115
14 Canning salmon, 2010 / 141
15 Pupils at Alfred Hall’s school, ca. 1880s / 145
16 G̱a’ax̱sta’las as a young woman / 156
17 Anglican Women’s Auxiliary, ca. 1910s / 174
18 Alert Bay, ca. 1900 / 176
19 Jane, G̱aga, and Stephen Cook, with children, early 1900s / 177
20 Cook family, ca. 1910 / 178
21 Stephen Cook’s mother, G̱aga / 182
22 Gĭga̱l̠’g̱a̱m clan / 184
23 “Hamasaka,” 1914 / 187
24 “Lagyus,” 1914 / 190
25 Cook family, late 1912 / 193
26 G̱a’ax̱sta’las, 1914 / 214
27 Pearl Alfred, 1974 / 235
28 Pearl Alfred and granddaughter Ashley, 1990 / 235
29 Industrial school students, ca. 1920 / 239
30 Allied Tribes of BC, ca. 1922 / 258
31 Stephen Cook, ca. 1930s / 307
32 Cook fleet at Alert Bay, 1948 / 312
33 Anglican Women’s Auxiliary, ca. 1930s / 326
34 Signature page from Reggie and Nellie Cook’s wedding, 1926 / 332
35 Michael Kamano, Annie Kamano, and Grace Scow / 340
36 Dog salmon on Cook’s Wharf, ca. 1920s / 356
37 Stephen Cook and Cyril, Reg, and Herbert / 360
38 Native Brotherhood of BC Convention, 1944 / 361
39 Emma Alfred, Connie Svanvik, and Florrie Matilpe, 2007 / 371
40 G̱a’ax̱sta’las at the Cook big house, ca. 1940s / 372
41 Charlie Newman and family / 376
42 G̱a’ax̱sta’las’s obituary, 1951 / 396
43 Stephen and Jane Cook, ca. 1940 / 401
44 William Wasden Jr., 1993 / 414
45 George Speck, 2006 / 426
46 Roberta Harris, Grace Stauffer, and George Cook, 2007 / 440

47 Protest at Legislative Buildings, Victoria, 1979 / 442-43
48 Chris Cook, Kelly-Anne Speck, Wedłidi Speck, and Pearl Alfred, 2007 / 443
49 Bear screen at the Kwagu'ł Gix̱sa̱m Feast, 2007 / 444
50 Singers at the log, 2007 / 446
51 Kwagu'ł ancestor dance, 2007 / 447
52 'Na̱mg̱is ancestor dance, 2007 / 448
53 George Cook dressing Wedłidi Speck as chief, 2007 / 451
54 Randy Bell, with William Wasden Jr., 2007 / 453
55 Feasting at the Gix̱sa̱m Feast, 2007 / 454
56 Family dancing at the Gix̱sa̱m Feast, 2007 / 460

Foreword

Who is Granny Cook? Why do I think I know her?
Was it my dad's stories about Granny Cook that sparked a loyalty and an allegiance in me to a woman I had never met? Or was it Granny Cook's whispering from the spirit world, planting the seeds of knowledge and inquiry into my mind?

I was born two years after Granny Cook passed into the spirit world.

While I was growing up in Alert Bay, we would attend Sunday school every week, and after Sunday school we would make our way up to Daddy Cook and Nana's for our family lunch. The Cook big house, as we called it, was always full of surprises. It was big and perched on the hill overlooking the bay, and there were always lots of nooks and crannies to explore and hide in.

I knew as a child that I would find a room full of leather-bound books and old dresses in the upstairs front bedroom. The old dresses provided hours of entertainment, and the books provided hours of reading and the desire to play school underneath the big house. I didn't really know who owned all of those books at that time. I only knew that it was fun to dig through them and then "borrow" a couple of books on occasion! I didn't know, at a conscious level, as a child, the legacy of learning and reading that Granny Cook had left to us. My dad, George Cook, spoke fondly of his granny. She was a woman who had sixteen children yet had time to sit and talk with her many grandchildren, nieces, and nephews. Dad saw Granny Cook as an understanding and caring woman. He could talk with Granny Cook about his problems and his challenges and always counted on her for valuable advice. She was also there to celebrate the good things in his life.

I never had the privilege of meeting Granny Cook in person; however, the imprint of her energy still permeated the big house in Alert Bay and was left on the pages of the many books stored in the front bedroom.

I grew up knowing the value of reading books and of education. Reading and learning were to be a very important part of my life; my parents reinforced these teachings continuously. Many of our extended family members are compulsive readers. Any chance we get we whip out our books, find a comfortable spot, and immerse ourselves in another world. We could be out on the fishing grounds waiting for the big fishing set, or we could be relaxing in the evening – whenever we had a spare moment, we would be reading. I grew up in my family knowing that women could pitch in and work as hard as any man, that women could do anything they wanted to do, and that education could provide the bridge to the mainstream world. Our Cook family was very involved in the commercial fishing industry, and my sisters and I were working on our dad's boat at a very young age. We worked hard and earned our own spending money.

When I attended the University of Victoria in 1972, I majored in anthropology and sociology. It was at this time that I began to read a lot of historical materials. One day, I was reading through Franz Boas's book *Kwakiutl Ethnography,* when I came across a quote that stated that, after the potlatch trials, people were laughing at Granny Cook, saying that she spoke Kwak̓wala like a baby. I was incensed, and it sparked my curiosity. Who was this Granny Cook, and what did she represent to our family? I remember quizzing my dad about Granny Cook, about who she was, and over the years I gleaned as much information about her as I could. I understood that she was an interpreter in the potlatch trials and was against the potlatch, but I knew that there had to be more to her story and we needed to hear that story. As a family, we have carried the social and cultural stigma that has emanated out of this time period, and we need to lift that stigma through the telling of her story.

In the early 1970s, the 'Na̱mgis band received the declassified potlatch files from the Department of Indian Affairs. I worked for the 'Na̱mgis band one summer as a student, and I started to pore through these files. They were fascinating and told a much larger story of what had transpired during those times. Tidbits of information began to unravel, and I became aware that Granny Cook had a very powerful voice in the political world, and it was more than being an interpreter in the potlatch trials. She in fact was a fighter for the women and the children. She fought to maintain our lands in our traditional territory with the McKenna-McBride Commission; she travelled to Ottawa with the BC chiefs to have their voices heard there. She was a woman before her time. Her voice couldn't be silenced.

As members of the Cook family, we have a responsibility to make sure that her voice is not silenced and her side of the story is told. Flash forward to the late 1990s, and we saw that books were still being published referencing the statement in Franz Boas's book about Granny Cook speaking Kwak̓wala like a baby. As members of the Cook family, we knew that it was now time to have Granny Cook's personal and historical story told. We could no longer stand back and let the legacy of her work be tarnished by these comments.

The research that has been conducted by Leslie Robertson has opened the gateway to increased understanding of a difficult historical time for all of our people. She has provided us with knowledge of the strength of Granny Cook in a time when women's voices were often silenced. Granny Cook's letters and petitions to the church and to government were done with one main goal in mind – to support our people, especially the women and children, and to maintain our sense of place and belonging in our families, in our villages, and in our traditional territory.

Granny Cook's legacy has inspired many of her descendants to support family and community, to stay connected to their traditional lands, and to use education as a bridge to mainstream society. Many members of the Cook family are now active members in our traditional ceremonies in the Big House and have now become the transmitters of culture and family history. There is no greater gift than to know from whence you came.

Nella Nelson, Victoria, BC
February 2010

Acknowledgments

This book is built upon an imaginative conversation sustained over a period of nine years. It is forged on the skills and knowledge generously shared by G̱a’ax̱sta’las’s descendants. Pearl Alfred is the rock of the work. Her hope, endless energy, and vision for change have fuelled it. Nella Nelson, Kelly-Anne Speck, George Speck, Wedłidi Speck, and William Wasden Jr. were also extraordinary collaborators (and untiring readers) whose fearless curiosity and expansive knowledge made for wonderful company on the way.

There are many whom we would like to acknowledge, some of whom have passed away since we began. We are grateful for the time we were able to share with family elders Nellie Cook and Ilma Cook, and we respect the support that Ethel Alfred, a great friend of the family, gave to us. Lorraine Hunt transcribed oral histories, offered invaluable advice on Kwak̓wala, and spoke often with me about the art and science of translation. Andrea Sanborn was very helpful with our research, assisting us with archival collections at the U’mista Cultural Centre.

Elders Emma Alfred, Rita Barnes, George and Ruth Cook, Gloria Cranmer-Webster, Doreen Fitch, Jeane Lawrence, Florrie Matilpe, Edwin Newman, and Peggy Svanvik shared their insights and recollections and we respect the time and care they gave to the project. Chris Cook Jr., Gilbert Cook Jr., and Bill Wasden were also generous contributors. We thank Chief Robert Joseph for his ongoing support of the family. We are grateful to Chief Bill Cranmer for translating Kwak̓wala speeches; to Diane Jacobson for fact checking portions of the manuscript; and to Patricia Shaw for offering her linguistic expertise during the production of the book. The labour of transcription was shared with Lori Speck and Geri Ambers. Lori also greatly assisted with the transcription of Alfred Hall's (less than legible) letters.

I would like to thank Jack Kapac, Kathy McCloskey, and Lynne Phillips at the University of Windsor for ongoing conversations about research, useful references, and the administrative and collegial support they offered. For honest conversations, insights, and all manner of different kinds of support, I thank: Alexia Bloch, Pam Brown, Julie Cochrane, Liz Furniss, Aaron Glass, Nan Hawkins, Dottie Holland, Jana Kotaska, Bruce Miller, Lee Montgomery, Paige Raibmon, Petra Rethmann, Pilar Riaño-Alcalá, Valerie and Gordon Robertson, Martin Silverman, Nancy Wachowich, and Wendy Wickwire. For her excellent mentorship, friendship, and ever-thoughtful encouragement, I thank Julie Cruikshank. Terre Satterfield's steady presence and always-engaging conversations have fed this work through the years.

Research was funded in part by a Postdoctoral Grant from the Wenner-Gren Foundation for Anthropological Research and a Phillips Fund Grant for Native American Research from the American Philosophical Society. Travel and research expenses were also supported by internal research grants from the Faculty of Social Sciences at the University of Windsor, Ontario. Our work was assisted by the Department of Anthropology at the University of British Columbia, which hosted me as a visiting scholar in 2008-09.

Archivists and librarians at the U'mista Cultural Centre, the American Philosophical Society Library, the Anglican Diocese of British Columbia Archives, the Jefferson County Historical Society, the Cadbury Research Library at the University of Birmingham, the Alert Bay Library and Museum, Library and Archives Canada, and the BC Archives were essential to realizing this work.

At UBC Press, Jean Wilson provided the first editorial eye and supported the project generously from its inception. We are grateful to Ann Macklem and staff at UBC Press and to the anonymous reviewers whose suggestions sharpened this work.

This book is infused with Dara Culhane's generosity, her friendship, humour, and intellect.

Finally, I must express my respect for the passionate members of the Kwagu'ł Gixsam. You generously guided me through your history and, with patience, led me through the remarkable story of Ga'axsta'las. Your project is a gift to those who seek a gentler way to move through difficult pasts. I have learned much from you. It has been a great honour.

Royalties from the sale of this book will go to the Kwagu'ł Gixsam.

G̱A'AX̱STA'LAS, JANE CONSTANCE GILBERT

"Old" Chief Wanukw,
Maxmawe'segeme*

Ṫłaḵwa'ił
(Bella Bella)

Tlaliłila
(son, became Chief Wanukw)

Ṫsa̱t'so'lał ('Walas Kwagu'ł)

'Nulis, Wakadzi
(Kumuyoi)

Ga'gwadi (daughter)

Hemasaḵa (son)

G̱a'ax̱sta'las
(daughter of Chief Siwiti of Da̱'naxda'x̱w)

(John) 'Nulis

G̱wa̱yuła̱las (Emily Whonnock)

William H. Gilbert

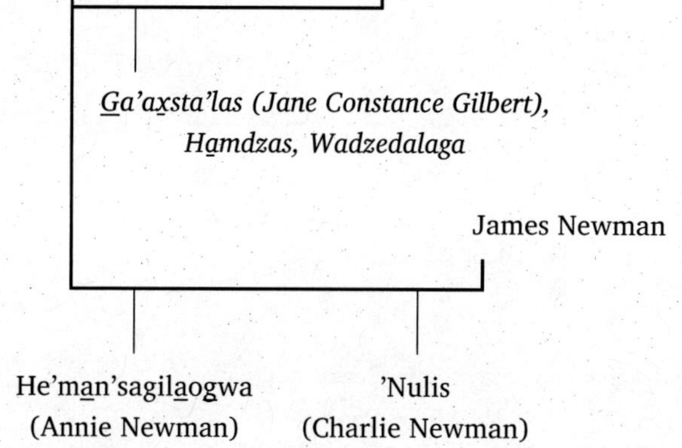

Note: dark line = marriage; light line = children.

* Married three times and had ten children. This is his first recorded marriage (Wedłidi Speck).

Source: Wedłidi Speck and William Wasden Jr.

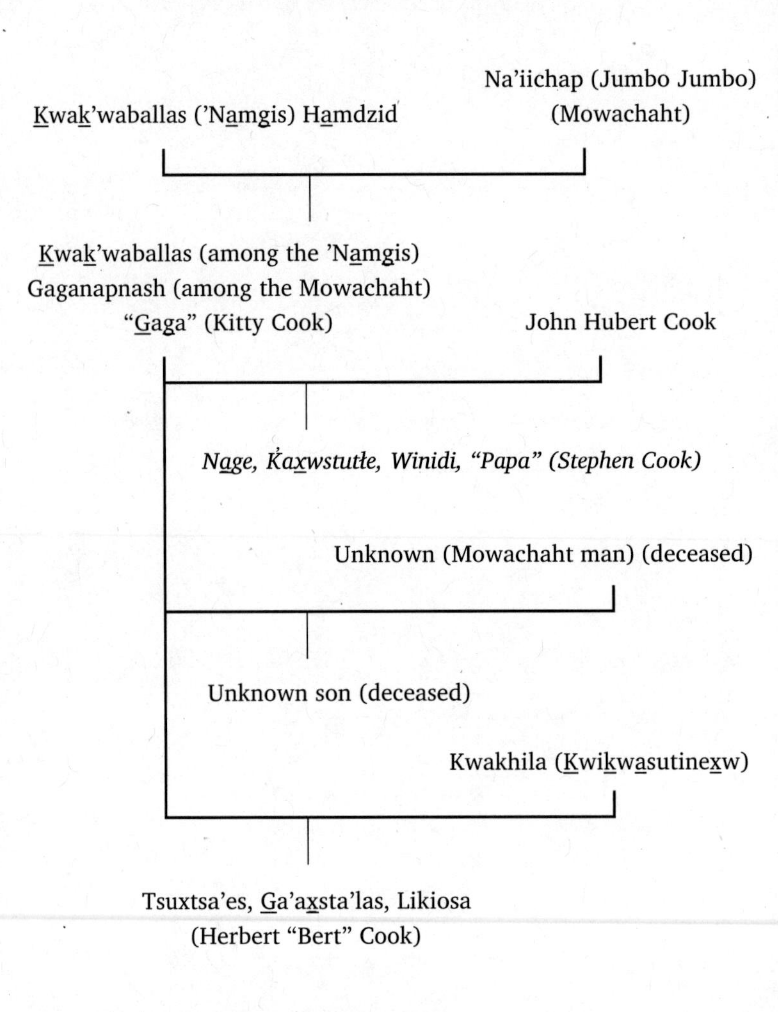

Note: dark line = marriage; light line = children.

Source: Wedłidi Speck and William Wasden Jr.

DESCENT FROM JANE AND STEPHEN COOK, including those who have contributed to this research

Jane Constance Gilbert (1870-1951) Stephen Cook (1870-1957)

- Elizabeth Grace Cook (1889-1927): daughter, Jeane Lawrence; grandsons, Billy Wasden and David Huson; great-grandson, William Wasden Jr.
- Alice Hope Cook (1891-1921, died of TB)
- William Alfred Cook (1892-1934)
- Stephen Gilbert Cook (1894-1911, died of TB)
- Emma Marion Cook (1896-1990): daughter, Doreen Kenmuir
- Victor Edwin Cook (1897-1918, killed in WWI)
- Alfred Hall Cook (1898-99, died of dysentery)
- Ernest Hall Cook (1900-31, died of TB)
- Samuel Reginald Cook (1902-75): married to Nellie Hamilton; son George, married to Ruth; daughters Pearl Alfred and Christine Zurkowski; son Reggie Jr., married to Maureen; grandsons George Speck, Wedłidi Speck, and John Nestman; granddaughters Kelly-Anne Speck, Nella Nelson, Dara Culhane (through marriage), and Lorraine Hunt (through marriage); great-granddaughter Lori Speck
- Cyril George Cook (1904-70)
- Gilbert Cook (1906-82): married to Ilma Wirki; daughter, Vivian; son, Gilbert Jr.
- Rupert Cook (1907-09, died from bronchitis)
- Herbert Timothy Cook (1908-73); grandson, Ralph Bell; granddaughter, Roberta Harris
- Pearl Cook (1910-97): daughters Florrie Matilpe and Emma Alfred
- Christopher Charles Cook (1911-99): son, Chris Cook Jr.; granddaughter, Shelly
- Winifred Ada Mary Cook (1912-70): granddaughter Diane Bell; grandson Randy Bell

Note: dark line = marriage; light line = children.

Source: Wedłidi Speck and William Wasden Jr.

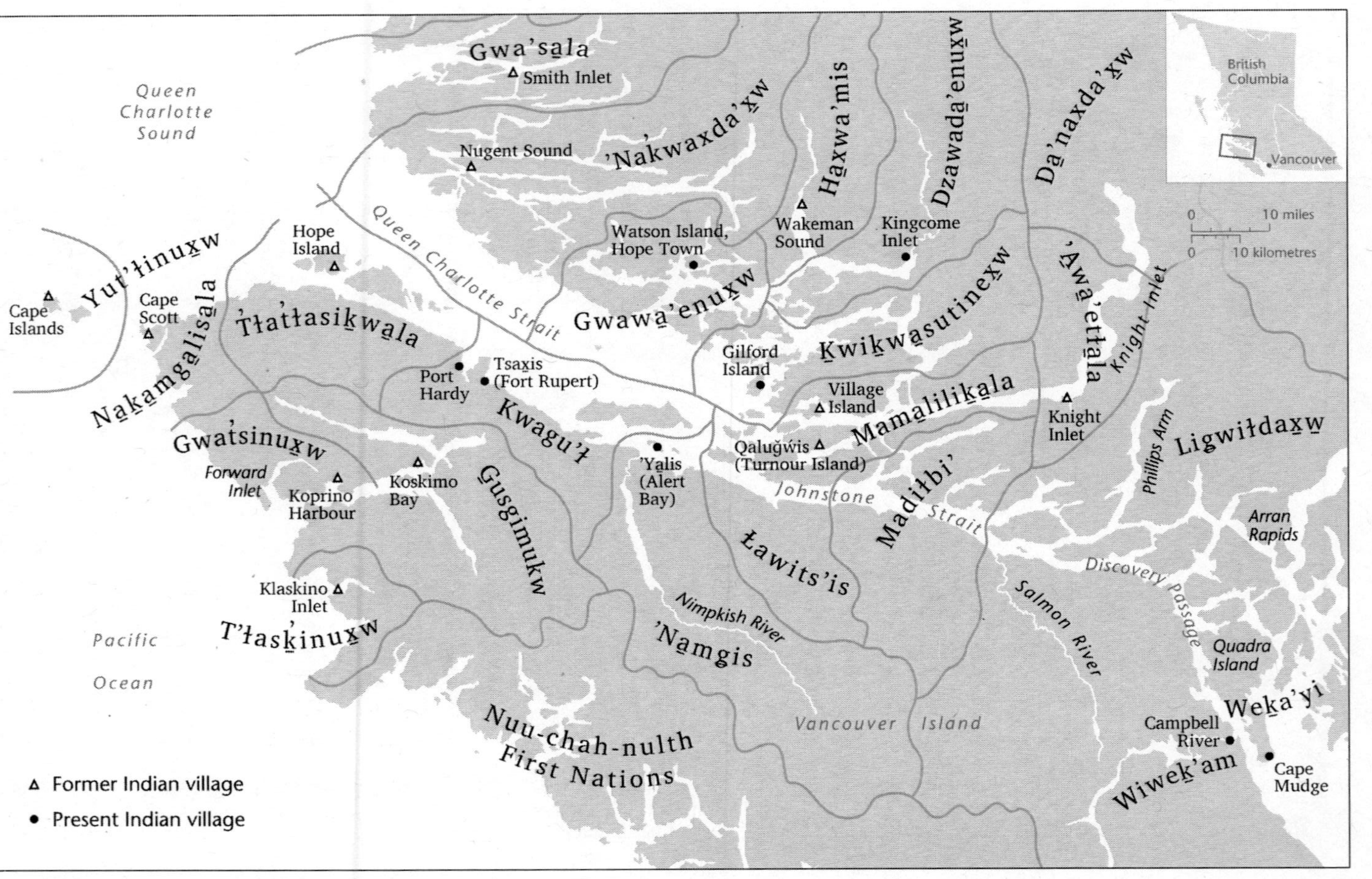

Kwakwa̱ka̱'wakw tribes and villages in British Columbia

Standing Up with G̲a'ax̲sta'las

Prologue

History makes people, but people make history.

– Sherry Ortner, Anthropology and Social Theory

Kwagu’ł Gix̱sa̱m Feast, ’Ya̱lis Big House
19 May 2007, 3 p.m.

Chief Robert Joseph, Kwa̱nkwa̱nxwa̱ligedzi
G̱ilakas’la!

The chiefs, matriarchs, my people, the Cook family welcome you here today, and they thank you for paying attention to your call for us to come here and to celebrate together their idea and their will and desire to be part of this great sacred circle of the potlatch and life itself.

They want you to know that they’re extremely proud to be Kwakwa̱ka̱’wakw, to be members of the ’na̱’mima that they are, and they respect all of the other ’ni’na̱’mima.

We are here today to commemorate the ancestors of this great clan, this ’na̱’mima, and to work towards bringing about the revitalization of this nation in full knowledge of all of the things that we need to do as Kwakwa̱ka̱’wakw.

Ladies and gentlemen, this is a great gathering.

This is a moment of reconciliation for all of us.

This is a moment when we reach out together and talk about being inclusive and being part of, so that we can become whole as the Kwakwaka'wakw.

So that we can become strong as the Kwakwaka'wakw.

That's how historic this moment is, this gathering is.

My brothers and sisters, I look forward to seeing you demonstrating the heart and the will and the spirit and the desire to welcome this great 'na'mima into the circle. So that when we look forward into the future, the future of our children is secure.

This great house has always been the place, my brothers and friends, this has always been the place where we right the wrongs and we correct the paths on which we've been, and where we make and create a world that is safe for our children, that is strong for our children.

Throughout the evening you're going to learn more about the purpose of this great gathering.

Gilakas'la.

This book begins at the end of the trail it travels, in the ceremonial realm of gukwdzi (the Big House at Alert Bay, British Columbia), where in May 2007 members of the Cook family were "standing up" to show their history. Here, high-ranked Kwakwaka'wakw lineages demonstrate lines of descent from a single ancestor, who represents their *'na'mima* (clan), which comprises several extended families. Just as "standing up" in gukwdzi represents 'na'mima history, this book shows how members of one descent group represent their past by revisiting the story of an ancestor named Ga'axsta'las or Jane Constance Cook, who was born in 1870 and passed away in 1951.[1]

The Gixsam Feast hosted by the Cook family is a significant public moment in the resolution of a difficult story that four generations of 'na'mima members carry. In welcoming guests to witness the feast, Chief Robert Joseph (Kwankwanxwaligedzi) of Gwa'yi (Kingcome) spoke about reconciliation. His invocation pertained not to relations with the colonial state (although they also are relevant) but to internal dynamics among Kwakwaka'wakw peoples.[2] The feast represented the awakening of the Kwagu'ł Gixsam 'na'mima, a clan that had been quiet for ninety years – since their ancestor had let go of her position in the potlatch.[3]

Like the feast, this work is grounded firmly in the here and now, yet it too references the past. The themes that run through this book reflect the organizing principles of the feast: attention to ’na̱’mima relationships and responsibilities, a desire to prepare the way for future generations, and the need to flesh out what has been an oversimplified public image of an ancestor. G̱a’ax̱sta’las lived through a period of intense upheaval for First Nation peoples. She was born during the late frontier era on the Northwest Coast, one year before aboriginal people were declared wards of the state in the new province of British Columbia (see map, page xxiv). In 1876, when she was six, the dominion government introduced the Indian Act, legislation that deprived aboriginal societies of the right to govern themselves; generated classifications that defined membership; racialized mobility and social behaviour; and sought to assimilate indigenous peoples. When G̱a’ax̱sta’las was eleven, an Indian Agent arrived at her mother’s village to enforce colonial policies. Her ancestors’ territories were appropriated and surveyed, and small portions were eventually reconceptualized as reserves. When G̱a’ax̱sta’las was fourteen, the state enacted legislation to ban potlatching – *the* complex of customary interactions at the heart of cultural and political sovereignty among coastal indigenous societies. The potlatch prohibition extended to the year of G̱a’ax̱sta’las’s death, and like others, G̱a’ax̱sta’las was embroiled in the fury of conflicts wrought by the ban. Her generation negotiated a world that called for daily acts of translation, for the honing of bicultural skills and the ability to respond to opportunities and obstacles. Her life was animated by Christian and customary cosmologies, and she acted consciously in a world that she knew as a Kwakwa̱ka̱’wakw woman of high rank and as an advocate for justice.

Standing Up with G̱a’ax̱sta’las attests to Jane Cook’s legacy, which is apparent in her descendants’ ongoing participation in the political struggles of First Nation peoples in Canada. As a work initiated by these descendants, this book includes their many voices alongside words written and spoken by G̱a’ax̱sta’las, words that have entered the historical record or have been waiting in archival repositories for consideration in the present. Our work reconsiders dominant historical and biographical portrayals that flatten the diverse motivations of aboriginal people and represent them as having naively consumed the colonizing project. We turn instead to a story embedded within the daily and ritual embodiment of one’s place in a web of ’na̱mi’ma relationships and within relevant social, economic, and political realities. Our collaborative, intergenerational approach seeks an intimate rendering of larger historical forces by focusing on family and community histories as they came to be governed by colonial suppression and by new forms of religious and political expression.

Briefly stated, the family oral history begins around 1869, when the warship HMS *Clio* sailed along the coast to the Kwakwa̲ka̲’wakw village of Tsax̲is (Fort Rupert) to arrest men suspected of committing a murder. During the skirmish, the village was bombarded. Kwagu’ł chiefs were taken to stand trial in Victoria, and Jane Cook’s grandfather John ’Nulis was among them.[4] His daughter, G̲wa̲yuła̲las (Emily Whonnock), accompanied him to Victoria. Eventually, the chiefs were released without charges, but it was in Victoria that Jane Cook’s mother, G̲wa̲yuła̲las, met William Gilbert, an English trader and sea pilot. Jane Constance Gilbert was born to them in Port Blakely on Washington’s Puget Sound, in 1870. G̲wa̲yuła̲las later married another man named James Newman, and they had two children – He’ma̲n’sagila̲ogwa (Annie Newman) and ’Nulis (Charlie Newman) (see Part II).

On paper, G̲a’ax̲sta’las’s story is difficult to trace until she appears, at the age of twelve, in the 1881 census at Tsax̲is, her mother’s village. Some in the family say that Jane, her sister Annie, and her brother Charlie were brought home by their grandfather John ’Nulis after the death of their young mother. According to other stories, after travelling for a time with her father, G̲a’ax̲sta’las was brought to Tsax̲is and later entrusted to the care of the Reverend Alfred Hall of the Anglican Church Mission Society (see Part III). Hall taught a few Kwagu’ł children in his home, and he later established a mission in ’Ya̲lis (Alert Bay), where he built Christ Church in 1881. It is likely that Jane Gilbert (G̲a’ax̲sta’las) met her husband, Na̲ge (Stephen Cook), at this time, as they were both missionary-educated. Through his mother, Stephen Cook had Mowachaht roots among the Nuu-chah-nulth peoples of the West Coast. His father was also European. At a young age, he received the name Na̲ge among the ’Na̲mgis.[5] Jane and Stephen married in Christ Church in 1888, and they raised their family in ’Ya̲lis. They were parents to sixteen children and grandparents and great-grandparents to many more.

Throughout their lives, Jane and Stephen opened their multigenerational home to those recovering from losses, to travellers, and to people who were ill or in need of shelter. Relatives and others remember G̲a’ax̲sta’las’s generosity. From her well-tended orchard, she distributed fruits, and her kitchen was open to visitors. They recall both the splendid Christmas dinners that spilled out over two rooms in the Cook big house and the more intimate sharing of seaweed and *t'lina* (eulachon grease) at the kitchen table. Those who lived with "Granny Cook" recall the occasions when she was called away at all hours to assist births, to tend those who were ill, and to comfort and prepare those who were dying. G̱a'ax̱sta'las is remembered as a woman of strength who demonstrated the importance of family relationships.

Together, G̱a'ax̱sta'las and Na̱ge and their children ran a general store in 'Ya̱lis, a salmon saltery, and net loft. Later, they and their sons built a successful fishing fleet and took on leadership roles in the Native Brotherhood of British Columbia. Their lives were touched by tragedy too. Before 1911, they lost three sons: Stephen Jr. (to tuberculosis), Alfred (to dysentery), and Rupert (to bronchitis). In 1918, they received news that their son Edwin had been killed in France while serving in the armed forces during the First World War. Daughters Grace and Alice died in the 1920s, and Jane and Stephen opened their home to their daughters' grieving husbands and children. Today, some of their descendants hold the title of hereditary chief; others have been initiated into the Hamat̓sa (Cannibal Society), or they are recognized and named performers of traditional expression who themselves host potlatches. Their descendants are also dynamic figures in First Nations structures of health, community and cultural development, education, law, resource rights, and local government who trace their passion for politics to G̱a'ax̱sta'las and her legacy of public engagement.

As president of the Anglican Women's Auxiliary for over thirty years, G̱a'ax̱sta'las ran weekly meetings in the village, offering women Christian teachings and support through often difficult circumstances. An avid reader and thinker, G̱a'ax̱sta'las's belief in education and literacy left an impression on her descendants and a trail in the recorded history of First Nations activism in BC. She translated sermons, speeches, and legal and extra-legal testimonies from English and her language, Kwak̓wala. Her letter writing began in the late nineteenth century, when she wrote to colonial officials at the request of community members (see Part IV). Sometime between 1911 and 1914, G̱a'ax̱sta'las translated traditional narratives told by Chief Lagius of Gwa'yi (Kingcome) for Edward Curtis, a photographer and researcher who worked to document the peoples of Native North America (see Part V). In 1931, she worked with anthropologist Franz Boas as he studied the Kwak̓wala language (see Part VII). Her services as a translator extended to the legal system, where she, and others, served officially as court interpreter for trials and hearings from the 1910s onward.

Ga'axsta'las was also an interpreter and representative of her people at government hearings for aboriginal rights. In 1914, she translated the words of Kwakwaka'wakw chiefs who made land claims before the McKenna-McBride Royal Commission, where she also testified as witness on behalf of the A'wa'etłala (Knight Inlet), Da'naxda'xw (New Vancouver), and the 'Namgis (Alert Bay) and made co-claims to resource sites (see Part VI). She was the only woman on the Executive Committee of the Allied Indian Tribes of British Columbia, in 1923, an early political organization composed of chiefs and other aboriginal leaders. Representing what was then the Kwawkewlth Agency, she spoke for commercial and food fishing rights and for nonracist health services – specifically, for Indian-only tuberculosis hospitals (see Part VII). Her words carried conviction, for she had already lost two of her own children and had nursed many others suffering with TB.

In her work with the Allied Indian Tribes, Ga'axsta'las represented potlatchers seeking compensation for property confiscated under the antipotlatch law, and she assisted potlatchers in scripting a petition to "relax" the potlatch ban. Some chiefs entrusted her to look after their ceremonial property, and she and Stephen were asked by relatives to hold money for them. Ga'axsta'las carried an abiding confidence in the law, and in the 1940s she stood with the Native Brotherhood in its fight for aboriginal peoples to benefit from the rights of Canadian citizenship without losing Indian status and hereditary privileges (see Part VIII). Too often, Jane Cook's contributions to the struggle for rights are overlooked. Many focus on her later support for the colonial ban on the potlatch, but simple versions of her story do an injustice to the complicated situations and events that she likely faced.

Although both of high rank (or perhaps because of this), Stephen and Jane Cook stood their ground on controversial matters, matters that would eventually leave them feeling – in Jane Cook's words – like "outcasts" (see Part VII). Ga'axsta'las's objections to some aspects of "the custom" had to do initially with questions about potlatch marriage and what she saw as women's limited choices. Potlatch marriage was a primary mechanism for the transfer of property and the naming of chiefs among high-ranked lineages. For colonial authorities, it was an obstacle to their attempts to control the political, legal, and social lives of coastal indigenous peoples. Positioned at a major intersection of the colonial and Kwakwa̱ka̱’wakw worlds, marriage was anything but straightforward.

When G̱a’ax̱sta’las advocated for women, she entered into dialogues that sometimes placed her in conflict with customary leaders and with colonial agents. Initially, she wanted officials to acknowledge the legality of Kwakwa̱ka̱’wakw marriages in the potlatch. Later, she asked them to legislate some kind of family support for women and children left destitute. G̱a’ax̱sta’las wrote and spoke about underage brides married without their initial consent, and about the specific situation of women who were converts, caught between Kwakwa̱ka̱’wakw and Christian norms. Eventually, she spoke about her own position within the realm of rank circumscribed by *gwa’ł* (the marriage contract). One of her letters about the potlatch stated that it was more than just a custom: it was a form of “government” or a “constitution” that affected all aspects of Kwakwa̱ka̱’wakw life. She was concerned that young women especially had few options but to follow customary authority.

In her early letters, G̱a’ax̱sta’las clearly supported the custom. As official prosecution of potlatching intensified, she took more decisive stances – against the social effects of long-term criminalization, against the financial burden faced by families, and against the more competitive aspects of potlatching that she felt affected village life negatively (see Part VIII). G̱a’ax̱sta’las communicated with powerful men in the colonial hierarchy: she wrote to and had meetings with bishops, senior Indian Affairs officials, police chiefs, and politicians in BC and Ottawa. Looking at archival materials, it is evident that she worked within a strong web of ’na̱’mima relationships, for many of her actions were directed to protect women and girls in her extended family.

Some stories about G̱a’ax̱sta’las charge that she informed on potlatchers during the colonial ban and that she mistranslated at the famous potlatch trials in 1922. These stories imply that she had a central role in the long sequence of potlatch prosecutions, the imprisonment of chiefs, and the appropriation of their ceremonial regalia (see Part VI). Although G̱a’ax̱sta’las was a woman with strong influence, these accounts underestimate the power wielded by Indian Agents, politicians, and police officials whose actions and decisions determined the outcomes. During the ban, potlatching stayed alive, but it went underground. The political terrain was shifting, and people found themselves in complicated positions given their allegiances to family, their membership in the Church, and their reliance on commercial sources of income.

In the last years of her life, Jane Cook made strong statements about the “awful results” of colonialism and the missionary condemnation of Kwakwa̱ka̱’wakw beliefs, about their continued lack of access to traditional resources, and about the “white man’s” misunderstanding of their “past.” Traced through her words offered up in varying contexts, the arc of her story still holds mysteries. What is clear is that G̱a’ax̱sta’las stood firm. She defied structures of customary authority at a time when senior, high-ranked Kwakwa̱ka̱’wakw women held power in their ’ni’na̱’mima but rarely throughout the public spectrum.

Jane Cook’s descendants do not intend to erase her involvement in colonial processes. They seek to contextualize her activities in the villages and in the wider political sphere (see Part I). By revisiting her story, they interrogate the historical record and seek to overcome a sense of stigmatization linked to her actions. They also “stand up” with G̱a’ax̱sta’las in a larger effort to reincorporate her descendants – especially younger members of their family – estranged from the potlatch system and from other sites of Kwakwa̱ka̱’wakw identity.

As a first-born child of a first-born child, G̱a’ax̱sta’las had the right to ’na̱’mima privileges that flowed through her Kwagu’ł grandfather, Chief John ’Nulis. Upon her marriage in 1888, G̱a’ax̱sta’las stepped out of her standing in the potlatch system. Her historical decision left some descendants without standing in that traditional arena. Many of Jane Cook’s descendants participate in this continual re-creation of identity, tracing descent through their mother’s and/or their father’s lines to ancestors from whose mythical encounters the symbols and stories of ’na̱’mima belonging are generated. Others are without this option. Among her potlatching descendants, there is a good deal of talk about young people who are without names, without the vitality of Kwakwa̱ka̱’wakw being.

This book documents ways in which one family has worked to resolve questions about the past. It is also intended to inform more distant relatives about a history to which they belong. The efforts of G̱a’ax̱sta’las’s descendants to include new generations in the cultural realm are documented in Part X, which includes discussions with two family chiefs about the potlatches they hosted in 2005 and 2006. G̱a’ax̱sta’las’s descendants also ritually reanimated the Kwagu’ł Gix̱sa̱m ’na̱’mima in 2007 at a feast where they bestowed over sixty names. This book concludes with an edited transcript of the feast through which the family stood up to reactivate dormant names and positions through one line of descent from G̱a’ax̱sta’las. In the welcome speech that opens this book, Chief Robert Joseph speaks of how the return of the Gixsam 'na'mima will strengthen the Kwakwaka'wakw as a whole, for the vitality of the potlatch system depends on a complex network of participating, interrelated clans. Evident at the feast was a palpable sense that Ga'axsta'las's descendants were stepping back into a relevant Kwakwaka'wakw history.

The words, actions, and embodied interpretations of the potlatches and feasts offered throughout this book address many angles of public and personal memory. The Big House in 'Yalis harbours an echo of the voices and movements of ancestors still alive in the recital of their origin stories, in the donning of their crests, in the bestowal of their names, and in the words and gestures that accompany their songs. Each of these prerogatives – these acts of remembering – is revealed to witnesses by retelling their paths of transmission. The tellings affirm links to the present; they are vital demonstrations of one's place within a 'na'mima and within the Kwakwaka'wakw world. To make the genealogical links explicit in the Big House is sometimes, as Chief Robert Joseph states, "to right the wrongs" and "correct the paths on which we've been."

Every potlatch or feast celebrates the continuity of a particular 'na'mima, and it is important to acknowledge that each lineage holds the memory of multiple histories that, over time, have woven themselves into the experiences and thoughts of individuals. The momentum of these histories generates shared ideas about the past, conjuring memories of collective struggle and colonial oppression and sometimes triggering the difficult stuff of belonging and exclusion. This book is a textual act of remembering that documents how some members of the Cook family use 'na'mima knowledge and historical analysis to "make and create a world" that is both safe and strong for their children.

Introduction: "Having Oneness on Your Face"

In 2002, I was invited by Dara Culhane to meet with Pearl Alfred, who was looking for someone to research and write a book about her grandmother.[1] My notes from that first meeting are a patchwork of annotations to published papers, to places and relationships to them, to names of people with whom to speak, and to some key details of a life lived. Pearl stated her convictions about the proposed research and the book that would follow. "Nothing is to be written," she said, "at the expense of anyone else." The first parameter set for the project indicated the extent to which this story not only intersects with but also belongs, in some way, to other Kwakwa̱ka̱'wakw people. This is important, for not everyone agrees with the decision to commemorate G̱a'ax̱sta'las.

Our book is not intended to weigh the polemics that surround interpretations of Jane Cook's actions. Rather, it is an account of how her descendants situate her story within particular historical contexts, cultural analyses, and their own family history. Given the nature of their ancestor's story, our work is intended to present details about her life not yet in the public record so that a more balanced conversation may follow. Because of their desire to address portrayals of G̱a'ax̱sta'las in the scholarly literature, it made sense to work with an academic (See Part I). I am a Euro-Canadian scholar drawn to this project for a number of reasons. As someone long interested in the imprint of colonialisms on settler and aboriginal worlds, I see the story of Ga'axsta'las and her descendants as a compelling narrative about the afterlife of colonization, a kind of "unfinished history" inhabited by the family.[2] As an anthropologist, I am intrigued by how this family's story folds into the history of my discipline while also having something important to say about real-world struggles with memory, the legacies of resistance, and histories of gender. Researching Ga'axsta'las's story offered the opportunity to collaborate on something that mattered to people, to build on the family's vision, and to improvise as our work unfolded. Such opportunities are rare. By writing about the process, I also hope to say something about the collective labour involved in collaborative work.

I was inspired by a project conducted with members of a Tsimshian community for the Royal Commission on Aboriginal Peoples' Life History Project. Margaret Anderson Seguin and Tammy Anderson Blumhagen worked to compile the life history of Louisa Anderson, a "little grandmother" who had passed away some time before the research.[3] Importantly, their work emphasized "communal memory" in the politicized context of contemporary social life. Like Seguin and Blumhagen's research, our work is also embedded in customary relationships – in ways that remembering extends through lineages, crests, and names and through colonial accounts and scholarly literatures. As a western genre focussed on an individual, biography is a somewhat limiting form. In this work, it is the telling of collective histories that offers the necessary medium through which an individual life is commemorated.[4]

Collaborative ethnography in aboriginal communities holds an uneasy place in debates about interpretation, voice, and the politics of colonial power. In our work, these contentious debates coexist with the more usual quandary of translation across historical boundaries. We sought a process that would include ongoing conversations about "academically positioned and community positioned narratives," and so we explore different forms of knowledge production.[5] We had explicit conversations about our approach, discussing the academic requirement (on my part) to publish articles and speak at conferences about this work and the importance of adhering to social and cultural protocols. While conscious of the need to work toward a much-sought-after decolonized methodology, I was guided by my collaborators into a research process that I came to understand was rooted in 'na'mima relationships.[6]

Researching the Story of G̲a'ax̲sta'las

Jane Cook's descendants drafted an initial list of participants who were chosen because of their desire to contribute and their experiences with and perspectives on their ancestor G̲a'ax̲sta'las. I was given a descendant chart compiled by the U'mista Cultural Centre in Alert Bay that documents the branches of Jane and Stephen Cook's sixteen children. Invaluable as it was for its orientation, the chart also cued me to the ways that the family was directing me to include members of each lineage and to acknowledge the convention of primogeniture (respect for the authority of first birthright). When sensitive issues arose, considerable effort was made to direct questions toward the eldest living member of that branch of the family in question. This was often dealt with by someone else.

Our methods included archival research, oral history, and family meetings. We co-analyzed anthropological field notes; police, church, and government reports and correspondences; private papers; news media; photographs; and archived transcripts from the McKenna-McBride Royal Commission, meetings of the Allied Indian Tribes, Anglican Church meetings, and a scholarly conference. Ethnographic participation at community and family events and potlatches and feasts hosted by family members complemented the textual approaches. I worked closely with seven or eight people noted for their expertise. Pearl Alfred was my primary collaborator in discussing the shape of the project as it unfolded.

Significant materials obtained through our research were distributed to G̲a'ax̲sta'las's immediate descendants: to her grandchildren (now elders), their cousins, and her great-grandchildren. It is important to acknowledge that many family members with whom I worked have considerable experience with aboriginal organizations and band administration. Some work to represent First Nations' perspectives within different branches of the federal and provincial governments. Already familiar with the body of documents that record the administrative history of colonialism in their villages, they sketched out for me a general terrain of topics and events that inhabit the archives. Additionally, several family members have conducted extensive research of their own, having interviewed elders now gone, read scholarly and popular works, and made their own archival searches – a far from unusual circumstance, given that First Nations are forced to engage with states on terms set by legalistic and bureaucratic regimes. My collaborators' familiarity with primary materials fed this research, making for stimulating dialogues and comfortable discussions about matters of interpretation.

Guided by the knowledge of what to look for, I consulted collections held by the U'mista Cultural Centre in 'Ya̲lis; the Church Mission Society Archives in Birmingham, United Kingdom; the Anglican Diocese Archives in Vancouver and Victoria; the BC Archives in Victoria; and Library and Archives Canada in Ottawa. Other repositories from which we obtained materials included the Washington State Archives, the Seaver Collection in Los Angeles, and local historical society collections in Port Townsend and Alert Bay. Many Kwakwa̲ka̲'wakw individuals also keep collections of their own, and family and community members offered photographs, letters, and media accounts from their personal archives. They include documents left over from the days of carbon copies and original handwritten letters that were later copied and sent to colonial agents. Some are "declassified" files. Made available in the 1970s, I have been unable to find some of these materials in public archival repositories. Deemed irrelevant, they might have been culled by archivists or perhaps lost in the shuffle of records. Much of the material included in this book comes from these family collections. Early in our work, we compiled a collection of historical documents that was distributed to members of each lineage of Jane and Stephen's descendants. It was exciting to see how these materials launched conversations about older interpretations, which acquired new meanings as they percolated through the family. Much of our work focussed on co-analyzing these documents.

We also examined the field notes and papers of Franz Boas. In April 2005, I travelled to the American Philosophical Society Library in Philadelphia with Wedłidi Speck, now recognized as chief of the Gix̲sa̲m 'na̲'mima, and William Wasden Jr., a potlatch chief and prominent traditional performer. Both men are descendants of Jane Cook and well read in anthropology; both were eager to comb through the archive's vast Franz Boas Collection. Boas recorded the names and stories of their ancestors. His papers include verbatim transcripts of their speeches and songs and descriptions of dances, feasts, coppers, houses, territories, and privileges. We found references here and there to G̲a'ax̲sta'las's grandfather John 'Nulis and to Boas's work with Jane Cook in 1931. Wedłidi and William repatriated previously lost 'na̲'mima names with the intention to redistribute them formally through potlatches and feasts. Our days in Philadelphia were rich with conversation. Listening to Wedłidi and William was like travelling through time to villages on the Coast. Their stories about conflicts, marriages, or births many generations past clarified, for me, large-scale changes in their society as well as how things work today. Such folding of the past into the present characterizes much that is at the heart of this book.

Research for what has from the beginning been called the "Granny Cook Book" began with speaking to individuals chosen by the family. Pearl Alfred initially accompanied me, but I later met with people in their homes, at restaurants and cafés, at homes where I was staying on the reserve, or in a rented cabin on the other end of Cormorant Island, on which Alert Bay is situated. Rarely did these meetings take the form of question-and-response interviews; rather, they were appointments with orators who often spoke for over an hour, until they had finished. We then had conversations about specific topics, about how they would like G̲a'ax̲sta'las to be remembered, about how they imagined the book, about the visual materials they would like to see included, and about why they wanted the book to be written. The initial list of participants expanded to include other community members and cultural experts (although these categories are in no way exclusive). Our meetings took place in 'Ya̲lis, in Comox, and in the cities of Vancouver and Victoria. The labour of transcribing audio recordings was shared with family members, sometimes younger people who did not speak for the book but who were interested in learning about their family's history. Individuals with expertise in Kwak̓wala also transcribed interviews. Nella Nelson spoke with her father, George Cook, in November 2009. A transcript of their conversation was sent to me via email so it could be added to relevant sections of this work. Transcripts were returned to people and, with their permission, they were sent to Pearl Alfred, who offered further directions to pursue and suggested other contacts or events to follow up on. The research process was discussed at family meetings held in 'Ya̲lis, often to share new information.

Jane Cook's descendants have for some time met regularly for family business – enormous reunions, family calendars, or loonie auctions. These meetings also came to include conversations about the book.[7] On the occasions when I was present, we discussed historical events and situations that invoked different interpretations, and we recorded these manifold perspectives. As individuals offered personal stories from childhood and adulthood, I heard about the sense of stigmatization shared by members of the Cook family (see Part I). Often, while discussing the research, conversation would turn to an explanation for why someone should be contacted. At these meetings, shared genealogical knowledge became a kind of matrix within which new information was continually absorbed and arranged. There were always new voices at the meetings as family visited from off island and as others dropped in when they had time. At one meeting, some questioned the family's intentions to publish a book, and this sparked conversations about difficult relationships, conversations that again emphasized the communal investment in G̲a'ax̲sta'las's story.

Writing the "Granny Cook Book"

Family history research in 'Ya̲lis often sparks controversy among those whose histories converge in the political arena that surrounded the potlatch during early colonialism, a time when "individuals were ranked within the 'na̲'mima consisting of the head chief, a direct descendent of the founding ancestor, lesser chiefs, commoners and their families."[8] As Joseph Masco writes, for Kwakwa̲ka̲'wakw people, "Rank is both a possession and a practice"; it involves active "negotiation between [community] structure and historical circumstance."[9] Negotiations among high-ranking families are often voiced through family-sanctioned biographies.[10]

Published works by and about Kwakwa̲ka̲'wakw peoples are rarely neutral.[11] Read through markers that are recognized internally, most have something to say about the histories of a specific 'na̲'mima or tribe, and they reflect the lively style of ongoing community conversations about the past. As is discussed in Part I, these works are central to the story of G̲a'ax̲sta'las because she appears in both early scholarly studies and in more contemporary literature about colonial history in Kwakwa̲ka̲'wakw territories.

Given these representational questions, I hold to the ethnographic responsibility of rendering collaborators' various articulations of the past in the present visible and understandable. Following anthropologist Richard Price, I agree that works by the "ethnographic historian ... must be animated by a constant attentiveness to meaning ... to processes of producing histories ... to processes of knowing ... and to problems of form."[12] Members of all societies understand that history making requires acts of interpretation and documentation that generate powerful images for present reflection. Indeed, the production of history here is, in effect, a long conversation with versions of literary and oral pasts suspended in the present for the purpose of telling G̲a'ax̲sta'las's story. This book offers a view of the ways particular "individuals represent themselves to *themselves* in history."[13]

I am self-conscious about my use of historical methods. Following anthropologist Peter Gow, “there is one point that must be made clearly: an anthropological analysis that uses historical methods must start from ethnography, and from the problems ethnography presents. Ethnography is to anthropological investigation what ‘primary sources’ are to historians.”[14] Our work rides the wake generated by people’s responses to oral and textual artifacts of the past. It represents the views of those members of one clan with whom I worked, not as “data” collected from “research subjects” but as the analyses, descriptions, and explanations of knowledgeable partners in research.

My collaborators sought to “set the record straight,” but there were varying opinions among them as to how that could be done. What everyone did agree on was protecting (when judged necessary) the anonymity of individuals whose presence is documented in written and oral histories. As an ethnographic history, this work seeks to be responsible to living participants, and so we take a stance that protects the anonymity of individuals to whatever degree possible. Thus, names and other identifying information are removed from discussions of sensitive topics. This stricture not only protects G̱a’ax̱sta’las’s descendants, it also extends to the ancestors of other families whose actions in the past may not be known to them or about whom we are not authorized to write.

Another realm of memory that is important to acknowledge involves the descendants of those people who were prosecuted and persecuted because of their defiance of the potlatch ban.[15] On one occasion, I was informed that G̱a’ax̱sta’las’s involvement in the potlatch ban should not be erased from any story about her. Clearly, she is a controversial figure, and this book does not shy away from critical information about her. It is narrated from the perspectives of those who both admire her and who sometimes struggle with her historical decisions.

Few readers will be indifferent to G̱a’ax̱sta’las. She worked in proximity to the agents of colonial rule, to the arbiters of Kwakwa̱ka̱’wakw authority, and to men and women and children whose daily lives were shaped by conflicting forces. Whether G̱a’ax̱sta’las influenced those who wielded political power, the potlatch ban followed a colonial script for the suppression of key indigenous institutions around the globe. Her actions were based in a faith that justice was attainable through colonial law, a position shared by the leaders of formal aboriginal organizations then struggling for recognition. Where she diverted from that position was in her confrontation with male customary power as it then affected the lives of women – and that stance challenged the potlatch practices of her day. As a living network of relationships continually re-created by each generation – responsive to local and external forces, to imposed structures and internal constraints – the potlatch is not static. Our work represents Jane Cook's stance on the social effects of the potlatch in the context of changing potlatch practices that she witnessed and that shaped to some considerable extent her early life experiences.

What is certain about G̱a'a̱xsta'las is that within Kwakwa̱ka̱'wakw villages her voice was (and still is) potent. She acted in a political realm where local demands were heard within national (and even transnational) arenas. Her bilingualism, her literacy, her economic security, and her position in the church cannot be separated from her high rank in the Kwakwa̱ka̱'wakw social world, all of which afforded her a powerful place from which to speak. But her location only enabled what was certainly a remarkable will to act and be heard. Readers will have to decide themselves where they land in the debates that her story rouses.

G̱a'a̱xsta'las's descendants stressed to me that although her stance on the potlatch ban is important, there is a woman at the heart of this story who was a village member, a wife, and a mother and grandmother whose busy household left an indelible impression on them. To remember "Granny Cook" properly means keeping an eye on the everyday and the mundane – meals, church activities, meetings, illnesses, and seasonal fishing activities. More importantly, Jane Cook's family members want to acknowledge the living legacy of her character in their lives, and so our story unfolds through the words of her descendants, accounts of their accomplishments, and their reflections on her life and times.

As we discussed writing strategies, people agreed that (anonymity permitting) Jane Cook's original words should be included whenever possible. We encourage her words be read not as timeless proof of her ultimate stance on a subject but as instances of active dialogue frozen in transcripts that do not convey the rich atmosphere or context of the original interaction. It is certain that much more exists "out there," in private or public collections. Like all histories, ours is partial. Written in a collage that privileges past-present voices and original texts, this book presents verbatim excerpts from historical sources, media tributes, official testimonies and letters written by and about G̱a'a̱xsta'las, and published interviews with her. Throughout, her descendants co-analyze these materials, explain aspects of their collective history, and tell stories that animate Ga'axsta'las's life. Some stipulated that ancestor legends be included as key orientations to who Ga'axsta'las was at birth and through marriage, and they also decided which narrator's versions of these stories should appear and where. I drafted an outline for the book with several options, and my collaborators decided on a chronological presentation of Ga'axsta'las's story.

We had many conversations about collaborative authorship and what it might look like. As is recognized in relevant passages throughout the book, family members have written sections on 'na'mima descent, Kwakwaka'wakw history and concepts, political rights, and customary privileges, and their titles, footnotes, captions, and co-analyses appear throughout the book. But there are other techniques of collaborative writing hidden in the text – continuous conversations about form and content and the wealth of shared interpretations.

Early in the writing process, we worked from the primary sources that were circulated among family members. They commented or expanded on the materials and focussed on whatever details they chose, usually through documented conversations, sometimes in writing or over email. Their analyses, descriptions, and speculations show historical imaginations at work, revealing the detail passed through oral histories. Our exchanges were "live feeds" to this book, and they were often elicited and included as I wrote about particular incidents or examined particular documents. All sources are attributed in the text.

Our dialogue about how to write about sensitive topics extended into the writing process, but I wrote independently and was not hindered in my interpretations. Indeed, engaging discussions often ensued. As I finished drafts of chapters, they were sent to family members for corrections and additions. Following a well-worn path of collaborative scholarship – and in accordance with the 'Namgis First Nation Guidelines for Visiting Researchers, the final manuscript was read critically by six family members, who reviewed the text, corrected names or Kwak̓wala orthography, and offered further details, often about kinship affiliations.[16] A few of the photographs that appear in this book I chose myself. Most were contributed by descendants. Interpretations of historical photographs illustrate another body of knowledge production through a close reading of material culture (clothing, construction techniques, or symbols).

We worked against a backdrop of scholarship that is a reminder of the degree to which Kwakwaka'wakw peoples have been documented.

I found an eerie similarity in representations of these peoples throughout time and in different places. Certainly, the rugged coastal beaches and lush rainforests of their territories remain recognizable, but the myriad ways in which people represent themselves and their histories often seem to be defined by the Boasian canon. The canon is impossible to avoid. An imposing literature, it has been trawled for over a century by successive generations of anthropologists. The gift of the literature is the rawness of the presentation, yet it holds its own secrets. Earlier texts were compiled largely by those whose interests in theory and ethnology revolved around precontact "traditional culture." Seldom do they represent topics that diverge from the well-worn pathways of scholarly interest.[17] My collaborators and I sometimes step off the path of accepted scripts, yet we too strive to maintain the clarity of primary sources.

Most work that seeks to represent Kwakwa̱ka̱'wakw peoples includes a linguistic note. Kwak̓wala has been textualized by explorers, missionaries, government agents, by Franz Boas, by subsequent linguists, and by the U'mista Cultural Centre in 'Ya̱lis. When quoting from various sources, I use the form used in the original. When there is confusion, I clarify the word or name in the text. Throughout, family members sometimes use Kwak̓wala words that do not conform to the U'mista orthography. We include those in the spirit of recognizing informal language conventions.

On Hope

All collaborations are unique, shaped by the desires, knowledge, and imaginations of those who are involved. Our research and this book are just one aspect of a larger process initiated by G̱a'a̱xsta'las's descendants to offer a more complete public record of her activities. I imagine our work within a larger chain reaction of activities, conversations, and decisions. In my struggle to describe this process, I was reminded of an early conversation with Wedłidi Speck and his use of the concept of *'na̱mała*. I contacted him to ask if he thought it could be applied to the way knowledge has been generated through this project. He responded with the following email: "The concept of oneness, of being in relationship with all things flows from aweetnakula.[18] It is held up by the 'na̱'mima ... people of one kind. When viewed together, fellows of the 'na̱'mima are considered 'na̱mwut ... those that are one. Kwakwaka'wakw cultural discourse could go no other way than to aim at 'namała, to have oneness on your face. I got that from Jimmy Sewid. He taught me 'namała; he told me a story about my great-grandfather, Chief Harry Hanuse."

"He was a strong leader, and when he wanted to discuss things with his 'namwut, he walked to one end of the village singing a song, his song, and the men of the village would come out of their houses and join him. He would walk back to the other end of the village and do the same thing. Soon, all the men of the village were walking together, singing his song. Then the men went into his big house. A mat was provided to each man to sit on. When they were seated, he discussed the contents of the song as the principles that would guide the discussion. His aim was 'namała."

"The key ingredient to 'namała was the place in which he (my great-grandfather) resided ... having oneness on his face. He started with it. This is seen in his desire to include all the men in the discussion. He also carried the spirit of sharing (providing the men with an opportunity to share his song [property] and experience ritual oneness). In walking through the village he also modeled transparency, openness and fellowship. 'Namała is connected to cultural discourse and is woven into the fabric of one's journey in life. It is only as good as the effort being applied. When a leader sets out to discuss things, he/she must know the place in which they are starting from. The meeting process is as valuable as the outcome."

Just as Chief Harry Hanuse "resided" in 'namała, from which place he gathered together his 'namwut and brought them into a shared realm of discourse, so too have members of the Cook family worked from 'na'mima relations to arrive at a oneness on the face regarding their ancestor's story. Wedłidi Speck's response reflects an analytic approach common throughout this book, one that works through stories rather than – or as – explanation and calls for contemplation rather than the acceptance of a truth.

Creating this book involved a collaborative, multimethod approach, but there was another process at work, one that attests to the ways that experience and knowledge and identity sometimes rub shoulders to let go a sea change. The process includes practices through which knowledge moves through different collectivities, generating fresh impressions and processing older interpretations in order to revisit the communal story of Jane Cook. Our research compiled *information,* but the *real* work of revisiting how Ga'axsta'las is remembered flows through relationships in the community that unite people in a shared – but sometimes contested – history. Potlatching and feasting are other realms of memory practice in which knowledge is transformed into ritual that sanctions certain kinds of information, creates new social networks, and modifies existing narratives. As new evidence moved through the family or as events in gukwdzi (the Big House) met with community approval, there was a palpable letting go of breath.

There is some resonance here with what others have named a "method of hope" that includes practices separate from our tasks as researchers, practices that go on – that have always gone on – in communities where we work. At the heart of this method, writes Hirokazu Miyazaki, is the mobilization of hope through what he calls "different genres of ... people's self-knowledge."[19] Evident here is the futility of separating scholarship from social relationships when the research is meaningful – that is, when it engages with deeply held convictions and carries a sense of movement toward a hoped-for outcome. Although research has a role, it does not constitute the whole venture.[20] In a place where relationships are everything, the desires re-presented in this work deserve consideration as part of a larger endeavour of hope.

PART I

The Living Text: Traces of Jane Cook

"She was a big woman. She was very buxom. And a very hardworking woman with big hands," Pearl Alfred held up her own hands as she spoke. "You just knew she was somebody who worked hard. Her hands reminded me of a man's hands – [a man] who worked hard."

"Granny ... yeah, she was a big woman," Ethel Alfred said quietly. "She was tall, kind of curly hair, too."

"Long braided hair. She'd undo it every night and brush her hair. Then she'd tie all of it in a bun," Pearl continued.

Ethel nodded, smiling.

"A bun that seemed to be all over the back of her head. She had lots of hair."

"I always thought, 'Gee, I wouldn't mind having one of those when I get old.'"

"Oh thick, thick hair. They never used to let us wear one braid. I used to have two big braids in school," Ethel Alfred said, laughing. "We weren't allowed to have it in one braid." She paused for a moment, "A nice-looking woman, tall. She always wore hats, you know, when she went to church she'd have a hat on."

"And cardigans, woolen cardigans," said Pearl.

In the years that followed this early conversation, I heard from many people about the iconic "Granny cardigans" that were sold in the Cook Store, located by the wharf below the family house in 'Y̲alis. For Jane

Photo 1 G̲a’ax̲sta’las, Jane Constance Cook, ’Ya̲lis, 2 June 1914. *Photographer unknown. Image H-07220, Royal BC Museum, BC Archives.*

Cook’s grandchildren, the cardigan was clearly a signature item in “Granny Cook’s” wardrobe. Early on, I had downloaded a photograph from the BC Archives’ website titled simply “Alert Bay, Mrs. Cook.” I took the photograph with me during interviews. G̲a’ax̲sta’las’s daughter-in-law Nellie Cook laughed when she saw the image: “I guess that was her dress-up,” she said, looking at the photo. Nellie’s daughter Pearl later told me that she rarely saw her granny without telltale stains from kneeling in her garden. Pearl’s sister Christine Zurkowski pointed out a Thunderbird brooch that G̲a’ax̲sta’las always wore and said symbolized her marriage to Stephen Cook because the Thunderbird was his crest among the ’Na̲mgis. In another photograph, hanging in a grandson’s basement, Jane Cook wears a silver grease spoon that invokes *t’lina* (eulachon oil). I was also told that she often dressed with a cross that her son Edwin had about his neck when he was killed during World War One.

The photograph from the BC Archives shows a woman standing, hands in cardigan pockets, purse hanging from her wrist. Behind her, hatted men walk toward the Cook family store, hands in pockets and coat tails flapping. It was 1914, members of the McKenna-McBride Royal Commission were in 'Y̲alis (Alert Bay) hearing testimonies for Aboriginal land claims, and Jane Cook was among those testifying (see Part V).

Regrettably, the image, which was taken at a significant political moment, has since been plucked from its context and appears in contemporary works that focus narrowly on Jane Cook. The omission of the photograph's setting erases the part that she played in key events, focusing instead on her role in the colonial ban on the potlatch. Such erasures are typical in the long stream of public representations of G̲a'ax̲sta'las embedded in scholarly practice and in community memory. These erasures have, in part, fuelled this work, inspiring her descendants to produce a fuller picture of their complicated ancestor.

In the photograph, there is a confidence in G̲a'ax̲sta'las's direct gaze at the camera, a buttoned-down certainty in her stance and her half-smile that would-be biographers could locate in the heady present, where a cult of individualism saturates activism. But this is a portrait of a forty-four-year-old woman whose granddaughters, Pearl and Christine; daughter-in-law, Nellie; and family friend Ethel Alfred describe in a way that is purely familial, in a way that attests to the memory of Jane Cook's physical presence in their lives. Their descriptions serve as a reminder of the flesh and blood behind all remembered events and actions, a point that G̲a'ax̲sta'las's descendants quietly stressed throughout our collaboration, one that speaks to the intended spirit of the book, to our research process, and to the writing strategies upon which we agreed.

In June 2003, Pearl told me why it was important to write this book about her grandmother. "I just think she never got a fair shake in terms of some of the things she said and did, which were to me quite remarkable in terms of a woman who had sixteen children, worked really hard from dawn to dusk, and was active politically. She was very active in the church ... did a fair amount of travelling in terms of what you hear today, being a court interpreter at a time when women's place was very obviously in the kitchen. How she got away with that always fascinated me," she said, laughing. "To me, a book acknowledges, somehow, a woman taking on issues that must have been horrific – I think."

Pearl's musings are not without substance. As the first female band manager of the 'Namgis First Nation, in her various roles as community activist, and during her long-standing service in the field of aboriginal health, Pearl Alfred confronts challenges not unlike those faced by her grandmother. At a later family meeting she elaborated on her vision for the book: "What *needs* to come out is *why* she took some of these stands. That it was not just a thing for her, that there were real people involved – children, women, sick people, fishermen, Nimpkish rights, fishing rights – stuff like that." I heard many express the sense that Ga'axsta'las "never got a fair shake."

George Speck also talked about getting to the heart of what his great-grandmother stood for and against. "I think that's part of the family wanting to revisit this whole thing, because it's time that people saw what she stood against for what it was. Perhaps it's time to hold a mirror up for people to look into and say, 'Not everything was good with potlatching. Not everything was good with the traditional culture.' It was a time of change, and she was a part of that change. We now have a different way of potlatching that everybody agrees with, that elders agree with. Elders don't want to talk about the burying of the slaves under house posts, or the slaughter of slaves for potlatch rituals, or the marrying off of young children. Nobody wants to talk about that now. Fair enough! But let's not pretend it didn't happen either at the expense of the Cook family *[laughs]*."

As the current band manager, hereditary Ławits'is chief, and a former graduate student of anthropology, George Speck is well situated to address the intersections of culture, history, and politics that have generated the silences that are so apparent to his family. "Growing up," he said, "the family never addressed that directly. I just learned it in my more adult years, what exactly her role was, what exactly she stood for and against around the traditional aspects of our culture."

As it appears in the published record, Ga'axsta'las's story is one of betrayal based on her support of the potlatch ban. But traces of the past portray a more nuanced story. Her descendants want to see a balanced portrayal that also depicts her commitment to aboriginal rights. Some express a double-edged sense of stigmatization linked to her participation in early colonial events and to her renunciation of the potlatch. Pearl Alfred noted that her sense of being stigmatized became obvious only in the late 1950s. "I don't think we were ever conscious of that until the potlatch started again," she said. "There was the revival, and then discussions came up, and you would hear her name mentioned as someone who took a stand against this and it was her fault that the dances died. You would hear all of this stuff, and you never knew whether it was true or not."

From some of Jane Cook's grandchildren (now elders) and great- and great-great-grandchildren, I heard stories that described a kind of separation in the social world of their villages, one that even carried into interactions among cousins. Their stories of exclusion often involved events as seen through their eyes as children and adolescents, but some extended well into adulthood. "We feel imprisoned," G̲a'x̲sta'las's grandson Chris Cook said at a family meeting. "For us, as the Cook family, we're imprisoned in the – I don't know the words, vacuum of guilt. For all these years ... We've always been looked at as the guys that sold out, the guys that sold the potlatch out. That's my feeling from growing up, like, *all you guys don't belong.*" I was surprised by these words from a man who has hosted potlatches and served frequently on the Native Brotherhood and the 'Na̲mg̲is Band Council. "I think that for our own selves and for our children – to make things right – it's the appropriate time to write a book." When I asked why this is the appropriate time, Chris suggested that "it's more open now," not like before, when "people were more set in their ways."

G̲a'x̲sta'las's descendants seek to make things right, but they also hope to clear the way for the youngest generations in their family, a point that great-great-grandson Randy Bell made explicit. "I wouldn't want to see kids ever have to worry about being told, 'You're just part of the Cook family,' and 'You have no right.' I don't want them to have to go through that. And for me, that's the passion motivating this book ... I never want to have them face that their great-great-great-grandmother was something that she was not. We're going to set the record straight on who she was and what she was about." When Randy expressed his worry about children being told "You have no right," he referred to experiences related by adults and children in his family who had been publicly called down, told they couldn't dance or shouldn't wear regalia or that they didn't understand what they were doing in the cultural realm. Given his experience as a youth worker in 'Ya̲lis, he is sharply aware of the role that cultural identity plays in the lives of young people who may be struggling.

It may seem contradictory that members of this high-ranking, economically and politically successful family express a sense of exclusion from the cultural realm, but the stigma follows from Jane Cook's decision to quit the potlatch and assumptions about her descendants' lack of cultural knowledge because of the decision. Some in the family did speak about their absence from ceremonial life, about being children in households that had little connection with activities in that realm. But family members also follow Kwakwa̱ka̱'wakw protocol by tracing descent through the line of their mother or their father or both, and many of these other lineages have maintained their participation in potlatching.

Not all of Jane and Stephen Cook's children followed their parents in rejecting the potlatch. Their daughter Pearl Mountain married into a strong potlatching family. She raised her young children in 'Mi'mkwa̱mlis (Village Island) with paternal grandparents Marion and Harry Mountain. One of those children, Florrie Matilpe, regularly attended family potlatches and speaks Kwak̓wala fluently. I asked her if she or her mother, Pearl Mountain, had experienced unease in their community because of G̱a'ax̱sta'las's activities. "I don't know if Mom did, because she went into the Big House," Florrie told me, "she was always there. She never said much, but she did go, and she'd take part. We had a memorial potlatch for our dad when he died – a few years after he died. So." We spoke for a time about the potlatch Florrie gave for her late husband and about changes in potlatching that she has noticed. "We go to nearly all of them if we can. That's why we're always saying Granny would be turning over in her grave, seeing us all sitting here *[laughs]*." Florrie's comment was echoed by some others in the family who wonder if the ceremonial reactivation of 'na̱'mima activities is appropriate given Jane Cook's stance against the early twentieth-century potlatch.

G̱a'ax̱sta'las's descendants express diverse opinions and are involved in various ways with cultural activities. Some have always participated fully. Many have one parent whose family participates in the Big House. Others, through marriage, have joined families active in the potlatch system. Some are members of clans such as the Gix̱sa̱m who have reactivated their positions in the system, and others spoke about being "looked after" by relatives who ensured that they received names.

Nine of G̱a'ax̱sta'las's grandsons, great-grandsons, and great-great-grandsons currently occupy the named standings of hereditary and potlatch chiefs. They and others have been initiated into the Hamat̓sa Society or they perform valued roles as singers "at the log" or dancers at feasts and potlatches. Women have mastered the seemingly endless labour and the subtle behind-the-scenes politicking required to host and prepare potlatches, and they instruct their daughters and sons to fulfill their responsibilities. Like many Kwakwa̱ka̱'wakw people, some family members move between 'Na̱mg̱is communities located on and off reserve. Several were raised in the more remote villages. There are also extended family members of this ’na’mima who have maintained but a thin thread of connection to ’Yalis. My collaborators hope that this book will offer these members a foundation for understanding family history and, perhaps, a sense of return to their ’na’mima.

Although many are aware of their noble ranking in the Kwakwaka’wakw social hierarchy – and they clearly enact the knowledge to participate – some in the family still carry with them a sense of unease. Yet the family’s absence from the Big House is not often explicitly noted by others. Instead, Ga’axsta’las’s progeny have worn a familiar constellation of labels associated with the taint of colonialism, with cultural assimilation, and with not being “Indian”: Christianity, whiteness, and economic prosperity. William Wasden Jr. spoke explicitly about these labels. “Well, I think it’s got a lot to do with the mixed blood and that they were very strong churchgoers, and they had a big house, which was a very Christian home. You look at the census of 1901, the long houses were still going, yet there were these modern houses and the [Cook] big house was a very prominent house because it was so big.”

Here and there, I heard the term *naxsoye’*, literally “fifty cents,” used to indicate a person of varied heritage. I do not know the extent to which others in the community also experience this form of racialization but, clearly, many count among their progenitors (mostly male) European traders and settlers. Some family members’ reminiscences were punctuated with stories about being labelled “white” and with insights into how the relationship between whiteness and church affiliation offered opportunities for economic success that might not have been open to others. Although Jane and Stephen’s family prospered through engagement with the church, many other families also secured economic success through alliances with missionaries, cannery and forestry companies, and museums and universities.[1] Such were the viable options – especially for high-ranking Kwakwaka’wakw people – during the nineteenth century. As the century wore on, these affiliations offered families of other social ranks the opportunity to participate in capitalist economies and in the potlatch system.

Anthropology and the Peoples Formerly Known as the Kwakiutl

The string of epithets carried by Ga’axsta’las’s descendants is mirrored in the litany of published accounts about Jane Cook, the most recent of which includes a half-page copy of the 1914 photograph of her as well as a letter (critical of the potlatch) she penned to colonial officials in 1919. The stigmatization felt by families whose ancestors played a role in colonial events is expressed, in part, through their engagement with works on Kwakwa̱ka̱'wakw life. In many ways, *Standing Up with G̱a'a̱xsta'las* is an interactive interpretation of what I call "the living text" of American anthropology and Northwest Coast historical scholarship. This includes not only the stories scholars tell about people and the ways other scholars reproduce these stories but also how these stories both describe and intervene in the lives of those whom they represent.[2]

Those who have written about G̱a'a̱xsta'las invoke three primary sources: comments written by Helen Codere in the introduction to Franz Boas's *Kwakiutl Ethnography* (1966); selected letters written by Jane Cook and included in archival collections focussed on the potlatch; and excerpts from a under-examined document in the Anglican Diocese Archives titled "Special Meeting on the Potlatch," recorded in 1936.The body of published works about G̱a'a̱xsta'las is haunted by the spectres of representation, authenticity, and agency – important sites of orientation for scholars and (in a different way) for her descendants engaged in the work of revisiting her history.

Recounted in conversations and regenerated in new publications, academic representations are alive. They are a potent medium through which people evaluate sometimes difficult pasts and re-examine individual lives alongside renewed customary activities. As subjects and as readers, Kwakwa̱ka̱'wakw peoples are no strangers to literature and scholarship. Indeed, a constructive dialogue about past events and persons in Kwakwa̱ka̱'wakw territories takes place, in part, by discussing the ways they are inscribed in published works. Perhaps several decades ago it might have been possible to ignore this shared literary sphere, but today scholarly works have a noted presence in public memory and in the lived experiences of 'na̱'mima members.

During interviews, I was initially surprised by people's engagement with anthropological and historical works. One family member referred to chapters in William Halliday's *Potlatch and Totem* (1935), the memoirs of an early Indian Agent. Many spoke with me about Charles Nowell's *Smoke from Their Fires* (1941) and James Sewid's *Guests Never Leave Hungry* (1969), works read and discussed. More recent publications mentioned were Judith Williams's *Two Wolves at the Dawn of Time* (2001) and Agnes Alfred's memoir, *Paddling to Where I Stand* (2004), edited by Martine Reid. In conversations, people referenced Douglas Cole and Ira Chaikin's *An Iron Hand upon the People* (1990) and Robert Galois's *Kwakwaka'wakw Settlements* (1994). Ruth Benedict's *Patterns of Culture* (1934) was mentioned late in the research process. In more than one household, I saw well-turned copies of *Chiefly Feasts* (1991), edited by Aldona Jonaitis, and I had several conversations about Volume 10 in Edward Curtis's *The North American Indian,* titled *The Kwakiutl* (1915). Not all of these works mention Jane Cook, but some position her as a vital node in village networks, and others discuss her roles as translator and advocate. Most conversations I had revolved around the many works of Franz Boas, including *The Social Organization and the Secret Societies of the Kwakiutl Indians* (1897), *Primitive Art* (1955) and, of course, *Kwakiutl Ethnography* (1966), edited by Helen Codere – an infamous volume for members of the Cook family. The thesis behind Codere's earlier work *Fighting with Property* (1950) was generally well known and came up in conversations about changing potlatch practices.

Many Kwakwaka'wakw people with whom I work have studied anthropology and BC history, and some are school teachers or instructors or students of their own collective histories and traditions. Ga'axsta'las's descendants strive to bring about innovations in museum practices and educational curricula; they work towards changing the justice system and mental, social, and physical health structures. Many are engaged in strengthening and reinforcing cultural identity, and that necessarily requires knowledge of colonial history. Descendants who are activists and politicians engaged in struggles for self-determination through claims to land, resources, and other aboriginal rights are likewise familiar with texts about BC history.[3] Indeed, First Nation scholars and students interested in British Columbia who study in many disciplines would have a difficult time avoiding the vast literature on the potlatch and early colonial relations.

That the social and scholarly realms overlap is hardly surprising given that the anthropological canon about the peoples formerly known as *the Kwakiutl* stretches for over a century into the discipline's past. In 1980, 'Namgis scholar Gloria Cranmer-Webster stated that the Kwakwaka'wakw peoples are among the "most anthropologized" in the world.[4] In 2005, I asked her if she thought people had been affected by that. "In a way I guess. I mean, I know the effect it had for me. I was away for thirty years, came home, and there was so much I didn't know. And Boas's stuff was there, and we were able to use that to develop curriculum, to teach language, this kind of thing. I think he's the only anthropologist who was able to help us in that way. The rest of them came and went and contributed nothing. Yeah, so I'm glad he came. I'm glad he stayed around as long as he did. I think it's an indication of how much was lost during the *dark years,* as the old people say."

Within anthropology, scholarship about "the Kwakiutl" punctuates key theoretical and conceptual shifts. Early works by Boas on Northwest Coast mythology, kinship, and diffusion were used to refute the evolutionary theories of universal development that fuelled Social Darwinism – a crucial ideological justification for European imperial projects. His later works were used by other scholars to think through some of the most charismatic ideas in the discipline: gifting and modes of exchange,[5] symbolic healing,[6] status and rank,[7] cultural personalities,[8] prestige economies,[9] and power and chiefdoms.[10] At the heart of over a century of theorizing is the potlatch, endowed with spectacles now embedded in European imaginations – cannibals who are tamed, extravagant displays of wealth, and cosmologies intricately woven through the nuances of social power.[11]

Early anthropologists interested in the Kwakwa̱ka̱'wakw potlatch scoured the Boasian corpus to generate what is now a mainstream body of theories and debates. "Scholars seem to have behaved like scavengers, tearing from the flesh of Kwakiutl culture whatever juicy morsel tempted them, ignoring the shape of the being."[12] In Irving Goldman's work *The Mouth of Heaven,* the true "shape of the being" was cosmology, but successive scholars have plumbed this corpus to also discuss cultural ecology and political economy.[13] Some theorists applied symbolic and psychological analyses,[14] and others examined the potlatch as an institution central to social integration and cultural identity.[15] In the more recently politicized context of land claims and sustainable resource management, a legalistic analysis of the potlatch has become apparent.[16] Contemporary concepts used in anthropological considerations of the potlatch include performative identities, authenticities, resistance, and cultural endurance.[17] In these works, colonial domination, cultural resurgence, and change figure prominently.

Like our project to contextualize G̱a'a̱xsta'las's activities, it is important to situate academic work within particular contexts of theoretical debate, disciplinary growth, and political awareness. Clearly, looking at early anthropological works about Kwakwa̱ka̱'wakw peoples, there was little expectation of a shared readership. The earliest studies were grounded in the assumption that indigenous peoples were destined to disappear in the coercive tide of "civilizing" progress. Widely acknowledged in anthropology as the period of salvage, this generation of scholarship extended from the mid-nineteenth century until well into the 1950s. It was an era when colonial and scholarly projects intersected but did not necessarily meet ideologically, a time that set the stage for the underlying principles of an emerging American cultural anthropology.[18]

Forging the Authentic: "Kwakiutlness"

> *Hybrid for whom, one might ask? ... This hybridity is simply* our *identification of "matter out of place,"* hybrids-for-us.
>
> – *Jonathan Friedman, "From Roots to Routes"*

There is an unsettling tendency in the history of anthropology to seek out pure forms of "culture" along with persons somehow uncontaminated by Europeanness.[19] Rather than looking to the ways people are forced to inhabit multiple realities and then fashion identities from within these circumstances, early scholars slotted people into rigid, often racialized, categories. Thus, academically trained scholars and field-trained collaborators worked during the salvage era to record as much detail as possible about aboriginal ways of life they assumed were slipping away. Disappearance was thought to be inevitable, but many sought to reconstruct an image of precontact societies untouched by the so-called civilizing project of missionaries or by the structures of capitalism that accompanied colonial incursion.[20] Imperialist nostalgia, a morbid longing for that which one has participated in destroying, contributed greatly to creating categories of persons based on imagined opposites.[21] So, nineteenth-century scholars and colonial administrators worked from ethnocentric ideas that imagined the opposites of "savagery" and civilization.[22] Although the salvage project was dependent on the assistance of bicultural individuals, early scholars, for the most part, did not depict people whose lives they felt were overly influenced by European contact.

While early anthropological works served to make "the Kwakiutl" (and others) into icons of a sort, they also cast into circulation images and ideas that judged customs and people based on what was (or was not) considered culturally authentic, pure, or genuine.[23] European "discovery," settlement, and state control set into circulation labels that were useful in maintaining colonial authority, then and now. The labels fell within categories thought to be opposites: Christian–pagan, traditional–assimilated, white–not white, reserve–urban, market economy–subsistence economy. For many, these opposites are experienced as a kind of oppressive authenticity.[24]

Not surprisingly, ideas about who is or is not real or authentic continue to be set in the triad of Christianity, whiteness, and economic prosperity. Christianity is associated with an imagined-to-be-complete loss of indigenous spirituality, with the extinction and replacement of languages and the imposition of European gender values and family life. Whiteness has, of course, long been an obsession in racist, colonial ideologies, which were popularly and administratively potent in the nineteenth century and had their genesis in scientific taxonomies of race, blood, and blood quantum, concepts still all too present in contemporary colonial relations.[25] When it comes to economic behaviour, there is a curious resilience in the idea that indigenous peoples who fully participate – or seek to fully participate – in market economies are somehow less authentic, that they have lost defining skills and the knowledge needed to prosper "on the land" and that this participation has somehow led to a loss of spirituality or customary knowledge about arts or technologies.[26]

Assumptions about who aboriginal people are figure greatly in how scholars have represented G̲a'ax̲sta'las. To work from them is to erase the realities (however vague they are today) of those born into life on the nineteenth-century "frontier," which was then already a marginal space of intermarriages, mixed economies, and conflicting political projects. Jane Cook's social, economic, and cultural context was overlooked by researchers more interested in what occurred before colonialism than what happened during it. In the face of accelerating colonial control, when the possibilities for livelihood depended on the ability to respond and cope socially and politically, assertions about authentic ways of being were inadequate. Researchers did later investigate processes of change but, ironically, it was during G̲a'ax̲sta'las's time (1870-1951) that they were collecting "data" that would contribute to a frozen, authentic image of Kwakiutl being.

A concept of Kwakiutlness emerged in anthropological works about Kwakwa̲ka̲'wakw peoples and places. This quintessential identity first appeared in Helen Codere's introduction to the edited works of Franz Boas.[27] In it, she refers to the "un-Kwakiutl life of a commercial fisherman," a statement that today would strike many as incredible. She was writing about George Hunt's refusal to work for the canneries, thus fashioning a figure who refused to participate in that economy and was instead commissioned to collect, compile, and preserve a record of Kwagu'ł life alongside Franz Boas. Hunt also translated for Department of Indian Affairs officials, served as interpreter on naval vessels, and translated for the missionary Alfred Hall and for provincial courts in Victoria.[28] As Franz Boas's lifelong collaborator, Hunt can be credited with generating the bulk of Boas's data, and Codere thought he epitomized Kwakiutlness.[29] As she notes, Boas and Hunt focussed almost exclusively on "non-Europeanized, traditional Kwakiutl culture."[30] In their careful observance of this protocol, their published work did not include the dramatic processes of change they were witnessing and that were taken up by subsequent generations of scholars, Helen Codere among them.[31]

G̱a'a̱xsta'las also appears in Helen Codere's introduction to *Kwakiutl Ethnography*. She describes "Mrs. Stephen Cook" as "a formidable super-missionized woman who was a matriarch of a large household, lay preacher and interpreter of the Bible, and a person of great influence among the Indian women of Alert Bay. She was dead set against all Indian ways, none of which she knew much about."[32] Boas worked with Jane Cook in 1931, during his last journey to 'Ya̱lis.[33] Retreading Boas's fieldwork path, Codere visited his early informants, who offered anecdotes about him and comments about G̱a'a̱xsta'las. Codere included these comments in her introduction, quoting another line that has haunted G̱a'a̱xsta'las's descendants for decades: "She talked our language just like a baby."[34] Like all signs of cultural authenticity, lack of knowledge of one's own language figures prominently in disparaging comments. The barb is particularly sharp, directed as it was at an individual who was an official interpreter.

Helen Codere's introduction was the first thing that Jane Cook's great-granddaughter Nella Nelson wanted to speak about when we met: "It really affected a lot of us. And maybe I got triggered so much because, when I was doing work for my degree, it was coming at me all the time, in those kinds of comments, in books, just studying it ... I think it's important just quoting from that continuous record. Boas's book – *Kwakiutl Ethnography* – I think it may be in italics at the beginning of the book. It's in his foreword. So, I'm thinking, that's probably the first way that that comment was recorded." Having studied anthropology, taught First Nations histories, and now having a leading role in First Nations education in the province, Nella is well aware of the social legacies of published representations.

That G̱a'a̱xsta'las spoke Kwak̓wala fluently is acknowledged by family members and by other residents of 'Ya̱lis. Thirty years after the publication of *Kwakiutl Ethnography,* linguist Judith Berman examined Boas's work and questioned Jane Cook's language incompetence, suggesting that Boas and Hunt had focussed more on ceremonial forms of Kwak̓wala, forms spoken at feasts and potlatches, rather than on the everyday language then spoken in the community.[35] Likewise, Charles Briggs and Richard Bauman suggest the Boas-Hunt collaboration was characterized by an urgency to collect the most "archaic" forms of expression.[36]

These published comments about G̲a'ax̲sta'las continue to haunt her descendants. The statement that "she was dead set against all Indian ways, none of which she knew much about" resonates loudly with those who experience stigma. It builds on assumptions about Christian conversion that set Kwakwa̲ka̲'wakw society somehow outside of history. William Wasden Jr., who travels the Coast a good deal, performing songs and dancing, told me: "There's a lot of people in the tribes that really have a lot of respect for her, and you keep seeing this very ignorant comment constantly being published. It kind of wears on you as a family, but to me it's just words. I know the difference of what I've been taught about her. You hear, 'Oh, they were the one's ratting on people for jail,' and stuff like that. That's why it's important for me for this book to come out, because I hear things. There's a lot of people that talk really well about her, too. You know, that she did a lot of good things for the people. And what a lot of our people are in denial about is what the potlatch became, why she went against it." As a composer of oral traditions, a researcher of Northwest Coast scholarship, and a student of tradition, G̲a'ax̲sta'las's great-great-grandson is familiar with the history of ceremonial forms.

Like Chris Cook and Randy Bell, William Wasden Jr. is also a descendant of the highly ranked Hunt family from Tsax̲is (Fort Rupert). Although they are "well looked after" culturally through the Hunt line, these men also reckon descent through G̲a'ax̲sta'las to an original ancestor. Randy Bell stated this succinctly: "I think this is true for a lot of Cooks – my grandmother was from the Hunt family, who are very traditionally strong, who maintained their cultural identity in the Big House. And our Cook side was never recognized and was always looked upon as something not positive. So, it was a real catch-22, and it was always a split for me. I was split in half between my grandparents." Negative portrayals of G̲a'ax̲sta'las affect her descendants regardless of their standing in the cultural realm.

Given anthropologists' attention to confidentiality, it is difficult to understand Codere's choice to name and describe an individual and then to publish opinions about her expressed by other members of her community. But Codere wrote at an important moment of cultural revitalization for Kwakwa̱ka̱'wakw peoples, a context quite removed from that within which Boas worked, one that called authenticity into the service of decolonization.[37] It is also relevant that the comments were offered by descendants of George Hunt, who would have known that Jane Cook had publicly expressed her opinion that he had "made up lots of new words."[38]

These portraits remain on the record, in what is perhaps *the* classical text of Kwakwa̱ka̱'wakw ethnology, read widely and praised by many people with whom I work. Books by disciplinary pioneers such as Franz Boas carry authority. His often-verbatim Kwak̓wala and English accounts are as close as people will come to their nineteenth-century progenitors. Franz Boas and George Hunt generated a valuable body of work that is consulted and referenced by Kwakwa̱ka̱'wakw people, but it is important to decentre their texts, to interrogate silences and assertions that may reflect more than the serendipity of research practices.

Kwakiutl Ethnography is difficult to avoid, and so too is its wounding portrayal of G̱a'a̱xsta'las. When Wedłidi Speck spoke about Helen Codere's introduction, he spoke from the position of a community organizer and a counsellor long engaged with the challenges of contemporary indigenous identity. He named a shift in community consciousness that occurred around the time the text was published, fifteen years after Jane Cook's death: "There's a lot of contradictions in peoples' criticisms of the old lady. For instance, all of them ... belonged to the Women's Auxiliary, which is the Anglican Church group. But see, that's what they did then. They were really moving in that direction, but then, at some point, younger leaders said, 'We're going to stop that and reclaim our culture.' They began to deny where they were, rather than saying, 'Yeah, we got sucked in too. Yes, we agree with you, we made mistakes, and we need to save the culture.' But what's happened is they've said, 'Oh yeah, that woman is a bad woman, da, da, da.' When they challenge her in the language, I think they feel a level of betrayal and hurt because they wouldn't have seen the old lady's letters or anything like that. They would have listened to her, and she would have spoken directly to their face, and they were afraid to confront her." Wedłidi described a gradual turn in the late 1950s away from the Anglican Church as a location of social solidarity toward a political movement to revitalize cultural activities.

What really stands out in Codere's description of Jane Cook is her engagement with Christianity. Indeed, there is little beyond that ascribed to her. Since the 1920s, when they began conducting their own fieldwork, anthropologists have had an uneasy relationship with missionaries. Alongside early disdain for lost authenticity was an interpretation of Christian conversion that flattened the motivations of culturally and biographically diverse people. Nuances of identity are rarely suggested in the bulk of anthropological and historical texts, in which Christianity is represented as the inauthentic opposite of the "traditional" person.

While early anthropology was set in the context of salvage, later works described societies within shifting historical and political contexts. During decolonization struggles from the 1950s to the 1970s, anthropology's relationship to colonial authority became explicit. The discipline's monopoly on working with colonial "others" was challenged by non-European activists and scholars.[39] By the late 1980s, anthropology had skidded into the slippery terrain now known as the crisis of representation. Characterized by calls to be attentive to the researcher's position (reflexivity) and to deconstruct power, researchers focussed their attention on their own authority, on the ways anthropologists, as writers, had actually created portraits of seemingly static, self-contained "cultures."[40] As Aldona Jonaitis wrote in 1991: "We now realize that such romanticizing of the 'genuine' Native person, immune to historical forces, coupled with the refusal to accept as 'Indian' cultural features that draw some elements from the dominant society, is tantamount to separating Native peoples from the common experience of all humanity, in effect, to dehumanizing them."[41] The focus turned to political identities rather than the multiple social positions generated by capitalism, colonialism, and indigenous resurgence.

In seeking to dismantle authenticity, Northwest Coast scholars focussed critical attention on George Hunt.[42] His great-granddaughter Gloria Cranmer-Webster spoke about this trend: "It ... annoys me when I hear graduate students or young anthropologists speaking at conferences and pointing out *yet again* that George Hunt was not Kwagu'ł, that his mother was from Alaska and his father was white. I mean, like this is some newly revealed secret? *We* always knew *[laughs]*." Rather than reproducing early Boasian types,anthropologists now challenge Boasian authenticities.

Christianity and conversion, though, are relatively new frontiers in anthropological analysis. Contemporary feminist and postcolonial scholars have taken on, as Bronwen Douglas suggests, "the need to problematize the romantic secularism that slights indigenous women's engagements in apparently banal Christian settings ... because they seem to advance ... missionary, male, and national agendas of conversion, domestication, and modernization, rather than empower women."[43] John and Jean Comaroff also identify the "murky business" of defining behaviour in the context of conversion and early colonialisms.[44] Within what they call the colonial "argument of images and messages," conversion, they say, generated new "forms of experimental practice," including political expressions.[45] By contextualizing G̲a'ax̲sta'las's activities, we hope to complicate ideas about identity well forged in scholarly and popular imaginations, to challenge conventions that have kept Christian and traditional social worlds separate from histories of anticolonial resistance.

Anthropologists have recently turned to documenting acts of resistance, to "highlight[ing] the presence and play of power in most forms of relationship and activity."[46] But as Sherry Ortner writes, few "go the whole way." We must recognize that within local worlds, people have "their *own* politics – not just between chiefs and commoners ... but within all the local categories of friction and tension," gender, age, religion, and so on. To ignore these tensions is in some way to "sanitize politics."[47] Our work should be read within the context of the debates and concepts that now surround resistance studies.[48] Although all historiographies are to some extent also salvage projects, contemporary works must also seek to address change through "the restless operation of both internal dynamics ... and external forces," to explore how knowledge is produced, to be conscious of erasures and current realities that inevitably shape our re-presentions of the past.[49]

Conscious of not portraying indigenous peoples as victims, scholars emphasize the enduring history of struggle against colonial oppression. But have we perhaps favoured a kind of David and Goliath backstory, one that overlooks the more nuanced responses and coping strategies used by people who acted *within* dominant structures of power?[50]

Agency in the Archives: Making Northwest Coast History

> *Agency is never a thing in itself but is always part of a process of ... the making and remaking of larger social and cultural formations.*
>
> – *Sherry Ortner,* Anthropology and Social Theory[51]

Harry Whitehead asks how it is that "individuals evolve into iconographic specters, haunting anthropological literature with an existence of their own; an existence which comes to relate little or not at all to their actual lives."[52] He refers to George Hunt, but a similar question must be asked about representations of Ga'axsta'las. As authors from other disciplines continued to reproduce iconographic descriptions of Ga'axsta'las, the binaries of authenticity persisted.

The work of historians needs also to be read through shifting scholarly approaches, most especially explorations of the archive that seek evidence of indigenous acts of resistance. Archives have long been recognized as "contested sites of power," as "dynamic technologies of rule which actually *create* the histories and social realities they ostensibly only describe."[53] But habits of archival reading also shape dominant narratives about the past. Advising scholars to "allow for different kinds of historical evidence," Ann Stoler warns us that our often selective search for colonial excesses may unwittingly silence other readings.[54] Such is the case here. Our work also engages deeply with the colonial archive, seeking ways to describe Ga'axsta'las's will to action within complicated political situations. Throughout our work, her descendants display a sharp eye for "tracking the effacement of archival traces and imposed silences" surrounding their ancestor.[55] Describing the Department of Indian Affairs correspondences known as the Potlatch Papers, Christopher Bracken writes that they "transmit the arguments and counterarguments, the errors and corrections, the recommendations, hatreds, and resistances of a whole canon of minor authors."[56] Within this fertile collection are the minutiae of administrative memos and the official bulletins and writs that preceded laws. Given the detail in these records, it is surprising to note the remarkable similarity in scholars' descriptions of Ga'axsta'las.

In Douglas Cole and Ira Chaikin's *An Iron Hand upon the People* (1990), Jane Cook is described as a "vigilant Native opponent of the potlatch" whose position on marriage throughout the tenure of the ban (1875-1951) is documented closely.[57] They write that she had a "white father," that she was raised by Reverend Hall's wife, and that "in 1891, she had married Stephen Cook, another half-blood, who had been educated in Victoria, Metlakatla and Alert Bay by Hall."[58] They also quote from the often-cited letter of 1919 in which Ga'axsta'las criticizes "the custom." "No missionary could have expressed the view with more sincerity or personal feeling" they concluded. Ga'axsta'las's motivations are seemingly transparent.[59] Their history of the potlatch ban is a close archival reading of the social responses and political moralizing surrounding the imposition of colonial law. They discuss governance through considerations of cultural relativism and its chilling counterpart – the imposition of nineteenth-century European values.[60] Importantly, though, these authors present some of the more uneasy details of conflict within First Nation societies, arguing against imagery that simply pits "white" against "Indian."[61] Subsequent works about the potlatch ban drew deeply on the recorded incidents and interpretations in *An Iron Hand.*

Later articles about the colonial history of BC and Kwakwa̲ka̲'wakw peoples reproduced Helen Codere's description of Jane Cook. (Codere was, of course, an excellent choice for historians to cite because her work was groundbreaking and occupies a noted position in anthropology.) Such is the case in a 1992 paper that examines law and agency through the now famous 1921 'Mi'mkwa̲mlis potlatch known ubiquitously as "Dan Cranmer's potlatch."[62] Tina Loo wrote that Jane Cook worked closely with Indian Agent William Halliday and again reprinted her letter to Duncan Campbell Scott.[63] Importantly though, Loo acknowledged that an individual's "motives are difficult to recover," and, citing G̲a'ax̲sta'las's own statements of 1936, concluded that she was "motivated out of a sense of frustration and marginalization within Indian society."[64] By 1936, G̲a'ax̲sta'las had already been involved for several decades in the struggle for aboriginal rights and for Kwakwa̲ka̲'wakw women's right to exercise choice in marriage.

In a later published discussion about colonial representation, the authors introduce Jane Cook as a woman of "mixed parentage ... raised by a Euro-Canadian missionary couple."[65] They quote Helen Codere's description and follow it with the powerful statement that Jane Cook's "efforts cannot be seen as attempts to reform Kwakwa̲ka̲'wakw society, but rather to destroy it."[66] Such portrayals reinforce a one-dimensional image of Kwakwa̲ka̲'wakw society that overshadows G̲a'ax̲sta'las's commitment to other aspects of Kwakwa̲ka̲'wakw well-being. By the mid-1990s, G̲a'ax̲sta'las had become a character whom scholars were able to conjure up as the personification of cultural breakdown.[67]

Writing about colonialism is politically charged, and scholars well attend to debates surrounding resistance and representation. Implicit in these debates in the 1990s was what Douglas Cole and J.R. Miller referred to as an "almost orthodox" interpretation that reproduced the binary of colonized-colonizer set in the bedrock of victimization and power.[68] The discussion is an important one for scholars who seek, on the one hand, to portray the devastating effects of colonial power and, on the other, to not propagate images of essentialized, authentic subjects.[69] Historian Jennifer Brown suggests a route through this quandary: "One means of self-correction," she writes, "is to situate as precisely as possible, in time, space, and context, all those whose voices we present. The more precisely we grasp who spoke when and why, and to whom, under what circumstances, and on whose behalf, the better equipped we are to analyze both the messages and their media."[70]

Subsequent scholars did seek to contextualize Jane Cook's actions and words by looking to specific political and social situations. In *Kwakwa̲ka̲'wakw Settlements* (1994), geographer Robert Galois describes G̲a'ax̲sta'las as "a mixed-blood woman raised by missionaries and married to a leading Nimpkish."[71] His description, in part, serves to explain why she was not only translating but also testifying on behalf of the 'Na̲mg̲is before the McKenna-McBride Royal Commission, in 1914. Galois's gazetteer is a layered compilation of information from several sources that reflects "adjustment and persistence, change and continuity."[72] It represents a kind of raw memory of geographical inhabitance, one that describes resilience *and* subordination and breaks with the pattern of either/or representations found elsewhere.

Margaret Whitehead's "A Useful Christian Woman," also published in 1994, describes the complicated positions of First Nation women who were Christian converts and active proselytizers within early Protestant missionary movements in BC. Jane Cook is portrayed in some detail, but Whitehead follows G̲a'ax̲sta'las's transcribed words through Anglican Church documents. She prefaces her use of archival materials with a warning about the hazards of interpretation. Ethnocentrism and "self-serving rhetoric" surely did shape materials written by church and colonial officials, as did their inattention to and lack of access to women's cultural worlds. Perhaps less evident, though, are the problems inherent in crosscultural translation pertaining to language, the role of interpreters, and the difficulty of reading across symbolic and cultural codes.[73] Concerning G̲a'ax̲sta'las, Whitehead attends closely to her testimony at the Special Meeting on the Potlatch in 1936. Unlike other authors who cite the record of this meeting, she tackles Jane Cook's status, describing her as a "Metisse" woman of high rank, a wife, and a mother.[74] As she notes, customary expectations regarding rank and gender are important dynamics in evaluating the positions of women on the Coast. Whitehead assesses how First Nation women were useful to the "civilizing" mission as role models, translators, and advocates, but her article works against assumptions that they were "passive recipients of Christianity."[75] Nor could it be said that women in Northwest Coast societies were firmly here or there in any simple binary of conversion, for as Whitehead shows, although many women who were early converts suffered the social stigma of marginalization, some also shared in the internal transmission and celebration of indigenous aspects of their cultures. They were also often politically engaged.

G̲a'ax̲sta'las's granddaughter Christine Zurkowski politicized Christianity when I spoke with her about her grandmother: "She was a tremendous believer – she was a tremendous Christian her whole life – to me, that was what motivated her. That motivated her into mercy and justice, because that's what Christianity is – mercy to have justice. And she was a woman who was motivated!" Others also suggested to me that, alongside the devastation wrought by the imposition of Christianity, missionaries encouraged the politicization of indigenous voices, and they publicized them. "I think the one thing she always felt bad about was that she was more involved with the community and maybe not so much with her more immediate family. That happens to a lot of people when they belong to the world ... and the ones at home." Christine's words petered out, suggesting that her grandmother was not the only one to pay a price for speaking out.

As Christine's brother George Cook told me, that toll eventually extended to Jane Cook's reputation in the larger community: "Granny was not really, in my mind, wasn't really liked in the village. I don't know, maybe because she was very outspoken. And yet, when anything went wrong in the village, she was always the one who they did call on. She was always there with the people. And so this is the kind of legacy she would leave behind – just knowing how much work that she did. She worked right up to the end." G̲a'ax̲sta'las certainly adhered to a model of labour and values that fit well within Christian tenets, but her story is complicated by familial circumstances and events that have escaped public attention. The scholarly project's tendency to portray general colonial processes often obscures the particularities of cultural expectations and 'na̲'mima relations so important in contextualizing G̲a'ax̲sta'las's actions.

Following John and Jean Comaroff, many scholars currently understand colonialism as a "plurality of forms and forces shaped by political, social and ideological contexts among colonizers and encounters with the colonized."[76] They call for consideration of historical and culture-specific contexts within which individuals and groups assess available options and opportunities. *Standing Up with Ga'axsta'las* depicts a history of activism, at times a divisive force within communities. Our collaboration revisits nineteenth- and early twentieth-century circumstances in which individuals could vie for power both through cultural channels and through alliances with colonial agents. We seek to understand the shifting contexts of gendered realities for women who negotiated rank, Christianity, customary male authority, and economic options.

Narrating from the Villages: Word Memorials

> *The idea of recording oral accounts to store in archives for future analysis ignores the way their social meaning is linked to how they are actually used to discuss contemporary events.*
>
> – *Julie Cruikshank et al.,* Life Lived Like a Story

The literature and scholarship written or narrated by Kwakwaka'wakw individuals themselves sit apart from the general goal of contextualizing colonialism but never outside of its harsh reality. Several of the early works were crafted in the genre of life history research. Life history research draws from the tension between history and living memory. As a method, it is riddled with questions about subjectivity (personal bias), interpretation, and translation – across cultures, from the oral to the textual, and within boundaries set by disciplinary interests.[77] As highly collaborative works, life histories are mediated by the perspectives of their editors, who are themselves embedded in particular visions of lives – in theoretical vistas and cultural terrains – that slant and order their subject's narratives. Early anthropologists saw individual lives as important for what they said about "culture." Personal motivations, social marginality, and creativity were problems without formulated questions. Feminist approaches to life history focussed on gender, diversity, and shifting subjectivities. They examined the relationship between imposed constraints and individual agency (the ability of someone to act).[78] Within a growing body of work that explores alternative forms of knowledge production, life history work that is consciously collaborative highlights collisions among differently ordered histories, cultural epistemologies (knowledge about what is "true"), and protocols for narrative.[79]

Life history work with Kwakwaka'wakw men began in the 1940s, when the psychological orientation of the "culture and personality school," which was interested in socialization, sexuality, and cultural adaptation, shaped interpretive frameworks. In 1941, Clellan Ford edited *Smoke from Their Fires,* a work that documents the life story of Charles Nowell, a contemporary of Jane Cook. Later, James Sewid worked with James Spradley to record details of Sewid's life in a book titled *Guests Never Leave Hungry* (1969). In their introductions and footnotes, Ford and Spradley focus on acculturation (the influence of outside forces), particularly how Nowell and Sewid negotiated and maintained "traditional" roles and customs in the face of large-scale change. Ford referred to Nowell as a "cosmopolitan," a lively personality who lived through an era of great "adjustment" among a people he described as "the remnants of a once powerful nation."[80] Like others of his generation, Charles Nowell was a culture broker who worked as a translator in colonial arenas and worked for missionaries, museum collectors, and canneries. Over twenty years later, Spradley worked closely with James Sewid's family. They provided extra material, clarified dates, and offered vital assistance translating names and songs. His work emphasized "biculturality." Spradley was intrigued by the seamless flow of identity markers in Sewid's narrative, including Christianity, participation in customary and market economies, and a full engagement with so-called traditional roles.

In *Assu of Cape Mudge,* published in 1989, Joy Inglis edited the life history of another Kwakwaka'wakw chief, Harry Assu. The absence of analytic attention to binaries of identity (so central in previous works constructed with anthropologists) stands out in this work. The foreword by Michael Ames includes a new vocabulary. Here, self-representation is "liberation" and "empowerment," and self-determination is attained by "asserting control over one's own history."[81] Understandably, to the members of a community being documented, details of lived experience are more relevant than theoretical and analytic frames imposed by outside scholars. My collaborators engaged with these texts through their sense of relatedness to families and individuals. Many are familiar with the events recounted by the narrators and have themselves experienced the legacy of the larger economic and social changes depicted.

Charles Nowell and Ga'axsta'las were both born in 1870. Given the depth of their interactions (evident in archival materials), there are surprisingly few references to her in *Smoke from Their Fires.* Instead,

Nowell mentions Stephen Cook often. Both men were educated by the Reverend Alfred Hall, and they were both sent for a short while to a school run by Bishop Ridley on the north Coast. As he narrates his adult years, Nowell formalizes his relationship with Stephen, referring to him as "Mr. Cook," the storekeeper, who ordered a coffin for his son Alfred.[82] Nowell's daughter Agnes married Jane and Stephen's son Herbert. At different times, Nowell stood as G̲a'ax̲sta'las's accuser and colleague. Their paths crossed in the official and unofficial arenas of the courtroom and church and in meetings and hearings for land claims. The importance of rank within the potlatch system is central in Nowell's narrative, evident in his recital of names and positions as they mark transitions from birth to puberty, marriage, and death. My research colleagues showed great interest in the genealogies Charles Nowell recited. A reference to the Thomas Nowell branch of the family connected the Cooks to Maligas, the youngest brother of Jane Cook's grandfather John 'Nulis. According to William Wasden Jr., a son born into the Nowell family "had the same scars as old 'Nulis when he died, so they believe it was him that came back."[83] Nowell's anecdote makes the family's lineage connection explicit. His account conveys a sense of the daily – but strangely apolitical – context of Kwakwa̲ka̲'wakw villages during G̲a'ax̲sta'las's lifetime.

James Sewid, on the other hand, did speak about his social relationship to G̲a'ax̲sta'las, whom he regarded as his godmother. "Mrs. Cook had been born in Seattle and was half-Indian and half-white. She was raised by the first missionary, Rev. Hall. She used to preach in the church in our language as well as interpret what the minister was saying by translating it into the Kwak'wala language."[84] James Sewid moved from 'Mi'mkwa̲mlis (Village Island) to 'Ya̲lis around 1920. His accounts come alive with the personalities and situations that animated colonial officials and other village members as they struggled not only with poverty and waves of colonial legislation but also through everyday losses and joys, including the internal politics surrounding rank.

When speaking about *Assu of Cape Mudge* (1989), members of the Cook family mentioned Jane Cook's daughter-in-law Nellie Cook and her relationship to the Assu family. Chief Billy Assu, Harry Assu's father, raised Nellie in Cape Mudge until she was brought to St. Michael's Residential School in 'Ya̲lis at age five. Nellie Cook's grandmother was Billy Assu's mother's sister. Her father, George Hamilton, was from the Comox people.[85] Family members told me stories about

Billy Assu's stays at the Cook family house. The warm friendship intrigued them, given Assu's early potlatching activities and his arrest for participating in the 1921 potlatch at Village Island. But Billy Assu and G̱a'x̱sta'las shared the arena of struggle for the recognition of Aboriginal rights. Later in their lives, they both represented the Kwawkewlth Agency as members of the Allied Indian Tribes of BC.

Accounts by Harry Assu, James Sewid, and Charles Nowell fit a defined niche in life history works focussed on the experiences and positions of "big men" in indigenous societies. But rank and position also figure prominently in *Paddling to Where I Stand* (2004), the published recollections of Kwakwa̱ka̱'wakw noblewoman Agnes Alfred.[86] In the introduction, editor Martine Reid outlines Agnes Alfred's motivations, which included the following: intergenerational knowledge transmission; "set[ting] the record straight about certain facts and their consequences"; documenting her "feelings about what happened to others"; and demonstrating, "particularly to the lower classes (xamala: commoners, lower class), how knowledgable she was about her cultural and personal history."[87] Few works make so explicit the relationship between the rank of the narrator and the right to public representation. Here, the published realm is an extension of the appropriate arenas in which people make assertions about genealogical privilege.[88]

Born twenty years before Agnes Alfred, G̱a'x̱sta'las first appears in Alfred's recollections in an account of a war and slave-taking raid in 1860 against the people of Gwa'yasda̱ms (Gilford Island). Jane Cook "looked after" a man named Cariboo Jack, Alfred's grandmother's brother, who had been sold to the Haida and returned from enslavement *("u'mista")*.[89] There is a kind of ambivalence in subsequent stories about G̱a'x̱sta'las. She was evidently the primary personality in the Anglican Women's Auxiliary, to which most 'Na̱mgis women (of all ranks) then belonged.[90] When Daisy Sewid-Smith asked her grandmother Agnes what she remembered about the First World War, she mentioned the death of Jane and Stephen's son Edwin Cook.[91] But Agnes Alfred also described G̱a'x̱sta'las as "anti-p̓a̱sa,"[92] as a devout Christian whose opinions extended even to criticizing the meaning of one of Agnes Alfred's names – Woman Lost to Gambling.[93] In a footnote, Martine Reid quotes in full Helen Codere's comments about Jane Cook written thirty-eight years earlier.[94]

Paddling to Where I Stand includes an appendix titled "Prohibition of the Potlatch" in which Agnes Alfred comments on the original 1922 police report on the arrest and trial of potlatchers from the 'Mi'mkwa̱mlis celebration.[95] The book also contains an excerpt from *Prosecution or Persecution* (1979), a book written by Alfred's granddaughter and translator, Daisy Sewid-Smith. Agnes Alfred was James Sewid's mother-in-law. His daughter Daisy had assisted Spradley with his life history, *Guests Never Leave Hungry*. Her work contains the most controversial portrayal of G̱a'ax̱sta'las.

I obtained a copy of *Prosecution or Persecution* from the Xwi7xwa Library at the University of British Columbia. The front cover includes a recognition card that shows that the book had been donated to the library by G̱a'ax̱sta'las's great-granddaughter Nella Nelson. The book follows the history of the potlatch ban through legal prosecutions and imprisonments to the eventual repatriation of regalia confiscated from chiefs in 1922. There is a visceral quality to this work that invokes a difficult period of struggle, for the potlatch ban not only pitted the Kwakwa̱ka̱'wakw against colonizing powers but also generated internal divisions within and between villages and families. Sewid-Smith's work includes oral histories by elders who were arrested in 1921, archived letters, and historical analyses from local perspectives. It reproduces a sequence of letters written by Indian Agent William Halliday; by the superintendent of Indian affairs, Duncan Campbell Scott; by chiefs of the Kwagu'ł, 'Na̱mg̱is (Alert Bay), Da̱'naxda'x̱w (New Vancouver), Matilpi (Estekin), Dzawada̱'enux̱w (Kingcome), and T̓łat̓łasiḵwa̱la (Nuwitti) bands; and by "Mrs. S. Cook."

In Jane Cook's two letters from 1919 (quoted so often elsewhere), she outlines significant rites of passage associated with potlatching and briefly explains the economics surrounding bride price and dowry in Kwakwa̱ka̱'wakw marriage agreements. She argues that potlatchers will never owe allegiance to the king. As will become evident in Part VI of this book, marriage, choice, and rank figured prominently in her public opinions about the custom for many decades. The bulk of Daisy Sewid-Smith's *Prosecution or Persecution* focuses on the convictions and the imprisonment of those who participated in the 1921 Christmas potlatch.

Sewid-Smith concludes her work dramatically with the following questions: "Was it right that they should appoint Jane Cook as interpreter [at the potlatch trials] when she had more contempt for the Potlatch than [Indian Agent] Mr. Halliday? This contempt was due to the fact that she knew nothing of our culture. Though born into a Kwakiutl noble family (English father) she was raised in a convent therefore was not taught the culture. She is the interpreter that Boas refers to as 'talking like a child,' meaning she knew very little of what she was talking about."[96]

G̲a'ax̲sta'las served as an interpreter at the potlatch trials, but Sewid-Smith does not mention that she and Charles Nowell were also asked by the convicted potlatchers to "engage the counsel" for their legal defence (an odd request from those who felt so betrayed by her).[97] Although she attributes the remark to Franz Boas, Sewid-Smith revives the comment about Jane Cook made by other community members and quoted by Helen Codere. She invokes Boas as the judge of authenticity and suggests that Jane Cook's desire to subdue the potlatch surpassed even that of the Indian Agent. Like the scholars who followed her, Sewid-Smith infers that a "convent" education had deprived G̲a'ax̲sta'las of the cultural knowledge that should have accompanied her standing in a Kwagu'ł "noble family." She, like others, acknowledges but discounts Jane Cook's rank.

G̲a'ax̲sta'las's great-grandson Billy Wasden drew an explicit association between accusations of mistranslating and Jane Cook's rank. "I was old enough to form an opinion. You know, I knew the lady, and I've always said, when they talked about her lying in the trials and the testimonies, that she would sooner die than lie. She was the most honest person that ever walked the face of the earth, and I'll tell the world that. But well, you know, she comes from a very high-ranking tribe, and all of this bickering that was going on – I mean it was a way of putting people down and practically taking their place." Rank surely played into the history of allegations and the mixed commemorations of G̲a'ax̲sta'las. One must wonder, though, how these histories unfolded during the important years of early revitalization and cultural renewal.

Prosecution or Persecution, a work about social memory, names individuals and makes allegations, some of which remain. Nella Nelson offered the following remark: "When I was teaching, I used that book. When I taught history, I always put my curve in there. I'd show the book because there's some good pieces in there, but I always talk about my granny and clarify that position. I'd say, 'Remember history is his story. Whoever wrote it, it's from their perspective. And this is my perspective, and this is my grandmother, and this is what we see.' So, it always gave them the lesson that not everything they read is as it should be. When I use that, I use it in that context. But of course, other people don't have the context."

Sewid-Smith calls her book "a memorial to those who gave so much of themselves in preserving our heritage."[98] Indeed, oral and written portrayals of the attempted eradication of the potlatch, the prosecution and imprisonment of potlatchers, are fixed for Kwakwaka'wakw peoples as perhaps the most potent symbol of resistance on the Northwest Coast. In *The Struggle for Survival* (1973), Forrest LaViolette suggests that the ban on the potlatch "became a major factor in the emergence of a sense of injustice and a knowledge of what Indian status means in the contemporary social organization of British Columbia. In reaction, a sense of unity, of being Indian, emerged among those groups which found it possible to maintain vitality and continuity in their changing social system."[99] The creation of the enduring categories "potlatchers" and "antipotlatchers," categories still used in a limited way among older generations, played a critical role.[100]

Ga'axsta'las was not the only First Nation individual to support the potlatch ban. Nor was she the only person to correspond with, interpret for, or provide information to the colonial authorities. As archival materials show, people were not simply Christian or traditional, potlatchers or nonpotlatchers – categories that emerged later. Instead, people's reactions to colonial law reflected their economic needs, shifting strategies of evasion or resistance, and the ever-present pull of 'na'mima loyalties. But Ga'axsta'las and her descendants carry this burden collectively. She was perhaps an easy scapegoat given her outspoken manner and her remarkable participation as a First Nation woman in high-profile events.[101]

Beyond any grounded reasons for vilification, though, Kwakwaka'wakw individuals had little authority relative to state agents – to soldiers, Indian Agents, missionaries, police officers, Department of Indian Affairs officials, and politicians, who were armed with military, legal, and civil powers. Nor could they assert economic sway, for they constituted the labouring class within ever-expanding mining, fishing, forestry, and cannery interests. Ga'axsta'las was certainly a high-profile participant, but her (or any other aboriginal person's) ability to assert authority on state bodies requires reconsideration.

By placing Jane Cook in the context of current critical, anticolonial scholarship, we do not condone the dark legacy of colonial interference. Nor do we rationalize or celebrate conversion. Rather, we offer an alternative view from the margins of a time when lives were more complicated than is often suggested today. Although *authenticity*, *representation*, and *agency* are part of an exclusive academic language, they are more than abstract concepts with literary lives. Debates about reality, about who people are, and what they are capable of, are loaded with their meanings. Like the descendants of Lakota holy man Nicholas Black Elk, members of the Cook family are affected by the social lives of academic dialogues.[102]

G̱a’ax̱sta’las was neither a victim nor a resistance hero. She had a deliberate, but at times faltering, confidence in her actions. Any consideration of her agency must take the challenges she faced internally and those she waged externally into consideration. G̱a’ax̱sta’las challenged customary authority, and in the latter part of her life she was engaged in a struggle to indigenize herself, to be seen as a member – by other members – of her own cultural community. In the realm of colonial power, she clearly counted herself (and was counted by others) as an indigenous “agitator.”

Memory in Practice

In an instructive letter written in 1897, Franz Boas suggests to George Hunt that he should represent their book to the people in Tsax̱is as a “box in which your laws and your stories are kept.”[103] The metaphor invokes a box of treasures, a singularly potent object (and idea) in which the masks, dances, songs, and privileges transmitted through ancestors rest. Charles Briggs and Richard Bauman suggest that members of the Kwagu’ł engaged in a dialogue with Franz Boas about the meaning of his work, that they were “socialized in a process of constructing texts” about themselves.[104] Although produced initially for an external academic audience, these texts also sometimes inform internal dialogues among contemporary Kwakwa̱ka̱’wakw peoples.

Social memory is embedded in political processes shaped by variable tides of power and by the more urgent necessities of present reality. But what is forgotten? What slips into oblivion in the face of such focussed remembering? These questions fall within what I call colonial memory, that is, a more or less shared – or at least understood – universe of narrated (and silenced) stories about colonial incursion. Dominant narratives frame, to some extent, the positionalities forged by historical colonialism as well as the rapid structural shifts it imposed, but my collaborators seek to widen the possibilities carried by those narratives to include innovations, resistances, and affinities borne of colonial processes. We suggest that the urgency to remember has “quieted” notable chapters in their public story. I heard about the silences that surround “what the potlatch had become” in the nineteenth century and how G̲a'ax̲sta'las had responded to the "exaggeration" of hierarchy, rank, and ceremonial conflict wrought by colonialism in her time. I heard that remembrance has "softened" the extent of Kwakwa̲ka̲'wakw historical participation in Christianity. What has been lost in the public story of G̲a'ax̲sta'las is her intense commitment to aboriginal rights – a vast omission.

Our work explores what James Werbner describes as the "passion in, for and against memory, keeping it alive, burying or killing it, disclosing, registering, textualising and recreating it," and we understand that these processes and practices are riddled with ambiguity.[105] We present this book as a kind of standing up, as an embodiment of memory practices among members of one family. In *Standing Up with G̲a'ax̲sta'las,* family history is a container for the story of an ancestor.

"Standing up – to me, it's like the family has been in shame. I think we've reconciled the fact that we made a choice about Christianity, and maybe some people feel that it wasn't our choice. Maybe some people feel that the cultural way of the potlatch was utopian, and on and on it goes ... We've journeyed around a void, and in that void we've researched, we've struggled, we've bitched, we've complained, we've done all this stuff. And now emerging is a new beginning, and I think that writing a book to tell someone's story is like an affirmation. 'Yes! I've made that choice.' This is what I mean by standing up. I'll crawl first, but I'll stand tall in the summer. As a family we need to do that." Wedłidi Speck suggests that G̲a'ax̲sta'las's descendants are engaged in a dialogue about their collective identity that must confront her choices. Standing up is a public act – in the Big House and in the literary realm.

PART II
Du<u>k</u>w<u>a</u>'es<u>a</u>la (Looking Around on the Beach): Ancestors[1]

"'You can't stop evolution.' That's what my grandmother says. 'We've always evolved from day one. You know, we had cedar capes, and then we had blankets. Then we had material clothes, and then we had electricity, and then we had running water.' And da, da, da, da. It just keeps going on and on and on, and today it's technology. Now we have the computer knowledge, and the only thing missing is the history, just telling it in our words, our own family's words. I think that's key." Randy Bell continued, "I think that's key for a lot of our history – it's been translated so much. And the problem – it's not the fault of anthropologists or any writers – but it's been done or said so many times over, it loses the essence of the real story. You know, it's 'So and so said, that so and so said, that so and so said.' And that's what we're living. It's because 'so and so' said that! It'll be nice just to live with the fact that this is the way it was, and this is who we are, and this is where we're going."

How change is recognized, and by whom, is a contentious topic in current dialogues about rendering indigenous pasts. No one denies that culture changes or that representations of change are knotted up in past imperial desires and current colonial structures. At issue is how to represent diverse views, how to assert the right to tell one's own story using imagery, ideas, and inspirations that make sense to the teller. Although cautiously absolving anthropologists and other writers, Randy Bell identifies a problem with the "translations" of history that have built the anthropological canon on Kwakwa̱ka̱'wakw peoples. At the same time, what I refer to as the living text includes a legacy of documentation that my collaborators also respect and draw upon.

Part II draws from the anthropological canon referenced by family members to create an image of the context into which their ancestor G̱a'ax̱sta'las was born. Boasian histories figure largely. They are not quiet records of the past; they are alive in current reckonings of ceremonial rights and in the ever-occurring creative moment where ritual performance is conceived. They are used to rejuvenate the language, to teach young people how to dance and how to behave. The works of George Hunt and Franz Boas have been trawled for toponyms – for the names of sacred sites, resource and village sites so key in current land claims negotiations. Fishers and lawyers have used their maps, and community artists and cultural researchers consider their drawings and photographs important references. Like performed genealogies, written records of the past serve as tangible resources. Most notably, family members contemplate the story of change proposed by Franz Boas, Helen Codere, and others whose work records shifts in the potlatch complex that figure centrally in G̱a'ax̱sta'las's story. Turbulent shifts in gendered activities, in the role of marriage and the acquisition of ceremonial and material wealth, initially set the stage for G̱a'ax̱sta'las's focus on the custom. Her descendants speak strongly about this context of change.

Through decades of study and attention to the oral and textualized pasts of Kwakwa̱ka̱'wakw peoples, individuals come to their own interpretations. They chart a course through multiple histories and land at sites that hold some meaning to them. I worked with those considered to be family historians – not scholars of the family's history per se, but historians and scholars of culture. Among these historians is Randy Bell, noted for his knowledge about the history of the maritime fur trade and the grease trail connecting Mowachaht and Kwakwa̱ka̱'wakw territories. Similarly, George and Wedłidi Speck, Kelly-Anne Speck, and William Wasden Jr. are respected as speakers on customary matters, on political histories and social realities.

In our dialogues about the past, George Speck spoke at length with me about what he called the "golden age," an ironic reference to a popular way of speaking about precolonial life that breaks collective history into defined and knowable befores and afters. His term invokes remembering and forgetting while acknowledging the complexity of how social history is shaped by postsettler realities. Similarly, George's brother, Wedłidi Speck, talked with me about what he called the "canonization of culture," a tendency to "filter" what is remembered and celebrated about the past "because you don't know your place in it." He used the Kwak̓wala word *t̓sa̱ndika* (fear or aversion) to characterize a selective celebration of the cultural past.

I return continually to this act of trying to locate one's "place in the past" – a seemingly common conversation in the international landscape of reconciliations, repatriations, compensations, and truth-seeking commissions. Across the colonial divide, most parties struggle. They defend, contextualize, or vilify the actions of their grandfathers. They ache for access to that past through startlingly different channels, including oral traditions, written histories and memoirs, archival traces, blurred representations, traditionalized social theories, and practised traditions. The problem with finding one's place in the past is that, for many, it affects where and how you stand in the present.

G̱a'ax̱sta'las's great-granddaughter Kelly-Anne Speck acknowledges the risk of depicting historical change in the politicized present. "When you see the kind of social upheaval that was happening as a result of the losses of hundreds of thousands of people, then any society that's going to survive on any level – you start making decisions that seem like the thing to do at the time. And it doesn't necessarily reflect old traditional values. I think there's a fear that people have that if we look honestly, or comprehensively, at what was going on at that point of time, it will somehow undercut a legitimacy of a claim we have from then going forward. I guess people have some reason to be cautious about that. But within that same time period and within [early] documents is also, if you will, the evidence that exists that, in fact, these claims do transcend that period of time, that, notwithstanding some of the social breakdown that was obviously happening, the community found a way to kind of meld together to survive through a mishmash of different societal values and come out the other end. So, I guess, maybe it's generational. I'm not as afraid to say, 'Okay, things weren't perfect.' How could they possibly be when you describe for anybody complete social structures and families, entire segments of communities, disappearing? How could that not have an impact?"

Part II offers impressions of life in Northwest Coast communities as imagined by G̱a'ax̱sta'las's descendants or as presented in on-the-spot descriptions by colonial agents or selected secondary sources written by Northwest Coast scholars. These impressions provide a sense of how memory is embedded in genealogical knowledge or, at the very least, how it finds meaningful expression in family history, in what Boas called *ninəwiləm.* "When the old people tell stories, it's not sequential," Wedłidi Speck once told me. "It goes off in all directions." So, too, our work reflects the many directions that people have taken into their past.

These narratives describe a period of immense change in the late nineteenth century, a period of intensifying European settlement, military coercion, legal constraint, and missionary influence. A time of frontier instability, the period was undeniably chaotic to First Nation peoples long accustomed to political and cultural autonomy – even within the fur trade. Gaps in early archival records and silences among some of Ga'axsta'las's descendants made our task more difficult. What follows is a collage of views from oral histories, written sources, and family commentaries on topics pertaining to early times in Tsaxis, 'Yalis, and along the Coast as they intersect with the known and surmised circumstances of Ga'axsta'las and her predecessors. Although sometimes hazy, traces of this past are contained in photographs, stories, and textual materials. The oft-told circumstances that surrounded the meeting of Jane's mother, Gwayułalas (Emily Whonnock), and her father, William Gilbert, is one example. We include key turning points in Emily's life, narrated by her descendants, alongside glimpses of William Gilbert found in archival repositories. Family members also vividly recount the circumstances surrounding the trek made by Stephen and his mother, Kwak'waballas, from the West Coast.

Hutłilala (Pay Attention): Genealogies

"She was from Fort Rupert."
"She was Kwagu'ł. Granny was from there."
"And he was from the West Coast – Papa was. We used to call him Nage. Yeah *[turning to Pearl Alfred]*, your granny's name was Ga'axsta'las. It's when people go for breakfast; that's what it means."
"Ga'axsta'las, you 'go Ga'axsta'las.' We say it when we were up for breakfast."
"Yeah, her name was Ga'axsta'las."

As she spoke, Ethel Alfred sat surrounded by framed photographs of her family – grandchildren and great-grandchildren dressed in graduation gowns and in button blankets. One photograph had been taken on her ninetieth birthday. Encircled by four generations, she spoke about where Ga'axsta'las "was from," mentioning key markers of

Kwakwa̱ka̱'wakw identity – village, tribe, and name – each a cue to 'na̱'mima membership.[2] But Ethel also spoke about her deeds, about the time when her family was away working in the canneries and "something bust" inside her. G̱a'ax̱sta'las sat with her in hospital every night for four nights. "I never heard anything bad about Granny in the years that she was with us," Ethel said. "She really broke a lot of hearts when she passed away." Like others who wish to commemorate G̱a'ax̱sta'las, Ethel, almost in the same breath, included Stephen Cook or "Papa," as he was known. Married for sixty-three years, until Jane's death in 1951, Jane and Stephen's partnership represents a solidarity that their descendants consider crucial to G̱a'ax̱sta'las's activities.

Formal Kwakwa̱ka̱'wakw introductions to individuals generally begin with a recital of their place in lineage relationships, particularly if they are *noxsola* (of noble lines). In what follows, family members introduce Jane; her husband, Stephen; and their predecessors. Those fluent in Kwakwa̱ka̱'wakw social organization hear in genealogies a sounding of villages tied to names, names tied to marriages, marriages tied to births, births tied to rights and prerogatives, and rights and prerogogatives tied to stories, crests, masks, dances, and songs – also called treasures. Each tribe or village includes several 'na̱'mima (clans), and each 'na̱'mima comprises several lineages. The core lineage of the chiefly line, directly descended from a first ancestor, holds the 'na̱'mima together. Other lineages in the 'na̱'mima descend from younger branches of the family (not first-born children), or they are associated through marriage – in their mother's or their father's line – to the extended family of the noxsola (nobility).[3] This is the formal scheme of rank.

The seemingly endless possibilities for strategizing descent often overwhelm those new to Kwakwa̱ka̱'wakw social organization. But these configurations are precisely what make genealogies critical. They are the raw knowledge from which Kwakwa̱ka̱'wakw people claim their position within ceremonial and, to some degree, social society. Individuals of noble lines have a procession of ranked names that indicate the lines of ancestry through which they reckon descent. These reckonings are an essential protocol in feasts or potlatches, where family members display the treasures to which they have rights as members of particular lineages. In the Big House, individuals literally embody their ancestor. They inhabit a name that has flowed through the generations before them. While feasting or potlatching, they declare which ancestral line of names and associated privileges they are "coming through." G̱a'ax̱sta'las's descendants trace her line

Photo 2 "Frame of a house erected in Dzawadi (Knight Inlet) by (Jane Cook's ancestor) Wanukw of the Wa'wa̲liba'yi clan of the 'Walas Kwagu'ł – when he gave a grease (*t'lina* oil) feast to all the tribes. The post to the right represents Wa̲liba'we', who is carrying the copper 'Maxt̓sola̲m (Cause of Shame), which was sold and the price given away to all the tribes who helped in erecting the house posts. The post at left belongs to Wanukw on his mother's side. She was an U'yala'eda̲x̲w of the Hiłdzakw (Bella Bella). The figure is holding the copper Na̲ngamala (Grizzly Bear on Face), which was broken and the pieces of which were put under the four posts of the house" (William Wasden Jr.). *Photographed by Oregon C. Hastings for Franz Boas. SPC Nwc Kwakiutl NM No # Boas 00069600, National Anthropological Archives, Smithsonian Institution.*

from her grandfather (John) 'Nulis; her mother, G̲wa̲yułalas (Emily); and G̲a'ax̲ta'la̲s herself. In what follows, I work from Wedłidi Speck's tribute to Jane Constance Cook, drafted for a booklet he prepared for the Gix̲sa̲m Feast in May 2007.

The House of 'Nulis (Grandfather)

G̲a'ax̲sta'las was a noble woman of rank among the Kwagu'ł, Da̲'naxda'x̲w, and G̲usgima̲xw (Quatsino) tribes. (Wedłidi Speck's feast booklet)

That is, through her mother and her mother's parents, Jane Cook could trace descent to noble lines in each of these Kwakwaka'wakw villages. To effectively hear genealogies, one hears affiliations to village, tribe (or band), 'na'mima (clan, house, or descent group), and ranked names. These attest to relationships of descent and constitute status in a society where each village, 'na'mima, and name formally occupies a fixed rank in the social hierarchy.[4]

> Jane's mother, Gwayułalas, was the daughter and only child of Chief 'Nulis[5] of the Kukwakum [clan] and Ga'axsta'las, who was the daughter of Chief Siwit (Munday) of the Ts!o'tsena [clan] of the Da'naxda'xw [tribe]. (Wedłidi Speck's feast booklet)

The convention of names skipping a generation applied to Jane Cook, who received the name of her grandmother. Jane's mother, Gwayułalas, also carried the name of a grandparent, her paternal grandfather.

> 'Nulis's mother, Ga'gwadi, was the eldest child of Chief K̓wamk̓wax'awidi (Wanukw), who had the name Gwayułalas when he distributed property. (Wedłidi Speck's feast booklet)

So, Gwayułalas received the name of her father's maternal grandfather, a name he used when he distributed property. High-ranking individuals carry several names: a name when feasting or distributing property; names used in the secular summer season and in the sacred winter, when important ceremonials are conducted; and names acquired through membership in (sometimes several) clans, reckoned through their mother's or father's lines or through both. Jane Cook therefore also carried the names Hamdzas and 'Wadzi'dalaga through other clan affinities, though she is primarily remembered as Ga'axsta'las.[6] (Individuals from different clans may carry the same name. When village affiliation is not recorded, confusion in the historical record may follow.)

Because of the fur trade, the increasing bureaucracy of colonial administration, and missionary interventions, Kwakwaka'wakw peoples also carried English names.[7] According to Wedłidi Speck, several chiefs took the name Jack or Jim or John, all variations on the English name James. Tapping with his fingers while we spoke, he named Captain James Cook, Captain James Hanna, Captain James Strange, Captain James King – traders and explorers who had significant and sometimes intimate interactions with Kwakwaka'wakw people. Jane Cook's grandfather's English name was John 'Nulis, but he also carried several other names. Her mother, G̲wa̲yułaḻas, was known also as Emily Whonnock, a variation on one of her father's ancestral names, Wanukw (River Owner). John 'Nulis was a hereditary chief, usually the first-born son in a line of first-borns linked directly to the first ancestor, keeper of the 'na̲'mima myth and holder of the ancestor mask.

In a report prepared for the Kwakiutl District Council in 1990, George Speck outlined the position of chiefs: "In a numaym ['na̲'mima] every house has a Chief and each Chief is ranked according to the ordering found in the spirit world.[8] Our numaym all have Head Chiefs who trace their rank back to the numaym ancestors who were themselves, before they became human, Head Chiefs in the spirit world. The Sub-Chiefs, and below them, the commoners, similarly traced their positions back to the positions held by their ancestors in the spirit world."[9] Head chiefs were endowed with supernatural power. They held responsibility for tending the reciprocal relationship between humans and the natural world, as renewed through potlatching during the Winter Ceremonial:

> Every numaym has a story that relates how and where its first ancestors became human. At the locations where the ancestors became human, the plants, animals, birds and fish agreed to allow the ancestors to capture and use them. In return, the ancestors promised to show them the proper respect through rituals such as prayers of thanksgiving and the Winter Ceremonial (i.e. feast and potlatches). Our ancestors were also required to use the proper harvesting and processing methods. In other words, humans had to prove to the animals, birds, fish and other beings of nature that they would honour their ritual needs. If humans failed to do so ... [they] would refuse to give themselves up for human use.[10]

Little is recorded from the house of 'Nulis in the Boas-Hunt record of nineteenth- and early twentieth-century Kwagu'ł life. But 'Nulis appears throughout Volume 10, *The Kwakiutl,* of photographer and ethnologist Edward Curtis's *The North American Indian.* Curtis portrays 'Nulis as impulsive, quick to lead his warriors in raids against other groups. In visceral detail, collected narratives describe 'Nulis as being among the first of the "Quaguyl" to be initiated as a Hamat̓sa or Cannibal dancer, around 1864. (In a booklet prepared for the Cook family reunion in 2011, it is "old chief Wanukw" (Jane Cook's maternal great-grandfather) who received the Hamat̓sa Ceremony, in 1856, through his wife T̓łak̲wa'ił's dowry.)[11] Curtis represents 'Nulis as a giver of great feasts to challenge his rivals and as a participant in the ritualized cannibalism of the Hamat̓sa Society.[12] Reading in the present, 'Nulis's descendant Wedłidi Speck views his distant grandfather as a "man of his times." According to oral histories, raiding, rivalry feasts, and secret society activities were vital chiefly pursuits in the mid- to late nineteenth century.

In a particularly vivid description of rivalry, Mary Hunt offered researcher Julia Averkieva the following account of a grease feast attended by Jane Cook's grandfather 'Nulis.

> One Ławits'is chief gave a grease feast. When the people were in his house he distributed the grease in kelp bottles to all his guests ... Then the host broke a copper and gave a piece of it to 'Nulis a Kwakiutl from Fort Rupert. Then 'Nulis got up and told his people to go after him. They took more than 200 blankets, tore them into pieces and threw them into the fire. Q!elxa – he wanted to put the fire out, that's why he threw them in. All the Ławits'is tried to keep the fire going by pouring more and more grease in it. Sometimes they poured the grease on 'Nulis ... After the blankets were burned he called the Fort Ruperts to go with him to the beach. They took a big canoe, $200 worth, brought it in the house and put it in the fire ... Then 'Nulis brought another canoe and put it in the fire. In the end he promised to [?] grease feast, and got the Fort Ruperts to sing for him.[13]

At the time I was revising *Standing Up with G̲a'ax̲sta'las,* William Wasden Jr. had returned from a research trip to Bella Bella with what he reasoned to be a photograph of John 'Nulis and Jane Cook's grandmother G̲a'ax̲sta'las. His interpretation of the image incorporates symbols of tribal and 'na̱'mima affiliation, read through material culture.

"I went to Bella Bella," William Wasden Jr. said, "searching for connections to our history, looking for the history of old Chief Wanukw's wife, T̓łak̲wa'ił. I was honoured to meet William Houstie and Elroy White. I found out that [T̓łak̲wa'ił's father's] name is Ha̱mdzid. He was one of the most renowned chiefs on the Northwest Coast. He had wives from many nations. For my research, we went to the Quay Café, William Houstie's dad owns it. They have albums with archival photos. I was looking through one, and this picture showed up. I got this weird vibe. She really looks like Granny Cook. His headdress *[pointing to the*

Photo 3 *From left to right:* Unidentified man holding a copper, woman who is possibly Jane Cook's grandmother Ga'ax̱sta'las, and a man who is possibly her grandfather 'Nulis. *Photographer and date unknown. Courtesy of Quay Café, Bella Bella.*

man on the right] caught my eye because I've held that headdress at the British Museum. It's in the Kwakwa̱ka̱'wakw collection. It's the work of Blunden Harbour artist Johnnie Davis. It's a Gix̱sa̱m headdress, and 'Nulis was head of the Gix̱sa̱m. The one in the British Museum was a headdress like that [in the photo], with a killer whale. It doesn't have the eagle on top – which shows when someone is an Eagle Chief. This one has ermine in its mouth, that signifies wealth. So, he is definitely the head of the Gix̱sa̱m: K̓wa̱mk̓wax'a̱widi, that's Wedłidi's name. 'Nulis's blanket looks like some kind of bird. He's got a neck ring with specific ties on it, which means he had a big role in the Cedar Bark Ceremonies. The woman next to him is clearly Kwakwa̱ka̱'wakw. You can see that with the buttons on her blanket. She has gold earrings – you're entitled to wear gold if your family's given gold away. In those days, only nobility wore button blankets – not just everyone could wear them. The man to the far left could be a relation of hers. He's wearing an imitation cedar ring and a headdress with a whale.

When I was in Berlin, I saw that same headdress that George Hunt collected with the same markings, but in cedar. His staff looks like silver with a ball on the end. They're obviously dealing with a copper. They've got a ribbon tied on it to represent the *T*. They could be paying back the dowry. In those days, they paid back several times, although they look quite old. Dan Savard had a look at the photograph, and he thinks it had to be taken in Alert Bay or Fort Rupert because of the milled lumber and the window in the background. The roof looks tiled, not shingled. So, it must have been after 1850. I think this is probably Jane Cook's grandparents 'Nulis and G̱a'ax̱sta'las, the daughter of old Chief Wanukw."

As first-born children in a line of first-borns, G̱wa̱yuła̱las (Emily) and her daughter G̱a'ax̱sta'las (Jane) were entitled to the high-ranking names and positions that flowed through John 'Nulis. Conventionally, positions of high standing would be transferred in a potlatch from 'Nulis to his daughter's husband at their marriage. Later, her eldest child would receive the names and the prerogatives that accompany them.[14] In the family histories that George Hunt compiled and Franz Boas edited, there is evidence that when a chief's first-born child is a daughter, she carries the chiefly name or names of a male ancestor. As Hunt wrote, she "is socially a man."[15] G̱wa̱yuła̱las (Emily) married a European man outside of Tsax̱is, and G̱a'ax̱sta'las (Jane) later renounced "the custom" upon her marriage to Stephen Cook. Some of these names therefore fell into dormancy, while others were transferred or passed through Jane's sister, He'ma̱n'sagila̱ogwa (Annie Newman), and her brother, Charlie Newman. Charlie carried the chiefly name or "standing" of 'Nulis. Today, his grandson Ed Newman of Bella Bella is 'Nulis.

Johan Adrian Jacobsen acquired 'Nulis's mask on his 1881-82 expedition to Tsax̱is. A replica of the mask is currently on exhibit at the Museum of Anthropology, University of British Columbia.

Franz Boas and George Hunt recorded a song that accompanied the double mask of the ancestor 'Nulis.

> "A bear is standing at the river of the Wanderer who travelled all over the world;
> Wild is the bear at the river of the Wanderer who travelled all over the world.
> A dangerous fish is going up the river. It will put a limit to the lives of the people.

Photo 4 Edwin Newman ('Nulis) with third-generation 'Nulis ancestor mask, U'mista, July 2008. *Photograph by Karen Duffek. Courtesy of Edwin Newman and the Museum of Anthropology, University of British Columbia.*

Photos 5 and 6 *(facing page)* 'Nulis mask collected by Johan Adrian Jacobsen during his 1881-82 expedition for the Ethnological Museum in Berlin. According to the museum, "This mask, from a potlatch in Fort Rupert, shows the rivalry in two phases: the closed mask shows a spiritual ancestor of a Kwakiutl tribe who is angry and wants revenge on a rival. When opened, the mask shows the opposite: a friendly ancestral spirit who gives away gifts with open arms to his guests." *Courtesy of Ethnologisches Museum Berlin.*

> Ya! The sī'siul is going up the river. It will put a limit to the lives of the people.
> Great things are going up the river. It is going up the river the copper of the eldest brother of our tribes."[16]

William Wasden Jr. offered me an excerpt of anthropologist Wilson Duff's handwritten field notes held at the U'mista Cultural Centre. They include a remark by Duff about "Mrs. Cook": "It's funny – some people used to be high rank, own things – Jimmy Sewid, Moses Alfred, Henyu boys etc. – same ones are well off today – low rank people have nothing, tho' nobody stopping them its not the custom holding them down. The same as Cooks – Mrs Cook was from almost the head of Ft. Rupert – (Gōxōmogut another name for Kwixa) (inft is Walas Kwag also called tsuntsuntgaiyū – just as gwĭtála is another name for Kwag. proper)."[17]

K̲wak̲'waballas and N̲age (Stephen Cook)

Stephen Cook's mother, G̲aganapnash, was a noble woman from the House of Na'iichap (John Jumbo) among the Mowachaht people of the Nuu-chah-nulth nations. Her family refers to her affectionately as G̲aga. Born into the Na'iitch'a'da'gum'ath clan of the West Coast Mowachaht, her mother, K̲wak̲'waballas, was 'N̲amgis. Stephen Cook's Mowachaht grandfather was one of Chief Maquinna's brothers. According to Wedłidi Speck, "His grandfather's house was next door to Chief Maquinna's, on the south side of the village. Papa Cook's grandmother was 'N̲amgis. She was from the Kunosila family. Papa's mother was known (among the 'N̲amgis) as K̲wak̲'waballas, after her mother, and G̲aganapnash among the Mowachaht. She had three sisters. Two married Nuu-chah-nulth chiefs (Johnston and Savey), and one preceded her to the 'N̲amgis and married a chief among the Si'santla."

G̲aganapnash married three times. Her first marriage was to Stephen's father, John Hubert Cook, a ship's carpenter from Shaldon, Devonshire, England. According to Stephen's obituary, published in the *Native Voice* in March 1957,

> Stephen was born in Esquimalt, near Victoria in British Columbia. His mother married again, a Native, one of her own people, from the tribe

> of the Motsadakw, west coast of Vancouver Island. Later, when her second husband died, she and little Stephen accompanied her father through the trail leading to Wask's Lake, coming down the Klaanch River by canoe back to Alert Bay. Stephen on his mother's side belonged to a noble family of high rank. His clan is the Thunderbird clan, Kwanosita. He was the nephew of Chief Dan Cranmer of the Nimpkish to which he rightly belonged ... His Indian name "Nega" means mountain.

Stephen was born to G̲aga and English shipbuilder John Cook around 1870. Perhaps after John Cook's death or for other unknown reasons, G̲aga returned to her village on the West Coast, where she married a Mowachaht man and had another son.[18] According to oral histories, her husband and second son died during a tuberculosis epidemic. G̲aga's 'Na̲mgis cousin G̲wi'molas (Dan Cranmer's father) then decided that the widow and her surviving child should be brought to 'Na̲mgis territory, likely to Tsax̲is (Fort Rupert) or perhaps to 'Ya̲lis (Alert Bay), then a Nimpkish winter village.[19] According to Dan Cranmer's daughter Gloria Cranmer-Webster, "[Stephen] was quite young, so was carried on people's backs."[20] To their descendants, the story of Stephen and G̲aga's trek across the northern part of Vancouver Island is loaded with imagery. It is a story that attests to their place among the 'Na̲mgis, for Stephen was adopted into the Gĭga̲l'ga̲m clan, where he was given the name Na̲ge.

Anthropologist Philip Drucker noted two primary trade routes that connect Nuu-chah-nulth and Kwakwa̲ka̲'wakw territories.[21] The Tahsis River trail begins at the head of Tahsis Inlet (*taci,* meaning door) and extends across mountainous terrain to Woss Lake and Nimpkish Lake.[22] Commonly known as the "grease trail," Kwakwa̲ka̲'wakw traders travelled the route to Nuu-chah-nulth territories. They wore around their necks coils of kelp bladders filled with precious eulachon oil, known to the Mowachaht as *ktl!inaqsit* and to the Kwakwa̲ka̲'wakw as *t'lina.*[23]

Randy Bell traces descent from Mowachaht people through his grandmother Emma Hunt (née Billy)[24] and through his great-grandfather Stephen Cook. He has been taking young people across the grease trail since 1998: "You know back in the 1700s – as far as the records that we have – that was a ten- or eleven-day trek. It's over 185 kilometres. Even for us today, with all of the technology that we have, it's pretty physically demanding ... They travelled this, if not weekly, biweekly. But they paddled and hiked during that part of the season because the trading was so heavy ... The grease came from us, making it up in Knight's Inlet and then being transferred by bull kelp over to the West Coast. One of the most significant trades was with the Mowachaht when they were receiving guns from the Spanish, and we started acquiring them in 1792 through the trade with them.[25] Utensils and blankets – those types of things that we traded with them – became more evident in our ceremonies. That's when the initiation of having blankets instead of having cedar robes [happened]."

"And then the Hudson's Bay Company was set up in Fort Rupert. So all of those things the Spanish and English traded [were] really significant in how our nations became ranked."

"When we went to Friendly Cove, being part of the Cook family, you sit with the Maquinnas.[26] Maquinna is the top-ranked chief in Mowachaht. It's really interesting how that is."

In 2004, Randy hiked the trail with some family members, carrying grease to his relatives in Friendly Cove. "I gave it to the Maquinna family, and I gave it to the Jacks and the Johnsons. And I gave it to the three higher-ranking families than my grandmother's – not giving

Photo 7 Wedłidi Speck, Nella Nelson, and Billy Wasden at the start of their hike along the Grease Trail from Woss to Tsaxis. *Courtesy of Wedłidi Speck.*

grease to our family, of course. But every time I go over there, I always do that, just because that's my granny's traditional teaching and also re-establishing our Cook connections because of where Jane and Papa Cook come from." Randy Bell walks and studies the grease trail, regenerating relationships among the descendants of those who passed there before him.

He attended a potlatch in Gold River in 1994, where, unexpectedly, he was given the "unused" name Kwinkalas, the supernatural Thunderbird. On that occasion, he was instructed by his grandmother Emma Hunt and by Daisy Sewid-Smith that it was a name that had originated with G̲aga's 'Na̲mgis ancestor. It had been transferred to the Mowachaht and was now returning to a Cook descendant. Several other family members carry names among the Mowachaht that were transferred to them in potlatches. Bill Wasden carries the name Na'iich'a, George Cook has the name Tlao'thla'thluk, and Wedłidi Speck has the name His'stoe'qwa'aa.

Sitting in Bill's Pool Hall, a diner run by Bill Cranmer and his family in Alert Bay, one afternoon in July 2007, Randy told me that there were a disproportionate number of First Nation youth in government "care" in British Columbia. He had already approached the Ministry of Child and Social Services to develop a program on the grease trail – a site where he imagines young people could become physically strong and (re)gain a sense of belonging by awakening their cultural identity. In this moment, and so many others like it, I was reminded that looking to the future through the past is a sensibility, a way of thinking and acting that attends to the now, a time when things happen again, a moment when the past rubs shoulders with the present and the aspired-to future. Randy's research extends backward to vital trade relations that began with the maritime fur trade.

"During the earlier part of the 1700s," he told me, "when the Spanish first came, when they were trading for those furs – just to give you an idea of what the Spanish and English were selling those furs for, like, between two hundred and three hundred dollars per sea otter pelt. So can you imagine how competitive that was?" "Spanish records," he continued, "talked about the Nimpkish supplying six thousand sea otter pelts per season over a ten-year period. Even though [European traders] were getting twenty thousand sea otter pelts per year on the West Coast, it still wasn't enough. So there was a lot of wars and a lot of infighting because of money. I think, back then, grease would be, like, ten or fifteen cents a gallon, and now, today, it's between three and four hundred dollars a gallon. But also, when we compare what the Spanish and them were doing with the sea otter pelts – compared to what they were giving us – they were giving us roughly fifty to a hundred dollars' worth of blankets and making thousands of dollars. For us, that was the first time that we started getting into the thing with money. Money was introduced to us."

By 1825, over two hundred vessels traded along the Coast. Kwakwaka'wakw nations had waged, won, and lost in international warfare. Their territories expanded and shrank as sites were abandoned after epidemics or as village groups relocated to form alliances with others. Primary trade sites also shifted as the Hudson's Bay Company built forts in rapid succession: Fort Langley (1832), Fort Nisqually (1833), Fort Victoria (1833). And aboriginal traders sometimes relocated their winter villages to gain the advantage of proximity. In Fort Rupert (established in 1849), four nations moved to Tsaxis, Beaver Harbour.[27] Kwaguł people became acquainted with the folding projects of labour, land, and the colonial economy. In a 1990 report for the Kwakiutl District Council, George Speck describes an early labour strike at the coal mine that inspired the Hudson's Bay Company to found Fort Rupert. Prior to establishment of the fort,

> the Kwakwaka'wakw produced many thousands of tons of coal for the HBC ... Despite this, the Company, realizing the potential value of coal, decided it wanted to mine and sell the coal itself. With this objective in mind the Company built Fort Rupert at Beaver Harbour in 1849. With the intention of working the coal fields as well as taking advantage of the opportunity to trade, four Kwakwaka'wakw tribes totaling approximately three thousand people, settled near Fort Rupert ... The Company, ignoring the Kwakwaka'wakw's earlier claim, brought in seven Scottish miners, who started to mine the coal almost immediately ... Our people became very angry. [They] surrounded the mouth of the shaft and protested that they would not let the miners out ... unless compensation was given them for their land rights ... Finally, in April 1850, the miners' frustrations came to a head and they went on strike against the HBC ... The Company Secretary wrote to ... James Douglas. He was told that "no time should be lost in purchasing from the Natives, the land in the neighbourhood of Fort Rupert." On these instructions Douglas signed two treaties with the Kwakwaka'wakw tribes camped around the fort in February of 1851. In these treaties the tribes allowed very specific tracts of land to be used by the Hudson's Bay Company, but retained the right to hunt

and fish on unoccupied land as they had always done. These were the first and only treaties ever signed by our people.[28]

It was at Fort Rupert, as anthropologist Joseph Masco notes, that the "first recorded gift exchange of Hudson's Bay blankets and the last recorded commerce in slaves" occurred.[29] The lucrative marine trade in sea otter pelts eventually melted away, but shingles and beaver, marten, and other inland furs became the new commodities of the land-based fur trade. For some time, descendants of Jane Cook have culled references relevant to their collective histories from the voluminous record of published and unpublished texts. From the archives at U'mista, William Wasden Jr. offered me an excerpt from Wilson Duff's field notes titled "The Village of the Kwakiutl Indians." "Old man Cook's m.[other] was Nootka ♀ over here – when came over to pay back her marr.[iage], 100 men came, wearing trade blankets under ced.[ar] Bark blank.[ets] – was most trade bl. [ankets] they ever had given in those days."[30]

William Wasden Jr. fleshed out the notes: "So, they didn't like the idea that their nephew was over there on the West Coast with different Indians. You know, by himself with his mother. So, they walked the grease trail, and it was Dan Cranmer's father, Jackson, his name was G̲wi'molas, and the other was [Stephen's] other uncle, who was Dan Cranmer's father's brother, they called him Lalakanidi. So, anyways, they went to the West Coast, and they packed him home. And they say it was Jackson, Dan Cranmer's father, that packed him on his shoulders all the way home. And that's not an easy walk. But those Indians were tough then."

"So they packed him home because there was a position for him to fill amongst the Gĭga̲l'g̲am, the Thunderbird clan here. They brought him home, and his mother came afterwards, when they knew what the intentions were – and they talk about this in the notes. So she sent West Coast warriors, a hundred of them, afterwards, to come on the grease trail, and they were all wearing cedar bark capes over the woolen blankets. They came over here to distribute that in [Stephen's] name. G̲aga sent them to come and bring the blankets. So they gave it away to the Nimpkish people for Papa to have his standing as Na̲ge, which means 'mountain.' And they say it was a real big deal because they never seen that many blankets before. So the people were really amazed. He was very young. That's how that story went. So he had Na̲ge. He had that chiefly position here, Papa Cook."

Photo 8 William Wasden Jr.'s family emblem includes the Thunderbird, Christ Church in 'Y<u>a</u>lis, the *Cape Cook* fishing boat, and the grease trail travelled by Stephen Cook and his mother, <u>G</u>aga, across the mountains from Nuu-chah-nulth territory to Kwakw<u>a</u>k<u>a</u>'wakw territory. *Courtesy of the artist, William Wasden Jr.*

Inspired to create something for one of the many Cook family reunions in 'Y<u>a</u>lis, William designed what has become a kind of family emblem that incorporates imagery from that story.

Those hundred blankets given at the feast by <u>G</u>aga's Mowachaht relatives validated N<u>a</u>ge's position within the 'N<u>a</u>mgis. George Hunt wrote in 1925 that "the giving away of blankets fastens the name on the child." By way of explanation, he added: "This is like a priest baptizing children to have their names."[31]

<u>G</u>aga married again to Kwakhila, a <u>K</u>wi<u>k</u>w<u>a</u>sutine<u>x</u>w (Gilford Island) man who was staying in the house of her uncle Chief Lalakanidi. They had a son named Bert (who also carried the names Tsuxtsa'es,

Photo 9 *From left to right:* Stephen Cook (Nage); his mother, Gaga; and his brother, Bert Cook (Tsuxtsa'es). Photographed outside the house of Gĭgal'gam Chief Waxawidi. *Photographer unknown. Courtesy of Reg Cook Jr.*

Ga’axsta’las, and Likiosa), and they lived together in the house of the Gĭgal’gam clan, which belonged to ’Namgis Chief Waxawidi. According to family histories, Gaga, by her own choice, lived her later years in what those who remember her call a “shack” adjacent to Jane and Stephen’s home.

Some say that the distribution of blankets to validate Nage’s position occurred around 1879, when he was nine years old. At this time, Mowachaht and Kwakwaka’wakw peoples had survived wave after wave of disease and were subject to ever-encroaching colonial law into their lives and their ways. Missionaries had arrived to stay in villages, commercial fishing was underway, and canneries dotted the Coast.

’Lul p̓adax’idan’s ’nalx (When Our World Became Dark)

It is perhaps one of the greatest injustices that people forced to confront acts of imperial incursion mark their pasts, in part, against shifting strategies and impacts of colonialism. Some Kwakwaka’wakw people refer to the nineteenth and early twentieth centuries as the “dark years,” an era branded by loss, grief, and monumental change.[32] The dark years encompass the epidemics that began in the late eighteenth century and continued well into the twentieth century, missionary interventions, and government restrictions on traditional resource use.[33] To Gloria Cranmer-Webster, this period corresponds with the 1884 ban on the potlatch, a period during which there was a “significant loss of knowledge.”[34] Other references to Kwakwaka’wakw-relevant periods include the maritime and inland fur trades and the grim years of coercive assimilation in residential schools and through legislation.

Darkness evokes forgetting, a past difficult to retrieve in the living memory of younger generations. For this reason, many are grateful to Franz Boas and George Hunt for their attention to precolonial lifeways. But what their texts portray is the complexity of the lived circumstances of Kwakwaka’wakw nobility, as expressed by Kwakwaka’wakw nobility. Through their speeches, dream narratives, songs, and histories, these texts provide a glimpse into the vitality of collective memory in the nineteenth century and early twentieth century. Although, as linguist Judith Berman notes, Hunt’s “compositions” were not verbatim accounts, the family histories and “Native texts” he wrote reveal motivated individuals dedicated to preserving bodies of genealogical knowledge, most especially knowledge about the transmission of ranked positions.[35]

George and Wedłidi Speck question what is often left out of tellings about their collective past. They seek to describe the cultural context within which their grandmother acted and to make visible the stories that have guided how she is collectively remembered today. "The one thing about history is that we all have our own sense of what that was. Mine has been cultural-spiritual." To Wedłidi Speck, the late nineteenth century involved a turn away from the cosmological grounding in *aweetna-kula,* a state of oneness that depended on balanced interactions between human and natural realms, on taking only what one needed from the ocean and the land. "We started harvesting our resources," he said, "whether it was fish or whether it was trees, whatever it might have been, to a scale that I believe changed the relationship between our people and the land and the sea and the air ... As a result of that, we could potlatch to a greater extent and have more prestige. In other words, we began to adopt a hierarchical, nonspiritual perspective. We started to climb and think that way. We created shame, competition, and all those things started to come out of the woodwork." To Wedłidi, significant effects of the dark years were an exaggeration of expressions of hierarchy and rank and rising conflict among Kwakwa̱ka̱'wakw villages.

Many in the family began their recitation of history at this point, often referencing Helen Codere's work about change that documents what she called a process of "secularization."[36] Working from the accounts of European explorers and from Boas and Hunt's records of family histories,[37] Codere traced changes in Kwakwa̱ka̱'wakw societies before and after 1849, what she named the "Fort Rupert subperiod" of "Kwakiutl" history. Perhaps most notably, Codere found that the fixed ranking of villages, clans, and individual standing within clans was not practised before then.[38] Scholarly research has focussed on the spectacular "rivalry potlatches" and the "credit potlatch economy" during the late nineteenth century in Fort Rupert.[39] The period was characterized by ever-greater ceremonial distributions of property, by an increased frequency in potlatching, and by a secular emphasis on economic status. Epidemics had so reduced Kwakwa̱ka̱'wakw populations that individuals occupied several high-ranked positions at once. Participation in the market economy opened vacant standings to those who might not have been of noble descent but were able to marry strategically or raise the wealth to host a potlatch and purchase ceremonial wealth. Codere argued that instability in the system of finite names or positions (usually cited as 658) ocurred so rapidly that Kwakwa̱ka̱'wakw people "admitted only a few talented individuals could keep all the details straight."[40]

Wedłidi Speck turns to oral traditions to explain this historical shift. "It was chaos," he said, "I believe we returned to the very state in which we, as the Kwakwa̱ka̱'wakw people, emerged. If you look at the origins of our people, all these old myths talk about the wind blowing all the time or the tides being controlled by one particular group of wolves, and out of that chaos emerged our ancestors. At that time, they took their costumes off and became human. In my way of thinking, they wanted to rid themselves of chaos, and they wanted to find peace. [They] found the vehicle to do that – the feast, where you had to remember to be inclusive, to feed one another, nurture one another. We needed to have harmony with the world around us. Our names will do that."

Ritualized gift giving (in feasts and potlatches) marks critical status changes in Kwakwa̱ka̱'wakw society. It validates existing relationships and forges new ones in an ever-extending web of 'na̱'mima connections. As George Speck noted in 1990, "By giving, a person shows he is a moral person ... At feasts and potlatches, guests witness the inheritance of, and validate claims to, certain ranks and their accompanying privileges and property. In Kwakwaka'wakw society rank, privilege and property are all represented in the eternal names of the ancestors. These names provide social identity for the Kwakwaka'wakw in that the individual who holds a particular name has the same rank, rights and responsibilities that every holder of that name has had since the beginning of time, when that name was first created by the spirits."[41] According to many, the balance of names and gifting was unsettled greatly during the early colonial period on the Northwest Coast.

"Then came a whole new chaotic world," Wedłidi continued. "We went full circle. The time of mythic chaos was now in our world here. It was almost as if, in order for things to change – we will have to take our costumes off again to become human ... There's a lot of indicators during that time to suggest that the cosmology of the Kwakwa̱ka̱'wakw was in absolute chaos. It had gone into every ceremony and social interaction that we had."

Codere called the years from 1849 to 1921 "the potlatch period."[42] Working from Boas and Hunt's materials, and from the accounts of Kwagu'ł and 'Na̱mgis people with whom she worked in the 1950s, she developed her thesis that the potlatch became an institution for "fighting with property," a new focus for the emotion and competition previously expressed through raiding and head hunting. Ga'axsta'las's story begins during this era of conspicuous wealth, in the year often cited as marking the end of inter- and intratribal raiding. It is evident, though, that colonial violence had not abated. In 1865, in a grim display of imperial might, the colonial authorities mounted a military attack on the four Kwagu'ł tribes in the village of Tsaxis. Ga'axsta'las's grandfather John 'Nulis was arrested in that raid and taken to Victoria for trial. His daughter Gwayułalas (Emily Whonnock) accompanied him to the city, where, according to oral histories, she met and married William Gilbert, an English sea pilot and schooner captain.

Interested in the responsibilities and obligations of women in high-ranking families, I asked Gloria Cranmer-Webster about their lives in earlier times. "I suppose [she would be] learning skills from her mother, her aunts," she said, "learning how to behave properly as the oldest daughter of a chief." In the nineteenth century, it was common for high-status women in Northwest Coast societies to marry European traders. Regarding Emily's marriage to William Gilbert (Jane Cook's father), Gloria told me: "I don't know about periods or years, but it seems that, at some point, young Kwagu'ł women, a number of them were married to white men. I think of George Hunt's sisters. All of them married white men, and I don't know whether that was just coincidence, whether it was a deliberate kind of decision by the parents. Or, if it was a deliberate decision in that case, was that a deliberate decision here?" These questions have no immediate answers. Indeed, for Jane Cook's descendants (and others) there is a somewhat haunting suite of unanswered questions about European male progenitors.

In what also appears to be the way of that era, Jane's mother, Emily, married several times. When Russian ethnologist Julia Averkieva accompanied Franz Boas to Fort Rupert and Alert Bay in late 1930, she elicited women's marriage histories, attending to a pronounced oversight in Boas's work. Women spoke about being married two, three, and even four times. Sometimes, women remarried after the premature deaths of their husbands. Sometimes they remarried because the unions were understood to be "sham marriages," annulled immediately upon the transfer of property and privileges from their father to the new husband. Women who offered marriage histories to Averkieva told her that sham unions were not consummated and that daughters did not leave their parental homes. They were marriages arranged by the daughter's father to enable the transfer of positions and privileges to a chosen successor.[43]

William Wasden Jr. told me about multiple marriages: "Yeah, that's what they say, 'When a woman marries four times, it makes four men chiefs.' That's when she can wear that big hat with the painting on it called *gwa̱nt'a,* which means 'four times big in the house.'" In Averkieva's papers, marriage histories narrated by women who became *modzil* (chiefs' wives) are punctuated by accounts of the transfer of names and named coppers, dances, and songs to the groom. Narrators such as Xemaxodayugwa recall in detail the number of blankets distributed to particular clans, and they describe the feasts held among women to validate the status of the new bride. Certainly, in these early accounts, men acquired standing or rank through the medium of marriage.

"I have to honestly say that I believe women's lot was probably pretty bad in our communities, comparatively speaking," George Speck told me. "There was certainly a hierarchy, and chief's wives probably fared better than others. But we were male-oriented. Our social structures were male-dominated. Women were married between wealthy families for status. There are people that wouldn't like to hear that."

G̱wa̱yuła̱las (Emily Whonnock) and Captain Gilbert

Perhaps the most-told story among G̱a'a̱xsta'las's descendants describes how her mother met her father in Victoria following the bombardment of Fort Rupert by a naval ship. The details are included in Jane Cook's obituary, written by her niece Ellen Neel for the *Native Voice.*[44] Neel's tribute first establishes Jane Cook's line of descent and then describes the circumstances within which Émily and William Gilbert met.

> Her grandfather was hereditary chief of Fort Rupert (Tsakis); Quatsano (Koskemug); Knight's Inlet (Denahaski). When her mother was a girl of 19, an Indian who was a stranger to the Rupert tribe had committed a murder, according to the white's idea, and took refuge with the Fort Rupert tribe. A warship was sent to ask the Fort Rupert tribe to surrender him. This they refused to do, although he did not belong to their tribe. The commander demanded surrender and started to search but the native women went into the old Hudson Bay Fort, sat down, spread their native blankets and hid the chief under their

> blankets. Later some of the chiefs, including the head chief, Mrs. Cook's grand-father, were taken to Victoria to be tried and punished – Governor Douglas released them. Mrs. Cook's mother followed her father to Victoria and when there met Captain Gilbert, and they were married.[45]

Notably, Neel writes of murder "according to the white's idea." Her comments raise questions about acts that were criminalized under colonial rule and those that were sanctioned by customary law long before the arrival of warships. In this account, women play a central role in resistance against military authority, hiding the stranger within their blankets, literally "under the nose" of colonial agents at Fort Rupert. Neel likely consulted family members about this account. Or perhaps it was a well-known story recounted by Charlie Newman, his sister Annie, or G̲a'ax̲sta'las herself.

On my first meeting with Wedłidi Speck, he told me about an incident that jigsaws into the larger puzzle of the past. "See, the story has it that there were three sailors who jumped ship and went AWOL, and the captain put a bounty on them. Well, I guess we sent our warriors out and just killed them and brought them back. Then we were charged for murder. They said they had brought certain people down to Victoria. Jane Constance's grandfather was one of them that came down. So what happened was this chief – his daughter went to support him. In any case, Emily met Captain Gilbert while the trials were going on, and they married. And they went down to Puyallup, where my grandmother was born."

Customary law and colonial law once again collide in this account. This incident took place in the early 1850s, when, according to historian Robin Fisher, British sailors deserted ship at Victoria and proceeded to Fort Rupert, likely in search of gold.[46] At Fort Rupert, as one account suggests, the young Hudson's Bay Company (HBC) officer George Blenkinsop issued a reward for their capture, perhaps even stipulating "dead or alive."[47] It was common practice "to offer the Indians rewards for bringing in deserting servants. Furthermore, from the time of first contact the Indians had assumed that ordinary seamen and, later, company labourers were slaves."[48] The three sailors were killed, but there was speculation about which village was responsible. Richard Blanshard, governor of Vancouver Island, was convinced that the people of Newitte, a Kwakwa̲ka̲'wakw village on the northern coast of the island, were to blame. He sent John Helmcken, an HBC physician, to investigate. No proof was found, but officials in Victoria were determined to punish the "murderers," and the HMS *Daedalus* was sent north. When the village refused (or could not) surrender the accused, Newitte was destroyed.[49] This incident and others like it demonstrate the arbitrary implementation of justice in a context where colonial authorities increasingly forced First Nation peoples to deal with militaristic rule.

Although family histories contain several versions of what happened at Fort Rupert, the order of events regarding the meeting of William Gilbert and Emily, Jane's mother, remains the same. At the American Philosophical Society Library, Wedłidi Speck, William Wasden Jr., and I found yet another version of the story of 'Nulis's arrest, this time in Franz Boas's typed notes titled "Kwakiutl Ethnography." Someone had pencilled in names and words (they appear below in handwriting).

> About 1865 *Q!5mena'qilla* of Newettee used to send his slave G'ōxu with red cod to Fort Rupert.[50] At one time three men went to waylay him and kill him. These were Nōlis and Nūte'wak' and their brother. However this is only surmised. The slave disappeared and a complaint was made in Victoria. The *Clio* was sent to Fort Rupert. They demanded that the man should be delivered up to them. He gave them ten hours to be turned over. Captain Turner landed one hundred and fifty men and gave them once more ten hours. The people refused to give up the three men and the captain had the village bombarded. It was burned except one house which was standing near the fort. One woman was wounded by a ball. After this Nōlis delivered them – *him* selves up and nothing could be *proved* against him and he was sent back on the Otter.[51]

William Wasden Jr. revised the above notations. The name of the chief from Newittee, he said, was K̲uma'nakwa̲la, and the man with 'Nulis was Nułi'wak̲w. I asked William about the "surmised" murder of a slave recounted in these notes. "I wonder where Boas got his story from?" he said, noting that 'Nulis's rivals had also worked with George Hunt and Franz Boas. His suggestion that information offered by and about competing chiefs might be "interested knowledge" is a salient reminder that research is rarely neutral.[52]

With that qualification, William continued: "I haven't really looked into it, but it was probably a strategic move in that somebody was offended. In them days, it was quite all right in Indian law – an eye for an eye. If somebody killed someone in your family, it was quite all right to pay back, and then it's done. I wonder what the slave was doing? Maybe he was in a restricted area, or maybe he had done something on behalf of the chief to the family. If you were caught in another person's territories, you would be killed. If you were accessing resources without permission, they would just bump you off, in them days ... It's considered stealing in our culture. It would probably have been taken to a higher level if the chief that owned [the slave] tried to retaliate. They probably would have brought it to the Big House, because they couldn't war at that time."

George Speck also responded to the account in Boas's papers: "Well, first," he said, "slaves were non-people, and maybe he wanted to fish?[53] Or maybe the fish was caught outside of Newittee territory? There's lots of stories like that. The first story I heard about the Hamatsa was about killing. My grandmother told me this story about how the Mama̱lili̱ka̱la caught a group of [other First Nation people] paddling outside Numas Island or somewhere around there. They killed them and found a box of treasures. And in it was the Hamatsa dance. That's how we got to do the Hamatsa.[54] I love those kinds of stories because they debunk a lot of the nonsense about the golden age of our people. It would have been a tough time. We were a tough people, and it was a way of surviving – not that we couldn't survive without slavery. But I think almost every culture has had it and gotten rid of it. There are things that you get rid of. You move on in your history. And cannibalism, ceremonial cannibalism, is different than cannibalism for the sake of nutrition ..."

"Everybody always looks back to their culture as the golden era of plenty, and the golden era of equal rights, and the golden era of looking after the land without any critical review of that. You start talking about slavery, ritual cannibalism,[55] and beheadings[56] – some of the less savoury parts of potlatch ritual – and people don't like that. They don't like to hear it. They don't like to talk about it. That was the *old way*."

As a scholar of Kwakwa̱ka̱'wakw culture and colonial history, George Speck is well versed in the written and narrated pasts of his people and well aware of the racializing discourses on savagery and civilization used to justify colonialism. He and others in his family acknowledge that the politics of representation carry political weight. But they also seek to describe their own histories on their own terms in order to contextualize the past. In another conversation, I asked him how he would describe Tsa̱xis in 1865.

Around 1865: Tsa<u>x</u>is

"1865?" George Speck began. "That was around the smallpox epidemics, that period of time. Well, I think that it was probably a pretty rough neighbourhood – the fur trade, trade with aboriginals during that period of time, alcohol. On the other hand, I've also heard that the Kwakw<u>a</u>k<u>a</u>'wakw in particular were pretty shrewd traders."

An 1862 witness to the smallpox epidemic in Fort Rupert wrote:

> Since our last visit to this place it is sadly changed; the once imposing looking village in all its rude uncivilized state is nowhere to be seen; the small-pox which went all through the Indian tribes about 3 months ago did not ease [?] off these poor fellows ... of the fine muscular stalwart fellows that 4 years ago numbered 400 men; now not fifty can be mustered & they are mostly middle aged or older men, disease appears to have principally attacked the Young and Strong, and those that it treated lightly, came to the same sad end through the alcohol supplied them by rascally traders; Disease in all its frightful forms and whisky have made sad havoc with these poor unlearned wretches.[57]

From 1862 to 1863, members of coastal communities were devastated by smallpox, what they called *kikinū'e* in surveyor George Dawson's vocabulary.[58] Their ancestors had already survived smallpox epidemics in 1785 and 1835-37, and they had endured measles and influenza in 1848-49. By 1865, Kwakw<u>a</u>k<u>a</u>'wakw peoples were drawing upon a heavy repertoire of grief. They were struck again by tuberculosis, measles, and influenza in 1868, and smallpox returned in the winter of 1876. Despite these devastating scourges, or perhaps in part because of them, Kwakw<u>a</u>k<u>a</u>'wakw peoples maintained dynamic economic exchanges with those they called Mamał'a, mostly European foreigners.

As early as 1792, these foreigners had noted that the purveyors of sea otter pelts were "well versed in the principles of trade" and that the "Nimpkish," in particular, were known to receive "more than double the value" ever seen "given for them on any other part of the coast."[59] Similarly, *kakilawilatsila,*[60] aboriginal traders who lived and traded at Fort Rupert, were described as "very relaxed, even jocular and matter of fact" in their interactions with Mamał'a traders.[61] At times, they were viewed as the HBC's competitors, people who served as middlemen in the lucrative north-south trade as they expanded their networks to include Fort Victoria and, later, New Westminster, as Vancouver was then called.[62] Travelling in 1862, Richard Mayne estimated the aboriginal population in Fort Rupert to be two to three thousand people, including visitors and residents.[63] The fur trade ensured the circulation of wealth and fostered a "peaceful and business-oriented" atmosphere at the fort, a place where traders apparently shared a common social sphere.[64] Liquor figured into the gendered norms of trade and sociality.

In 1863, the daily *British Colonist* reported that "one gallon [of liquor] was equal to two, three-point Hudson's Bay blankets."[65] As in other communities along the Coast, liquor "became a symbol of wealth," was integrated into ceremonials, and remained significant as a trade item despite the 1854 law "Prohibiting the Gift or Sale of Spirituous Liquors to Indians."[66] In the *British Colonist* on 28 February 1859, an ominous statistic appeared estimating that "full four hundred" aboriginal people had died within an eighteen-month period "from drinking whiskey prepared by the bush-rangers of Victoria."[67] The "Indian Liquor Ordinance" of 1867 likewise did little to curtail bootlegging activities. Nor did it interfere much with the ability to distill one's own whisky, called *nunkai'ma* in George Dawson's vocabulary.[68] Instead, "prohibition tended to put the trade into American hands."[69]

When George Speck continued his description of the late 1800s, he spoke about potlatching and offered the perspective of a chief from around that time: "Potlatching and what it was in terms of status, there would have been lots of competition for trading in furs or for trading in just about everything. My understanding is that it was pretty intense. Those were the days that coppers were broken.[70] Property was destroyed to show how wealthy you were.* There was a lot of

* According to Wedłidi Speck, "To give a potlatch, a chief had to own a *Tłakwa,* a 'copper.' The copper was the chief's entry into the potlatch system. In the old days, a chief announced to other chiefs that he is going to sell his copper. This was a signal that he is going to give a potlatch. Potlatches were given for a number of reasons – like birth of a child, coming of age, marriage, putting up a totem pole, and validating a claim to a seat or chieftainship. Now, back to the sale of the copper. The chiefs then assembled and bid for the copper. When the price was right, the chief sold his copper and, with the money he got from the sale of his copper, he purchased and distributed property to his village chiefs or to chiefs of other villages. The more potlatches a chief gave, the more

contempt for not being able to carry forward your ceremonial obligations. How wealthy you were was a reflection of the good favour shown you by the spirit world. And the converse of that, of course, was that if you weren't able to carry forward your ceremonial obligations, then you must be nothing as far as the spirit world was concerned ... In terms of the seats [ranked positions] that were opening up as the result of smallpox and things like that, there was a lot of turmoil in the potlatch, the taking of positions by people that didn't have rights to those positions. There was a lot of scrambling, and in that context there was, I guess, a lot of not-so-honourable things done. I don't know what the practice was prior to that, but there seemed to be a big issue around that in the 1800s and 1900s in terms of child marriages and prostitution, that sort of thing."

Marriage offered a direct avenue to rank through the transfer of positions from the bride's father to the groom. A particularly complicated set of practices from this period have been documented that exoticize potlatch marriages, most notably the marriage of a chief's body parts (declared daughters) to chosen male successors.[71] Older anthropological sources do not provide much detail on child marriage or on participation in the sex economy as it related to high-status marriages or to the gendered aspects of late nineteenth-century potlatching in general.

I asked family members about prostitution, a difficult topic but one that G̲a'ax̲sta'las confronted in her time. As Pearl Alfred told me: "Well, I only know her view that she thought it was wrong and that the chiefs thought nobody knew what they did to get their money. They'd send their women off, and then some of the women would come back sick. To hear her talk, she said the chiefs would send their wives – and I would think that they'd be women in their families because when you were having a potlatch everybody contributes money. I would think it wouldn't have just been the women: it would have been the women and their families. I think it was a lot different then, in terms of how strongly people felt about their positions in the potlatch. And that was determined, really, by how much you gave away, very important. It was important to have that money, and there

prestige he gained. This earned the chief a right to place replica canoes and coppers on a pole outside his house. It marked his standing in the village and in the spiritual world. He may have nothing left when he gave a potlatch, but he was wealthy in other ways."

were only a few places where you could get money. They went to Vancouver; they went to Seattle or Victoria or down south. Something I remember her saying – *"Sending women down south"* – was a bad thing. I think that's probably documented somewhere. I'm sure she wrote letters about that." In Jane Cook's letters, there is only one mention of prostitution, which is interesting given that many in the family stated to me that this would be the most controversial aspect of telling her story. What is certain is that G̱a'a̱xsta'las spoke often about her concerns.

Like others in the family, Nella Nelson explicitly tied the participation of women in the southern sex trade to changes in the potlatch, to what is commonly known as "rivalry potlatching." "I think, for myself, at the university doing anthropology, it really opened my eyes once I understood the chain of events that happened with the diseases through contact, the evolution of the potlatch, the rivalry, the movement of some of our women into the sex trade. And, actually, we haven't gone a long way in that, there's one person I know, Ron Hamilton, who did a couple of public presentations on our women in the sex trade. But it's not really talked about a lot."

I spoke with many about the need for delicacy when writing about this topic. On this occasion, I said to Nella, "I think it's going to be a difficult area to discuss in a book, right?" "It is," Nella said. "My thought is – hopefully, there are some written documents that Granny has done in relation to that. Because I think, from our perspective, it's sort of like what we've heard – hearsay? I don't know if you can call it hearsay when it's from different family members. So, hopefully, in some of her writings to government or to the church she does talk about that." Pearl and Nella expressed hope for some clarity on what G̱a'a̱xsta'las herself had observed and experienced in the late nineteenth century. Although official reports by colonial agents, missionaries, medical personnel, and anthropologists such as Franz Boas attest to women's participation in prostitution, at present there is no agreed-upon social language to approach the topic.

Records of the past are, however, passed on orally and through material culture. William Wasden Jr. connected the southern sex trade to ceremonial activity and also to changes in the potlatch complex: "There's carvings up and down our territories of chiefs ridiculing other chiefs because they did that in order to elevate the standings of their families.[72] My grandmother said to me that lots of chief's wives did that, and when they came home with all the money, their husbands would throw big potlatches. In our customs, they say nobody can talk about them after that because they gave big potlatches, which is sad, but that's where our culture was. Again, we go back to ... traditionally, would our noble ladies have been allowed to do that? I don't think so. It's what it had turned into – people trying desperately to keep their names and their positions."

Kwakwa̱ka̱'wakw peoples were, of course, not the only groups to participate in this economy. European women and others in financial need also resorted to prostitution in the demographic context of the frontier, where single males vastly outnumbered women. It is reasonable to assume that women then, as now, chose that labour reluctantly, as a means for survival or to provide for their needs.[73] To Kwakwa̱ka̱'wakw peoples, the potlatch has always been critical to cultural reproduction. In the context of the rapidly shifting economies of the late nineteenth century, that meant more pressure on chiefs and their 'na̱mima members to generate wealth for gifting.

In his 1921 analysis of Kwagu'ł family histories, Franz Boas also noted important changes after 1849. He writes that small-scale, reciprocal exchanges that had been continuous for several generations were dramatically "overwhelmed" in later accounts by an emphasis on potlatching.[74] The size and frequency of the ceremonials escalated as European trade goods – especially the blanket – replaced more stable and symbolic forms of gifting. "The Hudson's Bay blanket reduced exchange to a single unit; the older exchanges, as the records show, usually included an ensemble of properties – sea mammals, land mammals, human beings (slaves), yellow cedar bark, and an assortment of containers and conveyors, such as boxes, dishes and canoes."[75] The "Fort Ruperts" benefitted from their position as "home guard." They acted as interpreters, had the option to take up short-term employment with the HBC, and engaged in trade as middlemen or entrepreneurs in all activities surrounding the bustling fort. As "the south" became part of the Kwakwa̱ka̱'wakw sphere, regular visits by canoe and steamer opened other economic avenues.

George Speck continued his musings about life in Tsax̱is in the 1860s. "So, frontier life at that time – Europeans, I mean European traders, were a pretty shady lot. Hudson's Bay Company officials I can't speak too much of, and that was before the missionaries showed up on the Coast.[76] I would have thought there was very little constraint on the activities of traders as well as First Nation people. So the interaction must have been pretty intense."[77] Violence was a fact on the Northwest Coast frontier. During the maritime trade, it was common to hear of aboriginal people forced at gunpoint to deliver up furs. European traders also captured and ransomed aboriginal people for furs.[78] Historian Barry Gough reports that “Yankee traders” in the late eighteenth century “purchased slaves ... and sold their human cargo of two to eight persons ... for sea otter skins.”[79]

A number of modes of authority were then recognized in Kwakwaka’wakw territories. First, there was the ever-more-imposing rule of law meted out by colonial agents.[80] Within the far larger populations of Kwakwaka’wakw peoples on Vancouver Island, chiefs held power; they controlled access to resource sites and organized members of their ’na’mima for ceremonial gifting and internal and external trade exchanges. Their authority was invested with supernatural and, increasingly, economic power. They had a ceremonial obligation, as George states above, to uphold social and cosmological exchange relations by hosting winter ceremonies or feasts. Third, settlers then wielded limited authority, which was sometimes chilling, as they engaged in vigilante outbursts, mercantile activities, and the development of small land grants.[81]

The majority of newcomers to the Northwest Coast were young labourers who worked in all-male crews often a long way from the growing, but still limited, metropolis of Fort Victoria. They felled, cut, and transported timber; panned for gold; worked as stevedores in the busy harbours; built the infrastructure of the new colony; and hacked into hard seams of coal. Some, such as William H. Gilbert, worked on schooners or steamers, piloting vessels through a jumble of islands skirted by fast currents.

William H. Gilbert (Jane Cook’s Father)

According to Ga’axsta’las’s daughter-in-law Nellie Cook, Captain Gilbert was a fur buyer who travelled by sea, north to Alaska and south to Port Townsend. Over his several decades of research, Wedłidi Speck has asked his relatives about Gilbert. “He was a sea captain, and he was a trader. He traded materials like a merchant. There’s conflicting stories. I’ve heard stories that he ended up, when he retired from shipping, [that] he started up a saloon, like a hotel saloon. When he died, one of the boys was supposed to go and inherit it. And some say it was Alaska; some say it was Seattle. My grandfather apparently went to look at it and said it was too much of a saloon-type thing –

Photo 10 G̱a'aẕsta'las's father, Captain William H. Gilbert, master of the schooner *Winifred,* 24 September 1877. When this photograph was distributed to family members, many blocked off Gilbert's eyes, looking for family resemblances. The name *Winifred* is also significant. One of Jane and Stephen's daughters and several girls in subsequent generations carried it. *Photograph taken at Huntington Bros., Olympia, Washington. Courtesy of Jefferson County Historical Society, 2005.*

not our culture. I heard that partly through my mom, who's now passed on. Winnie Bell talked about that. She was one of my grandfather's sisters. It was also talked about by Pearlie Mountain. There were a few people. When I asked them, 'Where was he really from?'

they don't know these things. It's frustrating. Whereas in the oral tradition, we rely on it, right? The first thing we do is ask, 'Where are you from?' *[Laughs]* 'Who are you related to?'"

William Gilbert's birthplace in England, details of his life, and his eventual fate are unknown but for a few references in US court records and impressions of his life gleaned through family histories. In the 1870 census conducted in Port Townsend, Washington, one William Gilbert is documented under the categories "age at last birthday," "sex," "colour," and "profession" as a thirty-eight-year-old, white, male mariner.

I wrote to the northwest region of the Washington State Archives to inquire about William Gilbert. Archivists responded with civil court documents that provide some sense of the working conditions of a sea pilot in the late 1850s. On 4 February 1859, William H. Gilbert, then about twenty-seven years old, filed a libel suit against the schooner *Reporter,* upon which he had served as pilot from 5 January to 3 February. Proctor W.S. Spears documented the suit and requested immediate action because the *Reporter* was due to "proceed to Victoria, Vancouver Island forthwith." The "Libel & order of Wm. Gilbert VS Schooner Reporter" includes the itinerary of the Schooner and the cause for the libel action:

> On the 5th day of January 1859, said schooner then lying in the Port of Victoria and bound on a voyage to Steilacuvur and other ports on Puget Sound & back the said Master by himself hired the libelland to serve as Pilot on board said vessel, at the rate of $40 per month until the 18th day of January 1859 by verbal agreement, libelland having signed no shipping articles ...
>
> 3rd ... this libelland deserves to have [?] for said services at the rate of $65 per month that his services were worth said amounts.
>
> 4th That during the whole time he was on board said vessel up to the said 3rd Feb when he left said vessel ... he well and faithfully performed his duty as such Pilot and was obedient to all levels of command of the said Master, & the other officers of said Schooner, and was entitled to be paid his wages which were then on accounting $33.80 over and above all just deductions ...
>
> his
> Wm X H. Gilbert
> mark[82]

Action was swift. One day later, the court clerk returned notice that the writ had been executed "by seizing above named vessel & serv[ing] copy libel on Captain." Two days later, the court clerk received "the sum of thirty three dollars and eighty cents ... claimed on the above cause of libel." In 1874, William Gilbert showed up again in the Admiralty Court records of Washington State. At that time, he was an employee of the Black Ball Pilot Company. But other details about his life remain elusive.

A glance at the *British Colonist* from 1865 suggests the centrality of commercial marine intelligence in and around Fort Victoria Harbour. Each day, the paper printed a list of the brigs, barques, sloops, schooners, steamers, and gunboats entering and clearing port. Steamers fired their guns as they entered or left the harbour. The vessels carried lumber to San Francisco from the mills on Puget Sound or "precious cargo" to supply Hudson's Bay Company posts. Ships arrived and departed for Portland, Olympia, the Fraser River, Australia, Hong Kong, Tahiti, and London.

Pax Brittanica: The Bombardment of Fort Rupert

Manoeuvring the busy lanes of marine traffic were British naval vessels operating out of Esquimalt Harbour. Historian Barry Gough calls the man-of-war captains "amphibious sailor-diplomats" who served as "a world police force," investigating crimes and enforcing the rule of law with military might under the paradoxical symbol of *Pax Brittanica.*[83] Ordered to stem the trade in liquor and slaves on the northern Coast, the military missions more often than not dealt with the complaints of settlers, policemen, missionaries, or Indian Agents in remote villages. They responded occasionally to calls for justice by chiefs.

Such was the case when Captain Turnour sailed the HMS *Clio* into Beaver Harbour at Fort Rupert on 22 December 1865. According to the pilot's account, published in the *British Colonist,* "An Indian from Nawitta [sic] had been murdered by the Fort Rupert tribe and his people had refrained from retaliating at the request of Mr. Compton [the Indian Agent] until the arrival of Captain Turnour, to whom they desired to submit their complaint."[84] This description matches notes in Boas's papers about the murder of a slave. Gloria Cranmer-Webster was surprised by the complaint. "It seems hard to believe," she told me, "that anyone would go to the police about that at that time ... It seems very unlikely. When you think about the ranking of the tribes – you've got the Kwagu'ł way up here *[gesturing high]* ... and I just find it hard to believe that they would have gone to the police."

At the time, HMS *Clio* was returning from routing out whisky traders at Metlakatla, where missionary William Duncan, acting as the sole arbiter of justice, had tried and sentenced the offenders onboard. After providing an account of the wind and water conditions on the return voyage, the pilot wrote: "On landing we found that the steward of Mr. Compton (a Chinaman) had hung himself since our last visit. [He] accused himself of having committed murder at Cariboo, and said that the ghosts of his victims haunted him continually ... Next morning the pinnace and two cutters went ashore to demand the murderers, but met with obstinate resistance from the Indians."[85] Lieutenant Carry, in command of the shore visit, described the confrontation in his statement: "On landing, I was met on the Beach by 'Jim' the chief of the Tribe, who asked for what purpose we had landed. I told him to secure the 3 murderers, and destroy any Whisky we might find. He refused to give the Natives up, unless we gave 2 of our men as hostages, during that time about 50 Indians assembled on the Beach, and about the same number near the Ranch, armed with muskets, they continued yelling, and firing in the air, over our heads ... I told [Jim] he should have a certain time to give the men up, and if they were not then forthcoming, we should open fire from the ship and destroy the Village."[86]

The pilot, Captain Chambers, continued the narrative:

> When the boats returned an hour after, the ship came closer to the village and opened fire on it, throwing shot and shell amongst the villagers. The Indians took refuge behind the Fort in numbers, but did not fire on it as they had threatened, therefore, according to orders, the marines on the Fort did not fire upon them. After some few rounds the Indians gave in, hauling down four flags which they had defiantly raised and hoisting a white flag in their place,[†] but

† William Wasden Jr. commented on aspects of the account: "The flags probably represented the four tribes in Fort Rupert, the four head chiefs – to acknowledge that there was four tribes there, that they were all separate but they were an alliance. I know that Peter Knox and his family has an old Union Jack that they hang up as a dance curtain because it's so big. It was a gift to one of

though Mr. Compton urged them to give up the three murderers, they refused ...

We ascertained that a man and his wife were severely contused by the bursting of a shell in one of the houses ... Having permission to remain ashore all night, I spent an anxious time, as the Indians were on the alert all night removing their property from their houses and knocking at the Fort gates, endeavoring to induce us to sally out to get the men we wanted, as they said they were in a certain house. No doubt they wanted us as hostages had we been fools enough to have gone out, but the knowledge that they were packing off their valuables was sufficient to show they were prepared to fight on the morrow.[‡]

They require a salutary lesson not to play with a man-o-war as they boasted they were doing prior to the shell coming amongst them, and saying that they had seen plenty of men-o-war who always threatened them, but none of them ever fired on them yet. They will not forget the *Clio,* however.[§] It is the firm belief of men who know the Indian character that well that a severe lesson – no half measures – but sharp chastisement administered in earnest on one tribe alone will strike a panic among all the others and save the constant excitement and trouble connected with Indian outrages and audacity ...

Next morning early three boats, with tars and marines, were landed in charge of the First Lieutenant ... who required the Indians to do what was demanded of them, and on their flatly refusing, nothing

---

Peter Knox's ancestors, and he was the head chief of one of the tribes, a gift to make good relations, saying, 'Here's a sign of our good relationship. Here's a flag to hang over your house.' If they fly it, then they're saying their loyalty is to the flags and whoever gave it to them and that they probably had special privileges too, with the trading, they probably had advantages."

‡ "Their valuables were definitely coppers," William told me. "Because our people, when they [the coppers] weren't in use, they retired these things to caves. When you talk about burying things during the potlatch prohibition, it was to save things, especially the coppers, because coppers represented financial surplus. They represent a lot of material wealth. To bury a copper was saving a lot of potlatching power or feasting power."

§ "They wouldn't give up, the people who were accused, so I think they were very strong people," William told me. "There's a speech by O'wax̲alagalis, who was Tommy Johnson's father: 'Where was your Queen when the Creator gave us? They say if we continue our traditions, a man-of-war will come and bomb our houses.' And he says, 'Go ahead and do that, because we'll just build new houses. We'll just continue on.' So, the four tribes, especially where they were among the ranking system of our people, they were, in their minds, invincible. A man-of-war couldn't take them down."

more was said, but to work they went, and in a very few minutes the camp was on fire. The Indians, determined to resist our demands, had buried most of their valuables under ground during the night, inside their houses, and consequently lost most of their winter provisions. After firing a portion of the camp, the demand for the prisoners and the whisky was reiterated, and as sternly refused, though under the penalty of having the remainder of the houses burnt, and the canoes broken. Half-an-hour was allowed, and on a report being given at its end, the flames of the burning village again ascended. In searching the lodges a good quantity of rum was found and destroyed.[#]

The Indians, however, still obstinately refused to give up the remaining two prisoners (I should have mentioned that the other one was given up at an earlier period of the occurrence, who is supposed to be innocent himself of having perpetrated the murder, though no doubt an accessory.) We next came to the destruction of the canoes, a deed which affects deeply the avaricious and [miserly?] heart of the North-West Indians, viewing them as they do as the representatives of so many warm blankets, cans of liquor, &c. Still they stoutly refused to give up the culprits. So we had to single out six or seven prisoners as hostages for the good behaviour of the rest, as well as the last chance for them to deliver up the two for whom they had suffered so much; but their obstinacy ruled their judgment, and the *Clio* left early next morning, having done what was long wanted, and which, if well followed up for some time, will [not] only render navigation safe, but will allow traders to enter the port for the transaction of business, from which they are now deterred by the hostility of the natives ... Hoping you will excuse my inability to condense matters, and claiming the right to spin a long yarn, I remain, yours.

THE PILOT. (Captain Chambers)[87]

"Our people were definitely into liquor," William said. "We just had a potlatch here, and there was a dance that celebrated a whisky potlatch and a beer potlatch. There was a dance that was composed to celebrate that. I know that [someone] gave a whisky feast one time, and one of the men [from another village] died of alcohol poisoning, and there was a big rift for a long time because of that. But there was a lot of fun that went along with drinking as well. Our people were dramatic. I imagine for our old people, in them days, the fear of getting caught was an extra hype in itself. *We can do as the whiteman does too and get away with it.* Especially the Fort Rupert tribes, they were very defiant, a very proud people – and they still are today."

Lieutenant Carry concluded his official statement, writing: "We then made a prisoner of Jim and 10 other of the Natives."[88] Carry, Captain Turnour wrote, had deemed it necessary to remove the prisoners "for the present."[89] In Turnour's brief report, there is no list of prisoners from Fort Rupert, but it is likely that "Jim" is the Kwagu'ł chief remembered as "Captain Jim" and that John 'Nulis and his daughter Emily were among the eleven arrested – or taken as hostages.

Over a week later, the *Colonist* ran the following: "THE FOUR FORT RUPERT INDIANS:– The Indians brought down in H.M.[S.] Clio from Fort Rupert, having been discharged, indignantly ask why their property was seized or destroyed, themselves made prisoners, and brought to Victoria, if there is no legitimate charge against them. They think it hard that they should be thrown out on Victoria streets, and left to get home as best they can."[90] While in Victoria, G̲wa̲yuła̲las (Emily) met William Gilbert, who was in port. Family oral histories state that Gilbert was an acquaintance of ex-governor James Douglas, who was responsible for the release of those taken on the *Clio*. According to Boas's notes, the Fort Rupert hostages were eventually returned on the *Otter*.[91]

T̓SAMAS: VICTORIA

It is difficult to know what the prisoners or hostages taken from the ruin of the village endured in Fort Victoria. Were they already familiar with the streets and beaches of the small metropolis? Perhaps they made their way to districts near the beached canoes of their compatriots and sought out family members. These districts appear often in early European descriptions of Victoria, in the dark renderings of otherness used to describe reserves or what were then called Indian ranches. Governor Douglas had long been concerned with controlling the thousands of "northern Indians" who arrived yearly at Fort Victoria.[92] He had created a police force in 1855, and in 1856 he requested assistance from the Royal Navy.[93] Most residents were armed, and violence, gambling, and drunkenness figure largely in descriptions of Victoria street life in the mid-nineteenth century. Even before the gold rush, travellers noted that "the diseases of prostitution" (especially syphilis, long called "grand pox") were "epidemic" among Europeans and indigenous people.[94] Anglican missionary William Duncan noted conditions of squalor in the overcrowded

"Indian camps surrounding Fort Victoria."[95] He was soon bound to work with the Tsimshian people at Port Simpson, but at that time, Governor Douglas had tried to persuade him to stay in Victoria. "They care not one straw for the bodies or souls of Indians," Duncan wrote. "It is the furs they want ... and those places where the Indians cannot or will not procure them are just the places they would hand over to the missionaries."[96] Duncan predicted the colonial partnership between state and missionary that would be set in motion after the collapse of the fur trade.

Mrs. William Thain, who visited Victoria in 1858, reflected on labour relations within a colonial spatial regime in her account of the trip, written fifty years later: "We passed through part of an Indian village ... Crossing over a bridge by which we entered the city we saw no end of canoes, as some of the natives were allowed to remain on the city side, but later on as the population increased, all Indians had to go over the bridge before dark, and as they took the place in many families, of the chinamen of today; sometimes a pass was given to them, as they were afraid of the police. I do not know what housekeepers now would do with only Indian help, and they [had] to leave before dinner was cleared away."[97]

Haida, Tsimshian, and Kwakwa̱ka̱'wakw men, women, and children canoed the great distance to Fort Victoria to work and to sell their wares. Men found employment for about one dollar a day.[98] On the streets, women sold garden produce, berries, and clams. They worked as domestic servants, as kitchen workers in hotels and restaurants, and as laundresses. A large number also lived in Fort Victoria, either as wives of fur traders, both officers and labourers, or as part of aboriginal families.[99] Some women engaged in prostitution, but as historian Jean Barman notes, it is difficult to separate historical commentary on street work from the licence taken by European men who "had to portray Indigenous women as sexually transgressive in order ... to seduce them with impunity, without accountability."[100] Aboriginal women and men were clearly participants in both the informal and formal colonial economies.

The routes of First Nation people from northern villages did not terminate at Fort Victoria: their social and economic networks extended across the international line into Washington State, into Seattle, Olympia, and other ports on Puget Sound. According to family histories, G̱a'ax̱sta'las was born in the United States while her mother was working in the hop fields at Puyallup.[101] During the Gix̱sa̱m Feast in May 2007, David Huson, another descendant of G̱a'ax̱sta'las, gave me a copy of Stephen Cook's registered Indian record, which states that his spouse, Jane Constance Gilbert, had been born in Port Blakely, a township of Bainbridge Island, Puget Sound, a place of lumber yards, mills, and mercantile-shipping activity.

A̲wi'nak̓wa (Rocky Place): G̲wa̲yuła̲las (Emily)

Details of Jane Gilbert's birth and childhood are cloudy for many descendants in her direct line. As Pearl Alfred told me, "We know so little about her childhood. It's as if her life began when she married Papa! *[Laughing]*. It was never discussed, and we never asked. I can't believe that. It seemed as if we never dared to ask. We must have certainly been curious." Answers came from other branches of the family, from the descendants of Annie Newman, who had been told about the difficult circumstances of Jane and Annie's mother, G̲wa̲yuła̲las (Emily). Their candour in relating unfortunate events was interpreted by other members of the family as a plausible explanation for the silence they had grown up with. The family is resolved to make the story public as a piece of their collective history and as an episode in the family's past that likely greatly influenced G̲a'ax̲sta'las.

Annie Newman's great-granddaughter Doreen Fitch was born in the village of Gwa'yi (Kingcome). When I met with her in Vancouver, Doreen told me about a box of treasures that had been handed down from Emily (whom she called He'ma̲n'sagila̲og̲wa) to her daughter Annie. As Doreen moved several times with her family in Alberta, that bentwood box, carved in the style of the Bella Bella, served her children as a toy box. Doreen had recently taken the box to the Museum of Anthropology in Vancouver, where it is stored on long-term loan. Her mother's sister May had been raised by Annie Newman and her husband, Michael Kamano. As Doreen told me, she had bumped into her Aunt May on a ferry crossing to Alert Bay: "She started telling me about my great-great-grandmother who was Emily. Emily Whonnock was her maiden name. She had said that she was very young when she took off with that guy named Gilbert. Apparently he was the captain of a boat. She didn't tell me if he was part Native or if he was full non-Native. She didn't tell me that. She just said he lived in Victoria."

"Victoria or maybe Port Hardy, I don't know. It was probably Port Hardy if he was a skipper of a boat. I should have asked my aunt more *[laughing],* but I didn't. I just got what she told me, and she said that Emily had married this guy, and then they had Jane. Jane was their only child ..."

"And then after that man died – Emily's first man – Emily went to Port Townsend and met another man, who she was with, and he was a night watchman with the last name Newman. He was non-Native too. She said he was probably Scotch. This is what my aunt said."

"She said he went missing, being on night shift. And they don't know whether it was homicide or whether he just took off, but, apparently, he was a real gambler, and they figured maybe he was done away with for gambling money. This is what my Aunt May said."

"Then [Emily] went back to Victoria after that. But, I guess, she said, she had no reason to live. She went back to Victoria, and she got into alcohol and drank, and that's what she died from."

Doreen's sister Rita Barnes told me that Emily "was really young" when she had her children. "It sounds like she was about fourteen, fifteen when she had my great-grandmother [Annie]." There was some suggestion by another person that Jane had been taken from her mother because Emily was too young to care for her. But most stories suggest that Jane was with her mother when Emily met James Newman, the father of Annie and Charlie. Rita Barnes continued: "My understanding was, when Jane was born, she was taken by her dad and put into a mission place. She grew up and was educated in this little mission house, wherever this mission house was. And the mother wasn't there very long when she left with this Newman person. And he took her back to Port Townsend, and she had her two kids there."

Although some say that Jane travelled with her father, William Gilbert, on his schooner, others have heard that he placed her at a young age with the church. According to Wedłidi Speck, "Gilbert apparently brought her back and tried to put her in the Catholic Church here in Victoria. She couldn't stand the incense, was the story, and so they brought her to Fort Rupert. So, there was a crossover from the Catholic Church to the Anglican Church."

Searching under names that might have been used for her, I found no records of Jane in early Catholic institutions in Washington, Victoria, or Nanaimo. Jane's granddaughter Christine Zurkowski told me: "Now, this is only what I hear. I don't know for sure, but I understood that when her father went back to England, he put her in to the Reverend Alfred Hall and his wife to look after her and raise her. He actually supplied her a lot of books from England. She was well taught in a lot of ways." Whether William Gilbert died or returned to England is not known. A man by that name, listed as a pilot, appears on the Port Townsend census of 1887.

In Port Townsend, Emily lived with James Newman. As Rita Barnes explained: "He was a night watchman on the waterfront, and one morning he just never came home ..."

"And they're not really sure – I get different stories, a different story from my brother, different from my Aunt May. They don't really know what happened to him. Did he desert his family? Apparently, he was a gambler. Did he desert them to run away from his gambling debts?"

"And someone else suggested that he was killed because of his gambling debts. But, to me, that doesn't make sense. Why would you go and kill a person that owed you money? To me, it just makes more sense to keep them alive and keep them working and just take the money. Or he could have just drowned by accident ... Yeah, it's like we don't know anything about the Newman man. Who was he? Where did he come from? Where does the name Newman come from? I don't know. Nobody knows. But the mother stayed for as long as she could and then brought the children to Victoria, where she died an alcoholic, is what I hear. So, all the time she's in Victoria – and that's where she died – we don't really know: how did she live? We can only guess, and it couldn't have been good."

I had several conversations with the family regarding what is remembered of Emily and the likely circumstances of the last years of her life in Victoria. Visibly moved when they heard of her vulnerable situation, many felt that the story explained gaps in their own understanding of Jane Cook's life. Responding to the story, which she had never heard, Pearl Alfred suggested that her grandmother Jane must have struggled bitterly with this knowledge. "I don't doubt that's not true," she said, "just because [Emily] didn't exist for us. And when you think about somebody's grandmother never being spoken about! It must be so ... [Jane Cook's] weakness was her mother, and she couldn't deal with it. If she could, we would have known about it. If we knew, we would have thought *this poor little grandmother*."

When we spoke about Emily, Chris Cook, another grandchild, invoked a more collective history of survival and identity: "That's part of our history. That's part of where we were. I don't think it's shame; I think it's who she was ... I take a look at us, those of us who survived, maybe Granny's mom, whatever she did, whatever happened – she survived! And my Granny was a survivor. I heard an old man say one time, "We are the survivors of survivors. We are the survivors of the strongest. Everything happened – smallpox, you name it. But we are the descendants of those handful of people." I think that's why we are strong today, because we had somebody who made it up that river, who made it up that falls, who made it. And she made it, and she spawned. I'm part of that person who went through whatever she went through. [Emily] could have died like a lot of other people, but she gave birth to this woman who was even stronger."

We discussed people's level of comfort in making sensitive information public. "If you delete something from the story, it takes a part of the foundation out," Chris told me. All others with whom I spoke agreed. In subsequent conversations, Pearl told me that there are many people who likely know the story about Emily but, out of respect for the family, it was not circulating as common knowledge. Likely, Ga'axsta'las was acutely aware of her mother's unfortunate circumstances. Perhaps she was a young witness to that part of her life. Certainly, others in the villages knew the story. It is difficult to believe that these circumstances did not fuel Ga'axsta'las's later attempts to protect women from the liquor trade or from aspects of potlatching that she felt left women without choices.

Early in the research process, I sat with Gilbert Cook in his home in 'Yalis. He showed me Ga'axsta'las's death certificate. On this document, the name of Jane's mother appears as "Jenny." We recorded our conversation about that.

"I really have no idea," Gilbert said, "I don't know. I guess people just didn't know what her name was. It's hard to tell because by the time her death certificate came around, there was a gap of time there."

"So, it wasn't made out immediately?" I asked.

"No," Gilbert said. "From the time that she was a part of Jane's family until [Jane's] death, there was a long period of time. And who knows what she may or may not have told her kids. I don't remember ever having my dad mention his grandmother's name. She was just kind of an unknown factor, something from the past that really wasn't talked about a great deal. You know, he often talked about his mom [Jane], of course."

Gilbert also speculated about the death of James Newman: "My dad had a gold watch, just a cheap watch, a plated pocket watch that he'd been given. Charlie Newman gave it to him. And my dad didn't know the whole story or had forgotten it when he gave it on to me.

But he said he thought that it was the watch of the guy who had killed James Newman, who, as a result of that murder, had been hanged down there. And this is what he got from Charlie Newman. Now, whether there's any truth to that, or exactly what the circumstances were, I don't know. But that's the story that I got passed along with this watch."

According to Doreen Fitch, after James Newman disappeared from their lives, "[Emily] had the two little kids, my great-grandmother [Annie] and my great-uncle Charlie Newman. And somebody from Fort Rupert came to pick the two little kids up – brought them back to the reserve. Well, they had never been on the reserve before because they were born in Port Townsend. I guess that's just over the border a bit. They said if nobody had come to pick the kids up, they might have been just lost in the shuffle or maybe end up in an orphanage."

"[Emily] was from Fort Rupert. She was from a high-ranking family. This is why they wanted the kids back, the two kids."

Doreen's sister Rita Barnes also suggested that "someone from the Whonnock family came to Victoria, picked up the two kids, and took them back to Fort Rupert, where they were raised and must have got to know their older sibling, Jane."

Women were clearly accustomed to travelling to distant communities to work or to marry and establish families with European men. There are startling similarities in the story of G̲a'ax̲sta'las's early childhood and in the stories of others of her generation.[102] To what extent these expeditions were intended to be permanent is not clear, but in other work with Northwest Coast aboriginal women, there is a sense of the liminality, of transitional identities, they likely experienced.

Emily's seeming exile from Fort Rupert is reminiscent of those described in a paper by Marjorie Mitchell and Anne Franklin, who worked with Coast Salish women. According to their oral histories, "grandmothers" who married European men were viewed as "peacemakers" whose unions guaranteed important trade alliances. In Salish society, where descent through the patriline mattered, those women who left the partnerships risked losing the "paternal half of their children's birthright." They could return to home communities only in a state of "shame," which could be "wiped away" by a potlatch to "make their name good again."[103]

I asked William Wasden Jr. about this situation in the Kwakwa̲ka̲'wakw context. "Once you're married in our culture," he said, "it's shameful to return to your village. Once you're married, you go to your husband's village and you stay there. That was the tradition. I hear about fathers having to throw a big feast in order to wipe away the shame of [their daughter's] coming home. It was basically like you couldn't follow your obligations, you couldn't honour your marriage contract." He said the woman's father would likely have given the feast, because her children had no place in their social world without it. From 1869, under colonial legislation, women who married "non-Indians" lost their status upon marriage, as did their children. It is not known what effect, if any, this had on the internal prospects of return for women abandoned or widowed in exile.

According to research done on behalf of the Wasden family to regain their status, upon her return to Tsax̱is, G̱a'ax̱sta'las was formally adopted by her grandfather. William Wasden Jr. told me: "They were able to prove that she was legally adopted in the Big House by her grandfather John 'Nulis ... It's a thing that's going on right now with our people. People that aren't from the male lineage want to do [ceremonial] things, so the chief of the family adopts them and takes them for his own. I would think that's why 'Nulis adopted her, was to make everything official. In those times, there was probably criticism and a lot of putting down because our people were very shame-based in a lot of their teachings. Whenever they were talking to people, they did a lot of putting down because of the ranking system. 'Nulis did take her and adopt her as his own. Obviously, he was giving her cultural positioning, or grounding." Through her mother Emily, G̱a'ax̱sta'las likely assumed a place in the house of 'Nulis as the first-born in a line of first-borns. In this capacity, according to family oral histories, G̱a'ax̱sta'las later transferred the chiefly standing of Wanukw to John Hyałkin to facilitate his marriage to a woman of higher rank. Documented throughout the literature on Kwakwa̱ka̱'wakw peoples, the transfer continues to generate controversy.[104]

Family histories – textual and oral – clearly play a part in contemporary dynamics in the Big House. They are an important resource for entering into conversations about how history is told and the specifics of lineage or community identity. Genealogies, in particular, circulate as knowledge vital for knowing one's place in the world. They wind their way around material objects passed through family lines, and they offer a flexible set of ideas for social change, to mobilize members and, sometimes, to exclude others. The particular histories narrated here say something about how individuals view their place in history – as members of the Kwakwa̱ka̱'wakw First Nation, as members of the nobility, and as descendants of Ga’axsta’las. They say something about how they hope to contextualize her life.

We have yet to find any written evidence of Jane Constance Gilbert’s life before 1881, when, at the age of twelve, her name was registered in the Fort Rupert census. During the years between her birth and that census, many events occurred that shaped her life and the lives of those around her. Policy makers composed and then passed a startling succession of legislation regarding First Nation peoples. When Ga’axsta’las was in her first year, British Columbia joined Confederation. Indian agencies were formed, and Indian Agents were designated to manage them. When she was three years old, the canning industry began. Fort Rupert was sold to George Hunt’s father, Robert Hunt, and there were eleven houses in Alert Bay. At four, according to another document from Admiralty Court, her father, William Gilbert, worked for the Black Ball Pilot Company in Washington. In her fifth year, Alert Bay replaced Fort Rupert as the main economic centre on northern Vancouver Island. At six, the Indian Act became official legislation and attempted to assimilate aboriginal peoples. As part of the so-called civilizing colonial vision, government officials encouraged missionaries to move into indigenous villages. Like the naval officers before them, the missionaries arrived with a sense of duty to improve the prospects of so-called heathen peoples. Among them was the Reverend Alfred James Hall, who would play a central role in Ga’axsta’las’s life and the way she is remembered.

PART III
Stranger Than Fiction: Surviving the Missionary

On the morning of 20 May 2007, some of G̱a'a̱xsta'las's descendants met at Christ Church in Alert Bay for a special tribute. They had, the day before, publicly reanimated her clan in the Big House during the Gix̱sa̱m Feast. On this day, they met to remember her role in the church. Wedłidi Speck, newly recognized chief of the Gix̱sa̱m 'na̱'mima, spoke to the congregation.

"I'm here today to share a few words about my great-grandmother. We gathered over the weekend, and we celebrated culturally where Jane Cook came from for the sole purpose of wanting to build a sense of connection to people and strength and healing ... When I think about the church, it's my experience that you certainly have to look at the Cook family's contributions and the impression and the imprint they've left. You look around this house, and you'll see the fingerprint of the character of that family, our family. I didn't know my great-grandmother – she had passed on before – but I heard stories, and I was interested in people's stories."

"I remember one of our relatives – Lydia Whonnock. She told me a story about a time where she believed in her own heart that she was being attacked by angry people, and so she fell down on her left side. She was telling me ... she was walking down the road, and she was witchcraft – she fell over. And she knew the witchcrafter because the image came in when she fell over ... She went up to my great-grandmother, and she said: 'Look, this is what's happening.'"

"So, the old lady taught her how to pray. It's interesting. She taught her how to pray. She said that you could use that prayer, that belief, to ward off that projection ... The old lady was telling me this herself, and she said she's never been bothered by witchcraft since ... Granny Cook introduced her to a whole idea of faith, to an idea of believing in something that was greater, and something that was wonderful, and something that was more powerful. And that really helped Lydia, because when you have faith, [you are] strong. You never have to question who you are. That was a really powerful story."

"I've heard so many stories where Granny Cook – in church she was a pillar or a leader, and she organized women through the WA [Women's Auxiliary] and helped women to feel good about themselves, about being contributors to the culture and to the community and that whole way of life ... I've heard so many stories of her being a midwife and helping the birth of many, many children. Wow, sometimes, in the morning, I think of what two things I'm going to do today *[laughter in the audience]*, and I think about her, and I think about how powerful and how strong she must have been and how industrious she was and how committed she was to service ..."

"So, agreeing to speak today about that is a celebration of her, the wholeness of her."

"We did it culturally last night, and we're doing it in a different cultural way today. I think this is something also to celebrate. We have no shame on either side of that. When I look at Granny, she'd probably be the first bicultural person in British Columbia, someone who can transcend all the cultures. She practised the industry of our old people. She practised the building of community of our old people. But she also had a new way of expressing her faith in this world. And that's a very powerful thing."

Before and after Wedłidi's tribute to Jane Cook, the people gathered sang hymns and incanted prayers. Later, two children were christened. From my seat in a chilly back pew, I thought about the stories I had heard throughout our research, about how meetings of the Native Brotherhood had opened with "Onward Christian Soldiers" and about the first time hymns were sung in the Big House, at the memorial service for a woman who was strong in the potlatch, at her request. Wedłidi's comments about biculturality reminded me of the dedication in the *Kwa-kwa-la Hymnal* compiled by Alfred Hall: "To our ancestors who chose to encompass both cultures in their lives. G̲ilakas'la."

Engagements with both cultures are also graphically evident in the church itself. Near the entrance hangs a print by hereditary chief Tony Hunt Sr. titled *Baptism Mural* (ca. 1976). Elsewhere, on bronze plaques, are dedications to "devoted workers in this church" and to men who died in the world wars. Jane Constance Cook, Stephen Cook, and their daughter, Emma Kenmuir, appear with the names of others on the first plaque. Their son, Edwin Cook, and his namesake, their nephew Edwin Cook, are commemorated on the second. A stained glass window dedicated to the Cook family depicts Jesus at the helm of a fishing boat, the *C.N.,* with the inscription: "I will make you fishers of men." As Jane's great-grandson stated in his tribute, "the fingerprint of the character of the family" is certainly visible here.

Across the chapel, in a dark wood frame, a yellowed portrait of the long-bearded missionary Alfred Hall, with Elizabeth Hall behind him, hangs loosely from a nail. (When I see this photograph, I imagine eulachon oil dripping down Hall's beard, a vivid image that Charlie Nowell describes in *Smoke from Their Fires*.)[1] The window above the altar also bears a dedication to Reverend Hall. Interesting, I think, as I recall a letter Jane Cook wrote to church authorities in 1919, declining a window in his honour. What business lies between her decision and the installation of the window I do not know, but the letter attests to her influence within the church at the time.

Two years before the church service I had asked Jane Cook's granddaughter Christine Zurkowski if she had heard G̱a'a̱xsta'las speak about Mr. and Mrs. Alfred Hall.

"Oh yeah," she said. "She honoured them very much. She thought they were wonderful people ... She didn't say anything negative about them. I don't recall anything negative ... We had a picture of them on a wall in the dining room. This was the living room, I recall. There were two pictures up there *[gesturing high on an imagined wall]*. There was his wife, and him. She had them up on the top there. Then she had a lot of Bible verses. One in the dining room that said, and I can still [remember], "Christ is the head of this house, the unseen guest at every meal and the silent listener to every conversation." That was there *[laughs]*. She had that, and she had other Bible verses."

Christine turned to her mother, Nellie Cook. "What did she have on her walls in her bedroom?"

"The Rock of Ages," Nellie said.

"Yeah, that was her favourite song," Christine replied.

We looked at the often-published image of Reverend Hall and his wife.

"Yes, yes, that was the one," Christine said and showed it to her mother. "Who's that, mother?"

"Mr. Hall."

Photo 11 Missionaries Elizabeth Hall and the Reverend Alfred Hall, ca. 1870s.
Photographer undetermined. Image E-09190, Royal BC Museum, BC Archives.

"She had one of them separate [too]," Christine said.

"They look like pretty intense people," I said.

"Yeah, they look powerful. I don't know why they had to not smile in those days."

I asked Christine how she would like to see her grandmother remembered in a book.

"That was my question. How would *she* like to be remembered?" she replied. "I'd like her to be remembered for what she stood for, and I think her life and her faith, to me, made her who she was. I think that's how she would like to be remembered."

"For her Christian faith?"

"Yeah, although Christianity isn't always portrayed that way. It's a way of life. And a person should emulate that way of life. We all fail, but, you know, basically that's what it is. And I think that she did run a good race. She did do a good job. She did the best that she could. So, to me, I think she would like it to be remembered that she lived her life truly in what she believed. And she certainly tried to pass the baton. Unfortunately, none of us picked it up."

Jane's descendants stressed that Granny Cook's way in the world had been grounded in her faith and that she expressed her faith through *doing* and through socializing her children and grandchildren into ways of *being* in the community. Several of G̲a'ax̲sta'las's grandchildren were touched by what they called her teachings. As Chris Cook Jr. told me, "Granny and her beliefs – it seemed to me that she was well respected by my mother [a member of the Hunt family] and that the teachings that she had with the church and religion and the things that were happening with other people, you know, I think those passed down to us. I think maybe not directly from her but directly through her children and their children. We learned how to live, eh?"

When Nella Nelson interviewed her father George Cook for this project, she asked him about his grandmother's teachings, about how to treat each other or people in the village. "As far as the community," George said, "Granny always maintained that we always had to be kind and willing to help those that are in need ... I think of people that had no relatives ... That was her motto – "If you had, you could share." And that's one of the things she taught us – that we had to learn to share, and it was a good thing ... All I can recall is that she was very easygoing and open for discussion, and I know that we had discussions about other things. But since she was a Christian, she talked to us about Christianity."

Many of Jane Cook's grandchildren spent childhood years in the Cook family big house, as they call it. They heard her speak in church. They saw the comings and goings of chiefs and women and children and visitors from other villages. They noted her absences at all hours to care for sick and dying people. They lived with those who were offered meals, advice, and shelter in their extended family home. Some granddaughters attended the Women's Auxiliary, where they served women tea and learned to sew. They participated in preparing and distributing food for church bazaars. They also travelled with their grandparents to Victoria to attend Anglican synods. Grandsons contributed their fishing earnings to the extended family pot, they helped till the soil in G̲a'ax̲sta'las's garden, and they listened as she spoke to them about the importance of land claims.

Jane Cook's grandchildren who lived in 'Ya̲lis grew up at a time (from the 1930s to the 1950s) when most in the village, including those who potlatched during the ban, were participating members of the Anglican Church. Her great-grandchildren came of age from the 1960s to the 1980s, when there was a notable drop in the number attending church, a public reanimation of ceremonial life in the Big House, and a new politicization of colonial history. A researcher working in Alert Bay in 1966 wrote, "One Indian informant put it this way: 'Indians around here are married and buried Anglican. The rest of the time they're Pentecostal if they're anything – which most of them aren't.'"[2] By all accounts, in 'Ya̲lis from the 1930s to the 1960s, Christians and non-Christians were not bounded communities.

Several of G̲a'ax̲sta'las's great-grandchildren were born before she died in 1951, but few actually have firsthand memories of her. Instead, they recount stories told by their parents and by others in her community. Some great-grandchildren address their family's participation in the church through the idiom of biculturality (as Wedłidi Speck did). Others contextualize Granny Cook's Christianity by considering what was going on during her time and noting that their grandmother was among the first generation of strong Christians. Although her social position must have been challenging, her descendants face another kind of challenge because of it.

When Randy Bell spoke with me about the church, he invoked a sense of personal and familial identity: "The story I always share is that I grew up learning both sides of culture because I'm mixed-blood too – and that's a part of your identity. We're always told that you have to recognize your identity to move forward. But I think, too, there was a shame there. I know for myself, and for my family, that's the reason why we went to church. At least we had some dignity within the church. And they were recognized as noble community people. They weren't recognized in the Big House. So that's why our family, I feel, stayed going to the church – because they were accepted there. And now it's come full circle, where we're in the Big House, and we're accepted there." Our conversation was recorded after the Gix̲sa̲m

Feast, a point of departure for many in the family regarding their "acceptance" in the ceremonial realm.

Jane Cook's descendants expressed perspectives on Christianity that suggest both unease and affinity with the church. I often spoke with family members about how to represent Christianity. One afternoon, Pearl Alfred told me, "Everything she believed is in us. There's this sense that the church still has a place in our lives. I think we're all believers. We all seem to know that we are – her grandchildren."

Regarding missionaries, Pearl said: "These are people who influenced her. We have to see them for what they were and try to pick out what *she* believed. I'd like to think that, in spite of them, her beliefs were her own. There's no doubt about what she believed in – and made sure *we* all knew! It was as much a part of her life as her community life or her political life. But it's hard to think of how to do it." Pearl said the book should provide some sense of what Alfred Hall had thought, "something to show that she could live with someone like that and *still* come out a decent person, a very caring human being for all of her people." There was a pause in our conversation that day as I finished writing notes. "He believed they dug up bodies and ate them. Old chiefs used to laugh that they could convince people to do this. 'How gullible were the white people?'"

I heard Pearl's comments as a statement about surviving the missionary.

"Well, the whole purpose, the Christian purpose, was to civilize the savage right?" George Speck and I were talking about the missionary. "Of course, we fit that category at the time, with a lot of our ceremonies being quite repulsive to the Christian community. Yeah, they just wanted to eradicate any vestige of who we were and what we were doing. They thought they were doing us a favour."

Alfred Hall's letters are punctuated with a nineteenth-century racism that advocated what he called the "temporal and spiritual salvation" of Kwakwa̱ka̱'wakw peoples. Missionaries believed they would advance so-called heathen peoples within what was then widely accepted among Europeans as a universal evolutionary scheme that culminated in "civilization" – European Christianity, especially devotion to the one Christian deity, God. The Gospel (word of God) would "liberate" non-European peoples from an imagined spiritual "darkness." To missionaries, the singular truth of Christian scriptures carried the "light" of "eternal salvation." Proselytization and individual conversion were central to the evangelical practices of the Church

Mission Society.[3] Alfred Hall's letters, written from the field and now 130 years old, frame his intentions.

The proximity of nineteenth-century racism and Eurocentrism to aboriginal people who engaged with Christianity deserves delicate treatment, especially given the tendency to imagine it as a kind of contagion, to imagine conversion as the wholesale acceptance of colonial ideology and practice.[4] This assumption implies knowledge about the context within which predecessors lived, knowledge about their motivations to act and react, to be moved and to move others. Questions about choice and victimhood arise at this juncture, and no one I spoke with was willing to relegate G̱a'ax̱sta'las to the role of victim.

"It's never that simple, being a victim," George Speck continued. "It's too one-dimensional to see it that way. The aboriginal world was unavoidably changed when the first fort was erected, when the first pelt was traded, the first cutting tool acquired. Europeans didn't need to show up, things would have changed – production, potlatching, our own internal change. Just the introduction of metal tools brought a whole new set of wealth, social positions, authority. We'll never know. Colonialism did happen and colonization did happen."

Colonialism did not entail a total colonization of populations. Aboriginal peoples also indigenized colonial situations, commodities, and relationships.[5] Scholars have been warned of the dangers of reinforcing colonial categories and reproducing imperial fallacies by paying sole attention to colonial records. As many writers have shown, those who rely exclusively on missionary documents risk retelling a dominant history, one that obscures peoples' active role in "shaping the historical trajectories it narrates" by relegating aboriginal people to supporting roles, as "passive agents who merely accepted or rejected" Christianity.[6] Others remind us that we may read the colonial archive with the intention to "decenter colonial representations by identifying and decoding the traces of indigenous action and presence" without assuming the complete dominance of missionaries.[7]

With such risks in mind, I present excerpts from a number of Alfred Hall's letters, which offer varying images of encounters between 1877 and 1880. I am interested in the context of the early mission and in the imaginative tools that informed that interaction. G̱a'ax̱sta'las's descendants read for other details.

Alfred Hall's missives from Tsax̱is tell a story from the standpoint of a young missionary observer. Jane Cook's descendants, in turn, respond to various aspects of this encounter and its legacies.

Arrival: Alfred James Hall

At my first meeting with Wedłidi Speck, we drank tea in the lounge of the Bengal Bar at the Empress Hotel in Victoria. I brought photocopies of archival images, one of them the portrait of the Reverend Alfred Hall and Elizabeth Thimbleby Hall. Looking at the image, Wedłidi said: "You know my name was Alfred James? I was named after my dad's uncle, who was named after Hall. Yeah, I changed it to Wedłidi. I didn't want to have any connection to the missionary."

Reading vertically through the generations in the fifteen-page "Cook Family Descendant Report," I saw other instances of tribute through naming. In 1898, G̲a'ax̲sta'las and Na̲ge named their fourth son, their seventh child, Alfred Hall Cook. He passed away a year later from dysentery, and they named his younger brother, born in 1900, Ernest Hall Cook. Their first child, Elizabeth Grace, had been born in August 1889, and Jane and Stephen perhaps named her after Hall's wife. Although there is little oral or written evidence of G̲a'ax̲sta'las's time with these missionaries, we do assume that Elizabeth Hall was her principal teacher in the early years of the mission.

Hall's handwritten letters from his time in Metlakatla and Fort Rupert in the late 1870s offer a vivid portrait – through a young missionary's eyes – of the early interactions that constituted the mission as a historical process, as a gradual acceleration of political power attained, in part, through immersion in Kwakwa̲ka̲'wakw village life.[8] To me, Hall's letters to London visually evoke the coastal rainforest from which they were sent. They appear waterlogged. Ink bleeds through both sides of the thin-grade writing paper. Or perhaps this effect was the result of microfilming.[9]

Whatever the cause, it seems apt that Hall's words survive in a tangle of cursive, in a form that evokes the messiness of competing truths and what must have been the confusion of forms witnessed by this young English observer. Hall's early impressions conform to appraisals of the Kwakwa̲ka̲'wakw "character" disseminated by earlier explorers, traders, naval officers, journalists, and missionaries.[10] He sent his letters by steamer and "canoes going south." A lag of at least one month usually followed the inscribed date of writing and the date his letters were received by the secretaries of the Church Mission Society (CMS) in London.[11]

Hall worked in the context of an expanding British Empire and growing awareness of the destruction wrought by expansion. In 1836, for example, the CMS had joined with the Anti-Slavery Society, the

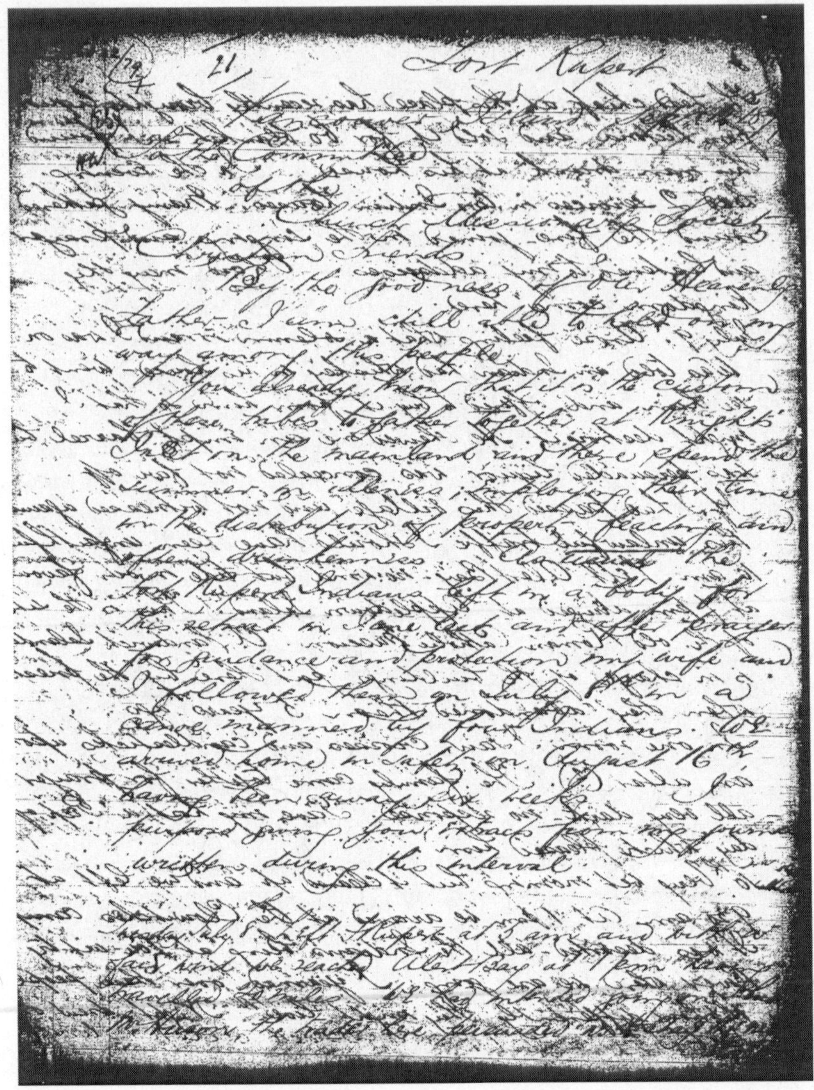

Fort Rupert

Vancouver's Island

To the Committee of the Church Missionary Society

Christian Friends

By the goodness of our Heavenly Father I am still able to hold on my way among this people. You already know that it is the custom of these tribes to gather together at Knight's Inlet on the mainland and there spend the summer [illegible] employing their time in the distribution of property, feasting and [illegible] drunkenness. [illegible] the Fort Rupert Indians left in a body for this resort in June last and after prayer for guidance and protection my wife and I followed them on July [illegible] in a canoe manned by four Indians. We arrived home in safety on August 16th having been away [illegible] weeks. [illegible] purpose giving you [illegible] from [illegible] written during the interval.

[illegible] left Fort Rupert at 3 am and [illegible] reached Alert Bay at 7 pm [illegible] travelled 20 miles [illegible] we had intended [illegible] the trader [illegible]

Photo 12 A page from Alfred Hall's letters written to London from Metlakatla and Fort Rupert between 1877 to 1890. *Church Mission Society Archives, 011/1-17, C C2/08/1-92.*

Aborigines' Protection Society, and other liberal and religious organizations in England to pressure the government for inquiries into the condition of "aborigines." Two parliamentary inquiries followed in 1837 and 1867.[12] According to anthropologist Jacob Gruber, "The awareness of the destructive impact of European civilization on native peoples and their cultures was both sudden and traumatic. As in the almost contemporary cases of urban blight and the desolation of the urban poor, the dysfunctional effects of the spread of European influence and power was dramatized as it was provided official recognition through the formality of parliamentary investigation."[13]

Official recognition did not result in attempts to halt the destructive impact of colonialism. One result of this awareness sparked the development of nineteenth-century salvage anthropology.[14] For missionaries, imperialism called for humanitarian projects to ease (through conversion) what they saw as the inevitable transition from "heathenism" to "civilization." Indeed, their goal during early missions on the Northwest Coast was largely to counter the effects of so-called white influence.[15]

G̲a'ax̲sta'las was seven years old when Alfred Hall, newly ordained and twenty-four years old, arrived in Victoria. His first letter to Henry Wright, secretary of the CMS, gushed with details about his adventure. He reported dutifully that on his journey he had been "called in to speak words of comfort to a dying man" and that he had also "prayed earnestly" for himself one night as his steamer to San Francisco "rocked and cracked" in a "severe gale." On his way from England to Victoria, Hall read the book *Stranger Than Fiction* and reported that he had found it "very valuable." It apparently "kept in good circulation all the way."[16] He likely referred to the 1858 edition of *Truth Stranger Than Fiction,* the dictated autobiography of Josiah Henson (1789-1883), an escaped slave, Methodist Episcopal preacher, Underground Railroad activist, and model for Harriet Beecher Stowe's *Uncle Tom's Cabin.*[17]

Indeed, slavery weighed heavily on the minds of eighteenth- and nineteenth-century missionaries, as did cannibalism and other so-called heathen practices. After the 1850s, Protestant, English-speaking missionaries had likely read in-house accounts about slave murder, cannibalism and secret societies, and what they called "blood feud," a seemingly uncontrollable propensity for revenge killings.[18] Barry Gough argues that although the British slave trade was abolished in 1807 and the empire-wide trade in 1833, frontier situations were approached on a "case-by-case" basis. In British Columbia, it was the "moral influence of law – and presumably of Christianity" that would eventually eradicate slavery.[19] Law was meted out heavily by the naval gunboats that plied coastal waters. Chiefs eventually agreed to stop participating in the slave economy if other tribes did the same.[20] But slavery – in practice and as a symbol – loomed large in the nineteenth-century European imagination.

Anthropologist Michael Harkin suggests that abolitionism became a kind of metaphor used by missionaries. In Methodist records from the early Hiłdzakw (Bella Bella) he found a tendency to conflate slavery with prostitution and with customary practices such as prestige marriages, child (or "sham") marriages, polygamy, divorce, and menstrual seclusion.[21] Alfred Hall used the idea of slavery to comment on perceived inequities in the highly stratified village of Fort Rupert. "They are all slaves of each other," he wrote in 1878. Some "live upon the earnings of the workers ... potatoes are always eaten at a feast less than a week after they come out of the ground."[22] Slavery, in his estimation, also referred to constraints on individual liberty enforced through the authority of chiefs by adherence to "the custom," as potlatching was then called.

Freedom and individual liberty also figured in Jane Cook's later letters, and, like many missionaries, her concerns were gendered. The important difference was that she spoke on behalf of Kwakwa̱ka̱'wakw women. In many situations, she served as an advocate for relatives struggling with customary marriage and gender values.

Tsaxis, 1878-80

Alfred Hall walked ashore at Tsax̱is on 1 March 1878. His first letter to his superiors describes his arrival in vivid detail: "200 men were seated on the beach when I landed. With scarcely an exception they had only blankets wrapped around them and they nearly all had their faces streaked with black, red and yellow paint which gave them an impressive appearance. Their eyes followed me as I marched to the Fort with my bag." He also reported that he had passed a "Romanish priest" "on his way to embark in the steamer."[23] (The presence of an Oblate mission at Tsax̱is and what Hall called a "substantial school ... built by the Roman Catholics" raises interesting questions about G̱a'ax̱sta'las's well-known revulsion of incense.)[24]

By page two of his letter, Hall had identified significant colonial institutions in the vicinity: the Hudson's Bay Company, the Roman Catholic church, and the CMS's North Pacific Mission. Nowhere in this letter or others does he identify Kwakwa̱ka̱'wakw persons by name. Often composed of multiple syllables, Kwak̓wala names were

Photo 13 Tsaxis village, photographed by Oregon C. Hastings for Franz Boas, November-December 1894. The image shows wood plank houses, totem poles, and canoes on the beach. Two of the poles on the beach are blanket poles between which blankets were piled during potlatch ceremonies. "This image is awesome. This is part of the Kwagu'ł village where the 'Walas Kwagu'ł are located. The 'Walas Kwagu'ł is the tribe the Tsuntsunqwa'U and Wa'waliba'yi come from. Counting the houses, Wanukw's house in the Wa'waliba'yi is second to last on the far side *[right]*" (Wedłidi Speck). *SPC Nwc Kwakiutl NM No ACC # Cat 175078 00057400, National Anthropological Archives, Smithsonian Institution.*

likely difficult for Hall to distinguish and document. Instead, he describes "them" by rank, as powerful chiefs, lesser chiefs, or chiefs' wives. Hall identifies people by gender, age, racializing categories (for instance, "half-breed"), and propensity for literacy or a perceived openness to the Gospel. In contrast, he names missionaries, traders, bishops, archdeacons, and officers in full. His descriptions of Fort Rupert, for instance, refer to George Hunt; his father, "Mr. Hunt"; Bishop Ridley; and fellow missionary, Mr. Duncan of Metlakatla.

Hall initially had little positive to say about the people he had come to serve and among whom he wished to live. But he was productive. Within eight days, he had conducted two Sunday services and, through George Hunt, had translated two "simple hymns" and the Lord's

Prayer. "Every day and night," he wrote, "the monotonous sound of the drum is to be heard accompanied with feasting singing and dancing." He had arrived in the midst of what he called "the season of pleasure," "the season of the year that they give away their property." He had already spent seven months at Metlakatla, which he called his "season of discipline," and was well acquainted with the missionary's struggle to combat the custom. His letters describe the ceremonial and economic activities that flourished around him. Hall referred to them initially as occasions for receiving and distributing blankets and later as feasts and potlatches.

"This property-giving is very dear to the Indian," he wrote. "It is the very last thing he would give up – it is one of the things for which he lives and even at the moment of death he will spend his last moments in giving away property and arranging his debts." Hall had witnessed the conveyance of "medicine" to a chief so that he could live two more hours to repay his debts. He seemed much taken by the Tsax̱is chiefs' deeds and wrote about one elaborate transaction in which one thousand blankets had been exchanged for a "copper shield" by a chief who "erected a pole in front of his house on the top of which was placed the figure of a white man."[25] After witnessing one copper transaction, Hall described seeing four canoes, lashed together and decorated with flags, in which Kwagu'ł men danced "in honour of the chief and singing his praises." "By the giving away of property an Indian maintains his rank and among some tribes can become a chief by his generosity – in this way there are no less than 21 chiefs at our village."[26] Like most European observers of his day, Hall most often noticed and recorded elaborate exchanges of property, acts that G̱a'ax̱sta'las spent much of her public life translating.

I asked Wedłidi Speck if he knew what age Jane Cook might have been when she arrived in 'Ya̱lis. "She went to Fort Rupert when she was about nine or ten, I imagine. Shortly after 1881, Hall went over to Alert Bay, so, within a couple of years." G̱a'ax̱sta'las was possibly in Tsax̱is the year of Hall's arrival. According to oral histories, her father, William Gilbert, was at this time "buying furs up north." Her mother, G̱wa̱yuła̱las, was in Port Townsend, Washington, for Jane's brother, Charlie Newman, was born that year.

"I do not think there are 30 women in the place," Hall wrote, "and certainly not one between the ages of 15 and 22 years. The steamer which brought me here took ten women to Victoria." He wrote that women were sent by their fathers and husbands to "make a gain of them." Yet Hall followed this speculation by stating, "I have not been here long enough to form an opinion of the people myself. I gather all my information from the Hunt family and think it very reliable."[27] Hall likely hesitated to proclaim himself an authority because his superior, William Duncan, had recently reprimanded him for causing "a fanaticism ... which threatened to jeopardize the whole mission" at Metlakatla.[28]

Prior to the incident, Duncan had left Metlakatla for Victoria for a few days, leaving behind the newly arrived Hall. He later wrote: "It appears that after my departure Hall began to give the Indians very passionate addresses in English. So alarming was this sermon that [a witness] declares that on some occasions he could scarcely retain his seat. As might be expected the Indians quickly caught the excitement and soon a fire raged which defied all control."[29] During the night, small groups of men and women met to exchange dream narratives. In the church, a "murmuring sound" emanated from the communion table, a sound they interpreted as the "Spirit of God." They launched canoes to carry the news to other villages. Girls declared that they had found "the cross of Jesus" in a "rotten branch of a tree." Some people saw angels, and others "presented the appearance of being possessed," at which time "one of the Native teachers set out to exorcize them." William Duncan was livid. "For his own sake as well as the people here," he wrote, "it would be wise to place [Hall] where he can begin again ... I have recommended him to go [to Fort Rupert] til you have communicated with him. Work among heathen will tend to sober his judgment and afford ample room for all his zeal."[30] Two days later, Alfred Hall also wrote from Metlakatla to the Church Committee in London. His defence provides some sense of the way that missionary work was done in the early days of arrival. "I am sorry to say that brother Duncan and myself have not yet been drawn together by the bonds of love."[31] Hall listed his mistakes, noting his "ignorance of the language," that he should have called upon the "energies of the [elderly] Native Christians" who generally "preached at the Sunday Evening services." His biggest failure, he wrote, was "allowing the Natives to hold meetings for prayer and reading the Scriptures among themselves." He had delivered his sermon through a "spiritually minded" interpreter named David, who was "able to bring home the truths written on my paper to the hearts of the people."[32] Hall described weeping, repenting, praying – all responses to what he felt truly was "God's Holy Spirit." The scenario strongly suggests that Alfred Hall was invested in a charismatic expression of Christianity. But it is obvious that the CMS set limits on the ways that members of the congregation could legitimately express their religiosity.

Metlakatla was a utopian Christian village established by the willing relocation of eight hundred or so Tsimshian people from nearby Port Simpson.[33] It became a kind of CMS blueprint for new aboriginal communities: located far from the influence of traditional authority and from seasonal, chief-centred rounds of resource extraction and distribution. Above all, Duncan imagined Metlakatla as a place for industry, a place where literacy, Christianity, labour, and commerce held equal footing (an arrangement that did not endear Duncan to church officials).

In 1878, Duncan was poised to initiate a mission at Fort Rupert and leave his community at Metlakatla. As Reverend Hall wrote, "Fort Rupert is looked up to by all the other villages and therefore it is the best place to start a Mission but Mr. Duncan told me it would not do to settle there (for one thing all the land belongs to the Hudson's Bay Company) his desire is to draw the people [of Fort Rupert] to a new settlement in the same way as he acted at Metlakatla."[34] Alfred Hall's stated intention in his first letter from Fort Rupert was to stay there for a period of three to four years to master the language, visit other Kwakwa̱ka̱'wakw villages, and choose a site for a new mission.

The "Gospel Plough": Conversion

In his "Cultural History of the Cook Family," which he distributed to his relatives via email, Wedłidi Speck describes the imaginative realm of his ancestors. "The view of the world when Granny and Papa were born was one that was influenced by mythology, legends, and folklore. Myths like those of the Nuxnemis (myth people), Tlisalagilakw and K̲anik̲i'lakw, the origin of the ancestors, ceremonies, and the flood structured Kwakwa̱ka̱'wakw thought." Alfred Hall inhabited (and attempted to persuade Kwakwa̱ka̱'wakw people of the existence of) another storied realm, one based on Old and New Testament Christian writings. As Wedłidi Speck commented: "Hall was using the language to convert, so he had hymn books done and a language book done."

The CMS emphasized language proficiency. In a letter dated 16 October 1878, Hall quoted Henry Wright: "As soon as it is possible, get among the people themselves, listen to the way they speak, and practice what you have learnt."[35] Hall clearly viewed Kwak̓wala as an important proselytizing tool. Hymns were translated into Kwak̓wala, and they endured through the residential school years, when the language was banned. People today know and sing these hymns, but in the late nineteenth century, the CMS's explicit goal was to adapt what was called "the new literacy." William Duncan underlined the term in an 1878 letter. "The progress the Indians are making in English will make it quite unnecessary to translate the scriptures into their tongue."[36] Here was a suggestion for an explicit program of linguistic assimilation. Alfred Hall acknowledged that he was working in a multilingual environment. All "Indians," he wrote, know the Chinook trading jargon and some members of more isolated tribes had already heard the Gospel in the language.[37] Hall thought Chinook was too awkward for the nuances of scripture, and over the course of several years began translating various genres of Christian thought into Kwak̓wala.[38] He discovered that Bibles had already made their way, through traders, to some outlying villages, where he met mostly girls and young women who spoke English as they had been taught by Methodist and Catholic missionaries.

Language was essential to what Hall called the "Gospel Plough," the spoken word through which he delivered Christian stories and teachings, the "seed sown" to "make this desert to blossom as the rose."[39] In his letters, Hall is invited, time and again, into houses to speak. Crowds gathered around him on the beach and at his "Indian house" in Fort Rupert.[40] At this time, it was customary for strangers, especially strangers of some status, to be invited to speak and share food at feasts. These forms of hospitality, like the detailed ceremonies, were likely misunderstood by Hall. In January 1879, he complained that people at Fort Rupert spent three out of every four days "feasting and speaking."

Hall's first audiences were with high-ranking men, whom he identified as "medicine men" or "sorcerers" or, by their presumed "mysteries," they were members of the dance societies, likely chiefs. Occasionally, chiefs' wives attended his addresses in full regalia, as when three "Officers of the Guards," whom Hall called "white chiefs," arrived from England to hunt elk and bear.[41] At first, when women attended his sermons, Hall wrote that, "as a rule," they sat at one side of the room and men at the other, "because they are not allowed to attend the meetings which the men constantly hold to talk over the affairs of the camp." People who came to Hall's sessions often attended with painted faces, and "all were clothed in blankets, some of them highly ornamented with needlework and pearl buttons."[42] Few in his audience were inclined to stand and sing when he played hymns on his English concertina. They followed their own protocol for public oratory.

The Kwakwa̱ka̱'wakw initially received Hall as a speaker, as a male of some status who interacted with them in a verbal medium they excelled at and valued. Hall wrote that people would not sit "upon the forms I had made; they prefer to draw their ... blankets tightly round them and to squat on the floor. When I am speaking they generally rest their head upon their bent knees and fix their eyes upon the floor. Not a muscle seems to move, and they appear to drink in every word that is spoken to them."[43] At other times, Hall spoke through his interpreter and noted that members of his audience "talk among themselves," either approvingly, he thought, or "more often because the truth spoken is a rebuke to the speaker in the congregation."[44] Hall had yet to master Kwak̓wala.

His language instructor was George Hunt, son of Robert Hunt, "the officer in charge." Together, the two men translated hymns, chants, prayers, and the catechism, which was modelled after that used at Metlakatla. Indeed, after two years in Fort Rupert, Hall still struggled with Kwak̓wala and depended on his translator. He wrote that his usual approach was to have his "addresses written before I enter church and read to the interpreter." As he became more organized, he wrote his sermons in English, had Hunt translate them during the week, and then read to the people from these translations.[45] It would be intriguing to ponder the exact meaning of the words and concepts provided by George Hunt (and possibly other interpreters), but the biblical stories that constituted Hall's "Gospel Plough" are mentioned in his letters.

"I have almost exclusively spoken to them from the book of Genesis," Hall wrote in June 1878. "These narratives ... have attracted them very much and they listen very attentively to my interpreter."[46] Old Testament genealogies; narratives about feasts, tribal congregations, and dissolutions; and streams of names and acts of naming must have resonated with Kwagu'ł orators, themselves invested in telling lineage histories. In his analysis of the "Kwakiutl mythologies" that he and George Hunt elicited almost a decade after Hall's arrival, Franz Boas notes: "In Kwakiutl imagination the interest in crests and privileges runs riot. There are tales that consist of nothing else than the enumeration of crests and privileges obtained by marriage or war ... The persons appearing in Kwakiutl tales are always named."[47] Alfred Hall wrote that the story of Creation and the Fall of Man also "appealed" to Kwakwa̱ka̱'wakw listeners. One wonders how such stories were received alongside ancestor narratives, an important genre, as Boas notes.[48]

Another kind of narrative opportunism is evident in Hall's choice of scriptures about healing, miracles, and illness.[49] He drew often from the Book of Matthew, which speaks of the twelve disciples' power "against unclean spirits to cast them out and heal sickness and disease." In one striking instance, Hall recounts a visit to Alert Bay in 1880: "The tribe assembled and our subject was Blind Bartimaeus – much attention and all appeared reverent during prayer ... I afterwards asked if they wanted a teacher among them and they replied in the affirmative."[50] How was the story of a blind beggar whose sight was restored received at a time and in a place where smallpox, syphilis, measles, and other ailments that caused blindness were commonplace? Hall's letters mention disorders caused by stagnant water and the high incidence of blindness, deafness, and skin disease.[51] Measles and influenza had likely swept through Kwakwa̱ka̱'wakw territories in 1868 and 1869. Along with the ravages of "the trade in rot-gut whiskey," epidemics caused an estimated population decline of up to 78 percent between the 1840s and 1881.[52] Nineteenth-century missionaries explicitly linked the provision of medical services to success in spreading the Gospel.[53]

Hall wrote that he passed his time learning medicine, visiting houses, teaching whomever would show up, and studying the language. At the request of individuals in the villages, and sometimes without such appeals, he attended to injuries, infections, and illnesses. He wrote about the work of Kwakwa̱ka̱'wakw healers with little apparent scorn, noting in one letter a rare interaction with a woman "practitioner":

> The medicine men still exercise much power. A few days since I went to see a sick woman I entered her house and heard strange noises. A medicine woman with her back turned to me was blowing scientifically on the breast of the sick woman and occasionally making a peculiar howl. I watched the practitioner unobserved and when she turned round and saw me she gave me a grin of recognition and then continued her blowing. For this she was paid two blankets [twelve shillings].
>
> A famous [doctor?] was recently sent for from a neighbouring village – I heard him blowing in the same way, and for his visit he received thirty blankets.[54]

Kwakwaka'wakw healers were either male shamans or elderly women healers. Shamans, as Dara Culhane notes, hailed from the nobility and were imbued with supernatural power. Both groups of healers sometimes worked together, and although they both used medicines, chants, rituals, and personal counselling, elderly women "could cure but not cause, disease."[55] Hall's letter suggests that "healing practices were ... public [in] nature and required the attendance of the elders of the village at curing ceremonies."[56] In the decades that followed Hall's encounter, the role of aboriginal healers was recast by missionaries and Indian Agents, often in derogatory terms. European medicine was regarded as an arm of the civilizing mission, intended to dispel Kwakwaka'wakw understandings about curing and illness, to break loyalties to healers, and to apply principles of hygiene deemed necessary for progress.

"Good Marriage Prospects": Hygiene, Domestication, and Women

As we engaged in conversations about the early years, I came across a newspaper article by Simma Milner, which had been saved by Sadie Thompson, secretary to Indian Agent M.S. Todd, in a scrapbook now held at the Alert Bay Library and Museum. There was no source or date provided, but the entry is included with other material from around 1949.

> "Mother Dedicates Life to Service"
>
> Story of an Island woman who was midwife and nurse to hundreds of expectant mothers within a radius of 20 miles of Alert Bay was told here last week.
>
> She assisted at her first birth at the age of 17.
>
> The woman is Mrs. Stephen Cook, 79, who was in Vancouver last week for the first time in 19 years to attend the Native Indian Affairs conference at Acadia Camp.
>
> Mrs. Cook recalls how her self-education in her isolated forest home on Queen Charlotte Sound helped her to deliver her own 18 children, gave her fundamental knowledge to treat the hundreds of tuberculosis victims who came to Alert Bay to die, and gave her background to be a lone nurse to 2000 Indians and many white people during the flu epidemic of 1918.

> She was born in the United States.
>
> Her father was a stickler for education and sent her to school in Victoria when the city was still mostly wilderness. She got as far as third reader when, for financial reasons, her father was forced to seek his fortune in the north.
>
> He took her into the wilderness with him and 5 other men. Her baggage was a big box of books.
>
> Still stumbling in her elementary reading education, she plowed through Scott, Dickens, Shakespeare, and the Bible. Then she found a big medical book.
>
> "Then I returned to Alert Bay. ... God seemed always to guide my footsteps back there through all of my wanderings," she said.
>
> One day when she was 17, a woman in labour came to the beach of Alert Bay. She could go no further.
>
> "I found myself taking over," said Mrs. Cook. "I gave her courage at the same time as I brought her baby into the world."[57]

Notably, there is no mention of Jane Cook's early life at Fort Rupert. G̲a'ax̲sta'las's descendants were interested in what the newspaper article *did* reveal about her early life. Regarding literacy, they spoke again about the impressive library in the Cook family home. Given the number of accounts that stress her childhood in a convent or other religious institution, it is interesting that G̲a'ax̲sta'las emphasized that she had had an intellectual rather than a religious upbringing. She was proud that she had "plowed" through several classics of English literature. Some family members questioned whether it had really been nineteen years since she had last visited Vancouver, although George Cook did mention that, by that time, her political career had ended and she spent most of her time in her garden.

Of course, Jane Cook, as far as is documented, gave birth to sixteen, not eighteen, children. Despite inaccuracies, this brief article is the closest we can come to hearing Jane's own account of her early "wanderings." But I wonder about the rest of her narrative, which was omitted by the journalist, as is implied by the ellipsis. There is a sense of strength and conviction in the verbatim comments. Certainly, there is an indication not only of her faith but also of her confidence in her ability to "take over" in an emergency, to offer "courage" and some skill in midwifery. Although medical care was an aspect of missionary training, Jane stated that she was self-taught from a "big medical book."[58] The headline of the newspaper article mentions "service," and, by all accounts, this was the most striking expression of G̲a'ax̲sta'las's Christianity.

The article refers to the 1948 Conference on Indian Affairs, held at the University of British Columbia. Transcripts of the meeting include clear statements by G̲a'ax̲sta'las about missionaries, "Indian" religion, and education. At that conference, her long-time colleague Chief Andrew Paull, then president of the Indian Brotherhood, addressed the subject of health and focussed on the topic of hygiene, which so occupied colonial administrators: "The fundamental code of the Indians was HYGIENE," he said. "The Indians were taught the proper use of herbs, after years of experience by their ancestors ... and to have frequent sweat baths ... Their code was cleanliness of their bodies, and changing their abode, so that dirt and filth would not accumulate. And so, while the peasant of Europe was wallowing in poverty and filth the lordly Indian of the forest was practicing hygiene in everyday life."[59] Paull discussed the criminalization of the "old customs" that followed the potlatch ban and extended to what he called "hygienics." He railed against the colonial program to force coastal people to abandon seasonal, communal longhouses.

In the nineteenth century, women in particular were seen to have a central role in the colonial program of hygiene, and missionaries believed domestication would bring about change. They expended their energies on teaching women literacy, influencing marriage customs, and shaping the composition and organization of households. Missionaries considered so-called domestication especially necessary for women, for literacy would give them access to the scriptures.[60] Gender relations figured into the choices that missionaries made about scripture and education.

Gloria Cranmer-Webster told me that she had been warned by her grandmother that literacy had an ill effect on women's participation in village life. "Several times my grandmother said, 'You shouldn't do that. You're going to get into trouble. It's not good for you.' And it wasn't until I grew up that I heard stories about girls coming out of St. Mike's [St. Michael's Residential School], back into their little villages, being completely unable to fit in. And they drifted away to places like Vancouver and Victoria. So it wasn't just the potlatch." She refutes the colonial agents' claim that Kwakwa̲ka̲'wakw women were lured to cities primarily to earn income to support potlatching males.

Nineteenth-century missionaries sought, in part, to use literacy to curb women's movements by replacing their veneration for "the custom" with the Victorian ethic of stay-at-home domesticity. Alfred Hall had a blueprint for women's role in his mission. "There is a marked contrast," he wrote, "between the women who were trained in the Mission house and others. The former are quite domesticated – many of them have clean homes and they exercise a good influence throughout the village. The girls enter the Mission house when about 10 years of age and remain if their conduct is good until they are married."[61] Hall admired Duncan's utopian Christian village. He likely followed this model of domestication aimed at girls but also intended to influence young men, who would find among the girls "good marriage prospects." When he first arrived at Tsax̱is, no women came to Hall's Sunday sermons. What started out as a crowd of 130 men soon dwindled to 50.[62] Later, his audiences consisted primarily of women.[63]

On 13 June 1879, Hall wrote to the CMS secretary, seeking permission to marry a Miss Thimbleby, who was a few years his senior. He mentioned that "married missionaries for the Pacific Coast were required," an edict on appropriate gender models, one that set an example of the nuclear family household.[64] Earlier that year, Hall's annual letter to the CMS had stated: "There are today 54 women from the place alone, living in Victoria or on the American territory, opposite to Victoria."[65] The seemingly unfettered mobility of Kwakwa̱ka̱'wakw women perplexed him. After the establishment of the Kwawkewlth Agency in 1881, mobility was also the focus of Indian Agents. Women who lived in cities and travelled throughout the territories had moved beyond the direct influence of the mission. When they returned with "bales" of blankets, Hall attributed their wealth solely to prostitution, erasing all other economic ventures in which Kwagu'ł women participated.[66]

Nineteenth-century missionaries of several denominations subscribed to the idea that women were more attached to the ways of their ancestors, that they essentially ruled households but had too much geographical mobility and social freedom.[67] The "remedies" (for "infectious disease was the model for all social ills") included moral and ideological persuasion to curtail women's physical and social autonomy.[68] "Marriage careers" (as Michael Harkin calls the successively higher, prestige unions among Northwest Coast peoples) figured prominently in the actions of missionaries. "I think everyone knows that [women] were very important in the potlatch scheme of things," Gloria Cranmer-Webster told me. "A chief or the son of a chief is not going to marry a nobody. It has to be somebody who can bring privileges with her. [She] can't come empty-handed." High-ranking women in Northwest Coast societies were important participants in the transmission of names and ancestral privileges. Missionaries viewed them as valuable subjects for conversion and literacy.

"With reference to school," Hall wrote, "I am sorry to say there are few Indian children to attend – the profligate lives of the women is the reason for their scarcity. I do not think there are more than twenty children under 12 years of age in this village – all these come to school and together with the young men and women I sometimes get an attendance of 40 or 50."[69] The missionaries believed that the time and spatial regimes imposed by school and by the adoption of nuclear family households with Christian women in charge would eventually break the pattern of multiple marriages and the frequent absences of women from the villages.

According to Wedłidi Speck, Jane Constance Gilbert arrived in Tsax̱is sometime around 1879 or a year later. Presumably, she was among the children who attended school at Hall's "Indian house" near the centre of the village. The 1881 census, however, lists her as not attending school. If Jane Gilbert did go to Hall's school, she would have learned the hymn "Jesus Loves Me, This I Know," the Lord's Prayer, and several Christian chants that had already been printed in English and Kwak̓wala.[70] Hall acknowledged that there was "no doubt" a "desire" among people in the village "to learn to read and write." "I know," he wrote, "the reason why they are anxious to learn is that they make a display of their learning, and this adds to their importance."[71] Clearly, the Kwagu'ł peoples attached some internal status to literacy. The distrust Hall expressed became exaggerated over time. Missionaries eventually sought excessive and exclusive displays of faith before conferring spiritual blessings such as confirmation. Of course, renouncing the custom was primary.

Given the Kwagu'ł peoples' thirty-year experience with external power, it is interesting that in a letter dated 11 June 1878 Hall wrote about a "deputation of the chiefs ... [who] told me they had waited a long time and now they believed something was going to be done for them. They also said French priests no good we want English priests all the Romanish priests are from France." It is reasonable to assume that Kwagu'ł chiefs were well aware of the language through which surveying lands, regulating trade and commerce, and allocating rights through treaty-making proceeded.[72] English was the language of the monarchy in whose name colonial agents acted, and members of the Anglican clergy (as well as their Methodist and Presbyterian counterparts) likely had easier access to aboriginal communities in British colonies because of it. Achieving literacy in English equipped individuals to communicate politically in a context where the autonomy of chiefs was increasingly challenged. For those not of high rank, English fluency enabled them to seek better opportunities at a time of dizzying change when wage labour was overtaking 'na̲'mima-centred economies.[73]

Reverend Hall wrote about – but did not name – chiefs whose opposition to his "teachings" obstructed the mission. "There is one powerful chief who is doing all he can to prevent the people coming to school and service."[74] John Tait, a "Native teacher," did note the names of three Fort Rupert chiefs in April 1877. Barry Gough lists them as Chief "Tsooachwiddy,"* who "said he would not follow Christian teaching"; Chief "Wahcahsh"; and Chief "Quahquahdahkallah," who stated that they would.[75] Misheard, misunderstood, or misdocumented names add to the difficulty of reading them across time, but the actions of the three chiefs in 1877 imply that there was no agreement among leaders in Tsax̱is regarding the potential damage or benefit of Alfred Hall's presence.

Hall wrote toward the end of his two years in Tsax̱is, "I cannot tell you yet these ... men who come to my services are seeking a better way ... I cannot tell you that I see any change in them. I know that some of them hate me and speak against it – but they come and hear the truth." Hall understood that his affiliation with Robert Hunt and the attendance of the "head chief" at his school "make the few who fear me hold their peace."[76] He patched together information about local leadership and rank from the Hunt family, from his knowledge of Tsimshian people at Metlakatla, and from his own observations. His narrated experiences suggest that he was invited into houses to observe ceremonials and, at times, asked to speak publicly. They leave the impression that his presence was not viewed as imposing.

---

* "I think Tsooachwiddy may be Owadi," Wedłidi Speck wrote to me about these names. "Owadi was 'Nulis's brother but also rival. 'Nulis had the name Wakius when sitting among the Koskimo. There is a picture of Wakius in Boas's book *Secret Societies* (1887) holding a copper. This is the picture that I showed you that really resembled Granny Cook and Hamasaga. Quahquahdahkallah is a common name among the Kwagu'ł. Gwagwadaxala, for example, was my uncle Billy Cook. However, in the context of this time ... I will scan my records." Many of our co-investigations into the past proceeded on these lines – through names. The holders of the names are located geographically (read genealogically, by village and 'na̲'mima affiliation) and temporally (by year) to clarify which holder of the name it might be.

"The Burden of Souls"

Alfred Hall embarked by canoe on his longest journey to the southern Kwakwaka'wakw villages in February 1880. His letters and itinerary include written observations about winter ceremonies and feasts – the constant flow of gift exchanges, dances, and songs and speech making that more often than not interfered with his delivery of the Gospel. In most villages, he and his five-man crew were, according to his own descriptions, accepted. But during the winter months he met with an impenetrable barrier of activities particular to what he called the "sacred season."[77] The young Alfred Hall likely had little sense of what was going on in this ritually charged context. Descriptions of his sojourn at one village portray his fatigue and his surprisingly casual manner:

> The people appeared fierce but were really kind. All wore turbans of red bark a sign that the winter dances were not over. Soon after our arrival a feast was given in the chief's house. Thirty men sat in front of me and sang, keeping time by striking boxes placed in front of them. Seals were boiled and eaten by the 200 guests.
>
> In the evening visited the Indians in their homes. In one house the head man seemed to receive the faith with gladness and explained my words to all present. While singing a hymn a message came from the chief saying it was unlawful to sing because of the red bark turbans they were wearing.
>
> When sitting in another house the same Evening I saw a strange scene. Whistling and growling were heard and then followed a terrible scratching at the door. It opened and in sprang a man naked, leaping on his hands and legs and tied round the waist with a long rope held by six men. After jumping across the fire two or three times he attempted to grasp all present as if desiring to bite them. He clutched hold of my coat but soon left the house. In a few minutes another medicine man held by five men in the same way went through the same performance. All in the house were frightened and ran away, and I heard afterwards that two men were bitten that Evening.
>
> Preparations were now being made in the house where I had to sleep for an Indian dance. About 9pm a large fire was lit in the centre of the large building and an audience of 250 were soon seated in it. The singers as before sang most heartily and made a deafening noise with their sticks. Several women stood up to dance; moving gracefully round the fire with their hands above their heads they kept time with

the singers. The dancers wore blue blankets decorated with pearl buttons and had crowns of red bark upon their heads. While this was going on out jumped the medicine man from behind a curtain – he was still naked and held in the same manner by 6 men and their object seemed to be to prevent him rushing among the audience or jumping in the fire – he danced with his hands on the ground in a most frantic manner and snorted like a wild bull.

About 11pm this was all over and then in the same house when all had gone out what a blessed contrast it was to read with my crew and a few other the words of our God to sing his praises and to kneel together in prayer.

Tuesday Visited a house this morning and found many preparing for a feast. About 30 gathered round me, and I began as usual with prayer. Was reading to this attentive group when the medicine man rushed in and all fled leaving me sitting alone. Felt my way barred from preaching the Gospel because of the excitement in the camp.

Wed. 11:30am Upward of 200 assembled and all were very attentive. According to their wish I refrained from singing. When I asked if they understood me several cried out "Yes! Yes! go on, go on we are listening. your words are good."

When the service was over a very old man replied he said his tribe were a hard working people and they were all glad to see a teacher among them.

He also said it was a pity that I have come while they wore the red bark turbans because that made them all crazy. When I asked if they wished a teacher to live among them the chief replied "you must please yourself."[78]

If anything, the chief responded with ambivalence. Yet, in other letters, Hall documented both explicit resistance *and* positive desire to having the Englishman among them. Perhaps the ambivalence reflected Hall's conscious decision never to speak "against the custom or ask them to give it up," although it is also evident that the chiefs with whom he met expected him to oppose their ceremonial practices.[79] This relationship would change with the establishment of the Kwawkewlth Indian Agency in 1881 and the subsequent enforcement of the potlatch ban.

Hall's letter portrays a community deeply engaged in public and secret-sacred performances. He was invited to witness ceremonies and stayed at a house hosting a Winter Dance, where he was subject to the strictures of the sacred season. He was, apparently, an easy mark for those he called the "medicine men" (likely Hamat̓sa initiates in an ecstatic state), who grabbed at his coat and danced about him in mock threat while everyone else knew enough to flee. Hall's description includes the gendered roles of dancers and singers, the presence and participation of audience members at feasts and dances, and the authority of chiefs.

"The children follow their fathers and grandfathers in the same way dance year by year," Hall wrote in another letter. He describes a ritual in which "the party – when they perform are hung up with hooks in a triangular frame: one hook being stuck into the back and two more in the legs, and suspended in this way they are carried through the village."[80] They were Hawinalạł performing the Warrior Hook Dance.

"You must have heard about Papa Cook being a Hawinalał – a warrior dancer?" William Wasden Jr. asked me in 2004. I hadn't, at that time. "In Daisy Sewid's book they talked about it," he said, "Granny Axuw talks about it in *Paddling to Where I Stand*. There's a part in there about Stephen Cook. My grandmother told me he was supposed to be a Hamat̓sa, but something went wrong, so they shifted him to a different society. And he was the last one in our village that they actually pierced. He was a little boy, and his uncle initiated him. He had the scars, and I guess he used to show it off when he was with some of the family. He was the last one to go through the whole ritual of being pierced and hung up in the long house by his – I think it was on his back and his collar bones."

In their books, Agnes Alfred and Charlie Nowell each describe the initiation of the Hawinalał within the Red Cedar Bark Ceremony. In Agnes Alfred's narrative, Stephen Cook is called by his secular or summer name K̓a̱xwstutłe (Whale Sticking Head Out of the Water, Looking).[81] His Hawinalał or Warrior Dance name was Winidi (One Who Wars). Stephen Cook was lowered through the smoke hole of the Big House. "During the ceremony they would pull the ropes until the flesh breaks ... Apparently it was real trouble for Q̓a^{x}wstuƛēy̓ [Stephen Cook]. He had his flesh pierced as a hawinalał. He was just a child. He would yell his hawinalał cry 'ay̓ ay̓ ay̓' and end with 'son of a bitch G^{w}ik^{w}iy' [or W̓asw̓as]. *[Laughter]* This was addressed to W̓asw̓as, who was initiating him ... I did not see this, I was just told about it."[82] When Alfred Hall witnessed the initiation of Warrior Hook dancers in 1878, he wrote: "By suffering in this way they keep up the dignity of their ancestors and are renowned for their bravery."[83] He had been in Tsaxis for six months, and the comment suggests some understanding of the importance of ancestral continuity.

Hall offered no cosmological explanation for the ceremonials he witnessed. One gets the sense that he was documenting exotica that bolstered his credibility, that he sought to persuade his superiors of his challenges. "Here I am and here I deserve to stay," he wrote in September 1878. "I heard this expression in England 'the burden of souls,' I know what this is now."[84] Many of Hall's letters ended with the words, "Believe Me."

When surveyor George Dawson arrived in what he called "Kwakiool territories," in 1878, his attention to "folklore" focussed on stories about the transformer, "Kan-ē-a-ke-luh," who, according to Alfred Hall, was "regarded as a deity and as the creator."[85] George Dawson was more nuanced in his statements about cosmology. He noted a pantheon of beings "attaching to localities" and an "unknown being of great power ... named Kī-ī," who "is respected, and petitioned in prayer." He also wrote about the sun (linked directly to Kan-ē-a-ke-luh and addressed in prayers as "our chief") and mountains, who were appealed to for "favourable winds" and addressed as "the ancients."[86]

The Church Mission Society had four principles: "to follow God in the same way as the missionaries of the early Church," "to begin humbly and on a small scale," to put money after prayer and study," and "to depend on the Holy Spirit."[87] After his embarrassment at Metlakatla, Hall was careful to encourage the "inward work of the Holy Spirit" rather than what he considered "the folly of expecting outward manifestations of God's presence."[88] How Kwakwaka'wakw people in the nineteenth century might have interpreted this spirit is a matter of speculation. Conceptually, the embodiment of different spirits was not at all foreign, but it was available only to high-ranking members of secret dance societies. The Holy Spirit was perhaps a way in for missionaries. But Hall was hesitant about allowing Kwakwaka'wakw people free charismatic expression, particularly given the representations of cannibalism in the Hamatsa performance.[89]

Reverend Hall seemed motivated to convey a "warlike" Kwakwaka'wakw past in his letters to the CMS. There is more than a hint of imperialist nostalgia in his description of the "Quaq-gulth" past:

> Twenty years ago there were 500 Indians at this camp but smallpox and the debauchery in which they have lived ... has left but a remnant of what they once were. Once it was the leading tribe among the

> Indians speaking the Quaq-gulth language famous for their warlike achievements, their bravery and wonton cruelty, so that Northern Indians were never safe in passing up and down this coast and on one occasion HMS Clio burnt down the camp because the people refused to deliver up two murderers who were in the camp. There are [few?] alive now, who can tell me of the triumph which was manifested when the war parties returned to the camp bringing with them the heads of their victims and placing them in heaps on the beach.[90]

Hall's description set the stage for an account of the Kwagu'ł's degradation, in good part because of colonial influences. Missionaries in late nineteenth-century BC sought to dissuade aboriginal peoples from travelling to the cities, to entice them to found new settlements away from the temptations of frontier society, but also away from the influence of the custom. "Our Society is for the express purpose of sending Christ's gospel to the heathen, to the dark corners of the Earth – permit me to say I do not think there is any corner of the earth where the Gospel is more need than here. The climate is beautiful 'the Prospect pleases but only man is vile' – I cannot call it a corner of the Lord's vineyard it is a desert a wilderness that has never been cultivated and rank [?] weeds have been germinated from other lands to make the wilderness more dense."[91]

By 1879, Hall's letters were focussed on the debt incurred through what he called "property giving." The practice, he wrote,

> makes the Missionary detest the "custom" ... it is a cause of endless jealousy, strife, hatred and Evil speaking ... The Indians know that I am opposed to this system, their consciences tell them this. They have already come to tell me they are willing to give up every other custom but this one. They are positive they must retain this or else the old men will starve. Of course such reasoning is false, it is the abominable system which enslaves them and keeps them lazy and consequently poor ... The time has not yet come to attack any of their customs directly. I am giving them the "light" of "God's Word."[92]

His decision not to attack any of their customs perhaps reflected a need to garner trust. Although he was not yet invested with state power, he knew that would soon change.

Letters from Hall's early years in Tsax̱is give the impression that he was in no position to declare anything with authority. Largely ignored by those with customary power, he was eventually haunted by his mission's failure. By his own account, the mission in January 1880 suffered from the prolonged absence of residents travelling to pursue economic activities, fishing and hunting, feasting, and potlatching. In March 1879, he admitted that the people of Tsax̱is had only been present in the village for five of the eleven months he had resided there. "When the time has arrived," he wrote, "and I have fixed on a desirable site, I shall propose to these people that we found a new settlement where all who wish to give up heathenism can come and settle."[93] Within the goals and projects of the North Pacific Mission, his scheme was predictable. His "desirable site" was Alert Bay.

August 20 1880

... Since I last wrote a school has been erected at Alert Bay 40 × 20 feet ...

For the last two months a Fort Rupert half-caste has lived with us and assisted in the school. He speaks and reads English very fluently and from what I have seen of him since his stay with me I have decided to send him to Alert Bay as soon as the Indians have finished salmon fishing.

Acting also upon the Bishop's instructions an application has been made to purchase 160 acres of land at Alert Bay (4/per acre) for the C.M.S. As soon as the purchase is complete it is proposed that our Mission house be built and the teacher William [Brotchi] will return to Fort Rupert. I find my message is accepted by most [of] the people, but they seem determined, led by the chief who opposes the Gospel, to continue their potlatching. They want to hold Christianity with one hand and still retain their potlatching by which they live ... The Indians are ready to make concessions in anything else but this is the monster evil and I have positively refused Baptism Marriage to those who refuse to abandon this practice ... My hope is in the young ...

For some time we have had four girls in our house and shall have a greater number when we can accommodate them. We are very anxious to save these girls. The training of them devolves upon Mrs. Hall a work she is adapted for and takes delight in. She joins me in Christian love.

Desiring Your continuous prayers
Believe me dear Sir
Yours Faithfully
Alfred J. Hall[94]

Hall systematically lays out the processes of missionization: an emphasis on bilingualism, the establishment of a school, the acquisition of land within a village site, training and "saving" girls, and a focus on the young. But the letter also describes resistance by local leaders. Although some accepted Christianity, none were willing to stop potlatching. Hall and other Anglican missionaries "refused Baptism Marriage" to those who would not abandon the custom. By many accounts, their prohibition was not a serious deterrent. Early missionaries also refrained from offering communion services. They considered the Eucharist (the ceremony commemorating the Last Supper, in which a wafer, symbolizing the body of Christ, is consumed) too suggestive of the act of cannibalism. Under no circumstances did they wish to promote any semblance of indigenous spiritual practices.[95] Missionaries sought to replace the central, sustaining role of the potlatch with settler capitalism.

"Extra Sight": Christian Capitalism

In August 2008, I had a conversation with George Speck at his home in 'Y_a_lis. There was a power outage. His four-year-old son Jack rode his small bicycle on the back deck, navigating around the outdoor table, a barbecue, and an impressive tableau of whale vertebrae. It was the time of year when families "do fish," and several coolers were near the back door, ready to distribute salmon.

"I'm starting to write about Alfred Hall," I said to George.

"He was an interesting character," George said. "He came into our territory at an interesting time, for sure. That was 1880? Well, Alert Bay – he started out in Fort Rupert before that. Yeah, *move the Indians to Alert Bay.*"

"What?" Jack asked.

"That was what the Reverend A.J. Hall wanted to do, was to get everyone over here."

"'Cause why?" Jack asked.

"So that we could go and work in the cannery," his father replied.

"Where?"

"Here."

"Where's the cannery?"

"It's not here anymore."

"Where is it?"

"It's torn down."

"What is the cannery, Dad?"

"Fish cannery."

"Where was it?"

"Across from Bill's." [Bill Cranmer's poolhall]

"Why it's not here anymore?" Jack continued.

"No more fish."

"Why it's not here anymore?"

"No more fish."

"Why it's not here anymore?"

"No more fish." George laughed.

"So, Dad, why doesn't anyone have no more fish now?"

"Global warming."

"Gogol warming?"

"Glo-bal, global warming."

"What's that mean?"

"That means it's warming up, and the fish are dying off."

"Dying?"

"Yeah." George paused and waited to see if Jack wanted to ask more. When Jack didn't respond, he said, "So yeah, Reverend Hall came at an interesting time, that's for sure, with the fish saltery down at the mouth of the river. That's an interesting coincidence, if you believe in that kind of a thing. You've got Spencer and Huson setting up their fish saltery and their projects sort of coincided."

George Speck linked missionary Christianity to colonial labour in the early fishery. This link is significant, for family and community histories are infused with stories about the aboriginal fishery. Indeed, successive generations of men and women in the family speak passionately about their participation in commercial fishing, in canneries, salteries, and on boats in the "Cook Fleet."

Most shocking, given this shared narrative of fish and family, of fish and community, is that this was the first year in living memory in which sockeye salmon runs were so diminished and fuel costs so prohibitive that the 'Na̲mgis Band Council was unable to provide members their allocation of food fish (according to residents, usually three hundred sockeye per family). George's refrain of "No more fish" and Jack's question "Why?" jolted me into the present. I had anticipated a conversation about conversion and cosmological violence (that did come later, guided by my questions), but George Speck's orientation to immediate reality was important. It highlighted the conditions of the present and the priorities of those telling their histories.

"Nobody seems to understand it, including the federal managers of the fishery," George said with a sigh. "Our guys have not had a salmon fishery, a commercial salmon fishery, in Johnstone Strait in years. Yeah, last year they had two or three days' fishing. But when I was a fisherman, a commercial fisherman, when I was a teenager, we were fishing four or five days a week. Now we're down to nothing. There's not going to be a commercial fishery in Johnstone Strait this year. I have never, ever, in my life not had sockeye out of Johnstone Strait. This is the first year that will happen. So, I don't know what's going on. We've seen the run downgraded from two million fish to seven hundred and fifty thousand. That's, like, what, two-thirds of the fish have disappeared, more than two-thirds? Yeah, that's something to be concerned about."

Everyone was speaking about salmon. "It's so bizarre," Pearl Alfred said. "You can't think that this would ever happen! We're a welfare community, for the most part. The sad part is that we're used to living off Kraft Dinner and bologna. We're used to living on $286 a month, and if you live in a home with several adults on social assistance, there's no shelter allowance, no $85. Fish sandwiches are still a big deal. It's probably where most of the protein comes from in families who are so used to living on next-to-nothings."

The reality of diminished sockeye runs stirred up other stories, particularly one by G̲a'ax̲sta'las's granddaughter Emma Alfred. I asked her if Jane Cook had encouraged girls in her family to be educated. "Oh yeah," she said, "she made sure that we learned what we needed to know. And she even told me, when my little boy was a month old ... At the Christmas dinner, he was lying on her bed. There was four new babies, and mine was there. She said, 'Which one's yours?'"

"I picked him up and gave him to her. She says, 'This poor little boy, Emma, your son.'"

"I'm looking at her, and I said, 'What do you mean poor?'"

"She says, 'You know, when he grows up there's going to be no fish, and there's going to be no logging. There won't be much jobs.'"

"She said that to me fifty years ago! I mentioned it to somebody, you know, 'Granny told me this when Bishop was one month old. She told me there was going to be no jobs, no fish, and our people are going to be poor.' I'm looking at Gran. How do you know? Her prophecy – it's true. It's true, what she said. It's all happening."

This was the first time I had heard about G̲a'ax̲sta'las's propensity for prophecy. What some in the family call premonitions, others call foresight. "Yeah," Pearl Alfred told me some time later, "she was kind of scary that way. There were times I remember that I didn't want to listen to her, because she was going to say, 'Well, this is going to happen,' or that was going to happen."

Certainly, today – and likely in the late 1940s, when Emma's son was born – people in Kwakwa̲ka̲'wakw villages have experienced failures in their fisheries. Almost total failures of the salmon runs were recorded in 1891 and 1898. In 1884, the failure of the eulachon fishery was blamed for malnourishment and illness. Gilbert Cook Sr. reported on hunger and poverty among people in 'Ya̲lis in 1927 and 1928, when the salmon runs failed.[96] Jane Cook herself had experienced the Depression, two world wars, and the advent of the welfare economy. Her words take on new significance given the startling failure of the sockeye runs in 2007. Apparently, some of Jane's children also shared her gift of foresight. "All his life, Gilbert Cook [Sr.] says he has seen and heard things more than other people. Once disturbed by an incident of 'extra sight,' Gilbert told his mother. She said not to worry, that one of his sisters was the same way."[97]

Growing up, Gilbert Cook Jr. listened to his father speak about his mother, G̲a'ax̲sta'las. His father's stories emphasized her determined vision toward the future. "They did all kinds of things, and that certainly rubbed off on my dad. And it was certainly something that Granny told my dad all the time as he was growing up – was to be working, looking to the future and making a place for himself somewhere. Being entrepreneurial was just a matter of course, as far as he was concerned, and he was passing this on to me as I was growing up." Gilbert Sr. did not encourage his son to be a fisher. "He didn't think there was a future in fishing," Gilbert told me. "As it turned out, there was. It was pretty good, darn good to us for a long time." Fishing provided an important context for the passing on of oral histories from father to son: "We got a lot of opportunity to talk about these old things when we'd be travelling, running back and forth, maybe to Vancouver in a boat or fishing, when we were sitting at the wheel together, and he'd chatter on about the old days. And the most important thing to him to pass on – which he said came from his mom – [was] a sense of morality and a sense of a work ethic. So he passed that along to us, and I think that is one of the things that me and my kids and everybody, my sisters too, have all received as a gift from Jane, is to look to the future. But she was also concerned about the past, and she was concerned about them, her sons particularly, worrying about their land claims, about their status as Indians here and the claims on the land that they had ... Jane was always telling the boys, 'Don't forget. Don't forget your land claims.'"

According to the varied corpus of stories that make up family oral histories, G̲a'ax̲sta'las passed on a moral code, an ethic, toward work and a concern for aboriginal rights, then and in the future. Kwakw̓a̲k̲a̲'wakw engagements with missionary Christianity had a good deal to do with altering aboriginal resource practices and politicizing aboriginal voices. But, in the history of missionization, scholars too often overlook stories about work and commerce and acts of resistance that coalesce around land, labour, and resource rights.

The Indian Reserve Commission was created in 1876 to address the impasse between British Columbia, which had ownership and control of resources, and the Dominion government, which had federal responsibility for those peoples "encoded in the Indian Act."[98] The 1879 census of the "Nimkeesh" lists over two hundred people at 'Ya̲lis.[99] The commission visited Kwakwa̲ka̲'wakw territories that year and recommended the allocation of Cormorant Island as reserve lands, with the exception of two leased lots, one for Wesley Huson and one for the Reverend Alfred Hall. Four years earlier, the surveyor general had sent a memorandum to the Land Office Division in Ottawa. It read, in part: "The practical value, in their civilizing influences, of religious Missions, is most strongly in favour of such establishments ... it would greatly strengthen the hands of the Government in administering Indian Affairs generally ... In such case, it would be better that the land should be given in the centre of such part of the Reserve as the Indians may be in actual occupation of, which would involve their being a direct party to the establishing of such Mission, and a surrender of the land required therefore."[100]

"On 10th August I went to the Nimpkish village in a canoe," Alfred Hall wrote in 1878. "This place is called Alert Bay and is about 25 miles further south. There are several white men living here salting salmon for exportation. I have reasons for thinking that in a few years my people will be surrounded by these men and that is another reason why the missionary should be among them."[101] Wesley Huson had just opened a commercial saltery at the village, which Hall called "Ilis."

George Blenkinsop, a former HBC trader, became the first Indian Agent at the Kwawkewlth Agency. In his 1881 annual report, he wrote:

> Visiting the Nimkeesh, at Alert Bay, on my way to Beaver Harbour, I there ascertained that the natives were somewhat alarmed at the extensive preparations being made by the Canning Company, for fishing the Nimkeesh River, fearing that the entire run of salmon would be secured by the nets of the company, and none allowed to go up river to spawn, and that they also would be deprived of their usual supply of summer food.
>
> I pointed out to them that the company were strictly prohibited from interfering with the established fishing rights of the Indians, and that ample time was allowed by law for a great portion of the fish to ascend the river to their spawning grounds. This reassured them, and they promised not to interfere with the work of the company.[102]

Kwakwa̲ka̲'wakw chiefs and lineages customarily claimed fishing stations. The stations were "distant from [winter] village sites and used most intensively for a brief period during the height of salmon and olachen [sic] runs."[103] In the 1880s, cannery owners exerted pressure on the Department of Marine and Fisheries, lobbying strongly for strict measures to curtail aboriginal fishing activities.[104] Within the colonial power hierarchy, individual Indian Agents held significant influence, negotiating free licences and often controlling access to fishing sites.[105]

In 1881, Blenkinsop wrote that he inspected other villages in the agency but was called back to 'Ya̲lis by the "Agent of the Alert Bay Canning Co. stating that the Indians had stopped two of their men who were fishing on the Nimkeesh River ... I proceeded at once to the spot and found that these men were, (not knowing the law) engaged in constructing a weir within the mouth of the river ... [I] requested them to confine themselves entirely to net fishing within the legal grounds, which Messrs. Huson and Spencer, the proprietors, readily agreed to do ... work was resumed and kept up without further trouble."[106]

Gilbert M. Sproat, the Indian reserve commissioner, had allocated more than one thousand acres of Cormorant Island as a reserve for the 'Na̲mgis in 1880. The allocation was "disallowed two years later by the Chief Commissioner of Lands and Works for the province ... one of the grounds being that the entire island had been leased" to Huson and three others. That lease had then been transferred to cannery operators Spencer and Earle in 1883.[107] In 1884, when settlers and commercial interests exerted more pressure to settle the land question, Peter O'Reilly, the Indian reserve commissioner, overturned Sproat's allocation on Cormorant Island, allotting two reserves consisting of the village and the burial grounds (totalling 48.12 acres).[108] When O'Reilly returned again in 1886, he "accepted three other sites recommended by Sproat," but he rejected or ignored other important fishing sites.[109] The collusion of capital, state, and church interests is clear.

As part of his tour for the Kwawkewlth Agency, Blenkinsop arrested whisky sellers and sought agreements from chiefs that they would prevent their people from going to Victoria. "During the past year the Alert Bay Canning Co. have afforded much employment to the Indian population, who are thereby induced to remain more at home. The Company contemplate enlarging their works, we may therefore reasonably hope, from the increased quantity of labour which will necessarily be required, that the natives will, in future, keep away from the haunts of vice at Victoria and Burrard Inlet. The latter of the places bears the reputation of supplying almost the entire quantity of liquors transported to the north-west coast by the Aborigines."[110]

Around this time, about forty men from the agency left for wage work in the Fraser River salmon fishery. The number doing so increased yearly. Long accustomed to profitable economic relations, men, women, and children took up new fishing techniques. They supplied fish to the saltery, "setting gill nets from skiffs, or hauling beach seines."[111] Wage labour for a day's fishing later shifted to payment by weight and then, eventually, to payment by piece.

Not surprisingly, Kwakwa̲ka̲'wakw people of high rank came to be the principal owners and operators of the seiners that supplied fish under commercial contracts and food fish for their families and other villagers. George Speck spoke about how the food fishery operates. "Well, it's evolving," he said. "Originally, when we had a bigger fleet of seine boats in the community, families would get their fish from family seine boat operators, and the community would benefit from that because they would get excess fish that was over and above family needs from the skipper. But as the fleet has declined, what we've seen is a greater need in the community and less access. So the band has stepped in. We started out hiring one boat. And we'd go out and get the fish, bring it in, and people would collect it at the dock, bring their buckets down and get it at the dock. And now we've evolved to where we take names of people that want us to deliver them fish. And the Band Public Works would gather the fish off the skippers. [In 2007] we hired two boats, two seine boats, but I think we only got

Photo 14 "Doing fish." Canning salmon at George Speck's home, August 2010.

about two thousand fish into our community. [In 2006] we got thirty-five thousand."

The band prioritizes the list of those who sign up for food fish. Elders and large families with children receive fish first, then it distributes fifty fish or more to each household and to off-reserve band members. "Now we need food fish regulations, it's never been an issue before," said Pearl Alfred. She referred, of course, to regulations *within* the band. The band has long contended with colonial regulations.[112]

Randy Bell described the labour of catching and preparing food fish when he was a younger man in Vancouver.

"Four or five of us would come every summer. We'd come back and do our fish, both here and at Fort Rupert. And there was a lot of boats that were here. Everybody had a job. There was a lot of money."

"Can you tell me what it means to 'do' fish?" I asked.

"We'd go out in a fishing boat and catch the fish. They commercially fish it the same way, the drag seine. And then we'd come in with the boat. We'd put the fish in totes with ice and bring it up to the house, and then the next morning, start cleaning it. And then our grandmothers would be on the canning machines, canning it. Then we'd boil it on the beach and boil cases, like, fifty to one hundred cases at a time. So, we'd be there for two or three days, and then after that, we'd put the fish up in the smoke house and smoke fifty to one hundred cases. And then we'd make our way back down island. Before 1980, when that bridge [over Nimpkish River] wasn't there, it used to be a full two days to get here. It used to be *[sigh]* long back roads, go through the logging roads, through Gold River, Kelsey Bay, then a five-hour ferry to Beaver Cove. Then another hour-and-a-half ferry from Beaver Cove to Alert Bay. We'd take turns between fishing at Alert Bay and at Fort Rupert. Our grandmothers would either come here, or they'd go over to Fort Rupert. Either/or. But the neat thing about it was – I think during that time the Cooks had six boats, six different boats, and so, besides doing the fishing, it was really a celebration, because it was kind of like a little family reunion. Everybody looked forward to getting out of school and coming up and doing that ... But when we start the talk of the fishery, the family that comes up when the fishery first starts is the Cook family. It's the foundation of commercial fishing in this area. That's pretty evident. Huson is a part of the family, too, so."[113]

In 'Ya̲lis, control over fisheries began with the establishment of Wesley Huson's saltery, which was soon converted into a commercial cannery. According to Blenkinsop, "An arrangement has just been fortunately made, principally through the exertion of the Rev. A. J. Hall, with the canning company, which will secure remunerative employment for a number of young men and women of this tribe (Nimkeesh) and consequently keep them at home; and it is in contemplation by the company to instruct them, hereafter, in the various branches of the work now performed by Chinamen, which will still further tend to bring about an improvement, both in their morals and habits of living."[114] When Blenkinsop wrote this report, in 1883, the headquarters of the Kwawkewlth Agency had recently moved from Tsax̲is (Fort Rupert, Beaver Harbour) to 'Ya̲lis, the site of the CMS mission. The bureaucracy encasing these organizations generated a seemingly endless stream of reports that contained, among other things, statistics that supported a new system of surveillance and auditing, the minutiae of minor administrative tasks and expenditures, and history-shaking pronouncements that continue to reverberate in aboriginal communities.

Jane Gilbert first appears in colonial documentation in the 1881 census of Fort Rupert's District 187d. Blenkinsop was the enumerator and Indian Agent of the "Quak-yohl Agency." Jane is listed among the residents of the fort in the village of Tsax̱is. A notation that she did not attend school confirms a statement she later made: "Our old people would not let us go to school because they were afraid we would drop the Potlatch."[115] Her religion was registered as "Anglican/Episcopal/C of E" (as it was for each resident of the fort). Following the nationality of her father, Jane Gilbert's origin is listed as England.[116] The census category "building" is filled with "house," and no "infirmities" are listed. "None or unknown" appears under occupations, and nothing is inscribed under comments. The census also enumerated two other girls aged fourteen and fifteen and without obvious parents. Blenkinsop was then a fifty-eight-year-old widower, Alfred Hall was twenty-eight, and Elizabeth Hall was thirty-five. In total, the census enumerated forty-six people at the fort, including a family listed as "Kamana" (from the "Sandwich Islands," Hawaii), the fifteen-member Hunt family (George Hunt was then married, aged twenty-seven, and listed under the occupation seaman), and William and Mary Weston (an English farm labourer and his "Native Indian" wife). Wedłidi Speck's research on the 1881 census reveals that G̱a'ax̱sta'las's grandfather, listed as "Noolish," was then fifty years old, while his wife "Kah ah sta lus" was forty-four. Within the 'na̱'mima of the Kwixa, in which they counted as members, eighty-two people lived in four houses in Tsax̱is.

George Blenkinsop's first report from Beaver Harbour stated that the census of ten villages or tribes would be sent after the "Southerly gales" had subsided. In the northern, more distant villages, he reported on "the contamination of those fearful diseases which have been and are now rapidly decimating most of the tribes on the coast ... Several ... had scrofula in its worst form, two or three were spitting blood, and the constant cough, heard in all directions" in one village "told but two [sic] plainly that consumption was doing its work."[117] Regarding the potlatch, he wrote that it "has, of late years, increased to a very great extent; and those most interested, who are principally old chiefs, have offered a most determined opposition." Blenkinsop also suggested that "the young chiefs in each tribe who have evidently all the authority needed," could be "assisted by the Agent, to work a change ... The Missionary establishment, under the Rev. A. Hall, is now located at Alert Bay." He continued, "Here a substantial house has been erected, also a schoolroom, the latter serving on Sundays for Divine service. The dwelling house affords ample accommodation for a number of young native females whom Mrs. Hall is striving hard to train up in a better mode of life."[118] Jane Gilbert was presumably among these young girls in 'Ya̲lis.

In *Smoke from Their Fires,* Charlie Nowell narrates stories to Clellan Ford. Some of these stories are about the mission school he attended in the 1880s. Many anecdotes include his childhood friend Stephen Cook. Nowell's reminiscences of boyhood portray a life in which customary practices and Christian discipline coexisted in the villages – although not easily. Nowell's rich accounts include descriptions of childhood activities such as play potlatches and play feasts, games involving physical tests of bravery, and boy marches to communal houses for food.[119] His descriptions focus on the socialization of high-ranked boys at a time when the potlatch was in full swing, when women often gave feasts, when members of different villages competed through *alaxwa* (*Lahal,* the bone game), when there were occasional accusations of witchcraft, and when interactions with the Indian Agent, fishing bosses, and missionaries were a daily occurrence.

In one story, Charlie Nowell and Stephen Cook hide from Hamatsa dancers. Nowell relates that a 'Na̲mg̲is dancer was "told by the old people to go inside the bedroom, where we were hiding, and to scare us ... He came to us and got a hold of Stephen Cook, who was also a little boy, and Stephen says: 'Sir, I am your friend.' And the Hamatsa let him go and came up to me. I didn't know what to say to him ... anybody the Hamatsa gets hold of, the Hamatsa is supposed to bite him. I was scared and said: 'Sir, I am just a little boy.' He went out laughing loud."[120]

At some point during their childhood, Stephen and Charlie were sent north to a mission post (at the "forks of the Skeena") to stay with Bishop William Ridley.[121] Nowell's account of their three-month stay describes inter-nation rivalries among two dozen boys from northern communities.[122] When Stephen and Charlie were sent home to Tsax̲is, Alfred Hall was conducting lessons in his own house. Charlie recounts that when he moved to 'Ya̲lis he was, for some time, the only boy at Reverend Hall's mission, which he shared with "two of old Mr. Hunt's daughters and one of George Hunt's daughters ... the others came in later."[123]

There is no mention of Jane Gilbert in Nowell's early accounts. "Two or three years after, Mr. Hall built another house for some bigger boys than us from Fort Rupert and other villages that came here

Photo 15 Pupils at Reverend Hall's school, Alert Bay, ca. 1880s. Stephen Cook is in the back row, *far right.* Jane Cook is possibly in the middle row, *fourth from right. Library and Archives Canada, George M. Dawson/Natural Resources Canada fonds/PA-037934.*

to school."[124] Hall routinely baptized the schoolchildren. When Charles James Nowell was given his English name, it was a name that a "Sunday School teacher in England" had requested be given to a child at the mission. Every Christmas, Nowell recounted, this "godfather ... used to send me presents."[125] Nowell recalled that they had received lessons in spelling and writing, that George Blenkinsop measured the children for clothing, and that Alfred Hall himself once tried to beat him with a walking stick but usually gave verbal shamings or held back food as punishment.[126] At the mission house, bells signalled lunch and supper. Aside from school, the boys also did chores and played football (soccer). If their families were close by, the children could visit them, but running away from the school seemed to be a regular occurrence. Charlie and Stephen were in cahoots for much of their time together and at loggerheads with Mrs. Hall, by Nowell's account a stern Christian woman frightened by thunder and gunshots.[127]

Nowell makes no mention of the measles epidemic that swept through Kwakwa̲ka̲'wakw territories in spring 1883, killing "sixty-eight children, of an age to attend school."[128] Many were pupils in Hall's mission. Among "this tribe, the Nimkeesh," Blenkinsop reported, "the mortality has been greater than in any other." Within the villages in the agency, 104 people had been lost, most to the epidemic, which had then "been raging severely" for three months "and is yet prevalent in some of the camps." Two people who had contracted smallpox were convalescing, and the Indian Agent attributed their recovery to swift quarantine.[129] In one sombre paragraph, Blenkinsop notes that, at Tsax̱is, people "were too despondent, on account of their losses by measles, to undertake any [garden] work."[130]

Indian Agent and missionary were invested with the power to attempt to alter the goals of productivity in aboriginal communities. In the midst of the measles epidemic, Hall wrote to the CMS about the baptism of his second convert, a schoolboy from Fort Rupert, and requested three hundred pounds to build a sawmill. Following the emphasis on work at the Metlakatla mission, Hall intended the sawmill to promote self-sufficiency and to facilitate the move from communal to European-style houses. In 1883, the Department of Indian Affairs annual report for 1883 noted that "Kwah-kewlth Indians" were working for wages at canneries and on steamboats and that many travelled to the hop fields in Puget Sound.[131]

Surveyor George Dawson visited the territories again in 1885 and probably stayed with Hall or Blenkinsop. His presentation to the Royal Society of Canada in 1887 included information about what were then the standard ethnological categories. From Blenkinsop and Hall, Dawson gleaned information about the ceremony referred to locally as the "pus-a or ya-hooit." Rather than using these terms, he instead used the "commonly recognized word *potlatch*." The potlatch, he wrote, was an institution to which "every member of the tribe is drawn ... If not themselves endeavouring to acquire property for a potlatch, everyone is pledged to support, to the utmost of their means, some more prominent or ambitious individual."[132] Blenkinsop told Dawson that "the custom was formerly almost entirely confined to the recognized chiefs, but that of late years it has extended to people generally, and become very much commoner than before."[133] Dawson saw chiefly rivalries and the breaking of coppers as "a means of acquiring and maintaining prestige and power."[134]

Dawson's report includes a section titled "Actual Condition of the Kwakiool People." In it, he writes that the "results of missionary labours ... are ... to all appearance, small."[135] "Food is abundant during the salmon run," but "they are restless and unhappy ... In some seasons, good wages are to be obtained by picking hops in the vicinity of Puget Sound ... They may be seen leaving their villages ... in their large well-built travelling canoes, whole families together with their household effects and children, and three or four paddlers to each canoe, setting out cheerfully enough on their voyage of two hundred miles or more."[136] "The problem," Dawson writes, "is fundamentally an industrial one, and is to be attacked, if successfully, from that side." Although Dawson made note of small-scale gardens in which the people grew potatoes, he imagined an industrial future in which they would be "boatmen and fishermen." He concludes: "The most essential step is the establishment of industrial schools ... where the younger people will be separated from their old associates and instructed in various callings appropriate to their condition and surroundings."[137] In Dawson's seven-hundred-word vocabulary, the term he inscribes for *church* is *tsā-ma-tse* (prayer house). He translates *schoolhouse* as *kīa-kā'-tuksi-lut-se* (book house).[138]

"Spirits Broken": Schooling in 'Ya̱lis

The hulk of a building that was once St. Michael's Residential School faces the water on the western shore at 'Ya̱lis. A pole from the former house of Ṫła̱kwudłas disintegrates at the edge of a circular drive that leads to rusting, hand-railed stairs.† White paint bubbles off red brick walls, which are spidered with crawling vines. Signs warn of falling bricks. Boards cover windows close to the ground. Yet, at the building's far edge, a sign warns "Carvers at Work." The U'mista Cultural Centre,

† According to William Wasden Jr., "The poles belonged to Chief Ṫłakwudłas of the Nimpkish people. He was the grandfather of Willie Harris, Ned Harris, Joe Harris, Phillip Harris. The design of U'mista – that was originally his longhouse before he started rebuilding this next house. But they never finished the house. Those were the house posts. So, those poles were there ready to build a house frame. They ended up just sitting outside of Ned Harris's. When his oldest daughter married Paul Rufus, for his daughter, Ned Harris gave those poles to Paul Rufus ... and names and lots of privileges to build him up because he married his oldest daughter. But he never did anything with it, never upheld anything. So those poles just became kind of insignificant. They removed them to St. Mike's for the entrance. They were farther down the village at one time."

adjacent to the old school, is a site of return and renewal, a place where the past meets the present in the creative celebration of self-representation. "Those who went there want it torn down," Pearl Alfred told me. "Others want money to have it fixed up, but it would cost millions to get it earthquake-proof. They say it should always stand as a memorial to what the church did. We shouldn't be allowed to forget."

In *Spirits Broken and Innocence Stolen,* Lori Speck traces the education project envisaged by early colonial agents. Her analysis includes legislation on Indian status, the potlatch ban, enfranchisement, and reserve policies, aspects of the past that she connects with voices today. "The first Industrial schools opened in upper regions of Canada in the early nineteenth century as a part of a government assimilation program. Together with the churches in Canada, the government formulated a program and the plan was to relocate the Indians to 'reserved' land, build schools and teach them to become 'civilized' Christian human beings while the Europeans continued to settle on the land that was once utilized by the Indians ... Thousands of Native children were displaced from the only homes they knew, abducted from their families and thrust into a cold, mean and unfamiliar world."[139]

These linked institutions in 'Ya̱lis had their origins in those attended by Jane Gilbert and Stephen Cook: the Indian Girls' Mission School and the Indian Boys' Mission School operated by Alfred and Elizabeth Hall from 1882. The Industrial School for Boys was established in 1893.[140] In 1898, "the Church Missionary Society placed the Girls Home (est. 1894) under the control of the Alert Bay Industrial School principal, Mr. A.W. Corker."[141] From 1912, a Girls' Indian Day School for local children opened and was staffed by a "Native teacher," William Brotchie.[142] St. Michael's (Anglican) Residential School opened its doors in 1929. It was one of eighteen residential schools in British Columbia.

English-language instruction was a primary tool in the attempted assimilation of aboriginal children. Steffen Nielsen estimates that the industrial school prohibited Kwak̓wala sometime between 1910 and 1920, long after Jane and Stephen had finished their schooling. The prohibition extended to the use of "Indian names." "By 1925, morning service was still held in Kwak'wala. It was in the 1940's that English became the dominant language in public discourse."[143] While children from 'Ya̱lis and other Kwakwa̱ka̱'wakw villages were sometimes sent to Port Alberni on central Vancouver Island, some younger children, such as Florrie and Emma Mountain from Mamalilikala (Village Island), moved with their families to 'Yalis, where they attended the original Indian day school. Children whose families did not relocate were often sent to St. Michael's.

Residential schools ceased operating in the 1980s. By 1999, a few ex-teachers had been charged and convicted of sexual abuse.[144] In the 1980s, Lori Speck writes, First Nation people began "open[ing] the doors of the past, revealing secrets of abuse that have broken the spirits and murdered the innocence of thousands of children."[145] But the doors of the past were not always open. As several people told me, for many former students, a coerced silence hangs heavy around that past.

Pearl Alfred spoke about this silence among an older generation of women: "We used to have these afternoons where we provided lunch for the older people, and we would talk about the old days, trying to record some of the history. Oh God, this must have been twenty-five years ago. We tried to bring the issue of sexual abuse up, and we got absolutely stonewalled. It was just a dead subject ... I think we had these five or six ladies, and one of them said, 'We are never to speak of those things. No. No. No.' She said, 'We are never allowed to talk about anything like that.' She said, 'Women don't talk about things like that.' Okay. We couldn't press the point, like, there was just no way." The woman's refusal to speak perhaps reflects the rhetoric of moral reform commonplace in the ideology of Anglican education. As historian Adele Perry notes, residential schools were gendered institutions seen by colonial agents as the mechanism to wipe out "disorder, disease and immorality." They would achieve this, they believed, by teaching industry to boys and domestic economy to girls.[146]

Pearl Alfred's daughter Kelly-Anne Speck also talked with me about the intergenerational differences she had encountered in approaching the past. "I think as any community, or society, when you look back, people of my generation go, 'Well, let's just put it all on the table, and whatever happened, happened, and we'll move on from there.' I know, for [some], trying to get them to talk about other things, like what really happened at residential school or what happened when things were happening around the Sixties Scoop,[147] things they would have to have seen because [they] lived through it in a very real way as respected members of this community. It's like, 'You just have to accept that it happened, and you move forward. And you live today in a more positive, better way.' I think there was sort of a desire to let sleeping dogs lie, if I can use that expression. Some things ... Forget it. We just move forward."

"In the beginning," Lori Speck writes, "the Indians accepted this program [of education] believing that it would help them learn the English language and improve their relationship with the white settlers ... Their objective was to maintain their cultures but also to be able to have control in communicating ... during these changing times."[148] In the early years at the Alert Bay Industrial School, language instruction was saturated with Christian moral teachings, an approach discussed in the Department of Indian Affairs (DIA) annual report for 1898: "All pupils have been carefully instructed in moral and religious truth. The Lords Prayer, Ten Commandments, and life of Christ have been taught in the classroom."[149] Christian discipline went hand in glove with early legal sanctions, as is evident in Alfred Hall's 1902 "Report on Missions": "Several [people] have been fined and imprisoned [for liquor violations] and thus the illicit trade checked. In the boarding schools 49 boys and girls have been carefully taught and trained and there are good results visible. The Sundays are now quiet and the services well attended."[150]

Increasing regulation of aboriginal education allowed colonial agents to realize their own programs for change. In 1907, for example, William Halliday, a new Indian Agent, wrote to William Sloan, MP. To deter potlatch marriages, Halliday wanted to extend the customary age of eligibility for marriage. "It is in order to counteract this," he wrote, "that I have ventured to ask the Government to build and equip a Good Girl's Home for the girls, and I would ask to be allowed the fullest latitude in taking the girls and placing them in this institution where they may be taught not only how to read and write but also how to keep house and a chance may be given them to arrive at maturity without being exposed to the evils of the potlatch system."[151] *Regulations Relating to the Education of Indian Children* (1884) already existed but Halliday sought power to "take any child not being properly educated and cared for and place him or her [in school] until the age of 18 years."[152] His goal was not realized until the 1920s, when residents were under "increased pressure from missionaries, governments, and law enforcement agencies to surrender children to educational institutions."[153]

When Lori Speck wrote about the history of colonial education in 1999, apologies were slowly issuing from "some of the churches and from the government."[154] G̱a'aẖsta'las's children attended the industrial school and the Indian day schools, which, by 1909, were overseen by Native teachers. Some of her grandchildren and great-grandchildren attended St. Michael's Residential School. One wonders about the conversations she might have had with her descendants.

Her granddaughter Emma Alfred attended the day school located near the council hall. In the late 1930s, the school was separate from the public school in Alert Bay. People called the public school the "superior school." It was "the white school" on "the other side," at the present location of the RCMP station. Emma told me about being strapped by a teacher for not being able to memorize something. I asked her if adults were aware of what was going on in the schools. "Well, I use to wonder about Mom," she told me. "Why didn't she step in and try to do something? If she did, then the Indian Agent would take our family allowance away from her, which she depended on. So you more or less had to keep your mouth shut. I remember her saying that. She says, 'Well, if I say anything, they're going to take the family allowance, and we need that to get groceries.' My mom and dad weren't rich, eh? Maybe that's why they kept quiet. But now, today, we can talk up now. We can stand on our own two feet. The Indian Agent, he had the upper hand."

Emma Alfred's reference to the present as a time in which First Nation people can "talk up" is important. When we had this conversation, First Nation communities and aboriginal organizations across Canada had long been demanding that the Canadian state recognize and take responsibility for violence, cultural loss, and the grief caused by residential schooling. The federal government implemented the Indian Residential Schools Settlement Agreement in 2006.[155] In 2008, it issued an apology to former students of residential schools. In his speech, the prime minister, Stephen Harper, described the system and its abuses:

> For more than a century, Indian residential schools separated over 150,000 aboriginal children from their families and communities ... Two primary objectives of the residential school system were to remove and isolate children from the influence of their homes, families, traditions and cultures, and to assimilate them into the dominant culture. These objectives were based on the assumption that aboriginal cultures and spiritual beliefs were inferior and unequal. Indeed, some sought, as was infamously said, "to kill the Indian in the child."
>
> Today, we recognize that this policy of assimilation was wrong, has caused great harm, and has no place in our country ...

> Most schools were operated as joint ventures with Anglican, Catholic, Presbyterian and United churches. The Government of Canada built an educational system in which very young children were often forcibly removed from their homes and often taken far from their communities. Many were inadequately fed, clothed and housed. All were deprived of the care and nurturing of their parents, grandparents and communities. First Nations, Inuit and Métis languages and cultural practices were prohibited in these schools. Tragically, some of these children died while attending residential schools, and others never returned home. The government now recognizes that the consequences of the Indian residential schools policy were profoundly negative and that this policy has had a lasting and damaging impact on aboriginal culture, heritage and language.
>
> While some former students have spoken positively about their experiences at residential schools, these stories are far overshadowed by tragic accounts of the emotional, physical and sexual abuse and neglect of helpless children, and their separation from powerless families and communities. The legacy of Indian residential schools has contributed to social problems that continue to exist in many communities today. Regrettably, many former students are not with us today and died never having received a full apology from the Government of Canada.[156]

By December 2008, some residential school survivors had received government compensation for their years of attendance in the schools.[157] During our research, advocates were vocal in defence of more vulnerable urban and reserve residents and about opportunists targeting individuals who had received compensation. I heard about aggressive car salesmen offering no-money-down deals with their showroom tours and free transportation to the venue. Some people talked about drug dealers and the profits they stood to make with the increased flow of cash in cities and on reserves. Two years after the settlement process began, I began to hear more about the thousands of former residential school pupils still awaiting compensation. Some had endured independent assessments in which they were asked to recall their experiences. Other survivors had died while waiting for compensation. In June 2008, the federal government established the Truth and Reconciliation Commission, which was "tasked with undertaking a truth-telling and reconciliation process, producing a report on the residential school system and its aftermath, and making recommendations to government based on its findings."[158]

"The closest other (residential) school would have been Port Alberni," Pearl Alfred said. "Some years ago, we were looking at some statistics. This particular school had the most students pass through. I don't know whether it was five thousand or seven thousand, something like that, a terrible number. And almost all of them, I would say 95 percent of them ... there were very few local [children.] One of my brothers was in there. I don't know if George [Cook] was ever in there. [It was] mostly for out-of-the-area children. I think it was part of DIA strategy – the further you took the children, the better it was going to work. A lot of kids that went through there were from the Nass Valley, the Bella Bella, the Bella Coola, all of that area. They all went to school there. They just sent them. Some of the kids that were here from Kingcome ended up in Port Alberni. One of my nephews was placed there. My mother came from Cape Mudge, up here. That always blows me away, thinking of someone taking a five-year-old child and plunking them somewhere. She was captured by the DIA and taken to residential school for eleven years. Her mother had just died, and her father had to go fishing. She was so tiny. Everybody protected her. She never had anything to say about life at the school."

PART IV
"Children of the Potlatch System," 1888-1912

X̱wâ'x̱was: Tradition of the Gĭlgilgam, a Clan of the Nimkish

In the beginning X̱wâ'x̱was was a salmon. When the Deluge came, it carried salmon up the mountains. When the waters subsided, the salmon landed at Flat Place (Ōdzâ̱'lí̱s) and began to build a house which he intended to name Only-House-on-Ground ('NemsgEmdzâlas). He searched for stones to make a stone axe, and found some on the bank of a river. Then he began to hew two heavy posts for his house. He had his hair tied up in a knot on the back of his head. While he was working, he suddenly heard a loud noise behind him, a short distance down the river. He turned round and saw a large thunder-bird which had alighted, each of his feet resting on one of two large bowlders [sic] that lay quite a distance apart. Then X̱wā'x̱was said, "O master! I wish you were a man, so that you might help me in my work." Then the thunder-bird took off his feather garment and his mask, and showed his face. He said, "I will help you." He flew up and took in his talons a large log which X̱wā'x̱was had cut for the beam of his house, and laid it on top of the post. Then he alighted again and took off his feather garment. He told his bird mask to fly back to the sky, and said, "You shall be heard when one of my descendants is about to die." Then the bird flew up into the sky. The man took the name Kunō'sila. He built a house at Flat Place, and both he and X̱wā'x̱was became the ancestors of the Gĭlgilgam. Kunō'sila's son was Ē'wagit, whose son was Wā'xowit, whose son was A'nx'anwísagamē, whose son was Ha'mdzid, whose son was Yā'goLas, whose daughter was NE'mnasâlaga. She was the aunt of NEg'ä, who told the story. One of the recent descendants of X̲wā'x̲was was Yā'qał'Enāla.

– Told by NEg'ä, a Nimkish (1910)[1]

Wedłidi Speck said that "'NEg'ä' was Stephen 'Papa' Cook, who was from the Kunō'sila family of the Gĭga̲l'ga̲m 'na̲'mima through his mother, K̲wak̲'waballas."

Ancestor stories are carried on the breath of the 'na̲'mima. They testify to an identity that marks one's place in the Kwakwa̲ka̲'wakw world. In my conversations with family members about the organization of this text, they suggested that we present some of these stories to mark important passages in G̲a'ax̲sta'las's life and the lives of her descendants. Like the silver Thunderbird brooch she wore, the story of the 'Na̲mgis ancestor Kunō'sila ties people to the Gĭga̲l'ga̲m clan. For her descendants, Jane Constance Gilbert and Stephen Cook's marriage is thus symbolized by the Thunderbird.

Part IV covers the years between Jane and Stephen's marriage in 1888 and the end of their child-bearing years in 1912. Between the ages of nineteen and forty-two, G̲a'ax̲sta'las gave birth to sixteen children, three of whom died before her youngest child was born. During that time, she began to write letters for other community members and served as an interpreter for the courts and as a translator in church. She became a central figure in the Anglican Women's Auxiliary and translated traditional narratives told by Dzawada̲'enux̲w chief Lagius for Edward Curtis's work. Like several other Kwakwa̲ka̲'wakw women, G̲a'ax̲sta'las was a midwife, and she accompanied missionary physicians to other villages, likely because of her language skills.

"We Are of the People, We Know the Custom": Marriage

On 7 August 1888, Stephen Cook left his job at the mission-run sawmill to attend his wedding. He returned in the afternoon to complete his shift. Alfred Hall married G̲a'ax̲sta'las and Na̲ge in Christ Church. Carey Kamana and Wesley Huson served as witnesses.

For some time, colonial officials had been observing and commenting on the lives of aboriginal women with a tenacity that reveals

Photo 16 Ga'axsta'las as a young woman. *Photographer and date unknown. Courtesy of Reg Cook Jr.*

imperial intentions. Indian Agents and missionaries sought especially to create what historian Adele Perry calls permanence. They wanted women to abandon mobility.[2] In Ottawa, Department of Indian Affairs (DIA) officials received report after report detailing the scarcity of wives in agencies across British Columbia. So-called domestic missionaries to the urban working class in Britain sought to "regularize marital and domestic relations."[3] In British Columbia, missionaries focussed on bride price and polygamy. The potlatch, so their reasoning went, *was* the mechanism through which these practices were upheld.[4] Anglican bishops in Britain began to meet regularly but informally at the Lambeth Conference.[5] In 1888, their business included one resolution that forbade divorce and another that excluded polygamists from baptism.[6] Given the organizational structure of church authority, these edicts would have been adhered to by those in the mission field.

Before he would baptize, marry, or bestow the "blessing" of confirmation on adult members in the congregation, Alfred Hall required them to renounce the potlatch system. It is difficult to say how, at eighteen, G̲a'ax̲sta'las would have expressed her separation from the potlatch. But almost forty years later, after her wedding, she did discuss her decision to leave the custom:

> I am Fort Rupert and being a Christian and my husband at the time of our marriage also being a Christian, although we were children of the potlatch system we saw even then that it was wrong and wanted to get out of it and we were married out of the Custom in the Church ...
>
> My husband and I found out in 1888, that we could not be true Christians and allow ourselves to be used in a custom that did not contain Christianity. My husband gave potlatches before we were married, the kind they were giving in those days and he came out of it to marry me and he saw for himself ...
>
> We know because we are of the people; we know the custom and we know where it is not consistent with Christianity.[7]

This statement, made during a 1936 church committee meeting, suggests the strength of Jane Cook's Christian identity and her adherence to church doctrine. Perhaps it was her commitment to a single marriage that was not wholly consistent with the custom. Not only was G̲a'ax̲sta'las stepping out of her standing in the potlatch complex, she was also defying customary gender expectations for high-ranking, first-born daughters. She refused to enter into a series of marriages that would bring prestige to herself and her family. But, by then, the Anglican Church had spoken against plural marriages for twenty years. According to Anglican Bishop George Hills in 1866: "A veil must be cast over the past, it must be viewed with regret & we must take converts as we find them & fix them from henceforth in a right course of principle and duty."[8] At Metlakatla, William Duncan had physically expelled and excommunicated residents he had charged with adultery. Other missionaries performed mass marriages and insisted on gold rings and white wedding dresses.[9]

Jane Gilbert and Stephen Cook appear to have made their choice consciously. It was a choice that, socially, seems to have distinguished them from their compatriots, who were also Christian but who had not wholly given themselves over to the conditions of marriage set by the church. In a conversation with Gloria Cranmer-Webster, I suggested that the first converts to Christianity might have had limited options. "I don't know whether it's a generational thing," she countered, "I mean, at her time, it seemed that it was either/or for her." Gloria suggested that subsequent generations had likely been subjected to the same edict to choose Christianity or the custom but that they made different choices. "I think of my aunt Axuw," Gloria continued, "and my mother, [and] various aunts who were quite comfortable being in both worlds. I mean, they were really strong supporters of the church, but they were also really involved in potlatches and stuff like that. They didn't seem to have a problem with that, and I guess Granny Cook did. I don't know." Having witnessed legal prosecutions for potlatching, the generations that followed G̲a'ax̲sta'las were also born into a new context of anticolonial resistance.

G̲a'ax̲sta'las and Na̲ge left the custom in the late 1880s, when the full weight of colonial law had not yet come down on potlatchers. The government banned the potlatch in 1885. At the time of their marriage, there had not yet been an arrest; according to colonial accounts, there was then a lively public dialogue about how Kwakwa̲ka̲'wakw chiefs could extract themselves without risk of economic or social ruin. Indian Agent Reginald Pidcock wrote to Indian Superintendent Arthur W. Vowell, in March 1888, complaining that he was unable to recruit "Indian constables" and that he had few "means" to "put in force the law regarding the 'Potlach.'"[10] Local chiefs had recently attended a meeting with the agent to address the government's new decision to enforce the potlatch ban. The meeting was the beginning of a series of negotiations and countertactics on the part of chiefs and DIA officials.[11] Pidcock mentioned a "Kwawkwelth" chief "whose word in some matters is almost law." At the meeting, the chief had asked, "Would the Government pay him for his 'Coppers,' which he has been buying for several years ... because if they would he would give up the Potlach; if he was to give up now he would have to lose many hundred blankets and he could not be expected to do that."[12]

Jane and Stephen Cook were also embedded in the system of reciprocal exchanges, of owing and being owed, that came with one's standing in the custom.

Wedłidi Speck contemplated the process whereby his ancestors extracted themselves from the potlatch system. "I believe that the front part of *Potlatch and Totem* – that's about her," Wedłidi said.[13] He continued: "There's two people who stood up and let go of all of their rights and properties. I believe that to be my great-grandmother and great-grandfather, because, on her husband's side, he was part Mowachaht from the west coast of Vancouver Island and part 'Namgis from Alert Bay. In Alert Bay, he had a chief name – Nage – which means 'mountain,' and he affirmed it by giving a big feast. If you're taking a position, then the person that had that name also had debts and also was owed. So you assume the debts, and you also assume the receivables. In this book, it talks about them having more receivables than debts. And when they were ready to quit, the chief said that they acknowledged what they did, that people were going to benefit by what they're doing, and to be grateful. One old chief stood up and said, 'Look! We have to treat them like we would treat some of our favourite animals, who we let go out, and we don't worry about them because we trust that they'll come back.' In my heart I believe that. I believe it's about them. Around that time there was nobody else doing that."

We do not know if, when Ga'axsta'las and Nage married, others also took such a public stand. Certainly, the Christian community was expanding. From 1879 to 1883, three aboriginal petitions – scripted and signed in support of the potlatch ban – had been filed with the dominion government. Two were written explicitly by Christian aboriginal groups.[14] Colonial agents encouraged vocal pockets of aboriginal Christians who supported the potlatch ban on the Northwest Coast.

By November 1888, Alfred Hall had just two communicants, members of the church entitled to receive the Eucharist or Communion.

To the Rev. A. J. Hall 16 Nov. 1888

My Dear Friend

It was indeed a sad disappointment that the newly baptized Mr. [?] joined in the heathen party at the commencement of '87. Or was it /88? Was the dancing accompanied with anything of a definitely heathen or quite heathen character? If so, did you execute any church discipline; and if you did what was the effect of it? Of course, I know that none of them were communicants as you only had two Indian communicants at the time that you wrote ...

The increased attendance at the services during the latter part of the year was encouraging, as also the dying out of superstitious beliefs. On the other hand, the condition of the younger women & the matrimonial customs are very distressing. Some of the latter must, I'd think be clearly illegal ... You are doubtless cautiously but firmly bringing the same power into action against potlatching.

I earnestly hope you will be able some time to draw away from [?] connections with secular earnings. As soon as possible get some Indian, or perhaps European, to manage the sawmill, & the store if you have any store. I should be very glad to know that you had no store. Let each abide in his own calling ... Trained native teachers are a necessity ... And when we have them, we must be quite determined (1) that their own country-men contribute to support them and (2) that they shall as they become more experienced take the place of Europeans ...

I wd earnestly entreat you to introduce religious self-support from the first. It is much easier to introduce at first than afterwards.

Let us all pray more, believe more, & expect more.
Affectionately Yours
Ch. C. Fenn[15]

Fenn's letter to Hall highlighted an economy of "souls" linked to the project to prevent converts from "backsliding" into "the custom." His underlined entreaty "to introduce religious self-support" reveals the fiscal interests of the church, which was then becoming a formal institution on the north Pacific Coast. Matrimonial customs continued to be scrutinized intensely by church and government. They also became central in G̲a'ax̲sta'las's struggle to negotiate customary power within the Kwakwa̲ka̲'wakw social hierarchy.

In the late 1880s, colonial administration of aboriginal peoples' lives was solidifying. High mortality in communities and the sharp rise in European settlement meant explicit struggles over land and resources, competition within an increasingly ethnic labour hierarchy, and new niches for culture brokers, who navigated multiple systems of meaning. The same year that G̲a'ax̲sta'las and Na̲ge married, George

Hunt met Franz Boas in Victoria, beginning a collaboration that continued until Hunt's death in 1933.

"What He Wants to Inform You Of": Witchcraft and the Potlatch

Alert Bay
Dec 24 1895

Mr Pidcock
Sir

[C] has asked me to write down for him what he wants to inform you of: thing's that have been brought to his notice, or that he has seen. He say's he has been told by a man that came down from [village name] expressly to see you,– but you were away –, that he wants you to speak about or take notice that a man that died up there, was killed by witch-craft by a man that was unfriendly with him because each were try to have a certain rank in the potlatch and this man that came down from there that he is afraid that the son of the man that died will be served the same way as his father. The uncle wishes you to speak to the man that is supposed to have killed him whose name is [T]. The man's name who came and informed [C] is [P]. And C says the same kind of case is in the camp here between [Kl] and [B]; they have quarreled about a rank that B's brother has taken; and as each nimkish has taken sides, it has caused a lot of bad feeling among them.

And he also wants [C] to tell you about a man named [M] whose money was stolen at Vancouver by a man named [Ku], a [village name] man. The son of [W], [M] was going to have him taken up at Vancouver. But [Ku] gave back part of the stolen money, he stole $390.00. He brought back 300 but kept the other 90, and gave a canoe instead which [M] brought up here but as soon as they got up here [Ku] took back the canoe. So [M] wants you to either get the canoe back or the $90.00 that was stolen. This was told to [C] in my hearing by [M] and his son and brother.

[C] wishes to tell you about a man [village] whose name is [Ki] who has had some (or brought up some), a [village] man name [Ka] bought a bottle from him which he paid, 6pr for or $9.00, and he is keeping it to show you. And he [C] wishes you to know what a hard time he is having from all the Indians as they blame him for the New

> Potlach act. The Nimkish is always sending him away as they do not want him in the camp because he tells you what they do. [K] is the worst of them,
>
> By Jane Cook for [C][16]

When Jane Cook wrote this letter, Christmas Eve, 1895, she was twenty-five years old and pregnant with her fifth child, Emma, born thirty-one days later. This is the earliest letter that we have by G̲a'ax̲sta'las. Like much correspondence of the time, it is handwritten. It is addressed to Reginald Pidcock, Indian Agent, at the request of a man we call "C," who was providing information to the Department of Indian Affairs. C reported an accusation of witchcraft associated with competition over a potlatch position, an accusation that had been referred to him, presumably as a representative of the colonial administration. He also made an appeal to the Indian Agent on behalf of a man named M in the hope that he would resolve a matter of debt. And he named a bootlegger in Alert Bay, someone also brought to his attention by another person. G̲a'ax̲sta'las's conclusion to the letter indicates that there is palpable animosity toward C from other "Nimkish" people, because of his role as informant in the community. Some people counted as members of the Kwawkewlth Agency evidently sought solutions to internal conflicts through the Indian Agent.

C's association with colonial authorities tied him to the "New Potlach act," legislation that was already contentious. As early as 1882, the superintendent of Indian affairs had proposed building lockup in "the most important Villages" "to prevent the recurrence of Indian Feasts (Tamanawas)[17] and Potlaches (donation feasts)."[18] The act referred to in the letter was one of eight amendments to the Indian Act in 1895. The government repealed section 6, "Celebration of Indian Festivals," and added Section 114, which expanded the net of legal prosecution to "any person who celebrated or assisted or encouraged another to celebrate any Indian festival, dance or other ceremony of which the giving away or paying or giving back of money, goods or articles of any sort forms a part, or is a feature, whether such a gift of money, goods or articles takes place before, at, or after the celebration of the same."[19] The response was swift. An aboriginal delegation visited Vowell in Victoria and submitted a "Petition of Rights" to the *Daily Columbian.* It concluded with the question: "Is it a chimera that under the British flag slavery does not exist?"[20]

The amendment followed on the heels of the failed prosecution, in 1889, of the first person arrested for potlatching under the ban – a

Mama̱liliḵa̱la man named "Hē-mā-sāḵ" who lived in 'Ya̱lis. Pidcock served as both Indian Agent and justice of the peace. The accused was arrested on 1 August and tried and convicted that same day. Pidcock sentenced him to six months in prison. The case was appealed under the Speedy Trials Act. On application of habeas corpus, Justice Matthew Baillie Begbie dismissed the charge and released the prisoner. In his "Bench Notes," Begbie wrote, "no evidence was called but the charge being read over to the prisoner with a woman interpreter, he was asked guilty or not guilty, and pleading guilty, and was immediately sentenced ... It is not alleged that the nature of the charge was explained to the prisoner and ... I think it would be very hard to explain... Until a defendant knows what those forbidden acts are, how can he say whether he has committed them or not?"[21] If that "woman interpreter" was Jane Cook, she would have been nineteen and a little over two weeks away from delivering her first child, Elizabeth Grace. The grounds for this legal dismissal reverberated in later prosecutions.

Before Hē-mā-sāḵ's appeal hearing, "a long list of Indians" had sent a typewritten petition to the lieutenant-governor. They charged that the Indian Agent had forcibly broken into Hē-mā-sāḵ's house at night, that the agent had been "falsely informed by two of the Indians ... who had apparently been made constables." The petitioners noted that these men had been "walking about our village saying they have power to arrest us for almost anything that we do and making us live in dread all the time. It is our nature to fear the law ... We are willing to give up all such doings but then we should be allowed something to help us live. Formerly we had plenty but now everything is being taken from us. Our rivers, our trees, our lands, even our fish are scarce among us, yet we are trying to live in peace ... but why should we be threatened with arrest all the time, when we do not know what is required of us?"[22] In response to the call to remove him as agent, Pidcock asserted that "not a single one of them can read or write," and he alleged that the petition had been written by "a white man or two and their [?] who are halfbreeds."[23]

The correspondence between Pidcock and Arthur Vowell provides a sense of what was then under bureaucratic consideration. In September, Vowell advised Pidcock to "use judgment to enforce" section 114: "when on these occasions they distribute food and clothing etc. among the aged and destitute of the people assembled, when no property is destroyed or otherwise wasted, such proceedings should not come within the meaning of the Section referred to."[24] Indian Agents were encouraged to hire interpreters to explain the "meaning and history" of "Indian Festivals" and to distinguish the potlatch from the "Tamanawas Dance."[25] In their attempt to have some "effect on the Potlatch habit" (in part, to curtail the travel of reciprocating 'ni'na̲'mima among various agencies), the DIA distributed posters that warned against trespassing on reserves.[26] "Weaning" the people from "superstitious belief" was on the list of agents' duties. Witchcraft was likely among those beliefs.

When family members read the 1895 letter, some connected witchcraft to potlatch politics. "Old stuff, lots of old stuff," George Speck said. "People joke around a lot about it," he said and laughed. "You know, 'cross me, and I'll put something in the crack of a cedar tree. And when the wind blows, look out.'" He laughed again. Lori Speck, George's daughter, was sitting with us: "Make sure you burn all your hair that you cut," she said, laughing. "Make sure that you don't leave any fingernails laying around."

"Yeah, you hear a lot of that stuff in early history and prehistory," George continued. "Stuff that I've read, anyway. And, it's by word of mouth. People talk about how it used to be. I've not heard of any case recently. Some of the guys talk about that in terms of certain individuals and why their names are no longer any good because the chiefs disowned them, or something like that. But usually, it's in the context of somebody talking about somebody in modern times, who've taken on that name, and 'Uh! Look at the name he took on! Little does he know that that name is dishonoured.'" George laughed. "So, you kind of wonder, what is the motivation? Anyway, it's interesting."

According to Charlie Nowell and Ed Whonnock, in the late nineteenth century there were 637 males, sixteen years and older, in all the Kwakwa̲ka̲'wakw villages. That number fell short of the potlatch places reserved for the hereditary standings of chiefs. In spite of objections, women began to inherit names, "small children were formally placed in statuses," positions went vacant, and adoptees or distant relatives of lower rank assumed names. Potlatch positions were refused by some while others "held several simultaneously."[27] Franz Boas documented two 1895 potlatches in Tsax̱is, and his list of the property distributed at these ceremonials attests to their scale.[28] As Charlie Nowell and Ed Whonnock made clear, "conflicts and stress" over standings had indeed intensified, and witchcraft was among the strategies available to the ambitious.[29] "There was a lot of dark witchcraft in those days," John Nestman told me, "so, Christianity would have been a lot more positive than that, something to promote over that."

When I spoke with Peggy Svanvik, an elder and Whonnock descendant, she suggested that witchcraft associated with the potlatch was the primary reason that her grandparents had left Tsax̱is. "My uncle was the heir to the chieftainship," she said, "and apparently somebody was doing the witchcraft on him. So, that's why they left Fort Rupert, because there was jealousy. My grandmother was higher ranking than my grandfather, but she didn't give [her chieftainship] to him – she gave it to her son. She was an only child, my grandmother, of a high-ranking father. So, she kept it, and she gave it to her son. I guess it was a little stubborn streak in her *[laughing]*, why she didn't hand it over to her husband. Apparently, when her father died, the chieftainship went to her. There was an uncle who didn't want her to have it. But, apparently, the people did not like the uncle, so they got together and had a vote – voted to keep her in as the chief, not the uncle. Mrs. Cranmer told me that story ... When I heard all these stories, that's when I started to think, that was why [Jane Cook] didn't want the potlatch, not because she didn't like potlatch for potlatching's sake."

Competition over potlatch positions served as a backdrop for many of Charlie Nowell's stories about his early life. He told Clellan Ford that people "often come to the Indian Agent and tell him someone is being witchcrafted, but the Indian Agent wouldn't believe it."[30] To colonial officials, witchcraft was associated with what they called Tamanawas or medicine dances. This association was made explicit in a 1908 letter to the attorney general by Dr. R.W. Large. In it, Large describes an incident from the community where he was working and inquires officially as to whether "the offense constitutes a practice of witchcraft as defined in Sect. 296 of the Criminal Code ... I would further ask if two Justices could try such an offense ... This old superstition is being revived, and in spite of argument and ridicule is believed in and dreaded by the Indians, to such an extent, that it completely nullifies Medical treatment in a number of cases."[31] The physician's rhetoric obscures the observation made by Helen Codere that "although [Kwakwa̱ka̱'wakw people] feared death by sorcery ... when additional medicines and treatments were made available to them they were prepared to accept them and did accept them readily."[32]

As Wedłidi Speck explained to me, "There's two types of medicine – *paxala* is where they do good medicine and *ē'aka* is where they do bad medicine – the fact that someone could influence the outcome of an individual. What they would do is they would take hair, where you pee, anything that was related to you as a person, they would take it, and they would use certain medicines to go after you that would influence, let's say, weakness of your spirit." He referred again to Lydia Whonnock's story about witchcraft in which G̲a'ax̲sta'las instructed her to pray. "It's almost as if – if you had your own inner strength, you wouldn't be susceptible to that," he said. "Granny Cook was having to face how much negativity there was, how much jealousy."

A determination of witchcraft called for the specialized skills of those who were versed in such matters – Christian and non-Christian. "I don't know much about witchcraft," Gloria Cranmer-Webster told me as we spoke about the letter. "I can just think of this story that my mother told. Her father became very ill, and the family suspected witchcraft. So, they sent for this guy from Bella Bella who was supposed to be an expert at dealing with that sort of thing. And he agreed, on the condition that if he cured my mother's father, that he got to marry one of these young women. My mother, her sister, and a cousin are all, I don't know, in their teens or late teens or something, and how horrible that must have been! Apparently, this guy was way older than the girls. *[Laughs]* They don't want their father to die, but they don't want to marry this old guy either. Yeah, in the end, he wasn't able to cure my grandfather, so nobody had to marry him. I don't know how often that kind of arrangement was made, but I remember her telling me that."

After a pause, Gloria continued: "I remember my aunt Axuw – I think she died before you ever came up. Anyway, when she was still in fairly good shape, she and my mother went to church every Sunday. And they'd stop by, and they'd have lunch. And about once a month, she'd fish around in her handbag, and she'd bring out one of those little change purses with a snap. It would be just full, absolutely full of hair. And she'd say, 'Here, take care of it,' because I was the only one she knew who had a wood stove who could burn the stuff *[laughs]*. You couldn't leave it lying around in case somebody got a hold of it. Yeah, so here she was, a staunch Anglican, but still believes quite firmly in things like witchcraft."

Indeed, it is difficult to state where Jane Cook might have placed herself on a spectrum of such beliefs. The Cook Family file in the Alert Bay Library and Museum includes excerpts from the summary of an interview conducted with Lucy Brown:

> She says that when she was younger she used to visit Mrs. Jane Cook and she once told Lucy that she dreamed about an old man who owned

> the house that was here (where Lucy Brown's house is now) who told her to go to Mrs. Whonnock's (she lived in the house then) and get a ladder and put it up and climb and reach with your hand (she told if it was the right or left hand but Lucy can't remember this exactly) and get a kettle that is there. One of those old big round kettles that we (our people) used to have. She dreamed of this twice so they told the kids, the boys to do this, to go climb and reach up (you couldn't see) and they did and there it was. So Jane told the boys to put it in a fire and burn it. So they did. This is how you give something to a dead person. You put it in a fire and burn it.[33]

The story is interesting for what it says about the complexity of G̲a'ax̲sta'las's beliefs. According to her descendants, Jane Cook also practised purification rituals. She smudged houses after a death with the smoke of burning hemlock boughs, and she told others about the importance of listening to ravens, a subject that came up in my discussion with her granddaughter Florrie Matilpe.

"My Uncle Tom – he was blind. He used to go and stay at the house with us – up at the [Cook] big house. He used to tell me, he used to say, 'Are the ravens still around?'"

"And I said, 'Yeah, why?'"

"And he said, 'Granny Cook used to say, your granny used to say, "When there's no more ravens, that's when the world's going to start changing around."'

"And then another thing he'd say was, 'Granny said our lives were like a totem pole.' He said, 'We're right on the top now, and it's going to keep changing as the years come and when we get to the bottom' – my Uncle Tom used to even do this *[gesturing below]*. I don't know why he used to see Granny do it, because he was blind! He said, 'When you get to the bottom of the totem pole, that's when you start worrying about the world. It's going to really change.' He used to tell me that."

"She told people, it's just like a totem pole – our world is. They get rotten I guess, is what she meant."

"I was really interested in my Uncle Tom when he used to talk. He said that to me so many times, 'Are the ravens still around?'"

"'Yeah, they're still around.'"

"'We don't have to worry about the world yet!' he'd say."

"She had so many visitors. That's the kind of woman she was. She never turned anyone away. Like, my Uncle Tom had a place to stay when he used to come from Village Island. So, he'd just come and stay with us up at the big house. And she used to talk to him there, too, just make him part of the family, which she did for everybody that came around."[34]

When I asked her about her grandmother's beliefs, Pearl Alfred replied. "Yes, not exactly psychic, or a prophet or anything like that. She seemed to know. She seemed to know, or have premonitions more than anything, of things that were going to happen. She seemed to always know when somebody was going to die, when something bad was in the air. But I shut my ears off at that point. When you're kids, you don't want to hear that stuff."

"Was she superstitious?" I asked Pearl.

"I don't think so. No, I don't remember her being superstitious."

"Work closely with Missionaries," Vowell wrote to agent Pidcock in 1895. He urged him to "wean [people in the agency] from superstitious belief and injurious habits."[35] These beliefs and habits likely encompassed all non-Christian ideas and practices, including those about ravens, witchcraft, and relations with the dead. But it was "cannibal rioting" – as CMS missionaries then referred to winter ceremonies – that was at the heart of such fears.[36] So-called injurious habits were approached through Eurocentric ideas about labour, productivity, and health. At the centre of the colonial gaze was the potlatch, which was seen as a site for redistributing and destroying property, spreading infectious illnesses, promoting gambling and liquor use, and contributing to the southern sex trade.

Later that year, Pidcock, at Alert Bay, received a copy of a circular sent by the Reverend M. Tate to police commissioners throughout BC. The circular advised authorities to "use all power to enforce" section 106, chapter 48 of the Indian Act (1886) and its 1887 amendment. The amendment pertained to prostitution and made it possible to charge Indian women working in *any* house, on or off reserves. According to Reverend Tate, women "now living ... in the cities would be forced to return to reserves and amongst their people lead better lives."[37]

Motivated to increase the number of eligible marriage partners, missionaries continued to press women to return to their villages. Reverend Tate aired his views in the newspapers of the day. On 2 March 1896, the *Victoria Daily Colonist* published a response written by Amos Gosnell and associates, who intended to:

> let the white people know our minds ... Mr Tate assumes the property taken by Indian women from the cities to their home are the proceeds of immorality, whereas they are mainly the earnings of these women

> at canneries, for sewing and gains at trading. He also assumes that all this property thus acquired is wasted in potlatching, whereas most of it is used by the families of the women who earned it, and only what can well be spared is given away to be returned hereafter with usury ... Mr Tate asks where certain stalwart Hydahs are. We anew they are dead. They died of smallpox and measles. They did not die of potlatch.[38]

Amos Gosnell, William Jeffrey, and Billy Williams, chiefs of the "Nass River Indians," had arrived in Victoria that week to present a petition and seek legal counsel to challenge the constitutionality of the potlatch ban as set forth in the Indian Act.[39]

About a month later, on 19 March 1896, the *Daily Colonist* published a letter by Reverend Hall, who wrote that he had counted "thirty-two women in one month who embarked by the steamers to bring back the coveted blankets. In my time fifty women under 25 years of age have died, all of whom have been sacrificed to maintain the potlatch."[40] Hall's letter also made his larger goals explicit: "It is to the interests of this province that we keep the Indians alive; they are worth preserving ... They occupy land the white man does not require. They love the white man, and their ultimate future must be absorption and assimilation."[41]

These letters were written during a time of intense public debate. Newspapers published letters for and against the potlatch by Christian, nonpotlatching groups; potlatching chiefs and their supporters; and merchants and settlers (both pro and con). In the years that followed, a series of petitions were sent to colonial authorities, and newspapers continued to publicize stories about aboriginal people "buying wives," prostitution, cannibalism, contagious diseases, destruction of property, and the whisky traffic.

The presence of women in the cities continued to preoccupy colonial agents in the late 1880s. Franz Boas's first book *Indianische Sagen von der Nord-Pacifischen Küste Amerikas* (1895) documents oral traditions elicited from members of several coastal groups then living in Victoria.[42] Writing for the German publication *Globus,* Boas described "Indian camps" in that city in 1891:

> The streets are lined with poor little huts which house the Indians who are temporarily in Victoria. The smallest of these huts are sheds of boards divided into rooms by wooden partitions. In each room a rough bed and a hearth are installed and it is ready to rent for about

> $2 a month. Such a wooden shack, twenty feet wide by sixty feet long, therefore brings the owner two hundred dollars a year and, since this income is gained practically without any initial expenditure, a great number of landlords have turned over their property for such use. In these huts the Indians who are in Victoria as temporary laborers live, often with their wives and children; in them also live Indian women who earn money as washerwomen or prostitutes and who plan to return to their homes with their savings.[43]

In the same article, Boas writes that prostitution "has been very destructive for many of the coastal tribes, since they lost almost all their young women ... All the measures taken so far to put an end to this pernicious practice have been fruitless and even the most remote tribes today send their daughters to Victoria to certain destruction."[44] The destruction to which he refers is likely sexually transmitted illnesses, which were "not only a direct cause of death but also contributed to the low birth rate and the high infant and child mortality."[45] Robert McKechnie's account of medical practices in Vancouver suggests that "gonorrhea and syphilis remained more or less commonplace and, at the turn of the century, there was still no specific treatment."[46] Of course, European men and women were also widely affected by such illnesses, just as they were also active participants in prostitution.

Several writers note a dramatic population decline in aboriginal villages on the Northwest Coast in the late 1800s, which they attribute to disease – to smallpox (which devastated coastal communities in 1862), measles (especially from 1881 to 1883), influenza (from 1890 to 1892), and the horrible advancement of tuberculosis (from 1881). Drucker and Heizer note that the toll from alcohol must also be considered a cause of high mortality: "Large amounts of alcoholic beverages brought from Victoria and Vancouver by free-lance traders and by the Indians themselves ... were the direct cause of a tragically long list of fatalities, chiefly drownings."[47] Although drinking was later popular at the canneries and fishing grounds, it is also important to consider the effect on health of increasing restrictions on the aboriginal fishery.[48]

The context is one of intensifying economic pressures. Commercial sealing – another occupation available to coastal workers – began to wane in 1895.[49] Chinese and Japanese labourers began competing with Kwakwa̲ka̲'wakw workers for employment in the canneries.[50] "The early canneries used manual labour in lavish amounts at every step of the canning process. Fish were unloaded, butchered, cleaned, and washed by hand. The carcasses were sliced into chunks and put into cans by hand. The cans were weighed, loaded onto trays, shifted through the steaming and cooking process, soldered shut, labeled, boxed and stacked – all by hand. Even the individual cans were initially manufactured by hand, in the cannery. Chinese men and Indian women were crucial to canneries along the BC coast during the first generation of operation."[51]

Under the notorious 1888 Indian Food Fishery Regulation, it was illegal to sell yield from the food catch.[52] The regulation also banned the use of spears and nets for salmon fishing, equated "fisheries strictly with subsistence harvesting," and ignored, in the words of Pam Brown, the value of "fish as wealth."[53] By 1894, aboriginal fishers had to "obtain the permission of the Department of Marine and Fisheries to fish for food."[54] The legal dependency on commercial fisheries and canneries and the criminalization of aboriginal fishing practices surely pressured families to move to ill-maintained facilities at cannery sites and to the southern hop fields.[55]

The Anglican Women's Auxiliary

For men, women, and children in the Kwakwa̲ka̲'wakw villages at the turn of the century, life to some extent was organized around these migrations. For those who were Christian, church meetings in 'Ya̲lis were a popular social venue where people came to hear speakers and organize church events. G̲a'ax̲sta'las translated English sermons into Kwak̓wala on the spot, and she orated her own interpretation of scriptural themes at separate Bible meetings. Young mothers such as G̲a'ax̲sta'las met weekly at the Anglican Women's Auxiliary, established in 1895.

Elizabeth Kasalas (Mrs. Sam Hunt) described the character of these meetings in an interview at the Alert Bay Library that is summarized below.

> Mrs. Cook, G̲a'ax̲sta'las, used to prophesize about things that were going to happen in the future. Mrs. Joe Harris, T'łaliłi'lakw, used to be the same way. Mrs. Sam Hunt, Pu'tsa, said, "I used to go to prayer meetings with my mom on Wednesdays and Fridays, the Anglican Prayer meetings. I really enjoyed what the older people talked about

and were preaching. If my mom didn't go, I would go with my aunty To'ti. It really amazed me. Mrs. Cook said one day, 'A one-eyed monster will be in every house, and you will see things in far away places. You won't even have to go there, but you will see it. These places are so far that we can't go there because these places, they are too far away.' Mrs. Harris said the world will have disobedient children and no one will respect the sanctity of marriage. The generations to come will be like *Sodom and Ghemmorah.*"

Mrs. Sam Hunt said, "These ladies foresaw things way before they ever came around our people. It was way, way back, before I was married. She (referring to Mrs. Cook) knew this before anyone could have known about these things.[56]

In 1895, G̲a'ax̲sta'las helped Mrs. Corker (wife of A.W. Corker, principal of the Industrial School for Boys) establish the Christ Church branch of the Women's Auxiliary, an organization that left an indelible mark on the social fabric of 'Ya̲lis society, particularly the women.[57] By 1896, the Union Steamship Company was delivering passengers and freight to Alert Bay every week. The day school operated by Alfred and Elizabeth Hall had twenty-three pupils, Jane and Stephen's children Grace and Alice likely among them. Their youngest, Stephen Jr., was less than a year old; their eldest, Grace, was seven; Alice was five; William was four; and Emma would be born that year. Each child had been baptized within three months of his or her birth. Their sponsors were married friends of the family, Native teachers, and missionaries. I was told that the Anglican Church Women's Auxiliary provided emotional, spiritual, and material support for young aboriginal mothers in 'Ya̲lis.

Connected through friendships and 'na̲'mima ties, women related to the Cook family offered descriptions of the "WA." Ninety-two-year-old Ethel Alfred told us that, "in her time," the group used to meet at the Council Hall, which also served as the Girls' Day School: "There was a group called ACW, and we used to love going to listen to her [Jane] interpreting the Bible for us. I never used to want to miss it – I dragged my boys. I had one girl, and I had four boys – five boys I had, but I lost one – and I used to drag them, and I used to teach them to sit still while she's talking, eh? You know, because I never used to leave my kids with babysitters. So, I used to just take them, so I could go listen to Granny ... The old people in the early, early years – she used to be a midwife, you know, she delivered babies. That's what I remember she used to do. And she was a wonderful person for us. She was a wonderful Christian woman, very Christian woman. She'd be interpreting in the church. And she always was there for anybody – you know, when anybody passed on, she'd be right there with the people ... She was always giving stuff away, food and that. I guess she would hear somebody is in need, you know, she would go and bring them food. Baskets of food, yeah." Ethel Alfred was a close friend of G̱a'aẖsta'las' daughter Pearl Cook (later Pearl Mountain). Both were born in 1910.

Jeane Lawrence and her five siblings lived with G̱a'aẖsta'las, her grandmother, in the Cook big house after the premature death of her mother, Grace, in the late 1920s. "She just was such a great lady," Jeane said, "we had to go to Sunday school and she'd take us around to some of her friends. She'd have a WA and we were allowed to go in on that lots of times, and help. You know, they'd be knitting wonder wool. I can remember using her spinning wheel."

"In those days she wound up her wool ... And she was a pretty good marriage counselor too, I think ... We used to go to her little WA, that used to be in the parish hall, because I remember the odd time when there was pictures taken and I don't think we were allowed in the pictures."

"Gosh," Jeane said, looking at a photograph of the WA, "I don't think there's any of those older ladies left, those grannies."

"Remember Miss Dibben and Miss O'Brien? They were missionaries. They'd come and go around the island, and then they stayed on Village Island."

"Oh God, yeah, [Miss Dibben] must have been here a hundred years!" Pearl Alfred exclaimed.

Following Jeane's statement that G̱a'aẖsta'las was a good marriage counsellor, Pearl Alfred spoke about the role of the group. "The WA they called themselves – those were the ones. We never did come across those minutes, those church minutes. The ones that I saw, there didn't seem to be anything about anything that was going on. There were these two big, long, black binders, which were the minutes of the WA and on all that very sheer – looked like tissue paper. It was all very fragile-looking stuff. They were planning things, mostly, like planning sales, or they were selling things, and people were donating stuff. But it kept a record, which I thought was interesting, of all the people that were there. So it was everybody. All the women in the community appeared to be there at one time or another. They were

Photo 17 Anglican Women's Auxiliary, 'Y*a*lis, ca. late 1910s. G*a*'a*x*sta'las is in the back row, *third from right. Courtesy of Pearl Alfred.*

all members of the WA. I think, for the most part, it was Bible study. But knowing my grandmother, I'm sure they discussed everything. But the minutes, I think, talk about what they're going to do and who's making the pillowcases for the tangle table and who's making the fish pond, or whatever it was they were doing. And she would read the lesson of the day. So, I think they always started off with a reading from the Bible. But Ethel said, at one point, she could hardly wait until she was old enough to attend one of those things. Everybody looked forward to becoming one of her group, the women. I guess it had some standing in the community, this ragtag woman with her." Pearl's words blended into laughter.

"I remember [the meetings]," she continued. "I don't know how old I would have been, but they gathered at our house. I think it was Wednesday afternoon, or something like that. Everybody came, and all these ladies trudged up the hill. Everybody had their – whatever they were working on, whether it was embroidery or some knitting or something. And then everybody had tea and biscuits. Or hot water! I can remember that, so. There had to have been [other things discussed at those meetings]. There just had to have been, but we've never come across anything." Pearl's sense that the WA dealt with other matters important to women is shared by many.

When the Women's Auxiliary was formed in 1895, Alfred Hall reported that 60 to 115 attended church, "mostly young people" at the morning congregation and 40 to 70 people at the afternoon Sunday school.[58] One hundred and seven years later, in 2002, Ethel Alfred told us that the church committee was deciding whether to renovate the vestry at Christ Church: "I said, 'What for? We're lucky if we've even got ten people who go Sundays.' When I went, there was only three of us *[laughs]*. We just went through the prayers though. We weren't good singers *[laughs]*."

The Cook Big House

> The principal buildings are the cannery of A.S. Spencer and the general store on the wharf, which is the landing place of the northern steamers. To the left of the cannery, which marks the centre of the village, is a terrace of cabins, where live the employees of the cannery, and further along are the dwellings of the provincial police officer and others, which reach for perhaps a hundred yards down to the Indian burying place. To the right of the cannery is the Indian rancherie, with its cluster of huts, many of which have immense totems in front of them ... At the end of the rancherie is the sawmill and store run by the Church of England missionary ... His residence, a two-story frame building, adjoins the little church ... the whole village consists of but a single line of buildings about two thousand yards long ... The Industrial School at the left limit of the village is also a large building in comparison with the size of the settlement ... The whole village fronts on the beach, and on a rising hill behind there is a dense background of Douglas firs. It is indeed a picturesque place.
>
> – *Victoria Colonist,* 11 March 1900

A tone of the ordinary predominates in this newspaper article, which reports on charges of cannibalism in 'Y̲alis.[59] The description also highlights the dominating presence of commerce, church, and state.

"Papa, we know him as being in his seventies," George Cook told his daughter Nella Nelson. "But I was looking at one of the pictures today and saw a big sawmill in Alert Bay. And he was a foreman of the sawmill for the Wastells 'til it closed down. At one point, the sawmill was right where Sam Hunt lived. So, you can see that Papa wasn't made a wealthy man – he always had to be working." Stephen Cook

Photo 18 General view of Alert Bay, ca. 1900. *Photographer unknown. Image E-07873, Royal BC Museum, BC Archives.*

adhered to a work ethic that had been encouraged by Protestant missionaries. He entered into the wage economy early on. He worked the books at the sawmill, which had been built by village labour but was run by the mission.[60] His language skills and long-term affiliation with Alfred and Elizabeth Hall no doubt offered him opportunities within several formal and informal economies. Like others of mixed ancestry, he was likely both disadvantaged and privileged by European and Kwakwa̱ka̱'wakw attitudes that racialized so-called half-breeds.[61]

Hand logging – an independent, self-employed occupation – became important among the Kwagu'ł and Ławits'is after the turn of the century. By 1908, though, sawmill companies and the provincial government had leased most of the timberlands and refused licences to aboriginal loggers.[62] According to the "Cook Calendar," compiled by the family for its 2001 reunion, "when BC Packers took over the mill, Stephen left and built himself a store and wharf ... He staked timber claims on the Klaanch River and later sold them for a large sum. He

Photo 19 Jane, G̲aga, and Stephen Cook, with children. Photographed at Ben Isaac's house, early twentieth century. *Courtesy of Ralph Bell.*

also staked copper claims at Quatsino and later disposed of them, too, for a reportedly handsome price."

"So this is where Papa built the house, made the store, and built the two boats," George Cook told his daughter Nella. "This all came from the money." Before he married, Stephen Cook lived in the house of 'Na̲mgis chief Wax̲a̲widi. Until the time they had fourteen children, Jane and Stephen lived in Ben Isaac's house by the 'Na̲mgis shipyards.[63] In 1907, Stephen and others built what came to be known as the Cook big house. It took two years to construct and had a veranda, two storeys, and nine bedrooms. It stood midway up the hill above the village.

Although there is no doubt about G̲a'ax̲sta'las's adherence to Christian marriage mores, her later domestic life defied the missionary design in interesting ways. She had married a young man who had participated in the custom and was also educated by European missionaries, yet the couple's household was anything but nuclear.

"Jane was very Native in her ways," John Nestman told me. "Just the idea of the big house, all the rooms, like in the old days, in the cedar big houses, they were partitioned off for the families. Upstairs

Photo 20 Cook family, ca. 1910. *Back row, left to right:* Emma, Edwin, Grace, Stephen, and Alice. *Front row, left to right:* Ernie, Cyril, Jane (holding Pearlie), Gilbert, Stephen (holding Herbert), and Reg. Willy is missing from the image. Alfred and Rupert died in their early years. Chris and Winnie were not yet born. *Courtesy of Reg Cook Jr.*

[in the Cook big house], there were six bedrooms. So, they had a family in each room – four beds, and three or four to a bed. Downstairs, there was the master bedroom and the kitchen and a large living room–dining room area." Economically, and in terms of extended-family residency, the Cook family big house resembled the multifamily domestic spaces of G̲a'ax̲sta'las's Kwagu'ł grandparents. Spatially, within the village, the Cook big house compared, in terms of elevation and size, with the houses of other high-ranking families.[64]

"They actually bought some land from the church," Pearl Alfred told me. "I think it was five acres that they bought. Their house is on the reserve. Our home – we lived on the reserve. But probably a foot of the dining room, we used to say, was not reserve. So, all of her garden and everything like that, was not reserve. The house was right on the top edge. It's a blue house on the hill. It's midway in the village, and you can actually drive right up there. It's a beautiful old place. I think my Dad said he was five when they moved into it, and he was born 1902. It just overlooks the bay ... That house was always overflowing with people."

"My family lived with her all our lives," Pearl told me. "My Dad [Reggie] was the oldest surviving son." By the time that Reggie and Nellie Cook began to raise their family, Edwin had been killed in action during the First World War; Stephen had died of TB (what was then called consumption), in 1911; and Ernie had passed away, in 1931, after a long bout with tuberculosis. Two years after the family moved into the big house, Jane and Stephen had lost their two-year-old son, Rupert, to bronchitis. As the eldest surviving son, Reggie had inherited the big house, ran the store, and was recognized as the family's leader.

"He always deferred to [his mother] in major decisions," Pearl continued, "which was always something big, because he was a big boss too ... I think we always had two settings of every meal *[laughs]*. It was not unusual to have fifteen people for lunch who were living in the house, twenty people. My parents, of course, had ten kids themselves. And we were there. So, it was a huge family. But I never had a sense that there was a lot of work involved in this kind of big operation. And it was huge, when you think about it now. She did all the cooking. That was something that astounded me. It seemed to me she just took anybody who was hungry or needed a place to stay. And in our family she raised – when one of her older daughters [Grace] died, I think she left eight children. And she took all those in, and another daughter [Alice] died and left two. So, she raised, I would think, ten children besides her own. Never mind anybody else."

"It must have been a tremendous responsibility for both of them to have all the kids up in the house, and to build that house up there," Pearl's brother George Cook told his daughter Nella Nelson. "Then, everybody thought [Papa] was crazy to build that big a house. But Granny must have foreseen what was coming, or something. It was full all the time."

For many in the family, the big house and the lives and activities that inhabited it are at the heart of the Granny Cook Book. Some felt that this work should comprise the stories about domestic and community life that flowed from this home rather than the political activities that came to overshadow their Granny's life. All however, expressed their sense of awe as they recounted the house's domestic rhythms. The big house's physical space was divided among lineages. Maureen Cook prompted her ninety-five-year-old mother-in-law, Nellie Cook, to talk about the big house.

"Did they have nine bedrooms upstairs?" she asked. "And they had to make another bedroom downstairs, because they needed it, out of the old dining room?"

"Yeah," Nellie replied. "That's where I stay when I go."

"They had to make another bedroom because there were so many families – so many kids in the house," Maureen told me.

"And then we had visitors, hey?" Nellie added. "And in those days, they brought their blankets, and they'd sleep on the floor."

Pearl Alfred also spoke with me about the economy of space: "We sort of lived in one room, our family and another family, sort of like a big house. And then, when somebody else came, we were stacked like cordwood. And meal preparations were just continuous."

"But she had a woman who used to help her. You had to have help with that much. And Lydia was another one, Lydia Whonnock. I remember her ... It just seemed to me [Granny] was always on the move. She was either at the stove, in her garden, or going out to see somebody through their last breath, or bringing a baby in ... And some kids used to just come for the meal. I don't know if their family situations weren't great. They just came for a bowl, and she always seemed to have this everlasting pot of soup. They'd come in for soup and bread, then leave. The old ladies would come for hot water and sugar."

Nellie Cook told us about the meals that Jane Cook prepared.

"Oh, maybe smoked salmon or fresh salmon."

"How did you store the salmon?" Maureen asked her.

"They had little cedar boxes. Those that were really dry. They had cedar boxes, and it preserved the fish. They used to go up the river and dry the fish. They had a place where they smoked it real dry, and they put it in cedar boxes."

"Did your family ever make grease?" I asked.

"They had a camp way up in Kingcome," Nellie told us.

Later in our conversation, Maureen asked her mother-in-law, "Did Granny knit a lot?"

"I don't think she had time to knit," Nellie said. "She was busy doing other things."

"I guess so," Maureen said, "keeping house and tending the garden and looking after friends. Did you say that Granny smoked? One cigarette a night or something?"

"A pipe," said Nellie. "She lay on the sofa when everybody was in bed. What memories, eh?"

"Our granny smoked?" Nellie's daughter Christine exclaimed.

"She said at night," Maureen added.

"No, that's G̱aga," Christine said. "Yeah, *she* did. No, Granny didn't smoke. Perhaps she's got it mixed up – the old lady did – a corn pipe, you know."

Many of the stories I heard about Stephen Cook's mother, G̱aga, referred to her "old time" ways. She lived until her death in what has been called a shack adjacent to the big house.

"I don't think she was comfortable living with us," Christine said. "She was more comfortable in this little house. She stayed very traditionally. So she lived here. And when we grew up, we used to be fascinated. She passed away there, and we used to, of course, go in there and have a look at her little house. It was small. It was very compact. It had everything in it. It was made for her."

"When you say she lived traditionally ... ?" I said.

"Oh, I meant she didn't want all the luxuries. She was just comfortable. Her house was very low-key. She just wore her blanket. She just was very, very low-key."

Christine and her mother wondered aloud if G̱aga could speak English.

"She must have understood it," Nellie said.

Several others speculated about G̱aga's ability to communicate with English speakers, including Stephen's father, John Hubert Cook. "Her husband – Papa Cook's father – brought the money home and told her to hang on to it," William Wasden Jr. told me. "I don't know how they communicated. Love, I guess. But, anyways, she would start the fire every morning with this money when he was gone. She didn't know what it was, and when he got home, most of his money was burned up. That was just my granny's story about her." I suggested she must have been at least bilingual. "You wouldn't be able to function here unless you could speak Kwak̓wala," William said.

Most oral histories about G̱aga recount her adherence to the old ways of living. As Agnes Alfred recalls in *Paddling to Where I Stand:* "When men went out halibut fishing ... their wives were told to eat a lot while they were out so that the fish would take their bait ... When [G̱aga's] husband Qʷaxila [Bert Cook's father], went halibut fishing, [she] took pilot biscuits, tied a rope to them, and hung them up. Then she would bite at them, just like she wanted the halibut to bite at her

Photo 21 G̲aga, or K̲wak̲'waballas, Stephen Cook's mother, n.d. *Courtesy of Ralph Bell.*

husband's bait ... She was told later that it would have been enough just to eat the biscuits."[65]

"Stephen's mother was ridiculed by other people in the 'Namgis," Wedłidi Speck told me. Gaga apparently had a heavy "West Coast" accent, even though her mother was 'Namgis. "So Lagius and T̓łakwadzi stood her between them in the village and said, 'You tease her about her language anymore, our coppers, we'll break them on you.' That silenced them. Sometimes you've got to use force. There's some kind of sanction."[66] The way Sam Scow presented it, they just said, "'This is our family. You talk to her that way, you talk to us that way.' So, as chiefs, they said that would be the end. They would be the principal chiefs of the village at that time." These 'Namgis chiefs were related to Gaga through her mother.

I heard Wedłidi Speck tell this story several times, always in the context of emphasizing social inclusion. "My grandmother Lucy Brown told me, 'There's no such thing as non-Status people. You have a name in my family – you are in my family.' She talked about her aunt Mayria Kamano, who said, '*I'll* tell you who my family is – this is *my* 'na'mima. I tell *you* who my family is.' As we've emerged, because we have less and less wisdom about it, we've handed responsibility for our 'na'mimas over to other people. In the [Goldthorpe] health inquiry [1980], Jack Peters, in his presentation, he said that what happened to us is that we turned our hands over, and we let go of the responsibility we had to be leaders. He said our strength was in recognizing that our power was more important than the power of others. So, when we gave our power over to them, we lost our strength, and then our health declined."[67]

Wedłidi discussed how the colonial system had claimed the authority to define people. He contrasted this power with the meetings of chiefs from different 'ni'na'mima and how they expressed authority over lands they owned: "This is where your property ended and mine began. That's all. If anything was wrong, they were really clear to stand up and say that. I think in our reclamation – it's really about taking power, our power, and going back into places like that where we can assert it." This repatriation of identity is at the heart of several current projects.

Just as Wedłidi Speck's account shifted easily from 'na'mima solidarity to colonial power to the relationship between 'ni'na'mima and the land, so too did Ga'axsta'las's advocacy. She served as an advocate for the women in her family and wrote and spoke publicly in favour of aboriginal rights and land title. Her career as a translator extended

Photo 22 Members of the Gı̌gal'gam clan, House of Chief Waxawidi. Jane and Stephen Cook and five of their children are at the far left. Charlie Nowell sits, with hat, to the right of Stephen Cook. Gaga stands behind Agnes Alfred (with baby at front). Bert Cook stands in the doorway (*back left,* with dark hat). His father, Ḳwakhila, stands at the doorway (*back, far right,* with striped shirt). *Courtesy of Wedłidi Speck.*

from the local church to provincial courtrooms and to working with leading ethnological scholars of the day.

Edward Curtis: Translations

Leslie,

So it turns out that Mrs. Cook also interpreted for Edward Curtis sometime between 1910 and 1914. In an unpublished

> *manuscript of stories recorded by E. Schwinke (Curtis' field collaborator) from a chief Lagius, likely in Alert Bay ... it mentions that she translated them. It only mentions that she is half-breed.*
>
> *The Ms. is in the Curtis Collection, #143, Box 10, File 14, in the Seaver Centre for Western History Research, Los Angeles County Museum of Natural History.*
>
> *Another piece of the puzzle.*
>
> *A.*
>
> – *Email from anthropologist Aaron Glass, 2006*

Helen Codere marked 1881 as the year "ethnological work" was counted among "Kwakiutl occupations." She included those who worked as "informants" or in the "manufacture and sale of ethnological goods for Museums and tourists."[68] George Hunt was contracted to work with English, German, and American collectors who travelled through Kwakwa̱ka̱'wakw territories during his lifetime.[69] Material culture (arguably, manifestations of 'na̱'mima identity through ancestral encounters) occupies much of the documentation of this history, but these "men of science" also collected human remains and documented oral traditions associated with "artifacts" that were then recontextualized as remnants of a soon-to-be vanishing people. Among those whose names are not often counted in the labour of ethnological translation is Jane Constance Cook.[70] It is unknown how much work she did in this regard, or for whom or when, although she was a primary informant for Boas in 1931, during his last field trip to Alert Bay. Charlie Nowell likewise worked with Charles Newcombe of the Chicago Field Museum.[71]

Edward Curtis (1868-1952) and his field assistants worked in and out of Kwakwa̱ka̱'wakw villages for four years. They generated material for Volume 10, *The Kwakiutl* (1915), of *The North American Indian* series and shot his ethnoromantic film, *In the Land of the Headhunters,* which premiered in New York and Seattle in 1914. Among the parade of characters who worked with peoples formerly known as the Kwakiutl, Curtis is a somewhat tragic figure. Bankruptcy, divorce, and poor reviews followed what can only be described as an ambitious and passionate dedication to documenting what he (and many others) saw as fading aboriginal worlds. According to George Horse Capture,

> Curtis made 10,000 wax cylinder recordings of Indian language and music. In addition he took over 40,000 images from over 80 tribes, recorded tribal mythologies and history, and described tribal population, traditional foods, dwellings, clothing, games, ceremonies, burial customs, biographical sketches and other primary source information: all from a living as well as past tradition. Extending the same principle to the photographs, he presented his subjects in a traditional way whenever possible and even supplied a bit of the proper clothing when his subjects had none. Reenactments of battles, moving camp, ceremonies and other past activities were also photographed. These efforts provided extended pleasure to the elders.[72]

During our research, Edward Curtis's photographs flashed up on my computer screen. At least two contemporary multimedia projects were then reanimating interest in Curtis and his work.[73] In people's homes in 'Ya̱lis, I was shown images taken by Curtis, including a portrait of G̱a'a̱xsta'las's great-uncle (grandfather in Kwakwa̱ka̱'wakw reckoning) Hemasaḵa.

When Curtis and William Meyers, his chief ethnologist, arrived in Kwakwa̱ka̱'wakw territories in 1909, they sought out renowned cultural broker George Hunt and arranged to work in Tsax̱is.[74] That year, Jane and Stephen lost their two-year-old son, Rupert, to bronchitis. Curtis and his team of fieldworkers began to compile texts and take photographs in Kwakwa̱ka̱'wakw villages in 1911, the year that Stephen and Jane lost their seventeen-year-old son, Stephen, to tuberculosis. As Shamoon Zamir makes clear, Curtis worked with a "variety of ethnographers, research assistants, academic advisors and editors, photographic technicians and printers. In addition, hundreds (if not more) of Native Americans participated in the construction of *[The North American Indian],* not only as photographic subjects but also as translators, informants and culture brokers."[75] G̱a'a̱xsta'las was among the translators.

It was likely that William Meyers arranged to collect the oral traditions and oral histories included in *The Kwakiutl.* Curtis himself was immersed in obtaining photographs and in planning and filming his musicale, *In the Land of the Headhunters.* Meyers had an eye for ethnographic accuracy and was close to prominent anthropologists of the day. One letter to Edmund Schwinke, written around the time that the writing of Volume 10 had begun, states that he had travelled with texts by Franz Boas.[76] He likely received the raw transcripts collected by others working in the villages and used them to write most of the

Photo 23 "Hamasaka in Tlu'wulahu Costume with Speaker's Staff – Qagyul, 1914." From Edward Curtis, *The North American Indian,* vol. 10, *The Kwakiutl.* *Courtesy of Charles Deering McCormick Library of Special Collections, Northwestern University Library, cp10005.*

final manuscripts. We do not know precisely when Jane Cook translated narratives for Curtis's assistant, Edmund Schwinke, but he joined their team in 1909 as a stenographer and photographic assistant.[77] It is interesting to contemplate if she also translated for her grandfather 'Nulis, who was included in Curtis's work. As Aaron Glass informed me by email, the English transcript of Chief Lagius's words holds few clues.

I spoke with Wedłidi Speck and William Wasden Jr. after they read the stories.

"Do you know who this Lagius was that Jane Cook translated for?" I asked Wedłidi.

"There was a Lagius in Turnour Island. There was a Lagius in Dzawadi. There were various Lagiuses. We heard the name last night being given to someone." (Our conversation took place in March 2009 as we spoke during a break in Dzawada̱'enux̱w Chief Frank Nelson's memorial potlatch that Wedłidi had travelled to 'Ya̱lis to attend.)

"I had a chance to look at the Lagius stories," he continued, "and the impression that I was left with was that Curtis had somehow asked for certain types of stories to be collected. So Lagius must have been known as a storyteller, as a myth keeper. And [Jane Cook] may have even chosen him because of that. When you're looking at the type of stories that have been included, they weren't necessarily ancestor origin stories. So, they weren't interested in that."

"Curtis was interested in myth stories and stories that certainly would influence the structure of the way we would think about the world. I guess, having to summarize it, they're asking him a little bit about the global mythology, a little bit about – let's say, some stories of ancestral heroes and some tribal events. He also focussed on war. I know in Curtis's Volume 10, he has a lot about the warrior. He was really interested in that. So, in the text of Lagius, it talks about the Dzawada̱'enux̱w and how the 'Na̱mgis and the Kwagu'ł and Ławits'is went to war with them. And that story I've heard from other people. I found the stories really interesting. Some of the stories of the wolf, the quartz crystal, the healing. There was a story that was collected that talks about the Thunderbirds who lived by Turnour Island, and I've heard that story from Lilly Speck":

"So, this particular Thunderbird village, they were in conflict with the myth people. And that was at a time when they were playing games, and they had a contest. When the myth people beat the Thunderbirds, Thunderbird gets upset and stole Kwixwaxawae's [Raven] *wife and took her to the upper world. So, now the myth people had to meet and talk about*

how they were going to fix it. So, Wren advised them to go to Salmon people and get their masks, because then they could go up and retrieve the wife."

"So, if I was thinking about this story, it makes sense that that was one of our foundation stories. It speaks to the chaos that existed in the myth world. It's similar to the chaos that existed then in our world, and there's a correlation in how to solve it. To address our chaos, we need to use the masks, or borrow the masks, and go to a place where we can find order and balance. That, to me, just makes sense. The story I was told about the Thunderbird was that they controlled different elements – like the rainbow or light and water, and things like that":

"And so, when they lost the game, they lost the rights to that. So the myth people took good care of those things after. Salmonberry Woman – who was the wife of Kwixwaxawae – she could sing a song, and out of this treasure box she had would come up a shoot, almost like a salmonberry. And then she'd sing a song again, and the next one came out with blossoms. And she kept singing different songs for that event. It brought salmonberries, to the point where they dropped in these baskets, and they fed the people, a salmonberry feast. And that's where Thunderbird took his opportunity. Lightning and thunder in the house, he knocked everyone over and grabbed her and took her above, because he liked the idea that this person could produce the magic of salmonberries out of a box."

"So that box of treasures is significant in that way. I'm wondering if, in terms of a theme, or a way of going to war, if we didn't apply that as well in our raids. When we go off and we would capture daughters of chiefs, we would take her like Thunderbird did. And we would then be able to have the wealth that came with the woman as a way of securing property ... I think, as a researcher or as an interpreter, Jane Constance was willing to do that work. I'm not sure why."

"She was translating," I said. "The guy who was interviewing Lagius – Edmund Schwinke – he was Curtis's still photographer. So, they were either working on the film or the book at that time. There's no date on the text."

"Ah, well, being the still photographer ... there's no doubt that Lagius of the Dzawada̱'enux̱w is the man. There's a really interesting picture of this man [in Volume 10]. He's a really kind-looking fellow. It would be lovely to put that picture to this piece of the story."

"Lagius, he's from Kingcome," William Wasden Jr. explained when we spoke about the texts. "Mike Willie and them figure that he is probably from the Toby Willie family. That's what they say. They know more about their history than we do. They think he was uncle to Toby Willie."

Photo 24 "Lagyus – Tsawatenok, 1914." From Edward Curtis, *The North American Indian*, vol. 10, *The Kwakiutl. Courtesy of Charles Deering McCormick Library of Special Collections, Northwestern University Library, ct10026.*

"So, what were your impressions of the stories? You seem to like them," I said.

"I do," William said. "I like Curtis because there's really particular details that we can draw from, details for our dances and our history, especially the Nimpkish stories."

"Curtis's work seems quite different to the Boasian work."

"Yeah, it's like a different angle on the way he writes, or maybe it was the questions he asked. I don't know. But it's almost a simpler, more personal view on our culture. Whereas Boas, a lot of it seems really influenced theoretically, whereas this stuff seems really plain and simple, really user-friendly." William laughed. "The stories were pretty consistent with how I know the legends."

"Do you think Curtis and Hunt and Boas talked to different people?"

"The Nimpkish stuff that I've seen, Curtis talked to a few different people, because we know the people they were using for Boas's stuff. We know who they were. I think what happened was that it came in, and it was translated. Whoever was translating – it was probably George Hunt – put his own slant on it."

"So how do you think it was for Jane to sit down and translate Lagius's stories?"

"I wonder why they were connected up. Just to gather information? I would wonder about her connections. I would have to say, to translate legends, they were talking in older languages than everyday Kwak̓wala. So, she must have been very good at that. She must have really understood the language. When you're dealing with legends, it's talking about ancient things."

By May 2010, Wedłidi and William confirmed with members in Kingcome that Lagius and G̱a'ax̱sta'las had indeed been relatives.

PART V
"We As the Suppressed People," 1913-18

"I just keep thinking about the context," George Speck said, "the historical and social context that she lived in. It blows me away because Alert Bay was the hub of the north island. This is where all of the freight came in. This is where all of the workers came to relax. This is where all of the fishermen tied up on fishing weekends. There was a cannery here. We had Native people coming from all over the Coast to work here. Then you had the boy's school and girl's school at that time, I guess the turn of the century ... There was no roads. There was just logging camps. Alert Bay was the entrepôt, the entry point of the north island. Everything came through here. If you see pictures of the harbour at that time, you'll just be amazed at the number of docks and steamships, and things like that. You'll see how much activity was happening."

"And there was Jane," I said, "writing to all these powerful men."

"There was Jane," he said, and laughed. "Well, it was very clear from the letters of the Indian Agent that she had a lot to say that he didn't like. From what I saw in one or two letters to the powers that be in Indian Affairs, she saw their duty as what it should be, and she wanted to know why they weren't living up to it. I can very well see her saying, 'You're our spiritual guides. Why aren't you ... ?' He laughs. 'You've taught me to be a Christian. Now, why aren't you acting like one?'"

G̲a'ax̲sta'las wrote to the powers that be, and they wrote back. Her letters make explicit demands for justice, particularly in the realm of

Photo 25 The Cook family, late 1912. *Back row, from left to right:* Willie, Alice, and Jack Warren (son-in-law, married to Grace), Grace, Emma, and Edwin. *Front row, from left to right:* Herbert, Gilbert, Cyril, Stephen (holding Chris), Pearl, Jane (with Winnie), Ernie, and Reg. *Courtesy of Reg Cook Jr.*

land, law, and marriage practices. In 1913, she penned a letter on behalf of the "Kwakwalla Tribes" in which she urged the Anglican bishop to use his influence in the struggle for recognition of rights and compensation for lands. In five letters written to defend a female relative in 1913-14, G̲a'ax̲sta'las questions the competence of the Indian Agent, whose application of colonial law, she felt, was affected by the sway of capital. These five letters, and two responses to them, provide glimpses of the imperial, legal, and social contexts in which she sharpened her focus on the material circumstances of women and children. In 1914, Jane Cook also translated the testimonies of Kwakwa̲ka̲'wakw chiefs and speakers at the McKenna-McBride Royal Commission. Because she was asked by some leaders to speak for them, she appears on commission transcripts as a sworn witness and interpreter.

Part V touches on particular moments in the ongoing struggle between colonial power and aboriginal societies on the Northwest Coast, sites of political engagement that remain relevant across the generations.

"We Are Agitating": Land

Alert Bay Jan. 11 1913.
Address To Bishop of Columbia

We thank Your Lordship for granting us our pray to tell you our troubles and asking Your assistance in this our cause. Your Lordship has probably heard that we are agitating that our Government in B.C. treat us fair. We feel that they have not done so, in that they have taken our Lands away from us without making *proper* payment to us or our Forefathers.

In time past we have trusted our Indian Agents and our Missionaries where they have told us that we have all we can ever expect from our Government. But now that we see how White Man and other Races are coming into our Country [and?] are given all kinds of Rights. But we who have owned these Lands from Time Immorial are not allowed to have any rights at all, in the Land of our Birth.

We feel it is time the Government of this Country takes up our case and give us some Compensation for our Lands, and also to give us, some rights that we may be able to compete with the Races, that are taking our place, in our Country.

There are good men that are helping us in this. But we would feel more confidence In you who are the Head of Christianity in this Country. We feel our cause is just and we do not want to impose on anybody. But we want our rights, as the proper owners of this Country that God Gave to us and our forefathers Years ago we felt helpless. But since we heard that there is a law, that treats of this subject, we feel, we ought to claim what this law gives us Now that we begin to see the time will come, when we will be strangers in this our own Country.

We have over and over again asked Mr R. McBride as the Head of the Government To take some notice of our case and he has always said that we have no right or lands or anything, and that he sees nothing to settled between the Government and us.

Will your Lordship look into our cause and if you see that it is Just, will you use Your Influence for us.

From the Kwakwalla
Tribes of B.C.[1]

Although not signed, this letter is in Jane Cook's handwriting. <u>G</u>a'a<u>x</u>sta'las was then forty-two and had given birth to sixteen children.

She had already survived three sons: Stephen (1894-1911), Alfred (1898-99), and Rupert (1907-09). At home, were six children under the age of ten; her youngest child Winifred was eight months old.

Paul Tennant describes a shift after the turn of the twentieth century toward First Nation political leaders who were fluent in both written and spoken English and who held traditional positions in their societies. Their predecessors had been limited to organizing on the basis of shared or closely related language groups and had thus been somewhat dependent on missionaries as intermediaries.[2] In the letter, the writer appeals to "the head of Christianity in this country," sidestepping local authorities – the missionary and the Indian Agent. G̲a'ax̲sta'las's generation – themselves educated by missionaries – were beginning to engage with the colonial legal system in written English.

Addressed to John Roper, the Anglican bishop of Columbia, the letter was signed by the "Kwakwalla Tribes," which I was told is a linguistic self-designation still sometimes used by the "old people." The term attests to their consciousness of rights, to a political climate in which agitating for fair treatment included demands for "proper payment" and compensation for land. "In 1908," writes Robert Galois, "the provincial government took a crucial step by declining to provide any more land for 'Indian reserves,' bringing the allotment process to a halt."[3] At the time of writing, aboriginal leaders must have been acutely aware of the recent push to cut back or eliminate "unused" reserve lands.[4] In the letter, the assertion of prior ownership is explicit and had already been declared by this time in dozens of arenas of protest.[5]

The Indian Reserve Commission was in chaos by 1913 – fiscal downsizing, resigning commissioners, and "uneven and inadequate" reserve allotments characterized the state of affairs.[6] The recognition of aboriginal title – a property right based on aboriginal people's historical use and occupancy of their lands – was then on the table. As Cole Harris notes, during the first decade of the 1900s the land question was characterized by a deadlock between the federal and provincial governments.[7] The pace of settlement was intensifying, and BC asserted its reversionary interest – the right of the province to claim any reserve lands "if a reserve is abandoned, or the Indians decreased in numbers."[8] Premier Richard McBride fiercely opposed the dominion government's strategies to have aboriginal title heard in courts: "new reserves could not be allocated; timber, minerals, gravel and often water on old ones could be minimally used."[9] Among the grievances voiced by aboriginal leaders was their opposition to the BC Game Amendment Act (1905), which had introduced fines and imprisonment for violations related to hunting, trapping, and fishing. Aboriginal people's access to and use of resource sites had been significantly curtailed, and letter petitions often cited overfishing, overgrazing, and the depletion of game by settlers as concerns.

At the heart of struggles for recognition of aboriginal title was the Royal Proclamation of 1763, an edict issued under King George III that continues to inform legal land questions. In 1909, the proclamation was the basis for the Cowichan petition, which asserted a strong case for title to lands occupied from "time immemorial" and never ceded.[10] Perhaps the proclamation is the "law that treats of this subject" referred to in the letter from "the Kwakwalla Tribes." One week after the Qa'wa̱tsa̱'n circulated the petition, the Nisga'a circulated their own petition, which also used the Royal Proclamation to assert title.[11]

Throughout the nineteenth and early twentieth century, opposition to colonial rule in BC took multiple forms: protest rallies, written and verbal refusals to accept the authority of Indian Agents, rejection of "reserved land" through the disruption or sabotage of surveyors' activities and refusals to fence such lands, and armed blockades or occupations to prevent entry into traditional territories.[12] Aboriginal delegations made nation-to-nation appeals to representatives at all levels of colonial officialdom – municipal (New Westminster), provincial (Victoria), dominion (Ottawa), and imperial (London).[13] By 1913, three important associations had been formed among dozens of First Nations along the Coast and in the Interior of the province: the Nisga'a Land Committee (1890),[14] the Interior Tribes of British Columbia (1909),[15] and the Indian Rights Association (1909).[16] The formation of a group called the Friends of the Indians in 1909 provides some sense of the varied nature of the land rights movement. In 1910, this non-aboriginal organization met with Richard McBride to press for aboriginal title.[17] Another strategy that emerged at this time was First Nation leaders' refusal to divulge "information about reserves and declar[e] their intention of adhering to this attitude until the question of Aboriginal Title had been settled."[18] Petitions were scripted to demand the return of lands, negotiated treaties, adequate reserves, and compensation for land occupied by settlers.[19]

"Petitions," writes Ravi de Costa, "are events ... every petition is an interaction of the identity of the petitioner and the authority being petitioned" within a known "moral world."[20] A petition is a written confrontation presented formally to a governing body. It is the culmination of processes of consultation that represents a group of like-minded dissenters. In the 1913 petition letter from the "Kwakwalla," the authority is the church, invested with power by the dominion government to convert, educate, and provide medical aid within agencies. Although the petitioners appealed to the morality of law or to humanitarian ideals, the moral sphere referred to in this letter is clearly Christianity. The author politicizes common religious values by writing about land as "this Country that God Gave to us and our forefathers."[21] That the petitioners appealed to the bishop to exert pressure on the provincial government raises questions about the relationships among the church and federal and provincial powers. Conflicts between the "Queen's law" and "church law" is a recurring theme in aboriginal protest rhetoric.[22] On the land question, some colonial churches pushed for recognition of aboriginal title while contesting the authority of Indian Agents.[23] Forrest LaViolette suggests that "the continued success of the missionaries appeared to be based upon the alignment of their political actions with Indian interests."[24] There is no indication that the Reverend Alfred Hall supported the struggle for aboriginal title; indeed, his early statements suggest he was aligned with the province.

Writing from Alert Bay, the seat of the agency and the mission, the author of the letter asserts "rights as the proper owners of this Country." Just three months later, the dominion and provincial governments arrived at an understanding to form a commission to provide a "final adjustment of all matters relating to Indian Affairs in the Province of British Columbia."[25] The McKenna-McBride Agreement of September 1912 put aside the question of aboriginal title and promised to "extinguish provincial interests in reserves, [and] allow more equitable distribution of reserve acreages." Notably, no reductions were to be made without the consent of those claiming title to lands.[26] Kwakwa̱ka̱'wakw representatives met with commissioners in June 1914. G̱a'a̱xsta'las was among them.

"Never Be Intimidated": On Activism

G̱a'a̱xsta'las's grandchildren and great-grandchildren speak often about her political engagement. As Pearl Alfred put it, "We learned that from her, somehow or other. We had to be strong. That's a word we associate with her always. Physical and mental strength – and never be intimidated." I asked Pearl about how the role of women had changed in the community.

"Well," she said sighing, "it seemed forever before anything really happened. But I think it is now. I think you can see what it looked like. It just seemed as if nothing was ever going to change." She laughed. "And I think a lot of attitudes still haven't changed, but the women have always been there. I mean, if you look at the political end of it, then the guys lead the politics. But it's the women who push. That's just the way it is. And then, if they don't behave, then we just push harder, until you end up more or less doing whatever, over the years. But in all of the land claim issues, I think women were a huge part of that."

"They're really left out of the written history," I said.

"I guess, yeah, when you come to think about it, eh? Kwakwa̱ka̱'wakw women were expected to be in the background ... There weren't many things that [women] were involved in, because there were no women's organizations or anything. There was only the church and the Native Brotherhood that you could be part of, and that was it. So, they could sit on the church committee, or something like that. But those that they were on, I think they worked hard on them. They were pretty vocal on the issues. So."

Women's strength echoes in stories about the family's political activities and community service throughout the generations. Jane and Stephen Cook's activities unfold in these pages, but their children, grandchildren, and great-grandchildren were also engaged (and continue to be engaged) politically. In adulthood, their sons – Reggie, Gilbert, Herbert, and Chris – were active in the Pacific Coast Fishermen's Association, and they and their sons held executive positions in the Native Brotherhood (see Part VIII). Like Reggie's wife, Nellie Cook, several women contributed to the Native Sisterhood. Stephen and Jane's daughter Emma ran the Girls' Auxiliary, and many mentioned her gift for music and her supervision of youth groups in the community. (As a young adult, Emma also guided Emily Carr on one of her painting journeys through Kwakwa̱ka̱'wakw territories.) Jane Cook's fourth-born daughter, Pearl Cook, opened her home at Village Island to anyone in need of shelter, especially during the winter clam-digging season. She travelled to other villages in the 1940s to assess the health needs of women. Pearl and Winnie carried on their mother's role at the bedsides of those who were ill, dying, or giving birth.

Several grandchildren were involved in the establishment and ongoing services of various aboriginal friendship centres on Vancouver Island and in urban Vancouver.[27] Granddaughters were leaders and key figures in the food fishery at 'Ya̱lis, in local band government, in aboriginal health organizations, and in hospitals, where some worked as nurses. Great-grandchildren continue this legacy in all manner of political and cultural arenas. For some, their engagement – picketing, erecting blockades, participating in occupations, negotiating formal agreements, and engaging in media and letter campaigns – follows the road paved by their ancestors.

Around the time that G̱a'x̱sta'las wrote to the bishop about the land issue, Christ Church congregants were approached about the "necessity of forming an Indian Parish Council." The protocol for establishing such a body reflected the chain of colonial authority, as documented in vestry minutes. "The Indian Agent was sent for, and on his arrival, after further discussion, he consented to call a public meeting to consider this matter."[28] I imagine this meeting was held among European members of the congregation, although it is difficult to say what their concerns might have been. That William Halliday, the Indian Agent, was called in for church business testifies to the fact of federal wardship. Later vestry minutes show that the topics brought forward at church committee meetings included a predictable list of social ills, the liquor trade being high on the list.

"Is This Justice?": Law, Liquor, and Power

At the close of 1913, Jane Cook wrote to Bishop John Roper. She was incensed about an incident involving one of her female relatives that had occurred a month or so before. G̱a'x̱sta'las sought assistance from several authorities stationed beyond 'Ya̱lis: the Anglican bishop, the provincial police chief, the attorney general of BC, and the superintendent of Indian Affairs. Her complaint, expressed in letters, was directed against the most powerful colonial agents at the village of 'Ya̱lis: William Halliday, the Indian Agent; BC Packers; Mr. Chambers, the sawmill manager; and a provincial policeman, Mr. Helmsing.[29]

G̱a'x̱sta'las's personal letter-writing campaigns were less visible than the strategies engaged in by mass protest movements, but they bring into view "moments where resistance crystallizes in individual acts or gestures," offering "critical, alternative perspectives ... on power."[30] Jane Cook's defiant acts certainly indicate the strength of her individual will. This moment cannot be torn from the chaos of colonial upheaval. It cannot be freed from the enormous structural and social upset experienced throughout the so-called colonized geographies. How could gender relationships not be affected in an indigenous world (or any world) experiencing high mortality, capitalist expansion, and intimate (as well as territorial) incursions?

Jane Cook's letters question colonial authorities about a liquor violation and demand answers regarding the legality of a female relative's marriage, which she feels is exploitative. Her letters render a male network of authority visible, a network that connected state power with the interests of capital on a local stage. Most profoundly, these letters attest to Jane Cook's growing sense of herself as an advocate, as someone who had a duty to demand justice. By July 1914, she explicitly addressed the material circumstances of women in Kwakwa̲ka̲'wakw villages. Her motivation to explore gender exploitation was grounded within the web of 'na̲'mima relations that constituted her world.

In respect for the memory of ancestors involved in these events and their descendants, who may now read about them, we have removed individuals' names and sensitive details deemed unnecessary to the story from the letters.

Mr T. Smith
Chief of Police.
Vancouver
B.C.

Alert Bay
Nov. 10th 1913

Sir.

I beg to bring to your notice what I and others here believe to be a breach of Justice.

Last Thursday a [man] ... was drunk on the Nimkish Indian reserve No. 1 with two Indian women ... to whom he had given liquor. On Friday afternoon last Mr Halliday Indian Agent and Mr Helmsing Provincial Police, on my information went to the Industrial School Indian reserve and saw [three women] drunk by liquor ... given [them] by [the man].

On Saturday the three women were fined $10.00 each. [The man] was missing, he was allowed to get away. On Sunday morning Mr Halliday accepted $200.00 bail on Mr Chambers the BC Packers Manager representing to Mr Halliday that he needed [the man] to do a contract of getting some logs out for him, in which both he and [the man] are interested.

As it depends on whether, they can get a freshet [spring thaw] in the Nimkish River, or not, it is uncertain if they ever can get the contract done. Are prisoners allowed out on Bail on the Sabbath Day because they have a contract to do? Is Justice to wait until an offender is quite ready and willing to be tried?

Some time ago, a Chinaman, cook of Mr Chambers sold liquor to an Indian and a complaint was laid before Mr Halliday, who told Mr Chambers about it, and Mr Chambers told his cook, and the cook ran away, after staying away for some time, the same Chinaman came back and is here now, and nothing has been done about him, although there had been a warrant made out for him, and I feel that the same will happen in [this man's] case. Is this Justice?

The same [man] was fined $75.00 about two weeks ago, for the same offence, and we have good reason to suspect and do suspect that the great amount of liquor that has been brought into Alert Bay the last two years has been brought here by the same [man], and now that we have really proved it by the evidence of the three Indian women that were fined. Why should he be shielded by the Packers Association? Why did not Mr Helmsing arrest and take him out of a single woman's house, when he said, she was dead drunk. And when he saw and also the Indian Agent saw [the man] drunk They would arrest any other offender if they found him drunk in the Indian Reserve.[31]

G̲a'ax̲sta'las emphasized the facts of the liquor violation, which had occurred on reserved land. She stressed that the police constable and the Indian Agent had charged and fined three women ten dollars each but had let the man who gave them liquor get away. In another letter, she wrote that she had paid her relative's fine. Her demand for justice hinged on the allegation that authorities, rather than adhering to the law, had a conflict of interest. The Indian Act (1906) stated:

135. Every one who by himself, his clerk, servant or agent, and every one who in the employment or on the premises of another directly or indirectly on any pretense or by any device, –

(a) sells, barters, supplies or gives to any Indian or non-treaty Indian, or to any person male or female who is reputed to belong to a particular band, or who follows the Indian mode of life, or any child of such person any intoxicant,[32] or causes or procures the same to be done or attempts the same or connives thereat; or,
(b) opens or keeps or causes to be opened or kept on any reserve or special reserve a tavern, house or building in which any intoxicant is sold, supplied or given; or,

(c) is found in possession of any intoxicant in the house, tent, wigwam, or place of abode of any Indian or non-treaty Indian or of any person on any reserve or special reserve; or,
(d) sells, barters, supplies or gives to any person on any reserve or special reserve any intoxicant;

shall, on summary conviction before any judge, police magistrate, stipendiary magistrate, or two justices of the peace or Indian agent, be liable to imprisonment for a term not exceeding six months and not less than one month, with or without hard labour, or to a penalty not exceeding three hundred dollars and not less than fifty dollars with costs of prosecution, or to both penalty and imprisonment in the discretion of the convicting judge, magistrate, justices of the peace or Indian agent.[33]

The terms of the Indian Act regarding the transport, provision, and use of liquor were unequivocal, well publicized, vigilantly enforced (as evidenced by the fines paid by the women), and, presumably, well understood.[34] G̲a'ax̲sta'las cited a previous incident in 'Ya̲lis where an offender was fined and another where an offender (also associated with Mr. Chambers) was tipped off by the Indian Agent to avoid charges. In the situation at hand, Jane Cook alleged that the intervention of Mr. Chambers – the leading capitalist figure on the reserve – was sufficient to delay the man's arrest, even on a Sunday, because he was invaluable to a logging contract. Jane Cook would have been acutely aware of the power of such interests.

A month later, at the McKenna-McBride Royal Commission, it became evident that access to timber had been strictly curtailed. Charlie Nowell stated on the record: "We have no place to log. Everywhere the land is called 'Claims' and we cannot touch them. If we cut a tree of them we would get into trouble."[35] The claims referred to by Nowell were timber limits, which were considered, as Commissioner Shaw later told Harry Mountain, to be "owned and paid for by whitemen."[36]

Testimony at the commission also provides a sense of Chambers's role vis-à-vis 'Ya̲lis residents. The BC Packers Cannery had dammed the creek that supplied fresh water to the village. Few fishers were granted licences after their traditional technologies had been prohibited. Cannery seiners blocked access to foreshore resources, and restrictions on selling fish meant that residents were hard-pressed to purchase other supplies from the cannery store. The interests of capital, implicated in Jane Cook's complaint, could only have exacerbated her sense of injustice.

Ga'axsta'las's letter both appealed to and exposed a network of power that included the bishop. She was likely aware that, in so small a coastal network of Europeans, these men were well acquainted. After receiving her letter, Bishop Roper wrote "unofficially" to Mr. Chambers that he was "persuaded that [Chambers] will always stand for decency and soberness ... If [he would] exercise [his] influence to the full."[37] To Ga'axsta'las, he wrote that her letters had "troubled [him] very deeply."[38] He also described having met with the man in question, who was with another woman. According to the bishop's letter, the couple had told him they were planning to be married.

Ga'axsta'las wrote to the attorney general of BC and questioned the legality of the man's marriage to her relative. He was, she argued, already married.

Alert Bay
Dec. 15 1913

To The Honorable
Mr Bowser
Attorney General. Victoria B.C.

Sir.

I was very sorry that I missed you in Victoria last Thursday afternoon, I followed you over to Vancouver, But you had returned to Victoria ...

I want you to know that at the time these things happened as stated in letter enclosed [the man] had a wife at home in his house who he had married in the Custom of our people the Indians, a day or two after these things happened, his wife left his house, as she got tired of waiting for her husband [the man] who had repeatedly told her to "get out"

On [date], Mr Halliday Indian Agent & Indian registrar of this place, married [the man] to [my relative] ...

Since then Mr. Halliday has had [the man] remanded twice at intervals of eight days. At your instructions or advice we hear.

I have stated the facts as plainly as I can to you. This is what we would like to know. Can Mr Halliday who is a registrar for Indians only marry a white man (as he says [the man] is) – to even an Indian woman, Is the marriage Legal? The Indian Department acknowledges an Indian custom of Marriage as legal.

Was Mr Halliday right in marrying a man who his Deptm. recognized as legally married. Was Mr Halliday, Justified in – under the circumstances – as Indian Agent – Bailing, remanding repeatedly, & marrying a man (already married) – to another woman who Mr Halliday knew had been tempted for weeks by [the man] before the occurrences related in enclosed letter (to C. of Police). I have seen Mr Campbell, C. of Police & Mr Ditchburne Inspector of Indian Agents & Mr Lindley Crease also Mr Smith C. of Police Van. And they all advised me to write you on the Matter. Hoping to hear from you on this matter.

I remain Yrs respectfully

Jane C. Cook[39]

Jane Cook set out "the facts" and questioned the legality of an Indian Agent marrying a man to her relative when the man had already been married "in the Custom of our people." Potlatch marriages, as Ga'axsta'las wrote, were recognized by DIA officials. Her question regarding the legality of a marriage performed by Halliday as registrar "for Indians only" hints at the colonial taxonomy of persons that was then coming into focus.[40]

Issued by the deputy superintendent of Indian Affairs in 1906, a circular sought to address "what seems to be more or less confusion or uncertainty in the minds of officials and Agents ... with regard to the law as to the recognition of Indian marriages."[41] The circular included the following legal guidelines:

(1) A marriage between Indians or between Indians and others solemnized or contracted in accordance with provincial or territorial law is valid.
(2) The validity of marriages between Indians contracted in accordance with the customs of their tribes has been established by the Courts, notably in the case of "Connoly vs. Woolwich and others" in 1867 nor does the fact that one or both of the contracting parties may profess adherence to Christianity affect the matter.
(3) It is particularly deserving of notice that the validity of Indian divorces has never been affirmed in Canada, and Indian marriages, if valid, cannot be dissolved according to the Indian customs, but only in such manner as other marriages may be dissolved.
(4) If an Indian is validly married to one woman and has gone through a form of marriage which would make her his wife but for the

> fact that he was already married he is guilty of bigamy and liable to the penalties for that crime (Criminal Code Section 276) and the Department of Justice has expressed the opinion that even if there were no valid marriage but the Indian intended by complying with the customs of the band relating to marriage to make more than the first married his wife or wives ... he may successfully [?] under Section 278 of the Criminal Code.[42]

In other words, unions between aboriginal and non-aboriginal men and women performed under church or registrar authority were valid. The courts recognized the legality of customary marriages, even by Christian converts. They did not, however, recognize "Indian custom" divorce.

Around the time that Jane Cook wrote these letters, Ethel Alfred attended the marriage ceremony of her elder sister Lucy to Alfred Nowell.

"It was getting less and less how it used to be, eh? I don't know how old I was. Maybe I was five when Lucy got married to Alfred [in 1915]. The marriage was done in Turnour Island, when she married Alfred Nowell. And they made this high stilt [platform]. High." She gestured. "And they had a plank going up to where she was sitting. Way up. Way up. So, young men had to run for her. And, so, she was dressed in her regalia, and Jumbo [Bell] was standing beside her. And every time the one that ran didn't get up to the top, he'd make a Turnour sound."

"That's part of the wedding ceremony," Pearl Alfred said.

"Yeah, part of the ceremony," continued Ethel. "Each tribe have four clans, and the kind we belong to is the Ta̲mta̲mła̲'ls. And that's how they got us to get married in the early days. They showed that when they were having the marriage. I can remember that day that she got married. And the one that got up to the top was from Alert Bay. I can't remember his name now. He was a young man that got up to the top. He was running for Alfred Nowell. He was going to get her for him. That's what they did in the early years."[43]

"There's lots of things goes on when you get married in the Indian way," Ethel Alfred said. "You have to have a copper. Your Dad has a copper, and they give it to the husband, eh? And they ask them, 'Do you want your copper back, or are we going to keep it?' So our Dad said that he wanted his copper back, and he had to give some money to Lucy's husband now. So, they gave it away to the people."

As William Wasden Jr. explained when he read these statements, "Marriage starts with an Indian name and a copper for the man. And then, whatever he sells his copper for – that he gets from his father-in-law – then, he gives that money away to sponsor the potlatch and a big feast that he has in order to lift his name. His first social standing, he gets from his wife."

"Yeah, it goes through lots of red tape," Ethel Alfred continued. "We just do it different. We just make it easier now, eh? An Indian marriage. And you have to pay the people that goes. It costs lots of money when you pay them two dollars each – people that goes out – and going to get the one that's going to get married. Yeah, it's lots of red tape to go through when you get married. There's lots of different things that's not being done the way it used to be."

Although marriage "in the custom" was recognized by the authorities, customary forms of divorce were not valid under colonial law. In Canada, in general, divorce was legally recognized only under contractual agreement, a process that was "virtually impossible for reserve residents and rare at this time for all Canadians."[44] Those who engaged in serial unions (even without formal ceremonies) were liable to criminal prosecution for bigamy.[45] An 1890 amendment to Canadian marriage law made a customary or civil bigamist liable to a five-year prison sentence, with or without a five hundred dollar fine.[46]

Jane Cook's next letter to the bishop referred to this legal context.

Alert Bay, 1914

To the Bishop of Columbia, Jan 5, 1914

Dear Lord Bishop

I received Your letter in answer to my Appeal to you and the Church in Victoria.

I think you will find that all I have written to you and others are the Main facts. Of Course I do no know, how Mr. Halliday will wriggle out of it, I know I have not much chance with him, as he is so plausibly and is not afraid to say anything to suit himself.

When I went I asked him, if he had really married [my relative] & [the man] though he must have Known that [the man] & [another woman] were married according to Indian Custom, he told me that [the other woman] herself had told him that she was not married according to the Custom here.

Now I can prove by at least 300 men who assisted at the Wedding that they were married according to Indian Custom!

Then when I asked him I asked him, how he could marry [the man] who was a white man according to him, he said he married [my relative] who was an Indian.

Of Course my point is this, that the officials have not been consistent in their duty or not doing it, is making the social life here worse.

Mr. Halliday you will have heard by now. Sentenced [the man] to the smallest penalty he could give him under the Circumstances ie 2 months.

Mr. Helmsing came back & said that [the man] will only serve 40 days.

[Another man] had 1 month when he was made drink by [this man] on the B.C. Packers property just about 10 days before he ... made the 3 women drink.

But still I suppose we have to be thankful he was sentenced to any thing at all.

Did your Lordship notice the piece that was in the Colonist on the 31st Dec. Where Mr. Halliday said that the Indians here exchanged their wives so frequently at the Potlaches, that it was impossible to keep track of them. Well if Mr. Halliday knows that such things exist here, should he not be all the more strict.

I Can inform Yr. Lordship for your own satisfaction, that Mr. Halliday cannot raise 1 woman or man who has exchanged their husband or wive of the Kwagult people here since he has been Indian Agent about 8 yrs. That article of Mr H reflects on the Churches work here, and I should like to have answered it but do not know to whom to send it to.

Because I feel more & more that it is my duty as the member of this Indian Mission to defend the Indian who in Justice is done to them.

I hope I have not imposed too much on your Lordship kindness.

But We as the suppressed people of this province feel we need every friend we can get, again thanking you.

I remain your very grateful.

Jane Cook[47]

G̲a'ax̲sta'las positioned herself as a petitioner among "the suppressed people of this province," thus reminding Bishop Roper of their subordination. She named another person "made drink" by the man whom Halliday sentenced to one month in prison. She noted that the bootlegger had served just ten days more in jail, again questioning a legal system vulnerable to manipulation. As a "member of this Indian Mission," Ga'axsta'las wrote, she felt it was her "duty" to "defend the Indian." William Halliday's inconsistency and failure to do *his* duty was, she wrote, "making the social life here worse." She had defended a relative whom she felt had been exploited and then fined for that exploitation. She was now reeling from the idea that Halliday had illegally married the relative to her exploiter.

Ga'axsta'las urged the bishop to act on the fact that Halliday had ignored a potlatch wedding witnessed by at least three hundred men. Like DIA officials, the Anglican Church recognized customary marriages. The church had resolved that bishops were "at liberty to adopt native forms of marriage and consecrate them to a Christian use" but that marriage was to be "lifelong and exclusive" and "free from idolatrous taint."[48] Jane Cook was eager to dismiss claims publicized by William Halliday in the *Victoria Colonist* about the frequent exchange of wives. She did so by stating that, because of the church's work, there had been no multiple marriages *through the potlatch* since the bishop had been appointed in 1906. Her assertions are all the more interesting in light of the missionaries' insistence that "the selling of girls in marriage ... is the great obstacle to be overcome" in 'Yalis.[49] The church had urged members of the Women's Auxiliary in particular to stamp out the "terrible evil," which it associated with marriage customs "on the Island of Vancouver."[50] Ga'axsta'las's appeal to recognize potlatch weddings at this time pushes somewhat against the official rhetoric of the church. She sought an official investigation into Halliday's actions.

Kwagutl Agency.
Alert Bay. Feb'y 9 1914

To the Supertendent of Indian Affairs.
Ottawa.

Sir:–

I beg to inform you of some complaints I have had to make of our Indian Agent Mr Halliday. I hope you will give me some help to have an investigation into these notions of his, that I have vainly complained about to the officials, and authorities in Vancouver and Victoria B.C. ...

Sir I feel that if you are going to take way all the Indian custom from them give them some kind of a law not like this what our Indian

Agent has made. This is worse than the Indian customs. If the Department is going to support Mr Halliday in the precedent what is going to be the social and moral state of this our Indian friends. I can prove that Mr Halliday married a man to another woman while he had two Indian wives married to him in the Indian custom .... [she and another woman] who was also married to him by church but he said he got a divorce from. I can prove that Mr Halliday knew that [the woman] was [his] wife. I can prove that Mr Halliday sent [her] home to her people to get her out of the way so that [he] could marry [my relative].

Our friends of the tribes who were present at the time of [her] and [his] wedding have begged me to present a petition to you signed by all the people asking that you give us some other Indian Agent, but I told them we would leave it to you after you had learned these facts I have related to you. I am sorry I have had to make it so lengthy but I had to make it clear to you, hoping that it will not be wasted time of your valuable time to peruse these pages and hoping to soon hear from you.

I remain your faithfully
Signed Jane Cook[51]

In response, William Halliday wrote two letters on 2 March 1914. In the one addressed to Bishop Roper, he stated: "I told you that [the man's] first wife from whom he had been divorced was dead. I find in taking my annual census that this was a mistake as she is still living ... I heard of her death I took it for granted without making any investigation."[52]

In a subsequent letter to the DIA's inspector of agencies, Halliday acknowledged the legal context of his actions and sought to discredit Jane Cook. For G̱a'ax̱sta'las's descendants, this letter is an artifact of colonialism that occupies a place in the repertoire of their family history. George Speck referred to it at the outset of research in 2002. "I do remember reading – when I was doing some anthropological research – that the Indian Agents were quite frustrated with her stand on a lot of the political land issues, as well, in terms of her involvement in advocating for our people and the fact that they took the potlatch away and didn't give anything back in return. The agent complained about her taking a stand and having bugs in her head because of that *[laughs]*."

Alert Bay B.C.
March 2nd 1914

W.E. Ditchburn Esq.
Inspector of Agencies.

Dear Ditchburn:–

I enclose for your information a copy of the complaint made by Mrs. Cook against both yourself and me which may interest you. The original was sent me and I took off two copies thinking you might be interested. I have sent in a report on the matter and only stuck to bare facts giving a denial of the charges laid against me and stating that instead of your trying to prevent an investigation that you had gone very fully into the matter, and I had no doubt would be ready to report if they thought necessary. I can not understand what motive I could have had to illegally marry [him] and [her] I would have been voluntarily running the risk of two years in the pen – for nothing.

Between ourselves I am of the opinion that Mrs C has to use a common expression bugs in her head. She has become possessed of the idea that the Indians are laboring under all kinds of oppression and unfair treatment, that they should own the whole country, that they should have the appointment of Agents, and is trying to make herself seem an authority on everything. It is too bad for up till the Indians rights movement commenced she was a splendid specimen and used her influences for good, but now that movement together with the prosecutions for potlatching seem to have put her beside herself.

Please regard this letter as strictly private.

Yours truly,
W.M. Halliday[53]

Addressing his superior, William Halliday sought to dismiss Jane Cook's complaint by citing her subversive involvement in the Indian rights movement and recent prosecutions for potlatching, which "seem to have put her beside herself." By all accounts, this was a time of prolific potlatching throughout Kwakwa̲ka̲'wakw territories, a time when there were so many Hudson's Bay Company blankets circulating that they were no longer accepted as legal currency.[54]

The government did not begin to prosecute potlatching "offences" in earnest until 1913. Halliday began his campaign by reading aloud the law and lecturing on the "evils" of the potlatch to a large gathering of people on their way to the canneries. "Johnny Bagwany, a

Nimpkish of Alert Bay, boldly stated that he was prepared to 'see the matter through' by calling the Indians from Cape Mudge, Campbell River and Salmon River to Alert Bay for a potlatch ... Halliday ignored a number of small potlatches." He compiled information against five men and then withdrew three of the charges to "concentrate on the one ceremony he had himself witnessed and could positively prove: that for which Ned Harris and Bagwany were responsible."[55] The two men pleaded guilty to the charge and were released until their jury trial the following spring.

"Ned Harris was head chief of 'Na̱mg̱is after Willie Harris," William Wasden Jr. told me. "They were always being tried in court for potlatching. They wouldn't stop. John Bagwany was first cousins with Ned Harris. *Bagwany* means 'skate' – you know the skate that floats through the water." William imitated a flat, moving fish with his hand. "It was like a play potlatch name. A lot of Nimpkish had really funny play potlatch names. They had all these sea animal names, but he would have had a big potlatching name, too. It's interesting ... a lot of other tribes try to condemn us for the whole tribe going Christian, yet there's proof there that one side of my family never ever stopped – Ned Harris and them. In [Philip] Drucker's notes, they've got the old man Wax̱a̱widi, Samuel Innes, saying to the Indian Agent, 'Who are you? You're just one man. You can't stop us from potlatching.'"

Harris and Bagwany were found guilty and given suspended sentences just a month before G̱a'ax̱sta'las testified alongside Harris at the McKenna-McBride Royal Commission.[56] She likely served as an interpreter at their trial. Perhaps it was her involvement in the first legal prosecution against potlatchers that "put her beside herself."

In the meantime, William Halliday wrote another official letter in response to G̱a'ax̱sta'las's complaint.

Kwawkewlth Agency.

Alert Bay

March 2nd 1914

I have the honor to acknowledge receipt of your letter of Feby 12 enclosing a seven page complain from Jane Cook of Alert Bay and asking me for a report on the same.

In the first place I would inform you that the complaint while not without a small foundation is so twisted and distorted as to be hardly recognizable ...

At that time I asked [the man] if he had ever contracted any kind of marriage with [the other woman] and he said the only thing that had happened was that after he had lived with [her] for over 3 years her father was giving potlatch and came to him and said that as he was living in disgrace with his daughter he had better give him something to help out with the potlatch and that would make things all right, but that there was no question or thought [of] marriage ...

With regard to the liquor charges against [the man] I would inform you that at the time [the man] had a contract with 9 Indians to run a boom of logs down the Nimkish River and at the time the water was rising fast and consequently Mr Chambers the manager of the Cannery and Saw Mill came and offered bail for [the man] and showed plainly that by taking him away at once it would seriously risk great loss to the B.C. Packers, the 9 Indians concerned and to the owners of the logs which were worth about $18,000.00 and I only used my common sense under the act which allows any registrate to allow bail for good reason, and [the man] appeared once a week for some time until the work was sufficiently finished as not to entail loss on others by taking him away.[57] He pleaded guilty and was given two months imprisonment with hard labor, which considering the way he had acted after his arrest and his previous good conduct, together with other extenuating circumstances I considered quite sufficient ...

The seat of the whole trouble is the fact that I have prosecuted some of the Indians for taking part in potlatching and Mrs Cook who until some action was taken on the matter always (to missionaries and Indian Agent) was opposed to the potlatch, now finds it polite to appear in the eyes of the Indian as an advocate of it in order to retain the influence she has with them, and because [he] had helped out in a potlatch therefore he was married according in potlatch customs.

J.D. McLean Esq.
Secretary Department of Indian Affairs.
Ottawa.

W.M. Halliday
Indian Agent[58]

By Halliday's account, Jane Cook did not imagine the legal prosecution of Ned Harris and John Bagwany. Nor was she, at the time, "opposed to the potlatch"; rather, she was an "advocate of it." Her letters calling for recognition of potlatch marriages certainly attest to her support.

"In This My Country": The McKenna-McBride Royal Commission

Oweetna-kula ... is our traditional statement of Aboriginal Title and means "one with the land and sea we own."

– *George Speck, "An Outline History of the Kwakwaka'wakw Struggle for the Recognition of Aboriginal Title and Self-Determination"*

On 1 June 1914, nearly a month after Halliday wrote to the DIA, Jane Cook was sworn in as an interpreter at the McKenna-McBride Royal Commission. Halliday also attended, and there was likely tension between the two. The enlargement and reduction of reserved lands was at the heart of the hearings, but concepts of title and customary mechanisms for the alienation of lands had always existed among the Kwakwa̲ka̲'wakw. "A chief could give any tract – a habituation site, a strip of beach and foreshore with all salvage rights ... a fishing place, hunting area, berrying or root-digging ground, etc. – to another clan, lineage, etc."[59] Transfers occurred largely through marriages at potlatches, where chiefs confirmed and validated their title to lands before witnesses.

At the "meeting with the principal Tribes of the Kwawkewlth Nation at Alert Bay, B.C. on the 1st. day of June, (Monday), 1914, the Chairman addressed the assembled Indians as to the scope and purpose of the Commission, and Mrs. Jane Cook was sworn to act as Interpreter."[60] As each hearing began, commissioners told the audience of chiefs, witnesses, residents, and colonial agents about the scope and purpose of the hearings: "to recommend the final configuration of Indian reserves ... enlarging or reducing existing reserves, and ... to eliminate the Province's reversionary interest so that [aboriginal people] ... could sell their land to raise capital if that was what they wished."[61] From 1913 to 1915, the five-member commission visited the primary villages of the so-called tribes, nations, or bands of BC.[62] Some of the early meetings were held aboard the CPR's *Tees,* a steamship that later transported commissioners to the West Coast and to the Kwawkewlth Agency.[63] Commissioners were "empowered to recommend specific tracts as reserves where lands requested by Indians (or Indian agents) were available – not pre-empted or under timber lease."[64] There was to be no discussion of aboriginal rights,[65] title, treaties, or self-government,

Photo 26 G̲a'ax̲sta'las/Jane Constance Cook, 'Yalis, 2 June 1914. This photograph was taken while G̲a'ax̲sta'las was an interpreter at the commission's hearings at 'Yalis. Jane Cook's descendants feel that the placement of the image here is important. The photograph is now in context, situated appropriately within the (reconstructed) arc of events in her life. *Image H-07220, Royal BC Museum, BC Archives.*

The expression on her face was for me – that she knew who she was. She knew what was right and wrong, and she was almost like a mountain, just standing there. She was going to stand there whether anybody said anything against her. Just like her life story. But her expression – it was very piercing. She had a very clear vision of who she was, regardless of what anybody else has to say. She was going to do what she had to do.

– William Wasden Jr.

a point recognized by several groups who refused to participate in the commission.[66]

Moving beyond "the reserve question," commissioners did ask witnesses about their access to physicians and hospitals in their territories. They inquired about the proximity of missionaries and about people's desire for schools. Almost without exception, aboriginal speakers sought better access to medical services and approved of education. They requested schooling for more of their children. At hearings with the "Tribes of the Kwawkewlth Nation," the commissioners also asked questions about marriage practices, which likely reflected media attention on Alert Bay. Chiefs and other witnesses stressed their rights to timber, hunting grounds, and food fisheries and their right to sell or exchange fish for money or other goods.

On the first day of hearings, several "Kwawkewlth" speakers prompted the commissioners to address the potlatch. Charlie Nowell argued that the potlatch was "Indian law," "a good Government" that "keeps them from doing wrong." He explained, in Kwak̓wala, that without the potlatch, there would be little "sympathy ... for the poor ones," that the potlatch feeds and clothes them and "packs them into their homes and keeps them there."[67] The commissioners responded that his words "will be taken down and will go to the Government" but that potlatching was illegal and not within their jurisdiction.

It is evident in the transcripts that interpreters were not required for each witness. Some chiefs, "sub-chiefs," and speakers represented themselves in English.[68] William Brotchie was among the interpreters employed by the commission. Like Jane Cook, he interjected and, when requested, offered opinions for the record.[69] At times, interpreters also translated shouts from the audience, some protesting what had been said, others calling for further evidence. Jane Cook translated for several Kwak̓wala speakers and, when asked, she spoke on behalf of individual chiefs. At other times, she was sworn in as a witness. Transcripts indicate that she had already, before the commission, pressured the government through letters and at meetings for the addition of a specific tract of land in 'Ya̱lis. And she is listed as standing with chiefs for several other land applications submitted to the commission. She stood with Chief Ha̱mdxid, who represented A̱'wa̱'etła̱la and Da̱'naxda'x̱w peoples, to claim eight named sites for fishing, clamming, timber, hunting, berry picking, eulachon fishing, cultivation, and village lands. G̱a'ax̱sta'las also offered information that led to three 'Na̱mg̱is land applications.[70]

Few identifiably female voices grace the transcripts of the hearings. G̲a’ax̲sta’las’s presence is intriguing. Her descendants suggest it likely followed from a combination of her standing, her language abilities, and her political prowess. “She held a position in this community that was strange,” Pearl Alfred told me. “I think that [role] was not a separation from her position in the aboriginal community. Nobody forgot that she came from a family of chiefs. I always think, how else would they have ever put up with a woman going to all these things? I’m sure it was part of it, had to have been, though Lord knows she was very well-spoken. When she talked, you had to listen. She was one of those women who, when she talked, you didn’t dare say anything until she was finished. She commanded attention when she spoke. You knew this woman knew what she was talking about. I hope she did anyhow *[laughs].*”

Reading through transcripts of the hearings, Wedłidi Speck spoke about his great-grandmother’s role by identifying her kinship connections to the territories represented at the hearings. “These are all Granny’s principal relatives,” he said, referring to the chiefs with whom she testified. Excerpts from testimony illustrate both the concerns of different Kwakwa̲ka̲’wakw tribes and the grievances they shared.

On 1 June 1914, a Monday, Chief Owahagaleese addressed the commission on the first day of hearings.

> I thank the Governments that have sent you here to listen to all of our grievances ... I will tell you all our grievances, and hope that you will be patient with us and listen to us patiently while we speak to you for all of our Tribes for we are in a bad condition of which I will now tell you ... We are beginning to see that we are losing our lands; not only our lands but all other things that would be good for our benefit such as fishing and trapping and all the places where we get our food which we have, in former days, been able to get – and all the fur animals. If we want to get any now we are threatened. We have no exclusive rights and privileges in our rivers, and our lands we are losing them, and we are losing the privileges among ourselves to have all the fish that are in the rivers that belong to our country – We have no friend to back us up in this matter in this my country for all the benefits of the country that I want to hold.[71]

As Wedłidi Speck told me, “Chief Owahagaleese was the head chief of the Ma’a̲mtagila clan – the head clan of the Fort Ruperts. That’s

Jane Cook's close relative." Like many who followed him, the chief spoke about the incursion of settlers and to his people's impaired access to fish and trapping grounds. "We have put down on paper," he stated, "what I want to bring before the notice of the Royal Commission. I want to bring to your notice the plan of my land that I have here in my band. It was only given to me on Saturday night, and according to this plan my land is too little; and I don't understand why the plan was given to me – Is it a sign of ownership, if it is, the land is too small. We have had our meeting and we have looked at the plans and the lands are not sufficient and not at all in the places that used to belong to us."[72] Chiefs were delivered official plans of their reserved lands often just a day or two before hearings began. They were instructed to submit their own plans – "petitions," in the language of the commission – for consideration or "approximate valuations ... without outside aid."[73]

On 2 June 1913, a Tuesday, "Chief Alfred Lageuse" of the 'Na̱mgis Band also began his address with the entreaty to be patient and listen, stating his expectations for the ensuing dialogue. "I am not afraid to tell you the names of my different fishing stations and homes and the lands that have always belonged to me and mine," he told the commissioners. "We are not foreigners – we didn't come from some far off country – we were born here and the country belongs to us, and here I was born and grew up. I will tell you straight and I expect you will be straight with me in all matters connected with my land, with my villages and with my homes."[74] According to Wedłidi Speck, Alf Lageuse was Chief Lagius, who stood alongside Stephen Cook's mother, G̱aga and Tłak̲wadzi, to defend her as a member of his family. "He was Charlie Nowell's father-in-law," William Wasden Jr. later pointed out. "Charlie Nowell named his son Alfred. I bet he's named after his grandfather."

Commissioner James McKenna asked Chief Lagius about fishing and the right to sell their catch, an activity crucial to the well-being of the coastal Indian agencies.[75]

McKenna: Can you catch them for your own food?
Chief: We are not allowed now because we are not allowed the traps.
McKenna: ... Do you refer particularly to the Nimpkish River?
Chief: Yes, that is my river. Our old trap grounds are in this river ... the cannery has been given the exclusive right to catch fish in that river ... We cannot use our traps, and we cannot get [sockeye salmon] from the men that use it for commercial purposes. The canneries are

fishing with the nets and they won't let us have any of the fish in the nets.[76]

Aboriginal fishers were forbidden from using traps, weirs, and spears. They had little access to cannery licences, which were issued almost exclusively to Japanese fishers, and they had no access to independent licences, which were only provided to white fishers.[77] Under fisheries regulations, aboriginal people were restricted from selling their catch, which provided income to purchase other foods, clothing, and supplies.[78] Since 1894, food fish permits had been issued only "to allow Indians to 'catch fish for the purpose of providing food for themselves and their families but for no other purpose.'"[79]

In this context, Chief Lagius was asked about access to fishing sites, and he was told that the cannery regularly forbade access to sockeye salmon. G̲a'ax̲sta'las, the interpreter, interjected and offered information about the history of access to the Nimpkish River and the difficulties 'Na̲mg̲is fishers faced in obtaining licences. Her perspective from within the early mission was evidently useful to the proceedings.

"The Chief does not and never could understand the situation with respect to the fishing. When the cannery had first got its fishing rights on this river, Mr. Hall, then resident missionary[,] to offset the injury to the Indians by the cannery fishing, secured for the Indians the right to fish in their own river on their own Reserve and established a small hatchery just to give them something to do and to show them that they might still fish. He had got some of the boys licences and they had got and salted a few salmon. It was to show the Indians that they still had the right to fish. There were others fishing for the cannery at the same time and in the same place and the two parties quarrelled and threw stones at one another. Mr. Hall afterwards drew out and the saltery was closed and since then the Indians had never tried fishing there any more, nor had they ever again been able to get fishing licences."

"In a case of that kind where stones were thrown, they ought to have gone to the police," the commissioner said.

"Twenty-four years ago," Jane Cook reminded him, "there were neither police or any kind of Government here then."

The chairman cut in. "We have a note of this," he said, "and will enquire into the situation, and Mrs. Cook I thank you for your statement."[80]

G̲a'ax̲sta'las referred back to 1890, to a decade (according to historians of aboriginal fisheries) characterized by a confusion of jurisdictions. She told the commission about Alfred Hall's influence among the first cannery operators, about his efforts to secure licences and fishing rights. DIA reports from the time make it clear that George Blenkinsop, the Indian Agent, was also sympathetic to aboriginal fishing rights. Both he and Hall likely saw these rights as necessary for the Kwakwaka'wakw's involvement in a future commercial fishery. They must also have recognized the social and material necessity of fishing.

Simply by virtue of being a member of the 'Namgis, Ga'axsta'las and her family were part of the experiential realm of fishing. Her son Gilbert told Gilbert Jr. that Jane Cook had taught him to fish. "When he was just a little kid, his mom would row him around, and they would trawl for Coho and whatnot, down in Blackney Pass, around the bluff. Stephen had a fish camp down there, buying fish, and so they were down around there. This would be certainly no later than 1915, or somewhere around there. So, she would row, and he would tend the line off the back. And then, eventually, he started trawling out of the skiff there for himself. He'd even sit on the corner of the bluff down there at high tide, so he wouldn't have to row and fish Coho off there – which we've all done over the years. And then he'd sell them for, you know, a little candy money, or whatever, to his mom."

As the 'Namgis hearing continued, Ga'axsta'las was sworn in as a witness to give evidence about land use. Her testimony suggests that, within her village, colonial property laws were not at all in focus. Ga'axsta'las wanted clarification of band members' rights to reserved lands. She wanted to know how the provincial and dominion governments defined land occupancy and use, and she sought to clarify the jurisdiction of the Indian Agent. After being sworn in, commissioner McKenna asked,

"When you were acting as interpreter a little while ago, I understood you to say yourself that the Indians were told that the Province claimed the Reserve and could at any time move the Indians off and take possession of the land – is that right?"

"Yes, we had been given that impression."

"What is your personal knowledge of the matter?"

"My impression was that the Province claimed the reserves and could at any time turn the Indians off, and the other Indians certainly had that impression; that is, that the Indians might stay on the reserves until the Provincial Government should want the land, and they would then be turned off."

Interpretations of the concept of reversionary right were in question – that is, the right of the province to claim unused reserved lands.[81]

It is implied that Halliday provided some information about this policy to 'Y<u>a</u>lis villagers and suggested that the province "could at any time turn the Indians off." <u>G</u>a'a<u>x</u>sta'las resumed:

"There is one case which affects myself. My husband and myself had been interested in having built on property supposed to be on the reserve and now claimed as industrial school reserve. The Indian agent had endeavored to put ways and a capstan on their enclosed home site thereby destroying our garden. We had been told that the Indian Agent was virtually supreme as to reserve properties, also that reserves were held as community properties, and a nice garden made by one Indian with a great deal of labour was therefore just as much the property of another who had done nothing towards making it, and that he might take the vegetables grown in that garden as freely as the owner."

"That does not in any way implicate the Provincial Government," Commissioner McKenna replied. He continued,

> Now about this Reserve here, it appears to have been bought for a school reserve, and with regard to the right of Indians claiming to have the right to live on that particular piece of land, of course that is a matter which will have to be settled between the Indians themselves and the Dominion Government; but you are entirely wrong and anybody is wrong who said that any Indian could go on to the land fenced in by another Indian and take vegetables out of his garden. Once an Indian or anybody else fences a particular piece of ground, the other Indians have not the right to go there and take the product of his labour at all.[82]

<u>G</u>a'a<u>x</u>sta'las asked about communal versus private ownership as she challenged the Indian Agent's virtually supreme power over reserve properties. Given the clashes she had had with the agent in the preceding months, and their personal conflict over property lines, Jane Cook's statements about her garden are interesting. "In the context of the commission where she was giving evidence," Wedłidi Speck explained, "she was laying out relations that women had to gardening and to their own property. She could speak to this. She was a wealthy woman because of her garden."[83] While in no way acknowledging the particular relationship that women had to property, the commissioner assured Jane Cook of her individual right to "the product of [her] labour." The fence, as a classical marker of British property lines, plays a key role in the exchange.[84] Commissioners clarified

provincial and dominion responsibilities for particular tracts of land, but they discovered that several witnesses wanted them, instead, to explain the difference between land held in common and private ownership.[85] When Moses Alfred was sworn in to give evidence, he, too, sought clarification on this issue. "I asked Mr. Halliday if I could build a house there, and he said I could not." The transcript of the hearing indicates that Jane Cook then explained:

"I understand you to say that because the land is held in common by all the Indians, they would not be justified in building a house there until they get their own piece of land with the title to same? It would not justify me in building a house on it if someone can come and build a house there. The Province claims that land, and they can come in at any time and claim that land."

"Who told you that?" asked the commissioner.

"I heard of that, and I went and asked Mr. Halliday about it, and he said it was true. Of course we have a general understanding about these Reserves here, but when I went to Mr. Halliday and asked him if the piece of land that I wanted to build my house on could be mine and mine only and not to the others, he told me it could not be because it was owned by all the Indians."[86]

Identified as a witness, G̲a'ax̲sta'las then sought further clarification of housing rights:

"Can any of the Indians, if they do anything wrong, can they be sent out of their house?" she asked.

"No," the Commissioner responded. "Unless they go to gaol. On an Indian Reserve an Indian who has his house and his ground fenced in no one can interfere with him."

"There is a young man who wants to build a house, and is afraid to?" Jane Cook continued.

"Well he need not be afraid," said the commissioner. "Not only that but if a railway came into an Indian Reserve, and that railway interfered with any of the Indians, they would get individual compensation apart altogether from the Band."

Lagius (recorded as *The Chief*), interjected, "Did I tell you that I wanted the Indian Reserves apportioned out to each member of the Band?"[87]

Chief Lagius later reasserted this request for family lots. He likely referred to the customary pattern of discrete sites for houses (arranged by 'na̲'mima) owned by chiefs. One imagines Commissioner McKenna leaning forward in his seat as he stated aloud for the record, "The witness is in favour of individual ownership." Given that they heard explicit statements of ownership, it is startling that commissioners did not appear to understand that exclusive title to land (owned and alienated by chiefs) was already practised through potlatching.

As the hearing with 'Na̲mgis representatives continued, several speakers told Commissioner McKenna which lands they wanted. After Joe Harris spoke about what is known as the Industrial School Reserve, McKenna rather impatiently instructed the representatives in proper procedure.

> Now that land was purchased by the Dominion Government, the Province has no claim to that land and makes no claim. This Commission has to deal really with the reserves in which there are dual ownership; that is those reserves in which the Province claims an interest as well as the Dominion Government. You people have got to bring this matter right through the Dominion Government: and set before the Dominion Government just what rights they should be protected in. The proper procedure for you to take is to draw up a petition setting forth how long you have been there and the rights you consider you have there, and ask the Dominion Government to secure you in such rights. If you will give that petition to Mr. Halliday, he will attend to it.

"We have been told," Jane Cook responded, "that [this land] was bought from Mr. Spencer a former missionary up here, and it is said that the Dominion Government bought it from him – Now we have a letter from the missionary who lived here over thirty years ago, and in this letter he does not say a word about selling it." Jane then handed the letter to the commissioners. "I have also written the Department about this matter myself."

"This matter is not within our jurisdiction at all," Commissioner McKenna responded. "In view of what you say, and your statement that you have been writing to the Department, this Commission will take this letter, and will also place on record what has been said about it, and will transmit to Ottawa an extract of same, and will ask that some definite action be taken, and that you be informed regarding the matter."

At this point, William Brotchie, identified in the record as "Indian Brotchie," joined the conversation: "We don't believe Mr. Spencer had any right to dispose of it – We don't believe that he had any pre-emption either." "You can find out all the information you want in the matter in the Land Registry Office," Commissioner Shaw told him. "Every Title from here is registered in the office at Victoria?" William Halliday asked. "Yes," Shaw replied, "but a copy of it is in the books of the Registry Office at Prince Rupert, and if they write up there for it, it will be forthcoming."[88]

G̱a'ax̱sta'las and William Brotchie referred to the Industrial School Reserve, land that had been allocated by G.M. Sproat in 1880. The allocation was then overturned by the province in 1882 on the grounds that the land had been leased by white settlers.[89] There was a good deal of speculation about the land leased by A. Wesley Huson, land that had allegedly been transferred to Earl and Spencer (cannery operators). Peter O'Reilly's allocation in 'Ya̱lis of two reserves for village and burial grounds excluded this tract of land.[90]

The reorganization of Native space, Cole Harris argues, fit aboriginal people into a compartmentalized world. Those who laid out reserves "intended almost all of the larger ones for farming or ranching, and the smaller ones to serve as fishing stations (or to protect village sites and graveyards), but had left Native people to test the validity of these intentions."[91] Such is the case here. Eighty-two years later (in 1996), George Cook, Ethel Alfred, and Peggy Svanvik were among those who testified at the Indian Claims Commission hearing for the settlement of the Cormorant Island claim. A letter from Alfred Hall to William Smithe, chief commissioner of lands and works, dated 27 March 1884, was among the articles of evidence at the hearing.[92]

On 3 June 1914, Jane Cook translated the testimony of "Humseet," likely the Da̱'naxda'x̱w (New Vancouver) chief, Ha̱mdxid.[93] "There is no English name for Chief Ha̱mdxid," Wedłidi Speck said. "We know that Bob Harris was the chief of Knight Inlet, so he might be known as Ha̱mdxid. No other person was the head. He's always been known." Ha̱mdxid's opening address to the commission discusses in some detail the ways in which Kwakwa̱ka̱'wakw territories were (and are) occupied and used:

> We are the Tanockteuch people and we are the people that own Tsawati. What the other Indians have said is all done – that is, they all have a part for the fishing places up there for the oolachans. They take part in the fishing for the oolachans at that place. Those words are done. I and my people are like a watchman for the other tribes – to be there and watch and let them know when the oolachan fish

> come ... Mr. Halliday knows that this country up there belongs to us and he knows also that it is dear to us. Why I am so glad of this chance of meeting the Commission here today is because I want the marks that are there to be taken off that place. There are posts there. I want them to be pulled up for I have a mark there myself; all the Indians have a mark there. The mountains itself on both sides of the place running up to the head at the source of the river. I work there on that river which belongs to me, and Mr. Halliday knows how we are up there. There are canoes up the lakes there which are there all the time and they have been renewed three times now, these canoes. When they get old we make new ones and it is three times to my knowledge that they have been renewed, and that is why I say that we own that place up there and it is valuable to us.[94]

The hearing transcripts leave an impression of Kwakwa̲ka̲'wakw chiefs observing the redefinition of borders and boundaries, imperial acts that did not erase their own physical and temporal markers in long-inhabited and deeply known places. Ha̲mdxid explained that he and his people *owned* Dzawadi but that "all the Indians have a mark there."[95] Laughing, Wedłidi Speck told me, "Every tribe married Knight Inlet – they wanted eulachon – several times they probably married Knight Inlet." Chief Ha̲mdxid and Jane Cook are on record at the commission claiming "the territory from the mouth to the source of the Klinaklini River for oolichans, salmon trapping, berries, and timber."[96]

As William Wasden Jr. looked over Ha̲mdxid's testimony, he remarked: "This old man must have respected her enough to allow her to speak. Obviously, they would have got someone else to do it. They were very cautious. In order to speak and claim things, you had to have a place somewhere. They wouldn't just let somebody smart do that. It had to be somebody with ranking that had a connection to it. I figure, she's probably speaking with Da̲'naxda'x̱w people because they respected her for a position her ancestor had." Wedłidi Speck made this connection explicit. "Jane Cook had a name at Knight Inlet," he said. "The family had titles, and there was a reason Granny was doing this at the commission. They were related."

Chief Seweet (Siwida'nakwa̲la), a cousin to Jane's mother, Emily, also stood up for Da̲'naxda'x̱w.[97] It is unclear in the transcript whether "the chief" speaking is Ha̲mdxid or Siwida'nakwa̲la.

"Now we will come to the applications for land," Commissioner D.M. MacDowell announced.

"I wish Mrs. Cook to speak to the Commission for me regarding Knight's Inlet," the chief responded.

"The Chief wants me to speak to you regarding this reserve. He himself has just a little reserve that he looks upon as his reserve, but he did not recognize the big reserve. He just shares a part of the reserve in his mind. He just knows that he has two little pieces that belongs to him."

Commissioner MacDowell replied, "Several tribes having their villages on this Reserve won't interfere with what we are doing in this way. We have to take these Reserves as they appear in the Government list, and we are dealing with the land and not with the distribution of the Tribes at all – That is a matter for the Department to settle. If we get the information we want about the land it is perfectly sufficient for us. If the two Chiefs will now give us the information about these lands there just in a general sort of way – we don't mind whether there is one village there or nine villages. What we want to do now is to find out the location of the pieces of land described on this paper which has been handed to us, and we shall be glad if one of the Indians will come up and point these different localities out to us."[98]

Commissioner MacDowell apparently had difficulty with Jane Cook's explanation that the chief "did not recognize the big reserve" but "shares a part of the reserve in his mind." Such conceptual statements did not fit the bureaucratic categories of tribes, villages, and reserves spatially defined in government lists and on cadastral maps.[99] Although "reserves held in common" provided access for several groups to a common resource, such arrangements were not the commission's business. Commissioners wanted only a definitive list of land parcels, and they had little interest in how the lands were accessed and owned.

After looking at the transcript, George Speck said, "I can just imagine people trying to explain what they meant by protecting their fishing stations. My great-great-grandfather made a claim here on Cormorant Island, a fishing station. Our big run is out of the Nimpkish, so, obviously, other tribes had fishing stations here. Mamalilikala, Ma'amtagila, I think, made claims here. Everybody had interests they were trying to assert to these commissions. And to explain the interest over title right, that's the difficulty [with these hearings] in terms of property and territory."[100]

On the last day of hearings, 8 June 1914, Chief Tsukaite from Blunden Harbour spoke eloquently:

> It is only now that I come to know that I have no country which I thought belonged to me ... I ask for the return of my country to me, and that the reserves be no more ... There was a time when there was no whiteman in the country, and in those times I had full possession of all the country. What has been done to me with my country would be the other way – I would have measured pieces off for the whiteman instead of the whiteman measuring off pieces for me. The one that is selling my country has never been here – they have never seen it, and they had no right to sell it to the whiteman.[101]

In addition to the land applications they filed with the commission, the Kwakwaka'wakw chiefs sought two hundred acres of land for each man. They wanted access to timber; foreshores; fishing, hunting, and trapping grounds; and freshwater sources. Chief Qua-wha-lagha-loose asked that William Halliday be removed as Indian Agent, "because we don't find much help from him." He also suggested that Halliday's gasoline boat be given to the physician.[102] Chief Lagius asked, "How many months or years before you can let us know when you can let me have all these lands?" The chairman replied, "Some time next year." The report, he said, would "go to the two Governments," and "it might be two years before they will be in a position to let you know."[103]

The findings of the McKenna-McBride Royal Commission were disappointing. The Kwakwaka'wakw tribes made 195 applications for land, 109 for fishing sites. "More than half were dismissed by the MMRC on the grounds that the site or area had been alienated."[104]

> In June 1916, when the commission made its final report ... Indian reserves in the province totaled 713,699 acres (or 1,115 square miles). The commission recommended that 666,640 (or 1,042 square miles) be confirmed as existing reserves lands and that 87,291 acres (136 square miles) be added as additions and as new reserves ... The commission recommended that 47,058 acres (74 square miles) be "cut off" from existing reserves ... almost entirely land regarded as desirable by white farmers, ranchers, developers, speculators and municipal offices.[105]

Following the final report, a province-wide aboriginal organization held a meeting to protest the cutoffs and the refusal on the part of both governments to deal with aboriginal title.

"We Who Wish to Uplift Our People": On Marriage

Both during and after the commission, Ga'axsta'las continued her campaign to ensure the well-being of women and children. On the fourth day of commission hearings, she wrote the following letter:

Alert Bay
July 4, 1914

To the Revd Lord Bishop of Columbia
Dear Lord Bishop

As you were so kind as to say, when you were here, that you would do all you could to help us for the good of our Indian people here.

I now take the liberty of bring to you notice a matters that has a very demoralizing effect on our people here, if allowed to go on.

I have taken this matter up before, but have not got any satisfaction, either, from the Dominion or the Provincial Government.

I am speaking of the loose custom of marriage allowed among our people, I will bring an instance that has happened here last year.

There is [a man] ... that has had 3 wives [in one year] each of these 3 wives he had married according to the Indian Custom of marriage. As there is no notice taken of these actions there are others men leaving wives since there was no notice taken of this mans marriage to his third wife ... about the end of [month]. [Another man] has left his wife & 3 little children this girl wife is not yet 23 yrs old.

[Another man] has left his wife and child.

We who wish to uplift our people are powerless to help them because neither the representatives of the Dominion or Provincial Government will stop these unlawful actions.

As there seems to be no law to restrain these men in leaving their wives & children and marrying other women.

Will you help us to try and get some kind of Legislation passed, that either this Custom be made binding, or that they be forced to marry in Church or by Register.

Also that these men, that leave their Wives & Children, without Cause be forced to support them.

We all feel that this is the great stumbling Block in the path of morality here, that this custom is allowed to go on.

I would be glad to give any information in my power to you or any one else that will interest themselves in a move to have something done to stop this.

Hoping that you will see your way to help us.

I remain Yrs. Grateful.

Jane Cook.[106]

G̲a'ax̲sta'las had been married for nearly thirty years. Through her weekly activities with the Anglican Women's Auxiliary (WA), she was closely acquainted with the concerns and circumstances of women in 'Ya̲lis. Her letter was dated the day after a WA meeting and three days into the commission's hearings, where she had already listened to three speakers explain "Indian custom" protocols for marriage and divorce. When asked about marriage, 'Na̲mgis chief Lagius testified that his people "follow the old customs mostly ... Half are christians, and the others adhere to the beliefs of their forefathers, and some of those that are christians still adhere to the old beliefs."[107]

On the first day of hearings, the commission had asked Harry Mountain to describe marriage protocol:

> The blankets or money is counted and is given to the father of the girl. One might give so much – it all depends on how much he can afford to give – some will give 1,000 some 1,500 and some 2,000 blankets ... And then when the blankets have been delivered to the father of the girl and the girl is brought out standing in front of all the people, then the girl is taken to the house of her husband, and then the father of the girl gives so much back to the husband of his daughter, and then the husband goes and buys grub and calls all the people into the house and gives a feast; and the women also has a feast, and the girl is called and sits in the midst of all the old women and she is told how she has to act now that she is married. When the feast and speeches are all over, they go home.[108]

When questioned further, Mountain described the completion of the marriage contract: "The father of the girl keeps these blankets [given to him by the groom at the time of the marriage], and when the boy and girl have been together for quite a while, the father of the girl gives these blankets back to the husband of his daughter in double." Commissioner McKenna then asked whether young girls, "say seven years or more," were purchased as wives. "No," Harry Mountain replied. "That is not the marriage contract – that is what they call the business contract, and the child will never be married to that man at any time – It does not mean that she will marry him at all."[109]

According to William Wasden Jr., "There were a lot of obligations in a wedding, and a woman was free to leave. Her family was free to buy her out in the end. It wasn't where the man had the choice of what he was going to do. It was the woman's family that had the privilege of fulfilling the marriage contract, and then what they called *gwał,* where she's finished, and they buy her back out so she's free to marry. It was she who was free to marry again. They loosely say *Indian divorce.* It's really completion of the marriage contract, where she's fulfilled her obligations to her husband and then free to marry again. But that's the wife's family's business. It's got nothing to do with the groom saying, 'I'm done with her.' It was almost the opposite."

Charlie Nowell was also asked about fulfilling the marriage contract or g̱wał.

"The whole essence of it," Commissioner McKenna inquired, "is that if a man and woman ... want to separate and take another mate they are at perfect liberty to do so?"

"They may have done that in the past," Charlie Nowell replied, "but in this time now their customs are changing. Myself and my wife have been married many years. She has paid me, but she and I will never separate ... [Divorce] is just the same as among the whites – they average just about the same – it is not as bad as it used to be."

"I think I ought to tell you," McKenna said, "that the whites cannot separate when they want to in Canada – In fact it is very difficult to get a divorce – They must go through a Court ... and if a whiteman and a woman have been married, and they separate without legal divorce they cannot marry again. If they did, they would be prosecuted for bigamy and sent to the penitentiary."[110]

This is the context in which G̱a'ax̱sta'las wrote the bishop about men remarrying and leaving their former wives and children without material support. She urged him to press for legislation to either make potlatch marriages "binding," or to require church or civil marriages. Her point was that not enforcing either was setting a precedent for abandonment. Although some effort had been made to compensate aboriginal women and their children abandoned by European men, no legislation existed to provide for Kwakwa̱ka̱'wakw women who had been legally married in the custom to Kwakwa̱ka̱'wakw men.[111]

The commission's hearings seemed to intensify Kwakwa̱ka̱'wakw resistance to the potlatch ban. During the hearings, they collected 165 names, signatures, and marks of potlatchers and their supporters to send to Ottawa.[112] In September, the government amended section 149 of the Indian Act to restrict people from wearing ceremonial regalia and to prohibit any Indian from taking part "in any dance outside his own reserve." The blow was aimed at curtailing the practice of hosting reciprocating clans and thus further limiting reasons for travel.

In a circular to the chiefs, Indian Agent Halliday wrote that the amendment was for their "advancement so that they are on the same footing as the white man."[113] A stream of written protests and petitions followed well into the New Year.[114] Early in 1915, Charlie Nowell described potlatching and feasting to A.S. Clements, MP, along with a list of the names and values of coppers owned by Fort Rupert and Alert Bay chiefs. Clements passed this along to Duncan Campbell Scott and wrote that he had "considerable sympathy in some of [the] grievances" told him by "some 65 Indians" during his recent visit to Alert Bay.[115] He included a petition on behalf of the "undersigned Indians of the Kwawkewlth Agency," dated 2 March 1915. After several meetings at Fort Rupert, the signators requested that "one or two commissioners from Ottawa come to this Agency to see these committees and look into the potlatch themselves."[116] The potlatchers believed that Clements sympathized with their cause. Rumours of his acquaintance with Scott, his support for the potlatch, and his desire to overturn the ban on it had spread throughout the agency. Jane Cook wrote a rather hurried note to Halliday stating that when Scott and Clements arrived in late June, "We non-Potlatchers want to interview him too."[117]

Canada joined other Commonwealth nations in "the Great War" in August 1914. Under the Military Services Act of 1917, men with Indian status were exempt from compulsory military service, yet those who volunteered "served overseas in ... numbers exceeding their proportion in the population."[118] Five men from the Kwawkewlth Agency enlisted. A sixth man returned because he was underage. Jane and Stephen's son Edwin joined the 102nd Battalion of the Canadian Expeditionary Force.[119] People in 'Y<u>a</u>lis once again witnessed the militarization of their waters.[120]

A few years into the war, 'Y<u>a</u>lis residents were struck by the Spanish flu. Gilbert Cook Sr. was twelve years old. He recalled that there were three funerals a day and that the "people of Kingcome Inlet drank warm oolichan grease and did not die."[121] Nellie Cook was eleven when the flu took away her father, George Hamilton. She recalled that Reggie, her future husband, had been working on one of the Union boats going to Alaska when his father, Stephen, "took him off, saying he was needed at home. There were a lot of people staying at the house during the flu ... A lot of people in Alert Bay died ... Reggie was running the *Howe Sound* then and used to go back and forth with the bodies and sick people from the logging camps."[122] Gerry Ambers remembers Lydia Peters telling her that she and G̱a'ax̱sta'las had visited ailing people in the village, where they administered doses of *t'łina* (eulachon grease) from a bucket.

In a petition sent to Ottawa in February 1919, the Kwagu'ł informed the government that Spanish flu "still prevails, many Indians were effected, fifty having died up to this time."[123] The number is astounding, given that population estimates for 1914 list only 137 members of the 'Na̱mgis tribes and 118 people among the Kwagu'ł.[124] Kwakwa̱ka̱'wakw people in general experienced a population decline of almost 90 percent from 1881 to 1924. As Wedłidi Speck told me, this reality greatly affected potlatching. Given that the transfer of titles, privileges, and property occurred largely through customary marriage contracts, the acquisition of dowries was inextricably linked to cultural survival. G̱a'ax̱sta'las objected to the multiple customary marriages that seemed to escalate during this population crisis. In the 1920s, she began speaking out against potlatching and challenging the authority of chiefs, with whom she had stood so closely in the preceding decade. As Peggy Svanvik, a family friend, told me: "She was really a strong woman and way before her time – as a timid Indian woman *[laughs]* – because in our culture, it's the men who are supposed to speak for us. But she was the one. She was the one. She was way ahead of her time. I believe. You know, she did what she thought she should do, and that was that. And too bad if you didn't like it *[laughs]*."

PART VI

"We Are the Aboriginee, Which Is Not a Citizen," 1918-27

The door in an adjacent room opens. Pearl Alfred gets to her feet and tells me she'll be just a moment. Someone greets her as "Auntie Pearlie," and she asks how they are, how a recent trip was, how someone in their family is doing. She pulls something from a tightly packed shelf, a packet of cigarettes or something sweet. We plan our visits around the operating hours of her store, usually when her daughter Lori or her granddaughter Ashley is there. Pearl is tireless. She will have had treaty talks that week. Maybe she just returned north from a meeting of the Intertribal Health Authority. Or maybe she is gearing up for a community forum, for elections of the 'Na̲mgis Band Council, or a visit to see someone in hospital. At her home, crackling bursts from the marine radio cross over soundless television images from somewhere else in the world. Her great-great-granddaughter lives with her mother at Pearl and Frank's. Teenagers come and go, and adults pop in to drop something off or pick something up. Some join our conversations about the book, or they join Frank in the other room. My eyes always find a drawing on Pearl's kitchen wall in a great-granddaughter's hand.

Arriving in "the Bay," my first visit was usually always to Pearl's, and she usually asked what ferry I had come in on. In 2007, she spoke about rising fares and in 2008 about the difficulties since the island's gas station had closed. She often had a new photograph or a letter or a book to show me, but she would always ask how the writing was going. And she responded patiently to my questions as I sorted out a timeline or sought guidance on what might or might not have been a delicate topic. Pearl always had something new to tell me about, often health-related: drug use or diabetes, the low catch in the current fishery, the fact that mothers now had to deliver babies off-island because there were no obstetric facilities in the Bay.

Whenever I asked Pearl if she would speak on the record about her own history of activism in the community, she replied that she did not want to appear too much in the book. More often than not, her stories melded into some episode in her grandmother's life as she traced a more contemporary concern to its roots in the past.

Pearl did sit down one day in August 2007 to tell me about a group formed in the mid-1980s called the Native Women's Alliance (NWA).

"At one point, we were a parents' advisory committee to the school – when the band didn't allow us to have a parent advisory group. My God! Things *have* changed somewhat. Oh, we were quite the gang. We had quite a thing. We'd plot what we'd bring to the band council," she said and laughed. "It all worked. *T Bags* – at first we were the T-School Parent Advisory Group, so they used to make fun of us and call us T Bags." She laughs. "Ah dear!"

"We put together this letter, which we sent to the band, telling them who we were, what we were doing, and who we were accountable to. We thought that since they were a band who hadn't had a public meeting for umpteen years that we weren't accountable to anybody. And we listed all of our issues from there. We had such a list of things – all the things we protested about – the elections and everything that we could think of. And we held meetings and invited [the band council] to come to our meetings. We were only accountable to the people that were part of our group, our membership and, of course, women and children."

"There was only about a dozen of us." Pearl laughed again. "But we sounded like a huge group. We were noisy and rambunctious. We brought some concert group in here, things our kids had never ever seen. The band wrote this letter to us, asking us who the hell we were, holding our meeting. So we took copies of that letter, responded to it, saying who we were. Then we went down to a big bingo that was happening in the council hall and gave them out to everybody that came in! Well, we felt that everybody should know what our council was saying about us. We were just this harmless little group of women."

"I doubt that," I said, laughing at her characteristic use of irony. "But the issues were mostly around women and children?"

"They were about women and the effects of Bill C-31 and what impact that was going to have on the band. It was becoming clear that the band councils weren't supporting them and that these women could come back – *But they're not having anything to do with any share of what we have.* So we took a position on that, that they were band members, you know, that whole big thing. That was one of the issues, and unemployment on the reserve, and no training for women.

We had this big long list of all the things – and health care. Depo-Provera? Yeah, we took a stand on that. And we actually went to a Native Brotherhood convention here and asked them to support us. Which they did!" She laughs. "We got support for it. But what we were trying to do was to stop the doctors who were putting everybody on the reserve on this injection. The doses that were given at that time were so large, and the test results – the women they had tested it on were in asylums. I don't know where we got the energy from, but that was a long time ago, yeah."

"So did it change things? Did they listen?"

"They had to listen to us. We held big meetings, you know? They called meetings they thought would be small little meetings, and we'd gather everybody that we could and take them down to where they held their meetings, in St. Mike's, down here, in the auditorium. And they were wicked! We got rid of someone at the school who was a sexual abuser. They didn't want to fire him. They didn't want to get him listed. Then they just turned around and accused the people who were the accusers. That kind of thing. That was a particularly ugly one. Yeah, but we *were* successful there. We were going all the way with that one."

We spoke for a while about the TB Preventorium located near St. Michael's Residential School and about how tuberculosis had touched Pearl's family. She often punctuated her history with descriptions of both physical and emotional scars, premature deaths, and extended periods of institutionalization. "Should we turn this off?" I asked. Pearl indicated that her store was due to open. "Sounds good," she said and rose from the table to unlock the door in the next room.

A few months after our conversation, Pearl gave me a copy of the letter that the NWA had sent to the band council in December 1987. The list of their past activities included bingo fundraisers, bake sales, bazaars, and the publication and sale of a hundred cookbooks. The women had screened films, arranged health workshops, and made a presentation to the Native Brotherhood Convention in 1986. Under

Photo 27 Pearl Alfred, 1974. "Stolen Land" protest in 'Ya̱lis. *Courtesy of Dara Culhane.*

Photo 28 Pearl Alfred and granddaughter Ashley, 1990, taken at a demonstration in 'Ya̱lis held in solidarity with Oka. *Courtesy of Dara Culhane.*

"On-Going Concerns," the NWA listed "continuing use of Depo-Provera as a contraceptive," local use of hormone injections, "lack of parental involvement in the operation of the community school" (noting that the DIA had funded school committees since 1954), drugs and alcohol use in the community, suicide, upgrading education skills for women, and housing and education for women and children under Bill C-31. Finally, they listed the need for "more adequate means of food fish distribution for single parents and elders," a need that could be met by a community smokehouse and "freezers for those too poor to buy them." "Current Projects" included hosting the Native Theatre Group for children in the community; co-hosting a book signing for *An Error in Judgement* (1987), authored by Dara Culhane Speck; arranging a province-wide breast-screening program for high-risk women; and organizing a support group for women in crisis.[1]

The formation of the NWA followed a long and bitter collective struggle to recognize 'Yalis residents' medical needs, a struggle that culminated in the 1980 Goldthorpe Inquiry, the subject of *An Error in Judgement*. As Dara Culhane Speck notes poignantly throughout the book: "No one in this Native community exists as an isolated individual. Everyone is someone else's mother, father, brother, sister, son, daughter, husband, wife, aunt, uncle, cousin, grandmother, grandfather, in-law. Experiences, no matter how personal in nature, are a property of the collective."[2] Activism is a double-edged sword that sometimes leaves scars in the relationships that *are* the stuff of community. Activities that are perhaps perceived to be a more "noble" form of anticolonial activism coexist with activities that challenge internal authority, putting stress on political and familial loyalties.

Like members of the NWA, and like those individuals who testified at the Goldthorpe Inquiry, Ga'axsta'las took difficult stands. She spoke out about thorny – even "ugly" – issues that affected the most vulnerable people in her community. Had she shared their vocabulary, Pearl Alfred's grandmother would probably have approved of the NWA's goals. Viewed from the present, Ga'axsta'las's activities during the 1920s were likely another turning point for herself and for her family. During this decade, she entered the public record as a supporter of the ban on the potlatch.

The 1920s were a painful period for Kwakwaka'wakw people. As Dara Culhane Speck notes, the decade encompassed "the stringent enforcement of the anti-potlatch law ... increased pressure ... to surrender children to educational institutions; a recession in the logging and fishing industries; and continuing sickness and high mortality."[3]

Wedłidi Speck described the 1920s from the perspective of chiefs and their families, people who endeavoured to keep the potlatch alive during a time when the Kwakwa̲ka̲'wakw population had reached a historical low: "The context of [population] decline would have placed the Kwakwa̲ka̲'wakw in a fear-based way of thinking. If you look at the 1881 census of the Fort Rupert *Kweha* – where 'Nulis and G̲a'ax̲sta'las came from – for the six clans of the Kweha there was only, I think, seventy something people. So, if you broke it down evenly toward those clans, there would have been fourteen to seventeen people in each clan. So, if every clan had fifty [potlatch] seats – you know? It radically changes the way people do things. It's like the Speck family. When you look at the Hunt-Boas material, you'll see there's some confusion in the stories about whether the chief of the Ławits'is [from Turnour Island] had the right to give a house away. In one case, they said this chief of Nu'nemaseqâlis gave away this house, and it belonged to the Si'senłe of that village, but yet, that chief was the chief of both clans. When they think too literally, then that's the problem."

"So, they're reaching out to grab people to come to be part of their clan, to keep the culture alive. Again, they're in survival. If you've got fourteen people, and people are leaving to become Christians, it's pretty threatening. So, like Granny Cook, who had all her children, they still gave them names. That's a big part of this context."[4]

Sometime between 1918 and 1931, Franz Boas noted:

> In the old days, as informants reiterated, it took years to save up the essential skins and goods, so that a potlatch was a rare event. Now a man can earn enough in a cannery in a single season for an elaborate ceremony. Accordingly, most of the old names have been duly validated, whereas long ago, some of them might have lain dormant for generations. The descendants of the old, influential families smile ruefully: "Now everyone is a chief" they say. Probably this facility for giving potlatches has increased the featyre [sic] of the destruction of goods.[5]

At the edge of the so-called Roaring Twenties, within the contexts described by Wedłidi Speck and Dara Culhane Speck, the Great War came to a close, potlatching continued unabated, and colonial officers sought intensely to quash it. The notorious assimilationist Duncan Campbell Scott had risen through the DIA's bureaucratic ranks from accountant to deputy superintendent general just as the Nisga'a and the Allied Tribes were formulating legal arguments for aboriginal title. The Anglican Church was, more than ever, interested in the role of marriage. In the media, sensational representations of the "sale of wives" at Alert Bay continued to provoke Indian Agent William Halliday. Church, government, and the agents of capital (fish companies) vied to establish different footholds on the so-called Indian question. The stakes were land, economic profit, and Christian morality – and they sought public aboriginal support.

Within Kwakwa̱ka̱'wakw villages, the social category "nonpotlatcher" seems to have coalesced in the 1920s. Although she was not alone, it is the singular voice of Jane Constance Cook that is now almost solely associated with this group. Her views on marriage remained consistent. She spoke out for young women and for families caught in the wake of shifting marriage practices. What had changed was the DIA's recognition of customary marriages. Aboriginal people were abruptly subjected to provincial marriage laws as the government began to enforce the potlatch ban in earnest. Perhaps inspired by 1917 legislation that gave European women the right to vote or by her affiliation with the church, G̱a'ax̱sta'las honoured the law.[6] Like other political leaders at the time, she defended the idea of equality through citizenship. Her role on the executive committee of the Allied Indian Tribes, to which she was elected in 1923, attests to her desire to obtain adequate material resources for sick people, fishers, and potlatchers. As Wedłidi Speck made clear, the potlatch should not be seen as a seamless, unchanging institution; rather, it is a deeply social set of practices and performances responsive to structural upheavals and to internal expressions of relationship and resilience.

Part VI revisits events in G̱a'ax̱sta'las's life in the 1920s, including the potlatch trials, a complicated set of legal and social processes that have come to overshadow what was a hopeful but ultimately frustrating political era for aboriginal rights activists. Within their family, the decade was also difficult for the Cooks. From 1918 to the close of the 1920s, Jane and Stephen lost three of their adult children: Edwin (1918), Alice (1921), and Grace (1927). The Cook big house expanded and contracted as grandchildren moved in to recover from the loss of their mothers. Some of the sons married and stayed on, while daughters moved out to build their own families in 'Yalis. Their younger

Photo 29 Industrial school students, ca. 1920. *Back row, six from left:* Ernie Cook. *Second row from front, second from right:* Reg Cook. *Second row from front, seventh from right:* Cyril Cook. *Front row, fourth from left:* Nellie Hamilton. *Courtesy of Wedłidi Speck.*

children attended the industrial school, which became the subject of official complaints in 1919.[7]

"We Whose Ancestors Made This System"

During the war, Edwin Cook was wounded twice and awarded the Distinguished Conduct Medal. He died from wounds received in combat in August 1918. Two months later, William Halliday wrote to Ottawa on Jane and Stephen's behalf: "About the end of April last [Private Edwin Cook] was married to an English woman who will now be left a widow, leaving one child. From his relatives here, they have not yet received any information as to the means or livelihood or income of the widow."[8] Consistent with her views on post-marital support, Jane Cook was concerned for Edwin's widow and child, whom she had not met.

The war and the war effort crept into Indian legislation in Canada. Patriotic duties included food production and conservation. To Duncan

Campbell Scott, the potlatch was both wasteful and detrimental to productivity in aboriginal communities. The “giveaway” and acts of “mutilation” had already passed into the list of activities prohibited by the Indian Act. Until 1918, however, they were indictable offences, which were heard in the higher courts and expensive to pursue. The result was a low number of convictions. The Indian Act was amended in spring 1918 to reclassify these violations as summary offences.[9] Andrew Paull of the Allied Tribes attributed the shift largely to agent Halliday’s persistence. The amendment, he wrote, “means instead of the case being tried before a judge it could be tried by a Indian agent or two justices of the peace Etc. which put the power more directly into the hands of the Indian Agent.”[10] According to Paull, Halliday was largely responsible for the strict interpretation of the antipotlatching law and was, almost without exception, the sole Indian Agent on the Northwest Coast to so passionately enforce it.

At the beginning of 1919, Ga’axsta’las was drawn into the first of a series of trials for violations of section 149 of the Indian Act. Lekiosa and Kwosteetsas were convicted before Halliday. At the schoolhouse-turned-courtroom, the two men were sentenced to two months at Oakalla Prison Farm in Burnaby. Their bail bonds of $1,000 each were put up by BC Packers, owners of the cannery at Alert Bay. An appeal was set in motion almost immediately, and the new trial was due to begin sometime in March. Like many of the cases that followed and resulted in convictions, this potlatch trial involved a customary marriage contract. Although there is little documented information about the bride, it was the groom’s third marriage. His previous two wives had already remarried under the laws of the potlatch system. The groom was Ga’axsta’las’s brother-in-law.

The case sent correspondences flying. Halliday wrote to Ottawa requesting top-notch legal representation for what he considered an important test case.[11] The Reverend F. Comley wrote to Bishop Schofield about a newspaper article on “the sale of girls ... BC Packers have gone bail for the Indians, you know what this means.” Comley continued, “the Potlatch brings thousands of dollars to their two stores ... Now is the time to demand where they stand on a moral question like this.”[12] Stephen Cook had operated his general store in ’Yalis for seven years. His daughter-in-law Nellie Cook told me that among his wares were “the big potlatching dishes – enamel.”

Ga’axsta’las voiced her concerns in a letter that described potlatch marriage at a particular moment when, for various reasons, some women were choosing not to marry again in the custom.

Alert Bay
Feb. 6 1919

Mr W. Halliday
Indian Agent
Alert Bay

Sir.

I am enclosing a Copy of a letter I am sending Mr DC Scott Ottawa. Re – Potlatch as practiced here by Kwaqutl Indians.

Will you please send a letter recommending this letter of mine.

Since reading my letter over to you. I have added "marriage not binding." I did not give Mr Scott an explanation of this expression. But I will give it to you & it may show you how difficult it has been to you to settle the "Legal laws of Canada" with the "Legal laws of the Potlatch." An Indian Marriage is carried through as an contract. Negotiations (to Kādsiklā) been carried on at this Ceremony. After the Sum has been paid the Couple are married. When contract has been fulfilled that is 100% double what was given for her at Wedding been paid back.

She can leave the husband, if she wishes leggally according to Potlatch laws.

But if she feels she is morally Bound *she will not* leave him or as the instances of converts to Christianity or fear of Public opinion or Maternal love for her Children begotten by this marriage. These are some of the reasons she will not take advantage of her freedom. But see how easy for them, if they are so minded to leave each other.

Yrs truly
Mrs. S Cook[13]

G̲a'ax̲sta'las tried to impress upon Scott (via Halliday) the diverse situations of women. She offered reasons why some did not remarry. Five years earlier, chiefs had testified before the McKenna-McBride Royal Commission that serial marriages had not been practised for some time, that most chiefs and men of high standing remained with their wives after their marriage contracts were completed. Jane Cook's letter stated otherwise. She wrote about women caught between the shifting mores of Christianity and the custom at a time when the frequency of strategic marriages was increasing to fill vacant potlatch seats.

The church and its associated organizations held some appeal for women who had been educated for several years by missionaries. On the other hand, women of high rank were important participants in customary transfers. Few would likely have resisted their family's wishes. As women moved into arranged marriages, their children "were placed either in the new marriage or taken by grandparents, aunts or uncles."[14] Ga'axsta'las's suggestion that some women would not leave a marriage because of "maternal love" perhaps reflected changing patterns in customary adoptions. She later argued that women should have a choice in marriage, but here she acknowledged why they might not exercise it. Perhaps her own situation as a woman without a Kwakwaka'wakw father gave her the liberty of speech and the possibility, as a Kwagu'ł woman, to define her own participation in the custom.

"A lot of [marriages] were arranged to deal with rank and status," Nella Nelson told me. "But when the church and Christianity came, they were really reacting to young women being married to old men. And I think that when more young women were exposed to a different way of life, there was more resistance to that. And the church did try to quell it. It was all done through families previously. My mom actually came to Victoria High at fifteen because the church or missionaries – godparents – got her here. [She] went home to work in the cannery, and her marriage was arranged with someone around the same age as herself."

"She didn't like it when they picked husbands for their children," Emma Alfred said about her grandmother: "She did not like that. She didn't think that was right. 'You should get to know him and love him first, before you do things like that.' Yeah, she used to say, 'When you get boyfriends, just make sure he's the guy you want to live with for the rest of your life.' But I didn't know too much about the ways of them picking husbands, and when I did, I thought, Oh, thank goodness, Gran didn't do that to me *[laughs]*. But, no, the type of woman that she was, she wouldn't have done that. 'You pick the man you want. And they will be happy with him if I am happy with him.' That [was a] type of saying of hers."

Emma's sister Florrie Matilpe suggested that her grandmother had had other objections to customary marriage: "The reason why she didn't like the potlatch – it's not just because she became a Christian. It was because of the things that they did to get to where they were, the chiefs. They actually did things wrong to become a chief, like marrying all these women just to get things [laughs]. That old lady Mrs. —— told me, 'Everybody was just getting married so they could get the stuff.'" She used to tell me, the old lady. I used to go sit with her for hours and hours and talk to her. I taped her a few times, but sometimes I used to take my tape recorder and forget to put it on.

Then she'd get mad at me, 'Don't turn that thing on,' she'd say to me *[laughs]*. But I think that's really why Granny didn't like the potlatch, was because of what the men did."

Pearl Alfred also spoke about G̲a'ax̲sta'las's views on customary marriage: "I always felt that she was offended that some woman could be discarded because she couldn't have children. That was the sense that I had. And I would have agreed with her *[laughs]*. Those are her issues, I think. And, then, the betrothal of children – that was something else that she felt was wrong. I heard her say that she picked her husband and that everybody should be able to do that – all women should be able to. Boy! To have said that. It's no wonder nobody liked her! Certainly, the chiefs – what was this woman doing? Destroying everything that was the basis of this male dominance here *[laughs]*."

"I find that that's probably the most amazing thing," George Speck said. "Thinking about her within that whole context – a woman taking a stand number one – against the chiefs, which is a fairly male-oriented and -dominated system, and taking a stand from a Christian culture, which was very male-dominated and -oriented, especially [in] the pioneer years, frontier-town kind of mentality, resource town, fishing town, logging town. But those kinds of attitudes she must have had to deal with, all at that same time, and still take the stands that she did. It's hard to fathom."

In her letter to Halliday, G̲a'ax̲sta'las expressed the difficulties of pitting the "Legal Laws of Canada" against the "Legal Laws of the Potlatch." Public debate was escalating. Halliday typed G̲a'ax̲sta'las's letter to Scott as it was "read over" to him. This letter, more than any other, appears regularly in print as evidence of her stand against the potlatch. Certainly, it was a departure from her previous entreaties to recognize the legality of customary marriage. Aside from his apparent lack of attention to spelling, one wonders how closely the Indian Agent adhered to her words.

Alert Bay B.C.
Feb 1st 1919

Duncan C Scott, Esq,
Deputy Superintendent General.
Indian Affairs. Ottawa.

Dear Sir:–

I take the liberty of addressing this letter to you because of the attempt being made by the authorities to enforce the Indian Act. Section 149.

Our Indian people feel that this act shouldnot be enforced, as it would do away with the system known as the "Potlatch" practised here by the Indians, and which has for its features the Festivals. Dances. Ceromonies. which cannot be conducted without giving or paying of money, Goods or Articles.

This Potlatch as practised among the Kwagults here, is a system governing all Indian Life, Every Indian man, woman or child have their part in it. each one has to be initiated into the Festivals, and Ceremonies, through the giving or paying of money or goods. into different Clans, Ranks, or positions.

I will begin with the birth of the Indian Child. Just as soon as the parents can collect enough money or goods to call a Band or Bands, together to have a Fest-ival, and Dancing and all the ceremony of naning and classing the child, it is done. If a sacred Red Bark Dance is on, the following winter, The Child has to be initiated into the Festival of Red Bark Through another Potlatch. It there received its Red Bark Name. Giving it the right of Belongng to the Red Bark System. which has its features. Often ounding or mutilation of the dead or living body.

When the child comes to an age when it can take a wife, which is as young as 14 in a Boy. or as young as 11 or 12 yrs in a girl. Money has to be collected by Parents or Guardians of Boy to be paid to the parents or guardians of the girl, as many as 3. 4. or 5, persons profiting by the transaction of the males party givingmoney or goods for the Bride, The amount depending on how high or low the standing of the family, of the Bride. The Bride and Bridegroom having no choice in the matter, only used as Pawns in a contract of the system called marriage.

(Marriage not binding)

All these Festivals, Dances, Ceremony contracts, giving and paying, is determining the future status of the child, Boy, Girl Man or Woman.

This is only a glimpse into the system known as the Potlatch There are many other features, Not anyone part can be pratised without Collecting or paying or giving away money, goods or Articles all worked on the 100% system. (All money, Good or Articles Borrowed, or given, has to be paid or given back double.) You will see how bound and tied every man, woman and child is to this system. They are slaves to it, all their time is devoted to it their mind and money has to be used for it, therefore there is no expansion of mind. Or Progress of any thing worth while.

The Potlatchers are sending Delegates to Ottawa, Presumably to ask you or Mr Clements, M.P. (who has promised to help them) to take steps to have this act 149 repealed.

Now Sir. We who have cast off the Potlatch System (Whom I represent in this letter) Wish to give you a few reasons why this Indian Act section, 149 should not only stand but to also be strongly enforced.

1st. The Kwagult people as a whole will never own Allegiance to the Government or King as long as they are allowed to practice their Allegiance to the Potlatch system, for to them this excludes every other Government. No Potlatchers volunteered to serve overseas.

2nd. It is because of this system that they will not marry according to the laws of Canada. Their system allows them to contract for a wife, and it being made so easy for them to cast one wife away and take another man's wife, according to the laws of Potlatch. Out of all this agency there are only five couples who have married leggaly by Church Laws, and these have left the Potlatch.

3rd. There is no liberty, in the Potlatch, No Choice whatever. They are all bound and have to practice all the different features of this system or they will lose their caste. Those who have left the Potlatch are looked upon as not Indians, or Have no standing or voice in any matters affecting their tribe or band. They are practically Outcasts.

4th This system keeps them form progress, every cent they have must be used to keep them in caste. There is nothing new done or allowed them. All must be done as their ancestors did. Therefore there is no progress on their lands and homes.

5th It hinders education, They would not allow their children to go to school, if it was not for the children wanting to go to school themselves.

Sir we feel hat the system has served its purpose. A Government to Govern Indians before the Canadian Laws were established in these lands, But now that Canada has Laws, These laws should be accepted and obeyed by all peoples in Canada.

We whose ancestors made this System, a constitution for the Indians, are sure we have a right, and are right in asking that this Indian Act section 149 be allowed to stand, and the Potlatch be Abolished from these lands and the laws of Canada take its place.

This only a few reasons why this Indian act section 149 should be enforced.

Begging your Indulgence.
I remain
Yours Faithfully
Mrs S. Cook[15]

A DIA memo was fastened to the letter. The memo hints at the first of many incarnations the letter would have beyond 'Yalis: "The attached letter ... is from an Indian school teacher ... the Department attaches considerable importance to [it]" as it was "written by one who is conversant with the situation and who is entirely opposed to the practice."[16] Little consideration was given then, or in recent publications, to Jane Cook's letter of 6 February, in which she presents a more nuanced account of the situation of women converts in regard to customary marriage.

At a time when the custom was being threatened, Ga'axsta'las had already felt the pressure of leaving the potlatch. Only five couples had been married by the church after leaving the system. Her strong words about the loss of "caste," about being "looked upon as not Indians" and having their political "voice" silenced, suggest that she was then experiencing a kind of social exile.[17] Refusing the position of outcast, Ga'axsta'las instead reasserted her rank and her aboriginal identity by signing off on behalf of those "whose ancestors made this system."

"They must have been pretty strong people to remove themselves from a system they were surrounded by," William Wasden Jr. said, responding to her letter. "My great-grandparents did that, too, Mr. and Mrs. Ben Alfred. They thought the same way. They said, *"It isn't what it used to be."* I take that with a lot of pride. It makes me stronger to know that I had ancestors that could say to the whole nation that was corrupting a system that was given to them – to say that they don't want a part of that."

Over the years, Ga'axsta'las's great-granddaughter Kelly-Anne Speck spoke with several generations of her relatives and revisited the story of Granny Cook. "I always thought it fascinating," Kelly-Anne said, "Granny Lucy [Brown] and Granny Ethel [Alfred], their ability to kind of balance off what was attributed to her, like saying she was really against [the potlatch]. And yet, at the same time, they both personally were really involved in the church and involved in the potlatching once it started again. They were right there, right involved."

"It's probably in the nineties when I was talking to Granny Ethel about this question, because she came to live with us when Gramps was ill and dying. She never believed that it was a contradiction. She sort of saw it as [Granny Cook] was really worried about what was happening to women and children. She would never talk about it in great detail. It was sort of like, 'Well, don't be stirring up things that have nothing to do with anything.' They actually, I think, saw that there were problems, but that that was in the past and the way that potlatching was happening – if you will, in the new era – was not what was happening when she was objecting to it."

The letter from 1919 leaves little doubt about Jane Cook's patriotism, a sensibility that could only have intensified after the death of her son Edwin seven months earlier. Her comments about allegiance to the government and king may reflect this loss, but she was writing to a representative of the Crown during wartime. Nor is her rhetoric unusual. During the war, women in Alert Bay joined with the Imperial Order of the Daughters of the Empire (IODE) and the Red Cross to sew hundreds of pairs of socks and make bandages and "belly bands" for soldiers at the front. In 1919, Ga'axsta'las purchased $500 worth of Victory Bonds. The Cook family prospered, and some family members suggest that their economic success was, in part, tied to circulating potlatch wealth.

"At one time, Papa had over five hundred potlatch blankets in the store," George Cook told his daughter Nella. "He would sell them for potlatches and then, after a potlatch, people would come back to the Cook's store and sell them back to Papa for groceries. He had his own potlatch economy going. Papa and Granny had huge ledgers of financial information where they had given people credit. Debts [were] repaid, but many debts remained unpaid, and they were write-offs. At the end, I think Papa had more write-offs than he was getting in. It made it hard for Cook's store to survive with so much money owing to it. The Cook's general store offered credit. The family looked after money for people before the advent of banks."

"The potlatch was definitely our governing structure, and a lot of the systems worked," Nella Nelson told me. "I am reminded of an occasion when I was speaking to a class at a local college. One of the students stated that they wanted to run their First Nations' student council in the traditional ways of our people, in a circle where everyone is equal. I let them know that not all traditional nations operated in a circle and were equal. As a member of the Kwakwaka'wakw nation, we were very much into rank and status. Everyone had their seat and place in the potlatch system. Everyone knew where everyone else fit in the tribal system, and we were very competitive." Nella Nelson's words reminded me once again that we were speaking about matters important to the Kwakwaka'wakw aristocracy. She suggested to me that her great-grandmother Ga'axsta'las had held the trusted position of confidante for many in the village. "So what began to happen, as

I understand, is that some of the people would actually come to talk to Granny about the fact that their parents had given away all of their possessions as well."

Like Kwakwaka'wakw chiefs, Jane and Stephen Cook were invested in the material well-being of their people. The ways that their investment was expressed, of course, differed. Ga'axsta'las argued that the potlatch kept people dependent, without the ability to exercise choice. To the chiefs, it was the potlatch ban that had brought about their inability to look after aged, sick, and poor villagers.

When Jane Cook wrote her letter, Charlie Nowell (Fort Rupert), Moses Alfred (Nimpkish), and William Roberts (Campbell River) had already gone to Ottawa to meet with Duncan Campbell Scott about repealing section 149. Their reception was, by all accounts, cool. Their "representations" reflect tensions that signalled a harsh turn in the potlatch ban. Ironically, as Ga'axsta'las had for several years been advocating, they too asked that customary marriage be legal and binding, that colonial officials disallow divorce "except in the same manner and legal form as now applies to the white man" and allow the bride and bridegroom to accept and give presents at weddings.[18] Nowell and his colleagues referred Scott to a newspaper clipping about the potlatch case against Likiosa and Kwosteetsas. They asked that the case not be pursued until an investigation could be held. "Investigate the fact that Mrs. Jane Cook, the official interpreter did falsely interpret the evidence. The fact is the said Mrs. Cook is the sister-in-law of the defendant Lakiosa, and they are not on friendly terms."[19] Finally, their petition read: "As wards of the government and non-treaty Indians, we want the same privileges as white men, the Chinese, Japanese and other foreigners. We are sufficiently advanced in the manner and customs of the white man to warrant full considerations and justice in this matter."[20]

J.D. McLean, assistant deputy minister of Indian affairs, responded the next day. "Provisions of the Indian Act have nothing to do with the marriage of Indians ... laws relating to the solemnization of marriage belongs to the different provinces."[21] The Kwakwaka'wakw delegation was instructed to await the results of the appeal in the potlatch case and advised that Inspector William Ditchburn would investigate the allegations against Jane Cook. Each of the eight points raised by the delegates were met with terse replies as to the law, most especially the firm hold of section 149.[22] That February, members of the delegation returned to the Coast dejected.

On 29 March 1919, Halliday wrote to Ottawa:

> I have just had a visit from Mr. and Mrs. S. Cook of Alert Bay, the parents of Pte. E.V. Cook ... who was killed or died from wounds and they gave me the enclosed correspondence from which it would seem that the widow is having some difficulty in receiving her pension allowance from the government ... It is implied that there are other heirs and Stephen Cook the father, has signed a relinquishment of any claim which he might have as the father of the deceased Pte. Cook. The father and mother have asked me to urge you to take immediate steps to see that the widow and child are properly cared for.[23]

The same day that Halliday wrote this letter, the provincial government amended the Marriage Act. The age for a legal union was set at twenty-one years, unless the consent of both parents or a guardian was given. If such consent was impossible, a petition for marriage could be sought from a judge of the Supreme Court or County Court.[24]

When Mamalilikala potlatchers Harry Mountain, John McDougall, Isaac, and Chief August of "Klawata" were charged under section 149, the appeal trial of Lekiosa and Kwosteetsas had not yet been heard in Vancouver County Court. In late March, they and the Mamalilikala potlatchers, along with "seventy five other Kwakiutl who crowded the court room," signed an agreement not to potlatch.[25] The chiefs' promises were given on condition that they could still "make representations to have the law changed."[26] Their hope was that Ottawa would send a commission to see and hear, first-hand, what the potlatch meant to Kwakwaka'wakw people. No such commission was ever struck. Instead, the DIA looked to Marius Barbeau to produce an anthropological report on the potlatch – a "confidential" document much sought after by lawyers over the next few years, one that was disappointing to the DIA because Barbeau was in favour of "an amendment to the said act."[27]

In April 1919, Halliday again wrote to Ottawa: "I have just called to see the father and mother of Pte. Cook and they informed me that by yesterday mail they received a letter from the widow stating that she was now in receipt of the pension as the fact had been established that she was the only dependent."[28] Edwin Cook's widow received a pension of forty dollars per month, with an additional eight dollars for her child. The pension took eight months to process because the paperwork, which included Stephen Cook's relinquishment, had to be administered through the Department of Indian Affairs’s Director of Estates and then passed back to the Office of the Agent-General for the province of British Columbia in London, England.

Toward the end of April, G̲a’ax̲sta’las travelled to Victoria as a “Native delegate” of the IODE. She took advantage of the journey to visit Bishop Schofield, and part of their meeting was spent discussing the potlatch. The church was being pressured by DIA officials to publicly declare their position.[29] Around this time, she was reported to have refused a commemorative stained glass window to honour Alfred Hall at Christ Church in ’Ya̲lis. Her actions did not conform wholly to the sanctioned wishes of the church.

The report on G̲a’ax̲sta’las’s actions as interpreter finally came available in June 1919. Having interviewed several witnesses, the report concluded: “Afterwards [Charles Nowell, Moses Alfred, and William Roberts] gave a written apology to Mrs. Jane Cook, who had interpreted at the potlatch case, for the statement they had made that she had wrongly interpreted the evidence given at the trial.”[30]

In the midst of these skirmishes, life in ’Ya̲lis went on. James Sewid moved to Alert Bay around 1920. In *Guests Never Leave Hungry* (1969), he describes his baptism at around age seven. He was walking with Jim Bell, his grandfather, and had forgotten entirely about the ceremony. At the last minute, he raced to the church, where Mrs. Cook and Mrs. Harris greeted him. They set up the altar for the baptism even though everyone had left. “After that I used to call those two old ladies my godmothers and they used to look out for me. Mrs. Cook would call me in her house to give me some shirts and other things that she had made for me, and Mrs. Harris also used to give me things, especially at Christmas time.”[31]

“Informations”: The Potlatch Trials

Some of Jane Cook’s descendants spoke about a kind of turning point when they learned about G̲a’ax̲sta’las’s role as interpreter in the potlatch cases. “That’s sort of where my journey started,” Nella Nelson told me, “when I understood that she was an interpreter in the potlatch trials. I understood that she was against the potlatch, because, when we were growing up, we couldn’t go to the dances in the Big House. That’s how my dad and his siblings were raised with my granny. What was really interesting was I became very active in the dancing and the potlatches and all of that. Some of our family members, a large number of our family members, are into the culture. And I'm trying to make sense of all of that."

Like other court interpreters, Ga'axsta'las received a little less than fifty dollars for two days' work at the County Court in Vancouver. She was likely sworn in with an oath to "well and truly interpret the evidence before the Court in this case, according to the best of your knowledge and understanding. So help you God!"[32] Witnesses later received a standard fee of $1.50 per day. The DIA paid for their room and board and for the gasoline required to get to the court in their boats.[33] Halliday later argued that if witnesses appeared in superior courtrooms (the County Court or Supreme Court in Vancouver), they should be provided "travelling expenses and a per diem allowance."[34] His correspondences indicate that the multiple witnesses who appeared at the series of potlatch trials often testified reluctantly.[35]

By January 1920, Halliday had eight new summonses for potlatching before him. A special police squad, newly named the Royal Canadian Mounted Police, had stationed a sergeant and constable in Alert Bay. "E" Division, under Sergeant Angermann, was dedicated solely to federal law. It quickly secured "informations" leading to convictions under section 149.[36] Like those before them, the eight accused pleaded guilty. But unlike the others, they were sentenced to two months at Oakalla Prison. Douglas Cole and Ira Chaikin suggest that the convictions shook 'Yalis, as evidenced by higher attendance in schools and at church and a sudden increase in church marriages. From 1919 to early 1920, eight couples were married at Christ Church.[37]

Apparently satisfied with what it saw as the effective deterrent of imprisonment, the DIA informally dropped its vigilance and allowed mourning ceremonies and distribution of food, as long as it was separate from dancing or the Cedar Bark Ceremonies. Some chiefs applied to DIA officials for permission to distribute *t'lina* or other customary commodities that supported 'na'mima networks.[38] It is unclear how many requests were approved. The following years set the stage for the creative logistics of the "sneak around" or "bootleg" potlatches, which were held at isolated villages during inclement weather or in 'Yalis, where the giveaway was often held at times and places separate from dancing and speech making.[39] Anglican Church ceremonies were one such alternative venue.

Christ Church Committee met in March 1920 and passed a unanimous resolution "that Section 149 of the Indian Act be not changed or altered."[40] Their stance reasserted objections to the potlatch made by Jane Cook in her 1919 letter, objections to the financial stress it caused, to arranged marriages, and to obstructing education.[41] But the church committee added two more objections that mirrored the DIA's wartime concerns about health and waste. Arranged marriages, they wrote, are "the cause of the loss of vitality, which is at the foundation of the grave percentage of Tuberculosis reported by the present doctor in charge here." Regarding waste, they pointed to the exposure of food and goods "to all kinds of weather" and referred to property "often broken at a festival to shame a rival."

Although the form of potlatching was altered to avoid the law, the reasons for potlatching continued. Charlie Nowell held a mourning potlatch for his brother Tom in January 1921. The event incorporated an Anglican ceremony, a totem pole raising, and the distribution of goods and cash. Nowell assumed the potlatch standing of *Owadi*. He too was charged, pleaded guilty, and was sentenced to three months at Oakalla Prison. His ethnological patron, George Newcombe, intervened, and the term was reduced to six weeks. At the end of the month, Sergeant Angermann finished collecting informations about a marriage potlatch that had occurred at 'Mi'mkwa̲mlis just before Christmas. His report gave details in the charge against Mrs. MacDougall and "Munday Seaweed."[42] Describing the case, Douglas Cole and Ira Chaikin write: "Mrs. Jane Cook of Christ Church, a vigilant native opponent of the potlatch, helped bring the matter to light."[43] But Angermann's report reveals the involvement of several informants, and it is not clear with whom the sergeant first spoke.

Jane Cook's grandmother, G̲a'ax̲sta'las, was Munday Seaweed's father's sister. Her mother, Emily, was first cousin to Munday; so, in European kinship terms, Jane was his second cousin. Likely because of their relatedness, she held money in trust for him. He had come to her for five hundred dollars. When G̲a'ax̲sta'las asked him what it was for, he said it was to marry Jennie MacDougall, who was, according to Angermann's crime report, "a girl of about 15 living on the Village Island Reserve." "Mrs. Cook warned him that he had better be careful as he might get into trouble." Another man was present during the conversation, and two others notified Angermann about the exchange of money at the wedding ceremony: "$1,000.00 in copper [was given] to ... Jennie MacDougall's grandmother, $500.00 in cash to ... Jennie's uncle, and $50.00 in cash to ... relatives of Jennie's, and the balance of $300.00 in goods to other relatives."[44] Munday himself later came to Jane Cook because he was worried that he would be arrested. "She told him that she had warned him and could do nothing." Angermann arrested Mrs. MacDougall and Munday Seaweed and issued summonses for eight witnesses, including Jane Cook. The accused pleaded not guilty and were set free on bail.

All witnesses said to be at the wedding, including Jennie, denied that any such event had occurred. The two men who had initially informed Angermann of the wedding said that they were not there but had heard about it from others. The man who witnessed the conversation between Ga'axsta'las and Munday Seaweed testified about what he had heard. The trial was adjourned for a week. When it reconvened, Jane Cook testified to giving Munday the money and to their conversation. Angermann reported: "I saw that there was no use proceeding with the case as the Indians had arranged to deny all knowledge of the ceremony, and the case was therefore dismissed."[45]

I sent a copy of Angermann's crime report to Jennie MacDougall's descendant Nella Nelson, who sent the following note to me in March 2007: "I talked to my mom about my Granny Jenny (Klaapa). I had shown her the article in *The Iron Hand* and I also believe Daisy Sewid-Smith wrote about it in her book *Prosecution or Persecution.* Mom is aware of all the kafuffle that was created with granny's arranged marriage to Granny's first husband Munday. My granny's parents were really strong into the potlatch so even if my Granny did not want to get married she would not go against her parents. My mom said that my Granny Klaapa really wanted her education and wanted to travel, she apparently had the most amazing voice and could have been an opera singer. She always instilled in my mom education and travel as well ... My mom's dad [Munday], was a lot older than Klaapa,[46] he worked on the sailing ships and would travel to China and India. He hurt his back and felt that he could no longer provide for Granny Klaapa and his children so that is when he released her to remarry my second Grandpa Bonsound. However [Munday] would row over from Village Island to New Vancouver to see my mom and her sisters, he was a gentle soul. My understanding is that Agnes Alfred helped to arrange the second marriage with Bonsound. Granny Klaapa was related to Agnes (Axuw). There sure were lots of things going on in the early days ... never a dull moment. I just talked with my mom and she has no problems with using the names, no secrets, put it all out there."[47]

It is easy to appreciate that there are secrets locked in past events – in archival drawers and in the spheres of personal memory. Spoken secrets circulate too as part of the miasma of social recall, but it is the steam of rumour that is most scalding. I heard my share of stories. Some were evoked only by a refusal to speak badly about someone;

some were articulated clearly and sharply. All were expected, given the controversial nature of this past today. Kwakwaka'wakw and other researchers constantly face decisions about disclosure. As one researcher told me, "If I was to say anything, I would say that people should be very careful where they throw stones. A lot of people were informing on each other. The more research we do, the more of this is coming out." Historiography is never complete. There will always be another document or file, a recorded or remembered history – a scar barely closed – that sends accepted interpretations spinning. This information is best sorted out among those to whom it matters most. It will unfold, as it always has, through dynamic social processes. The years of the potlatch trials and prosecutions weigh heavy in the memories of those whose ancestors were incarcerated. Given her views and her participation as interpreter, Ga'axsta'las inevitably figures into these memories.

"In terms of looking at the potlatch trials," Wedłidi Speck said, "she definitely had opinions about the potlatch, because she did give evidence in her own way – through letters. And she did try to influence an outcome. Part of it is that there's a question in the community, you know, if someone who has a bias can be objective in translating. What I would say to that is that she was of very high integrity and that she would do her job even though she had an opinion. I think there's a difference." When I spoke with someone noted for their translation skills, that person commented on the courage it would take for an official interpreter not to lie to protect the chiefs.

The year 1921 was an eventful one in 'Yalis. Jane and Stephen's daughter Alice Olney died on 26 February, and her surviving son, Silas, moved into the big house.[48] While Ga'axsta'las was likely nursing Alice in her last days with TB, George Scow, Johnny Scow, Chief Dick, Lagius, and Kesu were prosecuted and convicted for buying a copper at Gwa'yi (Kingcome). On the occasion of that exchange, there was no evidence of "feasting, singing or dancing ... [no] native costume, masks or headdresses were used or worn and ... [no] wand or staff of office ... [no] gifts were exchanged and ... there was [no] precedence in the order of their sitting at the gathering."[49] Legal arguments regarding what, exactly, constituted a "ceremony" followed for many years, but the sale of the copper brought the five men two months at Oakalla Prison each. In December 1921, the now famous Christmas potlatch was hosted by Dan Cranmer at 'Mi'mkwamlis, his wife Emma's village.[50] His daughter Gloria Cranmer-Webster recently wrote: "Our father, a Kwa̱kwa̱ka'wakw chief who carried the 'Na̱mgis hereditary name Pa̱l'nakwa̱wa̱la Wakas, had been previously married to Emma Mountain of the Mama̱liliḵa̱la, who was unable to have children. Because of our father's position in the potlatch system, having a son to take his place was important. So, Dan divorced Emma in the traditional way at the 1921 potlatch on Village Island."[51]

Angermann's crime report listed twenty-eight men and women, whom he charged for their involvement in the "repurchase" potlatch, the completion of the marriage contract, *gwał,* by Emma's family.[52] Two men who attended the potlatch had informed Angermann about it.[53] With the assistance of a male interpreter, the sergeant interviewed "a large number of Indians throughout the district" until he obtained "sufficient evidence to prove" the charges.[54]

In Agnes Alfred's account of the arrests, she mentions that Angermann "used to go to Mrs. Cook." On that occasion, she said, "He wanted her to look after Nora [Agnes' baby] when they put me in jail. Mrs. Cook told him that she could not handle any more children because she already had a handful to look after."[55] At that time, G̱a'a̱xsta'las was fifty-one; her youngest child, Winnie, was ten; Pearl was twelve; and Herbert was fourteen. She and Stephen were also raising their grandchildren.

In the 1922 potlatch trial, at which Jane Cook served as interpreter, "an agreement was drawn out by the Indian Agent and assented to by the counsel for the defense and it was done at the suggestion of Sergt. Angermann that in order that the Indians might show their good faith that they should voluntarily surrender to the Indian Agent all dancing masks, costumes, head dresses and other paraphernalia used solely for potlatch purposes. This was to be a voluntary act on their part and must be consummated on or before the 25th day of March."[56] So, at Angermann's suggestion, another agreement was drafted. In return for the "payment" of regalia, masks, and coppers, those charged from the villages of 'Mi'mkwa̱mlis, 'Ya̱lis, and Cape Mudge would not be imprisoned.[57] Kwagu'ł, Ławits'is, Da̱'naxda'x̱w, and Dzawada̱'enux̱w defendants refused to enter into the agreement because it was contingent on a promise to stop potlatching.[58] According to Herbert Martin's oral history, G̱a'a̱xsta'las was responsible for "recommending" the release of a man named "Goos-dee-jus (Japanese Charlie)" because he was 'Na̱mgis.[59]

"I think for it to be a complete story," Gloria Cranmer-Webster told me in June 2005, "you have to include all the other stuff. You know,

I remember being told that when she was the translator or interpreter at the potlatch trials, that when the magistrate would say, 'How do you plead? Do you plead guilty or not guilty?' to some guy who didn't speak English, her translation was, 'He wants to know were you there?' And, so, she would say, 'He's guilty. Yeah.'" From legal correspondences at the time, it is apparent that little more than one's presence at a potlatch was considered proof of guilt. This may perhaps account for the observations of Kwak̓wala speakers that Jane Cook did not ask if they pleaded guilty or not guilty.

Although accusations that Jane Cook had misinterpreted surfaced again regarding this trial, it is not clear that they were in circulation at the time of the trial, for G̲a'ax̲sta'las and Charlie Nowell were afterward asked by the potlatchers to "engage the [legal] counsel."[60] The following year, members of the Kwawkewlth Agency again chose G̲a'ax̲sta'las to represent them on the Executive Committee of the Allied Indian Tribes of BC. It was a time when specialist advocates for the right to potlatch were entering the public stage.

When Franz Boas addressed the Natural History Society in Victoria in late August 1922, the *Victoria Colonist* ran the story under the headline "Says Potlatch Is Not an Evil."[61] A few days later, William Ditchburn, secretary of the DIA, described the lecture to Duncan Campbell Scott: "[Boas] deprecates the action of the Dominion Government with regard to its attitude on the potlatch question ... If these people would mind their own business and keep their views to themselves without rushing into print it would not be so bad. Harland Smith, the Ethnologist of Ottawa, made like remarks with regard to the potlatch in an address to the same society last year while in Victoria."[62] It is not clear whether *these people* referred to US critics or anthropologists, but anthropology was assuming a public role at the time. At the Victoria Memorial Museum three months later, Edward Sapir, chief of the Anthropological Division of the Geological Survey, received "17 boxes of Indian curios" confiscated from the 'Mi'mkwa̲mlis potlatchers.[63] Halliday had already sold "paraphernalia" to the New York Museum.[64] Sapir was reminded that although other museums were also interested in the regalia, it was "to remain the property of the DIA."[65] Sapir valued the objects personally.[66]

Unbeknownst to the public, DIA officials had received Marius Barbeau's confidential "Potlatch and Dances File" in May 1921. Barbeau argued against the ban, using four categories that reflected colonial anxieties: "Economic Side of the Potlatch," "Sanitary Conditions of Potlatch Houses," "Initiative," and "Assimilation." "Poor Copy" is stamped at the border of the microfilmed print. Barbeau's recommendation rested on the conclusion that "deny[ing] the Kwakiutl Indians the institution of the Potlatch" would "force them to assimilate," which, in his estimation, was "impossible."[67] His obvious concern for what appears to be survival and cultural integrity likely only bolstered the DIA's aspirations to abolish the potlatch and force assimilation.

The years immediately following the potlatch trials saw the rise of new experts – anthropologists, lawyers, and aboriginal leaders – who now fulfilled the criteria for leadership beyond ranked positions in their societies. William Halliday continued to enforce section 149, but his efforts were stymied by the ingenious methods used to fulfill potlatch relations without overtly displaying interactions in public.[68] Dissatisfied with other tactics to repeal the ban, ten potlatching chiefs took their case to the 1922 Allied Tribes Convention in Vancouver.[69]

"Something Like an Equal Footing": The Allied Indian Tribes of BC

The Allied Indian Tribes of BC was organized in 1915 in support of the Nisga'a petition, which was, according to Philip Drucker, the "cause célèbre" of aboriginal title advocates. In 1919, objecting to the final report of the McKenna-McBride Royal Commission, the organization released a pamphlet with twenty demands, including access to and ownership of lands; fishing, hunting, and timber rights; individual ownership on reserved lands; and compensation for lost lands in the form of health care and education.[70]

Kwakwa̱ka̱'wakw bands joined the organization in 1922. At first, they elected ranking chiefs to represent them, but they soon turned to individuals skilled in English and who had an understanding of law, people who could communicate the organization's stand to villagers.[71] Each village chose one or two delegates to represent them at the Allied Tribes Convention in Vancouver in 1922 and during five days of meetings with DIA officials in Victoria the following year. Those elected to the Executive Committee, "worked with attorneys, developed tactics and met with government officials," and "drafted petitions, memorials, and statements sent to provincial and dominion governments."[72]

Like others who spoke about the Allied Tribes, Ethel Alfred mentioned that G̱a'ax̱sta'las had travelled to Ottawa with them. "You remember that picture?" she asked. "Yeah, all those men. She was the

Photo 30 Allied Indian Tribes of BC, ca. 1922. Andy Paull *(holding the brief-case, centre front);* Peter Kelly *(centre, with hands in pockets);* and Jane Cook *(behind Kelly).* Also present are Kwakwa̱ka̱'wakw Chiefs Harry Mountain, George Luther, John Nelson, Bob Harris, John Speck, John Scow, Joe Munday, and Billy McDuff. "All of these chiefs had regalia confiscated in the 1921 bust of Dan Cranmer's 'Mi'mkwa̱mlis potlatch" (Wedłidi Speck). *Courtesy of Wedłidi Speck.*

only woman amongst them with the land claims. Harry Mountain was among them there, and the old man Billy Assu. I guess she wasn't scared because there was quite a few of our people *[laughs]*. People from all over. All over, eh? Yeah, it came to my mind that she went to Ottawa too."

It is uncertain where G̱a'a̱xsta'las met Andrew Paull, a Squamish longshoreman and legal worker, and Peter Kelly, a Haida Methodist minister and schoolteacher. These leaders had visited the coastal villages in 1916. They had a good deal in common. They were educated, had acted as interpreters, and were experienced in the struggle for aboriginal land rights. In 1923, at the first meeting with Duncan

Campbell Scott, Peter Kelly spoke about members of the Executive Committee, about leadership and education. He explicitly acknowledged Jane Cook's presence on that body:

> If there is anything that would place the Indian on something like an equal footing with the white man, it is education ... Take the Executive Members of the Allied Indian Tribes – I don't say this in any way boastingly – but just pointing out a fact that I think in almost every instance a member was picked because his fellow tribesmen saw that he could present their views – I mean she included in that – present their views intelligently. Somehow, although it may not be admitted in so many words, they feel that one who has had educational training is able to bring any grievances before the Indian Department, or the Government, better than the one who has not.[73]

Although they were elected through a community process, members of the executive could not represent all views in their constituencies. Their letters of 1922 detail their discussion about whether the executive should take a stand on "the potlatch question." James Teit, former trader and ethnologist among Nlaka'pamux peoples, was then general secretary of the Allied Tribes. In May 1922, he wrote to Andrew Paull, the recording secretary, "Our tribes are of the opinion that Section 149 ... should be amended, as almost all of the tribes of BC consider this section of the IAct a standing injustice, they have resolved to do all in their power to have same amended."[74] The potlatch question arose again in the correspondence of Edwin K. DeBeck, legal counsel for the Kwakwa̱ka̱'wakw chiefs during the prosecutions.[75] "At a meeting of the convention of the Allied Tribes," he wrote to Scott, "Peter Kelly and one or two others who are connected with missionary work threatened to withdraw if that particular question were taken up ... they decided not to take it up by that organization but to take it up separately. You would find on investigation we believe, that at least ninety-five per cent of the Indians in British Columbia are vitally interested in the question."[76]

Kwakwa̱ka̱'wakw potlatch activists were later directed by their lawyers to avoid leaders who did not favour amending the Indian Act.[77] But Jane Cook, their delegate, took up the potlatchers' cause in a meeting with Scott after the 1922 convention. Her efforts to represent their grievances extended well into 1925. For the executive, the primary agenda was aboriginal title, access to resources, equitable participation in commercial fisheries, and control over food fisheries. Health and education were also on the table.

"When the Tide Is Out, Our Table Is Set": Fishing Rights

In 1980, the U'mista Cultural Centre worked with filmmaker Chuck Olin to document a community history of colonial persecution and cultural and material revival. In his first appearance in the film titled *Box of Treasures,* Chris Cook Jr. sits on a wharf's edge in 'Ya̱lis and mends a net. Behind him, the camera's eye opens onto a profile of fishing vessels set against the rising, wooded contour of the island. "You could call us more like the salmon people," Chris says. "That's all we ever depended on, and we still depend on the fisheries and the sea." To the mechanical beat of floats clanking on the stern gunwale and footage of his crew setting nets, he continues, "Our people have always fished where, when, and how they wanted. We can no longer do that. There's a moratorium on black cod, halibut. Next thing you know, it will be clams and everything like this." Chuck Olin's camera moves to the cabin of Chris Cook's boat, where he sits at the helm. "The ocean is our life," Chris says and looks out onto the water. "It's our whole lifeline. I think, you cut off the lifeline, like the salmon, the fishing, it's like taking the dirt away from the farmers. They no longer would exist."

In the scene that follows, Chris Cook speaks at a meeting at the 'Na̱mgis Band Administration Office. "We're now looking at hours in fishing, when we used to look at days. I think we should tell them, 'This is it. We're not going to be pushed anymore. We can't be pushed anymore, because we're right to the bottom of the row.'"[78] The voice of the narrator, Robert Joseph, resumes: "Many political battles are being fought these days in Alert Bay. Of all of the things that have been taken away from us, none symbolizes our loss more than the masks taken after Dan Cranmer's potlatch." In the narrative of *Box of Treasures,* access to natural resources folds into local initiatives to strengthen cultural identity through language programs and the establishment of the U'mista Cultural Centre, built to receive repatriated potlatch regalia. Cultural knowledge – which includes fish and language and potlatching – offers strong testimony to the ongoing struggle for aboriginal rights.

In 2006, when I spoke with Chris Cook Jr. at his home in 'Ya̱lis, he was still speaking about fishing and culture. "My Uncle Tommy told us, he told the young, 'If you don't learn these songs, we're going to take them home with us.' We were taught when the tide is out, our table is set, you know, because we've lived off the sea, and we just took for granted that this was our place and this was ours, all ours, eh?"

When William Wasden Jr. and I met in his home at 'Y̲alis in March 2009, his voice was hoarse from singing at a potlatch for which he had composed many songs. That afternoon, after the departure of his relatives, he carried the exhaustion of a three-day performance. Speaking about his great-grandmother's role on the executive of the Allied Indian Tribes, he said: "Everything is so connected for our people. Potlatching isn't the only part of our culture. Fishing is who we were. It sustained us. That was a part of our culture, our health. A lot of that was to do with the way our diet was changing. So, these are rights that our people needed to sustain and fight for, and here [Jane Cook] was doing this ahead of time. We're still trying to do that today. Everybody says, 'Culture isn't just singing and dancing; it's everything that we are.' So, to say that she wasn't a cultural person when she's fighting for the things that really mattered to our people ... You know, the singing and the dancing. It will go on; it will go on and on." We had spoken about culture so often over the course of this research. Here, as William invoked culture, he attached it to rights and health and activism – all expressed through the medium of fish. He identified G̲a'ax̲sta'las as a cultural person. "Fishing is who we were," he said to me, and I was reminded again of Pam Brown's concept of fish as wealth.[79]

Fish are for feasting and for ceremonial hosting. The potlatch itself derives from the cosmological imperative to honour reciprocating relations among fish, birds, animals, and chiefs. Fish are caught *with* relatives; they are prepared and distributed *through* networks of family affiliation. Smoked, canned, and frozen fish sustain communities over the winter months. Fish are sold to purchase food and other necessities. Simultaneously, fish are a medium through which Kwakwa̲ka̲'wakw people fulfill ceremonial obligations, meet their material needs, and sustain social and kin networks. The colonial attempt to define fish narrowly as food for subsistence has been an embittered political struggle for over a century in British Columbia.

In 1923, G̲a'ax̲sta'las was "delegated [by the Allied Tribes] to come down on this fishing question." Her testimony portrayed a vivid image of what concerned "the Rupert District and the Kwawkewlth Agency." Her testimony is included here in full.

CONFERENCE of Dr. Duncan C. Scott, Deputy Superintendent-General of Indian Affairs of the Dominion of Canada, W.E. Ditchburn, Chief Inspector of Indian Agencies of British Columbia.

WITH THE EXECUTIVE COMMITTEE OF THE ALLIED INDIAN TRIBES OF BRITISH COLUMBIA;

Held at Victoria, B.C., beginning on Tues., August 7th, 1923, at 11 A.M.

The following being present, composing the said Executive Committee:–

Rev. P.R. Kelly, of the Haida Tribe, Chairman,
Andrew Paull, of the Squamish Tribe. Secretary.
Ambrose Reid, of the United Tribes of Northern B.C.,
Alec, Leonard, Kamloops Tribes,)
Thos. Adolph, Fountain Tribes,) Representing
Narcissê Bapiste, Okanagan Tribes,) Interior of
Stephen Retasket, Lillooet Tribes,) British Columbia
Geo. Matheson, Lower Fraser Tribes,
Simon Pierre, Lower Fraser Tribes,
Chris. Paul, Saanich Tribes,
John Elliot, Cowichan Tribes,
Mrs. Cook, Kwawkewlth.
A.E. O'MEARA, of Victoria, General Counsel of the Allied Tribes.

(Proceedings reported by Mr. Justin Gilbert, Victoria.) ...

Mrs. Cook: I think that as I am delegated to come down on this fishing question, that I ought to say a few words in regard to our locality, that is the Rupert District and the Kwawkewlth Agency. We were asked to speak about our rights, on the fishing question. We are part of the country. It is the rights that we have been deprived of we want to speak of, not the rights which we have now. We have constitutional rights, our rights as Indians.

But we have to now speak about the rights that the Government, and the people of Canada have deprived us of, – our fishing for our food, in the old days when there were no white people in the country, but now today we say we should have had that same fishing privileges that we had in those days, for commercial purposes today. Because the Indian cannot live alone on the fish, as he did in those days; he has got to buy other kinds of food. Well, he needs that, he really needs that industry that he had, for today, just the same as he did in those days, for his livelihood.

Now in our part of the country I think there has a lot of injustice been done; and our people believe it; they claim it. I will just speak of one place there, called the Nimpkish River; and there I will bring in the view that our people have in that fishing ground.

Now, Mr. O'Reilly came there and asked our people, What land do you want?

Now our people are not agricultural people, they have no use, they don't know anything about that, they live altogether by the beach, and their livelihood is in the water. So when Mr. O'Reilly came there – and it was the same thing when the Royal Commission came there – they said, What do you want, what do you require?

Well, one old Chief said, This is what we want, we want the both sides of this Nimpkish River, that we have lived by; we have lived by the river, and we have lived on the river, on the fish in that river; we want both sides of that river, the land, for our purposes. And it was reserved.

Mr. Ditchburn will bear me out in this, that the reserve runs on both sides of the river, right down to the mouth of the river, right down to the fishing grounds today. And the canneries operate on the foreshores of this Indian Reserve on both sides of the river; they cannot operate anywhere else, and get one fish out of that foreshore at that reserve.

We did at one time agitate and try, these Nimpkish people, to get the rights of that foreshore, as they found themselves being crowded in; they lost the rights of that foreshore. At first the canneries did say, Well it may be the foreshores are yours, and we will treat you so well, and hire you to operate, because the foreshore [may] be yours. So that that Tribe operated on that river for forty years, some of the men fishing there today that fished on that river year by year for thirty years – operating for the cannery that is there.

Now this is their complaint: Just because they are not the citizens, or not reckoned as citizens, they are not allowed to buy a seine license; so they lose a lot out on that, because the canneries pay them. First the cannery had the monopoly of that license, but the last two or three years other canneries have come in there and operated on that little river, they have been allowed by the Government to get licenses out, and they are now fishing on that river, and the Indians are operating for them. And that is their complaint, that they cannot get seine licenses for themselves, after fishing there all these years. And they know how to fish; they learned the white man's way of fishing with the seine. But now they cannot buy their own license for that seine there and fish for the cannery, which the cannery would be quite willing for them to do, because they want the fish, and they don't care whether they have the license or not.

And cannery can go there and operate to-day, allowed so many licenses on that river. This year they were cut down to some number, but last year any white man citizen could go there, or a Jap,[80] if he got a license, go there and use a seine there, but Indians had to operate it. Well, that is their complaint.

And another complaint is this, that they have not got the foreshore there to fish, where these seines are dragged on the foreshores of their reserve. You see that is another complaint they have; – and the others have been allowed to come and fish there.

Now I know for a fact there is a company of Japs getting ready now to go in there; I came down on the same boat with the boss Jap of this company, on the boat when I came to Vancouver. And he told me, he said, I have contracted for so many thousands of tons of dog salmon, and I am going to operate; I have got the license, and I am going to get the fish.

Just look at all that. The Indians will stand by and see the Japs go in there with license and operate – in another three weeks, he told me. He may be up there now, and he will operate; and our people who have no other means of getting a livelihood, will be sitting down there and just watching them operate, on this foreshore of their reserve, and getting the dog salmon out of it, – right up to Beaver Cove, and all around that coast there.

I want to show you, and leave it to you to judge how our people feel about this fishing just there. And to show you that it is not the land that our people wanted in those days, they wanted the land on each side of their river so that they could have exclusive right to fish there for their food and for commercial purposes.

Now I will still go on with that river. Our people go away up the river there and get the fish for their winter supply. They have to get a permit now. They did not use to have to, but they do now. And they go up and fish right near that lake, up that river, for their winter's supply of food, or for the year round, really. And now if they go this fall will probably be the last year that they will be able to go there, because now we hear – I heard from good authority before I came down, that that river will be dammed before another year is out, for the Beaver Cove Cement & Pulp Company is going to be formed there, they have taken over the Beaver Cove, and they will make the biggest pulp concern on the coast, and they will dam that river, and use it for power for Beaver Cove. So that the Indians will not only lose their food, but they will lose the mouth of the river for commercial purposes. Because the Indians have told me that over and over again, there is not a river around this part of the coast – Scott Cove for instance, and Powell River – that when the companies have dammed it, that no fishes go up there, the fishes are just gone. Now then that is what they complain.

One complaint that was brought in to me last fall was this, that Scott's Cove behind Cormorant Island had been dammed, and dog salmon and other fishes that had always gone up that river, after the river had been dammed by a company to bring some logs in, the fishes ceased coming; and the company have gone away and left that dam there.

They left the dam there, and it has been there useless for years; they have finished operating there, and have left the dam there, and the fishes gone. They have never even taken the dam away so that the fishes can come back there again – because the Indians say the fishes will come back. Our people know this, that if they dam that river, the sockeye, which is a big industry up there, and the spring salmon; another big industry up there, and our dog salmon also, will be gone. Now, that is for the Nimpkish River.

And those are our people's complaint on that.

That the Japs go in, and they are allowed to have licenses, while an Indian is not allowed, because he is not a citizen, or something – I think it is because he is not a citizen. I think that Mr. Ditchburn has found out about it – you could not get that license for years; could not even for gill-net fishing; but now they can get gill-net license, but not seine fishing. And the Japs have now got the privilege, but the Indian, who was the original there, and to whom the reserve belongs, and who has had his food there from that river, cannot do so.

And you can understand the sense of injustice that he has in the matter.

Now that is what we contend, that these interests of ours should be protected, in the matter of the Indians' food, and in the matter of commercial purposes; and that we should be protected from the Japs; and that it is about time that the Indian – of course as I say, in another years time that river will not be there for either whites or Japs or Indians – but that we should be protected from the Japs somehow, we should be given a chance, anyhow. We do not ask anything too much; we are only asking the same privileges that are given to others – to citizens, so-called citizens of this country – we are the aboriginee, which is not a citizen. That will make clear to you in that particular instance.

And it is the same up at Kingcome Inlet and river, and it is the same at Knight's Inlet and river. The same complaint all around. Mr. Ditchburn knows well that localoty [sic], and he knows those three or four big portions of our country there, that is the main livelihood of our Indians there, our Indians do not get anything only by fishing. Our men cannot make a living, and there is no money, and they have got to go off to the logging camps and log for their livelihood. But all men that are old and middle aged, the only thing they know is how to fish; they go up to Rivers Inlet, they go and fish up there; and they say they are handicapped there. And then at home that is all that they do. They only work during that six weeks or may be a little more, and that is all the work they have for the whole year for their living.

So that you will understand how very important this is.

Now, this is their complaint on the trolling; that an old Indian will have a canoe, with the canoe and paddle he will go off with one and some-times two lines, that is as much as he can manage to drag, two lines with a paddle, and paddle along and troll.

Well, there comes along a Jap with a gas boat, a powerful boat, and he will have a twenty foot rod in the back of his powerful boat, and every foot of that rod will have hooks, and that Jap will go along and he will drag those twenty hooks along there, and pass this one man in the canoe; and you can just imagine, yourself, how much fish he gets; but the Indian has got to pay the same license for his trolling that the other man does.

That makes us have a sense of injustice, and it has made a lot of trouble up there with the men that are put there to look after the regulations. It has made a lot of trouble, and it would make more of that if it was not that some of us said, Oh well, just keep on, keep going, because I think we will get justice just as soon. If it was not for that, I think we would have an awful lot of trouble from that.

Just these few little things to show how we stand up there, the sense of injustice we have,– that just because we are Indians we cannot get licenses for seining.

Mr. Kelly: I think it is time to adjourn, but I would like to have this taken notice of; I do not wish to close this fisheries question up without arriving at something very definite. I would like tomorrow morning to have some very definite proposals in connection with the fisheries question recorded. We have been proceeding in the general way, and we could go on endlessly, because all the Indians feel the same way.[81]

Like many before and after her, G̱a'ax̱sta'las invoked decades of agitation over unsettled lands and rights. I heard an echo when I read O'Reilly's name and her reference to testimony at the McKenna-McBride Royal Commission hearings. O'Reilly had "explicitly included fishing rights" for each reserve allocation, and the commissioners had been sympathetic to calls for fishing rights.[82] In 1923, aboriginal fishers were still unable to obtain independent licences, in good part because cannery operators feared that they might raise fish prices and that such a move would "confirm [their] fishing rights."[83] The Department of Fisheries had moved away from cannery licences toward issuing independent licences. Although, by law, canneries were supposed to hire "Native" fishers first, most of the licences went to Japanese fishers, a point emphasized in G̱a'ax̱sta'las's testimony.[84] Her words attest to the ever shifting, racialized labour hierarchy in British Columbia. The Canadian head tax imposed on Chinese immigrants in 1900 and 1903 had reduced their presence at canneries where jobs were quickly taken up by aboriginal women. According to Douglas Harris, Japanese fishers "depended entirely on cannery employment and housing." In contrast to Kwakwa̱ka̱'wakw workers, who had footholds in 'na̱'mima-centred economies, these workers were vulnerable to coercive immigration policy and were thus a more malleable work force.[85] By 1923, the department's goal was to reduce the Japanese fleet by 15 percent, a move that reflected the government's "intention to encourage white settlement."[86]

G̱a'ax̱sta'las pressed the government to give aboriginal fishers access to seine net licences, which were then available only to cannery operators (Japanese fishers) and "white fish processors."[87] Since 1902, aboriginal fishers had been able to acquire only gill-net or drift-net licences. As Harris notes, during the 1915-16 season, no gill-net licences were issued in areas where seine nets were used.[88] G̱a'ax̱sta'las's emphasis on allowed technologies pointed to the inequalities. Her description of a powerful gas boat trailing a twenty-foot line threaded with twenty hooks evokes an image of a fisher paddling a canoe, dragging two lines in its wake. As G̱a'ax̱sta'las pointed out, the "Indian has got to pay the same license for his trolling" as the fisher in the gas boat. Her words on licensing seemed to contain a veiled warning that further confrontations with fisheries officers were likely.

As she did at the McKenna-McBride hearings, Jane Cook stood up again for rights to the Nimpkish River. Indeed, her testimony was, in part, a brief resource history of that river. Railing against the need for a permit to fish upstream, she noted that the Beaver Cove Cement & Pulp Company intended to dam the Nimpkish. As she stated, other rivers in their territories were already dammed, and "no fishes go up there, the fishes are just gone." The disintegration of aboriginal fishing rights was framed largely through the rhetoric of conservation, and Ga'axsta'las gave evidence about how industry was damaging salmon runs in her district. She appealed for removal of a dam at Scott's Cove "so that the fishes can come back there again."

Ga'axsta'las's testimony included the vivid image of Kwakwaka'wakw men sitting on beaches watching others fish their foreshores. The men had no hope of consideration for employment and were anxious about obtaining food fish and other staples for the following year. Despite testimony given during the McKenna-McBride Royal Commission, restrictions on food fish had remained essentially unchanged since the 1894 edict that fish could be caught "for no other purpose" than to feed fishers and their families. If "Indians" were caught selling fish, their permits would be revoked. By 1917, regulations were in place to "fix the places, methods, and timing of the food fishery." Fishers had the onus of proving that the fish they sold had not been caught under a food fish permit. Conservation measures were added for sites such as spawning grounds, and persons who bought fish caught with a food fish permit could also be found guilty of an infraction.[89] Localities, fishing methods, and times were at the whim of fisheries officers.

Ga'axsta'las's demands for the right to food fish *and* to participate in the commercial fishery were folded into statements about citizenship. Kwakwaka'wakw people had observed the success of non-aboriginal fishers, and their sense of injustice intensified in the knowledge that the situation existed "just because we are Indians." The dominion government made the franchise universal in 1920 but did not extend it to aboriginal peoples and selected minorities. The First World War had ushered in a public discourse about citizenship, and these leaders, in their struggle for aboriginal title, obviously tapped into it, emphasizing their native-born status at a time when "aliens," "Celestials" and "Bolsheviks" occupied the Anglo-Saxon imagination.[90] Perhaps it was more pertinent, though, that they were sitting at the table with the man who had singularly pushed for compulsory enfranchisement through Bill 14 in 1920.[91]

Duncan Campbell Scott's amendment allowed the DIA to cancel the status of "an Indian against his will following a report by a person appointed by the superintendent general on his suitability."[92] Media attention swelled, and the "Indian response" to the amendment was hostile. Among those who attended the seventeen meetings held in Ottawa to discuss Bill 14 was Arthur O'Meara, legal counsel for the Allied Tribes. Three months after these meetings, a statement by the Allied Tribes was read to Parliament: "The bill would break up the tribes, destroy Indian status, and undermine native land claims." They wanted "to obtain the vote and citizenship while retaining their lands and status."[93] Mackenzie King's Liberal government came to power in 1921. By June 1922, Scott's notorious amendment had been swept away.[94]

Douglas Harris has outlined the demands set forth by the Allied Tribes in 1923 regarding fishing. I paraphrase his work here. They sought the right to fish for food anywhere in the province, to troll for salmon in tidal waters without a permit, and to sell fish at will. They demanded seine-net licences with a half-price reduction on the licensing fee. They asked for exclusive rights to seine fish on foreshores and at river mouths within reserved lands. Regarding foreshores, Peter Kelly demanded that the Crown confirm title to the low tide mark at reserve beaches, noting that no residual discrimination should affect access to the foreshore.

In 1924, they won a partial victory when the government removed restrictions to seine licences. Three new reserves – fishing stations – were allotted in response to the Allied Tribes' conference, two in Kwakwa̱ka̱'wakw territories and one in Tsimshian territories.[95] Obtaining independent salmon and herring and seining licences was the only "concrete result coming from agitation and pressure." As Forrest LaViolette notes, "it was possibly the beginning of the change in the economic status of Indians on the coast, for they could now become independent fishermen and entrepreneurs in that industry."[96]

The decision paved the way for the establishment of the Cook fleet. Gilbert Cook's son told me that Stephen Cook "had a commercial concession for catching spring salmon on the mouth of the Nimpkish River ... it was the earliest time they were fishing over there for spring salmon with a drag seine. Then he was selling them, whatever he had, from the commercial concession there." According to the "Cook Calendar," "Stephen started fishing, acquiring the seiner, *Pearl C* [1924], later attaining a larger vessel the *Winifred C.* He started his sons in the fishing industry, Reg owning the *Cape Lazo,* Gilbert the *Cape Cook,* Chris the *Kitgora,* and Herbert the *C.N.* Stephen and his sons fished for the Canadian Fishing Co., Stephen himself being associated with that firm for 35 years." "Papa Cook," as he is known, eventually "had a wharf with a general store at the road end (later a saltery and a net loft also), an Imperial Oil station adjacent to the wharf and a fur-buying station. Buyers would come up from Vancouver once or twice a year. Cook also operated a fish-buying camp for mainly troll-caught salmon in Blackney Pass on the east end of Parson Island."[97]

Kwakwa̱ka̱'wakw chiefs came to be the principal owners and operators of the seiners that supplied fish under commercial contracts as well as food fish for their families and other villagers. As Paul Tennant notes, the social organization of fishing was an important factor "in shaping and supporting coastal political activity."[98] G̱a'a̱xsta'las and her family played significant roles in subsequent forms of political organizing around fisheries. "I think her influence over her family and the community was enormous," George Speck told me. "Her involvement with the Allied Tribes and land issues probably laid the foundation for her children's involvement with the Pacific Coast Native Fishermen's Association and, later, the Native Brotherhood. The Native Brotherhood was formed up north, but the Pacific Coast Fisherman's Association was on the central Coast here. They were very deeply involved in that."

It is difficult to ignore the contrast between the initial prosperity that came with participation in commercial fisheries and the present concerns of residents in 'Ya̱lis about failure of the food fishery. In our conversations, Pearl Alfred approached the fishery through health.

"What are the main health issues now?" I asked her.

"Well," Pearl began with a sigh, "I think that a lot of our issues are drug-related now. And I think that's going to be the norm until we get a handle on it. And the kids – I think, in a sarcastic way, we're used to being poor in terms of our diet, but we all love Kraft Dinner, and that's where the fish thing is important. When you talk about fish to kids, it's fish sandwiches that they want – fish and peanut butter. Kids are all going to school without proper breakfasts. What we're going to go without is the fish sandwiches. I don't think we're going to be in quite the same shape as some of the communities along the Fraser [River], where they would make a lot of money from selling fish, like whole families. Whereas here there might be half a dozen guys that are selling fish, there it's almost all of them. So, it's a different kind of scene at home. I think the kids will be the ones to pay."[99]

T̓sa̱ka̱'atsi (Hospital) – "For Indians Only"

Pearl Alfred's thoughts on health reminded me of aboriginal peoples' continuous struggle to attain adequate medical care in a white settler society, a struggle articulated during the McKenna-McBride Royal Commission and repeated by the executive of the Allied Tribes in 1923, when Pearl Alfred's grandmother spoke about the need for Indian-only hospitals. The Allied Tribes had agreed to accept the McKenna-McBride Commission's revised report only if a number conditions were met: general compensation for lands surrendered, the establishment and maintenance of an adequate system of education, and establishment and maintenance of an adequate system of medical aid and hospitals.[100]

Andrew Paull told Scott and Ditchburn, "the idea [is] that the money to be expended for medical attention will all be borne by the Government of Canada. That is what is in our mind."[101] The small missionary-run hospital at 'Ya̱lis had been destroyed by fire that year, and Paull spoke about the inadequacy of the single remaining hospital at Rivers Inlet. Ambrose Reid mentioned tuberculosis and noted that Indians were not welcome at Tranquille, the sanatorium near Kamloops: "I never knew of any one particular case where an Indian has been admitted to Kamloops, that is from the Coast," he said. "You are correct," Ditchburn replied, "they do not take them in they say they have plenty of white people on the road." Duncan Scott turned immediately to the question of title. "I understand from the remarks, and from the bearing of Sub-Section 2 of the 16th Clause, that you would expect the establishment and maintenance of an adequate system of medical aid and hospitals as part of the compensation of the cession of the aboriginal title?" "Yes," Jane Cook replied. "That matter would be given careful attention by the Government," said Scott.[102]

Scott reminded the Allied Tribes representatives about provisions in the Indian Act pertaining to health "and the treatment of communicable diseases." "Under the Act," he said, "we would have the right to – I don't want to use the word incarcerate – to take an Indian as having tuberculosis or any communicable disease and place him in a hospital ... we usually make use of the hospitals established for white persons. And upon the whole I think that is the best policy."[103]

Ambrose Reid told Scott, "They do not get very satisfactory treatment."

"My experience of the matter has been that," Jane Cook confirmed. "That is the policy of the Indian Department, that when an Indian needs medical attention, and it is a bad case, he will be sent to a hospital near by. And there is a grant given to that hospital; and the Indians pay for themselves in most cases. But we have found that they are not wanted there. They are not wanted in those hospitals; they may take them in for a few days, but after a few days they are told 'Well, you can go home as soon as you like' – and of course if you tell an Indian they are well enough to go home they will go home right away. But they are made to feel they are not wanted there and it is better for them to go home.

"I speak from experience, as we have a hospital at Alert Bay under the Coast Mission there. And we have found, and the doctors that have been in the hospital have told me repeatedly, 'Mrs. Cook, the only way you can do is to ask the Indian Department to put up a little hospital, it does not matter how small, even cottages, that will take in these Indians, because I cannot find nurses that will come in here and are willing to nurse the Indians in these hospitals.' And another thing, he says, we find that the white people, you see – that is central hospital in that locality – the white people coming in there are afraid of these contagious diseases that the Indians might have.

"And another thing is that they have to take in so many maternity cases, and the maternity cases are afraid knowing that there are Indians in the hospital. And so they find that difficulty. It got so serious at one time that we really thought of collecting money individually. Mr. Anthony made me offer that if I would collect the money he would furnish an outstanding that they have out there, where we could put the Indians cases, so they would not be in the same building with the white people's cases.

"And that is the way we have found it in our part of the country. And every doctor that we have had there has put that up to me, that I must start and try to get a hospital of our own, for Indians only; and he says that is the only thing that will work out, and the only way to do it. He said that nurses that come to such a hospital, understanding that they have to nurse the Indians, that they will stay there. That is why we have not found the hospitals satisfactory up there around that locality and Kwawkewlth Agency."[104]

"I wish to confirm what my lady friend has said," Cowichan representative John Elliot stated. "I took sick one time of Typhoid fever, and I was sent to the Nanaimo Hospital; I was sent there against my will, I knew if I went to the hospital I would not get attended as I ought to ... Honourable sir, I thank my lady friend for her stand; and in view of what she says, it ought to be attended to; and I think we ought to have hospitals on the Indian reserves."[105]

Such requests had been made before. In 1914, 'Na̲mgis chief Lagius told the commissioners that "although there is a hospital at Alert Bay, it is not an Indian hospital ... I have found from time to time that if one is too poor to pay for himself at the hospital ... that the Doctor is not good enough ... The Doctor don't appear to want to take them in."[106]

Throughout the early years of the agency, DIA correspondences focussed especially on the question of who would pay for medical attention. George Blenkinsop's expenditures list in 1881 included "shoes for a sick Indian," "milk for a sick child," and "rent of room for sick Indians for three months."[107] In 1895, agent Richard Pidcock was instructed to charge Indians a one-dollar consultation fee as well as the price of medicine.[108] In 1902, Kwawkewlth Agency residents were questioned by the Indian Agent, George DeBeck, about their ability to pay hospital charges. Doctors in Victoria received "so much a month to attend to the indigent sick Indians who may be in need of relief."[109] Arthur Vowell, commissioner, instructed DeBeck that "such an expensive place for treatment" (the hospital) was only for "grave cases or those of great emergency where life is immediately threatened."[110] On rare occasions, ill and injured people were sent to St. Joseph's in Victoria. Later, they were evacuated by steamer to Bella Bella, to the Rivers Inlet Hospital. By 1904, Alert Bay had a small Church Mission Society (CMS) hospital. In December that year, a voucher for cash was issued to Mrs. Kamano and James Provet "for services rendered in nursing and caring for a sick man" in the village.[111]

Financed by BC Packers, the provincial government, the DIA, the Women's Auxiliary, and by individual Kwakwa̲ka̲'wakw donors, St. George's Hospital opened in 'Ya̲lis in 1909. "Having no word in the Kwak'wala language for such an institution, the Indians called [it] *t̓sa̲ka̲'atsi,* which means "a container for the sick."[112] Dr. Anderson attended to patients at hospital, and Dr. Ryall visited villages along the Coast in the *Columbia,* the Anglican medical steamer. Testimony at the hearings indicates that the hospitals did not welcome Indians. St. George's had a separate ward. Tuberculosis, of course, also affected non-aboriginal people, but it is evident from G̲a'ax̲sta'las's testimony that the disease was racialized, leading to exaggerated fears of contagion.[113]

At the 1923 meeting with Duncan Campbell Scott, discussions about medical aid included personal anecdotes from several Allied Tribes leaders. Andrew Paull chastised what he called "Castor Oil Doctors."[114] Ambrose Reid suggested staffing the office of the Indian Agent with physicians. Peter Kelly recommended "that instead of the Department paying certain doctors so much per annum that they be paid for the visits they make, for the actual work they do." When Kelly later tried to add to the record "A Petition Sponsored by the British Columbia Anti-Tuberculosis League," Scott said, "Let us take it as read, and hand it in; because we have a copy of it too."[115]

Scripted consciously in the context of ever-expanding non-aboriginal settlement in BC, the petition appears in the transcript of the 1923 meeting as follows:

> "WHEREAS WE, the undersigned, view with greatest apprehension and alarm, the great amount of Tuberculosis prevailing in its different forms among the Indians of the coast of British Columbia, which has for a long time been a menace, both to Indians unaffected, and to the white people settled on this coast;
>
> "AND WHEREAS the Government of this Dominion and of this Province have in view extensive immigration plans for the settlement of this Province, as well as other portions of Canada;
>
> "AND WHEREAS there are no Tuberculosis Hospitals on this Coast for treatment and segregation of active cases particularly among the Indians and consequently such cases die in their homes surrounded by their families and many friends, who, through sympathy and long custom congregate about the deathbed some time before death, thereby being affected;
>
> "AND WHEREAS a careful report on this appalling condition of affairs compiled by the Medical Superintendent of the Alert Bay Hospital, covering the total population (men, women & children) of six tribes was sent to the late Government, and is on file for reference;
>
> "WE, the undersigned, consider that the bringing of such immigrants to the Province, and settling them on this Coast while the above

mentioned conditions are prevailing, would prove abortive if the public, both in Eastern Canada and abroad, became acquainted with the facts;

"WE, the undersigned, also believe that the establishment of such hospitals, exclusively for Indians would not only stem the spread of the disease among the Indians, but would also safeguard the lives of settlers who contemplate settling in the Province. Such hospitals, we believe, should be built on one of the plateaus on the Coast with which the Indians are familiar, and which are on their regular boat routes as it has been proved that it is difficult to get them to go to the Interior so far from their homes."

"BE IT THEREFORE RESOLVED that we, the undersigned, do most respectfully and earnestly petition you to use your utmost power to have action taken in this matter."

(Signed by 213 Indians.)

(*NOTE.* Signatures from the Naas, Bella Coola, Bella Bella, Powell River, Campbell River, Valdes Island, Churchouse, Simoen Sound and Central Vancouver Sections are still to come in, and will be added.[116])

According to a Canadian Tuberculosis Association survey conducted on behalf of the DIA in 1926-27, tuberculosis was five times more common among aboriginal people in BC than among the general population.[117] Oral histories attest to its lethal presence across the generations. "Oh, TB killed lots of people here. It killed a lot, a lot of people," Jane Cook's daughter-in-law Ilma Wirki told me. She was fourteen years old when she arrived in Alert Bay from the Finnish community of Sointula. It was 1929, and she worked in St. George's Hospital.

"Yeah, lots of TB. I guess that's about the only thing – the only disease that was killing people. The others, they were just measles and mumps and childhood illnesses, children's disease. Treatment was nothing different from somebody else. They didn't even isolate them. They were in the same room with other patients. And when a woman had a baby, they just took her from the case room into the ward, and there'd be TB patients in there. Until they built the preventorium – and then they were kept isolated. But that was years after. I don't remember when that preventorium was built – but after 1929. The [residential] school opened the fall of 1929, and they built that preventorium. And anybody that they even suspected of having TB went into that facility. Is that building still there?" Ilma asked her daughter Vivian, who was present.

"No. It was ripped down about fifteen years ago," Vivian said.

"It wasn't all Indian people that had TB," Ilma continued. "But it was very much so with them because they lived in very big families. They all lived together. Well, the Cook family, for example, they all lived together, and so many times there would be somebody that died – like Grace and Alice and Ernie. Grace, I think, passed on with heart disease, but I know Alice and Ernie died of TB. I think the hospital was there to treat acute cases. That's why they stayed at home all the time, because they preferred staying at home with their own families rather than laying [in] the hospital. And there was no pills to take, no nothing. Just lie in bed. So why go to the hospital? Just like my sister. She had TB, and she was in Kamloops – Tranquille, just outside Kamloops. They had a TB hospital there. She was there over two years. Yeah, all they did there, too, was just bed rest and then trying, of course, to see that they ate properly. They [also] removed the lung that had infection. Nellie [Cook] and Georgie [Cook] are both living with one lung. They were operated on in Sardis. Nellie was operated on in St. Vincent's Hospital in Vancouver."

"You said the other day that many people, they just cared for the people who had TB at home," I said.

"Yes, that's right," Ilma said. "My in-laws were one of the families. Lots of them stayed at home rather than go to the hospital. Lots of water gone under the bridge."

I asked Ilma about Jane Cook's involvement with medical care.

"Granny Cook visited a lot and interpreted. She had to interpret because the Indian people, the old ones, didn't know how to speak English at all. They didn't understand anything. I don't recall that she'd be visiting the doctor for any other reason except interpreting. I know Granny Cook used to go – if she was needed, she would go and look after a woman or stay with a woman who was having a baby. Her own children had babies, and she looked after everybody."

When G̲a'ax̲sta'las attended the Allied Tribes' meeting with DIA officials, she had recently lost her thirty-year-old daughter, Alice, to tuberculosis. Her son Stephen had also died of the disease in 1911.[118] The Allied Tribes' call for Indian-only hospitals on the Coast was not met. In 1938, St. Michael's Preventorium was built by residential school pupils as a manual-training project. The eighteen-bed facility became a home for too long, to too many children in 'Ya̲lis. Today, its presence is not acknowledged by the federal government.

Ilma Wirki was employed at St. George's Hospital after a new building was floated in from Port Hardy. "It was a very busy place, with the logging industry," she told us. "And there was no airplane service to get them to Victoria or whatever. So they had to go on the steamer – steamboat. You had to wait until they came from up north and they picked the patient up. And so many of them died on their way to Vancouver. But it was a very busy hospital – lots of babies being born, six or seven in one day, one twenty-four [hour] period."

During the opening ceremony of the hospital in 1925, the Reverend John Antle was presented with $1,500, cash donated by 'Mi'mkwa̲mlis and 'Ya̲lis residents to buy an X-ray machine.[119] A representative of the lieutenant-governor attended the ceremonies, and Chief Owaxa̲-laga̲lis "took the opportunity to implore [him] to restore the potlatch ... and delivered yet another petition on behalf of seven Southern Kwakiutl tribes."[120] Later that year, G̲a'ax̲sta'las wrote and submitted a petition on behalf of potlatchers asking for a "relaxation" of section 149 of the Indian Act.[121]

"After Consultation": Representing Potlatchers

Andrew Paull met with Kwakwa̲ka̲'wakw potlatchers a month after the Allied Tribes met with Scott in Victoria. Before his visit, Edwin DeBeck advised Moses Alfred that "[Paull] is just as much interested in the Potlatch as you are yourself, and is very strongly in favour of it."[122] Paull later appealed to Scott "to grant [Mark Seewid] permission to conduct a Potlatch, that is to relive himselve to his fellowmen by giving it back to them such articles as he formerly received from them..."[123] He included a list of the property to be re-distributed and wrote that "Jim Humchit is also seeking permission to give a feast to the people of his own tribe."

Obviously neither were granted because three months later, G̲a'ax̲sta'las wrote on behalf of the Ławits'is man.

Alert Bay, B.C. November 17 1923

Dr. Scott
Deputy Super. Indian Affairs

Dear Sir,

I beg to remind you that Mark Seewid is anxiously awaiting a letter from you to a solution of his potlach problems. This is the Indian who has a great amount of goods on hand, hundreds of Camphor Boxes, Embroidery Blankets, Furniture, Sewing machines, Gold Jewelery and crockery glassware and Enamel ware. Big portion of this he has been carting around for 6 yrs. preparing up to the time when the Sec 149 was enforced. You will remember that when I brought this case to you attention you agreed that something ought to be done about it and you kindly promised to consider this case and write me when you had decided. This man is patiently waiting, but tells me that he is tired of worrying about it and gets quite desperate sometimes.

If you will kindly consider this case and let us know he will appreciate it very much. As he says that to carry these goods over another Winter is too much for him as some of it is getting spoiled. I hope, you will be able to solve his difficulty for him for he has certainly tried to be loyal to the Law.

Yrs. Faithfully

Jane Cook[124]

Halliday was evidently approached to solve the problem, as he wrote to Ditchburn two months later: "Mrs. Cook, who was a delegate on behalf of the Indians to Vancouver, says that this matter was taken up personally with you and Dr. Duncan C. Scott and that you promised him that something would be done. I informed them that up to the present moment I had heard nothing about it but that I would write to you and see what promise you had made to him if any."[125] "In reply," Ditchburn wrote, "I beg to say that while I feel certain Dr. Scott had a discussion with Mrs. Cook in regard to potlatching material I did not take part in the same ... On the last day [he] remained for some time and I think it was then that he and Mrs. Cook talked over the potlatch material subject."[126]

Ditchburn advised Halliday to write to Scott. He did so a week later: "Mrs. Cook, who was the Interpreter at the time, says that she told you that even if this material was purchased that Seaweet could do nothing else but give away the money as he would feel that this property was not his own but belonged to the people who would in the course of affairs received it at the potlatch. Would you kindly advise me whether you made any such promise to him or not and if so what is intended to be done about it."[127]

A letter from Halliday to Scott written six days later reflects a turn in DIA policy. The bureaucrats were cautious not to leave potlatchers dependent on government relief.

In the usual manner of the Indians this man is wasting this time waiting for a reply ... personally I think it would be a great mistake to

> allow him any latitude ... He says that he is in duty bound to give this stuff to various people as he says it is a potlatch debt which he owes. I told him that if he wanted to do that there was nothing in the Indian Act to prevent him giving a distribution to each man individually, either by having him come and take his stuff away or by Seaweet himself carrying it to the individuals to whom he felt he owed it but I warned him that he could not call the people together and hold any ceremony or celebration in connection with it. I explained to him that in the payment of debts it was not necessary to do anything of that kind.[128]

Duncan Campbell Scott replied: "You may inform Seaweet that he may distribute these articles to the proper persons, it being understood, however, that no further obligation shall be incurred by the recipients thereof. Please make it clear that this distribution is to be absolutely final. I may add that this course has been decided upon after consultation with the representatives of the Allied Tribes who have been here."[129]

G̲a'ax̲sta'las was a diligent representative of the Allied Tribes and later acted as secretary and interpreter for "Indians of the Kwakwelth Agency who are asking for relaxation of the Section of the Act re the Potlatch."[130] She sent a detailed petition composed from a series of meetings to Andrew Paull, who in turn submitted it to Scott. According to the petition penned by G̲a'ax̲sta'las, the potlatch

> is a system for recording among ourselves the marriage names of the different Indians, and the means of declaring the standing socially of any individual, also the recording by witnesses of any important event in the course of our lives ...
>
> The enforcement of Section 149 of the Act ... leaves us all indebted to one another, and causes us to be ashamed to look at one another in the face all of which is no fault of ours which is very demoralizing according to our way of thinking ...
>
> To [give away] is considered criminal, the announcing of a marriage or a birth is considered immoral and a crime, and from the Indian view point we have no way of doing things in a highly moral way therefore we feel degraded and ashamed, as we have not yet attained the civilization that our children will attain and here is no hope for the old people to even attain that ...
>
> The relief that they get from the Indian Agent cannot keep them alive which amounts to about $2.00 per month also the orphans who would have received the benefits that their deceased parents would

have received are deprived of receiving the same, the ill and bed ridden have not the assurance of their livelihood, and we have no means of enforcing the Government to totally support these people ...

Our recreations that we used to practice, also the manufacture of masks, totem poles Etc. are on the verge of being forgotten because we are not allowed to practice the ceremonies which is related ... We are afraid that anything we may do may be interpreted as an infraction of Section 149 of the Indian Act ...

(After a series of meetings, the same being interpreted by Mrs. S. Cook, who forwarded the above to A. Paull.)[131]

G̱a’ax̱sta’las’s continuing respect for the law is evident in this statement and in her earlier support for Mark Seewid. Her keen ability to expose contradictions in colonial regulations and her focus on her people’s material circumstances were consistent stands that characterized her political career. By this time, she was particularly concerned about the criminalization of her people.

At their 1923 meeting, the Allied Tribes added to their list of demands the “provision of mother’s and widow’s pensions comparable to those provided for white women by the Province.”[132] Given G̱a’ax̱sta’las’s history of agitation, it is difficult to imagine that she did not have a significant role in drafting this request. By 1924, the federal and provincial governments had formally adopted the McKenna-McBride Commission’s report.

Like her colleagues on the executive, G̱a’ax̱sta’las’s public struggle to realize aboriginal rights seems to have been stalled after 1927.

The Allied Tribes sent a petition to Parliament for their case to be heard in the British Privy Council, but a joint committee found “no real basis in fact to the claims of aboriginal right in British Columbia ... [They] recommended $100,000 per annum ... be provided the Indian Department ... in lieu of ‘treaty monies.’” Most significantly, “the natives [were] advised that no further contributions of funds be made to continue presentation of claims now decisively disallowed.”[133] Section 141 of the Indian Act was amended in 1927 to make it a serious offence to solicit funds for the purpose of prosecuting an Indian claim against the government. Pushing for aboriginal title was criminalized.

The same year, Jane and Stephen Cook experienced the death of their eldest child, Grace (Ťłaḵwa’it), at thirty-eight.[134] Her eight children moved into the Cook big house until their father, Jeff Warren, remarried in 1929.

"There Was Eight of Us": G̲a'ax̲sta'las as Grandmother

"Well. It was a long time ago, I'm telling you." Jeane Lawrence sat with Pearl Alfred and me in November 2004. She is one of Grace Cook's daughters who, along with her seven siblings, moved into the Cook big house in 1927.

"When our mother passed away, we were young, the three of us, last girls or however you put it – Vera, Emma, and myself. I think we were two and a half, three and a half, and four and a half. She got very sick, and they took her to the hospital. And that was just what we were told. We never inquired into more in those days. There was lots of that TB but, as far as I gathered, it wasn't that. And then all of a sudden we were packed up to Granny's. So Granny, she just packs us all up, and away we go to the big house. We were just little fellas.

"We lived down in the village. Well, in those days there was BA oil dock and an old sawmill, but we stayed on with Granny. And she looked after us, just included us in the brood with all hers. There was eight of us. There was Girly and Stevie, Eddie, Mary, and there was a John that was lost, got sick, Emma, Vera, and myself. And, of course, Granny had her family too.

"Granny taught us all kinds of things. She had a big garden. You wouldn't know it today, though, would you? But, you know, we'd go and help her feed the chickens up there. We'd help her weed the garden. And she still had time to feed everybody. And Papa was there, too, but he always had his suit on and hands in his pockets. Papa always got our breakfast. He called us all boys, eh?" She laughed.

"We were all boys, and we'd have porridge and Cream of Wheat, or we even had rice. And there was whatever we wanted, butter and jam. 'One at a time,' he always said. We couldn't have the jam with the butter. It didn't matter. But we tried anyway. 'One at a time now, boys.' That was his big deed.

"Cooking breakfast for everybody." Pearl Alfred laughed too.

Jeane continued. "He was the boss, the chief I guess you'd call him. And then they had the store down below. He looked after that. And there was a saltery there, too. Japanese were running it at that time. But they had quite a business, mostly family business, I guess, with the store and people looking after it. I can always remember our Christmases there. It was nothing to have a hundred people sitting around the dining room table, eh? And we all would help get everything ready, and you'd all sit down, and there you are – the turkey, everything."

"Six turkeys!" Pearl called out.

"Oh! And did she ever smoke fish in that smokehouse! Sometimes you could hardly see. The fish was hanging in there, and they were really smoking.

"We were used to eating all that Indian food, eh? I remember sitting around the round table there, and the big pot there with the clams and seaweed and grease, and it was so good. But now I couldn't get to it again because it keeps coming up. It's because you get away from that type of food. I guess if I had to do it, I'd go and do it all over again." She laughed.

"There was always lots of good stuff, and we enjoyed helping, doing the tables. And I think Pearlie or Winnie or somebody would bang away a little bit and play a couple of little songs on the piano there. I remember the piano. We used to try to sit there ourselves, and still today I've got no tune. I can't play.

"And, of course, the family was getting bigger and bigger. Like her boys and Winnie and Pearlie, they were all having a family down the line. I can remember when one of Nellie's babies was born there – only we probably didn't even know then where these babies were coming from.

"But anyway, Granny said, 'I've got a surprise for you' one morning. We were pretty young, and it was Francis. She brought her out in a shoebox, wrapped in cotton batting, and there she was! No bigger than a pound of butter! Oh! It was so nice. And I don't even think that Nellie went to the hospital."

"Do you remember G̲aga?" I asked.

"I only just remember her. G̲aga was Papa's mother, but the one I used to remember more would be the old Mrs. Whonnock down the hill. See, I think older ones would remember G̲aga more than [me], because when you're only five years or six ... But this Mrs. Whonnock, I guess, would be doing the same things as G̲aga – like smoking the fish and doing all this around the fires. Now, she was such a nice old lady, too. I don't know whether you've ever heard or anybody has mentioned –"

Jeane turned and said, "You probably remember, Pearlie. If you needed an Indian doctor, or somebody like this, and especially when you've got something in your eye, then you had to go to Mrs. Whonnock. And they used their tongue to get it out, you know? And then you're all number one again. Away you go. But when I mention it again now, I think – Oh, never mind, we're all better. We're all fixed up, hey?" She laughed.

"That's just as good as how they treated thrush," Pearl said. "They took a fresh baby diaper and put it on the mouth, like the urine. I don't know what is in urine. Whatever it is, it worked."

Jeane replied, "In those days, everybody was pretty healthy then too. But I do remember when, if you got sick or something, there was a bed in Granny's room – Granny and Papa's room – and that was sort of, you might say, sick bay, where sometimes you'd probably try to make yourself sick to see if you could get in there. But I know, this one time, I had the whooping cough. They thought, the end of her is coming, but it didn't, and I got to go in there. And boy oh boy, you'd get special treatment in there. Just so affectionate and nice, you know, and she treated everybody like that – the same. Nobody was any better, all of us guys. And then, after, when you're kind of close to getting better – I do remember, she was great for making homemade brown beans and homemade bread, of course. I knew I was better then, because I could eat that.

"Yeah, oh gosh, her homemade bread. They were about this long, the loaves." Her hands gestured out two feet.

"And her daughter, I call her Aunty Emma, but Mrs. Kenmuir, lived down by the church. And so one of us or two of us would deliver it to her. I think once a week. And that was a big deal, too. We were allowed down the hill, and away we'd go. We could hardly pack this bread." She laughed. "But she made that bread for Aunty Em – up until the day that Granny died ...

"When Dad married Vera, I think it was 1929 or something, I think she came to work as a maid for the Indian Agent – Halliday in Alert Bay. They had maids, you know, for Mr. and Mrs. Halliday. You know, she'd get their meals or do this. She was very young in those days. Granny said, 'Today, you're going to have a nice lady come. And she's coming with your dad, and they have a place in Alert Bay. And you'll be probably going with them.' Of course, by this time *[pausing]*, my little brain is working away. 'Uh, I don't know about this.'

"And the old steamboat used to come into Papa's wharf. And when *that* steamboat came in, I wasn't anywhere. I went up those big tanks, those ESSO tanks. I thought, I'm not going. And there were those big ladders going up there, and I stayed up there. And they were looking for me. And, of course, by that time I was crying. And they found me. But the thought of going ...

"And Granny was just happy to see me. 'You just stay here as long as you like. You don't have to ... whatever.' I was happy then, so I stayed on. I don't know if Emma and Vera went right away. I think so. I don't know. I just continued on at Granny's, going to school and doing whatever, hey? Eventually, down the years, I was kind of thinking – Well, she's a pretty nice lady, too." She laughed.

"I don't tell that [story] lots of times. But I do remember that, and I was pretty young. And it's probably something that I should never have been doing because we were warned, 'Stay off those ladders.' But I just thought, my mind was thinking, 'What's this going to be?' I guess I was about five, maybe six."

PART VII
"With the Potlatch Custom in My Blood," 1930-39

"She's my great-grandmother," Kelly-Anne Speck began. "She died, obviously, many years before I was born, so there's no first-hand knowledge of her. And yet, when I was growing up, she was like this continuing presence in the family. People were always talking about her. People talked about her in terms of the family – typical stories about things that might have happened in a family event, or something, but there were other people who, obviously, had grown up in the house while she was alive. Emma, who came and lived at the house. Uncle Si used to talk about her all the time ... There was this, sort of, larger than life [pausing] ... And later, you came to understand that people were making comments and criticism about her involvement opposing the potlatch – or the ongoing potlatch practice at that point. That was something that really came much, much later."

"It was more her work as a member of the community and in the church. People would talk about her from the point of view of being with people when they were ill, actually going out to other villages and doing some of that work, being with people when they died. I can remember my mom saying, 'You know, we were there, and the message came that so and so was very near the end, and then she'd go off to be with them.' So, there was this sense that she had a role around caregiving for people that was recognized by the community."

Kelly-Anne and I spoke for a time about the criticisms of her great-grandmother that circulated as she was growing up. Like others, she commented on the power that the published record continues to have.

"There are a lot of people who didn't necessarily oppose the [anti-potlatch] laws, but they might not have been written up." She continued: "So, it's a little bit easier to not have to own that as part of the history, because it's just not written up there. But to me, that's actually some of the fascination I have for this person. How does somebody become this [pausing] lightning rod for these issues? It speaks to me of somebody with an incredible amount of courage – to be able to stand up and know that people are going to – I mean, I've seen some of the stuff that's written, about knowing that her children, her grandchildren, were going to be penalized by the community and were being treated differently because of what people thought about her. There's a couple of references in some of the material about people not willing to do things with her kids and extend to them the same opportunities. So there's a sense of that separateness there, and it's certainly something that I grew up being aware of."

During years of conversations and meetings with family members, I listened to a range of opinions and sentiments. We were each finding and placing pieces of the biographical jigsaw into spaces that made sense. For those whose lives fit into that larger jigsaw, G̲a'ax̲sta'las's eventual stigmatization is a living manifestation of what has been "written up." Kelly-Anne Speck calls her great-grandmother a lightning rod for issues, and by the 1930s they already included aboriginal title, the right to access and sell fish, and the provision of adequate medical care. G̲a'ax̲sta'las had agitated against biased applications of colonial law, for the legal recognition of customary marriage practices, and, later, against the exploitation and destitution of women as marriage laws solidified. The most difficult issues, the ones that required the courage about which Kelly-Anne spoke, were surely those that involved the ongoing potlatch practice at that point.

Those who publicly challenge traditional authority are often faced with social and political dilemmas, but as aboriginal women scholars today note, such challenges may turn bitter when traditions are cast as counterpractices to colonialism and racism.[1] Joyce Green writes about tradition in this context:

> All societies have them; all venerate them. Not all members of a society are similarly faithful to them, nor are all societies monolithic in their identification and replication of them ... But tradition is neither a monolith, nor is it axiomatically good, and the notions of what practices were and are essential, how they should be practiced, who may

> be involved and who is an authority are all open to interpretation ... Unless we can have conversations about what traditions are, how they affect men and women in their gendered roles and what the implications of this are, we are moving a powerful socio-political critique off the table.[2]

G̱a’ax̱sta’las’s story evokes such conversations. Was her opposition to potlatch practices in her day potent enough to somehow erase her voice from the record of the anticolonial, aboriginal rights struggles of her day? It seems so.[3] Her acts of opposition eventually affected her family’s standing. By the late 1930s, G̱a’ax̱sta’las spoke about herself, her family, and other nonpotlatching Christians as “outcasts.” During a series of recorded church meetings intended to address the potlatch question, there is a shift in her demeanour, a shift that her granddaughter Pearl Alfred perceived as anger attributed to an unknown situation or event. G̱a’ax̱sta’las’s comments at these meetings touch on the relationships among Christian nonpotlatchers and (Christian or non-Christian) potlatchers. More unexpectedly, they offer insight into Jane Cook’s personal investment in the gendered mores of “the custom.” In her late sixties, she expressed regret about her own noninvolvement in Kwakwa̱ka̱’wakw marriage practices, which had had repercussions for her children.

From this distant place and time of writing, it appears that the 1930s ushered in a sharpened politics of tradition among Kwakwa̱ka̱’wakw peoples. Colonial structures were shifting too as more and more non-aboriginal people settled aboriginal territories and as resource industries acquired more influence. The church and the former Department of Indian Affairs (DIA), which had merged with the Department of Mines and Resources (DMR), struggled to respond to popular opinion and to changes within their own organizations.

The Anglican Church debated its stance on a number of matters; marriage and adult baptism posed problems, and, later, clergy were divided over the potlatch ban. At this crossroads, Ga’axsta’las stood firm. She argued against lifting the ban on the grounds that the custom was not compatible with the gospel. Interestingly, she gave two interviews with newspaper journalists that offer few hints of her opposition. The new generation of clergy was sorting through legal, theological, and cultural questions. St. Michael’s Residential School had opened and soon had two hundred students, most attending for ten months of the year. As more children were sent to school, their families relocated from distant villages to live at 'Ya̱lis, where they could see each other regularly and participate more easily in economic activities. The aboriginal commercial fishery was under way.

Within the Cook family, Jane and Stephen's sons were almost all married, and some were parents. Ernest, Gilbert, Herbert, Reg, Chris, and Cyril became working fishers, and Stephen owned and operated several boats. Aboriginal women were an established workforce inside the canneries, and the men either operated and owned seiners or were employed by other skippers. Seventy-six salmon canneries operated in coastal BC in 1929, but following the stock market crash and the Depression there were just forty-four.

By 1932, William Halliday, Duncan Campbell Scott, and William Ditchburn had retired from the Indian Affairs Branch. E.G. Newnham replaced Halliday temporarily and was relieved by Murray Todd, an Indian Agent who shared Halliday's zeal for prosecuting potlatchers. A new generation of colonial committees was struck, expert opinions were sought on particular subjects, and reports were written weighing in on questions about the proposed assimilation of Kwakwa̱ka̱'wakw peoples. Franz Boas made his last field trip to Tsax̱is and to 'Ya̱lis as 1930 turned to 1931. Interested in changes in the Kwak̓wala language, he spent a week working with G̱a'ax̱sta'las.

Franz Boas and the "Official Lady Interpreter"

Given Franz Boas's almost career-long attention to Kwakwa̱ka̱'wakw peoples, it is remarkable to consider both how little time he actually spent in their villages and how little his published work reflected the political, religious, and economic realities of those with whom he worked. During his first field trip in 1886, as an associate with the Royal Ethnographic Museum of Berlin, George Hunt was likely translating for Alfred Hall; Boas documented the mask of 'Nulis, G̱a'ax̱sta'las's grandfather; Indian agencies had been established; and three land commissions had already divided and re-divided portions of Kwakwa̱ka̱'wakw territories into reserves. By the time of his second fieldtrip in 1889, the Anglican mission was well established at 'Ya̱lis, G̱a'ax̱sta'las and Na̱ge were married, the Nisga'a Land Committee had been organized, and chiefs from throughout the province had launched protests against colonial land allotments. When Boas studied "physical characteristics" with the Jesup Expedition in 1897 and then returned in 1900, church services in 'Y<u>a</u>lis were conducted in both Kwak̓wala and English, canneries dotted the Coast, steamers plied the waters, the industrial school was operating, and the sawmill employed Chinese and Japanese labourers. Boas returned in 1914. By then, Jane Cook had testified at the McKenna-McBride Royal Commission, translated narratives for Edward Curtis, and pushed for legal recognition of potlatch marriages. Interested in social organization and winter ceremonials, Boas was again among the Kwagu'ł in 1923. He does not, however, mention the First World War, the formation of the Allied Tribes, or aboriginal participation in fisheries and church organizations in his publications.

When he returned for four weeks at the end of 1930, the Anglican Church counted among its Indian congregations in 'Y<u>a</u>lis and Mam<u>a</u>lili<u>ka</u>la 487 people (of a total of 511), including students at St. Michael's Residential School.[4] Although he acknowledged the mission's influence on language change, Boas was not interested in Kwakw<u>a</u>k<u>a</u>'-wakw Christianity. Perhaps this was because there were no services held in Tsa<u>x</u>is (Fort Rupert), Gwa'yasd<u>a</u>ms (Gilford Island), <u>K</u>alugwis (Turnour Island), and T'sadzis'nukw<u>a</u>ame (New Vancouver).[5]

Soon after he arrived in Tsa<u>x</u>is, Boas received a letter from anthropologist Ruth Benedict. "Dear Papa Franz, your description of feasts sounds as if Kwakiutl life were far from dead. Is it really surprisingly in the old style? It would be almost too good to be true. Still I hope that interest rates have been enough modified so that the Acculturation appropriation won't sink completely out of sight. It probably has already!"[6] There is a tension in Benedict's message. On the one hand, she seems pleased that feasts were conducted in the old style; on the other hand, she hopes that Boas will be able to measure cultural and economic change, one goal of his field trip. Her use of the phrase *acculturation appropriation* is interesting. Acculturation implies imposed change on the people of one society by those of another. Appropriation is the active and creative uptake of social, technological, or economic aspects of another society for one's own uses.[7] Today, appropriation is largely applied to the intellectual and commercial theft of indigenous knowledge by members of dominating societies. In 1930, anthropologists considered the phenomenon from another perspective. Anthropologist Margaret Blackman suggests that Boas's project to "resurrect memory cultures" overlooked what were actually creative processes of appropriation among Northwest Coast peoples, particularly for those of high rank renowned for innovation.[8]

Boas had returned to study expressions and styles of storytelling and the effects of English on the Kwak̓wala language. Julia Averkieva travelled with him. The Russian exchange student worked with Kwagu'ł and 'Na̱mgis women to study string games and compile "autobiographical" materials. They spent three weeks in Tsa̱xis and one week in 'Ya̱lis.[9]

Before arriving in Alert Bay, Boas wrote to William Halliday for advice about whom to employ as an interpreter: "Mrs. Jane Cook, the wife of Stephen Cook, Is a wonderfully good interpreter," Halliday wrote back. "And Charles Nowell who by rights belongs to Fort Rupert, is pretty well educated, and acts very often as court interpreter."[10] Before leaving for 'Ya̱lis, Boas wrote to the governor of British Columbia to report on an epidemic of dysentery at Alert Bay. "Dying patients are turned out of the hospital," he reported, and he also described "disastrous health conditions" largely "due to syphilis." Boas suggested treatment by "inoculation ... as has been done in Europe."[11]

When he arrived in 'Ya̱lis, Boas stayed with Agnes Cranmer, George Hunt's granddaughter and Dan Cranmer's wife. The day he arrived, he paid a "polite" visit to Halliday and – as he wrote to his son, Ernst – "had a controversy over the fact that I notified Victoria" about the dysentery outbreak. "Then I visited the ... female interpreter ... Today I worked with her again and it went well, the only difficulty being that she is not familiar with some old forms."[12]

Letters provide few details about Boas's work with G̱a'a̱xsta'las, but his tone was increasingly critical. At the end of his week in 'Ya̱lis, Boas again wrote to Ernst: "I worked all week with the official lady interpreter and cleared up some items ... The people say of her that she talks like a child, and right they are, as she makes this kind of mistake."[13] Ronald Rohner, who edited Boas's letters and diaries, came across notes about Jane Cook: "The following material is a criticism of the interpreter which I can't read. [Boas] mentions that the woman systematizes the language improperly and somehow makes mistakes in English too."[14]

Given his own struggle with Kwak̓wala and his continuous critique of George Hunt's grammar, it is difficult to know what Boas expected.[15] He had written to Ruth Benedict from Port Hardy that "the language has baffling problems. There is no *good* informant because all of them are satisfied with a variety of forms."[16] A few weeks later, he wrote to her again about his difficulties with Kwak̓wala: "Most orators talk so rapidly that I cannot follow it, except now and then. Anyway, I have my troubles with ordinary conversation ... many have the Indian habit of slurring over the ends of their words."[17] Boas urged Hunt to use what he saw as the correct orthography, that is, Boas's own style for how symbols and letters represent sounds in Kwak̓wala.[18] Evident in the two men's prolific correspondence over their forty-five-year collaboration is the problem of how to standardize the language – in written form, through grammatical rules, and in terms of standard meanings of words and concepts used by speakers.

When I spoke with the late Lorraine Hunt, a Kwak̓wala expert, in 2008, she was translating 'Na̱mg̱is material compiled by Boas and Hunt into standard U'mista orthography. I sent her a copy of the notes Boas took while he worked with Jane Cook in 1931.[19] The notes consist of forty-six pages of word lists with ticks at the margin next to certain words. I asked Lorraine if she had trouble deciphering the words. "You can basically make them out *if* you can read his English," she said and laughed. "He's pretty good at picking out words because he's worked with it so long." I also sent Lorraine a copy of linguist Judith Berman's work about George Hunt and his Kwak̓wala texts.[20] "Judith Berman talks about [Boas] making fun of going to see [Jane Cook]," Lorraine said when we met again. "Why would he do that if he thought she didn't speak Kwak̓wala? It was a real puzzle."

Lorraine referred to comments in Helen Codere's 1966 introduction to *Kwakiutl Ethnography:* "Agnes Cranmer described how Boas got up from the table where he had been eating with them, and referring to his appointment ... smiled and said, 'Well I must go and increase my knowledge,' at which they and he all burst out laughing."[21] According to Judith Berman, the "joke" revolved around G̱a'a̱xsta'las's apparently not distinguishing among "shape classes" in Kwak̓wala – that is, the endings on words that describe whether an object is "bulky, long, flat, [or] dish-like."[22] As Berman notes, in everyday language at that time shape classes were already out of common use.

Upon returning to New York, Boas wrote to George Hunt: "As you know, I stayed for a week in Alert Bay. I was particularly interested to find out what has become of the language under the influence of English and so I spent quite a little while with Mrs. Jane Cook who is perhaps the best representative of that group."[23] Hunt replied soon after: "I was told that you went to see Mrs. Cook and I am glad that you found out that she knows lots of things of what she hears people talk about. But her Kwaguł language is Very short. I was told by her friends that she told them that I made up lots of new words. But I feels Proud that I know the old ways [then?] she is."[24] Revisiting these comments in 1994, Judith Berman suggested that the "made up" words might have been "old, disappearing words," words perhaps associated with "technologies and cultural practices" no longer in use.[25] Hunt used an "old fashioned," elaborated form of Kwak̓wala that he had learned from the age of nine by attending gatherings of chiefs and former chiefs in Tsax̱is. His letters to Boas suggest that it was the style of public oratory used at these early gatherings that shaped Hunt's Kwak̓wala repertoire. Certainly, everyday linguistic expression did not interest Boas until his 1930 field trip.

Lorraine Hunt told me, "There's a totally different language that you hear the chiefs saying in the Big House, in the old days, anyway, the chiefs that are gone now. But it's just changing all the time. It was all Kwak̓wala. People understand it, but they just use different words." Lorraine told me about going to a language workshop in Victoria called "The Ocean Is Our Highway." "They talked about the old days, travelling by canoe," she said. "There are lots of words that they used that are no longer used because we don't travel that way anymore. Winds, directions, the tides, that was language they used all the time."

Wedłidi Speck also spoke about technical vocabularies and used the example of legal terminology. "If you talk about basic right-and-wrong concepts in a community, and if you're talking about concepts that may be connected to constitutional constructs like usufructuary right and right of the sovereign, you know, it's different." His example is apt, for while Jane Cook had certainly been exposed to the legal vocabularies pertaining to aboriginal rights, her skills in ceremonial discourse suited a Christian context, where, as Wedłidi remarked, "she *was* unfolding the philosophy of religion in a significant way." Perhaps because he viewed it as inauthentic, Boas did not include the rhetoric of Christianity and political rights in serious study.

Several weeks after his return to New York, Hunt again mentioned G̱a'ax̱sta'las in a letter to Boas: "I am glad that you have found out the kind of woman Mrs. Cook is for she knows a lot. But she don't know a thing about the Potlatch for she never give once." What Boas might have found out about Jane Cook is unknown. Although he acknowledged that she knew a lot, Hunt criticized her lack of experience with the potlatch, his obvious advantage, given Boas's interest in the custom. In the same letter, Hunt told Boas about words he could not pin down, "for lots of the words is said means for lots of different meaning."[26]

Boas published a paper on Kwak̓wala language change a year later. "Most of my material was obtained from Mrs. Cook, who has been for a long time in close touch with the Mission and has talked a great deal about the language to the former missionaries without, however, having a very clear notion of grammatical concepts and of formal analysis. Her replies and corrections of texts were all given quite naively as a direct reflection of her feeling for correct usage."[27] Judith Berman found Boas's data "not sufficiently radical" enough to explain why contemporary speakers (from the 1970s to the 1990s) could not "understand Hunt's text material."[28] Looking at the Hunt-Boas correspondence, Berman suggested that G̲a'ax̲sta'las had likely not been fluent in the nineteenth-century formal vocabulary used by chiefs in potlatch ceremonials. It is difficult to speak with any certainty about the depth of Jane Cook's experience. George Hunt wrote that "she never gave a potlatch," and (following Helen Codere's comments) Berman noted that she was a "fervent Christian." "Even if she had been of high rank," Berman wrote, "these two conditions together effectively would have reduced her exposure to any special lexical domains connected to concerns of the nineteenth-century elite, as well as her exposure to oratorical style."[29]

G̲a'ax̲sta'las was sixty-one when she worked with Boas and sixteen years younger than George Hunt. The age gap placed her in another generation and within a different realm of experience, given her gender and the circumstances of her early life. Because the potlatch ban had been strictly enforced in 1920s, Berman reasoned that "even the children of chiefs probably had little exposure to a great deal of vocabulary." They would have had little access to the formal contexts familiar to their parents and grandparents.[30] By the 1930s, ceremonials that made up the potlatch were purposely disjointed.[31] Speeches and the "give away" were separated from the dances by periods of up to six months. Distributions of money, flour, and other gifts were disguised as Christmas presents as "charity for the benefit of poor people," or potlatch obligations were satisfied through house-to-house distributions.[32] Potlatches and feasts were performed in Kwakwa̲ka̲'wakw villages distant from the scrutiny of police and government agents – at Gwa'yi (Kingcome), Mama̲lili̲ka̲la (Village Island), K̲alugwis (Turnour Island), Wek̲a'yi (Cape Mudge), and Tsax̲is (Fort Rupert).

Alarmed as he was by the criminal prosecutions for potlatching, Franz Boas would surely have been informed of G̲a'ax̲sta'las's position on the custom. It is difficult to say whether he knew about her recent work with potlatchers seeking compensation for confiscated goods and petitioning the government to relax section 149. His letters provide no clues.

On Christmas Day 1930, Boas was approached by "all the important men" in Tsa<u>x</u>is to "intervene with the government so that they won't have to fear the government's interference with their feasts."[33] He wrote to the lieutenant-governor of BC to request an interview. At the same time, his books *Religion of the Kwakiutl* and *The Anthropometry of the American Negro* were being released. Remarkably, there are no references in his published texts to the substantial history of struggle for title and aboriginal rights. It was the potlatch that he saw as the vital point of conflict with the Canadian state.

The Great Depression hit the salmon fishery hard, and the fishery, in turn, influenced interactions and exchanges within the potlatch system. "Copper transfers almost came to an end," and the increasing debt of fishers made it difficult to potlatch.[34] In letters to colleagues and relatives, Boas hinted at changing conditions in Tsa<u>x</u>is, where there was "one still usable old house."[35] He wrote that a feast had been postponed because "there was not enough fish and oil."[36] In the same letter, he described one house, empty of furniture, as "only a shell ... The people are dressed like poor workmen."[37] Boas informed his son in mid-December 1930 that he had attended a feast where, in the chief's speech, the man could only invoke ceremonial bowls that were then "in museums in New York and Berlin."[38] "These people cling to the form, though the content is almost gone."[39] Boas clearly saw – and noted – changes in the ceremonial expression and material well-being of Kwagu'ł people. But these changes were not the focus of his work.

While in 'Y<u>a</u>lis in early 1931, Boas met the Reverend Arthur W. Corker, (whom he liked better than Alfred Hall), and "lectured him at length on potlatches and marriages."[40] St. Michael's Residential School had just opened, and Boas wrote that there were eighty children to a room, "packed like sardines, but the place is well ventilated."[41] His letter about conditions at Alert Bay sparked some bureaucratic activity, perhaps because it followed a verbal complaint by Bishop Schofield. Reports to Indian Affairs officials reveal that dysentery, tuberculosis, influenza, and syphilis were present in 'Y<u>a</u>lis but that dysentery had not caused any deaths. Influenza left "complications" in the form of tonsillitis.[42] <u>G</u>a'a<u>x</u>sta'las's future daughter-in-law Ilma Wirki was then a young attendant at St. George's Hospital. She may have witnessed the medical response to this wave of influenza. "So from '29, when the residential school opened, Mr. Anfield [the principal] had a truck that he used for the school down there, to take kids to the doctors or whatever. I remember them bringing those poor little things from residential school. All those kids. They had a day or two for taking out tonsils and adenoids, and all those little kids were scared and crying. It was so sad, poor little things. Yeah, I felt very sorry for those kids. I don't know whose idea that was – a doctor's idea – to take them all and have a day of operations."

Meeting G̲a'ax̲sta'las, 1930

In 1931, another son was cared for and eventually lost to tuberculosis in the Cook family big house. Ernest Hall Cook died on Christmas Day eight years before St. Michael's TB Preventorium opened in 'Ya̲lis. Stephen Cook's mother, G̲aga, also passed away that year, and her small shack adjacent to the big house was eventually converted into a smokehouse.

In November 2004, at her son Gilbert's home in 'Ya̲lis, I asked Ilma Cook if she would tell us about the first time she met G̲a'ax̲sta'las. It was around 1930. Ilma was fifteen years old:

"I didn't make friends or associate with the white people as much as I did with the Indian people like my sister-in-laws," Ilma told me. "We used to chum together, and Winnie worked with me at the hospital because Granny Cook didn't give her the money she wanted for something ... [Winnie] took me up to the house for dinner. Granny Cook always figured that guests eat at the first table – nothing but men around a big table, all her sons and son-in-laws and what have you."

She gestured to the large table where we were recording our conversation. "Papa Cook at the end of the table, and Uncle Herbert always on that side. Now *he* teased me all the time. He teased people all the time. Anyway, here I was, sitting at the table with all these guys, shy little me." Ilma laughed and turned to her daughter Vivian, "Can you imagine?"

"So the women sat at a different table?" I asked.

"Well," Ilma said, "the second table was a mixture – only so many would fit around it."

"Where did Jane Cook sit?"

"Oh, she and Papa Cook – most of the time they had grease. They ate eulachon grease, and they would sit in the kitchen. But if they weren't eating fish and grease, Papa would sit at the end of the table. I don't think I ever ate with Granny Cook. She was always busy waiting on everybody, seeing if there's food on the table enough for everybody, filling the vegetable dishes, that kind of stuff. Being a waitress ... But she used to have some of the Indian ladies come up and help her, either in the garden or whatever. They would stay there and have lunch. But there were three big meals a day. Breakfast, dinner was in the middle of the day, and supper was in the evening. But she was never available for the first sitting. I think that's what I'm trying to say."

By all accounts, Ga'axsta'las was fully in charge. Her granddaughter Pearl Alfred wondered aloud about her relationship with her other daughter-in-law, Nellie Cook. "My mother is a very quiet little soul," she said, "and I would have thought she had a difficult time in a household with a woman like my grandmother who was – must have been quite dominating. So I asked her, 'Did you ever have any real arguments?' 'Oh, no,' she said. 'We never had an argument. She was always the boss'" *[laughs]*.

Nellie Cook herself spoke softly about living with her mother-in-law. "She had a few boys," she said, "and we had to get someone to come in and help with the washing of the boy's jeans because my hands were so soft. She worked in the garden – had a nice raspberry patch. People used to come and pick in buckets. And she had some spuds – potatoes – but they didn't do very good because it was too wet and muggy. But the raspberries did very well, and she used to have the other berry – loganberries – too. And in those days, when the boys grew older, they used to take bales of hay for the animals."

Nellie's granddaughter Kelly-Anne Speck noted how often family reminiscences were tied to that garden: "It was funny. People always talk about the garden. There was only the remnants of the garden left when I was a kid. You could see the orchards – the trees in the back yard – but the whole garden that had to be there to sustain a very large household was pretty much a thing of the past. I had this picture of this woman who had this larger-than-life presence not only in the family but also in the community. Very clearly, her place in the church was there. We all grew up going to church, and there was this sense – there were always these references to her and my great-grandfather being involved in supporting the church and everybody being involved in – not only the religious part of it but the ACW and kids' groups, whatever. So it was very much something that she participated in herself but also expected, and everybody else had to go. My fondest memories of growing up were – we used to go to church, and Sunday afternoon you'd get to go have dinner at Nanna's [Nellie Cook's]. By that time, she's not there, but we'd go up the hill to the house, and we'd all have dinner – lunch together. They'd prepare it all before church, and we'd all go sit there and have a meal together afterwards."

"What Is a Parson to Do?": Church and Custom

A number of controversies were brewing in the Anglican Church in the early 1930s. Perhaps most threatening was the competition from the Apostolic Faith Mission, which was based in Vancouver but had begun to flourish in 'Ya̲lis.[43] As Agnes Alfred said, "I continued to go to the Anglican Church with Mrs. Cook. Some of these religions can be so different. They told us that some children had fainted in the new church ... They said they really went overboard with wailing ... As a result, the Nəmǧis decided at a meeting that the representatives of this new church should leave. They were asked to leave on account of the children who had fainted during the wailing. Our church did not like it."[44]

While church officials revisited their stance on the potlatch, they debated the sensitive issue of performing adult baptism at the request of dying patients. They also struggled with the question of whether men and women could be married by the church if they had already married different partners through the custom. Church marriages had increased throughout the 1920s, and young people were choosing their own partners in the 1930s.[45]

At the 1930 meeting of the Provincial Synod, the archbishop, bishops, clergy, and other attending members (possibly Jane and Stephen Cook) participated in "a considerable discussion" about the potlatch. "Very different views were expressed as to the place and value of the institution."[46] They consulted missionary opinions and scholarly texts, but "the truth [was] extremely difficult to arrive at."[47] Among the evidence was information about the function of the potlatch and its shifting form, given the "changing status of the Indian" and their "exploitation" by the "White race." The committee reflected on the church's own history of responsibility for the potlatch ban: "The first missionaries ... assumed a harmful attitude. Reflecting the current theological conceptions of their day, these missionaries placed all men's social activities into one or two categories, Christian or heathen. The potlatch was obviously not Christian ... and forthwith it was condemned ... Later this attitude was carried into active opposition when seemingly the Church sought the aid of the law ... The

Government was guided into declaring 'the Potlatch' illegal by the pressure of missionaries and Church authorities."[48] But the committee report concluded that "the time is too late, and the complications too many, to attempt to save the 'Potlatch.'"

Its single example of "things that are harmful" reflected escalating economic crisis. "The standard expense has grown to such a degree that today the Indian who gives a 'Potlatch' is beggared for the rest of his life ... The Church should urge upon Indian converts to renounce the Potlatch," the report stated, "and should press for the definite gradual preparation for the enfranchisement of the Indian adult and for the education of the children to be planned with this end in view." Regarding marriage, the committee report suggested that existing "Indian marriages" should be "solemnized by a Government agent," that the unions should be blessed by the church, and that the church will continue to marry its own members. This final consideration reflected a growing tendency "to 'play off' between marriages in 'The Potlatches' and marriages under provincial law."[49]

G̲a'ax̲sta'las had written to church authorities about these strategic marriages as early as 1913, but she consistently framed her protest in the context of Kwakwa̲ka̲'wakw women left destitute by shifting laws and practices. She initially appealed to officials to legally recognize *K̲adzitła* (potlatch marriages). When the provincial Marriage Act came into force, she sought legislation requiring men to provide support to former wives and their children. Church deliberations, however, had little to do with the material circumstances of women in Kwakwa̲ka̲'wakw communities. Instead, church leaders became enmeshed in questions about morality and in the rules of faith and ritualism that defined Anglican fellowship.

Apparently, G̲a'ax̲sta'las *was* consulted about other matters. Unlike their predecessors, the new church officials in 'Ya̲lis did not speak Kwak̓wala, a situation that affected their ability to work with older people in the villages. When Reverend Prosser refused to baptize a dying man, George Luther, a Kwakwa̲ka̲'wakw teacher and prominent church committee member, complained to the bishop. He stated that all clergymen before Prosser had performed adult baptisms when requested by ill and dying persons. According to Bishop Schofield, the rite required the "repentance and faith of a patient," but he suggested that Prosser could "look upon the older Indians as special cases." He wrote: "I wonder if you ought to have taken an interpreter, such as Mrs. Cook, and have been guided by her in some measure; always recollecting however, that the Church places the final responsibility with you."[50] Ga'axsta'las was a trusted advisor, but the bishop reminded Prosser of his ultimate authority. Ironically, this man, who was stingy in admitting dying people into Christian baptism, eventually became a primary advocate for the potlatch, or at least for modifying the laws against it.

When the marriage question emerged again in 1931, an unnamed writer submitted a handwritten summary of the opinions of clergymen at Alert Bay, beginning with the newly appointed vicar of Christ Church: "*Rev. C.K.K. Prosser* Rector Alert Bay. *Writes* 1931 – Potlach means various things & comprises numbers of Indian ceremonies. Probably P. was method of public transaction of business or family records. Some communicants still practice the potlach – Says purchase of wives at potlach is untrue. Thinks potlach may be utilized for Christian teaching."[51] The memo included views on marriage (and potlatching) by Charles de Veber Schofield, the bishop of Columbia; by John Antle, founder of the Columbia Coast Mission; by the Reverend F. Comley, principal of the industrial school; and, by Archdeacon W.H. Collison. Their statements suggest that the ground had shifted. Communicants in their parish were potlatching, a situation not tolerated by Alfred Hall.[52] Here, too, Jane Cook was mentioned.

> *Rev. A.W. Corker* – Agent C.M.S. 40 yrs. exp. w Indians. Arr. Alert Bay 42 yrs ago ... "Only recently an Indian rebuked Mrs. Cook (Xtian Indian) that she had not done *her* duty as an Indn; only once married, sh[ould] have been earning money by "marrying" men that her family might be glorified by holding potlach – and have a great name. Indians borrow to pay, but have to pay 100% – He who gives expects *double* back – It is demoralizing, and leads to destitution. Law agst potlach is good, but is badly enforced."[53]

Corker's statements indicate that Ga'axsta'las had been criticized for only marrying once. As the eldest daughter of a noble line, there was clearly some expectation that she would enter into a series of marriage contracts.

"Looking at this system of marriage in the economy," Wedłidi Speck noted, "women would have married several times. That would be connected to the idea that the father of that woman had accumulated more wealth. So, as a result of her marrying someone else, more dowries would be given and more wealth distributed. It would guarantee that there was a venue for the release of material goods. She would [have been] criticized because she would represent a woman becoming powerful. That's the other side of it. So people start shaming her. It's like saying ... that would be detrimental to other women because if other women thought they could be where you are, they would only be fooling themselves. So, the dialogue is about dragging [women] back down."

The gender expectations and responsibilities that women of rank in G̲a'ax̲sta'las's generation carried are evident in a marriage history elicited by Julia Averkieva in 1930. Xe maxodayugwa's story of her four marriage contracts emphasizes the many events wherein acts of gifting to the groom indicated her family's high standing. According to the woman, her fourth marriage had been conducted "in the 'white' way because the agent was very strict that no Indian should marry in the Indian way. He threatened the Indians with arrest." As she told Averkieva: "For about five years the Indians have married only in the white way, so nobody knows how much they pay for their wives. We do not want to be unpain [unpaid] of course."[54] Evidently, among women of the nobility, being paid for and reciprocating secured their own and their family's high standing in Kwakwa̲ka̲'wakw society.[55]

G̲a'ax̲sta'las and Na̲ge's single church marriage likely had repercussions, and their descendants continue to imagine them. "If she hadn't gone to the church," her grandson Gilbert Cook told me, "and if she hadn't been opposed to what it was taking to put the money up for potlatches ... Aside from the women's issues of how women were being used in that regard, aside from that, just in putting everything that your family had into [the potlatch] and not preparing your family for the new reality of a new century. We're talking a hundred years later, dealing with very similar issues, issues of being able to provide for your family in regard to work, jobs, education, all of those things. Those are still issues within our family today, and I imagine they will continue to be so. But, no, if she had carried on and exercised the rights and traditions that were passed down to her, through her mother *[pausing]* and Stephen, if he had continued the rights that were passed to him through *his* mother, things would have been *very* different in regards to this family, very, very different."

Beginning in 1931, the Indian Affairs Branch of the Department of Mines and Resources officially denounced "Indian custom marriage." A circular sent to all Indian Agents from the new deputy superintendent of Indian affairs, Harold McGill, stated unequivocally: "From now on, no marriage celebrated according to Indian custom is valid ... after the passing of marriage laws in a province or territory, no marriage according to Indian custom or per verba de praesenti[56] is valid unless such took place in a part of the Dominion so remote from a person duly authorized by law to celebrate a marriage."[57] Chapter 41 of the BC Marriage Act (1930) sought "to appoint Indian Agents [as] marriage Commissioners," so the circular read "it is unlikely that any valid marriage according to Indian custom or by necessity could occur in British Columbia."[58] McGill advised agents not to announce the change. He also stated: "The Indians should conform to the Provincial Marriage Laws ... to avoid the difficulties that otherwise arise in determining who are members of a band and in distributing the property of deceased Indians." The department took even firmer legal control over those areas of descent and inheritance formerly decided through relationships in the potlatch complex. According to the 1931 circular, anyone born within the British dominions was "a natural born British subject." It declared that aboriginal peoples "no longer possess an Indian nationality" because they had all been born since "acquisition of this country" in 1763.[59]

Although considered British subjects, those classified as Indians under the Indian Act had no rights as citizens. As wards of the government they were subject to legislation that overdetermined their mobility, education, and employment options; their access to physicians and hospitals; where they lived; and the political, legal, and economic processes that governed their lives. "Indians" had no right to vote in provincial or federal elections and, since a 1930 amendment of the Indian Act, were prohibited from entering poolhalls.[60] The prohibition exaggerated an already established form of social apartheid. In the fishing industry, where so much ground had been gained, it further racialized fishers.

Outside of relations with the Canadian state, class and rank – social phenomena Averkieva pressed Franz Boas to recognize – also figured into relationships in Kwakwa̱ka̱'wakw communities. Averkieva kept in touch with Boas from Leningrad, where she worked at the USSR Academy of Science. In October 1931, she told "Papa France" of her decision to study from a "Marxian ... point of dialectic materialism ... I have a question," she wrote,

> In the secret societies people were divided according to there class principle – rich and poor. Initiations were connected with distribution of much wealth ... Those who did not have neither fishing places nor gardens for digging roots, could not obtain much wealth as they always were poor. As a result of the whole – winter ceremonies ware characteristic not for the whole tribe, but only for the upper class ... How

> it was with the common people we do not know, perhaps they had had very [few?] relation to that ceremony. I write that to you as first impressions, I did not go in deep yet.[61]

While Boas publicly supported the right to perform potlatching ceremonies, he paid little attention to the so-called common people. Boas did not write about the ongoing struggles that aboriginal agitators waged against colonial regulation of their lives. He was interested in reconstructing the imaginative and behavioural worlds of precontact "Kwakiutl." Economic activities played an enormous role in his investigations, just as they did in the opinions of Indian Affairs officials and missionaries who sought to quash the potlatch during the Great Depression. Several anthropological works about the Northwest Coast were published during the 1930s. Most focussed on historical descriptions of rank and social prestige at a time when Kwakwa̱ka̱'wakw villages were being relocated, when increasing numbers of aboriginal children were entering and staying at residential schools, and when membership in Christian social worlds was increasingly common. The economic grind of the Depression sharpened the socioeconomic distance between aboriginal and non-aboriginal societies.

"A System That Works Right Around in a Circle": The *Christian Science Monitor*

In 'Ya̱lis, some church and some state officials voiced fears about the social impact of economic choices, including ceremonial activities. They noted the impoverishment caused by the perpetual accumulation and distribution of property and money that crossed generations. Jane Cook was among those who expressed similar opinions, but her tone was accepting in 1932, when she met with a journalist from the *Christian Science Monitor*. Stating predictable concern in the midst of the Depression, G̱a'ax̱sta'las described the symbolic and material property at the heart of potlatch exchanges. The article likely includes a transcript of a conversation between Ta-de-win (a.k.a. Mabel Knight) and G̱a'ax̱sta'las.[62] Perhaps because of her recent acquaintance with Franz Boas, G̱a'ax̱sta'las uses the term *Kwakiutl* to identify her people and she speaks of totem poles and coppers as existing within a "system" of exchanges.

Mabel Knight opens the article with a description of 'Ya̱lis.

ALERT BAY, BC – On Cormorant Island, opposite the northeastern part of the Island of Vancouver, is the intriguing village of Alert Bay. Just one main street follows the shore for two miles, sometimes with houses flanking both sides, sometimes with open spaces affording a view of other Islands and sea green water disturbed only by the fisherman's boats and occasional steamers that dock at this small town.

One is told that Indians and whites dwell at Alert Bay, but according to that classification the whites include Japanese and Chinese who live at the southern end of the Island. The Kwakiutl Indians have full sway over the other end, and a large sign reading "Speed Limit, Four Miles an Hour" lets the stranger know when he reaches the Indian section of the village, and the 12 automobiles of which the Island boasts must obey that sign; while at the "white" end of the same street automobiles are held in check by cows who sometimes step obligingly aside when an automobile "honks" ...

The first time the stranger wanders down to the Indian part of the village, the swaying clotheslines hung with a complete line of dry and drying goods stretched from totem pole to totem pole extend a cordial welcome like banners floating in the wind ...

One-third of these Indians have withdrawn from this potlatch and totem pole system and under the leadership of George Luther, the Indian school teacher, and Mrs. Stephen Cook, official interpreter of the tribe, are leading the ordinary life of their white neighbors on the island.

Mrs. Stephen Cook, the hereditary chieftainess of the Fort Rupert Band, for there are 20 other bands on the adjacent Islands under the jurisdiction of the Alert Bay Agency, is a witty and intelligent Indian and to her is the writer indebted for the intimate account of this social system. Looking around her comfortably furnished living room, Mrs. Cook laughingly remarked:

"Now if I were still in the potlatch system I wouldn't have an article of furniture left and I have so many things the Indians would like that they wish I were back in the old life."

Preferred the Money

It was Mrs. Cook who arranged for the sale of the totem poles standing in Stanley Park, Vancouver, and why not, she said, since the Indians [who] owned them preferred the money to the totem poles. However, no more poles can be removed, is the official decree. There are enough left, though, to make Alert Bay attractive. The twin poles showing so prominently as one walks down the street picture the eagle and the bear; a very tall pole has carved on it the whale and the wolf, while there are plenty of less imposing ones in front of the Indians' houses. "But what do all these poles in the villages signify?" remarked the visitor.

"In the first place," began Mrs. Cook, "totem means emblem, and before an Indian can show that emblem he must give a potlatch, or a big feast, if the pole is an elaborate one."

"Just what is a potlatch?" inquired the visitor.

"Well, there is the modest potlatch that may be given for $150, and then again a potlatch may cost the Indian who gives it $2000. When there is a potlatch the author of it invites the tribe to attend, displays the things to be given away, and the Indians receive gifts according to their rank. The Kwakiutl doesn't mind disposing of his possessions thus, because at the next potlatch he himself will receive valuable gifts, for it is an unbroken rule that one Indian must give to another more than he has received from him. At any rate," laughed Mrs. Cook, "It keeps the property in circulation, for suppose a man gives a phonograph set away, in the course of a few years he is liable to receive it back.

"If a Kwakiutl hasn't money enough to give a potlatch he borrows what he wishes from the Indians and pays back at the rate of 100 per cent; that is, if he has borrowed a dish of one Indian, he must give that Indians two dishes before the debt is canceled, and there is a public accountant who inherits the task, and he must keep a strict account of all property transfer and money are loaned and to whom. It is a wonderful system but then, don't some go in debt today among the whites to give Christmas presents!"

Potlatch Events

"When is a potlatch given?" asked the guest, while Mrs. Cook paused for breath.

"A potlatch is given at the birth of a child, when a girl reaches a marriageable age, when a man desires to have a son vote and take part in the councils of the tribe or when he wishes to erect another totem pole and display more crests, for with any act of distinction like the giving of a feast or potlatch he can assume more emblems. Once gray blankets from the Hudson Bay Company used to represent a man's wealth. Such an Indian would spread the blankets on the ground and erect two potlatch poles at each end of the blankets to show the extent of his wealth and then he would give those blankets away at a potlatch.

"One potlatch pole like that is still standing. You passed it when you came to see me. It is a pole with a grinning figure at the top. A Kwakiutl may not own an article of furniture after he has given a potlatch, but at least he can erect a totem pole thus publicly displaying his emblems, speak in council and he is happy with a grin like that on the potlatch figure."

Before the writer was able to think over all these remarkable facts, Mrs. Cook continues:

"Important as the potlatch and the totem poles are, there is something even more important and that is the 'copper.' My people first obtained that shield-shaped piece of metal from a tribe in the north long before the whites came to this section. There is a rib-shaped T in that shield which the Kwakiutls will tell you is the life of the 'copper.'

"When I was twenty-one years old an Indian brought me his 'copper' to care for while he was away and he had it wrapped in a blanket and that blanket was none too clean so I suggested that he take the blanket home and leave the 'copper' with me. But he was startled and told me that 'copper' must be kept warm. That just shows you how these Indians here regard that piece of metal. It is just like a $12,000 bond.

Bestow Anything

"With a 'copper' a man can give a potlatch, for he can borrow anything he wants when he owns a 'copper.' If no one else in the tribe owns a 'copper' he can become a chief. The more 'copper' a chief owns the more powerful he is among the other tribes, so the people always help the chief to get another 'copper,' for that will make the tribe more important along with the chief. A man will marry his daughter to anyone who will give him a 'copper.' A stranger coming into the tribe cannot buy a 'copper,' no matter how rich he is, until he has given feasts and one potlatch after another and even then he still may be regarded as an outsider.

"Even stranger than all this, if a chief breaks a piece of his 'copper,' never breaking into the T and gives that piece to another chief, it proves him the best man unless the chief who has received the piece gives the donor two pieces of his 'copper,' and perhaps that chief has none and can't do anything about it, so the tribe with the chief owning a 'copper' is declared the mightier one."

> "Oh, it is a system that works right around in a circle," Mrs. Cook said, in conclusion. "A man may give everything he possesses for a 'copper,' then he can buy much and give a big feast as well as a potlatch, then erect a totem pole and declare himself chief. He may not have anything but the 'copper[,]' his debts, his authority as chief and his smile left, but being chief he will receive the lion's share at the next potlatch and soon his house will be refurnished and he will be casting his eye around for another 'copper' so as to give another potlatch and erect another totem pole, having by this time enough family crests to cover it from top to bottom."[63]

It is difficult to know how readers of the *Christian Science Monitor* received G̱a'ax̱sta'las's description of the potlatch. Her tone does not condemn the system; rather, she understates the negative economic aspects. She compares the potlatch to debt at Christmas time and calls it a wonderful system of crests and other symbols of prestige that "works right around in a circle." In reference to her "comfortably furnished living room," she remarks somewhat lightheartedly that others felt she should be participating in the custom. Her sons were then living at home, and her daughters and their families occasionally moved from the villages to the Cook big house during the hard times. Nellie Cook recalled that "the Depression was dreadful! ... The boys all worked hard, hunting for venison and fishing halibut as well as salmon. At one time, there were thirty-three people staying with the family ... They ate a lot of fish and canned venison. Jane Cook did most of the canning. It was very difficult to make boat payments during the Depression."[64]

It was surprising to read that G̱a'ax̱sta'las had arranged the sale of the totem poles to the City of Vancouver. At that time, there were two house posts and two totem poles at Stanley Park, part of the Art, Historical and Scientific Association of Vancouver's vision to build a "model Indian village."[65] The two poles belonged to Chief Wakius of the 'Na̱mg̱is and to Chief Sisa-kaulas of the Dzawada̱'enux̱w, respectively, both of whom were elderly and lived at 'Ya̱lis. Wakius was blind, and Sisa-kaulas was paralyzed.[66] The Reverend John Goodfellow acknowledged the "assistance" of Jane Cook, George Hunt, and the Reverend Arthur Corker in *Totem Poles of Stanley Park*.[67] George Hunt recorded the ancestor narrative for what is known as the "Wakius Talking Stick Pole." Jane Cook translated the narrative about Chief Sisa-kaulas's ancestor See-wid, whose underwater supernatural encounters his pole depicted.[68] No owners or meanings were offered for

Photo 31 Annually, Stephen and sons would go to the Nimpkish Lake to a traditional site and hunt geese and ducks (ca. 1930s). *Courtesy of Wedłidi Speck.*

the house posts.[69] By this time, journalists noted that fewer poles stood in coastal villages because they had been acquired by museums, public institutions, and by private collectors intent on preserving what they saw as a disappearing art form.[70]

Although totem poles were less visible in the skylines of Kwakwa̱ka̱'wakw villages, the ceremonial occasions from which they were generated continued. Doreen Fitch told me in passing that her father, Albert Dawson, had hosted a potlatch during the Depression.

"So your father had a potlatch in the thirties?"

"Yeah, I don't really remember, hey? I just remember missing a lot of things in the house. We ordered a real nice chair from the catalogue – I think it was Woodward's or David Spencer catalogue. And some other things that were really nice they had ordered – they were gone! They had given it all out at the potlatch *[laughs]*. I must have been about six. There's still some little things I remember ... I remember part of a potlatch, other people's potlatch. I guess what I liked is what I remember, something that fascinated me. I remember seeing somebody on a canoe on the beach at Gilford Island, and they were pretending to talk Chinese – two old ladies, two elderly women. It was part of a potlatch, hey? There's little things I remember. I can't remember the whole things."

Such impressions are the substance of revisited collective histories. Kwakwa̱ka̱'wakw researchers who listen to the oral histories of the current generation of elders hear stories specific to the Great Depression. "Even in the thirties and the forties," William Wasden Jr. explained, "there's some people you could interview who say, 'We had nothing because our parents gave everything away. We were sleeping on the floor.' Things like that. They gave even their furniture away, and there was just little, empty Japanese orange boxes to sit on for furniture. And, so, the children weren't being thought of. They were suffering, going without, hungry sometimes, because their parents were trying to uphold something they couldn't afford." William Wasden Jr. understood that poverty was a part of his great-grandmother's objection to the potlatch. "So that, to my understanding, that's why she was against it. Because that's what it had become. I've heard stories from other families – not even regarding Granny Cook – that their parents did that to them, and that's why a lot of them they won't go [to potlatches], because of how they suffered on account of it. People were doing things out of their means."

On Giving, in 2008

As we worked to understand G̱a'ax̱sta'las's life and times, I was reminded of recurring themes in her story and in the portrayal of

Kwakwaka'wakw peoples. In December 2008, one reminder arrived via email in the form of a *New York Times* article. In it, journalist John Tierney posed the question, "Now that hard times have arrived, now that we're being punished for our great credit binge, what are we supposed to do for the holidays?" His answer came from "the Kwakwaka'wakw Indians, the world's most experienced gift-givers," who have "learned that exchanging presents is too important to be discontinued in any kind of economy."[71] Tierney and I write in the midst of the economic crisis that began in 2008 with the collapse of the subprime mortgage market in the United States and reverberated around the world. Tierney's piece follows a deep trail of media attention to the potlatch that began in the nineteenth century. Whether the focus is on exoticized behaviour, sanitary conditions, criminal charges, or gender relations, the economic aspect of potlatching has rarely been overlooked.

Like me, Tierney looks to the past through the lens of the present, and his vision includes anthropological works. From Ruth Benedict's 1934 *Patterns of Culture,* he quotes a nineteenth-century chief who made a speech about his "groaning" copper. Tierney compares nineteenth-century "nouveau riche leaders vying for prestige" with "Wall Street's nouveau riche," who fell from grace as their financial base melted. Invoking the Great Depression, he emphasizes the endurance of the potlatch and mentions the ingenious strategies that the Kwakwaka'wakw used to conduct their "underground ceremonies." Tierney quotes 'Namgis chief Bill Cranmer on the social aspect of potlatching: "Even in hard economic times, the potlatch has always been the structure that enables people in our society to work together."

Titled "Tips from the Potlatch," the article suggests that gifters should buy in bulk and not be afraid to re-gift (with interest). "Control your animosity" is another tip, but don't break coppers or engage in one-upmanship in family gifting. Finally, the journalist suggests that we should not forget our enemies, advice that anthropologist Aldona Jonaitis also endorsed. "Besides strengthening the bonds within a family," she said, "potlatching enabled people to establish bonds and obligations with potential enemies outside the family." In the article, anthropologist Aaron Glass suggests that the potlatch can be viewed as a kind of "trickle-down economics ... Although elite chiefs controlled the fishing grounds and the trade networks, everyone had enough fish and ... excess trading wealth was redistributed to the entire community."[72]

Ga'axsta'las's 135th Birthday: The Cook Fishing Fleet

Social rank, control over resources, and ceremonial privilege swirl in a kaleidoscope of impressions about Kwakwaka'wakw life and livelihoods throughout the generations, and fishing figures prominently. By the 1930s, Ga'axsta'las had agitated for the right to fish in local waters, to make one's livelihood from fishing, and to have access to fisheries for what would today be called "food, social and ceremonial purposes." In the late 1920s, her husband, Stephen, had entered the commercial fishery on the Northwest Coast. His sons joined him soon after.

On that part of Cormorant Island where homes look onto the narrow, kelp-filled channel north of Johnstone Strait, Gilbert Cook Jr. told me about his life on the water. It was 3 March 2005. Jane Cook's grandson told me that it would have been her 135th birthday. We talked about canoe travel. Gilbert told me about how closely navigators would have watched the tides, about how long a paddle to Victoria would have been. Our conversation moved from canoes to early seine boats to tugs, from Jane Gilbert's childhood, to his father's fishing career, to Gilbert's own days as a fisher, to his sons' careers on the sea.

"The first involvement in commercial fishing would have been – from Stephen's point of view – as a buyer and processor with the saltery there. He was a fish buyer to begin with, and he had a boat, one of the Howe Sound boats. I don't know how many smaller boats that he had. Mostly they were packing, not fishing, boats, but packers. The *Howe Sound IV,* I believe, was one ... And they also used to ferry guys back and forth across to the logging camp ... the guys who were working over there. I guess they would just run them back and forth. [But] he was a fish buyer, big time. He was buying them from whoever was catching them.

"I know they had a fish camp that carried on until late down at Parson Island ... and just at the time that BC was considering, or they actually had already, a few fish traps, salmon traps, built on the Coast. Then it became obvious, by what was happening in Alaska, that that was not the way to go. So, the government dropped that idea and banned the fish traps from here. But, at that time, the family was just going to put in a trap again, down there by Parson Island, what's called 'the Bank' now, in between the bluff and the bank. So, they had an involvement in fish buying and, by then, processing.

"So, Papa [Stephen Cook] was buying fish, and, of course, as the boys got older, they were fishing with other people. And my dad's [Gilbert Cook Sr.] first fishing experience came on a boat called the *Red Wing*. I'm not sure who owned it, but I believe Michael Kamano may have owned or been running it ... It was one of those small little boats ... They'd have a small table seine on it, and everything pretty much by hand. And then, when he was sixteen, he got an opportunity to run it as a skipper for a while. I don't know what the circumstances were that led to that. And then he decided that was the way he was going to go. And within a couple of years, he got together with his brother Ernie, and Stephen – Papa Cook – chipped in. Gilbert managed to get the other guys to chip in to buy a boat, to have a boat built, actually. So, they had the *Pearl C* built. And then, after the *Pearl C* was built, then a couple of years later, they had the *Winifred C* built.

"The *Winifred* was built, and Reg was a partner in that. They all chipped together to get the money to do these things. And then, later, much later on, in 1931 when my dad's brother Ernie died – who was his partner – my dad bought out all of the other shares of the boat from his dad and his brother Ernie. So, there were the three of them that chipped in together in the first place to get the first boat built. And what the circumstances were with the *Winifred C,* when they had that one built in the early days, I don't know. As they went along, the *Kitgora* was owned by Chris and Steve Warren, and the *C.N.* was a packer and also a dispatch boat. Herbert was the Canadian Fish dispatcher with that. The *Cape Cook* was my dad's second boat. He sold the *Pearl C* to Silas Olney, his nephew, and then the *Winifred C,* which Reg started out with. He ended up buying the *Cape Lazo*.

"So, the boys were the ones who sort of developed the fleet amongst themselves, eh? And then others in the family. Chris ended up the half-owner of this one, the *Kitgora*." He gestured to a photograph of the Cook family fleet. "Steve Warren would operate that one, and Chris would operate a company boat. There were all kinds of them, different boats that were run by different members of the family. Cyril Cook, I believe he had the *Menzie's Bay* for a year or two. He didn't care for it – he didn't like running a boat. He'd rather just work."

"What companies would have been operating then?"

"This was Canadian Fish mostly. I'm not sure when they started calling it Canadian Fishing Company, but it was [out of] New England. We're talking about the thirties and forties, and like that, when the boys were grown up. So, the commercial industry and the various

Photo 32 Cook fleet at Alert Bay, 1948. *Left to right:* the *Kitgora* (Chris Cook Sr. and Stephen Warren), the *C.N.* (Herb Cook), the *Cape Cook* (Gilbert Cook Sr.), the *Winifred C* (Stephen Cook), the *Pearl C* (Stephen Cook), and the *Cape Lazo* (Reg Cook Sr.). Stephen Cook is standing at the end of the dock. *Native Voice,* May 1973. *Courtesy of* Native Voice.

companies were pretty well developed by then. Anyway, that's how the fleet started – was the boys getting involved in it and then getting together as partners and scraping together what money they could to get a start with a boat. And in those days, if you did that, you could start with a new boat, you know, build your own boat. Stephen Cook was the business end of it, and the boys were the production, the fisherman end of it. And they made their own way with those things, still working together as a family, but they did it their own way. It's sort of a family affair all the way along, and the idea that family heads – the father of the family – is kind of the boss of things is really not the case at all. If there is a boss that way, it will probably be the mom." He laughed.

When I asked Gilbert whether he thought that Jane and Stephen's children felt the repercussions of her choices, he replied: "I think so. You know, there was certain resentment in the community over those things, and not only resentment in the community over the cultural issues – which is sort of what you're dealing with – but this kind of thing. The entrepreneurial side – 'them that's got and them that ain't' kind of thing. I mean, there was a lot of resentment over that, as there is right to this day. I don't think that that's any different than in any community anywhere on this coast or in this country, regardless of your ethnicity. I think it's an issue, something that is common to all humans and all societies."

R v Stephen Cook et al.: Taxing Fishers

In 1933, the Cook family faced yet another struggle over fishing and rights.[73] Stephen Cook, Alvin Alfred, Moses Alfred, Oly Shaughnessy, and William Dawson were charged and convicted for not paying a provincial tax for drag-seine fishing on the Nimpkish River.

Since Kwakwa̲ka̲'wakw fishers had obtained independent commercial licences, many were in debt to fish-packing companies who extended credit to purchase and maintain the boats, buy gear and supplies, and pay crews.[74] As a ward of the government, an aboriginal fisher "could not be sued and therefore no bank would risk making him a loan."[75] At first, fishers borrowed money from canneries to purchase cannery-owned boats, paying off the debt through successive seasons; later, canneries extended loans to fishers to build their own boats. Kwakwa̲ka̲'wakw fishermen likely had contracts or arrangements with one of three major fish-packing companies: the Canadian Fishing Company, the British Columbia Packers Corporation, and the Anglo British Columbia Company. These companies typically paid owners in advance to cover start-up expenses. They also paid licence fees and taxes that were then deducted from the final payment for the catch at the season's close.

Over twenty canneries became idle after the 1929 stock market crash. Among them was the Alert Bay Cannery, which had been established in 1881. The salmon run was abundant in 1930, but it was difficult to sell the catch given the condition of world markets.[76] "Fishing and cannery incomes were almost cut in half during the early 1930s" and fish prices fell with them.[77] Drag-seine fishers who worked on the Nimpkish River in 1933 had a disappointing salmon season and found it difficult to cover their operating expenses. Among them were two drag-seiners who worked under independent licences bought by Stephen Cook. He worked with the Canadian Fishing Company, selling to the Bones Bay Cannery at Cracroft Island near Knight Inlet.

By then, he had drag-seine and purse-seine operations. His sons skippered boats on which they employed aboriginal crews.

At the end of the 1933 season, provincial police constables charged Stephen Cook and four others with not paying a twenty-five dollar drag-seine tax, as was required by the BC Fisheries Act ("Fisheries Regulations," chapter 92, part 2, section 10). The charge had the potential to accelerate into a test case that would pit corporate interests against provincial authority over fisheries.

According to the Canadian Fishing Company, because "Indians" were not subject to taxes, and because these men fished on the Nimpkish River on Cheslakee Reserve Number 3, they should not pay the tax. According to the Provincial Police, the drag-seine tax was imposed because they were commercial fishers who sold or traded off the reserve to a cannery. They were seen as competing with "white" fishers and subject to taxes.[78] Perhaps Jane Cook's arguments in favour of the right to fish the Nimpkish River had paid off, for at this time only aboriginal fishers were allowed to work there. They were also the sole operators of drag-seine boats at a time when the federal Fisheries Department was attempting to permanently shut down the aboriginal food fishery.[79] Stephen Cook had already bought a federal independent licence, but the province threatened to fine him and the others for separate offences and for each day they had fished without paying the tax.[80]

During the trial, G̲a'ax̲sta'las served as the court interpreter. E.G. Newnham, the temporary Indian Agent, presided over the court as judge. The accused were asked if they understood English, if they wanted an interpreter, and whether they wished to make their statements on oath. When asked to plead guilty or not guilty, Stephen Cook replied,

> I suppose you call it guilty because we never pay that tax before we started fishing ...
>
> Well, I been fishing about 15 years and they never asked me to pay this tax before I start fishing ... And the last few years there was nobody collected it. Of course we thought it was Indian Reserve and the buyers come take the fish from the reserve ground. I understand that Indians don't have to pay the tax on the Indian reserve so I wired down below when I heard about it and I got this.

He produced a telegram, which was read in court by the magistrate:

THERE IS CONSIDERABLE DOUBT AS TO WHETHER OR NOT PROVINCIAL AUTHORITIES CAN LEGALLY TAX FISHING OPERATIONS BECAUSE PRIVY COUNCIL HAS RULED PROVI[N]CIAL AUTHORITIES HAVE NO JUSRISDICTION OVER FISHING STOP WE UNDERSTAND NAAS RIVER GILL NETTERS REFUSED PAY PROVINCIAL TAX ON THIS GROUNDS AND PROVINCIAL GOVERNMENT DID NOT ENFORCE COLLECTION STOP IF COURT RULES AGAINST YOU PLEASE ADVISE ALL DETAILS AND WE WILL SUBMIT ALL FACTS TO OUR LAWYER FOR HIS CONSIDERATION AND RECOMMENDATION.

The Canadian Fishing Co.

The advice in the telegram stirred up controversy about whether or not the fishers had been misled by cannery operators.

Mr. Dorman, who represented the company, was called to testify. He and Jane Cook entered a "protest" that, by court order, the boat was ordered to remain in dock. Speaking for the Canadian Fishing Company, Dorman argued against taxation for Indians on the grounds that, under the Indian Act, Indians on their own reserves were exempt from poll tax, income tax, and land tax. He stated: "Last spring in the House there was talk of enforced enfranchisement in order to collect taxation from them." He objected that the Indian Agent was acting as a magistrate rather than defending the fishers' interests. Newnham responded: "The Indian Agent does not have to help Indians break the law. We see that you get a square deal and you will get a square deal." Still, he did write to his superior in Victoria seeking advice about whether to step down from the case.

One by one, the accused testified and pleaded guilty. They either stated that they had not paid the tax before or were unaware that it existed. As Newnham continued his investigations, it became clear that even the federal Fisheries inspector was unaware of the provincial tax.[81] The fishers handed over their books, and each man confirmed that he was "in the hole" to the company. One drag-seine captain said that his catch of one thousand sockeyes did not even cover his operating expenses, never mind paying his crew. When the prosecutor noted that Stephen Cook had not paid his purse-seine tax that year or the year before, he replied, "Nobody made any money. Lots of licenses for different people on my name, I have to collect it from other people first."

The court, represented by agent Newnham, said that it would be an injustice to send the accused to jail for six months. "You have not got the money [to pay fines and the tax], and you are all in the hole."

Newnham referred the final decision to the BC attorney general and berated the Canadian Fishing Company, which, although not bound by law to do so, had not paid the fishers' fees, as was common practice. Newnham noted the confusion caused by the message the company had wired to Stephen Cook, and he found the story about Naas River gillnetters not paying provincial taxes to be hearsay.

Newnham heard back from the attorney general's office in September 1933: "These Indians, on the material submitted, acted quite bonafide on the stupid or malicious advice of a white man as to the state of the law, and were therefore not willfully guilty." The attorney general noted that "circumstances change cases."[82] A week later, Stephen Cook wrote to Dorman: "Attorney Generals letter blames Canadian Fishing Company for malicious misleading of Indians. Judge says must pay. Be here when others come up."[83] It is not clear who the others were or what Stephen Cook intended when he wrote the note, but he heard from the Indian Agent a day later. Newnham wrote, "It is possible that this action of the Canadian Fishing Company will make it necessary for a law to be passed controlling the relations between canneries and fishermen."[84] Newnham thought the Canadian Fishing Company had "counseled the Natives to commit offenses in order to test the validity of a certain Act."[85]

These documents, which put aboriginal fishers in a passive role, do not do justice to the long history of protest and proto-union activity among aboriginal fishers on the Coast.[86] There is a pattern of aboriginal fishers being intimidated and abandoned when others broke strikes and resumed fishing. At Rivers Inlet in the 1890s, for instance, Kwakwa̱ka̱'wakw fishers struck to raise the price for sockeye from five to ten cents a fish. They loaded their canoes and left with Japanese fishers, but local aboriginal fishers along with "white men stayed and fished at the original price."[87] In 1912, according to Percy Gladstone, Nimpkish drag-seiners demanded higher fish prices from canneries, but when non-aboriginal fishers accepted cannery prices, the Nimpkish had no alternative but to drop their demands.[88] Given the ethnic composition of commercial fishing, racialized politics often favoured the canneries.

As Stephen Cook and the other skippers faced charges, representatives of the newly formed Fish Cannery Workers Industrial Union were demanding an end to the "contract system of hiring Indian fishermen and cannery workers."[89] Aboriginal commercial fishers were engaged in long-term economic relationships with fish-packing companies.

Their financial obligations made them loyal to particular canneries until their debts were paid. In return, "in years of heavy salmon runs the cannery was likewise under an obligation to accept all the fish of these regular fishermen, though it might refuse to accept, or accept only part of a transient fisherman's catch."[90]

Although aboriginal fishers might have had more secure relationships with fish packers, their families were not eligible for the provincial government relief that proved to be a benefit to other communities during the Great Depression. Thomas Gosnell testified before Parliament: "An Indian either has to be sick or there had to be some actual starvation and destitution before he comes under relief, which calls for approximately $4.00 and some odd cents ... $4.00 per month and not per week ... The problems concerning Indians cannot be dealt with by one individual village ... The birth of the Brotherhood took place about six months following."[91] According to Gosnell, the Native Brotherhood of British Columbia began in Port Simpson in 1930.[92] It was what Percy Gladstone calls a "fraternal group, with the aim of furthering the general welfare of the British Columbia Indians."[93] Within the early organization, a Fishermen's Joint Committee was struck. Its purpose was to "co-ordinate ... negotiations of organized fishermen with cannery operators."[94]

Up against a Stone Wall: Potlatching in 'Y̲alis

Union formation and labour action intensified during the 1930s, a decade when ideological movements based on economic, class, and "race" theories were generating steam around the world. Julia Averkieva wrote to Franz Boas on 9 October 1933:

> Papa Franz I am so glad of your attitude toward our [Soviet] ideals. Of course the Nazis never came to them. At present Germany is taking much attention of the world ... Germany is now the most hostilcountry to us. You put our oppression and the oppressions of Nazis in one line [like?]. I thing that is impossible. They are quite contrary things. Their oppression is against the oppressed people and we suppress the oppressors ... In our country people is now busy with gathering of the crop, and with the question of its transportation. Besides that is going on the kleaning of the party ranks. This is also not less serious matter which takes much attention of the people.

"In ethnographic work," Averkieva wrote, "I want to study the clan or social organization of the Kwakiutl with use of texts ... From materials I have read on that question, there does not exist blood relations between the clans of that particular tribe, and between the tribes of the Kwakiutl. Is that so? What then unites them?"[95]

How Boas answered Averkieva is unknown, but he, too, noted the flexibility of 'na̲'mima bonds outside of the nobility. I imagine that Boas likely read Marcel Mauss's 1923-24 "Essai sur le don" (An essay on the gift). Perhaps he also considered the circulation of symbolic and material property as a unifying force.[96] Mauss was building his influential theory about exchange relationships. In *The Gift* (1950), he writes that "system[s] of the gift," such as the Northwest Coast potlatch, establish "mutual ties and alliance ... that are comparatively indissoluble ... subgroups in these ... societies ... feel that they are everything to one another."[97] Norman Hacking, who wrote for the *Vancouver Province* in 1935, likely agreed: "The spirit of the potlatch is as strong as it has ever been," he wrote. "The entire tribal and social system of the Indians is so inseparably wound about this ceremony that all combined opposition to church, school and the state have been unable to stamp it out."[98]

Like many journalists before him, Norman Hacking described 'Ya̲lis: "At first appearance Alert Bay is a typical coast fishing village ... [that] boasts such modern innovations as motor cars, beer parlours and talking pictures. It is the site of a large hospital and a residential school for Indian children. The only reminders of the past are the famous totem poles that decorate the cemetery and line the street through the straggling Indian 'rancherie' ... The vast community houses are also being demolished."[99] Marriage was in the air, and Hacking described the "lavish" wedding of a chief's daughter, a wedding that boasted a five-tier, eighty-pound cake graced by a one-foot-tall thunderbird totem pole; four bridesmaids; an Anglican service in both Kwak̓wala and English; a dance at the parish hall; and distribution of flour sacks filled with "apples, sandwiches, cake and other edibles for home consumption." The new Indian Agent, Murray Todd, cut the cake, and the bride's grandfather gave a speech "explaining the family pedigree of his clan." Afterward, a feast was held upstairs for four hundred guests. Hacking's description is strangely at odds with the headline: "Barbaric Potlatch Still Survives among Alert Bay Natives."

"I have had the potlatch system carefully explained to me by several authorities in Alert Bay," Hacking wrote, "but opinion differs on so many points it is almost impossible to attain a clear perception." "Mrs.

Stephen Cook" eventually gave him "the clearest picture of what a potlatch entails." The explanation shared much in common with the description of coppers that G̱a'aẖsta'las had offered Mabel Knight two years previously, but in 1935 she also described the crest system to Hacking. It was customary, she explained, for the man giving a potlatch

> to point out to the assembled gathering the story of his family. Each clan is claimed to be descended from a distinctive bird or animal, such as the bear or raven. As intermarrying occurs, the various emblems of the clans are combined ... Having no written history, the potlatch gives an opportunity for the donor to point out to the people the history and significance of his particular family. The tribal dances are part of this ceremony, in which younger members of the clan use the dance as a medium to imitate the various animals from which they claim descent.[100]

The final words in Hacking's article give some sense of perceptions about the future of potlatching in 1935: "The potlatch is an anachronism," he wrote. "It still flourishes, but under present conditions it can last only a few more years and will then become a relic of the past." The reality was something different.

The potlatch trials during the 1920s, and the 1927 law that criminalized fund raising for land claims, had created "hostility ... prompted by resentment of the potlatch legislation and its ... enforcement."[101] A sense of solidarity galvanized Kwakwa̱ka̱'wakw peoples, and the police and the Indian Agent found themselves "up against a stone wall" when they sought information about clandestine ceremonies. "No-one turned witness."[102] Christian potlatchers, Christian non-potlatchers, and non-Christian nonpotlatchers remained silent. The church was under pressure from the Indian Affairs Branch to support the potlatch ban. There was no longer an RCMP detachment at Alert Bay, and there had been few successful prosecutions. "Blocked in such efforts at enforcement, Kwakewlth Agency officials sought scapegoats. Public opinion, lenient judges, and, after 1929, missionaries were seen to bear some responsibility for the Kwakiutl remaining outside the law."[103]

Officials in the Indian Affairs Branch also disagreed. In 1935, at the department's request, potlatchers met with Colonel George Pragnell, Ditchburn's replacement as inspector of Indian agencies, to discuss acts of giving and receiving at the potlatch.[104] Pragnell wrote to Harold McGill, deputy superintendent of Indian affairs, that "it might ... be in the best interests of all to allow things to slide." His letter suggests that he did not support Todd's zeal for prosecution and saw harm in it, for "if the prosecution fails, the Indian Agent is the one who gets the blame and it destroys his influence with the Indians as a whole."[105]

Rector C.K.K. Prosser was not convinced that people's adherence to the custom was a sin.[106] He generated controversy in 1933 by attending a potlatch at Mamalilikala, where he reportedly wore regalia.[107] The following year, he married twenty-eight couples in a mass ceremony. The media reported that many of these couples had been married in the custom but were ineligible for relief until wed legally under the Marriage Act.[108] "Disgusted to see such blatant distortion of facts," the church denied that the couples had been married to get relief. Reverend Anfield wrote to the *Vancouver Sun* and explained that people in Alert Bay had "repeatedly requested work for their food alone rather than accept direct relief."[109] Controversies and pressure from the Indian Affairs Branch of the Department of Mines and Resources led the Anglican Church authorities to again take "the whole subject into advisement ... to gather sufficient data to make some corporate conclusion" about "all these old Indian customs."[110]

"We Are All Indians Here": Special Meetings on the Potlatch, 1936

The Anglican Church eventually supported adherence to the law. The Provincial Synod had met in 1930, and members of the Christ Church Committee in 'Yalis held special meetings in 1936 and 1937 to discuss the potlatch. At these meetings, Ga'axsta'las spoke boldly against aspects of the custom that, from the strength of her words, were crucial to her family's well-being as they affected work, marriage, and children's legitimacy. She negotiated Christian conflicts with Kwakwaka'wakw cosmology and escalating tensions between nonpotlatchers – both Christian and non-Christian – and those who practised the custom.

Two of the special meetings were held in 'Yalis, one on 31 May and the other on 1 June.[111] At the first meeting, church officials, missionaries, and parish members met to discuss "what the custom represents." The transcript of the meeting opens with Jane Cook stating: "The word 'potlatch' is used to mean 'giving away' but it is no such thing.

Potlatch is a word from the lingo known as Chinook used between the whites and Indians in the early days. The white people saw the Indians apparently to them giving away articles wholesale and they asked them what they were doing, and they replied, 'Potlatching' ... But there is a lot more to it than merely the giving away; that is only the sealing of the potlatch or the custom."[112] She continued by describing the importance of the transfer of high-ranking names. "This is what white people cannot understand, the name must live for ever. The custom has to live for ever. If one person drops it somebody else picks it up, whether they are related or interested; they take it on for gain sometimes, but they carry it on for the good of the tribe. No name can go out of existence."[113]

By this time, G̲a'ax̲sta'las had been working with church authorities for forty years and with aboriginal rights organizations for at least twenty years. As the archival trail suggests, she was a mediator-interpreter who actively translated meanings across cultures in formal and informal arenas. Here, she referred to ancestral names being inhabited by successive generations of men and women of the Kwakwa̲ka̲'wakw *noxsola* (nobility). The names carry title to territories, defining access to resources and ceremonial privileges central to well-being. For the 'na̲'mima, names constitute "inalienable wealth ... retained ... through the ... process of paying witnesses."[114] To G̲a'ax̲sta'las, the transmission of names was a crucial and dominant form of government among her people.

Missionaries and the archbishop of New Westminster had recently circulated letters supporting aboriginal peoples' right to potlatch. The 1935 salmon run had been excellent. According to agent Murray Todd, potlatching had "reached serious proportions" with this boost to the cash economy.[115] He had earlier argued forcefully for an amendment to the Indian Act that would allow department officials to confiscate "goods and supplies in excess of immediate family needs."[116] The proposed amendment was taken up by some, but Todd's so-called seizure amendment had not been passed into law. He was furious. At the meeting, he wanted answers and support from the church.[117] G̲a'ax̲sta'las addressed him directly, but diverted the focus instead to the church's interests:

"We are met here tonight as Church members for the sake of Church and missionaries, not for what we can do in supporting the law, but for the sake of our Church. I think every loyal citizen ought to judge for himself how he should act when it comes to a question of the country's laws ... But we are up against a bigger thing than law amongst the Kwawkewlth people; the gospel is taught differently at Kingcome, Mamalillikulla and Fort Rupert than it is at Alert Bay. They say 'you can be a Christian and break all the laws you like.' We want to know what the heads of the Church think. We want to know where we stand in the matter of teaching the Gospel of Christ to these people."[118]

Just that week the archbishop had been in a village performing the rite of confirmation. He told candidates they had to "drop the custom" to be eligible, and several were not confirmed because of the stipulation. Ga'axsta'las clearly remained loyal to her vision of a law-abiding society, but what she emphasized here was the responsibility of the church to uphold Christian ethics. "If any ... have the courage to leave the Custom they are hated and there is great division amongst us and they have great persecution. The Clergy preach 'be at unity, be at one with each other'; this is utterly impossible where you have some who are still practicing this heathen custom; they are suspicious, jealous of each other and us, and it is absolutely impossible to be at unity with each other as Christians."[119]

The word *heathen* jumped out at me from the transcript. I had not seen Jane Cook use it before. She was clearly emotional as she spoke about suspicion, jealousy, and divisiveness. Transcripts of the church meetings imply her sense of frustration as she spoke to the audience of missionaries. She was joined by fellow parish committee member George Luther: "This custom is compulsory among our people whether they like it or not. In regard to the law it is the duty of Christian missionaries to stand by that law ... You have not asked us why we have come out of this Custom, why we have suffered so to embrace Christianity. We want to speak to these Missionaries here so that they will get to know the true facts."[120]

"Unlovely Things": Christianity versus the Custom

While Murray Todd pressed church representatives to support enforcement of the law, George Luther talked about spiritual and educational "progress," and Jane Cook discussed ethical social behaviour.[121] They focussed on what the winter ceremonies "represented," on the imagery let loose by the dances and carved on memorial poles. Luther stated: "I would like to give you some details" about the Red Cedar Bark Dance, and he described the winter ceremonial – the Hamatsa in particular – in terms of the Christian idea of spirit possession:

> They dropped what we call the "red bark dance" for some time ... When they stard [sic] this red cedar bark dance they start worshipping it; they put the bark on their heads and the moment they put it on their heads they become witches, witchcrafters, sorcerers and all sorts of evil things; they change their names because they are all supposed to become wild, supernatural and they represent what St Paul talks about ... A person becomes wild and he will act the creature he is to represent, if it is a wolf, he acts wild and fierce; the raven is reckoned to be a liar ... In these dances a certain amount of people are supposed to disappear; that is supposed to be done by supernatural means; the man is supposed to come in touch with spirits and he becomes wild; he lives on human flesh while he is away from his own people. Then the time comes when he is to return and when he comes back he is wild, a cannibal.[122]

Luther himself had moved in and out of the custom. By 1936, he was clearly concerned about the non-Christian elements of dance society rituals.

To initiates of secret dance societies, spirit is central. "I've been told that Baxwbakwalanuksiwe' was the most feared and most evil spirit we ever had to deal with," William Wasden Jr. told me, responding to Luther's statement.[123] "And that's why the Hamaṫsa rose to be the highest of our spiritual dances. It was basically the dance that, through long rituals, had to be followed right to the tee – it was an exorcism of this most dreaded spirit. But it was to prove to the people that good will always overcome. Like I said, a lot of ancient teachings around the world – you could relate that to the Bible pretty fast." Both Wedłidi Speck and George Speck commented that the pantheon of spirits associated with Hamaṫsa ceremonials were relatively new to nineteenth-century Kwakwa̱ka̱'wakw cosmology and that these performances were likely regarded by village members in various ways. Following Luther, G̱a'a̱xsta'las let loose with words that were in sharp contrast to the temperate explanation of the crest system she had so recently given to journalists:

"Some years ago the whole village of Alert Bay had been invited to go to Village Island to attend a red cedar bark dance. The night before was the night of our bible class, and when I saw them all there and knew what they were going to the next day, it was an inspiration to me to tell them what I thought of it all. I said to them, 'I am going to talk to you tonight about your trip to Village Island. You are all going there and are going to take your little children with you; you are going to impersonate and personify dreadful things. There are indecent things, horrible things, done in public, and you are going to teach your little children all these most unlovely things in the world, cannibals, witches and murderers. I defy one of you to tell me of one lovely thing that you are going to personify in those dances. Tell me one thing that Jesus mentioned that a Christian ought to be that you are going to show to your children.' They just kept quiet. I said, 'I have never been able to find even one thing; you never mention love or any of the wonderful things that Jesus wants us to learn.' They left the next morning."[124]

Ga'axsta'las had spoken her mind to a group of potlatchers at a Bible meeting some years before. It is possible that her words preceded a potlatch that was reported to police and that this speech had led some to assume her involvement. *Unlovely things* refers to the imagery and acts portrayed in ceremonial performances, to the things people personify and impersonate in dances. "This makes perfect sense," George Speck commented. "She was against cannibalism and slavery and slave killings. This is all about possession. Christians are always against that, the possession of the body by the devil or the cannibal spirit. All of these figures represent spirit beings, and the dances are part of that – they're enactments of possession." Ga'axsta'las knew that many missionaries had observed but did not understand the meaning of these performances. While George Luther quoted the Bible, she talked about Christians not perpetuating what she felt were central Christian values.[125]

In August 2008, holding the transcript of the meeting, Pearl Alfred responded to her grandmother's statements: "Holy Smokes! Bad day! She's so angry. You can really feel it. But she never strays from what she believes. Common sense tells you that on a daily basis things must have been hot and heavy. But it would be interesting to know what brought on that. In terms of her whole life story, there must have been something that would bring that on. That's the first time she's been hateful. You've never had that sense before. At times, she must have been at her wits' end! There must have been personal attacks. It is a part of her life. We'll deal with a lot of things out there [that are said and written about her], and we're open [to that]. Why would she not be human? It's that effect on her life that still evades us – and her childhood – we still have nothing to ..." Pearl's words faded as she acknowledged the mystery surrounding Ga'axsta'las's early life.

"You have to look at this in its contemporary context," Wedłidi Speck said as he contemplated the transcript: "That's the difficulty when we take a piece out of time – we take a piece of a conversation – we're trying in modern times to look back at that period and understand it. I go back to Jane's experience of the changes in the potlatch, how people were upholding what they believed to be true about the potlatch. She was in Fort Rupert when Hamat̓sas were involved in ritual cannibalism. She obviously feels powerless. She hasn't left her position that the potlatch of that day was inappropriate."

"I can talk about that in the context of my father, when he was a little boy – about five years old. He witnessed a Tuxw'id ceremony where a woman's head was cut off. They were in a canoe on the river, and her body was thrown over the canoe, and she drifted down the river. He was crying. And then, through the course of the next few days, she came back to life. But the experience that my father had – he never, ever forgot that. When you look at the impressions that are left out of context – that's horrifying. If my father was allowed to stay in that cultural context, he would have been healed. But out of that context, he was traumatized. As an elder, he still spoke about that. Having a counselling background, I understand what that means."

Like his brother, George Speck also spoke about historical interpretation: "It's difficult to look back at something, seeing it with today's eyes. Definitely the mood had changed in the wider world, about potlatching. The world was becoming more liberal, and she just wasn't. What *are* we descended from in her eyes? The potlatch wasn't just a social system: it involved marriage, birth, and death – and rivalry. She was talking about spirit possession. It *was* possession for her. The potlatch wasn't just folklore. Nowadays, we don't see spirit possession anymore. Nasty stuff in the potlatch disappears with today's eyes ... None of us will really understand what it was like to be a true Hamat̓sa in 1860 on Village Island. Imagine when there was a deep, dark forest full of beings waiting to devour you."

Not long after G̲a'ax̲sta'las spoke at the special meeting, Annie Kamano's granddaughter Rita Barnes attended a potlatch in Gwa'yi (Kingcome). In 2005, at her home in Vancouver, she recalled the vivid imagery of that performance, which had taken place around 1940. I asked her what had changed most in potlatches. "Well, a lot of the drama," she said. "It's not as dramatic as it used to be. I remember them cutting off a head in the Big House. It was my aunt. I remember this when I was a little girl – they cut off her head and put it on the

Photo 33 Anglican Women's Auxiliary, 'Y̲alis, ca. 1930s. G̲a'ax̲sta'las is in the back row, *fourth from left. Courtesy of Wedłidi Speck.*

bow of a canoe. Seeing her head there for four days. I don't know how they did that, with all the blood and gore, and then hearing her voice singing from everywhere, coming up from the ground, from the walls of the Big House, from the ceiling. You could hear her voice in stereo! *[Laughs]* I don't know how they did that. And then she comes in on the fourth day. You hear her voice first from everywhere, and then she comes dancing in with her head intact. I'm thinking, how did they do that?"

By 1936, G̲a'ax̲sta'las had also expressed her concerns to members of the Women's Auxiliary. She spoke about the social repercussions of evading the law as well as the effects of criminalization on children in the village.

"You know the time I had here this last winter with our W.A. women, it came up so often, and I said to them, 'I just want to show you what you are doing. You are busy gathering up dishes to take to Village Island, Fort Rupert or Kingcome, you are calling in all your debts and sending your little children secretly out at night to take these dishes from one house to another.' Our W.A. members are hiding them under their shawls on the street. What kind of people are the next generation going to be when they see deceit, slyness, jealousy and lying going all around them in childhood?"[126]

Just as she had some years before, G̱a'ax̱sta'las also stated her opinion to potlatching members of the auxiliary. Perhaps these and other episodes fed antagonism toward her and other nonpotlatching Christians in Kwakwa̱ka̱'wakw villages. The next day, when potlatching chiefs joined the conversation, G̱a'ax̱sta'las spoke about that antagonism.

The meeting began with testimony from a man who had left the custom: "It filled my mind," he told those present, "[but] my ambition, my love of the Custom has gone ... I have publicly renounced the Custom, and have found that my mind has steadied itself." When asked what he thought was "anti-Christian in the Potlatch," he listed pride, ambition, and supernatural worship in "the part of the Custom you call our dances."

Another man, listed as "anti-Potlatch," was asked about "Indian contract marriage." This question opened discussion about women's ability to leave a marriage and about brideprice. At the age of sixty-six, having married once, G̱a'ax̱sta'las expressed a sense of regret, particularly for her children, who were evidently most vulnerable to the politics surrounding *Ḵadzitła* (marriage contracts). At the meeting, she addressed a young man: "We are all Indians here, we all know the customs ... Is it not a disgrace for a man or a girl to choose and live with a man or a girl without some sum of money being paid ... Is it not true that it is the certain sum of money that is paid over that makes it respectable?" He replied that he was not able to answer because he was not a chief and had no right to speak on behalf of his village. But G̱a'ax̱sta'las continued: "You know that any Chief, any decent man, cannot live with a woman as his wife without a price being paid, even if they were married in the Church. I am talking about those that are practicing the custom. To be respectable, and to be legally joined in the sight of the Indians, there has to be a price paid over between the parties, and this is still held today."

Charlie Nowell was present. He asked Jane Cook:

"When your son Herbert married my daughter Agnes was there any price paid for her?"

"Certainly there was no price paid for my son's wife; we would never allow any price to be paid for anybody belonging to us. My son chose his wife himself and they were married in Church as Christians ought to be without the transaction first ... It is no use talking about people who are definitely out of the custom as we have been for years; we would not have anything to do with a price."

"That is true," Charlie Nowell said, "but I could have refused my daughter."

"Yes, we give you credit for that," G̲a'ax̲sta'las replied. "I should like to declare here, that as an Indian with the potlatch custom in my blood, that no respectable Indian man will live with a woman without a price being paid; the price makes the respectability... Every man present here, every respectable Indian, must have had somebody pay a price for his wife... It would be a disgrace to them if there was no price paid; there must be a contract."

Another Kwakwa̲ka̲'wakw man agreed with Jane Cook's declaration.[127]

Missionaries asked Charlie Nowell about the legitimacy of children. Nowell told them that children from church marriages "still belong to us." G̲a'ax̲sta'las also spoke, offering herself as an example. She said that without the marriage contract her children would be considered illegitimate:

"I am Fort Rupert and being a Christian and my husband at the time of our marriage also being a Christian, although we were children of the potlatch system we saw even then that it was wrong ... Of that union children were born, 16 in fact. My children are illegal in the eyes of the potlatch system or custom; for years it was my shame that my children were illegal and would neither have been considered of the tribe from which my husband came ... Some of them are married; the boys that are married are still not recognized by the Indians in the Nimpkish tribe. Had it not been for the Indian Agent and our determination to have them classed and fight this point in the custom so that our children in the books of the Department were put down as Nimpkish, none of them would be recognized as Nimpkish today. That shows how the Indians look at a marriage that is contracted only in the Church."

"Are they illegal in the sight of the Indians?" an unnamed person asked.

"Yes," Jane Cook replied, "because I was never paid for and did not go through an Indian custom marriage. It was only through the respectability of my connections and my husband's connections that we were countenanced in the country."

"Are they still looked down on today?"

"Yes," Jane Cook replied. "They were boycotted for years, my boys were boycotted from work in any industry in this district for years by their own tribe because they were illegal in the eyes of the Indians."[128]

One chief said that people were married in the church so that they could be "publicly acknowledged as man and wife" but that "children have legal status under the Indian contract marriage; they do not go to church to make it legal."[129] The chief referred to *gwał* (fulfillment of the marriage contract, repayment from the bride's family).[130]

Although the conversation took place in a colonial context within the Anglican Church, those who spoke discussed legitimacy through a Kwakwa̱ka̱'wakw idiom that revolved around gwał. Their language completely ignored the state categories that legally defined "Indians" and their children through the criteria of blood and the patriline (the father's line of descent).[131] Instead, it was the potlatch system or custom that was the social and legal institution defining membership and exclusion. There is a strong impression that as G̱a'a̱xsta'las asserted her own identity as "Fort Rupert" (Kwagu'ł) and as Indian, she was urging those present to acknowledge her children's place among her husband's tribe, the 'Na̱mgis. Interrupting the Kwakwa̱ka̱'wakw conversation, Principal Anfield warned those present that "the day is coming when it is going to be absolutely imperative that your children have legal parentage and legal status; enfranchisement is coming ... and you owe it to your children." His words sounded the toll that state institutions were moving away from any recognition of indigenous knowledge systems, especially those through which *K̲adzitła* sanctioned membership.

Despite their withdrawal from the potlatch, as G̱a'a̱xsta'las stated, she and her husband, Na̱ge, were recognized for "the respectability of their connections," a point in part evidenced by their relationships to the potlatching chiefs present. G̱a'a̱xsta'las's son Herbert Cook was then married to Charlie Nowell's daughter Agnes. Her daughter Pearl Cook was married to Chief Harry Mountain's son Robert. Marriage among members of the Kwakwa̱ka̱'wakw nobility, was arguably, the best proof of one's standing in society. G̱a'a̱xsta'las's admission of shame because she was "never paid for" suggests the social power of customary unions.[132]

"It kind of flies in the face of what she was working for – for women not being objectified. In terms of some of her sorrows, listening to her words, there was definitely some injury there," Wedłidi Speck told me. "And she would have been drawn into some of that old thinking, even though she was aspiring to be outside of that. I often wonder who would have benefitted from that. You have to ask the question. Stephen. So, by not [being paid for], did she see that he was demasculinated? If it's about power, then you have to ask what power a person would have. So, she could then say, 'Look, this was transferred. The debts were paid. I'm free.' The only time that you would make reference to that is if you had a root or a connection to the culture. So, she still has a foot there, and she is struggling with that."

Given the criticism today that Jane Cook was not cultural, several of her descendants were struck by her 1936 admission of shame. "There was enough cultural stuff in her for that to bother her," one of her grandchildren said to me. "We might have to pay that debt for her someday." The comment was not meant lightly. Many aboriginal communities "already have ways of understanding how historical grievances should rightly be handled."[133]

George Speck spoke about the Christian critique of Kwakwa̱ka̱'wakw ceremonial practices and his great-grandmother's admission of shame: "Potlatching and participation in potlatching and the dances and the stories that go with them – like the Cannibal Dance and the representations in that particular ceremony – do speak about certain spirits and supernatural beings. We do it. I do it. I'm a Hamat̓sa. Do I believe in Baxwbakwalanuksiwe'? Probably not. Although I like the idea of being a cannibal *[laughs]*. Yeah, so all of those kinds of things, and how people explained their world then, and how people explain their world today are significantly different. A lot of the symbolism and the characters that occupied our world in those days helped us to live in that world. So, with the coming of Christianity, colonization, and a new economy, everything was changing. Lots of people were adapting, and new explanations were probably useful. But you've still got Jane saying, 'I never got married in the Big House,' which probably speaks to having her relationship recognized the formal way or Indian way. I got married in the Big House, but I also got married in a civil ceremony. There's two ways of people recognizing that. In the civil ceremony, the people involved were much closer to me – family. Whereas in the Big House it was all the tribes. So, I guess that would probably be much, much more significant for Jane at that time, because I think the hold that potlatching had and the meaning that people attached to potlatching was much more significant in those days."

Today, some of Jane Cook's descendants are surprised to hear that her sons were ostracized from various industries. "I never heard about boycotts," Pearl Alfred told me. "They were so active in the politics, in the fishing and the Native Brotherhood. Reggie Cook was the contact for the Canadian Fishing Company, getting contracts, and for BC Packers it was Moses Alfred who would get boats. They had power. They were heavy-duty business people. The boys dabbled a bit in logging in the valley, but then fishing was their whole life, and they were so successful, in spite of this. I think the ones that suffered were their kids. A couple of them moved away. There were two, I think, who enfranchised, which wasn't unusual in those days because you couldn't get a job. It was just a way of saying, 'Okay, you enfranchise, you will get a job.' They were the only two, I think, who moved away. The rest lived here."

Commercial fishing was and is an independent, competitive enterprise in which each boat vies for the same run of fish during a limited opening of the fishery. It is difficult to say what might have happened given the rivalries within the industry during the 1930s. Although hard hit by the Depression, the relative prosperity of fishers likely tightened lineage support networks, perhaps even Christian networks, at the expense of others. In 1934, fishers had difficulty accessing food fish permits. The successful salmon season of 1935 was followed a year later by two strikes at Rivers Inlet and Smith's Inlet, actions that left Kwakwa̱ka̱'wakw fishers without adequate means to purchase winter supplies. The 1936 strike at Rivers Inlet resulted in the complete loss of the fishing season.

In response to reading G̱a'a̱xsta'las's comments about her sons, I was sent a copy of the signature pages of guests who attended Reggie and Nellie Cook's wedding in 1926. "In my Mum and Dad's wedding," Pearl Alfred told me, "anybody who was anybody, the entire community, was there. At their wedding, almost all the chiefs were there, and all the bigwigs of the community were there. I found that really fascinating ... I thought, well, if she was really outside of the social, why would anybody have come?" Ninety-three signatures fill two pages, among them the leading chiefs and their wives from several Kwakwa̱ka̱'wakw villages. To family members, this documentation of attendance speaks louder than any other evidence. It is a manifestation of social relationships and social standing in 'Ya̱lis that seems to challenge Jane Cook's description of boycotts and illegitimacy.

At the meeting in 1936, G̱a'a̱xsta'las described her own sense of marginalization:

"Most of our people are baptized Christians; many of them are confirmed and communicants, yet they are practicing this custom and

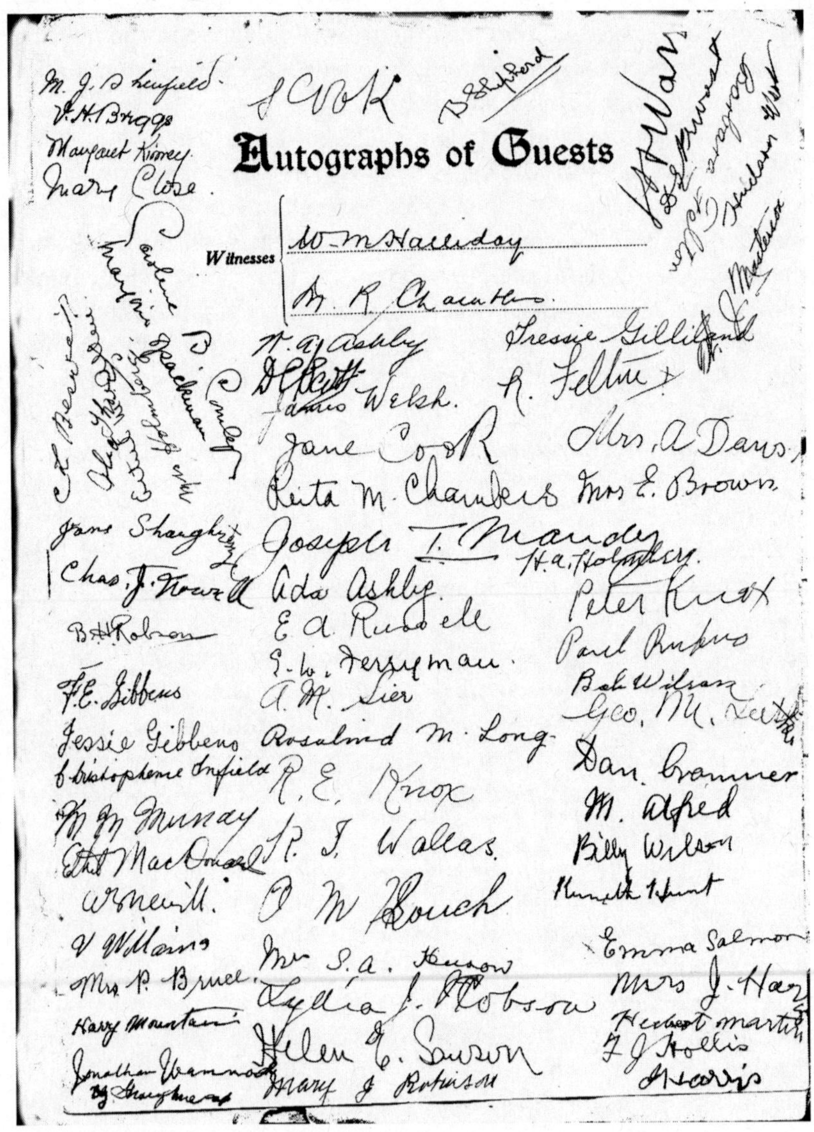

Photo 34 Signature page from Reggie and Nellie Cook's wedding, 1926.
Courtesy of Reg Cook Jr.

cannot feel one with us. Why? I would like these young men who have been called to this meeting to understand it is out of good feeling and it is out of love for our work here of the Church amongst our Kwawkewlth people that we brought this matter forward ...

"I know from experience I could tell a lot more because I have gone through it. I have tried to live a Christian life amongst my own people, but you all know how they feel towards me and how they have treated us as outcasts ...

"I know you look on me as your enemy, you who love and stock to the custom, because I have been interpreter for the Government for one thing and because I do not tell you you can practice the potlatch and be a Christian. The more I learn the more I see that we were right when we broke away from it and had nothing more to do with it."[134]

Wedłidi Speck thought through his great-grandmother's statements: "Stephen – Nage – was 'Namgis. He had a root there. That was understood. He has a name. And Chief Lagius and Chief Tłakwadzi stood up for Stephen's mother to lay rest to any criticisms that were there, that would speak to her point about being outcasts. It was maybe that people were being made fun of. I also think that we have to remember that we weren't Canadians; we were Indians until, what, 1963? We weren't Canadians. So, as a result, you had to enfranchise in order to work anywhere. It was fortunate that Stephen had the ability to buy boats and claim timber and do salteries and all the things that he did commercially. That allowed him to have the independence. He was a self-made man. But his family also has boats – *his* boats ... I think that comment [about feeling like outcasts] was probably emotional. I think we could easily say, 'It's hard to be a leader. It's lonely. You signed up for it, Granny' *[laughs]*."

Ga'axsta'las evidently believed that people had to choose either Christianity or the custom. Given the number of active Christians who were potlatchers, her views must have been controversial. "Think over this one thought," she said at the meeting, "and say to yourself truly whether you can follow Him and follow the practices of the Custom, whether you can follow the Cross and follow the Potlatch in the sense that we all know it." When one chief said that the potlatch had been given to them by God, Jane Cook translated his words: "This custom was given by God to them and he does not know whether we are right or they are right. He means the Government ... He says we are wrong in saying that they worship idols. He means me personally ... [He] and I are connected but there is always strained feeling over this matter ... I have often told our people that our forefathers did worship a God but they did not realize that this custom was worship because they did not realize then what true worship was."[135]

Ga'axsta'las suggested that the custom, as practised by her forefathers, had become something other than what it was – "the Potlatch in the sense that we all know it." As the meeting progressed, it became clear that she saw in the potlatch division rather than unity, and she stated that the outlawed custom had propagated a social climate of deceit. She again talked about how the potlatch ban had influenced church membership, suggesting that people were joining the church with the incorrect assumption that they would be protected. She stood for an expression of Christianity that was, she felt, in conflict with the custom:

"We wanted to have this Conference ... to see if we can go to the Kwawkewlth people along this coast ... Can we say to these people "Come on, be baptized, join the Church, be confirmed, and still stay in the potlatch ... I think it is a pity because the Government enforced this law so many of our Indians came and were baptized because they thought it would protect from ... the penalties of the law and that the Church would stand by them. We did not call you here to argue with you or try to argue you out of the potlatch."

The meeting's transcript gives the sense that, although (as G̲a'ax̲sta'las herself stated) "this is a conference of missionaries," the real dialogue was occurring between Jane Cook and the chiefs. They were age mates who had grown up together and stood beside one another in anticolonial arenas. At this meeting, they were hashing out an internal debate about tradition that was both personal and ideological.

In 2010, as we were again discussing this difficult chapter in the story of his great-grandmother, Wedłidi Speck said, "The Native Women's Association of Canada could be Granny. Granny and them could be saying, 'This is what is really important – the way you're marrying our daughters out, the way you're treating our daughters, the way you're not paying attention to the gardens, all this stuff. Step up!'"[136]

"A Glory Rather Than a Sin"

Word was out that the Christ Church committee had held a conference in 1936, and people in Gwa'yi (Kingcome) asked that the report be sent to A.W. Neill, member of Parliament for Comox-Alberni.[137] Neill wrote to Agent Todd, and the church authorities, in turn, replied that the "private meeting called by the Bishop of Columbia" was an internal matter. They denied that the church "force[s] any bereaved Indians to have a Church funeral" or "any couple to seek matrimony within the Church." They also denied refusing confirmation to a girl because her father and grandfather were potlatchers. Neill's subsequent demand to allow moderate potlatches to "preserve the so-called aesthetic" parts of ceremonies was refused by the committee.[138]

The Indian Commissioner for BC was pleased by the finding. He thought that strict supervision of "potlatches in moderation" was impossible.[139] However, he did approve of Neill's recommendation to allow the following: dances not part of the potlatch, funeral obsequies, and "the Indian form of marriage," which would "follow our own forms of marriage by recognized authority."[140] At the same time, the Anglican Synod of the Diocese of British Columbia passed a unanimous resolution that "it would be against the best interests of our Indian people to change the existing law regarding 'The Potlatch,' so-called, without very careful thought and study of the situation on the ground by experts."[141]

Responding to a call for information from one of Neill's opponents, Jane and Stephen Cook sent a letter to the member of Parliament for Nanaimo, James Taylor.

COPY of a COPY

S. COOK

Alert Bay, B.C.,
April 15, 1937

J.S. Taylor, M.P.,
House of Commons,
Ottawa, Ontario.

Dear Sir,–

We have received your letter dated April 6th and will try to set forth for your information the true facts in regard to the customs commonly known as the "Potlatch."

It is noted in your letter you refer to this as a "tribal custom," but I would like to call your attention to the fact that it is much more than just a tribal custom; it is a "native government" or constitution by which the lives of the native people are entirely governed and controlled. This control starts from the birth of a child, through every stage of phase of his life, and continues not only to his death but long after, when the debts and obligations left by him are passed on and carried on and paid by his heirs.

This government or constitution is the only government or control recognized and adhered to by the Indians who practice this custom. This is a fact not generally understood or appreciated by the white people, who look up to our Dominion Government and our Parliament as the means of control and government in our country. To those who are engaged in the potlatch custom this government means nothing; the only control they recognize is their own native custom as explained above, and until this is abolished there will never be any whole-hearted co-operation or loyalty to the Government or the Crown from these native people when their interests and loyalty are claimed by the native custom. As you can readily see, to the mind of the native people the Government of Canada is there-fore only a means of assistance and holds no respect for them and the laws of the Custom mean more to them than the laws of the country.

You wish to know whether the custom is increasing or whether it is in common use. The Custom itself has never abated in any way, but the practice of it more or less depends on circumstances at the time. For instance, when the Potlatch Law was first enforced, and several cases were brought up and prosecuted, the practice of the custom quieted down for the time being, although it was practiced secretly and not openly and so part of the glory was taken away. Then when the depression came along and money was scarce amongst the Indians, this also had a quieting effect on the practice of the Custom, although even than the hold of it was as great as ever in the minds of the people and some effort was made even in a small way to carry out their obligations.

As pointed out in the first part of this letter, it should be remembered that each event in the life of an Indian is governed by the Potlatch, and has its part in it; therefore a birth, death or marriage requires the practice of the custom by the paying or giving away of money and the other parts relative to it.

During the last few years since public opinion and persons in influence positions have seen fit to encourage the Indians in this custom, and have held out hopes to them that the potlatch law would be repealed, giving them full liberty to practice the customs openly, it has increased, and has been carried on more openly than in the past when it was hidden through fear of the actual consequences of being caught.

You wish to know if any abuses develop out of the practice of this Custom. Surly it is clear to anyone that a custom that controls every phase of a person's life and every event in that life, cannot be helpful or progressive. The practice of the custom is one of *force,* thus destroying all personal liberty. When a death occurs in a family, the bereaved ones are met by the Indians who "mourn" with them until the bereaved one makes the promise of his potlatch. Whether he is financially able or not makes no differences; he must raise the money somewhere to fulfil his obligations.

Children are forced to take part in [a] practice they may have no desire to take part in, but are forced to by their parents who are called upon to fulfil the obligations through them. At any time in his life an Indian may be called upon to repay potlatch debts (or "gifts" as you call them) which have been handed out to him at a previous potlatch, thus crippling him financially and making it impossible for him to progress in any way, either by helping himself or his family or improving his home or living conditions. That is the reason why even though the Indians have earned thousands of dollars in the past through good fishing seasons, they have today homes that are only shacks, no furniture, and no advantages for their children; even the effects they do have in their houses may be called on at any time to be used as repayment of debt.

This brings us to the methods of raising funds when they are forced to repay debts. Every means is used to obtain money, and this is where the selling and bartering of women plays a large part, either by marriage or by prostitution. In regard to the latter, it is not generally known, but payment for prostitution of women makes a wrong right, and anything that is done to help the Custom is a glory rather than a sin.

Sometimes the marriage is cloaked with a civil or a religious ceremony, which of course later complicates the affair as then a legal tie binds the parties together where as they have probably no intention of staying together except for the completion of the contract made of their behalf. A marriage in the Indian custom has no responsibilities or vows as our marriage has in the Church. The results of this can be readily seen; the marriage tie is not considered in any way sacred or binding, and results in broken homes and wrecked lives as we have today.

The conflict of the Potlatch Custom results in prejudice, jealousies, rivalry and hatred for the whole practice is one of the competition and rivalry, each one trying to outdo the other by any means whatever in order to make himself higher in the standing of the tribe. This of course results in no co-operation for any tribal benefit or progress in any form, and it will readily be seen how this works to the detriment of the Indian people as long as it is practiced.

The Indian Department is encouraging education and has provided Day Schools and Residential Schools for this purpose where young Indian boys and girls are placed and educated for a few years of their lives. When they return to their villages they are immediately forced by their parents or guardians to take their part in the practice of the custom and before long they are so involved in this practice that the high ideals with which they left school are immersed in the jealousies and hatreds of the custom.

It is said by many in support of the practice of the custom that it is not today as it was in the past, but the spirit and foundation of the practice is still living in its oldest and strongest form, and would be carried out.

This is only a general outline of what the custom represents in its general form in the lives of the people and the results it has on them. We have not given or gone into the various forms in the custom, the dances and orgies that are carried on in connection with them, the spirit of which has never died out, but this general outline may give you some idea of what it truly represents and now the Indian people can never make any real progress so long as it continues.

In our opinion the Government was quite right and justified in making the Potlatch Laws, and doing their best to abolish this heathen custom and make loyal citizens of the native people, and we hope that nothing will ever be done to upset it.

If you should be in the neighborhood of Alert Bay, as you suggested in the last paragraph of your letter, we would be very pleased to see you.

Yours respectfully,

(signed) Stephen & Jane Cook.[142]

Jane and Stephen Cook wrote that "the spirit and foundation of the practice is still living," that it was a system of *control* and *force.* Their letter emphasized G̲a'ax̲sta'las's concern for material well-being by outlining the intergenerational repayment of potlatch debts that kept people poor, despite money earned in the fishery. But they also brought up social issues in the villages, particularly "broken homes and wrecked lives," which they linked to arranged marriages. Although G̲a'ax̲sta'las objected to colonial representations of the sale of women, she explicitly mentions the "selling and bartering of women ... either through marriage or prostitution" in this letter. It is, as far as we know, the only written statement by G̲a'ax̲sta'las on prostitution, although she spoke often about it. Relationships between potlatchers and non-potlatchers were clearly uncomfortable enough that the Cooks were willing to write openly about things "not generally known."

In 1961, Helen Codere summarized the state of potlatching in 'Yalis during the Great Depression:

> Even when sufficient wealth was accumulated for a potlatch distribution ... recipients were unable to raise the funds for a potlatch with the necessary increase in return gifts. Those few who stubbornly potlatched became self-righteously embittered at the failure of their debtors to repay them and refused to continue to "just give away property for nothing." Those unable to potlatch rankled at reminders of their debts and felt the bitterness of their dilemma. The younger people who had not yet taken a place in the potlatch saw the system as the source of all troubles and unhappiness around them.[143]

Codere concluded that by the time "prosperity returned in the forties, the potlatch as a system was broken."[144]

Colonial relationships were coming into sharp focus in unlikely places. Jane and Stephen Cook likely attended the Synod of the Diocese of British Columbia in 1937. One wonders what they made of statements such as this:

> The supremacy of Europe and the white races is now definitely questioned, and the world system based on their privileges has definitely disappeared. We are face to face with the emancipation of the coloured races of the world. They have copied our science and our technique, and imitation and revolt go hand in hand. The other things we have taught them are going to be a potent weapon in their hands towards our overthrow ... this crisis opens up, with an utterly new urgency, the whole question of spiritual leadership in the world.[145]

"Better to Prevent Than to Cure": The TB Preventorium

In January 1939 the Indian Agent, Murray Todd, threatened to cut off potlatching chiefs from government relief.[146] The following month, St. Michael's TB Preventorium opened. According to one newspaper article, the fourteen-bed facility "work[ed] on the theory that it is better to prevent than to cure open infection in Indian children and young people."[147] The compelling demand for Indian-only hospitals, made in 1923 by Ga'axsta'las and other members of the Allied Tribes executive, was ignored. "Open cases will be hospitalized in different units in Vancouver and in other hospitals," a situation that

Photo 35 Michael Kamano; Jane Cook's sister, Annie Kamano; and Grace Scow at Gwa'yasdams (Gilford Island). *Courtesy of Doreen Fitch.*

left aboriginal sufferers and their families vulnerable to a racist medical system and responsible for the care of people in their homes.[148] Built as a manual-training project by twelve boys aged fourteen to sixteen who attended the residential school, the preventorium would also provide "older girls of the school ... practical training as ward maids, giving them a greater chance to be of use in home nursing when they return to their villages."[149] An unreferenced study had found that 50 percent of the 823 "Indian deaths from tuberculosis" in 1937 had been "natives under twenty years of age."[150]

In December 2004, Doreen Fitch showed me a photograph of her mother, Grace Scow, and Jane's Cook's sister, Annie Kamano, taken at Gwa'yasda̲ms (Gilford Island). "My great-grandmother, she died of TB," Doreen said. "Same with my mother. My two aunts died of the same thing." Like many people with whom I spoke, tuberculosis punctuated Doreen's genealogy.

"Funny *she* didn't have that," Doreen said, pointing to Annie Kamano. "She looked after my mother when my mother was really sick, and I was put in a preventorium, which I still get angry about today."

"In Alert Bay?"

Doreen nodded. "It was 1939 I went in that preventorium. It was a church thing called St. George's Preventorium. I went in with my cousin Amy – my mother's sister's oldest daughter – went in the same day! We went in together. We stayed there for four years! We never went to school. I had just turned eight. Four years I was in there, with no schooling! For about two years, or a year and a half, I wasn't even allowed out of bed, and I didn't feel sick at all. They gave us treatments where they put us on, like, a stretcher, and they had this lamp that looked like fluorescent lights, but the colour was different from the fluorescent lights.[151] We had to put sunglasses on, and they put a towel here *[gestures across her chest]* and a towel there *[gestures across her thighs]*. They assigned that light on us. It was only for maybe five minutes – maybe not even that. Then they'd turn us over – put the towel in the back of us. Then you had to put lotion on after we got off the stretcher. That actually made our skin chapped. I don't know what it was. Now they've got pills and shots for TB. And it wasn't a sanatorium. It was called a preventorium."

"What gets me is that I didn't go to school all the time I was there, and not even feeling sick. Just mostly religious stuff was taught." She laughed. "Yeah, and my cousin and I, we came out exactly the same day! If we were sick and put in there for something – how could two people get better from whatever it was at the same time?"

"What was an average day like in the preventorium?"

"Well, a lot of us stayed a year or two years, the ones that I went with. I think my cousin and I might have been the longest there. I think we had our breakfast around 8:00 a.m., lunch, dinner, to bed about 7:30 p.m. At 7:00, we had a prayer meeting before we went to bed. We were just stuck in there! There was a girls' ward and a boys' ward. The first year I was there, there was no boys' ward, and then the second year – I think it was 1940 – when they had the boys' ward. They had a little room which was maybe the size of that living area with three beds in there, and they said those three women who were in there – well, they were teenagers – had open cases of TB. I think one of them stayed there a long time who was from the Queen Charlotte Islands. A lot of them went to the residential school and then they'd put them in there. I don't know if they were really sick or what." Doreen laughed again. "But nobody seemed sick when I was there. Even those three people that they said had open cases of TB, even they didn't seem sick to me. It was part of the residential school – St. Mike's. Pray morning and night!"

Seven months after the preventorium opened, Canada declared war on Germany.

PART VIII

One Voice from Many: Citizenship, 1940-48

"I moved in with Granny and Papa, and Granny was a real hard worker. She had this big garden that she looked after herself, and Papa worked in the store. And the meals! She'd get up at five in the morning! I'm still asleep, and she goes up to the garden. She's there from five, and then she comes back down about seven-thirty, eight o'clock to put the porridge on for us and the cereal and makes her homemade bread, then goes back up to the garden again. Ah, she was a hard worker. Awesome ... She brought us up quite well."

In her office at the Alert Bay Medical Centre in 2002, Emma Alfred spoke about her grandmother's presence in her life, which inspired her to work with people affected by drug and alcohol use. Emma conjured the rhythms of the Cook family big house:

"When I moved in, I was going to church with her, Sunday school. They used to have Bible class, and I think I was the youngest one doing Bible class. Most of the Christian stuff she had us attend, which we did enjoy. We did enjoy going to church and learning from her and sitting in church and listening to her talk our language and interpret what the preacher had said, interpret to our Native people all sitting there.

"They used to have people coming from different villages up there. I never knew until I got a little older that she was counselling these people. They'd come up there and talk with her about their problems, and she would help them with it. More Gran than it was Papa. Papa was more a businessman in the store all the time. But Gran always had visitors, and they talked the language. So, that's where I got to understand it, just from listening to them talk."

"What sort of problems do you think she was helping people with?"

"Probably home problems, money problems, you know, somebody being really ill. Yeah, she really helped people. I think that's where I get this idea for my job – working for the alcohol and drug people ... She was a midwife too, eh? I asked her once, 'How many kids?' I said, 'Granny, tell me how many kids you've delivered all these years.' And she couldn't go back, and she just said, 'Oh, hundreds of them.' And she was hauled out of the house in the middle of the night to go and sit with a person who was dying. She stayed right with them until they died, and she even dressed them for the family. She was quite the woman in those days.

"I think I was about five years old when I moved up and stayed with them because I was scared of potlatches. It scared me at my age – you know, being so young. I guess it was the big fire. There was a big huge fire and the yelling that goes on, and I didn't know anything about potlatches at that time. Being five years old, it just bothered me. And yet it was never mentioned to me that I had to be scared of potlatches. None of my other brothers and sisters were. I was the only one. Uncle Reggie [Cook Sr.] brought me home. I was crying when he came to deliver food to us. We were in an isolated village, and he brought some groceries to mom, and he heard me crying away. And he said, 'What's the matter with Emma?'

"And they said, 'She's scared of the potlatch. She's been crying since yesterday.'

"He said, 'Okay, get her clothes ready.'

"They threw my clothes in a box and brought me home, and I stayed here ever since. I was just happy to get on a boat and get away from that racket, which scared me. So, then I lived with Gran, and she brought me up ...

"There were eight, nine, ten, eleven, twelve, thirteen, probably about fifteen of us in one house, but she had an upstairs and downstairs. Every morning that Bible was on her desk. When I wake up in the morning, here's Gran, reading the Bible. And then Papa would ask her to tell him what she was reading, and she would tell him. I'd sit there and listen to her. Yeah. But she had books galore that she used to read.

"I mean the radio was nothing to her. That was all that we had was the radio – we'd be all sitting by the radio, listening to the Lone Ranger." She laughed. "And then we'd all go to bed after. But Gran read. Ten o'clock was lights out. Off to bed her and Papa would go. She used to laugh when Papa used to say things to her. I stayed in her bedroom. I had a bed in the corner, and they had a big bed on the other side. When Papa used to say goofy things to her, she used to just giggle away. I stayed up there right until I was twelve, thirteen years old, and I had to move back. The only reason I moved back home was because my mom had all the kids, and I had to go and help her. And it was a real different atmosphere than what Granny and Papa had. I wasn't used to that. It took me a really long time. Every now and then, I had to just go back home to Gran and stay a night or two nights and then I had to go back with Mom and help with the kids. I was the second oldest. It was really hard getting used to Mom and Dad's ways, because I was used to Papa's and Granny's. Everything just seemed so easy for me up in Gran's."

"How would you describe Alert Bay in those days?"

"It was a big, huge place to me," she said. "It was just awesome because, where I came from, Village Island, it was just a small, little place. I guess that would be my Vancouver, coming here. There was a lot of different things, though, in Village Island. They did have Christian people there, too. Those people, they had a church there. Then coming back to Gran's, it was different. I don't know. She just knew how to make your life so important, like, 'There's nothing wrong with you. You're okay.'"

Many of G̱a'ax̱sta'las and Na̱ge's surviving grandchildren remember the 1940s well. They travel another avenue of memory through G̱a'ax̱sta'las's books, some of which survive as respected mementos circulated after her death in 1951. "She was very interested in other cultures and in religious worship," Pearl Alfred told me when I asked about these books. "Whenever you crawled into her bed, there were always stacks everywhere." She remembers a book on Egyptian archaeology and books on Hinduism, Buddhism, and Islam. "'You have to know about everything,' she would say. 'You have to know about all religions.'" Pearl kept her stamp collection in one of her grandmother's books, John Steinbeck's *The Wayward Bus,* and she remembers *Gulliver's Travels*. She showed me Jane's copies of Ralph Waldo Trine's *The Greatest Thing Ever Known* (1898), a tract on Christian "New Thought" philosophy; H.P. Thompson's *Worship in Other Lands* (1933), a missionary guide to crosscultural religious practices; and *The Iron Heel* (1908), a dystopian novel about socialist revolt.

I wonder what Jane Cook's response to *The Iron Heel* might have been. Jack London's mildly futuristic novel is notable for its descriptions of poverty in America through the rise and fall of unionism under a repressive and brutal oligarchy. Although we do not know when Ga'axsta'las read the work, in the late 1930s and the 1940s Jane and Stephen and their children were certainly embroiled in labour politics. Stephen was a central figure in the Pacific Coast Native Fishermen's Association (PCNFA) and, later, their sons were active in the Native Brotherhood of British Columbia (NBBC).

The Alert Bay Cannery reopened in the 1940s. Kwakwaka'wakw fishers and others benefitted from increased fish prices and from government war measures that encouraged aboriginal participation in commercial fisheries. Mechanization in processing plants meant that fewer Chinese and aboriginal workers were guaranteed employment, but the Second World War brought an economic boom to 'Yalis.[1] When the PCNFA united with the NBBC in 1942, they stood in solidarity to protest the taxation of Indian income. Later, the NBBC fought against conscription and organized around better cannery housing, equal pay, old age pensions, family allowance, and improved medical and education services.

In her seventies, Ga'axsta'las was still called to Kwakwaka'wakw homes – to assist births, to sit with people who were ill, and to comfort those who were dying. When I asked Emma Alfred if her grandmother ever went out on the fishing boats, she told me a story about the death of her paternal grandmother.

"[Granny Cook] had to go to Village Island to look after my other grandmother, my dad's mom. She was dying of cancer. So, she stayed at the village for a whole month while my granny was dying. She stayed right there with her ... My granny called for her, so she went. And that's when she went on a boat. She went on her own son's seiner boat."

"When would that have been?"

"My other granny must have died when I was about five – it was before I moved to Alert Bay. I remember lying beside her in bed, wondering why she never got up. I didn't realize she was sick, and they had to remove me from her every now and then. And the next thing I knew, Gran was there, my other granny, and she stayed and looked after her until she died. A month she stayed. And they brought her here because she wanted to be buried here in Alert Bay. So Gran brought her home and buried her here."

"It's pretty amazing to hear how she was called out to these villages."

"And she went. She just dropped everything and went. And if somebody was dying in the middle of the night – two, three, four o'clock in the morning – she just got dressed. Never said, 'No, I can't go. I've got lots of work to do,' or anything. She was gone. Especially when she was delivering babies, she'd come back and say, 'Oh, it was a little boy,' or 'Oh, it was twins,' things like that. It was just the job for her, and she enjoyed it. I used to want to ask her, when people are dying in front of you, doesn't it bother you? But I heard her talking once to one of the people from Kingcome, one of the ladies, and she said, 'They know where they're going. They're in good hands, and they're not suffering anymore. They're in God's hands, so why should we feel bad? Instead of having them suffering on earth, and we can't do anything about it.' Just hearing her say that made me really think, yeah, it's okay to die. And the way she explained it – it was all right if you weren't going to get better. She used to be out almost every night ... She'd up and just leave."

The rhythm of the Cook big house was punctuated by G̲a'ax̲sta'las's comings and goings, seasonal fishing activities, Brotherhood meetings, illnesses, soccer tournaments, and, to some extent, by the Anglican Church calendar, as Jane and Stephen's relationship with the church continued. By all accounts, G̲a'ax̲sta'las's religious study intensified in her later years. She analyzed Christian texts and focussed on scriptural prophecy. One descendant remembered her corresponding with other biblical scholars, but there is now little to show of these dialogues, for, as is customary, her clothes and some personal papers were burned in a fire on the beach after her death. She and Stephen travelled to the Anglican synod in Victoria, taking with them each year different granddaughters, each of whom vividly recalls these journeys to the city. As Emma mentioned, church officials were among the couple's many household visitors. "The bishop, I was so scared of him," she told me. "Big ring on his hand, and the way he dresses. But she treated him like he was this ordinary man, which he was. He was one that came once, twice a year here."

During our early conversations, most of G̲a'ax̲sta'las's descendants eventually came around to the topic of the potlatch. As Emma told me: "Once I heard Gran say about potlatches, 'All the money that they use went to potlatch, never mind their family, never mind their kids.' And that's one time I heard Gran saying that that's why she disagreed with the potlatch, because of things like that and how people sought to be higher than the next person. Instead, 'We're all equal. Doesn't matter what we do' and 'Everyone wants to be chief.' That's the only time I ever heard Gran say something about the potlatch. I really agreed with her when she said that to me."

In the 1940s, the Anglican Church revisited the question of amending the potlatch ban, which then inhabited sections 140 and 142 of the Indian Act. Discussion still focussed on the compatibility of Christianity and the custom and on material security, but missionaries in villages beyond Alert Bay were sympathetic to the continued calls from potlatchers. As during the First World War, government anti-potlatch rhetoric was grounded in patriotism and warnings against waste.

Potlatchers in 'Y̲alis had lived under strict surveillance and official pressure for over twenty years. They had manoeuvred around two Indian Agents, who were zealous enforcers of the ban. Charges or indictments had been laid against 164 people; some of the accused had experienced the humiliation of imprisonment. Sustained tensions led to improvised forms of potlatching that fulfilled ceremonial obligations. For those in 'Y̲alis, however, performing the full program of dances that constituted the winter ceremonial was both dangerous and logistically difficult. In more distant villages, potlatching continued, and it was from these sites that the persistent call for an amendment of the ban came.

Aboriginal rights activists in BC during the 1940s strategically dropped the right to potlatch from their central demands. During the Second World War, there was renewed political organizing among BC First Nations, who again sought to unite diverse peoples in the province. In an atmosphere of war and heightened nationalism, First Nation leaders pushed the state for equal rights and political representation – without enfranchisement. They wanted the same freedoms, privileges, and protections granted to Canadian citizens without having to be assimilated (or enfranchised) into the Canadian state. Dropping the potlatch question would help obtain these goals.

Early in the decade, nonpotlatching Christians in 'Y̲alis opposed an amendment of the potlatch ban. They raised questions about governance and sought citizenship rights. Alongside G̲a'ax̲sta'las, other high-ranking women argued for their daughters' rights to choose their own marriage partners. In the last decade of her life, as her children assumed roles of leadership and support, G̲a'ax̲sta'las retreated from the political stage. But in 1948 she spoke out against colonial incursions, their destructive effects on earlier expressions of "Indian religion," and the ignorance of early missionaries. In 1949, Status Indians became eligible to vote in BC elections, and Nisga'a activist Frank Calder was elected as a member of the Legislative Assembly in Victoria. Jane Constance Cook died on 16 October 1951. In December of that year, the potlatch ban was simply removed from the Indian Act.

"The Dead and Their Debts": Revisiting the Potlatch Ban

"Kingcome was one of the last holdouts on potlatching," John Nestman told me, "because it was so hard to get to. They potlatched long after communities closer to the mainstream stopped. It's quite a ways up the Coast, and then it's about two and a half miles up the river." Potlatchers in Kwakwa̱ka̱'wakw villages such as Gwa'yi (Kingcome) and Dzawadi (Knight Inlet) continued to perform the ceremonials of the custom relatively unhindered. Far from the surveillance of colonial authorities, they had advance warning if anyone entered the rivers leading to their villages.

It was from Gwa'yi that another sustained effort to overturn the potlatch ban came in the early 1940s. During Easter celebrations in 1939, Gwa'yi potlatchers invited colonial representatives to witness ceremonies at their village.[2] Wasting no opportunity to gather legal evidence, Murray Todd, the Indian Agent, later took statements.[3] Reverend Greene of the Columbia Coast Mission, obviously moved, promised Dzawada̱'enux̱w (Kingcome) potlatchers that he would secure a meeting with Indian Affairs officials of the Department of Mines and Resources and with representatives of the Anglican Church.[4]

When the delegation arrived in Gwa'yi for a three-day conference a year later, the eulachon were running.[5] "The river banks [were] covered with these small fish stranded on the falling tides," Reverend Anfield wrote. "Hundreds of huge sea lions ... sw[am] lazily along with their mouths agape scoop[ing] up huge and delectable feeds of the little fish."[6] Potlatchers wanted members of the delegation to "hear their requests for amelioration of section 140 of the Indian Act, to enable them to practice customs at present forbidden by that section, and Section 142 of the same act."[7]

Fifty people received Communion from Archbishop A.U. de Pencier, and ninety people were present for services in the small congregation-built church. Over three days, nine hundred meals were served. As Anfield wrote, they received "genuine, well-planned and splendidly executed hospitality." A petition was drafted and debated "until its final form received unanimous support." Signatures were added, and the petition was turned over to Inspector J. Coleman to give to the BC Indian Commissioner. Dzawada'enuxw petitioners proposed changing the nature of their dances and changing "the name of the potlatch, to call it something else."[8]

Weeks later, at Christ Church Rectory in 'Yalis, a meeting was held to hear "the other side."[9] Not long after Ga'axsta'las turned seventy, nine high-ranking men and women who were nonpotlatchers met with local clergy and the Indian Inspector. According to Anfield, they were "Indian men and women, young and old, who have left the Indian 'custom' within a year, and up to twenty years past."[10] They had prominent social standings among the Kwakwaka'wakw and, as Ga'axsta'las had done for some time, they spoke about the negative social and religious effects of the custom. Like Jane Cook, they also maintained the importance of adhering to the law and trusting in the Canadian state to better their lives.

Inspector Coleman directed most of his questions to the high-ranking men. Almost to the person, the nonpotlatchers stated that the custom, as practised, and Christianity were incompatible. Although no one described an earlier form, they implied that it had become something other than what it had once been. When Coleman asked what would happen if the act were amended, one man, who had been out of the potlatch for four years, said, "Even if only a Tribal affair, it will run wild." He told Coleman about a recent "fix[ed] marriage ... every winter they have rows ... When I was growing up I had to give a potlatch to name my children. I cannot afford it today, so it is better to quit it. The same when one dies, if you haven't got it, you borrow it, and repay with 100% interest. If the thing is re-opened, they will start to recall the debts as far back as the great grandfather. The future welfare of the young people cannot be helped by changing the Act."[11]

In Anfield's notes, Ga'axsta'las spoke little. But she did interject to question a man of her generation who had left the potlatch in the 1920s.

"Is the custom an Indian form of government?" she asked him.

"Yes, it is the form of law the Indians abided by in the old days. It is still regarded as the form of law today."

"Is every Indian a citizen of that Government in the Custom?" Jane Cook asked.

"Yes, all were a party to it in the past."

Inspector Coleman interjected, "Do the custom practicers consider that they are a law unto themselves today?"

"I cannot say," replied the man.

"The reserves are under the Government, which protect them," Jane Cook said.

The man responded, "The Indians in the custom consider the Canadian Government has no right to interfere with the Government of the Custom."[12]

As G̲a'ax̲sta'las spoke, aboriginal rights activists were gearing up to push for the rights and benefits of citizenship. She compared the custom – as practised – to a competing form of government and asserted the responsibility of the Canadian state to "protect them" on reserves. She invoked "legal principals of trust" that, although consistently violated, were historically central to political relations between aboriginal peoples and the state.[13]

I asked Wedłidi Speck about G̲a'ax̲sta'las's faith in the government. "If you think about what she would have learned through the land commissions – the fact that we had a protected relationship – my sense would be that, as we go through the changes in frontier territory, the government was seen as the container to hold us during those changes. We know full well now that we've experienced the government, that that's not necessarily true. All they want to do is assimilate us and steal our land *[laughs]*. That's been the case forever. I think that in terms of where Granny was, she was a bit naive. As brilliant as she was, she was a bit naive. But back then, I imagine that was her vision and that was her hope."

At the 1940 meeting, discussion focussed on the discord in the villages caused by potlatch competition. Two women present spoke against the non-Christian character of the custom and, like G̲a'ax̲sta'las, they addressed its effect on their children. "I want my children to grow up in the teachings of Christianity," one woman said, "to choose their own mates in marriage." She was followed by a more senior woman, who had taught the first woman the ways of the custom. "Both my husband and I put on potlatches against the law," she said. "Today I have learned better things ... I am responsible for a lot of children. I would not feel justified in bringing back the custom and spoiling the lives of children. I know the old way ... There is no reward in practicing the custom in life. I feel a responsibility to point out the right way, and away from the old way."[14]

After everyone else had spoken, George Luther stated: "The custom is compulsory ... It is the duty of every Indian, for death, joy, sadness, disgrace, injury, birth, marriage. An Indian cannot get out of it, either directly or indirectly ... There are just two or three children in school when potlatches are on ... There is a need for social life among all people. Many of the dances are very enjoyable. It is up to the Government and the Church to point the way to better social conditions."[15]

"Mrs. S. Cook" spoke next:

"It is a big question. If any amendment is made I would not like to answer for what will happen. The dead and their debts will come to life again. It is an Indian Government. In it are the dances and all other customs of the potlatch. It controls everything. It is their religion of the spirit. A man had to be enfranchised into the tribe by a potlatch, without it he could do nothing. Potlatch is the enfranchisement of the man, the child, and all must work towards it. If the Department sees that, the Department will never attempt to repeal the law. As long as an Indian is in the custom, he cannot be loyal to God or the State. No potlatches can be loyal to the Government. The custom is higher than the Government. [...? say] 'White men are fools – they have nothing like we have.' They may say so, but it cannot be. The custom is worship according to the Indian Government. You should hear the interpretation of the songs.

"My [female relative] was sold to a [village] man, and now the child cannot look at me. A Sports meeting is warfare on a different plane."[16]

G̲a'ax̲sta'las again referred to potlatching as a form of government that activates social, political, and economic status, without which a man can do nothing. Her use of the term *enfranchisement* seems to mean, literally, "to entitle or privilege." As G̲a'ax̲sta'las had already stressed in 1936, attaining social status through the transfer and legitimation of 'na̲'mima names and privileges was at the heart of the custom. Like names, economic transactions among potlatchers were remembered across generations, and she and others at the meeting feared resuscitating the debts of the dead if the potlatch law were amended.

"This is because we represent our families, and what we invest into the potlatch is inherited," William Wasden Jr., Jane Cook's great-grandson, wrote to me in November 2009: "If our father has a debt, our family has a debt, if it is not paid or settled with honour, it reflects on the whole family. The potlatch is our celebration of life. It is an investment system; to receive you must first give. Not everyone had the right to feast and potlatch, it was inherited from your ancestors if they had the knowledge to do these things or were groomed to understand the complexity. It is just like insurance, if you pay in, when you retire you will still receive and be taken care of, even if you can't attend ... The dances have spirituality and teachings, they are not talked about outside of the families normally ... [Some of the songs] are up for debate, when we look deeper into the symbolism and metaphors; there are real stories, history and spirituality."

Writing about this dialogue, I was reminded of what Florrie Matilpe had told me about her childhood in 'Mi'mkwamlis as part of a potlatching household. "That's another thing Mom [Pearl Mountain] used to say, why Granny didn't like the potlatch, because they just went broke. In those days, they used to try to beat each other. I remember my grandfather. His house was completely empty! My granny – in those olden days, you know, they had those cabinets, all glass. She had three of them in the house, and she used to tell me, 'One's yours, and one's your Auntie Annie's, and the other one's Emma's,' I think she used to say. That was all gone. Grandpa took it all and gave it in the potlatch *[laughs]*. It was really amazing because he was such a big chief ... We saw everything go. That's why Granny [Cook] didn't like the potlatch. Well, it's probably a lot to do with the faith, too, her being a Christian. A lot of people here who are Christians don't go into the Big House. But some of them go in there because the potlatches today are not like the potlatches they had in the olden days. They used to fight, you know, argue about the one who'd be the highest chief. I know my grandfather had about four coppers, and he had a couple that were broken. He'd break it for somebody, you know, to be higher than him. See, that's another thing Granny didn't like – they were trying to be the best – because it's a sin to be higher than God. And this is what they were trying to do, I think, in her eyes. So."

Before the meeting in 1940 adjourned, Inspector Coleman told the group that "the Department is concerned with the freedom of the Indian to choose his way of life and religion. It felt the 'custom' is spoiling the economic welfare of the people. They are free to choose their own religion, but the Department is interested in seeing that the religious life is a happy and successful one."[17] The colonial government unrelentingly encouraged total assimilation, but here its stand was veiled by the rhetoric of freedom and choice.

Perhaps indicating a tired scribe, the last lines in Anfield's notes on Ga'axsta'las's statements at the meeting seem abbreviated. She was evidently still commenting on arranged marriages and speaking out for a woman in her own family. Responding to her words, William Wasden Jr. focussed on the groom's family, who, by offering a bride price, were "investing in [their] son by securing a position through the bride and surplus wealth to validate and uphold the position from her family." His perspective shows the gendered nature of the debate about marriage. On the one hand, Ga'axsta'las and others spoke up for women to be able to exercise choice in marriage partners; on the other hand, those who fought to maintain the custom were upholding the central institution of cultural reproduction "for the good of the tribe."

Jane Cook's statement that a "sports meeting is warfare on a different plane" is intriguing. Whereas Helen Codere saw "fighting with property" as a replacement for intertribal warfare, perhaps Ga'axsta'las was suggesting that sporting events were displacing antagonisms generated in the custom. "She is referring to the rivalry between our tribes that soccer became the venue for," William Wasden Jr. explained via email: "The 'Namgis were always champions and were victorious in most meetings on the pitch. Lower ranking tribes obviously, would take great pride in defeating the 'Namgis on occasion and felt on top of them even if it wasn't in the potlatch tribal standings. There was a war that took place years ago between the 'Namgis and numerous Kwakwaka'wakw tribes, the outcome was revenge by the almost-annihilated 'Namgis, and the bitterness has never left the memories of the tribes they slaughtered in retaliation."

Soccer was definitely one beat in the rhythm of the Cook big house. Jane and Stephen's sons – Chris, Gilbert, Ernie, Reggie, and Cyril – played on the first Cormorants team in the 1920s.[18] As William Wasden Jr.'s father, Bill Wasden, told me in 2006: "The soccer team, the Cormorants, you know, it was basically started by the [Cook] brothers, and we've had descendents on that team ever since the day it started ... The girls made the uniforms, of course, out of the old flour sacks, and they played the Navy, for years." During the Second World War, men in 'Yalis played soccer with other village teams and with the navy. Married women in 'Yalis later formed their own soccer team called the Flying Hens, and unmarried women had a team called the Screaming Chickens. In the 1960s, Stephen and Jane Cook's granddaughters – Pearl Alfred, Emma Alfred, Frances Speck, and Shirley and Grace Bell – played their first match against the Kingcome Wolverines.

Reminded of the war, elders in the family recalled placing tarpaper on windows for blackouts. "Someone would come around to check if there was light coming out of windows," Ilma Cook told me. "And we had one gas mask for six people!" she said and laughed. "There were Japanese families – our barber was Japanese. It was a sad time. Unfair." Japan joined the war in 1941. Canada's response caused a shift in the social world in 'Yalis, and the war also affected the balance of labour in the commercial fisheries. According to historian Rolf Knight,

> The entire Japanese-Canadian fishing fleet was confiscated and the Japanese-Canadian population in BC was interned. When these expropriated fishing vessels were later auctioned off, more than three-quarters of them were acquired by and added to the cannery fleets. This provided a large number of cannery vessels available on a rental basis, which benefited native fishermen who were prominent in the cannery fleets. Japanese-Canadians were not allowed to return to the BC coast or enter fishing until 1949, and some native spokesmen were vociferous proponents of Japanese-Canadian exclusion.[19]

The persecution of Japanese Canadians was felt by members of the Cook family. As George Cook recalled, "Papa had Japanese partners that were involved in the saltery at the wharf. They would get the chum salmon and salt it at the Cooks' wharf. The Japanese preferred Viner Sound and Nimpkish River salmon. After it was salted, it would be shipped out and sold, and Papa would get a percentage of the sales. Our family had a fish camp in Barnett Pass, and our relationship with the Canadian Fish started there. Our family sold fish to the Canadian Fish Company. The fishing companies in Alert Bay were BC Packers, Nelson Brothers, Canadian Fish, and a Japanese company. Sukiyama and Fugiyami were the managers for the saltery at the Cook Wharf."

Reggie Cook Jr. offered more details about Mr. Fugiyami, as told by his brother: "A story from George last week. As he was over visiting, he told me that Fugiyama, who was operating the fish plant on Cook's Wharf, was taken away during the Second World War apprehension of Japanese people. He said they came and got them and paraded them away, leaving everything as it was, and just left. For years Papa left all their equipment untouched, but they never returned to the Bay to resume their fish buying after the war. They did rejoin the fishing fleet as gillnetters. I myself remember them coming to visit my dad in the latter 1950s and maybe early '60s and visiting and bringing sake and having a good time together. Sake will do that. I remember tasting it. Thought it was terrible stuff."

During a conversation with Jeane Lawrence and Pearl Alfred, Jeane also recalled wartime in and around the Cook big house.

"Yeah, I remember that saltery down at the dock ... dog salmon I believe it was, because that's the time when there used to be lots of

Photo 36 Dog salmon on Cook's Wharf, Alert Bay, ca. 1920s. "When the old saltery was down at the end of the wharf ... A Japanese family operated the wharf for many years, the saltery and the netloft" (Jeane Lawrence). *Photographer unknown. Image H-06867, Royal BC Museum, BC Archives.*

dog salmon out the Nimpkish River.[20] And that faded away, I guess, probably about the time – maybe when the Japanese had to go. I remember when we went to school, and we knew these little Japanese girls, and all of a sudden they were taken away from us. Our friends Yoko and Sissy and all those – they had to go. You know, they just, 'Off you go.' And that's it at that time. I missed them all. I actually still have pictures taken with them. I can remember Fugiyama."

"And I understand there was a Chinatown in Alert Bay, early on?"

"Oh, when the canneries were there, they worked down by the BC Packers. They had a family – a row of houses where they worked in the fish cannery that was there many years ago. Yeah, and then I can remember them in the evenings. I guess they'd come down our way, to Granny's way and down. And they would sell peanuts wrapped in a cone."

"Of newspaper," Pearl Alfred added.

"'Oh, here they come.' They'd be nice and warm, those peanuts. They were only ten cents a bag. But, yeah, those were the days, too. They'd come, and we'd be waiting for them." She laughed.

As I listened to these conversations, I was continually reminded of how deeply memory is tied to the senses, to the feel of warm peanuts, the anticipation of a newspaper cone in a child's hand, or the sensation that passes among family members when something extraordinary occurs. When I asked Pearl Alfred about the war, she recalled a moment that had passed between G̲a'ax̲sta'las and her father, Reggie Cook Sr. At the time, the family had once again experienced the uncertainty of one of their own enlisting in the armed forces. Following his namesake, Edwin Victor Cook, the son of Bert Cook, was killed in action on 30 September 1944. Silas Olney, the grandson whom Stephen and Jane raised, had also joined the navy.

Pearl recalled: "I remember during the war, or when she was talking about wars, I always had a sense that she knew what the hell was going to happen – it seemed to me. What do you call people who sort of have some sense of what's going to happen? I remember one of the children that she raised was in the navy. I still remember my dad's reaction – he was shocked. Her coming in from her garden and saying that Si was coming home. And she knew it, she said, because of the way the birds were out in the garden, the ravens or whatever it was. She just said, 'He's coming home.' And he came home the next day *[laughs]*."

Throughout the war, aboriginal leaders from the northern branch of the NBBC opposed "drafting Indians."[21] They argued that because they "did not possess full and equal rights of citizenship, Indian people should not bear the responsibility of full citizenship."[22] The protest was unsuccessful – Indians were required to register. But the Brotherhood was "successful in obtaining deferments for Indian fishermen as they were engaged in the essential occupation of food production."[23]

"We'll Knock at the Doors": The Native Brotherhood of British Columbia

"We'll knock at the doors
We'll knock at the doors
We'll knock at the doors
'Til one day our children will walk through."
Our grandparents opened the doors a little.

– *Pearl Alfred, NBBC chant*

The Native Brotherhood of British Columbia was formed in 1931 in Lax Kw'alaams (Port Simpson). Within a decade, it was known for its strike-breaking activities.[24] According to Harry Assu, Ligwiłdaxw chief, the more southern Kwakwaka'wakw fishers also organized. "After the 1916 strike our people got together at a big meeting at Alert Bay, my father [Chief Billy Assu] and Dan [Assu] went up, and an association for native fishermen was formed. [They] went to all the villages in our area and on the west coast and told our people how to protect themselves with their own association. Later, in 1936, we widened the membership to include seiners, gillnetters, and trollers. It worked well for us."[25] Assu refers to the strike at Rivers Inlet in 1936, when "Indian cannery workers were returned to their homes by chartered steamers ... [and] Native Brotherhood members as well as white fishermen came from the Northern area and broke the strike."[26] Nuu-chah-nulth and Kwakwaka'wakw fishers lost their entire season.[27] When families appealed to the Department of Indian Affairs for relief, William Halliday and the cannery operators opened Johnstone Strait to gill netting.[28]

In fall 1936, 'Yalis fishers organized the Nimpkish Fisherman's Association, which later became the Pacific Coast Native Fishermen's Association (PCNFA).[29] Among its first challenges was negotiating to "extend credit for Cape Mudge fishers ... in peril of losing their boats."[30] Given their close association with the Assu family, Jane and Stephen Cook must have fallen into easy collaboration with the Cape Mudge organizers. Chief Billy Assu frequently stayed at the Cook big house and was an early delegate for the Allied Tribes. He also took responsibility for their daughter-in-law Nellie Hamilton after the death of her young mother. Of course, relations among kin crisscrossed all of the villages. Economic hardships in one locale were felt in extended households throughout Kwakwaka'wakw territories.

In the 1940s, cannery operators dealt with the Brotherhood as a negotiating entity and consulted with the organization about fish prices. The war, however, brought with it new complications that united aboriginal fishers on the Coast.[31] When "Indians" became subject to income tax by an Order-in-Council in 1942, Andy Paull (Ga'axsta'las's former colleague in the Allied Tribes) approached the PCNFA to join the NBBC.[32] He travelled to coastal villages and set up branches in Kwakwaka'wakw, Salish, and Nuu-chah-nulth territories. He eventually opened a small office in Vancouver.[33] Percy Gladstone described "the PCNFA faction" as mostly Kwakwaka'wakw members who were "more aggressive and more experienced in fishing matters [and who] soon became the dominant group in the Brotherhood."[34] Between 1938 and 1944, Moses Alfred, Dan Assu, Frank Assu, Stephen Cook, Harry Mountain, Alfred Scow, and James Sewid of 'Ya̲lis and Cape Mudge helped co-found the NBBC's Southern Area.[35]

As business agent for the Brotherhood, Andrew Paull was again at the forefront. He presented a petition to Ottawa opposing income tax under the slogan "No Taxation without Representation."[36] Kwakwa̲ka̲'wakw fishers largely funded the delegation, which argued that it was unjust to tax Indian fishers because fishing occurred off reserve lands.[37] They lost their appeal and agreed to pay income tax to support the war effort. After the war, however, their push against taxation resumed.

As George Cook recalled, the NBBC's opposition to income tax was in the tradition of previous demands for aboriginal rights. Jane and Stephen's grandsons had entered the commercial fishery. George Cook – long recognized as the current head of the family, long-time president of Native Friendship Centres, and former elected chief – was among them: "My dad [Reg Sr.] was involved in the Native Brotherhood of BC. He worked with Reverend Peter Kelly.[38] They were constantly fighting for our rights, and one of the stands they took was not to pay income tax on our fishing income. Their position was that the fishing was our right. We followed their direction for a few years. When we didn't pay tax, things were good; however, the Brotherhood didn't win their case, and we had to repay the tax money. That put us all into really rough times. I owed ten thousand dollars, and it took me years to pay it off. Since that time, I always pay my taxes. Money was so tight that [my wife] Ruth and I had to dig clams for $1.50 a box. One Christmas, Dong Chong gave us a turkey. It was a blessing. We also had a herring and a fishing strike the next year. So, it was really, really tough. We learned a lot through that time, finances, et cetera. It was so tough."

"By 1945," Percy Gladstone writes, "the Brotherhood was officially recognized by the British Columbia Department of Labour as the bargaining agent for all British Columbia Indian Fishermen."[39] While fishing was a central focus of the organization, the NBBC's constitution expressed wider goals:

> To work for the betterment of conditions, socially, spiritually, and economically for its people.
>
> To encourage and bring about a communication and cooperation between the white people and Native Canadians.

Photo 37 Stephen Cook and his sons with a sunfish. *From left to right:* Stephen, Cyril, Reg, and Herbert. *Courtesy of Wedłidi Speck.*

> To join with the Government and its officials and with all those who have at heart the welfare of the Natives of British Columbia and for the betterment of all conditions surrounding the lives and homes of the Natives.[40]

The public political agenda of the Brotherhood was silent about aboriginal rights, a deliberate strategy to avoid prosecution following the government's decision, in 1927, to criminalize the collection of funds to pursue land claims.[41] At meetings and conventions, members discussed aboriginal rights explicitly, but on the record, they phrased their goal as "to better the socio-economic position of Indian people."[42]

At the fifteenth annual Native Brotherhood Convention, which was held in 'Y_a_lis in 1944, delegates

> resolved that Indians should be consulted on anything that affected their lives. They also passed resolutions stating that they were against drafting of Indians, impositions of income tax, that the Department

Photo 38 Native Brotherhood of British Columbia Convention, 1944, Council Hall, 'Ya̲lis. Jane Cook is in the second row, *centre.* Also present: Herbert Cook, Charlie Nowell, Billy Assu, Dan Assu, Joe Harris, Andy Frank, John Hanuse, and George Alfred. "I wonder if that was the first convention here? There's [another] photograph of my father [Dan Cranmer], Ed Whonnock, Charlie Nowell, and this handsome young man Bill Reid, who was a CBC reporter. Yeah, that was kind of funny because my father and those other men had decided that they were going to perform dances for the delegates. So, hardly anyone showed up. They all went to the hospital to watch a film about TB or something. People were really scared [of the law] still!" (Gloria Cranmer Webster). *Courtesy of Wedłidi Speck.*

> of Indian Affairs account for its money, better cannery housing, and "equal pay" for equal work for cannery workers and Indian farmworkers of the lower Fraser Valley. They also resolved that steps be taken to obtain old age pension, family allowance, and better education and medical services. In education they wished to see better and increased provisions for Indian people to obtain a secondary and post-secondary education.[43]

Among the delegates and members were Jane and Stephen Cook and their sons.

Aboriginal activists wanted adequate medical care. Canada introduced Family Allowances late in 1944 and "baby bonus" payments to mothers the following year.[44] The programs, however, were coercive. They threatened to cut benefits to aboriginal parents who did not send their children to school. In contrast to the Native Brotherhood, several unions were opposed to a universal allowance on the grounds that it would undermine their efforts to attain livable wages. Regarding education for children, the NBBC stood firm in its demand for equal access to the same quality of education as other Canadians. Its members were also outspoken in their support of secular rather than religious schools. Although the Canadian Old Age Pensions Act had been passed in 1927, persons classed as Status Indians were exempt.[45] Given the lack of conventional employee protections and benefits, the Brotherhood's demands spoke to the historical invisibility of the aboriginal labour force.

The war brought new opportunities in the logging industry and for fishers at 'Y̲alis and Bella Bella who seined herring.[46] George Cook recalled that racism again became a force among competing factions of fishers. "I remember herring fishing in Butedale one year. There was literally a line drawn across the middle of the hall on the floor.[47] Indians on one side; whites on the other. The same with the groceries. The racism was so strong that you would walk away from each other so as not to touch each other. During the herring season, when we would go to deliver our fish, the people at the packers would unload the non-Natives' fish. But when we arrived, they would move away, and we would have to unload our own fish. During the strikes, we would be corking each other and cutting the cork lines. It was not good."

When George Cook recalled his start in commercial fishing, he talked about negotiating the entry of women into the fleet: "Papa, Granny, and my dad (Reggie) were all active and connected to the Canadian Fishing Company (CFC). But I was closest to my granny, so I went to talk to her first about skippering a boat. I went to see my granny [Jane], and I asked her if she would support me to talk with the Canadian Fish Company to skipper a seine boat. Her words were, 'Do you feel responsible enough to be a skipper of a seine boat, realizing that you have the responsibility of five men under your hand? If so, then you are ready to go fishing.' I then met with Jack Dorman, Bones Bay [of the CFC], and said I was ready to go fishing, and could I skipper a boat. I assume that Jack Dorman went to speak to my dad.

My first boat was the *Qualicum L.* It was good to us. It loaded me up with salmon a few times.

"My first crew was Sonny Brotchie, Peter Coon, George Scow, Ruth, and one of the Quock sisters. When I first started fishing, there was a bit of resistance from some of my crew to having my wife, Ruth, get a fishing share for her work on the boat.[48] So, I held off for a couple of years. Ruth says she was really irked about it, as there were already some other wives on crew shares. However, as time moved on, she was put on full share and was part of the crew. As things changed, so did the attitudes, and the expectation was that my children – Geri, Nella, Wayne, and Cindy – were expected to put their time out fishing. They would be earning money for their clothes and school supplies. They would learn independence. They started at half shares and then moved up to full shares. They were around ten when they started fishing. They would cook, pitch fish, and other fishing duties as required. We worked to support the family. Before I became a skipper, all the money I made went into the Cook family pot. I was a skipper at twenty-six years of age. All of the halibut money made by my uncles also went into the family pot."[49]

Women became full-share crew members on fishing boats, but during the war they were the primary labourers in canneries and net lofts.[50] Following the initial meeting of the Brotherhood at Port Simpson in 1931, the first branch of the Native Sisterhood was formed and operated through the "Village Women's Auxiliary." Women paid a three-dollar "sisterhood fee" to support negotiations with canneries on their behalf. "Wage scales set for net women are arranged only with the Brotherhood," Philip Drucker notes, "since it is said there are no white women who do this work."[51] At first, women prepared feasts for the meetings. At the 1933 convention, the Native Sisterhood was "established as the Indian women's auxiliary of local Brotherhood branches."[52] The women's role shifted to fundraising for annual conventions. Women leaders emerged who are well remembered today. Brenda Campbell, for instance, was elected first president of the Native Sisterhood.[53] And two Kwakwa̲ka̲'wakw women, Kitty Carpenter and Vera Cranmer, took over the presidency in later years.[54] Eva Cook is also often recalled. In the early 1950s, the Native Sisterhood played a central role in the assessment of schools and health care delivery in the villages. Its members also negotiated day care for shoreworkers' children. Kitty Carpenter and Jane and Stephen's daughter Pearl Mountain took midwifery courses together and travelled to villages to assist mothers. In 1954, Jane and Stephen's daughter-in-law Nellie Cook was elected vice-president.

Cook men were likewise well represented among elected officers of the Brotherhood. From 1944 to 1948, Herbert was the general secretary. Reggie was elected treasurer in 1954, and he held the position until 1961, when Frank Calder succeeded him. Chris Jr. and Gilbert Jr., Jane and Stephen's grandsons, were elected vice-president in 1974 and 1977, respectively. Charlie Newman's grandson Ed Newman was elected president in 1977, and Bobby Duncan was elected vice-president in 1981.

Some of Jane Cook's descendants wondered about her involvement with the NBBC and the conflicts that might have arisen for her, given her stance on social issues. "I often wondered how she dealt with that," said Bill Wasden, "because the Native Brotherhood was instrumental in the rights of aboriginal people to access alcohol. But I don't know that it bothered her one bit, because it was a right that every other Canadian had. No matter what the fallout would be, the Natives had to have the same rights."

Her grandson's wonder made me think about G̲a'ax̲sta'las's early battle against the whisky trade and the exploitation of women on the reserve. But in the 1940s, as she had always done, G̲a'ax̲sta'las stood in solidarity with those formally agitating for structural change and recognition of equal rights for aboriginal people. She was not alone. "Although some Brotherhood leaders were strongly opposed to the use of alcoholic beverages, they took a strong stand against the discriminatory law that forbade Indians (and Orientals) from consuming [alcohol] ... in public licensed premises and to purchase liquor."[55]

Prohibitions of alcohol had long roots in colonial thinking, and the legacy of yet another layer of criminalization is well remembered. "The police were everywhere when we were young," Peggy Svanvik told me and laughed. "They didn't even have to have a warrant to come into your house. They would just burst into your house if they wanted to. They were running after somebody who had the beer *[laughs]*. That was horrible. You know, people went to Oakalla – the prison – for having a beer! They didn't steal anything. They didn't hurt anybody. But they just had a beer, and they were sent to prison. So, they've got lots of Native people on their records at that time. Just for having a beer!"[56]

Given G̲a'ax̲sta'las's ideals it is difficult to say how the struggle for the right to legally consume alcohol meshed with her ethics. Her granddaughter Christine Zurkowski suggested that she was broadminded.

"One day, I was walking with Granny to the church, and one fellow was hanging on, you know, to the railing going up to church? He was drunk. He was very drunk, and everybody passed him by. Everybody walked in the church, and he just hung there – stood there. We came along, and she walked up to him, and she put her arm on him, and she took him into church, and he sat with us."

"You know how Granny always sat in the front seat?" Christine said to her sister-in-law Maureen Cook. "He sat in the front seat with us through the whole service. And he rested his head on her shoulder and kind of passed out." She laughed. "Then she picked him up after, and she took him out. This was her thing – if this man wants to go to church, he goes to church. That spoke to me as a child. Those little things really affected my life, because she valued people. She really valued people, and there is no difference. She had no difference for anyone. She just loved them."

I had asked Emma Alfred if her grandmother had had any sayings: "She taught me a lot about caring for myself, to look after myself. A lot of us forget that ... 'Remember who you are' and 'You're never mean to your next-door neighbour. You don't talk about them, because you don't know anything about them. You don't live in their house.' She used to always say that. And we used to say, 'Well, what's she saying that for?' You do not live in their house. You don't know that much about them, so you don't talk about them. Even if we saw somebody drunk, she said it was not our business. We don't pay attention. We turn our head the other way. 'No. It's not for us to judge this man.'"

As Wedłidi Speck noted, his great-grandmother's stance reflected the political strategies of aboriginal activists in her time. "I approached the late Bill Scow," he told me. "We used to sit together and talk. And I asked Bill, I said, 'You were with the Native Brotherhood and with the Union of BC Indian Chiefs.' And I said, 'Why did you guys fight to have a right to drink?' He said, 'What we were really fighting for was our right to vote, but what came with that was the drinking. We knew, in getting the package, there were pieces of the package that wouldn't work for us. Our vision was that at least we had a voice.' So, he was looking at a time where at least we had a lawyer to speak for us. We couldn't hire a lawyer for land claims then. So Granny Cook sees citizenship as having a voice, and if we were able to [attain the right to drink], then we were able to have a voice. But there would be no voice if there wasn't the collective will to change things. Resistance would mean fragmentation, and fragmentation would mean that we wouldn't become citizens."

Life with Granny Cook in the 1940s

Throughout the war, G̲a'ax̲sta'las continued her work as president of the Indian Women's Auxiliary of Christ Church. In October 1945, she received a letter from Murray Todd: "I am writing on behalf of the Indian Affairs Branch to thank all members of the Indian W.A. for their loyalty and help in every way to the Allied cause during the dark and uncertain days of 1939-1945, and to request your continued support in the days that lie ahead."[57] Todd mentioned the "instruments and results of war" and the "sorrow, tragedy and unbelievable suffering" faced by millions who were homeless and without food, clothing, and medical supplies.[58] He appealed to the organization's members to purchase Victory Bonds to help the government "bring our boys and girls home and properly re-establish them in civilian life." The letter is also notable for its mention of the recent Family Allowances Act. "It will mean," he wrote, "that approximately $50,000.00 a year will be distributed as a gift to the Indians of the Kwawkewlth Agency." G̲a'ax̲sta'las must have received the news as a victory.[59]

Several women shared their impressions of G̲a'ax̲sta'las in the 1940s.

"She was just a powerful woman. Dynamic," Peggy Svanvik said. "She was a big woman, tall, and she had a very interesting face. She was a matriarch! She was a very vibrant lady. I often think, people go to war for their land, and we've been fighting for our land for over a hundred years. I would've loved to have seen her in Ottawa. When I think about her – we used to always go to church, and what amazed me was how she could interpret the minister's sermon word for word in our language. I used to be, I guess, what you call mesmerized. I used to sit there, and I used to think, 'She's talking to me.'" Peggy laughed. "It just seemed that way. She was very strong in what she did. She had nothing written down. She remembered it all ... But like I say, she could interpret the minister's sermon word for word. He did the whole sermon. He didn't stop until it was done. Then he sat down. Then she stood up and interpreted his whole sermon."

"How was her Kwak̓wala?"

"Well! Excellent! Yeah, I don't think anyone could speak as well as she did. That's what we spoke at home. I didn't go to residential school. Thank goodness!"

According to many of their grandchildren, Jane and Stephen spoke Kwak̓wala at home – to each other. Christine Zurkowski heard them "when they had visitors, and when they didn't want to you to understand." Several of their children understood Kwak̓wala, and their daughter Emma Kenmuir was a fluent speaker. When Emma Alfred lived in the Cook family big house, the Women's Auxiliary meetings were a regular event. "Yeah," Emma said, "they read the Bible, and they talked about it. I think, after that, they were starting to make things and helping people outside. There was a lot of the elders in there, and they'd go from house to house. It was never in one place. They would always move around. Different houses used to invite us every week."

Emma's sister Florrie Matilpe lived at Mama̱lilika̱la (Village Island) until 1943. She was thirteen when the school there closed, and her family moved into the Cook big house. "Granny had a church service," she told me. "It was so amazing. She'd read from the Bible, and then she'd translate it into Kwak̓wala. I used to understand her more in Kwak̓wala than in English. It seemed to have made more sense to me than in English. Well, at Village Island, in my [paternal] granny's house, that's all we spoke was Kwak̓wala. If I went from my granny's house to my mom's house, then we'd speak English."

"Yeah, I remember her," Gloria Cranmer-Webster told me in June 2005. "I mean, this church was very much a part, a big part, of everyone's lives when we were young, and I remember her translating at the preacher's sermons. I think there were times when she figured it wasn't really good enough, so she'd give her own." For many women with whom I spoke, their memories about the WA and the church folded into stories about the presence of G̱a'a̱xsta'las in their lives. "We would have parties at the big house," Gloria continued, "and she never seemed to get impatient with our noisiness. She was a very kind woman because, when I went away to school, travel was a lot harder in those days. So, I had to get shipped off to Victoria in September, come home at Christmas, come back, come home for the summer, and not see anyone in between time. But Papa and Granny Cook would attend these Anglican synod meetings, and they always took me out for dinner, and we always had good visits. Yeah, it meant a lot, because I was pretty lonely down there. *[Laughs]* I remember one time, we're having dinner at the Empress [Hotel], and it's all terribly fancy. Here's this finger bowl – and I can't remember what we had been served – but, at some point, Papa Cook picked this up and drank it. Well, shoot! Granny Cook elbowed him in the ribs *[laughs]*. Yeah, that was kind of funny."

I asked Christine Zurkowski about going to Victoria with her grandparents. "They occasionally took us ... Of course, we were just children. We did lots of crazy things because we weren't used to city life ... I came down twice with them for the synod. They took different grandchildren with them every year to Victoria, and we stayed in the Empress. And, of course, it's such a cultural difference. We can always remember my grandfather washing his teeth. You know the water to wash your hands? He must have thought that little water container was for washing his dentures *[laughs]*. I'm sure they must have been mortified there, now I think back. But as a child, we all just got the giggles. I think Granny came every year, but she chose different people to come along with them. They both were involved with that. He was a warden in the church all his life."

Here and there, other stories about Jane and Stephen's trips to the city emerged. "My father [Gideon Whonnock] and his brothers, they all respected Jane," Peggy Svanvik told me. "He was telling me about a time when he and his brother were in Vancouver, and they picked up girlfriends, and they went to a movie. They were sitting there with their arms around the girls, and somebody behind them spoke Kwak̓wala and said, 'You're crazy.' They turned around and saw Jane, and they jumped up and ran out and left the girls there *[laughs]*. He said, 'Boy, did we jump fast,' he said. I think she just wanted to bug these guys *[laughs]*."

As our work unfolded, I was struck by how people spoke about Jane and Stephen Cook's attention to kin ties and obligations. Rita Barnes told me that her grandmother Maggie Scow was G̱a'a̱xsta'las's niece, the daughter of Jane's sister, Annie Kamano. When Rita's grandmother was ill with TB, she moved into the Cook big house with her daughters, Grace and May. G̱a'a̱xsta'las nursed Maggie until she passed away. According to Rita Barnes, Jane Cook was responsible for maintaining the bonds between their families. "You see, the connections just keep happening between the families, and I really think it was all her influence. First, caring for – taking my mother [Grace] in ... But, you know, had it not been for her influence, if we were a different family without someone as strong as she, would we still be – after generations going down the genograph – would we still be connected in any way? ... So many of us. Had she not kept track of her sister's children, would we be as connected today as we are? ... My mother died when I was four. She also died of tuberculosis. I asked my dad once, I said, 'How come my mom was buried in Alert Bay? Why wasn't she buried in Kingcome?'

He was silent for a long time, and he said, 'The old lady G̲a'ax̲sta'las wouldn't allow it,' that she had to be buried in the Anglican Church cemetery with her family ... way up the hill."

There are stories about G̲a'ax̲sta'las reminding her children and grandchildren about the ties that bound them to others in the community. In some stories, she warns them about their relatedness to people they may choose to date, but many stories reveal the emphasis she placed on the obligation to support kin. I asked Gloria Cranmer-Webster about G̲a'ax̲sta'las's attention to this. "I think, certainly, Papa and Granny Cook taught their kids – or their kids knew a lot more about kinship ties – because I remember when my father died, the first person who came to my house at two o'clock in the morning, or something, was Herbert, one of their sons, who said to my mother, 'Don't worry about anything, Agnes, I'll take care of it.' Yeah."

Some who grew up in the Cook big house marvelled at its organization. "At one point," George Cook recalled, "we had Robbie Mountain [Pearl's husband] there. And then we had Daddy Cook [Reggie] and Mom [Nellie] there. And we had Robbie Bell and Winnie [his wife] there. And we had Si [Olney] there, and their families were there. There was a huge gang there. Everyone had to work together. Each one of us had a chore to do. This is how we had to live in the big house to survive. So, there was a law that the work that was done, everything went into the pot. Part of it went into the store, because that was where the grub was coming from. That type of lifestyle now is gone. There's no such thing as anybody putting money into the pot anymore. It's everybody for themselves. I was eighteen before I could have three hundred dollars in the bank – and I had been making big money. Granny never went out and spent money, and she was the backbone." Her grandchildren note that their parents called G̲a'ax̲sta'las "Mamma."

"You know, the people more or less came to her," Jeane Lawrence told me. "She had *lots* of different visitors that came up to visit her, that came from other islands."

"Going way back to childhood," Emma Alfred began, "I can still see ourselves again. Sure, there was lots of playing and fun in our lives, but there was also work. We had to pack wood up from down the hill, all the way up under the house. Pack bags of sawdust and bring it in for the kitchen stove. Things like that. But we had a real beautiful life at Gran's house. It was such a warm home. You walked in, and you could smell jam. Or you'd smell her bread or her fruitcakes at Christmas, always a smell. And then her soups. You knew what we were going to have for lunch because you'd smell it walking up the hill and down the hill *[laughs]*. We did our own canned fish and smoked fish. She did that all. And the boys would go deer hunting, and she'd put it away in the root house. That's where she put the preserves and stuff."

Everyone spoke about Papa's breakfasts: "Of course there was mush every morning," George Cook recalled. "And Granny had the stew every night, every day. There's always different kinds of smoked fish, any kind of fish that was around at the time. And I know that Daddy Cook [Reggie] and Stevie and Chris and all them – they used to go out halibut fishing in the middle of winter."

George Cook told his daughter Nella Nelson about coming home one day from fishing. His grandmother placed a bowlful of raspberries in front of him for his sixteenth birthday. George's sister Pearl Alfred smiled as she recalled a dark night when her grandparents woke them up to watch shooting stars from the verandah of the big house. Inside the house, Jane and Stephen's descendants recall, there was a framed photograph of Edwin Cook, killed during the First World War, and an image of two women standing, looking out over a moonlit sea waiting for the men to return from war. Another image depicted a scene of two stags in the forest, and an oval frame surrounded the photograph of a young Stephen Cook. Annie Kamano's great-granddaughter Rita Barnes spoke fondly about running down the stairs to get to the fireplace in the big house because there was no central heating. Jeane Lawrence loved it when they cooked clams in that fire. The house was filled by music because most of the children played instruments and sang. Emma Alfred vividly described evening hours with her granny, darning a seemingly endless array of socks. G̲a'ax̲sta'las walked everywhere she went, Emma told me, and she wrapped hot, wet bread poultices to their chests when they had pneumonia.

Illnesses of all kinds punctuate her grandchildren's reminiscences. "I remember always being around TB," Emma Alfred told me, "and it never got to Gran. It's like she was covered when she was doing her rounds. She did [and] she saw lots. Even one of her son's little boys died of diphtheria, and she sat with him. I happened to be in the house at that time, and we were quarantined. I couldn't go home. I had to stay in Uncle Herbert's house because I was there with the kid that had diphtheria. We were all quarantined in that house for two weeks. Nobody else got it, but they wouldn't take that chance. She'd come down every night and be with this little boy [who died]. His name

Photo 39 Sisters Emma Alfred, Connie Svanvik, and Florrie Matilpe at the Gi<u>x</u>s<u>a</u>m Feast, May 2007. *Courtesy of Christina Cook.*

was Gilbert. Stayed with him through the night and through the day, and then she'd go home. She could go home, and I couldn't go home *[laughs]*."

"I don't know if anybody talked about our quarantines?" Florrie Matilpe asked.

"Gee, we were quarantined for so long one time. My mom and my cousin Billy Cook – that's Pearlie's brother – had got typhoid fever. They were in the hospital. So, we were quarantined, and Doctor Ryall and the nurse – he only had one nurse – used to come up and give us a needle every Sunday! We'd all go and try to hide. Granny would be looking for us and getting mad, 'You've got to have this shot.' We used to get them here," Florrie said and gestured to her neck.

"I can't remember how long it went on, but, anyway, we were in quarantine, and after we came off quarantine, it was May Day. I'll always remember this May Day. We were all standing on the porch, all dressed up. Everybody here used to dress their kids up for May Day, you see – new shoes, new clothes. We'd all have new runners – big thrill with new runners – new dresses, skirts." She laughed. "Because pants weren't in in those days."

Photo 40 G̲a'ax̲sta'las on the steps of the Cook big house, ca. 1940s. *Courtesy of Pearl Alfred.*

"What year might that have been, Florrie?"

"I must have been fourteen – fifteen – then, and I'm seventy-four right now. So, about there. Then we were all dressed up, standing on the porch, waiting to go down to watch the parade. And then Auntie

Nellie – Pearlie's mom – came down and said, 'Nobody's going anywhere!' We all looked at her. Francis – Pearlie's sister – had broken out in the chicken pox." She laughed. "And, in those days, they used to put the quarantine sign – Granny's house is up the hill there ... so, just before you take the first step, was this big sign 'QUARANTINE.' So, we stood on the porch and watched the parade go by." She laughed. "[We were quarantined] until every one of us had it, or if we didn't get it. We were quarantined for a long time! It seemed like years to me. We could stay around the yard, but we couldn't go past that stairway. Yeah, that was really something."

I asked Florrie's cousin Jeane Lawrence if she remembered the preventorium. "Uh huh, yeah, that was down by St. Michael's School, down there. We were never allowed to go down there. But the St. Michael's School – some of the kids from out of town, like, say, from Masset and up Bella Bella way, they had nowhere to go. And on Saturdays, they could go out to different places, and Granny would take two or three of them in. They could come out for the afternoon – not overnight, I think – but for a few hours, and then they'd go back to the school. We had met lots of good friends like that when we were growing up, and had softball teams, and everybody got together. And they had the theatre in St. Mike's in those days."

When great-granddaughter Nella Nelson spoke about the Cook big house, it was G̲a'ax̲sta'las's orchard that was the object of her fascination. "The cherry tree was beyond the beyond! Even as a kid, when she'd been gone a few years, there was still huge cherries and gooseberries and raspberries and apples in there. My husband said they would go steal from there. He was in residential school, and the big thing was to go steal from the Cooks' orchard."

Unnatural Circumstances: Schooling

Few ruins of history compare with the menacing brick edifices of Canada's remaining residential schools. They are the relics of an experience that runs deep into the histories of aboriginal families throughout Canada. However brief, a story about education in 'Ya̲lis must acknowledge how the past accordions into the present, revealing the imprint of colonialism on people's lives. Although children from 'Ya̲lis and other Kwakwa̲ka̲'wakw villages were sometimes sent to school at Port Alberni, on central Vancouver Island, some younger children, such as

Florrie and Emma Mountain from Mamalilikala (Village Island), moved with their families to 'Yalis, where they attended the original Indian Day School. Children whose families did not relocate were often sent to St. Michael's Residential School in 'Yalis.

In the early 1940s, Rita Barnes was sent to the residential school from Gwa'yi (Kingcome). "Well, you know, when I went to St. Mike's, I really wanted to go," she told me. "There were no kids in Kingcome. Everybody had moved out of there. I think, at the time, there was a big push to relocate people from Kingcome to Gilford Island, probably to keep track of potlatching and all that. But there were five families who refused to move – that was the Dawsons, the Nelsons, the Dicks, the Webbers – so, there were only a few houses and no kids. And I wanted to go where everybody went."

"When I got there, I screamed the place down. They brought my brother over to try to reason with me. That didn't work. They must have told him to just go, 'You're not doing any good here.' When he tried to leave – I'm holding on to his shirt, and he's trying to get away, and I'm sliding across the floor, holding on, because I wanted to be with my brother. I cried so much they had to send for my cousin Lilly, Alfred Scow's daughter. She's Lilly Alfred today. They sent for her to come and settle me down, and she sat on my bed until I fell asleep. She had to do that for several nights, and then she would pick me up every Saturday morning ..."

"I was seven years old and sitting in the classroom, not understanding a word, I think, just bit by bit. There were letters that I had a hard time with. We don't have *r* or *sh* in my language. So, *r* came out like *w*. So, *really* would be *weally*. They had an older girl from Masset – her name was Beatrice. She married Wilfred Hanuse eventually, from the village of Alert Bay – who was always coaching me. She was the one who would have me all ready with my tam and everything, waiting for my cousin Lilly to come and pick me up ..."

"At least I went to relatives in the village on weekends, when I first went in there. I was really young, seven, eight, nine, you know? I'd go to my granduncle Charlie Newman's for lunch, but [my friend from Haida Gwaii] was just *there*. Her culture shock was going home to Masset at age sixteen, never knowing anything outside of that place."

"When we were – what? – about ten years old, I guess, [her] and me, our beds were side by side. My bed was right in the corner. She was there *[gestures]*, and there was a window over me that overlooked the roof of what used to be the infirmary. Our dormitory was here *[gestures]*, and then there was the boy's dormitory *[gestures]*. But the latches [between them] were always kept locked. I woke up when someone stepped down on the head of my bed. I looked, and then four boys came in very quietly – big dormitory. They went straight to the corner there – moonlit night – [my friend] and I staring at each other. And some girls got up, and they held each other, and they all cried. It turns out there was a death in their family, and they needed to get together to mourn together. They couldn't wait – this was a Tuesday – they couldn't wait until Sunday. Every Sunday we were allowed on the boys' side to play, and these kids couldn't wait until Sunday ... They must have just written notes back and forth ..."

"But, you know, the strangest thing is, [my friend] and I never talked about it. We never said a word. The boys quietly left again after they cried together. So, I think about it today. I think it was a part of how we survived together under very unnatural circumstances – how they survived, because they were there ten months out of the year, not seeing their parents. *We* were just a small group of who they called the *local girls* – the Kwakwa̱ka̱'wakws there – and we were kind of bullied. We were picked on. And when [my friend] and I talked about these things – why that was – she said, 'Probably everybody resented that you were in your territory, that your family came to visit. You were taken out to dinner. You went to restaurants. You had relatives that you went to.'"

"I had lots of relatives, but I only favoured two places to go – that was my granduncle Charlie Newman's and Mrs. Whonnock's. And that's where – that was my only experience with G̱a'ax̱sta'las, in my granduncle's place. When I'd go for lunch – his wife was already bedridden. I'm not even sure what was wrong with her, tuberculosis probably. Her bed was just in the living room."

Rita recalled one meeting with G̱a'ax̱sta'las: "One time, G̱a'ax̱sta'las came in with food, with a pot of something, I guess, because my grandaunt was bedridden. And she spoke a time, and they were talking about me. My uncle Charlie Newman was telling her that my uncle Alfred had told him that he should talk to me because every time Lilly, his daughter, would take me back to Saint Mike's, I'd start crying. And she lectured me – well, a little lecture. She said that I had no reason to cry. I shouldn't be crying. I should be happy to be going to school and that it was a good thing I was in there. Did she say, 'Being given a good education'? Or did she just say, "Learning to read and write and to be a good Christian'? I didn't understand the *Christian* for a while. Of course, I got to know the meaning of that. So, she gave me that. 'So you go and be a good girl, and you go back to the school.

Photo 41 G̲a'ax̲sta'las's brother, Charlie Newman, and his family. *Standing:* Herbert and Carey Newman. *Bottom row:* Charlie Newman (holding Margaret); Ellen (Neel) *(standing);* Charlie's second wife, Lalaxsa; and Louisa (Hunger). *Courtesy of Wedłidi Speck.*

And no crying.' And I nodded my head *[laughs]*. This was a lady of authority, right?"

Grandson Chris Cook Jr. attended the Indian day school, which had, by then, moved to the present location of the 'Y̲alis Apartments, across the street from the soccer field and the Big House: "I started school here probably about 1947. I think I was five years old. And my mother, who has blue-green eyes from the Hunt family in Fort Rupert, grew up with the potlatch, with all the customs. She spoke fluent Kwak̓wala, and my dad [Chris Cook Sr.] understood it. It was just the start of the Indian day school. We started school there. But when we went to school, I really felt sorry for the kids who came from a lot of the villages, because all they spoke was Kwak̓wala, you know. And they get strapped on the hand. But we talked a little bit of Kwak̓wala. And then the kids would have to write "I must not talk Indian in school. I must not talk Indian in school" five hundred times. We'd get caught speaking the language in around the school. They warned you that you could get the strap. So, I believe that was the first time for me, being ashamed of who you are, or all of a sudden there's somebody starting to mould you."

"So, you know, when you start to go to school, you start to feel these things. You come in, in the morning, and there's times that they check your hair and your fingernails and make sure you are not dirty. Some kids wouldn't have as good a place as I did, and I felt kind of sad for some of them, with the clothes they had. But that's the first time I started, I think, I started to change, you know, try to enunciate my words. Well, I was an Indian. So I think I started to have a lot of anger within myself, and my racist – maybe the racist part of believing – Jeez, these white guys. Who the hell are they? You know, they come in here, and they want us to be like this, and they want us to be like that. My mom would tell us, 'This is our way,' you know, 'This is our Indian way.' My mom always talked about the potlatch and our way and our names. But my dad, on the other hand, he'd say, 'No, that's all bullshit,' you know, 'That's not our way.' It was part of the way *he* was growing up. So, I had two sides – the capitalist, I guess, part of it, and growing up and trying to take that in balance."

"A Shining Quality": The *Native Voice*

Obstacles in the day school recounted by Chris Cook Jr. were echoed in the public discourse of the Native Brotherhood of British Columbia, which sought "a change of attitude on the part of whites and their governments."[60] The term *racism* emerged after the Second World War to describe the ideology that had propelled the German National Socialist Party's genocidal project, and aboriginal activists used it. They called for "racial tolerance," for "a re-adjustment of Canada's own domestic, racially based politics."[61] When aboriginal veterans returned from overseas service, wartime food production had waned, so "the fishing industry no longer had a preferred place in the economy of the Dominion ... In the spring of 1946, Parliament appointed a committee to investigate Indian problems in preparation for a thorough revision of all Indian legislation."[62] While officials were organizing the committee, the Brotherhood published the first volume of its newspaper, the *Native Voice: Official Organ of the Native Brotherhood of British Columbia.*[63] According to Forrest LaViolette, the paper represented the continuation "of the old protest movements." It focussed in particular on garnering public support and building awareness of the political situations faced by aboriginal peoples in Canada. Included in the first volume is a tribute to Jane Constance Cook, written by Maizie Armytage-Moore, renowned rights advocate and publisher of the *Native Voice.*[64]

> When I arrived at Alert Bay I looked forward to being received by Jane Cook. Immediately I was struck with the force of her personality, for she is a leader. Now 77 years of age, she is much respected and beloved; though when she willingly renounced the ancient customs of her people and found it hard to explain to the older people how much she loved them still and sympathized and respected many of the old customs, but she knew she was created by God and must follow His teachings. This responsibility was impressed on her by her father, and she was spurred on when she saw the great suffering around her, particularly among the women. She worked for years nursing them through sickness and teaching them the Word of God.
>
> Mrs. Cook's father was Captain Gilbert, a rugged sea captain and trader along the Pacific in the days of Sir James Douglas. Her mother came from Fort Rupert and was the daughter of a powerful hereditary chief. One of her family names is Warnook, meaning the possessor of a river. The Indian name for Fort Rupert is "Tsakis," meaning the spiritual bird, more powerful even than the thunder bird, and seldom spoken of because of his great power. Tsakis was the ancestor of Mrs. Cook's family, but before he became a man, Tsakis waltzed like the sand bird up and down the beach at Fort Rupert and that is why

> Rupert is called Tsakis by the Indians. Her grandfather was Hereditary Chief of Fort Rupert (Tsakis), Quatsano (Koskemug), and Knight's Inlet (Denahaski) ...
>
> Outstanding was Jane Cook's position as interpreter for the allied tribes. This work she carried on for many years. Today this quality of leadership is born in her children, one of her sons, Herbert Cook, is secretary of The Native Brotherhood of British Columbia.
>
> Jane Cook has great faith that someday her people will enjoy equality in their own country. One point she reasons is unfair, that is, why should an Indian have to become enfranchised at all to vote. Any British subject coming to this country automatically votes without enfranchisement, only subjects foreign to British soil must become enfranchised to vote, and the Indian is placed in this category – a foreign subject.
>
> Jane Cook could not work unselfishly for many years and think great thoughts without having shining quality about her. Jane Cook has a shining quality about her.[65]

Since the 1857 Gradual Civilization Act, persons considered by colonial authorities "to have acquired the qualities of a good citizen could be deprived of ... Indian status, so as to be thereafter legally treated for all purposes as a non-Indian."[66] Losing one's status meant that one could vote, own individual property on band lands, and legally consume intoxicants. Enfranchised individuals, however, had to give up all hereditary rights.[67] Historically, both compulsory *and* volunteer enfranchisement were met with persistent protest from aboriginal peoples, not least because they meant the eventual dissolution of collectively held lands, as well as the loss of treaty rights and other rights guaranteed under the Indian Act.[68]

The right to have political representation and the vote was a matter of intense debate in the late 1940s. Activists argued in favour of retaining status and including aboriginal peoples in the body politic at a time when the federal government was thickening its roster of citizens through new legislation that excluded "Indians." An editorial in the January edition of the *Native Voice* reported: "With the birth of the New Year all peoples residing in Canada regardless of their birthplace ... are entitled by law to call themselves Canadians ... under Canadian laws INDIANS ARE NOT PEOPLE."[69] Later that month, at a briefing before the Special Joint Committee on the Indian Act, Chief William Scow, president of the NBBC, issued a declaration to the premier of BC, John Hart: "We in the name of Pacific Coast bands do hereby declare the white chieftains to immediately surrender their false authority to an all Indian committee which we will form shortly. This proclamation will inform you that your government which has not seen fit to permit the owners of the Pacific coast lands a voice in their control, namely by voting, has no longer any standing."[70] Chief Scow also addressed the situation of women who had "married out" and were either widowed or deserted. He asked for a provision to grant Indian bands the power to reinstate their status.[71] The NBBC focussed on achieving an effective political voice.

"Let Us Go Forward, to Survive the Times": The BC Indian Arts and Welfare Society

In *Tales of Ghosts,* Richard Hawker defines the 1940s as the beginning of the Indian art revival. Monumental carvings from Northwest Coast nations signify the histories of particular clans and chiefs linked to specific territories and ceremonial rights. In the context of dealing with imperial officials on celebratory occasions, carvings are strong symbols of aboriginal sovereignty. During the late 1940s, however, museum professionals and academics promoted an apolitical craft industry as a "viable response to economic dire straits." The intention was to support aboriginal art co-ops and to foster interest in a general market for "handicrafts."[72]

In April 1948, the BC Indian Arts and Welfare Society and the BC Provincial Museum co-sponsored a conference on Indian affairs at the University of British Columbia. Several speakers expressed concern about the lack of protection for First Nations' designs created for the "curio trade," and so-called experts sought ways to assess the "authenticity" of works. There was no acknowledgment of aboriginal peoples' authority over their own expressions.[73] Theories of social evolution still dominated academic dialogues about art. Aboriginal peoples and their "artforms" were seen to be disappearing in the face of assimilation, a point that Kwakwa̱ka̱'wakw carver Ellen Neel addressed at the conference. "If our art is dead, then it is fit only to be mummified, packed into mortuary boxes and tucked away into museums. Whereas to me it is a living symbol of the gaiety, the laughter and love of colour of my people, a day to day reminder to us that even we had something of glory and honour before the white man came."[74]

Ellen Neel was the granddaughter of famed carver Charlie James and the niece of artist Mungo Martin.[75] Daughter of Charlie Newman and Lucy James, she was also Jane Cook's niece. Although they addressed different subjects, both aunt and niece spoke at that forum.

During the conference, G̲a'ax̲sta'las offered what were perhaps her last recorded public statements. The agenda set by organizers was broad and included education; arts and handicrafts; health and welfare; and the training of teachers, welfare workers, and nurses.[76] Following a public display called "Arts and Handicrafts of the B.C. Indians,"[77] eighty-four speakers from throughout the province discussed topics (called "problems" in the official report) in an atmosphere described as informal and friendly.[78]

Andy Paull, president of the North American Indian Brotherhood, gave an impassioned speech on the second day of the conference.[79] He spoke about health and welfare and about the potlatch, which he described as a constitution or law that included good features and bad features. The latter, he said, should have been "eradicated by the government." His point was that the good features were necessary to the health and well-being of aboriginal peoples.[80] He asked, "in the name of humanity," that conference organizers send a message to the Canadian government, that they demand progress on several fronts, including a "well defined housing program," an adequate domestic water supply in "Indian settlements," and an immediate extension of the Old Age Pension. His demands on behalf of women are worth quoting: "that mothers and deserted wives and widows be included in all benefits enjoyed by their white sisters under similar circumstances, because in many cases the white people are responsible for these conditions." Paull concluded by stating, "Let us go forward, not backward ... You can re-write the infamous history of the treatment of Indians of Canada which is one of sweat, blood and starvation, by doing something for the Indians now."[81]

At the morning session the next day, G̲a'ax̲sta'las spoke about education. But R.F. Davey, inspector of Indian schools for BC, spoke first. He offered statistics on Indian education in the province.[82] The Indian Affairs Branch, he stated, was paying the fees to "secure the admission of Indian pupils to 'white' high schools" rather than developing Indian schools.[83] The rationale for residential schools was to give priority to children whose "circumstances require ... they will receive adequate care," to admit pupils from communities too distant for educational facilities, to accommodate those attending "white" high schools, and to educate pupils "whose parents wish them to attend a Residential School."[84] All schools were operated by the churches. Day school teachers were nominated by church authorities. Many were not certified at a time when the department was investing in new day schools rather than residential schools.

The next speaker was the superintendent of Indian missions from the Diocese of Victoria. Although Father Bradley stated that he would rather "speak about the man in the moon" than talk about Indian Catholic schools, his presentation emphasized "Catholic faith as a fact of knowledge."[85] "If a man is a Catholic," Bradley said, "he will only be a good citizen so long as he is a good Catholic." Acknowledging the anger he was likely to stir up, he asked to be left alone by both Protestant and secular authorities: "Don't crush us," he said, "you who are not Catholic help us to make our ... schools really efficient."[86] Harry Hawthorn, an anthropologist who was chairing the session, thanked Bradley for his "honesty ... in discussing a subject which lies deep in human belief and is not discussed lightly among those who disagree."

When Hawthorn introduced the next speaker – Dr. Raley, a former principal of the Coqualeetza Institute – he praised him for his "unrivalled knowledge of the coastal Indians of B.C." Raley's presentation began with the observations of early explorers who were impressed by the "advanced" state of arts and customs on the BC Coast. He quoted anthropologists who spoke of the equality of Europeans and "Indians" in areas of intellect, art, vocational training, ethics, faith, and "native mythology which is also native science."[87] Raley gave a history of "Indian education" traced through missionary activities and government aid.[88]

"While others can speak of working *in* this field," Harry Hawthorn said as he introduced the next presenter, "Mr. Scow can speak of being worked *on*." Bill Scow, president of the NBBC and a Kwakwa̱ka̱'wakw chief, told his audience that the Brotherhood then covered twelve districts. He asked for "up to date educational facilities and more teachers," and he spoke about his own struggle to support his son, a student at UBC.[89] Scow discussed the formation of the NBBC eighteen years earlier and praised Alfred Adams, its founder from Masset, for choosing the term *brotherhood* with what he called the "far-sightedness of a Christian man." "We have had real Cristians who started us, and we appreciate what the missionaries have done in the past. If we had no contact with the missionaries in the early days, I would not be able to stand before you and speak your language. We have a dear lady here who has done so much for the Indians. It was through the help I got from her that I was able to carry on this work. Let us carry on."[90]

Chief Scow ended with a story:

> I am reminded of a story of the first contact of my people with the white people. A ship had come into the harbor at Masset. The Indians were curious. They had never seen a white man before in their lives. The whole tribe stood on the beach watching the unloading of the cargo, which consisted mostly of farm implements and cattle. One of the Indians walked over to one of the animals and took hold of one of the horns, and said "What is this?" The white man replied "It is a horn." The cow let out a "moo," and the Indian said "Which horn was that?" Let us join together, and let the authorities hear but one voice, and let us not give them cause to say: Which horn was that?[91]

According to the transcript, Harry Hawthorn did not introduce Jane Constance Cook. But Chief Scow's comments about a dear lady likely referred to G̲a'ax̲sta'las. Her statements follow a long and complicated dialogue on the interpretation of meaning across cultures. That her views shifted over time is undeniable and expected, for Jane Cook was engaged in a politically charged communication that was generated and responsive to shifting internal and external contexts.

❧

MRS. S COOK, Alert Bay

The discussions I have heard about the Indian problems are so important, it gives me pleasure to talk about my people: their ideas – how they were brought up before, and how they were brought up today, and what we hope will be the result of today's education. So many points have been brought forward. I think Father Bradley brought out a main point. But it does not matter if you are a Roman Catholic, an Anglican or United Church. As the people of the Brotherhood told us, we must unite as one. There is one thing that I must stress, because I have been brought up in this way – and that is Christianity. As one Anglican minister said to me: "Do you know Mrs. Cook, I don't know what you are. You are not an Anglican. You are really cosmopolitan in the way of religion." Religion must come first in the training of the Indians. If a missionary comes into the country, he has come for a purpose. And what is that purpose? In our area first a Catholic came, but he couldn't stand it. He had to get out. Then came the Anglicans. They had got out of some place before and finally landed in Alert Bay. One of the main things they came for was to bring God to those people. But we have a religion, as we have heard from Dr. Raley. It was pagan, of course. The Missionary comes in with the one God. It doesn't matter whether you are Roman Catholic, Anglican or United Church, there is one God. That's what they came with.

You can't make a good Indian without religion. You can't make a good Indian without God. You can't make a good citizen without making a good Christian.

What has grieved me all my life is the ignorance, the misunderstanding about the Indian's religion. [Captain] Vancouver found that already before the white man came the Indian had their laws, and respect for authority, they had their religion. The Indian saw God in nature – the sun, moon and stars he worshipped and practiced his religion. He was a good Indian. I was old enough to see the tail end of that era. Everything that an Indian man or woman could be – honest, courageous. It was the thing that came after that I saw the awful results of what the other nations brought into the country to the Indians. It was not God – it was the Devil.

What we are struggling with today is the teaching of the white man who did not understand the Indian and taught that these things which were good were bad. They did not understand his past.

We have a display of handicraft here, but it is nothing to what I saw as a child. My people cannot do that today. They have not the materials. The Government has sold the material; the woods and the big cedar tree. Now he can't go out to the cedar tree to get the bark he needs for his art. He can't go to the woods and kill the deers for the skins. If he tried to get his materials today as he used to, he would be put in jail. How is he going to get materials to do his art?

There is another thing which the missionary didn't understand. He couldn't see the beauty of a totem pole. He discouraged the Indian from making them. They didn't recognize what the totem poles meant. At the foot of the totem pole you see an animal with outstretched hands. Who understands what this is? That represents death. She is holding out her hands to you. She is saying "I am going to get you some day." The missionary didn't know what that figure meant. We buy totem poles for curios, but don't make the children carve them without knowing what they are doing, what it means. We don't know what the controlling thought of the Indian will be. Let us have one idea – the idea of the Indian in religion. Let us educate the young people, the future Indians, in the life which has to be lived today, to survive the times.

I would like those who want to keep these things of the past to know what they mean. I know an Indian who says: "I come from a bear." He is a Christian. He belongs to a church. He believes a bear became human and that is why he is here. Is that right? No. We want them to say that they are created by God. Can't you see it, missionary? Can't you see it, all you teachers of the young people, what the people believe and what they go back to? Take them into a village where they are not getting Indian instruction. What do you expect? We are thankful that we had the church early.

Do learn what the customs of the Indians mean. Do learn what it means and you will know there is only one thing – a faith in God.[92]

G̱a'ax̱sta'las qualified her comments on education by positioning herself as a Christian. Her statements offer insight into how she envisaged the Kwakwa̱ka̱'wakw – past, present, and future. Like Chief Scow, she viewed Christianity as synonymous with political solidarity. Indeed, G̱a'ax̱sta'las's testimony must be read in light of the politicized Christian idiom through which she expressed herself. "We must unite as one," she said and, like Chief Scow, her opinion about education pushed back a little against the public stance of the Native Brotherhood, which opposed religious education.

I asked Wedłidi Speck about this aspect of her testimony. "So that's a stand," Wedłidi told me. "There's an assumption that the Native Brotherhood were a homogeneous group. The Brotherhood are from the Nisga'a. They're from the Queen Charlottes. They're from the Tsimshian. They're from the Coast. We've never got along in a unified, mono, holistic kind of way. It's about the push and the pull and the tug, and it's about trying to persuade. And those who are going to be more persuasive get the motion passed. To me, that's just the way it's always been. I think in terms of the Brotherhood, she would be lobbying here." G̱a'ax̱sta'las identified herself as "cosmopolitan in the way of religion," and Wedłidi saw this as significant. "I think that cosmopolitan is an important thing here," he told me. "That's a whole bunch of things together. That's the first clue from an outside perspective – that people see her as bicultural or multicultural and that she obviously did some cross learning." The books in her vast library certainly attest to her lifelong interest in expressions of belief around the colonial globe.

Jane Cook offered a brief chronology of the missionaries who came to Kwakwa̱ka̱'wakw villages and emphasized that they brought one

God. In our discussions, George Speck spoke about the Christian introduction of a single deity: "I'm not even sure what people think about Aboriginal spirituality and that whole concept of a single being. I think that's kind of an accommodation from a Christian tenet. There were lots of transformations that occurred or people that had the ability to transform themselves and everything into spirit. This whole 'the creator' is a Christian creation. That's kind of – what do you call it? – syncretism? *[Laughs]* How to fit an aboriginal concept into a Christian mould. I wouldn't be surprised if it was around Jane's time they tried to do that. The history of Christianity in non-European societies has been pretty common integration of local forms with the Christian thesis. When I was doing some work for the KDC [Kwakiutl District Council], I did some research on origin stories. It was funny how the origin stories changed with different tribes. Raven in one story was the major change force, and in others it was individuals making themselves into rivers for the people, and others were trees or fish or whatever."

In 1948, George Speck's great-grandmother said that "the Indian saw God in nature," in the pre-Christian beliefs and practices of her people. Perhaps her theological studies had led her to a more abstract conception of God, one not confined to Christianity. Referring to Dr. Raley's talk, G̲a'ax̲sta'las spoke about pre-European cosmologies and the ignorance of Indian religion, laws, and respect for authority, a misunderstanding that had grieved her all her life. Throughout her public career, Jane Cook referred to the custom not being what it used to be. She now implied that what had been lost was the grounding of religious expression in nature.

Equating good citizenship with good Christianity, G̲a'ax̲sta'las reasserted the demand for equal rights. Reading the words *good Indian,* Wedłidi Speck heard a tone of impatience in her voice. "She was expressing that her people were faith-driven people. I imagine sitting and talking to her – she could give the roots of her faith, where she came from." He spoke again about biculturalism, about his own mother, who was "rooted in Christianity," and his father, who was "rooted in feasting."

During her presentation, G̲a'ax̲sta'las positioned herself as a witness who "was old enough to see the tail end of [the] era," a time when her people were "everything that an Indian man or woman could be – honest, courageous." And then she mentioned "the thing that came after," "the awful results" of colonial incursion. Like the discourse in early written petitions and testimonies, she expressed her political views through a Christian idiom. She asserted that colonial incursion "was not God – it was the Devil." For several decades she had argued for adequate services and legislation to protect vulnerable people from illnesses exacerbated by poor living conditions; from uneven, Eurocentric applications of justice and enforcement; and from negative changes in the social organization of her own community caused by "what ... other nations brought into the country."

The contemporary struggle that G̲a'ax̲sta'las identified was "the teaching of the white man who did not understand the Indian and taught that these things which were good were bad." Her comment evokes a parade of the powerful white men with whom she dealt throughout her life. Was Reverend Hall included? Did William Halliday, Murray Todd, or Duncan Campbell Scott fall under this umbrella? "They did not understand [the Indian] past," Jane Cook stated, and her words reverberate today in the context of reconciliation, racism, and abuse in residential schools. But her critique also included European ignorance about the symbols and meanings embedded in totem poles, in what were then commodified as handicrafts.

G̲a'ax̲sta'las said that the display at the conference was nothing like what she saw as a child and that her people were severely constrained by the government. They could no longer access cedar for carving or their hunting territories, where they obtained deerskins. In the midst of a seeming celebration of aboriginal peoples' artistic expression, G̲a'ax̲sta'las reminded conference attendees of the colonial legislation that prevented access to lands and imposed yet another layer of criminalization on First Nation peoples. Just a year before the conference, at the 1947 annual convention of the NBBC, delegates had rallied for compensation for lands and timber alienated from reserves. It is difficult not to hear an echo of the testimonies about timber leases given at the McKenna-McBride Royal Commission, an echo that reverberates today.

When George Speck spoke to me about the band's access to timber in 2007, the situation had not changed: "To get tree farm licences under the Forestry Act, we have to make applications. Now we can get wood for 'community purposes' under the watchful eye of Forestry. It's inconvenient for them if we use logging roads; so, if we want to make a canoe, they supply the wood and have it exempted from our stumpage fees. The cost is considered to be a donation from the forest companies. Last year, we had a meeting about acquiring wood on an ongoing basis – 1,200 cubic metres annually. That's twenty-five truckloads. The cost would have to be carried by the community – about

$40,000. Jane Cook was saying, they can't just go out there and get wood. She'd have gone through commissions where land and wood was always an issue."

"There is another thing which the missionary didn't understand," G̲a'ax̲sta'las told her audience in 1948. "He couldn't see the beauty of a totem pole. They didn't recognize what the totem poles meant." Along with George Hunt, G̲a'ax̲sta'las had worked with Reverend Goodfellow in the late 1930s to translate ancestor stories associated with the poles acquired for Stanley Park in Vancouver. Her comments about the female figure at the bottom of the pole likely refer to Dzunuk̲'wa, the almost iconic form of the cannibal woman, with her round, open mouth and outstretched arms. "Who understands what this is?" Jane Cook asked. "That represents death," she said. "She is holding out her hands to you. She is saying, 'I am going to get you someday.'"

Given that G̲a'ax̲sta'las knew about her heart condition, it is difficult not to read her comments through an awareness of her own mortality, but according to William Wasden Jr. the figure of Dzunuk̲'wa is imbued with many meanings. We were speaking about marriage contracts, when he mentioned the use of Dzunuk̲'wa poles to shame those who had not paid the marriage debt. "A lot of marriages were just for rights," he said. "They have a Dzunuk̲'wa totem pole outside the house with its arms open like that *[gestures out before him]*. What that symbolized was that the father of the bride hadn't paid the marriage debt back for his daughter and that they were waiting to receive it. That was a shameful thing for someone to have that put up against them. They never face it toward the water, though, because that was inviting death into your village. They always had it facing another way. That's a real strong custom among our people. Sometimes ... they have coppers in its hands, which were added later, after it was paid." We spoke about his great-grandmother's statements at the conference. "Everyone knows that [open arms invite death]. That's still going on today," William said. "When a pole [like that] went up [in the village], that's when all these stories came up. We also say that the bottom figure represents the ancestors, that your grandfather's holding the rest of the family up. So, for us, the bottom figure is the most important figure."

In 1948, G̲a'ax̲sta'las spoke about the translation of totem poles into curios – commodities carved without knowledge of the meanings attached to them.[93] She addressed members of the museum and anthropology community directly and said, "I would like those who want to keep these things of the past to know what they mean." Her brief portrait of a Christian man who claimed descent from a bear seemed to illustrate the complexity of the meanings attached to totem poles and the challenges of mainstream education. "Can't you see it, missionary?" she challenged. "What the people believe and what they go back to? ... What do you expect?" It is difficult to interpret her intent, but G̲a'ax̲sta'las's final statement was certainly clear: "there is only one thing – a faith in God."

Jane Cook stated that she did not know what future ideologies and beliefs would take precedence among her people, but, for her, the "idea of the Indian in religion" was clearly linked to education, to "the life which has to be lived today, to survive the times." This theme rings loudly in the testimonies of many of her descendants who admire her literacy.

"She became a teacher," Wedłidi Speck told me as we were discussing Jane Cook's presentation, "and there were key things that she wanted people to think about. So, she offered questions, and she wanted you to answer them. It's different than reacting, defending, and protecting. That only comes from taking the journey. So, a person that walks through this life – at the end of it, you will definitely know where you've come from. I don't think her journey ever ended. I don't think she ever stopped learning. There are pieces [of her] as a visionary that she was so brutally honest about – like knowing that when Emma's son becomes a man there would be no fish left – to know that and yet to still persevere with hope. That's amazing."

PART IX

A Tower of Strength: Word Memorials, 1951

Ga'axsta'las lived to see the provincial vote granted to aboriginal peoples in March 1949. But that June the federal government recognized only selected Indians as eligible for the federal franchise.[1] Frank Calder became the first aboriginal representative in the legislative assembly. In January 1951, an article appeared in the *Native Voice* titled "Full House for Cooks." Jane and Stephen had celebrated Christmas dinner with seventy members of the family. "It was necessary to have two sittings," the article stated. "Had all the family been able to attend, there would have been 104 present." The year before, the couple had celebrated their sixty-second wedding anniversary.[2]

Jane and Stephen's sons Reggie and Herbert appeared on the front page of the *Native Voice* in May 1951 as president and secretary-treasurer, respectively, of the new Native Vessel Owners' Association of BC.[3] Members of the Native Sisterhood went on strike the same month, withholding fees to attain voting rights within the Native Brotherhood of British Columbia (NBBC).[4] The *Native Voice* also reported in April that Jane and Stephen Cook had attended the Anglican Synod in Victoria, taking with them Dorothy Mountain, Gracie Cook, and Christine Cook. At the time, their daughter Pearl Mountain and Mrs. Willie Cook "were visiting villages ... getting the ladies organized," and their son Reggie had one of the first cars on the reserve – a Morris.[5] Forty percent of aboriginal children were reportedly not attending school because there were not enough schools, and of those who were attending, less than 1 percent had received schooling beyond Grade 8. The *Native Voice* contained detailed reports about the ongoing protest against Bill 76, which would drastically amend the Indian Act.

In June, the *Native Voice* reported on a victory in negotiations over salmon prices and listed soccer scores from 'Yalis under the heading "Alert Bay News."[6] In July, Ellen Neel appeared in photographs, with her children, carving miniature poles at her workshop and sales booth in Stanley Park. In August, the paper reported that Canada, the United States, and Japan were negotiating a treaty to conserve and protect Pacific Coast fisheries.[7] On 4 September 1951, the federal government amended sections 93 and 94 of the Indian Act, allowing Indians to enter beer parlours. People were still being arrested and fined, however, because the province had not yet issued its own proclamation.[8]

Ethel Alfred recalled a time in September or October of that year: "There was one thing that really stands out in my mind – is when I got sick. Nobody was here. Everybody was away working at that other place – the canneries. And [Ga'axsta'las] heard about me getting sick because I came home. We were at Steveston, eh? And then I got sick when I was here for a week. I thought then I was going to go back, but I just got sick ... We had sawdust burning in the house, and I went out and started the fire before the kids came. Then I started breaking some peach boxes. I preserved some peaches when I came. So, I left them beside the stove, and I broke some up to start the fire. So, I came in, and something seemed to have really bust inside of me, and I had awful pain. So, I just went to bed."

"I just want to tell you how it stands out in my mind – what Granny did for me. My eldest daughter and my sister Stella told me to get up. 'I don't know. I'm sick,' I said. Every time I lift my head up, my head would just swim like that and get unconscious ... So they must have phoned the hospital for me to be brought in, and that's who told Granny what happened to me ... [Nellie Cook] went and sat with me, and Granny was there for four days with me. I always felt bad when I think about her, when I tell her that the water wasn't cold enough during the night when she would be sitting with me. She'd get home, and *[turns to Pearl Alfred]* your mom *[Nellie Cook]* would go and sit with me during the day. And Granny said, 'It really makes me good, Ethel, that Nellie phoned and offered to come and sit with you during the day.' The doctor didn't want me being alone, said I might hemorrhage again, because it wasn't coming out of me. It was just inside. That's why. Yeah. So that really stands out for me all the time – how wonderful a person she was to do that for me."

"I always think of that Reggie. It was about September or October when I had that happen to me. So I ordered a dressing gown for Granny for Christmas *[laughs]*. And after that, after that, Reggie said, 'You shouldn't have bought Granny a dressing gown. She's been sick ever since you gave it to her!' he said to me *[laughs]*. 'Why? Well, I thought it would be nice.' It was a winter one, eh? *[laughs]*. I always think of that. That wasn't too long before she passed away."

Narratives about G̲a'ax̲sta'las's death form a collage of voices.

❧

Ilma Cook: "She had a big garden. She looked after that, and that's how she landed up in the hospital. She died on my birthday, which is October 16. She was outside, cutting up the fish to smoke. Those guys, big men, they used to just bring the fish in coal sacks, because they used to burn coal on the boats. There was no propane stoves and things like that then. So, they had just small, little stoves that they could fry anything on, like bacon or pork chops or a steak or whatever. Everything was fried. What was I saying?"

"You were talking about Granny. They brought the fish up to her."

"Oh yes, in these coal sacks. Are you going to carry two fish at a time all that distance from the dock up to the house? No. They wanted to carry as many as they could handle and had the strength to pick it up. So, they put them in coal sacks and brought them up and just left them there. What do you do? What's going to get done with that fish? So, here she was, all wrapped up warm with a hat on. Yeah, she got a real bad cold. I guess it was pneumonia. The last trip she made to the hospital, and she died there. It's cold out there this time of the year, wet and damp."

❧

Emma Alfred: "She had a heart attack, and that was it. I don't think she was with us very long, and that was a shock. I was out for a walk with my little boy, and we saw the ambulance going by and never thought anything of it. And somebody said it was Gran, and we all tried to get to the hospital. But just so many of us were allowed to see her for a few minutes. It was really heartbreaking."

❧

Pearl Alfred: "We were in the hospital. There were so many of us just crowded in there, standing around Granny. You could hear her voice.

I was standing, and she was singing "Rock of ages, cleft to me," and she died singing that. Then she was bathed and dressed and carried home."

ꕥ

Ilma Cook: "In those days, you know, people used to take their family members who died into their homes in a coffin. And Granny was no exception. Her body was taken up, and everybody in the family came who wanted to see her for the last time. Yeah. Everybody mourned her loss, her death."

ꕥ

Peggy Svanvik: "She passed away, and it was really hard to believe that she could – she could do that *[laughs]*. Of course, we all do that, but it was really hard to imagine that *she* could do that. Yeah, I remember poor Papa standing there crying. He was so sad when she died."

ꕥ

Emma Alfred: "They took her body straight up to the house. As soon as she died, they went right up to her home. No morgue. She never believed in that. And people phoned from all over the country, and Auntie Winnie told me to answer the phone. And that's when Granny's body was in the dining room. Gran's body was there, and I don't know why, I was a little bit nervous of it. So, it was one of these hand phones. I answered it and turned around and glanced at Gran in the coffin. They just said they wanted to send their condolences, and I had to write on this pad who was phoning – if they were coming or not coming. And I turned, and I glanced at her while she was talking to me about how she knew Gran so well, and all this, and all of a sudden, Gran got a smile on her face. She just started smiling *[laughs]*. I said, 'Okay,' and I hung up. And I said, 'Auntie Winnie, come here!' I said, 'Look at Granny's face.'"

"'Oh my God! She's got a grin on her face.' It was just awesome. I looked at her, and I said, 'Is it all right?'"

"And she said, 'Yeah, it's all right, Emma. It's all right. Granny's happy where she is, and she's letting us know.' So, I've never forgotten that. And then I couldn't remember the lady who was phoning *[laughs]*. But she got phone calls from all over when she died. It seemed like somebody sent a telegram out, and everybody knew, because the phone never stopped ringing."

"As we grew older and thought about her ways, it seemed so easy. It just seemed like she just knew what she was doing. I mean, there was always a good day with her. It was always a good day. Very strong. Very strong."

❧

Pearl Alfred: "I was sixteen the day she was buried. So much for my birthday that year *[laughs]*. I'll always remember that. Probably one of the biggest funerals there ever was here. She was just known near and far, and people seemed to come from everywhere. One of the things that I remember was – and I always think of this – there was a big roll of thunder, and someone at the cemetery said, 'Somebody big from the 'Na̲mgis has died.'"

❧

George Cook: "I remember going to her funeral. One of my uncles said to me at the funeral, 'She's gone. Shed no tears' ... That's the Cooks, you know, we never cry... [But] Granny showed emotion, and Papa was very emotional on the morning after Granny went. He walked up the garden and wailed. Every morning. But that was his way. He'd go up every morning after breakfast, wail, and then he'd come down and walk off down the street. That's it. Every morning."

❧

Emma Alfred: "I remember hearing Granny say to Papa Cook, 'You know, I really hope you die before me,' she says, 'because I really know how you are going to be.' And I'm sitting on my bed, and I was thinking – Gee, Granny's mean. She wants Papa to die. So, when Granny had the heart attack and Papa was left behind, every morning he'd go in the back and look at this big garden and cry for her. He called her Mamma, and he'd yell, 'Mamma! Why did you leave me?'"

"And I thought, okay, now I understood Granny, because it was too much for him if she left. Granny would have held up better than he did if she stayed behind. She was right, and she knew what she was talking about."

❧

Nella Nelson: "My mom says they were staying at the [Cook] big house then with us, because my dad was away for TB for a couple of years, in the hospital in Nanaimo. He was in there, and then he was in quarantine in that little room at the top of the stairs in the big house. Yeah, so my mom says she remembers when Granny died, that Papa would get up early in the morning and go out on the stairs and just wail and wail and then come back in and start his day. He just released his grief every morning."

Pearl Alfred: "Papa said he had a dream, and she came to him at night and said she was hungry. So, we built a fire and burned some steak."

Christine Zurkowski: "My grandfather, although he was a believer, he wanted to make sure. In the afterworld – they kind of believe that they should get some stuff to you. So, when she died, I remember Pearlie and I burning steak, and, of course, we were just children ... He'd asked us to build a fire where Gaga's fire was. Do you remember?"

"They used to burn all their clothes on the beach – in the bay," Nellie Cook, her mother, replied.

"Yeah, that's what they'd do. They burned everything. So he burned her things, and he gave her meat – Pearlie and I did ... Well, *he* fed it. We just thought – he wants it done. We'll do it. It was funny because it was like I said, he was putting one foot in this world and, just in case, another over here *[laughs]*. Yeah. I remember him doing that. *Us* doing that."

Jane Constance Cook passed away on 16 October 1951. She was survived by her husband, Stephen Cook; her sister, Mrs. Annie Kamano; her daughters, Emma Kenmuir, Winifred Bell, and Pearl Mountain; and her sons, Reggie, Cyril, Gilbert, Herbert, and Chris. Ga'axsta'las and Nage at that time had fifty grandchildren, twenty-six great-grandchildren, and many nieces and nephews.

In her obituary, which appeared in the *Native Voice,* her niece Ellen Neel wrote that her funeral had been attended by relatives and by hundreds of friends from Haida Gwaii, Port Simpson, Prince Rupert, Bella Coola, Bella Bella, Fort Rupert, Vancouver, and Victoria. Neel praised "this great Christian Native lady who fought for the freedom of the Natives of BC." She was praised as a secretary and interpreter for the "Kwawkiutl Agency" and as a "member of the allied tribes of British Columbia in their long fight for justice, fighting shoulder to shoulder with her native brothers ... She nursed the sick, comforted

October, 1951 The NATIVE VOICE Page 9

Beloved Native Lady Passes

Alert Bay Mourns Death of Mrs. Cook

MRS. JANE CONSTANCE COOK
Irreparable Loss to Alert Bay.

Mrs. Jane Constance Cook, beloved wife of Stephen Cook, died at Alert Bay, British Columbia, in her eighty-second year on October 16, 1951. She leaves to survive her three daughters, Mrs. Emma Kenmuir, Mrs. Winnifred Bell, and Mrs. Pearl Mountain and five sons, Reginald, Cyril, Gilbert, Herbert and Christopher, fifty grandchildren and twenty-six great grandchildren, one sister Mrs. Michael Kamano and many nieces and nephews.

In addition to her relatives, hundreds of friends, white and natives will mourn her passing up and down the coast from the Queen Charlotte Islands, Port Simpson, Prince Rupert, Bella Coola, Bella Bella, Fort Rupert, Vancouver and Victoria. British Columbia has lost one of its most colorful links with the past.

This great Christian Native Lady has fought for the freedom of the Natives of B.C. This outstanding woman, as secretary and interpreter for her people of the Kwakiutl Agency, Alert Bay district, B.C., represented them as member of the allied tribes of British Columbia in their long fight for justice, fighting shoulder to shoulder with her native brothers.

A life-long member of the Church of England, she was educated at Alert Bay by the famous pioneer missionaries, Mr. and Mrs. Hall. Her Christian life was an example to all, both whites and natives, since she was 15 years of age. She nursed the sick, comforted and helped her people to overcome the terrible conditions forced on them by the coming of the early white settlers in the wild pioneer days of British Columbia.

Kindly, understanding Mrs. Cook generously gave of her love and great wisdom to her people. Always, she had faith that some day the British justice she honored would prevail and give her people the equality that was their right as owners of this country. One point she reasoned was unfair and unjust, that was, "Why should an Indian have to become enfranchised to gain citizenship and vote, when any British subject coming to this country automatically voted without enfranchisement? Only subjects, foreign to British soil, must become enfranchised before voting and the Indian was placed in this category."

Married at 15, she had 16 children, eight now survive her. Many of her sons and grandsons and nephews served in two world wars. Her beloved son Edwin gave his life in the First World War. She bore her sorrows bravely, her faith in her Father in Heaven carried her through her sorrow.

Mrs. Cook's father was Captain Gilbert, a rugged English sea captain, a great Christian gentleman who traded along the Pacific Coast in the days of Governor Douglas. Her mother came from Fort Rupert, the daughter of a powerful hereditory chief — chief of three tribes. One of her family names was Wonook, meaning the possessor of a river. The Indian name for Fort Rupert was "Tsakis," a spiritual bird even more powerful than the Thunder Bird and seldom spoken of because of his great power.

Tsakis was the legendary founder of Mrs. Cook's family. The legend said that before he became human, Tsakis waltzed like a sand bird up and down the beach of Fort Rupert, and that is why the Indians called Fort Rupert Tsakis.

Her grandfather was hereditary chief of Fort Rupert (Tsakis); Quatsano (Koskemug); Knight's Inlet (Denahaski). When her mother was a girl of 19, an Indian who was a stranger to the Rupert tribe had committed a murder, according to the white's idea, and took refuge with the Fort Rupert tribe. A warship was sent to ask the Fort Rupert tribe to surrender thim. This they refused to do, although he did not belong to their tribe. The commander demanded surrender and started to search but the native womne went into the old Hudson Bay Fort, sat down, spread their native blankets and hid the chief under their blankets. Later some of the chiefs, including the head chief, Mrs. Cook's grandfather, were taken to Victoria to be tried and punished—Governor Douglas released them. Mrs. Cook's mother followed her father to Victoria and when there met Captain Gilbert, and they were married.

Her father gave her a Christian up-bringing. She gave up her hereditary rights as chieftain to her nephew. Her long life was devoted to the service of her people.

Calm, serene dignified, a tower of strength to all who knew her, her loss is irreparable—there is no one to take her place. It is hard to think of Alert Bay without her, but one thing is certain, her memory will never die. Her teachings and work will live like a great shining beacon to guide us in the years to come, a great noble lady has gone to her rest.

The Native Voice extends deepest sympathy to Mr. Stephen Cook and family in their great loss in the death of our great leader, Mrs. Jane Constance Cook, Mother of Alert Bay.

Charlie Williams Dies In Accident

Charlie Williams of Soloose Indian Reserve, Lower Nicola, died as the result of injuries received in an automobile accident recently.

He was the son of the late and famous Chief Johnny Chilliheetza. Our deepest sympathy goes out to the family in its loss.

Photo 42 Ga'axsta'las's obituary. Written by her niece Ellen Neel. *Native Voice* 5, 9 (1951): 9. *Courtesy of* Native Voice.

and helped her people to overcome the terrible conditions forced on them by the coming of early white settlers in the wild pioneer days of British Columbia ... Always she had faith that some day the British justice she honored would prevail and give her people the equality that was their right as owners of this country." Neel also cited

G̱a’x̱sta’las’s line of descent from the “legendary founder Tsakis,” who, before he became human, “waltzed like a sandbird up and down the beach at Fort Rupert.” She wrote about G̱a’x̱sta’las’s grandfather ’Nulis and how Jane’s mother, Emily (G̱wa̱yuła̱las), had met William Gilbert in Victoria. “She gave up her hereditary rights as chieftain to her nephew. Her long life was devoted to the service of her people. Calm, serene, dignified, a tower of strength to all who knew her, her loss is irreparable – there is no-one to take her place ... Her memory will never die. Her teachings and work will live like a great shining beacon to guide us in the years to come, a great noble lady has gone to her rest.”[9]

The same issue of the *Native Voice* reported that Peter Kelly, chair of the legislative committee of the Native Brotherhood, was negotiating Old Age Pension benefits with the BC attorney general and the minister of labour. In December 1951, major revisions in the Indian Act were passed in Ottawa. The new act brought in a legal definition of “Indians.” Indians were given the right to drink in beer parlours, but under section 95 it was still illegal to possess, supply, or sell liquor on or off the reserve.[10] The status and enfranchisement clauses remained in the new act. When women married non-aboriginal men, they were immediately enfranchised and lost their status as Indians. The voluntary enfranchisement of adults came through application to the minister and would be determined “on satisfactory evidence that he or she ‘is capable of discharging the duties and responsibilities entailed.’”[11] The *Native Voice* reported that five hundred BC Indians were then hospitalized with tuberculosis and that an estimated two hundred others were living with the disease in their communities because they refused to go to the “Indian TB hospitals.” Prohibitions against potlatching were removed from the act.

As G̱a’x̱sta’las’s great-grandson John Nestman told me, life continued in the big house. “One of my first memories was going to the big house to eat. It must have been just after she died. There’d be huge bowls full of seaweed and corn. They’d have these big wooden ladles, Native ladles, and smaller Native spoons to eat the seaweed with. Stephen – Papa – he used say, ‘Bring the fish heads over here! Johnny and I, we’re going to eat the fish heads.’ *[Laughs]* Fish heads and eyes dipped in eulachon oil. Auntie Shirley told me that Granny used to go down to the beach, in front of St. Mike’s there, and harvest eelgrass. They’d just eat it raw – peel down the outer leaves and eat the sweet root ... The Cook’s Wharf, down there, the family used to go down and work on their nets, and at lunchtime they'd all walk up the hill and have dinner. All the ladies would be cooking. Papa, he used to be walking up and down the wharf with his cane. I'll always remember that."

Word Memorials

Ethel Alfred: "She was a wonderful Christian woman. Very Christian woman. And she always was there for anybody – she'd be right there with the people."

Pearl Alfred: "I think she really believed. She believed that life would be better for Indian people if they got away from the potlatch, if they got into what we call the white man's world. And that never happened. She was, I think, a very smart woman, and she would have figured that out before too long. And I'm sure she would have been very disappointed in the role of the church in terms of land claims and things. I mean, she was a hundred years too early! She should have been around now *[laughs],* when we need her."

Rita Barnes: "I think she should be remembered for her strength. Even though she might have played a big part in potlatching being banned, she did it because she so believed that she was doing the right thing. You know, when you believe in something and you believe in it enough, shouldn't you? She really thought she was doing it for the good of all. She didn't know. She had no idea it might be damaging to some. Yeah. She had to be a strong woman to go against all these chiefs."

Randy Bell: "It's funny. When you say something bad about someone, many times that's all people remember. They don't remember the other things that Jane Cook did. And I think the thing that I see the more and more that I study her history is that she was trying to teach us so that we could adapt into this society. And if people would have seen that early on, we would have been that much further ahead because she had, at that time, extraordinary vision. And to be able to translate our language, that just says enough on its own. Never mind all of the other gifts she had and the high ranking and, I mean, a pretty humble person on one side. So, I look forward to the story being told of what and who she really is and was."

∽

Nellie Cook: "All I can say is she was a wonderful lady. In the early days, she'd help at birthing. She went to help people that's having the baby in those early days. Both she and her husband were Christians."

∽

Gilbert Cook: "The picture I have of her, of course, comes from my dad and also from my mom, because she knew her and thought the world of her. The picture I have of her is, as I said, a person with a conscience. Everything that she did, she did for a reason, a well-thought-out reason. And she stood for things – and that was it – she did stand for things."

∽

Ilma Cook: "[She should be remembered] as a beautiful, wonderful person – and I don't mean in looks and things like that. I mean inner self. Yeah, I can't pin anyone down here that could step into her shoes. Not anybody. Not anybody in the family, not as far as gardening and stuff like that, cutting fish up and smoking fish."

∽

Jeane Lawrence: "I'd want her to be remembered because she helped so many people with everything, you know, church work and to get along together. And voicing her opinion when she did in politics, to get people straight. She was a very even person, and she always helped people out. What more can you say? Right down the line. And even after I left to get married, I just kept going up to visit, and I always took my kids up there to remember. She just should be remembered, I guess, as being a great woman for voicing her opinion on different things and keeping everybody together, church and people, in Alert Bay. And she'd keep us in line too!"

∽

Florrie Matilpe: "Well, she was such a wonderful Granny to us all, really a beautiful Granny. There was a lot of bad things said about her, and I know they weren't altogether true because she had her own way of thinking and her own way of being a Christian. And what she taught us was really good. I thought of her as a very great lady because she looked after us all in hard times, bad times, and I never saw Granny get mad. I never heard her get mad."

❧

Nella Nelson: "Let's tell the story in context. Let's talk about her as this mother, this woman who had sixteen children and, God knows, was lucky to sit down with less than twenty-five people at any given meal ... I think it's important to look at her as a whole woman in the various roles that she played, not just as an interpreter at the potlatch trials – this woman as a political activist, this woman as a mother and a matriarch, this woman as a community person, this woman as a church person."

❧

George Speck: "How would I like her to be remembered? As a leader. Generous. I think that's probably what a leader in my mind is – somebody that is able to see what people need and able to act on it, and to be generous and honest. She was all of those. I think she was firm in her conviction. I think those are all good things, and perhaps if there was any negative, I would just say that perhaps it was her – zeal? *[Laughs]* I'm just thinking that she must have had a hell of a backbone to do all of that at that time. So she had a conviction or a vision of what was right and wrong that just could not be daunted by anything that stood in her way. She stood for a lot of good things at a time when it was needed. The fact that the potlatch was banned was not any fault of hers. There was another agenda that the government had. They were looking for a workforce. They wanted people to be good, productive Canadian citizens and work for peanuts."

❧

Wedłidi Speck: "I think synonymous with Jane Gilbert Cook is the idea that she's a pillar. She's strength. She's a visionary. She's a spiritual warrior. What it means for me is that she was a woman walking the road less travelled – and in that, it's a chance for us to have pride ... I believe she made up her mind. I believe she was reconciled."

❧

Peggy Svanvik: "I really think that we owe it to her to tell that story about why she was against the potlatch. They were high-ranking people,

Photo 43 Nage, Stephen Cook (1870-1957) and Ga'axsta'las, Jane Constance Cook (1870-1951) on the steps of the Cook big house. *Courtesy of Pearl Alfred.*

and she willingly gave it up. It wasn't taken away from her. Well, it's like I always talk to people, 'You know,' I says, 'Nelson Mandela was in jail for twenty years. He was probably the freest man there was around because he would not give up his beliefs for anything or anyone. He stood by his beliefs and had to spend that time in jail for it.' This is why I think he was a free man. So I guess I could compare him and Jane Cook together *[laughs]*. I thought the world of her. I listened to every word she said because it just amazed me how she did it. I happen to think a great deal of Mrs. Cook. Jane Cook, I respect her and honour her memory. And if others don't, that's too bad *[laughs]*. I think most people do. I've not seen another person like her since she's gone."

ഗ

William Wasden Jr.: "I would like for her to be remembered as somebody who knew where she came from, but, yet, was willing to put her title and whatever aside to stick up for what was right. You know, to be what everybody else in our society wants a person to be but to truly believe in something more important. That's just basic respect."

ഗ

Christine Zurkowski: "I'd like her to be remembered for what she stood for, and I think she really stood – her life and her faith, to me, made her who she was. And I think that's how she would like to be remembered. What she did do was all done because of what she believed, and I truly believe that. Yeah, and from there, that's what she lived."

ഗ

PART X

Dłax̱w'it̓sine' (For Your Standing), Feasting

Gix̱sa̱m Ancestor Legend

Gix̱sa̱m, the ancestor of the Giksum, the second clan of the Kwakiutls – which means, "where you believe you are going to get the blankets from that were used in the early days" – went out fishing, not with gun but with spear and harpoon. He went northward on Vancouver Island, and then he went past Shoshade Bay to a nice beach and camped there. Early the next morning, before daylight, he heard a sound on front of him in the water that made a terrible noise. He knew, when he heard it, that it was a hok-hok – a bird kind of like a crane. He looked toward the water to where the noise was and saw it was a thick fog. When he saw a shadow like through the fog, he covered his face again with his Indian blanket made out of cedar bark. Then he heard another noise which sounded like an eagle. Every time he take his blanket off his head, the noise seems to stop. Then he knew he shouldn't look at it, and then he covered his head up again. The hok-hok still make the noise, and the eagle, and there was a grizzly bear noise added to them. Then he took his blanket and bit a hole through it, where he could put his eye to look through the blanket. Every time the shadow became higher, the fog lifted higher. Soon he could see the thing plainly. Then a whale came up on the bottom, and it was a pole with a hok-hok on top and beneath an eagle and beneath that a grizzly bear. When the whale was up, a wolf came up under – a sea wolf. Last of all was a sea monster, which was a large bullhead. The bullhead was a house under the pole. The mouth of the bullhead was so wide that it reached from one side of the house to the other. Then he saw people and fishes going inside as the bullhead's mouth opened, and then the mouth goes down again. Then he spoke while his head was still covered. He saw a man outside the house, and spoke to all those who went inside the house. He says to this man in a loud voice: "I have been watching you since the top of this totem pole appeared, until now, and I have seen what you have done. Do not move, for I will go inside the house to see what I can get out of the house." The man outside the house says: "Come, my friend, for you have done well when you did not disturb all these things that you saw while they were coming up. You will be welcomed by the rich chief that owns the house."

So he got into his canoe, and he watched the mouth as it opened and closed. He was near to the mouth, and the water was running into the mouth of the house very strong. As he was near the mouth of the house, he was backing his paddle not to get too close; as soon as he saw the mouth opening, he paddled as hard as he can to get in before the mouth closes again. When he got inside the house, the canoe landed on a dry place, and he stopped there still sitting on his canoe. Then the Chief "Rich Man," spoke to one of his servants that hears everything, even your thoughts, and the servant came up to him and stood beside him. "Rich Man" says, "What does our friend want in coming into my house?" Gix̱sa̱m thought he would like to have the house and pole and what is in the house. The little man that was beside him spoke before Gix̱sa̱m spoke saying, "our friend wants to own your house and the pole and what is in your house." The "Rich Man" replies: "He shall have the house and the totem pole and this little box that contains riches. All that there is in this box, although he takes them out of it, the box will be always full. If he wants blankets, he will put it inside this box, and there will always be more and more. Now you will stay here four days until I show you all the dances of my people, and you will get whichever dances you like to have."

So he stayed there four days. He got hungry and the "Rich Man" says, "Our friend better come to sit down by the fire, and we will give him something to eat." So he got out of his canoe, but his steerman had stayed on shore and never knew what had become of him. When he saw that Gix̱sa̱m was nowhere, he walked back to Shoshade Bay. After Gix̱sa̱m sat down, ready to have his meal, "Rich Man" said to his servant, "Take down what is in the bag hanging there." So his servant took it down and poured it into a dish. The dish was a seal, and it moved itself. Gix̱sa̱m looked in the dish and saw it was dried frogs, and he thought to himself, "I have never eaten frogs in my life." This little man that always stood by him says to the chief, "He thinks he has never eaten these things before in his life, and he doesn't want to eat them." "Rich Man" says to this little man, "What does he want to eat?" He saw a lot of seals crawling along the floor, and he thought to himself, "Seal is what I would like to eat." The little man says to the chief, "He says he would like to eat one of your dogs." So "Rich Man" told some of the servants to club the seal's head. They burnt the fur off the seal, opened it, washed it out, and then built up a fire and put stones into the fire until it was red hot. Then they put kelp on top of it, and put the whole seal on top of the stones, and covered it with kelp. When it was cooked it was put in a dish, and this dish was a sea otter. Every time "Rich Man" gave him something to eat, and it was a different kind of dish – a porpoise, sea otter, beaver, and other things. And every time he finished eating, "Rich Man" says, "You will keep that dish; it will be yours." That was why the Giksum clan had the most dishes.

At the fourth night, all the fishes came together and made a dance of their own dances. He like the Rock-Cod dance, and he also like the dance of the Blackfish, and some of the dances they showed him he didn't like. Every time he thinks that he like one dance, the little man beside him says, "He like that," and every time he think that he don't like that dance, the little man beside him says, "He don't like that one." Last of all, there came a dancer with four ghosts or skulls on the head and four skulls on the neck ring, and on her blanket there was a skeleton of a man. When the dancer gets to the rear end of the house, the people that went around covering the dancer opened up, and then the hok-hok on top of the pole begin to say, "Hau-hau-hau-hui-hui." He says to himself, "I like that." The little man told the chief, "Our friend likes that, and he wants to own it." The chief says, "He shall have it." Then he saw in the rear end of the house a harpoon; the ends of the harpoon keep shooting out, for it was a magic harpoon. He says to himself, "I would like to own that harpoon." The little man told the chief his thoughts, and the chief says, "He shall have it. But do not throw it when you want to kill anything, or else it will only turn to stone, but simply aim it without throwing it and whatever you aim it at will be dead."

So all these things that he liked was put in a box. It was a small box, and they took the totem pole down and folded it up and put it in the box. And all these things that he liked was folded and put in the box excepting the house. The chief says that as soon as he gets home to take out this totem pole and just put it on the ground, not too close to his house, and, when this is set up, it will all come to life again and make all the noises. He must put it up the same time – early in the morning before daylight – and after it is put up the house will be there.

He was taken home to Fort Rupert by a blackfish. When he got there, he saw that his father's house was falling to pieces; his father had built a little shack to live in, for he thought that Gixsam was dead. He put up the pole, and it made all that was in the totem pole; the hok-hok, the eagle, the whale, the grizzly bear, the wolf, and the sea monster was making a terrible noise so that it waked all his tribe. When he had called all his tribe to come to the house, there was one man standing in front of the house telling the people when to get in, for if they are too slow in getting in, they will be chewed up by this bullhead.

He found out that he had been gone four years instead of four days. He made a winter ceremonial and showed everything that he saw as it was done by "Rich Man," after that the ghost dance. That is why the Giksum owns all these – the totems, the house, the dances, and the dishes. The people didn't know what to think how he get all these things, for when he put one in the box in the night it get full. The box was small when it was given to him, and when he put it inside the house it became a large box. Anything that he put inside this box, this box would be full of it in the next day. So he gave a potlatch all the time, and he was the biggest chief that ever lived.

– Narrated by Nowell, as told to him
by the old man called Wakius[1]

In February 2010, when I asked where the book should end, Wedłidi Speck replied: "At the Gixsam Feast, because we are her story. We're her promise. Her journey is reflected in the well-being of her family. There are people who are caught in Granny's story as a young woman. There are people who are living Granny's story as an older woman, as a wife, as a leader, as a healer. This array of descendants, this landscape, we are all living her story." Wedłidi Speck told me that as you enter gukwdzi (the Big House at 'Yalis), you move into the body of the ancestor. The doorway represents the mouth both symbolically and figuratively. Inside, the beams are spine and ribs, and the fire at the centre is the soul. We were speaking again about memory. "The Big House is where we revisit the dances, songs, stories that have their place in our cultural archive, where we refresh the cultural memory of our people. Children used to walk into the house and never question the memory of the ancestor. It connects us to a consciousness before our time."

In the Big House, most attend as relatives, and many perform as descendants. Those who embody names carry the substance of their ancestors. They are all part of the social web of connected 'ni'na̱'mima. I open this section with a strong personal impression invoked as just one moment in this eternal inheritance. It is a moment when the seemingly insulated past flung itself upon the wide-open present. I was attending my first T̓seka̱ (Winter Ceremonial) at gukwdzi, hosted by William Wasden Jr. Of the thousand or so guests, many were from 'Ya̱lis; others were near and extended family members who had travelled from cities or from neighbouring Kwakwa̱ka̱'wakw villages; and some represented other First Nations on the Coast. We had already witnessed the mourning songs.[2] Singers struck at the log – the beats and their voices beginning a new cycle. As dancers wearing button blankets entered and moved around the fire, some women stood in their seats, moving in rhythm. As more dancers entered, more women rose to their feet, creating a patchwork of standing and sitting witnesses. In some areas of gukwdzi, there were rows of six or seven women whose turning bodies and extended arms marked a synchronized collage of gestures.

The standing women honoured the dancers with whom they shared an affinity, a lineage, or a 'na̱'mima relationship. Barriers between performer and audience dissolved as connecting threads were spun through these dynamic tributes. The threads fastened the standing women to individual dancers but also secured them to a sequence of names, traditional narratives, crests, sounds, movements, ideas, and objects vitalized by each generation. This moment of standing and dancing and demonstrating relationships continues to move me. It represents much that is at the core of the story of G̱a'ax̱sta'las and her descendants.

But G̱a'ax̱sta'las's story is not only about ancestral tributes and powerful continuities, it is also about the ruptures and conflicts wrought by colonial interventions in vital political and cosmological systems. In these early years of the twenty-first century, there is a sense of immediacy when people speak about preceding centuries, a passion in their voices that should not be reduced to theorizing about the obligatory gestures of nobility and rank. For some, this passion folds into questions about colonial relationships and inspires them to seek their place in history, to learn about their ancestors' multiple positions along the colonial spectrum and among the social divides born of it.

In Canada, it is commonplace to discuss reconciliation in the context of unequal structural relations between aboriginal and non-aboriginal peoples. In British Columbia, the conversation has a particular tone, given the treaty process that began anew in the 1990s, the prime minister's apology for residential schools in 2008, and the Truth and Reconciliation Commission that followed from it. But reconciliation is also a social process that inspires questions about one's own (read: one's ancestors' or one's predecessors') place in the politicized past. It is important to look not only to *information* about the past but also to the passions generated by the making of histories.[3]

How and why people in aboriginal societies seek to find their place in history are questions complicated by colonial strategies intended to instill a kind of amnesia.[4] Early colonialism was the conscious administration of technologies aimed at erasing culture by interrupting the transmission of knowledge and acknowledgment. On the Northwest Coast, the strategy to sever inter- (and intra-) generational links focussed especially on the complex of ceremonies and exchanges that constitute the potlatch and feast – institutions at the heart of social, economic, and political reproduction. The potlatch is clearly a vital symbol of resistance and belonging that has come to stand for the resilience of aboriginal nations on the Coast. Its strength is in the tapestry of relationships animated by the women who stand and dance.

I am uncomfortable generalizing about the pattern of silence and utterance I read in histories of colonialism, for the patchwork of official history and social memory that make up the past (in any society) is dynamic and belongs to every individual who enters into it. Conversations about such things did indicate to me that there is a lot at stake. I heard stories about distant events and people that summoned tears for the speaker or brought an instant flush or pallor to a listener's face. Among the people with whom I worked, the however-defined past seemed linked to an intimate sense of nearness to ancestors.

On 8 June 2005, I spoke for several hours with Chris Cook Jr. at his home in 'Y̲alis. During the conversation, he told me about the first potlatch he had hosted in the late 1970s, when he assumed the name Na̲ge, one of the names carried by Stephen Cook. It was the first time a member of the Cook family had stood up in gukwdzi to host a potlatch. In 'Y̲alis, potlatch protocol includes a chiefs' meeting, often the night before a potlatch or feast, where the planned program is presented for discussion. Other chiefs either speak in support of the family or enter into dialogue about the proposed dances, the display of ancestral privileges, and the transfer of names. In this way, feasting and potlatching are "perilous" and "open-ended," for "crucial to this system is the constant possibility of failure."[5]

Chris Cook Jr. spoke with me about the chiefs' meeting that preceded his potlatch. "When I got into that room, there was just a welling-up of tears that were inside of me that needed to come out. I listened, and I had pride in everybody that was sitting there. And what I was looking at was a room full of people who were the glue to our culture. They were from different tribes, all these people who were sitting in that room. And my Uncle Tommy got up, and he started to talk. And he started to cry, and he was saying, 'Really proud of my nephew; my nephew, my sister's son, is giving a potlatch. He's holding up our culture, and it makes me really happy.' Those were part of the things he said. And he cried, and he said, 'These aren't tears of sadness, these are tears of joy.' And another guy got up – Joe Sewid got up. He got up, and he gave me a song, and he said the same thing."

"See, I was only in my twenties, twenty-nine maybe, something like that, and they saw this coming, and they basically said the same thing – that what they have is dying and that the young people have got to grab onto it. And they all knew my granny, and they all knew my grandfather – Stephen Cook and Jane Cook. They all knew where she stood. You know, like she stood in the Kwagu'ł from Fort Rupert. They knew her standing, where her high standing was. And Stephen Cook, from the Nuu-chah-nulth, and my grandfather, from Fort Rupert, they knew who I was, eh?"

"I felt like it wasn't really me that was sitting there. I can't explain it. I felt like there was a thousand me's in me, you know? I was overwhelmed. I guess it was my ego, my sadness, my happiness. But I believe it was supposed to happen."

Chris's words suggest a powerful way of experiencing the past that reminds me of Marshall Sahlins's work on the "mutuality of being ... how it is that relatives live each other's lives and die each other's deaths."[6] Some scholars call this the intergenerational I, a sense of oneself in the present but at the same time carrying the experiences of those who came before you.[7] During our work together, I heard what may be called an "intergenerational we" when people spoke about their family, regardless of which generation they were talking about. When (mostly) men spoke of the past deeds – heroic, violent, or ordinary – of their ancestors, their stories were often followed by statements about a collective we. Naming is at the heart of this deep sense of continuity. It produces what anthropologist Christopher Roth calls "immortal subjectivities that make histories."[8] To Irving Goldman, 'na̲'mima "names are like masks whose bearers are privileged to wear them, but who are not themselves 'real' persons ... the person holding the name is only an impersonator."[9] Names are infused with an emotional and existential charge deemed critical – as G̲a'ax̲sta'las stated, "for the good of the tribe," and they are everywhere in written works by and about Kwakwa̲ka̲'wakw peoples. They are "considered vital to the well-being of all descendants."[10]

I heard people speak of regular names, chiefly names, potlatch or giving or big names, disgraced names, copper names, active or inactive or dormant names, ancient names and derivative and root names, winter names, secular names, and feast names. People speak about having, touching, or hearing names, about giving, assigning, reactivating, taking, receiving, or transferring names, about putting names on people, and about names coming down, coming through, or falling onto someone. People spoke to me about names being where you are from and what you represent, about having to uphold a name or stand up a name and the rights that flow from it, about the rights dying or just lying there (when lineages are broken.) I heard people speak about inactive and quiet 'ni'na̲'mima, about people getting built up or looked after in the Big House through the transfer of names and dances, about putting dances on family members, and about women bringing names and dances with dowries and carrying chieftainships.

People speak about names in a way that evokes a particular view of the past, a certain knowledge. Names carry an understanding that one's place in history exists and that one need only step into it by standing up in the Big House – that is, by mobilizing genealogical knowledge to publicly claim and occupy a standing. "As long as you know your history, you can bring it back. It's done," Wedłidi Speck told me. "It's just about backing up what you've got to say. Your history – that's what the potlatch is all about."[11] In gukwdzi, chiefs, speakers, dancers, and singers ritually reanimate their ancestors. All who are present feast and bear witness as host families demonstrate house histories.

"Standing up – that's your identity. That's where you come from. That's where you are," Randy Bell told me. "Back in the day, when someone was doing something, everybody supported one another, because every time you bring a family up in a Big House and you stand them up, you make your nation stronger. Well, that philosophy got lost somewhere. It got lost before the residential schools. The next generation needs to work more and more together for us to survive as a people, not only in the Big House but in society. We're gaining strength to get above what happened and those conditions that our people are in. But it's up to the generation now and the generation coming up to make that change so that we are all supporting one another. That's the end goal."

Potlatching and feasting reconfirm relationships among 'ni'na̱'mima and tribes. By correcting, validating, and legitimating Kwakwa̱ka̱'wakw pasts, potlatches both confront and conceal colonial memory. Anthropologist Johannes Fabian writes that rituals are more complicated than the "mere enactment of a pre-existing script"; they are about "making, fashioning, and creating" what he calls "sociality," people "working together to give form to experiences, ideas, feelings, projects."[12] Potlatching and feasting generate new stories and legitimate old ones. They are physical and emotional and material and symbolic performances that enact belonging (and exclusion) – individually, politically, and within 'na̱'mima webs.[13] They are weighty occasions that offer the possibility of shaping identities independent of the state definitions and the legal processes that so often intrude in people's lives.[14] Such is "the simultaneity of colonialism and tradition" experienced by many First Nations' peoples.[15]

For G̱a'a̱xsta'las's descendants, part of the intention of writing her story was to examine the context within which she let go of her place in the eternal flow of names. Of course, she was not alone. Within the silence that surrounds the potlatch is a social history that generated colonial categories of "Indian-ness" – potlatchers, nonpotlatchers, and antipotlatchers, non-Christian potlatchers and Christian potlatchers – historical divisions that defy the contemporary binaries of colonizer and colonized, Indian and white, and Christian and traditional. These categories are remembered by older generations, but, as I was reminded, they are not familiar to all.

Many today do not know about their predecessors' stands for or against or outside of the custom. Given the potency of the intergenerational we, this book does not seek to reveal who these people were in the past. Working with oral histories and archival documents to patch together impressions, we may only speculate about the motives of people who stepped out of the custom. Epidemics, illness, and resulting high mortality rates may have prevented 'ni'na̱'mima from having the strength to potlatch. Some might have been unable, materially, to realize their reciprocating obligations as Northwest Coast peoples became impoverished and were prohibited from accessing resources in their territories. Perhaps a few opted for enfranchisement. Maybe others renounced the custom during the ban for religious, economic, or political reasons. Certainly, legislation defining Indian status set successive generations of women and children adrift from local systems of descent.

Billy Wasden suggests that many left the potlatch because of changes wrought by colonial processes. "There are numerous families in Alert Bay, Fort Rupert, all around the country that left the potlatch system for the same reason. I don't believe they ever, ever really stopped believing. But they stopped following what had become different than the potlatch system that was there before. It was a good thing before contact, before money became involved, before the epidemics came – the influenza and the smallpox – and the people died off ... It had changed a lot from what they understood as children."

Billy's son, William Wasden Jr., was explicit about what to do with the past in the present: "For me, Granny and Papa left the system, and that was their personal choices. But what they belonged to ... We were always taught that family was bigger – we represent our families, and when we do things in life, we're representing a bigger entity than ourselves. So, they made their personal choices, but we are still representing John 'Nulis, old Chief Wanukw, and our ancestors before that. So, if those people believed in it, we still have the right and the choice to follow what our ancestors did, even though three generations back – or four for me – decided to leave it. There was still those generations before that who upheld and followed those practices. So, just as they had their choices, we have our choices. For me, I don't think we̱ can let our history go because we can't think in the way our ancestors Granny and Papa felt. They had their own reasons, and we feel differently today ... If things are going wrong in your culture, then you've got to do something about it. Sometimes, if you don't have enough power, then you just have to remove yourself ... But in this day and age, I think that the generations we have, and the strength that we have as a people, we have the ability to put it back."

Since the 1970s, there has been, and still is, the will and energy to ceremonially reanimate names whose transfer had been interrupted. Today, families dislodged by early colonialism are stepping back into the Big House. They are feasting and potlatching through ancestors who temporarily released their links in the chains of descent. As they do so, 'na̱'mima members rebuild relationships with those "lost" or "marginalized" through assimilationist practices. Feasting and potlatching offer possibilities for resolving these difficult histories, particularly the histories of religious conversion, loss of children through fostering, and the painful assimilationist legacies of residential schooling. G̲a'ax̲sta'las's descendants are among those who are reanimating dormant names. During our work together, there was a good deal of talk about young people, about those who live in socioeconomic difficulty in Vancouver and those who are struggling to imagine for themselves the goals of employment, education, or of realizing roles in their communities. They are descendants of Jane Cook who do not have the option of being ceremonially incorporated through other lines of descent. The family gave them names by ritually reactivating a dormant 'na̲'mima traced through G̲a'ax̲sta'las.

On 19 May 2007, descendants of G̲a'ax̲sta'las hosted their first feast and "awakened" the Gix̲sa̲m 'na̲'mima. Recognized as the family leader, George Cook passed the rights to the 'na̲'mima chieftainship to Wedłidi Speck, who assumed the feast name K̲̓wa̲mk̲̓wax'a̲widi and the potlatch name G̲a̲yuła̲las. During our work together, two other chiefs in the family hosted potlatches. In November 2005, William Wasden Jr. hosted a T̓sek̲a (Winter Ceremonial) by which his family reanimated the 'Na̲mgis chieftainship of Wax̲a̲widi, a standing left dormant when his great-grandparents quit the custom. In October 2006, George Speck hosted a memorial potlatch for his father, George Speck Sr., Claire Culhane, and Lou Ambers. The potlatch fulfilled his obligations as hereditary chief of the Ławits'is and ensured that a new generation of children would "have a place" through receiving names. Part X is made up of the words of G̲a'ax̲sta'las's descendants as they speak about their future and their past through potlatching and feasting. Her story concludes with an English transcript of the Gix̲sa̲m Feast, because, as Wedłidi Speck stated, "her journey is reflected in the well-being of her family."

Wax̲a̲widi, Wasden T̓sek̲a (Winter Ceremonial), November 2005

William Wasden Jr. and I met in August 2007 to talk about the potlatch he had hosted in November 2005 in 'Ya̲lis. We sat in the front gallery at the U'mista Cultural Centre. Wrapped around us on the walls were powerful photographs of Kwakwa̲ka̲'wakw elders, some

Photo 44
William Wasden Jr. on the Tribal Canoe Journeys paddle to Bella Bella, 1993. *Courtesy of Wedłidi Speck.*

of whom trace their descent from G̲a'ax̲sta'las.[16] Glass cases containing Hamat̓sa whistles and delicate regalia reflected the faces of those elders, evoking a kind of all-present past that resonated in William Wasden Jr.'s words. Over a year later, we met at a house on the Capilano Reserve in North Vancouver to edit the transcript of our conversation.[17] William was there to participate in a ten-month-old's naming ceremony, a ritual, he told me, now becoming popular. William offered grammatical and spelling corrections. He also chose to expand on some topics and shorten or delete others. In notes, William (designated as WW) explains or adds further detail to his commentary.

Before our initial interview, we had discussed including narratives by family chiefs who potlatched during the course of our research. William Wasden Jr.'s potlatch is important for many reasons. It represents another family reentering the potlatch complex after seventy years of ceremonial inactivity. It speaks to the passion that surrounds cultural and ritual identity and to the enormously creative endeavour of hosting over one thousand guests and thinking through a deep history of cultural forms and social relationships. We began by discussing when and how William made the decision to potlatch.

"What instantly comes to mind is that I was thinking about the things that I was told my great-grandparents had, and then, when I researched it, finding out that I could go so many generations back and that they had a lot of history that was still laying around."

"What kind of research did you do?"

"Research was pretty much through potlatch ledgers, from old potlatch books that the old chiefs used to keep, Boas's notes, the origin stories. I would only know that my great-grandfather had an Eagle position because I knew his name was Wa<u>xa</u>widi, the only one in Nimpkish.* But thank goodness that the Salmon family's ancestor told the legend in 1900 and connected the names straight through the male lineage coming down to wherever we're at now. So, it's all through the research."

"I thought about this. I went to my grandmother. Well, my uncle Stevie Beans, first of all, sat me down on the banks of Knight's Inlet when we were there at eulachon time, and we had a really serious talk. It was important for me to get his opinion on it and his backing. And he said to me at that time, he said, 'Let's quit talking about it and do something about it, before it gets sour.' That was his exact words. So, in his way, you know – the saying in our culture is 'If you're going to talk about being cultural, then you be cultural and do it in a potlatch.'"

"So, I went to my granny and asked her if it would be all right if I picked up what the family had. And she said, 'You have to talk to the older sister.' My Auntie Mary, because she's older than her; she was following the birthright respect for that."†

"So, I went to my Auntie Mary, and my Auntie Mary said, 'Well, what did your granny say?'"[18]

"I said, 'She said it's up to you.'"

---

* "I was working with Boas's field notes, and you can see George Hunt's handwriting for names. He wrote *w*'s like *n*'s. And, so, Boas has, for example, the head chief of the Nimpkish – Ṫła<u>k</u>wudłas – his rival was Wa<u>xa</u>widi – but it looked like *Wakanidi* in Hunt's writing" (WW).

† "The oldest birthright is so important. If you're from the oldest birthright, oldest lineage, you're always going to be from the chiefly lines. It's the second and third children that come that create the other families but that aren't from the original nobility. That's where your ranking comes from" (WW). In anthropological terms, *birthright* refers to the rule of primogeniture.

"She says, 'Well, if it's all right with Granny, it's all right with me, too.'"

"So, I went with it. But the way I explained it to my granny, I said, 'I know that the family is not really into the culture – you know, the way I am. God or our Creator – whatever you choose to call the higher power – made me this way ... I have a lot of capabilities in the culture. I can make songs. I can dance. I can transcribe songs. I can learn old songs. I can do whatever. I'm an artist. I can carve. I can paint.' That's how I said it."

"My grandmother agreed with that. She said, 'Yeah, well, if you want to do it, do it right and make sure things are done properly.'"

"Her parents ended up leaving the potlatch, Mr. and Mrs. Ben Alfred. They left the potlatch because it had evolved into something that it wasn't. And my great-grandmother was concerned about who was touching her rights and where they were going among the extended family. My great-grandfather used to always say to her, 'Why are you worried about it? It isn't what it used to be anyway.' And my great-grandmother was literally in tears because she wanted to carry on with her rights."

"So, I thought about them. They were real powerful people to be able to just leave the culture that they were born into and that they invested in."

"The last potlatch my great-grandfather threw was in 1935, on Village Island, so it was shortly after that where he just gave it up. His eldest daughter, her name was Dorothy Alfred, she died of meningitis at sixteen, and he was so broken that this was his final reason to leave. My grandmother said that my great-grandfather Ben was very upset with God, or the Creator, because the birthright is so important, and when his oldest daughter died, he was questioning why the Creator would do that to him – 'I have no eldest now, so I might as well just call it a day' – that he was so destroyed that he just said, 'That's it. I'm finished with it.' I guess because they did a lot to build her up in the Big House, this young lady."

"I know that Christianity played a big part. They did turn Christian. But I know that from the stories I hear that my great-grandmother was always concerned with her rights. So, it's hard for me to accept that it was Christianity that forced them to change. And my great-grandfather was not strongly Christian. He was a Christian, but he wasn't full-blown." He laughed.

"Yeah, but there *were* the extreme people, where they burned everything, and they were holy rolling for the rest of their lives. And then there are some people that despise the church because of what it had done. I know that there was a lot who could function in both places and had no problem with it."

"I think that it was to do with the changing times. I heard that my great-grandfather was cheated with the dowry that was promised to him, that he had invested quite a bit with the marriage arrangements – his family did – and when it came time to return things, there was a lot of dishonesty. So, I think that had heartbreak in it, too. So, they just removed themselves."

"I think about the people that have told me stories about my great-grandpa – Dadax̱alis, Ben Alfred Sr. My great-grandfather followed the protocols, and when it was being made into something that was more of a mockery, he just didn't want a part of it anymore."

"So, I thought that was pretty powerful and that if we were going to do something, that we would follow the protocols as best we could, to honour how they felt about the system. So, that's why. When people say that we did things differently [in the potlatch] ... those differences were in hopes of following protocols from the way we understood it, what was told to us."

"Why did you want to potlatch?"

"Because there was a deep part of me that said, you know that your family had rights, and yet they're not active in the Big House. And it was always other sides of my extended family taking care of me.[19] Whereas I wanted to have my own feet on the ground and know that my family would also have their feet on the ground, in the Big House, in the cultural place. A lot of them, I know, felt that they had no real sense of belonging to the culture because they didn't have a dance. A lot of us had names, but a lot didn't have dances. And when you have a dance, it really validates your place in the Big House, because, with dances, there's a social standing that comes along with it among your family. So, unless your family is participating in dancing and showing their dances and putting dances on their family members, it's like they don't really have a place within the Big House as a whole."[‡]

"The dances [we showed at the potlatch] are all dances that were either transferred from my great-grandmother to my great-grandfather

‡ "Dances and songs connect to Winter Ceremonials and secure you a place in the Big House. The Big House is not a building but all of the people who participate in the Winter Ceremonies" (WW).

or dances that my great-grandmother's father or grandfather or uncles owned. It was all from one treasure box."[§]

"My grandmother said it in a real nice way. She said my great-grandmother was so concerned with their family rights dying – these things that were her possessions – that she had transferred to my grandpa and things that she had still owned. After we had finished, my grandmother said that she knows that in the spiritual world that our great-grandmother had come back for a while and knew that the family had taken care of the business and that she was really at rest now, on the other side, that these things hadn't just been lost on the wayside – because our rights were no longer flowing through our family. That's how she said it. So, it was very heavy spiritually for our family."

"You know, there was a time when our culture was about, 'Oh, I do this dance because I'm higher ranked than you' or 'I'm a better dancer because of this' or whatever. Yet there's strong teachings that have been lost along the way, and I think it has a lot to do with the colonization of our people. The spirituality of our people had been stomped on and changed. Not all the families are like that, but I know that a lot of people think that the potlatch is about being better than each other and that there's a lot of rivalry. I strongly believe that that only came about when there was an opening of positions and people were able to compete for positions because there was no one to fill them."

"So this potlatch was the reactivation of your grandmother's 'na'mima?"

"It was a reactivation of the chieftainship of Waxawidi.[#] Waxawidi was my great-grandmother's paternal grandfather, but the chieftainship was also passed to her father. My great-grandmother came along and broke the male lineage because she was the only child. So, she broke that lineage coming from the first ancestor, who was the Thunderbird named Kwanu'sila. He became a man and continued on with the name Kwanu'sila as his chieftainship. Then he had a son called K'wiladzawikama'yi, and then his son was Waxawidi. And here

§ "When a family has a treasure box, it doesn't just necessarily mean this physical box. It represents all the names and privileges and songs and dances and history and territories, and everything that belonged to that family is within a treasure box. And it's like we all belong to it. We all draw from it. We get our strength and our spirituality from it" (WW).

"This name means: *canoes come to him, people are always travelling to him*" (WW).

we are today after so many generations from the flood hearing Waxawidi."¶

"There's so many more names that came down as chieftainships and people changed their names, but that's where *we're* at. So, it would have been the grandson of the original Thunderbird that the name came from. That's where this chieftainship came from. And he was the Eagle position at one time, head chief of the Thunderbird clan.** When we say *Galaxa,* meaning Eagle, which is *the* first one down, it means that we can trace our descent through a male lineage to the first ancestor – except when it came to my grandmother, when the lineage was broke. So, it filters through grandchildren, and we picked it up again."

"They married my great-grandfather to her to get the chieftainship because my great-grandfather was the younger brother to Moses Alfred and wasn't in line to get what Moses would receive. So, they strategically married him to my great-grandmother, who was this only child, the daughter of a big-time chief, sitting there with an abundance of rights. And her uncles kicked into her dowry as well. So, he received a treasure box for her, received Red Cedar Bark Dances and Peace Dances (Tłas'ala). He received both types of ceremonies for her."

¶ "All Indians alive on the Coast are descendants of ancestors that survived the flood. We all have our flood stories. One of my elders, Basil Ambers, who I really enjoy listening to, he said: 'You know, so many people today try to shut each other down and say that they're not this and they're not that, and, yet, we're all survivors of the Great Flood. And according to our beliefs and our tradition, the Creator chose people to survive the flood because they were worthy and they had a purpose.' So, he sent messages to different ancestors to prepare themselves. Every Indian that you see in our tribes today survived that flood. So, they all descended from original ancestors – they all descended from survivors, and everybody came from nobility somewhere. The key to it today is to be able to trace your history and connect yourself to those original ancestors, because that's where the hereditary chieftainship comes from. If you're from the direct descent of the first ancestors, you're connected to traditional, hereditary title" (WW).

** "Eagle position is the head of a clan, and the reason for that is we can still tell the story right back to the flood time, when our ancestor became a Thunderbird transformed into a man. At this time, there probably was no Winter Ceremonies. When the Thunderbird came down, then his son – that's way before the Winter Dance probably started up. Feasting was, I've always been told, the most ancient giveaway" (WW).

"And the story is, when she was being brought in by her tribe, here at Alert Bay, the 'Namgis had four canoes tied together like a catamaran, and she was sitting in the bow. One of the headdresses she was wearing I still have. The eagle down was blowing out of the headdress, and it was symbolic that she was bringing the chief the Tłas'ala or Peace Dances. Those dances were really rare at that time, amongst our tribe. It came through her grandmother's Bella Bella heritage. So, it was a prestigious thing she was bringing, that a lot of chiefs didn't have."[††]

"So, when there's only a female [child], she can carry a chieftainship. Or, if she is married, she can transfer a chieftainship. When a son shows up in her lineage, then it goes back to the male lineage. She had an oldest son who was the Hamat̓sa and who would have technically been the chief. His name was Billy Alfred, but he died, and that's why we took his daughter Mary and made her the Hiligax̱ste'. And she danced in front of the Hamat̓sa. Then the next oldest – they had a sister who died of meningitis – and she would have been older birthright. She died. So that eliminated that line. Then my Auntie Mary came along, and that's why her oldest grandson was chosen for Hamat̓sa. We're respecting her place in the family – that she's the oldest member of our family now. The oldest male had only a daughter, so she was dancing in front of the Hamat̓sa. And then the next lineage with no male went to the oldest grandson. He danced as a Hamat̓sa."

"I guess there could have been room for people to contest me being chosen to be the leader, but I was initiated as a Hamat̓sa by my grandpa Jimmy Dawson.[‡‡] You have to be a Hamat̓sa to be able to distribute property through potlatches. I was the only one, along with my brother, that had a Hamat̓sa position. If we were to follow old tradition, we were the only ones that would have had a right to do that.

†† "Every chief holds a key to the ceremonies and the rituals. One chief doesn't hold everything. There's different ceremonies that came through different origin stories, creation stories, different encounters. So everybody holds a piece of the puzzle in order for things to work in the winter ceremonies. If one chief died and there's no one to fill that role, there'd be a loss or a missing link in the ceremony" (WW).

‡‡ "When I was taught to be a Hamat̓sa by my Grandpa Jimmy, he always said, 'When you first come out, you're facing the four directions in a ritual sequence going around to welcome the people. Even your dance movements are to show the people that you're so honoured that they've come that you're going to share your spiritual dance with them and share all that you have and all that you are'" (WW).

So, it all fell down that way, and nobody really argued with it. They just felt that I knew what I was doing. I've been involved in the culture for a while."

"How would you describe your potlatch?"

"That the people were united. Well, you saw how the Hamaťsa [Society] was acting, how the Hamaťsa was all together.[20] The singers were one. My Alfred family was all united.[§§] And just the way the chiefs came. My Hunt family, all the chiefs from the Hunt family, came. So, for me, if I could explain the feeling, it was that there was a real oneness with the people, that people went there to share in a traditional style of a potlatch – a Ťse<u>k</u>a, a Winter Dance. That's what it was. It was strictly just a Winter Dance. The Winter Dance is most sacred to us. I think that the people really feel the power of the winter ceremonies when it's done with strong intentions. The values and the teachings of our dances, they have spirituality in them – the dances, the people. The people dancing are dancing for their ancestors and guests, and when they understand that, they put their spirit into it."[##]

"You had the potlatch filmed."

"I had a friend named Judy Hoffman who is a professional filmmaker, and she said she would do it, her and my cousin Barb Cranmer, because they worked together over the years. I didn't want filming, or videoing, or cameras, but my mom and my granny said, 'Well, what if you were to die?' which is just speculating that this might happen suddenly one day. 'Who will be able to run the program? Or who will be able to explain what had happened?' That's why we wanted photos

---

§§ "You know, Vera [Newman] and Eva [Dick] really took a leadership role [at a time] when there is no older lady in our family that really runs the floor because we've been inactive for so long. So my grandmother's nieces really took charge. My cousin Maxine Matilpe was in the back [room] with Pewi Alfred, and that's our extended family again. So, they took care of the back. Beau [Dick] was in the back, and my Dawson family was there: Uncle Charlie, Uncle Tom, Auntie Doreen, Auntie Rita, and Auntie Gerry, the older family members. The whole works of the younger ones were there too. They had given me strength when it seemed that I might have been alone in the potlatch system" (WW).

"You may receive monetary gifts or actual material things. But when our people dance, there are gifts that the dancers bring for the people. So, you have to be very careful about how you're presenting yourself, because you're not dancing for yourself. You're dancing for your guests and for your ancestors. You're repeating what they have done, and you're making sure that you're doing it in a real respectful way. You're representing your ancestors first. But I don't know if a lot of people believe in that anymore" (WW).

and one video set of this. So, out of respect for my granny and my mom, I let them override my yearning to keep those ancient ceremonies sacred. It was more to document what had happened, because, in this day and age, you know, our people don't sit in the Big House and grow up with it every winter for months, understanding what goes on. So, it was done for the next generation – that there would be something for them to follow. Yeah, and I didn't want anybody taking notes. I was guarding our traditional names because a lot of our names are really old. A couple of elderly ladies from Kingcome said they were really happy to hear some of those names because they hadn't heard them for so long. Yeah, it really touched them that way, that there were some really old, unique names coming back out."

"And these old names have come through oral histories?"

"Some of them. There were some that I had taken from the 'Na̲mugwis story recorded in Boas. There was some there. The potlatch ledgers. There was some names that we knew. Birth certificates, death certificates, baptism records – you can go back from your parents. A housing census had a lot of names that were from the house, and you could tell that those were our great-great-grandparents, their children's names. I knew some relationships to Kingcome and Gilford, so I connected with one of my cousins from Kingcome who looked at the housing census and was able to pull a few more children's names out from our family, children that had passed on, but we never knew about them. And my grandmother was very good with Indian names, my grandmother and my last great-aunt that I have."

"So, is there anything more about your potlatch that you think should be said?"

"Well, I think that the beauty of it was how well the speakers and especially my uncle, Robert Joseph, spoke, because he learned the history, and it's so much more powerful hearing the history leading up to the dance. It's so common now, when you go to Winter Dances, that people present a dance, and then they just call it a name, and that's the end of it. Nobody understands the history of it. So, you could feel the power of the dance when the story was told – even people that spoke English and couldn't speak our language. [Uncle Bobby] would do it in Kwak̓wala, then in English for people that didn't speak. So the speakers explained where things came from and who had it before you. And that way there's no room for any kind of confusion or any conflict. And there's so much more meaning to the dancer when they know that that dance belonged to their ancestor and who it came from and what it's supposed to represent, the real teachings and the values behind the dance that they're doing."¶¶

"How long did it take you to prepare for this potlatch?"

"I would say it took a good two-and-a-half years. Two years to save. I had saved for two years with my mom, keeping up with her because I didn't want her to pay for my name. But in the end, I couldn't keep up with her. The carvers in this town are very, very generous. I gave them a list because they had asked me for one. I was overwhelmed that they said that they would do all the carving for free. So, all the masks that I have are really treasured, wrapped up, and they're only shown during ceremonies – the majority of them. It's just the way the culture is, though. It all comes back. What you invest in people – time, monetary things, even just respect and helping out – those things come back when your turn comes, if you invest in the system properly, in a good way."

"How did it feel to give away?"

"I was overwhelmed at how much my extended family gave to build up what we gave away under our family. It was a real overwhelming gesture on behalf of my extended families, that they just kept bringing stuff to add to the room for our giveaway. It was really quality stuff, that's for sure. And the cash ... I don't even want to talk about how much cash was on the table. Extended family bringing money – it was overwhelming. I was directed by my grandmother to keep a running score of who gave money because you have to pay that back whether they said it was for love and not to be paid back. My grandmother is very traditional. She says, 'You will pay that back.' It was part of the system where the money keeps flowing. I have a running score of who contributed. So, when their turn comes, we pay back. I've almost covered seventy-five percent of the list now. Where most of the money's gone back, that's all done behind closed doors."***

¶¶ "I hear stories about how the chiefs would speak for hours and hours, and sometimes a dance might take five minutes. But they would speak for nights and nights on something, and then it would take five minutes to complete it. It was a lead up to what was being presented, and then, afterwards the names were announced and how they were being transferred" (WW).

*** "The chiefs used to have meetings behind closed doors. The other chiefs would put money down and say, "I'm going to give this much to help out." Then they'd start writing the ledger, and when the next time comes, if the chief couldn't pay it back within a certain amount of time, then the interest was added to it. That's how the whole investment system was done. If you couldn't pay it back within a year, then it was double. It was a hundred

"Now, we pretty much go double because it's been over a year. Some of these families kind of get upset and say, 'Well, we don't want double because it was done just because we love and respect the family.' So they just want to accept half of it back."

"What does it mean for you to have assumed the role of chief?"

"It means that I have to be very honest these days. I can't be a fence-sitter, because there's a lot of Indian politics that go around. So, I have to speak up now, and I have a voice. I'm not allowed to make speeches in the Big House because my mother said I'm not allowed to until I can speak Kwak̓wala fluently, and I've agreed to that. I believe that that's a sacred place, and only our language should be spoken first and foremost there. But there's a lot of responsibility. I have to make sure that, first, my whole family is taken care of, and if there's family politics, I have to go and smooth that out. And then, after my family is taken care of, then it's the clan that I worry about, then the tribe."

"Your family being ...?"

"My immediate family, my great-grandparents' children's children's children coming down. We just took care of the first four generations. That's who we technically took care of at the potlatch."

"When you say you were looking after these generations, what does that mean?"

"Well, with their spiritual things and their cultural stuff. I can't financially look after them. It's impossible in this day and age. But, you know, a lot of my cousins come to me for advice because I do ceremonies, too. It's not involved with the potlatch, but it's spiritual – cleansing ceremonies, stuff like that. I think, also, with being put in a leadership position – I hate to say chief, I like family leader – when the tribe's doing something, we want things done properly. A lot of families are asking for help regarding research, and I have to tell them, 'I don't know much about your family, because there isn't much out there.' You just have to be straight up ... I know that a lot of our people are searching, and that's a good thing because it opens up cultural discussions and, most importantly, family history. Family is the most important teaching for our people. When they dig in and find information and the information gets out there, it starts to spread, and everybody gets involved somehow, and pretty soon everybody

---

percent interest. And if it was just a short loan for a couple of weeks, it would be not even a hundred dollars interest, on whatever the amount was" (WW).

realizes that they're all connected, one way or the other. So that's a good thing."

"I think that if you make marks in your life, potlatching is one way to do that. For my family, it was a big ending of a chapter but an opening of a new one. Like my grandmother said, her mother is spiritually at rest now that we had solidified and validated everything that belonged to us. We had a history and a story that went with it. But now, the new chapter is opening. Where are we going with this now? We have to decide new successors to the dances, to the chieftainships. I have no children. I have not married yet. These questions all arise. What's going to go on with it further down the road? So, it's a real responsibility, and it also leaves you with a whole bunch of obligations that you have to take care of."

"I know for sure that a lot of our family feels that they have a place in the Big House, and they're more comfortable going there again. So that, for me, was what it was really about – was making sure that they were taken care of and that we could find some sort of balance within ourselves, that we could all feel safe, comfortable going there, that they have a treasure box and a copper and a talking stick that will defend them if anybody has any negativity toward them. My great-uncle said, 'Because of what you've done, now your family will take their rightful places, and they'll never have to look at the backs of other people's heads in the Big House.' Coming from him – he's a real old Indian – I didn't want to hear that. But in this day and age, that's a part of it too. To take your rightful place, you have to be strong, and in order for your family to have seats in the Big House and positions and names, you have to be active in the potlatch. So, you have to give in order to be able to receive. That's the whole culture. I know a lot of my family are more comfortable about being who they are now that they have names from the family. That's lifted a whole new spirit up for them, knowing that these names come from their own treasure box and that our names are not shared with anybody. There are a lot of families that do that now."

Yakudłasdzi, Speck Memorial Potlatch, October 2006

Almost a year after William Wasden Jr.'s potlatch, George Speck, a hereditary chief of the Ławits'is, hosted a memorial potlatch for his father, George Speck Sr.; for his mother-in-law Claire Culhane; and for Lou Ambers. The potlatch included a *<u>K</u>adzitła* (marriage ceremony),

Photo 45
George Speck at his memorial potlatch, October 2006. *Courtesy of Wedłidi Speck.*

before which his wife, Beth, and daughter Cullen were adopted by another family. Whenever we met in George's home, there were people coming and going, and his son Jack and his daughter Lori were often present. In conversations that spanned several years, I asked him to speak about this potlatch and his general sense of what it means to host one. He answered several questions with his characteristic sense of humour. In footnotes, George (designated as GS) explains or adds further detail to his narrative.

"Do you want to talk about why you gave your potlatch?"

"Why I gave my potlatch? Why I gave my potlatch? Why do we potlatch?" He laughed.

"Well, number one, it'd been quite a number of years. I can't remember the last time, probably going on to ten years. So, there were lots of kids without names."

"My dad had passed away. The normal thing to do around here is to wait at least a year.[†††] We did that, plus some. There was Mom [Claire Culhane]. When she passed, we said we would honour her in a potlatch. So that was outstanding quite a number of years. And I did include Lou Ambers in my Sa̱ntła [mourning] ceremony. There were those reasons for potlatching."

"Personally, I find that part of the potlatch – whether it's ours or anybody else's – it's a moving part of it. It's part of the grieving process. You sit. You're sitting in the crowd. Everybody – chiefs, elders, everybody – is just sitting quietly in the crowd. And I think everybody is doing what I'm doing – just reflecting on the people that have passed. The songs are mourning songs, and you get that sense from them even if you don't understand. You get that sense. And then it ends. You're done. Let it go. Get rid of it. You're putting it away, putting your grief away. It's almost surgical." He laughs.

"It could have greater uses. We run counselling out of our Health Centre, but I never participated. Whereas I have no difficulty sitting in the Big House and listening to songs and thinking. And then it ends. I find that lots of people still hang onto their grief for people that have passed. They haven't done anything like that in the Big House for the people they have cared about. I think it would help them, those people, to go through that process."

"And I think I already said it – a number of kids had been born. You hear it often enough – 'They are the future.' The reality is, you don't involve them, and they don't have an enthusiasm for it. It's going to go the way of the language. We're having a tough enough time right now just figuring out a way for the language surviving.[‡‡‡] So, there were those reasons for potlatching."

"Why do you give children names?"

---

††† "We don't participate in ceremonies for that year. You're mourning, so celebration isn't appropriate. But we do attend. By attending a potlatch, you're acknowledging the right of the people that are giving the potlatch to do things. You're bearing witness" (GS).

‡‡‡ "It's good that they do that in the school, the dancing and singing. And there's now a language program, although it's a very small group. The success is, I guess, going to be determined by what happens to those kids ten years from now. It's always the test. We've run our band school so long now, and the true success of our cultural program is the dancing and singing. A lot of our kids participate – and they participate without a second thought" (GS).

"To make them people. They're nothing without a name." He laughed. "You have no place. Yeah, you get new names and become a part of the process, and there's lots of kids that want to. It's a big deal for them. Lots of kids want to be able to participate in the potlatch. Not everybody gets to. You get a name when you participate." He paused. "I wouldn't ask you to dance without giving you a name, or you already having a name."

"You had said that for a few years now you've been looking out for the Cooks in that way – some people who didn't have the opportunity to participate."

"Well, I'm half Cook-ed?" He laughed. "Pearlie [Alfred], she's my mother's sister. Her family, my Aunt Shirley and their kids, they're Alfreds. Yeah, all those people participate in my potlatches and in my dad's potlatches because of our relationship to that side of our family, the Cook side of that family. And the Cooks up to now hadn't potlatched.[21] That will change when Wedłidi takes his seat, but up to now their names have either had to come through marriage from the other side, which is the Alfred side, or my side, the Speck side. A lot of the Cooks who are married to or related to the Specks have Speck names."

"Speaking of Wedłidi, something that seemed to be happening at your potlatch was that he was transferring a lot of names."

"Yeah, he was giving up his chief's positions, or chiefly names, so that he could take on a Cook chiefly name. That was my understanding. Although I do know that others have a couple of chieftainships. They gather their chieftainships together to one person. I never really asked Wedłidi, but I would suspect that he wanted to start off with a clean slate and take on the things that came through the Cook connection. So, it depends, it depends on whether he wants to capture more names and he's a bigger chief."

"Capture?"

He laughed. "Take on chiefly names from other areas, or houses."

"Who do you talk to about names?"

"My brother, Wedłidi, he's the keeper of that kind of stuff. He keeps track of and knows the history of the family as well as other families, and we've got our own list of names, available names. So people pass on names. Family members will contact us and say, 'I'd like to pass on my dad's name, and what goes with it, to another family member.' You start getting lists like that together and what's going to happen during the potlatch. We've done it so many times that our program's pretty much set ... "

"So, we made a decision to do it and then started organizing around it. Sat down and set a date. People start figuring out what they're going to do. Family members start saving potlatch goods, money, and that sort of thing. And we talk about names and talk about who's going to do what – assign jobs, assign Pearlie the food job." He laughed.

"I did have three meetings, three family meetings to talk about the potlatch. We had family members come about and discuss our program and what we were going to do and who we were going to get to do what dances. There are special events within the potlatch that we decide on beforehand. A wedding, for instance, if that's going to happen; if we're going to do an additional dance that we haven't done before. We have other dances that we haven't done before – Loon Dances, for example."

"And, yeah, in this potlatch, we decided that Beth and I would be married. So that was something different – off the agenda. I've seen marriages before, and it went well. Some of it was kind of funny, you know, like the wooing, the whole wooing process and the various chiefs trying to get Beth to come over to my house. But, yeah, it was fun." He paused. "I think Bethany was a little stressed by it and the whole adoption thing too.[22] It was kind of a double whammy."

"Yeah, so you just make your decision about your program and talk about who your attendants are going to be and who's going to be your dance program organizer, who you're going to ask to be the speaker at the potlatch, that sort of thing. Like I said, we've done it so many times before that I already know who I like, and I like Tee Dee to be our dance program organizer. She's very efficient and understands what needs to be done. And bang, bang, bang – things happen in a very orderly and organized fashion when she's in charge of the dance programs. Bill Cranmer I've got a lot of respect for, so he's our speaker. And Bobby Joe Joseph, I like him to assist Bill. They have a good rapport, an interplay between them. They understand what's going on. They've always been very supportive of what we do."

"How long beforehand do you begin planning?"

"Just about a year, just about a year. We've had a couple of false starts where we've said, 'Oh, we're going to have a potlatch next year' and something's happened. Somebody's died or something like that. So we put it off. Or an event happens where people just can't do it when we want to do it. But, yeah, about a year. And then you start buying, buying, buying. That's a process in itself. Potlatch goods. Blankets, for one. It's kind of a traditional item that's given out. Anywhere from, I'd say, about a hundred and fifty, I guess, a hundred and fifty blankets. About average, yeah. You've got to get a picture – if all the chiefs get blankets and then the chief's wives and other elders, yeah. And then just cups, plates, and who knows." He laughed. "Just lots and lots of different stuff – household wares, that kind of thing, but also smaller potlatch goods that target guests that you want to make sure that you get gifts for. Special gifts for the chief's wives, for instance, or notable elders in our community or visitors that are going to be here that we know that are going to be here. We make sure that they get appropriate gifts. And, of course, you always want to make sure you've got something for the kids. And laundry baskets. It's the container that carries the gifts to the guests. It's kind of become a staple. In terms of chiefs, we try to get better baskets for them, either more expensive storage containers or wicker baskets."

"Is there a process for inviting the chiefs?"

"You do that at other potlatches. I'll remind people or make a formal announcement. I'll make that at a potlatch. Your Hamaťsa will dance and go around to announce that beforehand. You see somebody from a particular family do that, then you go, 'Oh, they must be potlatching.' And then, of course, the speaker for that potlatch will announce why that person's gotten up and danced ... But yeah, the announcement is done that way."

"So, you're a hereditary chief?"

"My position was handed down from my father. My father – his oldest brother decided to pass over the seat to my dad, and that's how that came down to me. His older brother had no interest in carrying it forward. I had no problem with it. I wanted to do it. I think I needed to assert myself in that area somewhat. But that was okay. Sometimes, I have a bit of a quiet disposition." He laughs. "I think there was an assumption that maybe I might not want to do this or want to be in the forefront. I disabused them of that in short order. And here I am." He laughed again.

"What's your philosophy as a chief?"

"What's my philosophy as a chief? Well, the role of chief has changed quite considerably from precontact times, for sure. I think that the position was – for us, the Kwakwa̱ka̱'wakw – it was a fairly autocratic but ... a very, very responsible role in terms of maintaining a community, maintaining the economy and social life and the ceremonial life of the community. It required an expertise that placed a huge, huge burden on one individual in terms of making sure there was enough food to last the year, in terms of the right people being placed in the right position, in terms of accessing the resources that they needed to maintain the community. And then, just in terms of the ceremonial life, the planning ahead that had to happen in early times in terms of the perishability of goods. I mean, can you imagine trying to preserve food for a couple of hundred people coming to your village to spend several months, [people] who were living with you while you carried out your ceremonial obligations?"

"Today, I think it's more focused on the ceremonial area. You don't get to allocate the resource sites or fishing spots. Well, with treaty now, the whole concept of property has changed. We've been required to define what our traditional territories are. Whereas there was a lot of overlap, a lot of spots that were isolated. Say, I had a little spot over in White Beach Pass, and surrounding me were the Mama̱liliḵa̱la, the Da̱'naxda'x̱w and the – you know, it could vary. The map was a lot more cut up than it is now. Now, you've got very distinct, hard lines drawn around our territory. There's pockets of traditional territory surrounded by other pockets of traditional territory. In our current situation, we can't think that way except for the fee simple property of families on the reserve. But territorial property, we know where those are."

"So, contemporary chiefs, yeah, it's largely focussed in terms of the ceremonial life of our families. It is *totally* focussed on the ceremonial life of our families. That's where our cultural life is right now. It's in the potlatch. The family's connection to traditional, ceremonial activity is through the potlatch, and some of our younger members carry it on, I guess, in more extra-community ways. Community life is not really focussed on the – in quotes – 'traditional culture.' I'd say that our community life just tends to be more Western-oriented. But then you've got individuals. Wa [William Wasden Jr.] is an example. He does a lot. My brother [Wedłidi] is another. They do a lot of work around the culture that's outside of the potlatch in community life on a day-to-day basis."

"Do people come to you as their chief?"

"I just had a fellow show up a couple of hours ago looking for some money to buy cigarettes." He laughed. "I gave it to him. Sometimes there are family members who phone up and say, 'Hey, Wees, I've got this problem ...' They're family members, but I'm also band manager, so it's hard to distinguish that. In terms of our house, they come to me around potlatch time if they want to do something with their kids or the dances they've had – they want to pass on to a niece or a daughter or something like that. We accommodate that for sure. People like to make sure that their family continues to participate."

"Your son Carey was your Hamatsa at your potlatch."

"Yeah. When he first did it, it was quite neat. Nobody really knew how he would do because he wouldn't come to any of the practices. The first time I saw him dance was at the practice two days before the potlatch, and it was like, holy — ! He'd been practising in secret. He didn't want to practise with anyone else. He just wanted to do it on his own. Yeah, I was quite proud of him."

"And there's something else that my dad instituted right from the very beginning. He always put aside a part of the potlatch for a play dance for the kids, so the school kids could come out and show their stuff. Some of the elders frowned on that. They wanted to say, 'This is a serious event, and all the dances should be like this.' And my dad said, 'I don't care. I'm a chief, and this is my potlatch, and we're going to do it my way.' I actually said that, too, at one of our family meetings for this potlatch. I said, 'Yeah, I hear a lot of these people saying that certain dances happen this way, certain dances happen that way, but what keeps coming to mind is my dad saying, 'You know, all those other tribes, they have their own way, but the Ławits'is have their own way. We're going to do it our way. I don't care how they dance it.''" He laughed. "So, everyone kind of nodded their head, 'Oh yeah.'"

"How does nobility play out now?"

"That's funny. We had that conversation on Thursday when we were coming across on the ferry with the [grand]kids, Justine and Jordan. I could hear them talking in the back there, and Jordan leaned across and said, 'Grampa, you're the chief, eh?'

"I said, 'Yes, I am.'"

"He says, 'Well, what does that make me?'"

"I said, 'You're a prince.'" He laughed.

"Justine says, 'Well, what does that make me?'"

"Um, a princess."

"'Well, will I be chief?' Jordan says."

"Well, maybe one day. You know, you've got to earn it. But maybe one day."

"'Well,' Justine says, 'Well, what will I be?'"

"I said, 'You'll always be a princess.'" He laughed.

"So there you have it, although I do have relatives who are female who would love to be chief."

"I was actually thinking just the other day and trying to compare the difference between this potlatch and the previous potlatch. And the first potlatch, actually, I was less of an authority figure in that potlatch than I am now. It was a more level playing field for family members, and that had to do with my lack of experience, I suppose. I think knowledge has a lot to do with it, and experience. I acted a lot more independently in terms of the potlatching, deciding when to have a potlatch and what's going to occur. Family meetings – I can stand up and say, 'No, I don't want that to happen. I've already decided that this is what I'm going to do,' and that puts an end to any discussion around it. If people are adamant, then I could, at the end of the day, say, 'Okay, well, then we're not going to do it at all,' and that would put an end to it. Although the people *can* argue, you know, it's not authoritarian by any means."

"A lot of people talk about the shift in potlatching around the competition."

"Yeah, elders frown on breaking coppers. I know that there are disputes that do happen about dances. People have made comments about us, for instance, and some of the stuff that we've done. But these are isolated individuals. I mean, most of the time those people have no leg to stand on because all of the chiefs agreed that our family was one of the richest in terms of ceremonial dances and the things that we owned. So, somebody would say, 'Well, those guys grab everything. They want to do everything.' And I've had chiefs stand up and counter that by saying, 'The Specks own these, and the Specks have done this, and this family has always had all of these things, and it's wrong for these people to say that they grab too much. They have a lot more.'" He laughs.

"But that's about the level that it's at. It's about who owns what, and there's still a little bit of that intercommunity rivalry. There's lots of tension leading up to the potlatch within families, too. That's not a smooth ride either. There's lots of rivalry in terms of positions. In the last potlatch, not the recent potlatch, but the potlatch before that, [I had to say to someone] I said, 'I own all those dances. We've got lots of family members. You don't own them. You dance them and, if it's available, you can dance this dance. But the dance that you've had from the previous potlatch has got to go to another family member because we want to make sure that everybody participates.' I don't let people accumulate them. It's my box of treasures."

"Do you see Christianity having shaped the potlatch?"

"Oh, definitely. I remember Bobby Duncan, when he potlatched. He had his Slave Killer Dance, and they'd had this mask carved with hair on it, and there was blood painted onto the mouth, dripping down to the chin. And the dancer had a sword, and he was going around pretending to be chopping the slave's head off. I watched a lot of the elders, and they just dropped their heads. I loved the dance myself." He laughed. "I kind of like that stuff."

"So, Christianity, in terms of the appropriateness of certain activities and how people view them, dispute resolution in Big Houses are frowned upon. I think that's a Christian kind of thing, you know, elders frown on breaking coppers now. We don't do that any more, and I think that's got that English, WASPy, Christian kind of *[laughs]* – 'keep your disputes private or take it to court.' Whereas, I think, traditional potlatches, you just brought it out in the open and some of the speeches were just like, you know, if somebody made a speech like that today – about how great you were and how bad so and so was." He laughed.

"Yeah," he sighed. "I think Christianity has had a huge impact on the shape of what happens in the Big House and how the stories play themselves out, how the Hamaťsa is talked about."

"You are a Hamaťsa."

"Yeah, I learned to dance, and I danced. I'm not bent toward the spiritual. I don't set out to insult anybody for their beliefs. There are many beliefs in this world, and if you spent your life trying to feel better than the Christians or the Hamaťsas or the ..." He laughed. "I guess my view is very anthropological – that there are so many human societies that have invented ways to explain their world that it'd be patronizing to think that there was one that was better than the other. Take your pick or none at all. I mean, really, every society's had some form of animism in their spiritual beliefs, all of it aimed at explaining their natural world. And what if you don't need the natural world explained to you?"

"I was a teenager or preteen with a chip on my shoulder. I think I was about thirteen years old when I started saying I don't believe in God. I was called on it by a teacher who gave me a book on religion. He says, 'Well, if you're going to say that, at least you should have some information to back you up.'" He laughed. "It was basically unreadable, but I got the gist of it, and I've built on it since then. Not to say that I don't have a sense of spirituality. I mean, when I go up to Knight Inlet, sitting on the deck of a seine boat, just the immensity of the mountains and the cliffs and the air inspires a very, very intense emotion. You see something very, very beautiful and moving, and, okay."

Kwagu'ł Gixsam Feast, May 2007

At the Speck Memorial Potlatch, Cook family members gathered to announce that they would host a feast. "This is a great family standing here," the speaker said. "It's a much larger family than are here today. George Cook will pass his title to Wedłidi – the many privileges, names, and positions from his father and grandmother. He will come to feast on May 19." The following day, at a family meeting, Chris Cook said that he had almost lost his voice, and Wedłidi spoke about his research, how it started from a "place of embarrassment." "But that's not going to happen anymore ... The announcement was made with a confidence in who we are," he said.

"Yeah," Florrie Matilpe affirmed.

"When I left the Big House last night," George Cook said, "someone said to me, 'It's about time the Cooks are doing that.' When we feast, a lot of people out there will think, 'Those Cooks have nothing.' We have to give the history of where the Cooks are from. There's a lot of history lying dormant, just lying there. We have to bring it to the surface. This is where we're coming from."

At a later meeting, we decided to record the process of preparation, and family members discussed the meaning of a feast.[23] "I've always been told the most ancient giveaway is the feast," William Wasden Jr. began:

"Feasting is a spiritual giveaway. My uncle the late Peter Cook, Chief Lalakanx'idi, he said that the old people always said that our souls are in our stomachs, as Indian people.[24] And that when you care for people and your guests come, that you take them in and feed them. Even if you're not hungry, old people would feed you, put something on the table and feed you anyway. If your soul is open – which is referring to your stomach, where your soul resides – then you're hungry, and you're weak and weary and vulnerable to bad spirits and bad energy. But when you're full, then it's been taken care of, and nothing can come in and take over your being. They're spiritually taken care of, covered, and protected. That's why the feasting was so big for our people. A lot of people think it's about being great – having a big name, blah, blah, blah – but there's spirituality behind the things our people used to do."

Wedłidi Speck continued the discussion. "A feast is about food and relationship. We can do what we want – honour the people with gifts, celebrate the amazing things people in the family have done. In a potlatch, there's strict rules – you're showing treasures, and the secret societies are dancing. The feast is more informal. It's for your house. That's where we present our history – how we got all our treasures. We have to think about who to invite and feed, what tribes."

Chris Cook responded, "We have to have something for the kids. This is more for the kids than for the elder generations in the family. A short while ago, none of us had blankets or knew songs. We'll make a statement to all the Kwakwa̱ka̱'wakw. After this, we'll yell and shout. There's nothing to be ashamed about what Granny and Papa did."

There was some discussion about the importance of including Nuu-chah-nulth relations, and the discussion turned to the logistics of gifts, fish, and finances. Each person was told to put aside five sockeye salmon. There were varying opinions about what to give to guests as a small token of the feast: a T-shirt, a family poster by William Wasden Jr., perhaps a coffee cup.[25] We discussed giving out a chapbook that would include a brief family history. The family set up a bank account for those able to contribute. They would need cash for the "chiefs' wages"; for the speakers, the singers, and the witnesses; and for the fire tender. Because they were naming a chief, they would also have to decide whether to give away flour or sugar or coffee.

In January 2006, they discussed names. They would be naming Wedłidi, and they talked about how to include each line descending from Jane and Stephen's children. One month before the feast, the family was clear that their purpose was to honour Jane. Women were setting the menu and making arrangements to prepare the Big House. They were thinking about who would dampen the sand, look after the washrooms, attend the fire, and cook. (In my mind, I heard Pearl's voice reiterating that the greatest shame is to run out of food.) The planners estimated the number of guests to be around one thousand people. They were not daunted by this, as they had hosted and fed up to seven hundred people at their family reunions.

"One of the things that always strikes me," Kelly-Anne Speck told me, "is there's never really one person in charge of preparing a potlatch or feast. It always amazes me how things just get prepared. At various times, you'll step in. Some people who are really knowledgable, they just keep working, and all of a sudden it comes together. It's not really a hierarchical process, where one person is designated. So, many of the people who participate either in the preparation of all the food or starting to think about the dances are people who have been participating through other families."

"A big thing will happen in the Big House," Randy Bell told me in February 2007. "We don't have to say much. Our presence will do it. We're not creating anything new. It's been there waiting." The plan was to keep the dance program simple: welcome songs, two or three dances, supper, and fun dances. At a meeting in February, the family decided to serve breakfast the morning after the feast, followed by a special church service to honour G̱a'a̱xsta'las. Discussions about food took into account the health needs of their guests. The Traditional Food Project, supervised by Dr. Jay Wortman, was then popular in 'Ya̱lis, and the hosts prepared to set tables for those living with diabetes or committed to the diet. George and Cornie Speck would supply the elk and deer. Someone joked, "A feast is a way of bragging that you can provide *more* food." Leaders in the family were making arrangements to travel to the villages to invite chiefs.

The family met regularly throughout May 2007. They had already purchased five hundred fifty-pound bags of flour and sugar and had raised thousands of dollars to pay out. Twenty singers had been invited to sit at the log, and the family had invited chiefs representing the Mowachaht, Kwagu'ł (Fort Rupert), Dzawada̱'enux̱w (Kingcome), A̱'wa̱'etła̱la (Knight Inlet), Mama̱lilika̱la (Village Island), Ławits'is (Turnour Island), and 'Na̱mgis. The family were "coming through" the Kwagu'ł Gix̱sa̱m 'na̱'mima, and they received support from Peter Knox in Tsax̱is (Fort Rupert). They had sockeye, halibut, prawns, five forty-to-fifty pound sacks of clams, and herring eggs from Bella Bella. But the "oolies from the Nass Valley" were running a month late, so there was uncertainty about the amount of *t'łina* (eulachon grease) they could serve. William Wasden Jr. was composing a welcome song and had begun to paint the grizzly bear screen for the Big House.

An email call was put out to the family for those who did not have names. They received about two hundred responses and intended to stand up adults and children in each of those lines. An extensive, up-to-date family tree was also underway thanks to the family email network. Filmmaker Barb Cranmer was asked to record the feast on video. Women continued to sew button blankets for people who would receive important names and for children who had grown or who had never worn a blanket before.

Pearl Alfred was preparing blankets; she told me that one of her strategies was to recycle cloth from other blankets, that children were thrilled to see the stitch outlines from former crests worn by their older relatives: "We've always worked for other people's potlatches, but this is our feast. This one is our own. We've been talking about this for so long! I can't believe we're actually doing it! The benefits are yet to come. The kids will learn the story and the struggle leading up to the feast and this history. You see someone young being asked questions and not knowing the answers – the old ones know it – they need to know the story."

Thursday night, before the feast, family members met at the Big House. They spoke first about costs, recognized those who had paid for the flour and the breakfast, and then asked that people give only what they were able to afford. They said they would make up any shortfall in a family bingo, if necessary. The menu was presented, and people were told that fish and game were being donated by 'na̲'mima members. Wedłidi Speck and William Wasden Jr. went through the four-hour program of dances and names and told those gathered that the feast would begin with mourning songs and then move to two welcome dances by women representing the Kwagu'ł and the 'Na̲mgis.

A tribute to Jane Cook was planned, and after Wedłidi was "dressed" as chief, they would distribute flour and sugar in a feast dance. After supper, the different branches of 'Nulis's grandchildren would dance in order of birthright: descendants of Jane Cook first, followed by the descendants of Annie Kamano and Charlie Newman. There would be a thank-you song and then the naming ceremony. As he spoke about the program, William Wasden Jr. connected names and dances to other families in 'Ya̲lis and Tsax̱is to whom they were related. "We're always making connections," he said, "to show we are family." Chris Cook said it was especially important to invite their youth, that they would help out by seating people and distributing the flour and sugar. William spoke about the breakfast planned for Sunday morning, when "the young will cook for the old" and honour G̱a'ax̱sta'las's name "Breakfast Giver." He told everyone that he had composed a song around the imagery of sandpipers lifting off the beach in the shape of a larger, unknown bird. They asked again at that meeting for children and adults without a name to come forward. "It's important to give people a connection to what we're doing and how we're coming through." Someone asked about the protocol for special announcements, and William told them, "We do our own thing. That's what Granny Cook is all about." He announced a cleansing ceremony strictly for family members and assured people that it wouldn't be strenuous. Anyone who wanted to attend was welcome, and they would meet at the Big House at sunrise.

The floor was opened for everyone to speak. "I'm proud to be here," Diane Bell said. "At our reunions, everyone got to dance – it was so inclusive. This is exciting. There's a good, happy feeling about seeing all these relatives." Billy Wasden acknowledged those who chose not to attend. "There's people in the family not ready to take this step with us," he said, "but the door is always open. The point is inclusion, not a threat to Christianity. It's up to us. We're the old ones now. This is a giant step toward keeping this family one. That's what Jane and Stephen are about. They took in families."

"I've been away for twenty years," Roberta Harris, the granddaughter of Herbert Cook, told everyone: "It's an honour to be involved in this, to come home and be included in the high ranks with Pearlie and Grace. I didn't know our culture ... but I have pride. You can't know where you're going until you know where you're from. For the kids, my own son, in Maple Ridge, people were racist against him, and that hurts.[26] Now, at home, we're accepted, hugged. We all need that. It's important to embrace our culture. I'm grateful to Wa and Wedłidi for their knowledge, for pulling us in and not letting us forget who we are ... My son and his son will know where they come from. We're honoured to be here to help. There's no looking back. This is all about being family."

Chris Cook's daughter Shelly said that she, too, was grateful, and she thanked Wedłidi Speck, "who I believe was born to do this – lead the family. I'm proud of you." "I'm ashamed to say that I was not proud of the Cook family because of the stories of Jane Cook. But now I'm proud. We had these gifted and powerful ancestors, and I'm blessed by that. Being a part of this, for me, is a gift. I've been at the meetings and learned so much about what happened. It's time to heal the grief and pain put on us. Once we become one, we'll heal fractures and become whole. My love for Pearlie, Kelly, Satch, they opened my heart to different members of the family in a way that's not happened before. *[Laughs]* Hey, they're our cousins – they're related – they're going to make sandwiches! The closer the day comes, the more emotional I become. Thanks for being part of this, for sharing and letting me speak. I want to thank my father. It's been hard, but he kept moving. Like Granny and Papa, just keep moving."

Kelly-Anne Speck spoke about her work with the many First Nations people passing through the penal system, about how the rituals and ceremonies she witnessed had "stretched" her "because of the involvement of Christianity *and* the culture. I've had to accept that as part of history," she said. "It's not one or the other. I hope others come to

Photo 46 Roberta Harris, Grace Stauffer, and George Cook cutting salmon in preparation for the feast at Gukwdzi, May 2007.

understand that as important to the family identity. In twenty years, as elders see this as an important point, we can work to document our relationships. The younger people will be able to see that Jane Cook was about responsibility and acknowledging relationships."

"I really appreciate what I'm hearing here, speaking from the heart," Wedłidi Speck said. "What draws us here is Granny Cook. The stories about her are so powerful. I've studied her, tried to understand what kept her strong. She never lost herself in the midst of the craziness of times in her community. We have the strength to share that story about what Granny and Papa represent. Their courage and strength will bring us out on Saturday. We're not interested in ego. We will take lessons from Jane Cook. The family is strong and alive. You have to say this is yours – ours. You have to let all of the family know that there are no one-sixteenth Cooks here! We are who we are."

Preparation of the Big House began a day or two before the feast. Children and adults worked together to carry sacks of sugar and flour from a back room and stack them in an arch around the main entrance. Women and men and children cycled through the kitchen on Friday and Saturday morning. Fish and meats thawed as people dropped off utensils and cooking equipment. The culinary aspect of the feast involved an extensive chain of labour as the family cleaned and prepared 150 sockeye salmon and other seafood, fed and tended soups, washed and peeled tubs of potatoes and buckets of carrots, boiled eggs, prepared elk and beef roasts for the oven, cooked special dishes, and washed and prepared salads. The kitchen was energized with laughter and conversation as drinks and desserts and plates and coffee urns materialized.

I had lively conversations with women in the kitchen. Dianne Bell told me about one of her ancestors, "a chief who gave away everything – even the shoes off his feet, his mother's slave, and his daughters' slaves!" "In the old days," she told me and laughed, "the *feast special* was soup and a bun and twenty-five cents." At my prompting, Dara Culhane and Pearl Alfred told me about a time in 1975 when they had seized the Nimpkish Bridge.

"We wrote this declaration of sovereignty over the whole valley," Dara said.

"It was to do with the logging," Pearl added. "We stopped all of the logging trucks from going through."

"The CBC phoned and wanted to confirm whether there was a battalion of AIM [American Indian Movement] warriors on their way to Alert Bay, and we said, 'No, we don't need to import militants. We have a whole community full of them,'" Dara said and laughed.

"We were protesting the land that was confiscated for the bridge. They took that and gave us a cheque for $480, something like that. So we decided to take it back and invited them to come and get their cheque. And they did come. And we did present it to whoever he was. Who was that?" Pearl asked Dara.

"Oh, that was after the blockade. That was Dave Vickers, the attorney general. We went over there and stopped everything for the day. Of course, we were going over, and the herring punts were running out of gas. We were making this great declaration of sovereignty and no one remembered to get gas!" Dara laughed.

Pearl and Dara talked about the demonstration of women and children at the Legislative Buildings in Victoria, where they demanded a "sober doctor." And they spoke about when they blockaded the main street in Alert Bay in protest of "Stolen Land." "We had a sign coming off the ferry saying 'Nimpkish Land,' pointing to the reserve, and 'Stolen Nimpkish Land,' pointing to the valley."

Friday night, before the feast, the family served coffee and snacks to people coming off the ferry. The customary meeting of chiefs and elders was held at 7:00 p.m. in a back room of the Big House. Eighteen

chiefs were present. George Cook welcomed them, and they then listened as William Wasden Jr. presented their intended program of dances and their naming protocol. Called to speak according to their village affiliation, each chief stated his support of the feast and talked about his experiences with Jane and Stephen and other members of the Cook family. Statements about "making our nation stronger" and "looking after the next generations" were prominent.

At 5:00 a.m. on Saturday morning, twenty family members met with William Wasden Jr. for a cleansing ceremony. "People are carrying whatever from their past history," he told me. "This will help them move forward, find connectedness." By 3:00 p.m., women had dropped off thirty salads, the sockeye had either been barbequed or prepared teriyaki style, and three hundred crabs were ready to be served. The menu also included one gallon of eulachon grease, roast elk and two small deer, one hundred and fifty pounds of halibut, forty pounds of roe and kelp, six sacks of clams in seafood chowder and clam fritters, roast beef and roast ham, asparagus, sixty loaves of bread, ten dozen cupcakes, fruit salad, twenty dozen cookies, cakes, fresh coffee and tea, and dozens of bottles of water.

Photo 47 Health protest by women and children at the Legislative Buildings, Victoria, July 1979. *Courtesy of Pearl Alfred.*

Photo 48 Chris Cook, Kelly-Anne Speck, Wedłidi Speck, and Pearl Alfred in the kitchen at Gukwdzi, May 2007.

Kwagu'ł Gi<u>x</u>s<u>a</u>m Feast

3:00 p.m., 19 May 2007

Photo 49 Grizzly Bear screen at the Kwagu'ł Gi<u>x</u>s<u>a</u>m Feast, video still, May 2007. *Artist, William Wasden Jr.*

Chief Bill Cranmer, Kwax<u>a</u>la'nukw<u>a</u>me' 'N<u>a</u>mugwis

We ask you please to settle down and get seated ...

I invite the singers to come forward now. They're a very important part of our ceremonies. I invite the singers to come to the log.

<u>G</u>ilakas'la![27]

It's been my pleasure to welcome you here on behalf of the Cook family.

Before we start, we're going to sing one song just to wipe the tears away before we start. This is when we weep for our loved ones who have gone before us.

You've been called here to witness some of the many prerogatives of the Cook family from the 'N<u>a</u>mgis and the Kwagu'ł. You will be seeing that today. So, we welcome you, and we know we're all going to have a great time.

<u>G</u>ilakas'la.

[S<u>a</u>ntła Ceremony, Washing of Tears]

So, what we have done, as I said before, we've wiped away the tears and put away the sorrow for the time that we're here in this Big House.

[Introduction of Chief Robert Joseph]

Chief Robert Joseph, Kwa̲nkwa̲nxwa̲ligedzi

G̲ilakas'la!

The chiefs, matriarchs, my people, the Cook family welcome you here today, and they thank you for paying attention to your call for us to come here and to celebrate together their idea and their will and desire to be part of this great sacred circle of the potlatch and life itself. They want you to know that they're extremely proud to be Kwakwa̲ka̲'wakw, to be members of the 'na̲'mima that they are, and they respect all of the other 'ni'na̲'mima.

We are here today to commemorate the ancestors of this great clan, this 'na̲'mima, and to work toward bringing about the revitalization of this nation in full knowledge of all of the things that we need to do as Kwakwa̲ka̲'wakw.

Ladies and gentlemen, this is a great gathering.

This is a moment of reconciliation for all of us. This is a moment when we reach out together and talk about being inclusive and being part of, so that we can become whole as the Kwakwa̲ka̲'wakw, so that we can become strong as the Kwakwa̲ka̲'wakw.

That's how historic this moment is, this gathering is.

My brothers and sisters, I look forward to seeing you demonstrating the heart and the will and the spirit and the desire to welcome this great 'na̲'mima into the circle, so that when we look forward into the future, the future of our children is secure.

This great house has always been the place – my brothers and friends – this has *always* been the place where we right the wrongs and we correct the paths on which we've been and where we make and create a world that is safe for our children, that is strong for our children.

Throughout the evening, you're going to learn more about the purpose of this great gathering.*

G̲ilakas'la.

---

* "I'm always fascinated to listen to how things get portrayed. So, you had Bobby Joe leading off, talking about this being a moment of reconciliation. And, to me, that's a very interesting word to use. To me, there has been – within a certain part of the community that pays attention to this – a perception of apartness. So, this is about bringing in a group who had this label, if you will, of not being part of the cultural life of the community. When he used that word, I thought it wasn't entirely clear to other people. I actually took it almost as a message that he was giving to other clans, saying, 'Now is the time we go forward. We stop trying to say or perpetuate the view that this family has not got a rightful place in this house' ... I thought that the whole notion that it's

Bill Cranmer

[Calls the tribes and chiefs from the audience]

We're inviting the chiefs of our different First Nations to honour our guests by sitting up front here.†

Photo 50 Singers at the log, at the Kwagu'ł Gix̱sa̱m Feast. Video still, May 2007.

[K̲ak̲usa̲lał, Kwagu'ł Welcome Dance]

That was the Welcome Song from the Kwaguł, which belongs to Chris Cook from his Kwagu'ł side. That was a dowry from the Kwagu'ł when he got married.‡

['Ya̲witła̲lał, Welcome Dance of the 'Na̲mgis]§

been sitting there, and now they've chosen to reactivate it – I'm not sure how people will see that in the future" (Kelly-Anne Speck).

† "Some of the people sitting at the chiefs' tables are people connected with the family in one way or another. It's like this thread that was there connecting all of us just wasn't recognized" (Kelly-Anne Speck).

‡ "This was from my grandfather Dadata's (Sam Hunt's) Kwagu'ł side. It was his dowry from Badidu the Da̲'naxda'x̱w when he married her" (WW).

§ "This came through marriage as part of a dowry from the west coast of Vancouver Island" (WW).

So, that last song was a welcome song from the 'Na̱mgis and the ladies, most of whom were 'Na̱mgis. There were some who weren't, but you see our great strength on the floor, of the 'Na̱mgis women.

Robert Joseph
Chiefs, matriarchs, friends and relatives, sons and daughters of the Kwakwa̱ka̱'wakw, as the evening unfolds, you will hear the stories of some of the first ancestors. You will hear the relationships between some of the 'na̱'mima and the clans, and that's how – through our oral history – we were strong. That's how we knew we were connected.

So, pay attention as these events unfold this evening, so that we all begin to learn and understand how we are connected and how we need to respect each other and to support each other. Everyone in this room belongs to this great culture, to the great ceremonies and rituals, and we have to be more inclusive than ever before.[28]

The Welcome Song by the 'Na̱mgis said that: Ya a heya a ha heya, "You are going to listen. You will listen to me." So please pay attention.

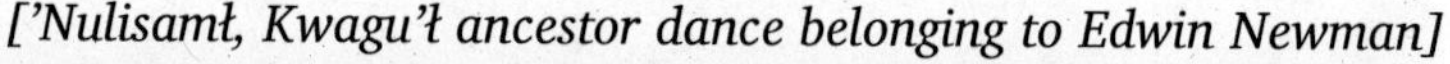

['Nulisamł, Kwagu'ł ancestor dance belonging to Edwin Newman]

Photo 51 'Nulisamł, Kwagu'ł ancestor dance belonging to Edwin Newman, May 2007. *Courtesy of Christina Cook.*

Edwin Newman, 'Nulis

Chiefs, ladies of high rank, relatives, ladies and gentlemen, that mask belonged to my grandfather. This is an ancestor mask, and it shows 'Nulis. When he's angry, it's closed. It shows him in an angry situation. When it's open, it shows him in a happy manner, when he's busy passing all his goods to his guests.

The original mask is in Berlin, Germany. Hank Speck is the one who made that mask for me, for a potlatch in Bella Bella. We're very happy to show it on behalf of our relatives here tonight.

We're very proud to be a part of this great standing.

My grandfather and Jane Cook were brother and sister, and the people who are standing here tonight represent our family as a whole. The family are related to the late Jane Cook, the late Charlie Newman, the late Annie Kamano. We are a huge family here. We're very proud to be part of this great gathering today.

I'd like to thank all of you for coming out here tonight to support us and to represent us, because it's important for us to do what we

Photo 52 Thunderbird Kwa̲nu'sila, 'Na̲mgis ancestor dance, belonging to William Wasden Jr., May 2007. *Courtesy of Christina Cook.*

have to do tonight. It's important for our children and our grandchildren that we do this. They're very much a part of the culture of the Kwakwa̱ka̱'wakw people. It's important for us that they feel the strength that we all have when we gather in this great house.

We'd like to thank all of you on behalf of the family for being here to support us tonight.

G̱ilakas'la.

[Thunderbird Kwa̱nu'sila, 'Na̱mgis ancestor dance, belonging to William Wasden Jr.]

Wedłidi Speck

The chief here asked me to share a story that the late Sam Scow shared with me.

I used to visit the old man to ask him questions about some of the old people and relationships. One day, I was talking with him, and he said all of what our chief has said. That the old man Stephen Cook – his mother was half-'Na̱mgis and half-Mowachaht. That her mother came from here, from the Gĭga̱ḻ'g̱a̱m and was really closely related to the Cranmer family, to the Scow family, and other 'Na̱mgis chiefs, to the Cook family – the Johnson Cook family, Lagius. And so, as he was telling this story, he said, "But she had a real strong West Coast accent." And I guess some of the people – our own relatives – used to tease her about that.

On account of that, T̓łak̲wadzi, Sam Scow's grandfather, and Lagius called the tribe together. And he stood her between them, and what he said to the people was that, "It stops now." He had a talk with them and said, if it didn't stop, then they would use their coppers to stop them.

It was a way in which, sometimes, we had to solve problems and remind people of how important relationships and family was and that we shouldn't lower ourselves to look for fault in people, that what we had to do was stand tall and live large in the world and celebrate our greatness rather than try to pull people down. And, so, therefore, she became really strong amongst the 'Na̱mgis.[##]

G̱ilakas'la.

"Because of this story. That's where we got the idea at the feast to put the people between Ed Newman and me as they were being named. It was on the spot. We decided. It just happened" (Wedłidi Speck).

Robert Joseph

I just mention to everyone that the story that was just told is a story of great teachings, and if we observe carefully all of the songs, all of the dances, all of the rituals of the Kwakwaka'wakw – they are all embedded in our teachings. So we want us to pay attention. Like the 'Namgis Welcome Song says, "You will listen to me."

This is part of our gathering today. The most important part of the purpose of our gathering together today is going to be the conferrance of a chieftainship title to Wedłidi. I need a lesson on the microphone. *[Laughter]*

The family has put a great deal of thought to this matter and originally it was supposed to be George Cook that was going to be conferred the title. But because of George's health, he's not comfortable assuming this position and responsibility. So, with George's blessing and the consent of all the family, they want to confer this title, the chieftainship, to Wedłidi, because of their tremendous respect and love and admiration for Wedłidi.

Most of us in this great house know that Wedłidi is a *noxsola,* a very wise man, that he has learned many things from our elders. I have watched him for the last twenty-five years speaking to all of our elders from all of our tribes, learning about our ways, learning about our history. So, it is fitting and appropriate that he takes this position.

And to the 'na'mima – all of the relatives of Wedłidi – you will respect this decision today and allow Wedłidi to lead and walk with you in our house and in our community. And wherever he is, he will carry this title well, and he will represent you well, as well as representing all of us here.

I'd like to ask all of the Cooks to come and stand around the perimeter for this part of the ceremony. Probably, when we have you all, there will be no one left sitting there.¶ *[Laughter]*

[People stream from the seats to the floor]

This position of the head chief of the Gixsam of the Kwagu'ł proper, that's where this standing originates from.

¶ "This is the beginning. Here we are as descendants of Granny. Here we are in 2007, giving a feast for the people coming up. This is where we are today, because of her fight. What we're doing is putting the light on the eight hundred descendants" (Chris Cook Jr.).

Photo 53 George Cook dressing Wedłidi Speck as a chief, in his blanket. The blanket was made by Grace Stauffer. Video still, May 2007.

I wanted to tell you that the clan – this great clan of the Cooks – and George, who was originally going to inhabit this position, decided that he was not well enough. So George, in consultation with all of the family, have reached a consensus that Wedłidi would take on this position, and for a number of reasons. He is very well loved by his 'na̲'mima family and by many of us. Wedłidi is a well taught and noxsola person, who has a great deal of passion and care for our culture.**

So, I think that while the 'na̲'mima of the Cooks is very happy that this has transpired, we all should be happy that this has transpired because, when our ambassadors – the chiefs – are out in the big world, out in the community representing us, they truly do that.

** "I throw myself into the story of my ancestors. And when they use a word like *'na̲'mima* – *'na̲'mima,* to me, means that I have to stand up and I have to work as a leader to ensure that there is 'na̲'mima, that people are included. With *'na̲mała* – "oneness on your face" – it means that, when I'm finished, we'll have that oneness. When I was talking to elders in the seventies, those were the questions I was asking them, because it wasn't working – the way we were thinking, the way we were speaking, the way we were trying to solve it. What I was trying to understand was the space we create and what we put into it. What we put into it shapes our relationship between our family and our clan. We have to ask, have we done our job of including everybody?" (Wedłidi Speck).

And I know that it gives us inspiration and strength when we see our chiefs conducting themselves in the way that they do with great dignity and respect.

[Wedłidi dances with George and Ruth Cook, followed by the whole family]

Bill Cranmer

We'll ask you to be seated again.

We're now finished with the [dressing]. We will be distributing flour.

We'd also like the children of the Cook family to go and stand in front of the flour, and they will all be receiving names tonight. We'll be singing a few feast songs, and then we're going to have dinner. Will all the youngsters who will be getting names please go sit by the flour for a photo op? This is all part of the business of recognizing our new chief.

Okay, this is how it's going to work. All the family that are going to be distributing the flour, grab a sack of flour, and the first feast song will be just standing on the spot, dancing on the spot with your flour. And then the second song, you'll start to distribute the flour. Distribute the flour first to the chiefs, here in the front of the building. Okay, grab the flour.

[Family members of all ages dance with sacks of flour and sugar and then distribute them to the chiefs and then to other witnesses]

[Ladies' Dance and feast songs of the Kwagu'ł and the 'N<u>a</u>mgis]

That song that was sung belongs to Chris Cook Jr. It came from his grandfather T̓ła<u>k</u>wagila T̓łasuti'walis (Sam Hunt). It was composed by Mungo Martin when he gave flour to the Dzawad<u>a</u>'enu<u>x</u>w (Kingcome).

Robert Joseph

[Calling tribe names]

I just wanted to point out the connections between all of those ladies that were just dancing. All of them came from so many tribes, even though they belong to specific tribes. It's essential to all of our teaching as Kwakwaka'wakw to know how we are related, so that we can begin to build the family ties that will make us strong again.

So, when we point out these things, it's important for you to remember them.

Bill Cranmer

We'd like to call all those descendants of Winnie Bell to come forward. There's a special presentation that's going to be made.

It's my sister Florence's birthday – seventy-two years old. *[Applause]*

The Cook family wants to just recognize what a very special person she is. She's one of the very good in-laws that have married into the Cook family.

Photo 54 Randy Bell *(centre),* with William Wasden Jr. *(at right),* at the Kwagu'ł Gixsam Feast, May 2007. *Courtesy of Christina Cook.*

[Singers at the log sing "Happy Birthday" in Kwak̓wala, then in English. Randy Bell presents a gift to Florence Bell]

We're going to ask Ruth to say grace.

Ruth Cook
I'll just ask you to stand up, please.

Father, God, our Creator, we thank you for being in our midst while we're having a good celebration. We just ask for your blessing upon each one of us and especially as we share our food and we share good words and love with one another, and we give you all the thanks and praise for gathering us together.

All my relations.

[Women set up the long tables and bring out the food. They serve chiefs and elders first]

Bill Cranmer
So, when Chief Bob Duncan had his first potlatch, Skyce – our new chief's dad – gave Bob a headdress. And at that time, it was a great

Photo 55 Feasting.

gift to our chief, Bobby Duncan, and he wants to give that back – not the headdress that he got – but he's giving you *[gestures to Wedłidi]* a headdress that he made especially for you.

Bob Duncan

We want to thank you all for your attention.

My sister, here, is the blanket maker in our family, and I commissioned her to do this blanket for our brother, here, to show our love, our respect, and our appreciation for all they have done for *our* family.

Uncle Skyce was always there. He treated my own children – these are my children here, my grandson *[gestures]* – like they were his own. I'm very happy and proud and pleased to be here to say this to my brother. When we wear glasses, we look alike *[laughter]*. It never worked in my favour when we were younger. We were always getting into trouble. *[Laughter]*

I just want to say these words and stand Satch and Wedłidi up to show that we are all family, and we're here to share this day with all of the rest of our family here, share and show our appreciation and love for what they have done for our family.

G̱ilakas'la.

[Song]

Bill Cranmer

So, I will ask Jane and Papa Cook's descendants to go to the back room. You're going to be doing the next two dances. All of Granny Cook and Papa Cook's descendants to the back room.

To the cooks and the great food that they served us – let's give them a big hand.

[Applause and log beats]

Robert Joseph

Chiefs, matriarchs, friends, ladies and gentlemen, guests, this is a wonderful occasion when our hosts are demonstrating the connections that they have between each other. They're showing us how they validate their descendants and their children.

All the groups that has come out are branches of this great family, this 'na̱'mima. You must be proud to see this – from the old days – to see the descendants, to see the children here, celebrating with all of us. This is why we have this culture that we have, so they will validate each other, honour each other.

We need to get beyond simply enjoying watching what we do. We need to understand why we do it so that we can begin to open our minds, entrench our minds, with issues that are so important, especially now when we have to look forward to the future because we're broadening the circle in this community.

All the children of all you who are chiefs, your chieftainship will be stronger and you will be greater. All of the clans, the clans will be the same – growing bigger and stronger. We have much to be grateful of this evening, much to celebrate.

These are all the descendants of Na̱ge, Papa Cook, as he was formerly known. And, as you look at this great circle of descendants this evening, you cannot escape the added power and inspiration that all of these descendants will give to all of us in this great house.

These are the descendants of Na̱ge, of K̓ax̱wstutłe. For generations to come, children will be born to these people around this circle, and our future is stronger – brothers and sisters – because of Na̱ge, because of K̓ax̱wstutłe, and especially because of these descendants.

They want to honour someone this evening that I haven't met. Someone who is a friend of the family and, I gather, is doing some historical research and writing about this family. This family greatly appreciates that, and they want to extend to her – this person that I have not yet met – an invitation to be a part of this family ...

[Leslie Robertson is given a name by the family]

[Introduction to Nella Nelson]

Nella Nelson

I'm really honoured to stand here and talk about the story of how Leslie came into our lives.

For many years, as a member of the Cook family and certainly in my experience when I was going to school, I always heard about Granny Cook. I was born after, but I do remember Papa – in that brass bed, and that hook he always used. I must have been –

But I always heard about Granny Cook.

Many times, when I was doing my education, I would come across the information about Granny Cook, about her as an interpreter in the potlatch trials. And, often, that message would come across really negatively. I knew from the stories that I heard from my dad and from other people that there was more to Granny Cook than being a translator at the potlatch trials.

I remember when a book came out a few years ago, and I picked it up again and I started to read, and there was the same reference to Granny Cook – about her not being able to speak Kwak̓wala very well and other things. And it really bothered me.

I phoned my Auntie Pearlie, and I remember phoning Billy, saying that "I really feel that Granny Cook's story needs to be told. We need to do something, because Granny Cook was more than that."

This is how Leslie came into our lives, with the help of Dara [Culhane]. And we really want to acknowledge Dara, because she searched for a researcher that would be able to do all of the work we needed to do to tell Granny's story – G̱a'ax̱sta'las. So, Leslie came into our lives, and things have been falling into place. And she's done a lot of research, and now we're getting close. The University of British Columbia Press has agreed to publish the book once Leslie is finished. And she's finding out some absolutely amazing things.

As I look around this circle, I am reminded that Granny Cook's and Papa's genes have laid the foundation for many people in this circle who work hard at the community level, at the provincial level, at the international level, and they have carried her messages.

She was a woman before her time, and we have to admit that Papa was pretty liberal to let her whip all over the country in 1915 with the Allied Tribes of British Columbia. She was the only woman standing there, with her tight jacket and her hat, and she stood in the middle of all of the men and the chiefs of British Columbia. So Papa was pretty liberated, even though, I guess, for some of you who knew him, he seemed a little bit staunch at times. But she truly was an amazing woman. I'm not saying that it's all perfect, but I think the story in the book will tell us about G̱a'ax̱sta'las as a mother, G̱a'ax̱sta'las as a community member, G̱a'ax̱sta'las as a church person, G̱a'ax̱sta'las as a politician. That's the story that Leslie's going to share, and when we get that book published, we'll be here to celebrate again.

So, I would just like to thank you on behalf of the family, and their support in the meetings that we've had – everybody's excited. We just wanted to make sure that everyone knew that is what we're going to do – to tell her story. Oh, I missed one chapter –

Ga'axsta'las in her hereditary, traditional position, which, of course, is why we're here.

I just want to say on behalf of our family, Leslie, that we're really honoured, and we know that when the book comes out, it will be awesome, and it will leave a legacy for every single person standing in this circle of the Cook family.

Gilakas'la.

[Everyone moves into the back room and prepares to dance in order of birthright, through the three grandchildren of 'Nulis. Jane Cook's line comes on to the floor first – the Hamatsas and initiated dancers lead, followed by the women. Descendants of Annie Kamano are followed by the descendants of Charlie Newman.]

Bill Cranmer

I have to announce that our Chief Siwiti, Pat Taylor, just passed away, and we want to have a moment of silence ... Thank you. If you'll just remain standing please, we're going to sing one song to ask the Creator to just watch over us and to look after the Taylor family, and then we'll ask for a moment of silence again.

Robert Joseph

We want you all to pay attention to this very important function. We're going to be placing names on the children now. And to the people who don't have names, the first batch of names we're going to assign you will go to Grace Cook's family, her descendants.[29]

Just while we're getting ready, we want you to think about using these names in our everyday, daily lives. Even the young children, remember your names and then call each other that on the playground. The others, call your names to each other at home or in the community. Think about that really hard.[30] As soon as your name is called, we want you to quickly come forward.

Grace Cook's line. *[Nine people receive names. One is a baby]*

We're now going to Alice Cook's branch of the family. *[One person receives a name]*

Now we're going to Reg Cook's line. *[Twenty people receive names]*

Now we're going to the Gilbert Cook family line. *[Two people receive names]*

We're going to Herbert Cook's family line now. *[Five people receive names]*

Auntie Pearlie's [Pearl Mountain's] line. *[Eight people receive names. Three are babies, and one is an unborn child]*[††]

Now, Auntie Winnie's [Winnie Bell's] family line. *[Four people receive names]*

And now the Bert Cook branch. *[Three people receive names]*

Gig̱ame' (chiefs or elders) names:[‡‡]

[Names are given to Edwin Newman, Chris Cook Jr., Bill Wasden Sr., Pearl Alfred, Emma Alfred, Flora Cook, Florrie Matilpe, Nella Nelson, and Stephen Cook]

Xamag̱ame' Gig̱ame' (head chiefs) names:

[Names are given to Wedłidi Speck, Randy Cook, William Wasden Jr., and Randy Bell. Each receives a feast name and a potlatch name]

Just very briefly – because this 'na̱'mima have been quiet for a long time and not fully active – in consultation with each other and with bestowing Wedłidi, they wanted to be sure that everything was done right, that all of the seats that they want to acknowledge and recognize and would be fully activated would be announced this evening.

That's why we brought these people here to stand before you, so that we can tell you who they were and the names that will go to them when they feast and when they potlatch in the sacred Cedar Bark Ceremonies. So, that was what this part of the ceremonies were this evening.

I wanted just to pass on in English that Auntie Doreen – Doreen Fitch, Doreen Dawson – holds the treasure box that came down

†† "This is the first time we'll have children who won't have any baggage. It's all they will have known – that they are *in*" (Pearl Alfred).

‡‡ "From ancient times, the 'na̱'mima clan is made up of head chiefs, chiefs, nobility, and commoners. The head chiefs had specific duties and worked in council with the chiefs or lower chiefs. The head chief held the office of inviting the tribes for feasts, potlatches, and breaking coppers. The number two chiefs invite the tribes from time to time and are responsible for protecting the 'na̱'mima as the war chiefs. The third and fourth chiefs did much the same. All are defenders of the 'na̱'mima" (William Wasden Jr.).

from Chief Wanukw from Bella Bella. That particular box is at UBC right now, and when this great band decides to move forward in the Ṫsek̲a [Winter Ceremonial], that box will be there, and Auntie Doreen will be there, and, of course, all of these people and others who are not here. And we hope that, in that time, all of you who have celebrated this great day with this ’na̲’mima will come back and bring your other families and friends with you.

Bill Cranmer
Everyone on the floor!

[Two fun dances are performed]

[All three lines of descent from ’Nulis dance to thank everyone for witnessing the feast]

Breakfast is going to be served here for those going to church. The heathens, don’t bother coming! *[Laughter]* A breakfast for the *Breakfast Giver,* G̲a’ax̲sta’las!

Photo 56 Members of the Kwagu’ł Gix̲sa̲m, dancing at the feast, May 2007.

[The feast concludes with speeches from chiefs representing the Kwagu'ł, Mamalilikala, Ławits'is, Da'naxda'xw, Dzawada'enuxw, Ligwiłdaxw, Gwawa'enuxw, and 'Namgis. As they speak, they hold the talking stick. Most speak in Kwak̓wala and English. Some speak only in Kwak̓wala]

Kwagu'ł Ma'amtagila Gixsam Chief Edwin Newman, 'Nulis
Relatives. Friends.

It's been a great day for the family. I thought about my grandfather, who, I know, if he was here today, would leave here with a good feeling in my heart for what he saw the family do here today. As I said earlier, it is very important for our children and our grandchildren to do this, for my grandfather to be part of this family, to be part of what you have done here today. Today is just the beginning of what we have to do according to the customs of our people.

I'd like to thank the chiefs for being here to witness the things that happened here today.

I'd like to thank all of you for coming here to witness what the family had to do. Thank you from the bottom of my heart. Gilakas'la!

Bill Cranmer
Gilakas'la 'Nulis.

[Invites the Mamalilikala]

Mamalilikala Chief Arthur Dick, T̓łakwagila
[Translated from Kwak̓wala][31] Welcome, people of the potlatch. We've come to witness this great family. We've been waiting a long time to hear your position. We've had the opportunity to see who they are, and also, by being here, we have the opportunity to tell people who we are. Our children will be proud to know who they are and where they come from, to lift our children up. We thank the wise ones who are singing the songs.

[In English] I'd like to thank the family, the Cook family, for what they've shown today. In the words of our elders that went on before us – to uphold our children, to name them, and to hold each other up in times of need. I remember the uncles that went on before me on both sides of the family – Uncle Skyce and Uncle Jim – and I remember Reggie insisting on me calling him "Uncle." You know,

we see the extended family we haven't seen for many, many years come together. That's the power of our culture. Bring everybody together and have a good heart while we're doing it. In the words of my grandmother Axuw, "To love one another," this is what I've witnessed tonight. Without that love and without that care, we wouldn't be half as strong as we are today. What I see here today only strengthens us as a people in our daily dealings with the outside world. When I hear our speakers talk about the strength of what we have here, there's no law that supersedes our family ties and what our chiefs say here in the Big House.

G̱ilakas'la. G̱ilakas'la.

Mama̱liliḵa̱la Speaker Robbie Mountain Jr.

Hello, everybody.

I'd just like to thank everybody for showing up. I stand before you to speak on behalf of Chief Bobby Mountain, who couldn't be here. He's my dad, and we're descendants of Pearl Cook. My dad sent his regrets. He wishes he was here and the rest of my family that's still in Vancouver. There's another forty or fifty in Vancouver that couldn't make it. I'm so honoured to be here on behalf of our chief. I see the strength that the chief was talking about in our family here, the Cook family. Every year, every time we get together with the reunion, I'm amazed at how many people we have, and all the new children ... We have a family that's growing, just growing every day. I'm proud to be part of this family and just like to let you know that I loved my Granny Pearlie so much. I lived with her most of my life, and I'm proud to be here and thank you all for being here for our chief.

Thank you.

Mama̱liliḵa̱la Chief David Mountain Sr., Na̱gedzi

[Translated from Kwak̓wala] Welcome. I'm from the Mama̱liliḵa̱la.

My name is Na̱gedzi.

It makes me happy to be here to witness what you are doing. Continue on with what you are doing, everything is for the children.

[Bill Cranmer invites the Ławits'is]

Ławits'is Chief George Speck, Yakudłasdzi

G̱ilakas'la.

Chiefs, guests, friends, tonight we did a great thing. I would just like to say to my family, I'm very, very proud of what we've done tonight. I come from two brave lines, the Specks and the Cooks. Tonight, you have made me whole, and I thank you for that. And I thank you for witnessing what they have done, what we have done.

Gilakas'la.

[Bill Cranmer invites the Da'naxda'xw]

Da'naxda'xw Chief Bobby Duncan, Wałolas

Gilakas'la Gigame' [Welcome Chiefs].

I'd like to say that I'm very happy to be here tonight to celebrate this great family and to honour a great woman and all of the things that she's touched in all of our lives. The seed started there for many of us in this room here tonight. The bloodlines obviously run through us all. I think we all carry a piece of that history with us every day, and I'm very happy that we're honouring not only this woman but the many women among our communities, among our tribes. We don't honour our women enough, and it's been a great pleasure to witness tonight what we've done here. Tonight is just a part of the three-day weekend that this family celebrates every ten years. I was at the very first celebration. I missed the second one, and it would be remiss to miss this one. I'm very happy to be here, and I'm happy all of the tribes were able to share in that, to know how big this family is and how far the branches go through all of our communities, the Kwakwaka'wakw, and other parts of the world. I'm very happy that our brother has taken the position that he has. It's about time, and I'm very glad that he's done that. He's always one that was very well versed in the history of this family but also in the history of our people and always lent a helping hand to make sure those stories are not only told but preserved in the part of our history that goes with that. I'm thankful that my brother has done this well.

Gilakas'la.

Da'naxda'xw Chief Jack Nolie, 'Maxtsolam Kamg'id

[*Translated from Kwak̓wala*] Welcome, chiefs. Everything has gone well.

Welcome Wedłidi and his family.

Thank you, singers, for working hard to remember the old people's songs.

Da̲'naxda'x̲w Chief Norman Glendale, Ṫła̲k̲wadzi
[Translated from Kwak̓wala] Thank you, chiefs, loved ones.

G̲ilakas'la to Wedłidi and his family.

What you've done here today is great. This is what you've worked for, for the children. Let's just say good things when we're in this house. Be careful in what we're doing and only say good words. Be strong together.

Thank you, people of the potlatch.

'Ma'a̲mtagila Speaker Greg Wadhams, Ha̲mdzidag̲ame'
G̲ilakas'la.

G̲ilakas'la, chiefs, all the people.

My chief just went home. He was tired and had to go home and have a rest. He said his cheeks were pretty sore, that it was a really good day. I really respect what's going on here. Our family are really closely knit with the Speck family. Skyce stayed with my mother for quite a while when he was young, and I think Wedłidi and myself kind of carried it on after that because we were pretty close friends. I know all of the knowledge work Wedłidi's been doing, all the stuff he's been looking into with his culture and his background. It's really inspiring to see what the Cook family is doing in honouring Wedłidi and his knowledge and making him head speaker of the family.

G̲ilakas'la. G̲ilakas'la.

[Bill Cranmer invites the Musga̲'makw][32]

Dzawada̲'enux̲w Chief John Moon, Ma̲kwa̲la
[Translated from Kwak̓wala] Welcome, chiefs.

Thank you for inviting us to witness this great family gathering.

G̲ilakas'la.

Dzawada̲'enux̲w Chief Beau Dick, G̲a'ax̲sta'las
G̲ilakas'la.

Thank you very much everybody for being here today. I'd like to share a little bit of the history that I know of this family and of or people, of Jane Cook and how she got the name that I was given. I feel very connected to the Cooks not only because of blood but for other reasons. But I wanted to talk about the history and about where Jane Cook came from. I'd like to talk about her grandmother

Anislaga Ebbets-Hunt and her father, Chief Shakes, the seventh from the Tongas people from the Bear House. The history goes way back from that house to a time – long, long time ago – when there was a big glacier that held the rest of the world back. And the very first man that came through the Stikine Valley encountered a grizzly bear that he wrestled with for four days. And he couldn't beat the grizzly bear, and he eventually made love with her and had children. And, hence began this Bear House of the Tongas-Tlingit. There was a name that started at that time – the origin of that name in the Stikine Valley, way, way back – Edensuk. Along with all the spirit, that name also came with Anislaga. In the 1800s, the Hudson's Bay Company was holding hands with the government and coming in here and laying claim to their new territory. And one of the policies was to marry into the high-ranking families so that they could have a good business relationship with the local Natives. That was why Mary Ebbets was given to the Hudson's Bay Company. It was a nice arrangement, because it was marrying into another tribe that had a lot to offer. She had also two sisters, Emily and Annie. Emily was given to the Haida people, to the principal chief, Albert Edwards. She also brought that name with her Edensuk, and Albert Edwards named his son Albert Edwards Edenshaw. That's our family. There was another girl. Her name was Annie, and she was given to the Nass people at Port Simpson, who are also our family. This goes way back, and I wanted to mention that. We come from great people, and we're all connected. These little tidbits of history should be noted and remembered.

In 1850 they built a Hudson's Bay fort in Fort Rupert, and Robert Hunt and his wife – Mary Ebbets-Hunt, Anislaga – moved to Fort Rupert. They had two kids, George and his sister, who was given to Jonathan Whonnock. That's a little bit of the background that I wanted to share with you tonight, because I just wanted to reaffirm our connection, not only between my family and the Cook family but also with the rest of the Coast. It's an important connection, because all of our tribes up and down the Coast are like trees whose roots are all intertwined, and we all need each other to stand together.

So, thank you for listening and thank you for being here. I'm very honoured and privileged to share this.

<u>G</u>ilakas'la.

Dzawada̲'enux̲w Chief James Speck, Lagius
G̲ilakas'la, chiefs, singers, the Cooks, and the people in the back who are working so hard – and to all of you who came to witness this great thing that happened here today.

Thank you for bringing us together and holding themselves up and ensuring that the children have a place. This is an amazing thing. It really lifts my heart to be here. I'm so proud to be part of this culture and glad to be a part of you and everything you've shown here tonight.

G̲ilakas'la.

[Bill Cranmer invites the Ligwiłdax̲w (Campbell River)]

Ligwiłdax̲w Chief James Quatell, Kwaxiladzi
G̲ilakas'la.

I stand here and thank the Cooks for their family. I see the strength – that you're going forward, how Wa has put this all together. It was an honour to see what was put on Wedłidi to carry. From my heart to each and every one of you, myself and my family congratulate you for this day. We're honoured to be here to participate in this event you've put on here. I wanted to be here to hear the courage of the family.

[Bill Cranmer invites the 'Na̲mgis]

'Na̲mgis (Sisa̲ntłe') Chief Pat Alfred, 'Na̲mugwis
[Translated from Kwak̓wala] Welcome chiefs, people of the potlatch.

Thanks to our host, K̲̓wa̲mk̲̓wax'a̲widi. We are amazed at what you're doing. You're a wise young man. From what I know of your family, I'm impressed.

[In English] Chiefs, I think I should speak English so that everybody can hear that this is probably the most important part of the day – to say thank you to the Cook family and to the chiefs of the Kwakwa̲ka̲'wakw. Last night, I heard some wonderful things in the other room when the chiefs got together. One of the chiefs said, "Tomorrow, we will *I'tusto,*" that is – "to be rising upwards, giving a u'mista." I heard that coming out. I heard talk of how you did things today that brought to mind that, when we talk about uniting and respecting each other, you and your family have done this – how it has to be done. You touched every corner of our family, of

the Kwakwa̱ka̱'wakw nation, excluding no one. And I respect you for that. It's an honour to speak on behalf of my family.

I remember the old people, not that well, but I remember spending a lot of time in Papa Cook's store. And how he told me –

I'm glad I'm with you while you're doing this, because some of you are too young to remember this – that Papa Cook, K̓ax̱wstutłe, told me he was the last man ever in this Big House *[gestures to the smoke hole]* to come through with eagle claws in his body. He was Hawinalał.

Remember that.

And Granny Cook. She had a garden. We all hung out up there, and when she wasn't looking ... Instead of bawling us out she would always say, "Come in, you children. I will give you jam and strawberries. You don't have to come and steal anymore." I'm speaking about your family, the Cook family. The economic development that family brought into this community – Bones Bay, ten seine boats, employment for all of our people.

Remember that.

A great family. It's good to see. My grandmother told me that Mrs. Cook taught all the people how to understand the Bible and how she travelled with my grandfather Moses [Alfred], for they were the two head speakers of the village to go to Ottawa to represent you. Be proud of that. I was. I really want to say thank you to you for showing us the wonderful time we've had. And I can hardly wait for the T̓seḵa. When you're ready, we'll be there. All the families and all the Nimpkish chiefs will be there to support you, and you know that. I thank you, all of you.

G̱ilakas'la.

[Translated from Kwak̓wala] My uncle Chief Ha̱midi [Alfred Hunt] didn't come today because of his wife passing away.

[In English] Chiefs, and to the Cook family, my chief could not be here today because he's grieving for his family that he's lost. He's lost his sister, his brother, and his wife. It's hard for him to be here today because they were going through his wife's possessions. The reason I raised that is – I'm really glad that Wedłidi asked me to walk with these people, to show the people they're connected to your family. Why I'm saying that is, in this Big House, the Ḵ'umu'ya̱we' never disappeared. The Department of Indian Affairs took my family, took them off the charts, yet this Big House where I stand before you today recognized the family and the Ḵ'umu'ya̱we' clan.

Gilakas'la.

[Bill Cranmer announces that Chief Pat Alfred was also speaking on behalf of his uncle Chief Sonny Alfred, Udzistalis K'wixalagi'lakw]

'Namgis Chief Don Svanvik, Ho'miskanis

Gilakas'la Gigame' [Chiefs].

Gilakas'la to the singers.

Gilakas'la to the people of the potlatch.

Gilakas'la K̓wamk̓wax'awidi.

First off, I'd like to tell you that our family are a little bit shy here today, because a lot of them are down in Victoria with our auntie. But she's slowly doing better, and they'll be home soon. They send all their best and wish that they were here with you. It's been a really wonderful day. Today, I saw the joy on people's faces the first time they danced with their family in the Big House. I know that's a wonderful feeling. And the happiness you see on people when they're getting their name, even a lot later than maybe they should have, but it's a good thing that they're getting names, because that's what we're supposed to do. I want to thank you for sharing that joy with us, and I'm sure that they have ancestors who are sharing that joy with them tonight, too.

Gilakas'la.

'Namgis Chief Al Wist, 'Namugwisamdzi

[Translated from Kwak̓wala] Welcome, my tribe, 'Namgis, gathering at this Big House to witness what's happened here. It makes us happy following in the footsteps of our old people. It makes our bodies feel good. Everything that's happened here is good. We've been fed, so we will be happy as we go home.

'Namgis Chief Chris Cook Jr., T̓łakwagila

Yo, Gilakas'la!

Hello, gang! Hello, family! I want to thank you for our great day today. I'd like to thank you chiefs for being here to witness today. I'd like to thank the singers. I'd like to thank the whole family. And I hope, today, when you see our family, you'll see that the Cook family goes into many, many families on this Coast. We will all come together. This was just a dream thirty-five years ago, when I had my first potlatch, the Cook family. When we got together, one of my cousins passed away, Silas Olney, and we got together with Cornie, and we said, "One day we should get our family together. They're all over the place. Some of us don't even know each other." It wasn't long after that my Auntie Emma passed away, Emma Kenmuir. So, I told Billy Wasden, we were sitting having coffee, and I said, "We've got to get our family together." So, Billy and I went to our cousin Pearl, who's never, ever short of words, like Granny Cook. So, there we decided to have a Cook reunion in 1991. All those at the head table are gone now. In 2001, we had another Cook reunion, and we talked about how we have to get our family together to have a feast, have a potlatch. And that's how it started. We got together the last three or four years, and we said, "We're going to do it." So, I'd like to share that with those [other] families – that it's possible, when you get all the parts of your family together and say, "We're going to do it."

This, today, is such a happy day for me and my children, my grandchildren. I'm not as old as Bill Cranmer or Ed Newman, who's eighty-one years old. So, I'd like to thank all of the people here today. Thanks to Robert Joseph and Bill Cranmer, and I'm glad to see that my papa and my granny had so many children – or we wouldn't have been here.

G̱ilakas'la.

'Na̱mgis Chief Bill Cranmer, Kwaxa̱la'nukwa̱me' 'Na̱mugwis *[Translated from Kwak̓wala]* I'll say a few words on behalf of 'Na̱mgis Chief Charlie Beans, T̓łaḵwagidakw and also Chief William Wasden Jr., Waxa̱widi, to thank the family for what we've seen here tonight. We're glad that they're holding on to their history.

On behalf of all the 'Na̱mgis chiefs and all who are here, I'd like to thank all who are responsible for bringing us to this day. I want to thank Wa and Wedłidi for what you did in putting together the history of the family. When we see our relatives, the Cook family, in our language, "awaken to open their history," we are honoured to witness that history. It is our strength as 'Na̱mgis that, by their doing so, we're made stronger. I want to thank the singers for making it possible for us to carry on what we have to do today. Without them, it would be impossible. I'd also like to thank the co-speaker, Kwa̱nkwa̱nxwa̱ligedzi, for his expertise in moving things along.

The name must live for ever. The custom has to live for ever. If one person drops it somebody else picks it up, whether they are related or interested; they take it on for gain sometimes, but they carry it on for the good of the tribe. No name can go out of existence.

– Jane Constance Cook, 1936

Notes

Prologue

1 Pronounced "Ga-aax-sta-lass," her name translates as "Breakfast Giver."
2 Kwakwa̱ka̱'wakw First Nations comprise seventeen tribes that share the Kwak̓wala language. See the U'mista Cultural Centre website.
3 *Kwagu'ł* is pronounced "Kwa-gee-you-l-th"; *Gix̱sa̱m* is pronounced "Gi-yik-sam."
4 The Kwagu'ł tribe is associated with the primary village at Tsax̱is (Fort Rupert).
5 The 'Na̱mǥis tribe is associated with the primary village at 'Ya̱lis.

Introduction: "Having Oneness on Your Face"

1 Dara Culhane is a member of the family through marriage; author of *An Error in Judgement: The Politics of Medical Care in an Indian/White Community;* and an anthropologist at Simon Fraser University.
2 Ann Stoler, "Imperial Debris: Reflections on Ruins and Ruination," *Cultural Anthropology* 23, 2 (2008): 195. See also Laura Bear, "Ruins and Ghosts: The Domestic Uncanny and the Materialization of Anglo-Indian Genealogies in Karagpur," in *Ghosts of Memory: Essays on Remembrance and Relatedness,* ed. Janet Carsten (Malden: Blackwell, 2007), 36-57.
3 Margaret Anderson Seguin and Tammy Anderson Blumhagen, "Memories and Moments: Conversations and Recollections," *BC Studies* 104 (1995): 69-83.
4 For another example of approaching individual histories through family or clan history, see Jennifer Nez Denetdale, *Reclaiming Diné History: The Legacies of Navajo Chief Manuelito and Juanita* (Tucson: University of Arizona Press, 2007).
5 Luke Lassiter, *The Chicago Guide to Collaborative Ethnography* (Chicago: University of Chicago Press, 2005). Perhaps the greatest challenge here is not to overly impose scholarly frameworks that obscure what it is people want to say. See

Vine Deloria Jr., *Custer Died for Your Sins: An Indian Manifesto* (Norman: University of Oklahoma Press, 1973), 130-37. See also Luke Lassiter, "From 'Reading over the Shoulders of Natives' to 'Reading alongside Natives,' Literally: Toward a Collaborative and Reciprocal Ethnography," *Journal of Anthropological Research* 57, 2 (2001): 137-49; Wendy Wickwire and Harry Robinson, *Write It on Your Heart: The Epic World of an Okanagan Storyteller* (Vancouver: Talonbooks/Theytus, 1989); Julie Cruikshank, in collaboration with Angela Sidney, Kitty Smith, and Annie Ned, *Life Lived Like a Story: Life Stories of Three Yukon Elders* (Vancouver: UBC Press, 1990); Jonathan Friedman, "Myth, History and Political Identity," *Cultural Anthropology* 7, 2 (1992): 194-210.

6 Linda Tuhiwai Smith, *Decolonizing Methodologies: Research and Indigenous Peoples* (New York: Zed Books, 1999).

7 In 'Y̲alis, families and organizations hold loonie auctions to raise funds for a number of reasons, including to pay for travel, expensive medical treatments, or larger events such as reunions.

8 See Kwakiutl Indian Band, "Our Land: In the Beginning," http://www.kwakiutl.bc.ca/land/beginning.htm.

9 Joseph Masco, "It Is a Strict Law That Bids Us Dance": Cosmologies, Colonialism, and Ritual Authority in the Kwakwa̲ka̲'wakw Potlatch, 1849-1922," *Comparative Studies in Society and History* 37, 1 (1995): 844.

10 See Bruce G. Miller, review of *Paddling to Where I Stand: Agnes Alfred, Qwiqwasutinuxw Noblewoman,* edited by Martine Reid and translated by Daisy Sewid-Smith, *American Indian Culture and Research Journal* 29, 2 (2005): 149. Martine Reid and Daisy Sewid-Smith, for example, acknowledge that their collaboration with Agnes Alfred was forged through motivations on Agnes Alfred's part that included "clear[ing] up community rumours and set[ting] the record straight about certain facts and their consequences": see Martine Reid, ed., *Paddling to Where I Stand: Agnes Alfred, Qwiqwasutinuxw Noblewoman,* trans. Daisy Sewid-Smith (Vancouver: UBC Press, 2004), 193.

11 For a discussion about similar research dynamics in her home community, see Audra Simpson, "On Ethnographic Refusal: Indigeneity, 'Voice' and Colonial Citizenship," *Junctures* 9 (2007): 67-80.

12 Richard Price, *Alabi's World* (Baltimore: Johns Hopkins University Press, 1990), xvi-xvii.

13 Maurice Bloch, "Internal and External Memory: Different Ways of Being in History," in *Tense Past: Cultural Essays in Trauma and Memory,* ed. Paul Antze and Michael Lambek (New York: Routledge, 1996), 230. To Jonathan Friedman ("The Past in the Future: History and the Politics of Identity," *American Anthropologist* 94 [1992]: 837), the construction of history includes the simultaneous act of self-identification involving "the inevitable confrontation between Western intellectual practices of truth-value history and the practices of social groups or movements constructing themselves by making history." As he writes, "The latter is by no means a unitary or homogeneous process, since it depends upon the ways in which agents are situated in a larger social context."

14 Peter Gow, *An Amazonian Myth and Its History* (Oxford: Oxford University Press, 2001), 20.

15 I reference Daisy Sewid-Smith's title *Prosecution or Persecution* (Cape Mudge: Nu-yum-baleess Society, 1979).

16 On collaboration in First Nation communities in British Columbia, see Ron Ignace, George Speck, and Renee Taylor, "Some Native Perspectives on Anthropology and Public Policy," in *Anthropology, Public Policy and Native Peoples in Canada,* ed. Noel Dyck and James Waldram (Montreal and Kingston: McGill-Queen's University Press, 1993), 166-91. The "editorial board" included Pearl Alfred, George Speck, Kelly-Anne Speck, Nella Nelson, Wedłidi Speck, and Dara Culhane.

17 For a discussion about the political contexts of scholarship to which I refer, please see Sherry Ortner, "Resistance and the Problem of Ethnographic Refusal," in *Anthropology and Social Theory: Culture, Power, and the Acting Subject* (Durham, NC: Duke University Press, 2006), 42-62.

18 In a paper prepared in 1990 for the Kwakiutl District Council titled "An Outline History of the Kwa̱kwa̱ka'wakw Struggle for the Recognition of Aboriginal Title and Self-Determination," George Speck writes that "oweetna-kula ... is our traditional statement of Aboriginal Title and means 'one with the land and sea we own'" (p. 3).

19 Hirokazu Miyazaki includes activities as diverse as gift giving, archival research, Christian rituals, and business practices. See Hirokazu Miyazaki, *The Method of Hope: Anthropology, Philosophy, and Fijian Knowledge* (Palo Alto, CA: Stanford University Press, 2004), 3. Māori scholar Russell Bishop similarly writes about something he describes as a "non-accountable, non-describable way of knowing" characterized by "connectedness and engagement by kinship." He invokes the Māori concept of *whanaungatanga* in his discussion of culturally relevant research methods. See Russell Bishop, "Freeing Ourselves from Neo-colonial Domination in Research: A Kaupapa Māori Approach to Creating Knowledge," in *The Sage Handbook of Qualitative Research,* ed. Norman Denzin and Yvonna Lincoln (Thousand Oaks, CA: Sage, 2005), 118. Similarly, Cree scholar Shawn Wilson writes about the bedrock of "relational accountability," about recognizing relationships as a guiding principle to research with and by aboriginal communities. See Shawn Wilson, *Research Is Ceremony: Indigenous Research Methods* (Winnipeg: Fernwood, 2008), 77-78.

20 One such larger endeavour may be internal reconciliation. See Val Napoleon, "Who Gets to Say What Happened?" in *Reconciliation Issues for the Gitksan: Intercultural Dispute Resolution in Aboriginal Contexts,* ed. Catherine Bell and David Kahane (Vancouver: UBC Press, 2004), 176-95.

Part I: The Living Text

1 See Aaron Glass, "From Cultural Salvage to Brokerage: The Mythologization of Mungo Martin and the Emergence of Northwest Coast Art," *Museum Anthropology* 29, 1 (2006): 20-43.

2 The living text may be counted among what Stoler calls the imperial debris that "saturate[s] the subsoil of people's lives and persist[s], sometimes subjacently, over a longer durée." Ann Stoler, "Imperial Debris: Reflections on Ruins and Ruination," *Cultural Anthropology* 23, 2 (2008): 192.

3 In British Columbia, given the current bureaucratic structures for filing land claims and the legal protocols through which aboriginal rights are challenged, historical and contemporary scholarship figures prominently.

4 Quoted in U'mista Cultural Centre, *Box of Treasures,* Chuck Olin, director and producer (Watertown, MA: Documentary Educational Resources, 1983). For an analysis of the role of this history of representation in the solidification of Kwakwa̱ka̱'wakw identity, see also Barbara Saunders, "From a Colonized Consciousness to Autonomous Identity: Shifting Relations between the Kwa̱kwa̱ka'-wakw and Canadian Nations," *Dialectical Anthropology* 22, 2 (1997): 137-58.

5 Marcel Mauss, "Essai sur le don: Forme et raison de l'échange dans les sociétés archaïques [An essay on the gift: The form and reason of exchange in archaic societies]," *Année Sociologique* 1 (1923-24): 30-186.

6 Claude Lévi-Strauss, "The Sorcerer and His Magic," in *Structural Anthropology,* vol. 1 (London: Peregrine, 1963), 167-85.

7 See, among others, Tom McFeat, ed., *Indians of the North Pacific Coast* (Toronto: McClelland and Stewart, 1996), 134-66; Wayne Suttles and Aldona Jonaitis, "History of Research in Ethnology," in *Handbook of the North American Indian,* vol. 7, *Northwest Coast,* ed. Wayne Suttles (Washington, DC: Smithsonian Institute, 1990), 87.

8 Ruth Benedict, *Patterns of Culture* (Boston: Houghton and Mifflin Company, 1934).

9 George Dawson, *Notes and Observations on the Kwakiool,* Transactions of the Royal Society of Canada, vol. 5, sec. 2 (Montreal: Dawson, 1888); Edward Curtis, *The North American Indian,* vol. 10, *The Kwakiutl* (Norwood, MA: Plimpton Press, 1915); Homer Barnett, "The Nature of the Potlatch," *American Anthropologist* 40, 3 (1938): 349-58; Stanley Walens, *Feasting with Cannibals: On Kwakiutl Cosmology* (Princeton, NJ: Princeton University Press, 1981).

10 Vernon Kobrinsky, "Dynamics of the Fort Rupert Class Struggle: Fighting with Property Vertically Revisited," in *Papers in Honour of Harry Hawthorn,* ed. Verne Serle and Herbert Taylor (Bellingham, WA: Northwest Scientific Association, 1975), 32-59; Eric Wolf, *Envisioning Power: Ideologies of Dominance and Crisis* (Berkeley: University of California Press, 1990).

11 For summaries on the state of theorizing the potlatch, see Thomas Irvin, "The Northwest Coast Potlatch since Boas, 1897-1972," *Anthropology* 1, 1 (1977): 65-77; Marianne Bölscher, *The Potlatch in Anthropological Theory: A Re-evaluation of Certain Ethnographic Data and Theoretical Approaches* (Nortorf, Germany: Volkerkundliche Arbeitsgemeinschaft, 1982); Suttles and Jonaitis, "History of Research in Ethnology," 84-86; Joseph Masco, "'It Is a Strict Law That Bids Us Dance': Cosmologies, Colonialism, and Ritual Authority in the Kwakwa̱ka̱'wakw Potlatch, 1849-1922," *Comparative Studies in Society and History* 37, 1 (1995): 41-75; and Isabelle Schulte-Tenckhoff, "Misrepresenting the Potlatch," in *Expanding the Economic Concept of Exchange: Deception, Self-Deception, and Illusions,* ed. Caroline Gerschlager (Boston: Kluwer Academic Publishers, 2001), 167-88.

12 Irving Goldman, *The Mouth of Heaven: An Introduction to Kwakiutl Religious Thought* (New York: Wiley, 1975), ix.

13 See Walens, *Feasting with Cannibals,* and Judith Berman, "Red Salmon and Red Cedar Bark: Another Look at the Nineteenth-Century Kwakwaka'wakw Winter Ceremonial," *BC Studies* 125-26 (2000): 53-98. On cultural ecology, see Stuart Piddocke, "The Potlatch System of the Southern Kwakiutl: A New Perspective," *Southwestern Journal of Anthropology* 21 (1965): 244-64. On political economy, see Helen Codere, *Fighting with Property: A Study of Kwakiutl Potlatching and*

Warfare, 1792-1930, Monographs of the American Ethnological Society 18 (New York: J.J. Augustin, 1950) and Melville Herskovits, *Economic Anthropology* (New York: Knopf, 1952).

14 Benedict, *Patterns of Culture;* Alan Dundes, "Heads or Tails: A Psychoanalytic Study of Potlatch," *Journal of Psychological Anthropology* 2, 4 (1979): 395-424; Mark Fleisher, "The Potlatch: A Symbolic and Psychoanalytic View," *Current Anthropology* 22, 1 (1981): 69-71.

15 See Barnett, "The Nature of the Potlatch," 349-58; Philip Drucker and Robert Heizer, *To Make My Name Good: A Reexamination of the Southern Kwakiutl Potlatch* (Berkeley: University of California Press, 1967).

16 In these works, the potlatch complex is approached through kin-based access to and ownership of specific territories and resource sites that are intimately tied to 'na̲'mima histories and may form the basis of legal arguments. See D. Bruce Johnsen, "The Formation and Protection of Property Rights among the Southern Kwakiutl Indians," *Journal of Legal Studies* 15, 1 (1986): 41-67; Ronald Trosper, "Northwest Coast Indigenous Institutions That Supported Resilience and Sustainability," *Ecological Economics* 41, 2 (2002): 329-44; Dianne Newell and Dorothee Schreiber, "Collaborations on the Periphery: The Wolcott-Sewid Potlatch Controversy," *BC Studies* 152 (2006): 7-34.

17 See Isabelle Schulte-Tenckoff, "Potlatch and Totem: The Attraction of America's Northwest Coast," in *Tourism: Manufacturing the Exotic,* ed. Pierre Rossel (Copenhagen: International Working Group for International Affairs, 1988), 117-47; Aldona Jonaitis, ed., *Chiefly Feasts: The Enduring Kwakiutl Potlatch* (Seattle: University of Washington Press, 1991); Masco, "Competitive Displays," 837-52; Anne E. Guernsey Allan, "All the World's a Stage: The Nineteenth-Century Kwakwa̲ka̲'wakw (Kwakiutl) House as Theater," *American Indian Culture and Research Journal* 21, 4 (1997): 29-73; Ira Jacknis, *The Storage Box of Tradition: Kwakiutl Art, Anthropologists, and Museums, 1881-1981* (Washington, DC: Smithsonian Institution, 2002); Aaron Glass, "The Thin Edge of the Wedge: Dancing around the Potlatch Ban, 1921-1951," in *Right to Dance: Dancing for Rights,* ed. Naomi Jackson (Banff: Banff Centre, 2004), 51-82.

18 See Jacob Gruber, "Ethnographic Salvage and the Shaping of Anthropology," *American Anthropologist* 72, 6 (1970): 1289-99.

19 What Robert Paine calls "cultural counterfeit thinking," a view that "has to do with the relation of past to present in which the present is 'counterfeit' if it is not in the likeness of the past." See Robert Paine, "Aboriginality, Authenticity and the Settler World," in *Signifying Identities: Anthropological Perspectives on Boundaries and Contested Values,* ed. Anthony Cohen (Routledge: New York, 2000), 88.

20 What emerged as the early culture concept was in part the result of Franz Boas's critique of social evolutionism, a move away from universalizing theories of human development toward a consideration of societies in their historical, geographical, and "psychological" particularity. His standpoint was known as historical particularism.

21 Renato Rosaldo, "Imperialist Nostalgia," in "Memory and Counter-Memory," special issue, *Representations* 26 (1989): 107-8.

22 These categories are still evident in the popular use of labels that contrast "traditional" with "acculturated" or "assimilated" types of persons. See Roy Harvey

Pearce, *Savagism and Civilization: A Study of the Indian and the American Mind* (Berkeley: University of California Press, 1988).

23 See Michael Harkin, "Ethnographic Deep Play: Boas, McIlwraith, and Fictive Adoption on the Northwest Coast," in *Strangers to Relatives,* ed. Sergei Kan (Lincoln: University of Nebraska Press, 2001), 65, for an interesting discussion of adoption practices on the Northwest Coast that extends to the political, legal, and social practices that surround naming. Regarding ethnonyms, names for groups of people, Harkin notes that Boas named the Kwakiutl. For a diverse selection of works by aboriginal and non-aboriginal scholars regarding identity, representation, and authenticity, see Vine Deloria Jr., *Custer Died for Your Sins: An Indian Manifesto* (Norman: University of Oklahoma Press, 1973); Robert Berkhofer, *The White Man's Indian* (New York: Vintage Books, 1979); Marcia Crosby, "Construction of the Imaginary Indian," in *Vancouver Anthology: The Institutional Politics of Art,* ed. Stan Douglas (Vancouver: Talonbooks, 1991), 267-91; Daniel Francis, *The Imaginary Indian: The Image of the Indian in Canadian Culture* (Vancouver: Arsenal Pulp Press, 1992); Kateri Damm, "Says Who? Colonialism, Identity and Defining Indigenous Literature," in *Looking at the Words of Our People,* ed. J. Armstrong (Penticton, BC: Theytus, 1993), 9-26; Gail Valaskakis, "Rights and Warriors, First Nations, Media and Identity," *ARIEL* 25, 1 (1994): 60-72; Paine, "Aboriginality, Authenticity and the Settler World," 77-116; Bonita Lawrence, *"Real" Indians and Others: Mixed-Blood Urban Native Peoples and Indigenous Nationhood* (Vancouver: UBC Press, 2004); and Paige Raibmon, *Authentic Indians: Episodes of Encounter from the Late-Nineteenth-Century Northwest Coast* (Durham, NC: Duke University Press, 2005).

24 Jeffrey Sissons identifies three primary axes of oppressive authenticity: eco-authenticity, biological authenticity, and tribal authenticity. See Jeffrey Sissons, *First Peoples: Indigenous Cultures and Their Futures* (London: Reaktion Press, 2005), 37-59.

25 See Leslie Robertson, *Imagining Difference: Legend, Curse, and Spectacle in a Canadian Mining Town* (Vancouver: UBC Press, 2004).

26 Jeffrey Sissons calls this complex of inscriptions eco-authenticity. See also Raymond Hames, "The Ecologically Noble Savage Debate," *Annual Review of Anthropology* 36 (2007): 177-90.

27 Helen Codere, introduction to *Kwakiutl Ethnography,* by Franz Boas, edited by Helen Codere (Chicago: University of Chicago Press, 1966), xxx.

28 See Ira Jacknis, "George Hunt, Collector of Indian Specimens," in *Chiefly Feasts: The Enduring Kwakiutl Potlatch,* ed. Aldona Jonaitis (Seattle: University of Washington Press, 1991), 181; and Charles Briggs and Richard Bauman, "'The Foundation of All Future Researches': Franz Boas, George Hunt, Native American Texts, and the Construction of Modernity," *American Quarterly* 51, 3 (1999): 489.

29 See also Harry Whitehead, "The Hunt for Quesalid: Tracking Levi-Strauss' Shaman," *Anthropology and Medicine* 7, 2 (2000): 149-68.

30 Codere, introduction, xxiv.

31 Boas did write about the effect of current conditions and political issues on Kwakwa̲ka̲'wakw people, but these topics appeared only in personal correspondences, newspapers, or letters to colonial bureaucrats. They were quite separate from his "scholarly" publications.

32 Codere, introduction, xxvii.

33 See Franz Boas, "Notes on Some Recent Changes in the Kwakiutl Language," *International Journal of American Linguistics* 7, 1-2 (1932): 90-93.

34 Codere, introduction, xxvii.

35 Judith Berman, "George Hunt and the Kwak'wala Texts," *Anthropological Linguistics* 36, 4 (1994): 483-514.

36 Briggs and Bauman, "The Foundation of All Future Researches," 489.

37 As Julie Cruikshank's work reminds us, there are no pure narratives. Stories have social lives. As local knowledge is performed and translated, it becomes entangled in other powerful narratives, including the narratives scholars tell about others. See Julie Cruikshank, *The Social Life of Stories: Narrative and Knowledge in the Yukon Territory* (Lincoln: University of Nebraska, 1998) and her work *Do Glaciers Listen? Local Knowledge, Colonial Encounters, and Social Imagination* (Vancouver: UBC Press, 2005).

38 Berman, "George Hunt and the Kwak'wala Texts," 504.

39 See Kathleen Gough, "Anthropology and Imperialism," *Monthly Review* 19, 11 (1968): 403-35; Deloria, *Custer Died for Your Sins.*

40 James Clifford and George Marcus, eds., *Writing Culture: The Poetics and Politics of Ethnography* (Berkeley: University of California Press, 1986); Lila Abu-Lughod, "Writing against Culture," in *Recapturing Anthropology: Working in the Present,* ed. Richard G. Fox (Santa Fe, NM: School of American Research, 1991), 137-54, 161-62. From the centre of this so-called crisis, Edward Bruner suggested that dominant narratives shape ethnographers' texts, guiding the way other societies are portrayed: "The dominant story constructed about Native American culture change saw the present as disorganization, the past as glorious, and the future as assimilation. Now, however, we have a new narrative: the present is viewed as a resistance movement, the past as exploitation, and the future as ethnic resurgence." See Edward M. Bruner, "Ethnography as Narrative," in *The Anthropology of Experience,* ed. Victor W. Turner and Edward M. Bruner (Urbana: University of Illinois Press, 1986), 139.

41 Jonaitis, *Chiefly Feasts,* 31. Anthropological work about Kwakwa̱ka̱'wakw peoples continued to revisit earlier works, paying particular attention to how anthropological knowledge is produced and to constructions of cultural authenticity. See also Masco, "It Is a Strict Law," and Glass, "From Cultural Salvage to Brokerage," 20-43.

42 Janine Cannizzo, "George Hunt and the Invention of Kwakiutl Culture," *Canadian Review of Sociology and Anthropology* 20, 1 (1983): 44-58; Judith Berman, "The Culture as It Appears to the Indian Himself: Boas, George Hunt, and the Methods of Ethnography," in *Volksgeist as Method and Ethic: Essays on Boasian Ethnography and the German Anthropological Tradition,* ed. George Stocking (Madison: University of Wisconsin Press, 1996), 215-56; Briggs and Bauman, "The Foundation of All Future Researches," 479-528; and Whitehead, "The Hunt for Quesalid," 149-68.

43 Bronwen Douglas, "Christian Citizens: Women and Negotiations of Modernity in Vanuatu," *Contemporary Pacific* 14, 1 (2002): 2. See also Michael Harkin and Sergei Kan, eds., "Native American Women's Responses to Christianity," special issue, *Ethnohistory* 43, 4 (1996).

44 John Comaroff and Jean Comaroff, *Ethnography and the Historical Imagination* (Boulder, CO: Westview Press, 1992), 259.

45 Ibid., 260. See also John Barker, "Tangled Reconciliations: The Anglican Church and the Nisga'a of British Columbia," *American Ethnologist* 25, 3 (1998): 433-51.

46 Sherry Ortner, *Anthropology and Social Theory: Culture, Power, and the Acting Subject* (Durham, NC: Duke University Press, 2006), 44.

47 Ibid., 46.

48 See, for example, Michael Brown, "On Resisting Resistance," *American Anthropologist* 98, 4 (1996): 729-35; June Nash, "Defying Deterritorialization: Autonomy Movements against Globalization," in *Social Movements: An Anthropological Reader,* ed. June Nash (Malden, MA: John Wiley and Sons, 2004), 177-86; Anna Tsing, "Indigenous Voice," in *Indigenous Experience Today,* ed. Marisol de la Cadena and Orin Starn (New York: Berg 2007), 33-67; and Kay Warren, "Perils and Promises," in *Engaged Observer: Anthropology, Advocacy and Activism,* ed. Victoria Stanford and Asale Angel-Anjani (Newark, NJ: Rutgers University Press, 2008), 213-27.

49 Ortner, *Anthropology and Social Theory,* 9. For a compelling, contemporary view on salvage, see Virginia Dominguez, "For a Politics of Love and Rescue," *Cultural Anthropology* 15, 3 (2000): 361-93.

50 See Anne Marie Hilsdon, "Reconsidering Agency: Feminist Anthropologies in Asia," *Australian Journal of Anthropology* 18, 2 (2007): 127-37.

51 "By 'agency' I mean not a naturalized notion of the bounded, autonomous individual, but a presumed general human capacity to choose and act strategically, within the limits of local, gendered conceptions of subjectivity and unstable constellations of culture, religion, structure, personality, and circumstance." See Douglas, "Christian Citizens," 25.

52 Whitehead, "The Hunt for Quesalid," 149.

53 Joan Schwartz and Terry Cook, "Archives, Records and Power," *Archival Science* 2, 1 (2002): 1-19.

54 Ann Laura Stoler, "Colonial Archives and the Arts of Governance: On the Content in the Form," in *Refiguring the Archive,* ed. C. Hamilton et al.(London: Kluwer Academic Publishers, 2002), 83-100.

55 Ibid., 88. Stoler quotes Michel-Rolph Trouillot, *Silencing the Past: Power and the Production of History* (Boston: Beacon Press, 1995), 55.

56 Christopher Bracken, *The Potlatch Papers: A Colonial Case History* (Chicago: University of Chicago Press, 1997), 1.

57 Douglas Cole and Ira Chaikin, *An Iron Hand upon the People: The Law against the Potlatch on the Northwest Coast* (Vancouver: Douglas and McIntyre, 1990), 117.

58 Ibid., 132. For the record, Jane and Stephen were married in 1888.

59 Ibid.

60 Ibid., 181-82.

61 Ibid., 180.

62 Tina Loo, "Dan Cranmer's Potlatch: Law as Coercion, Symbol, and Rhetoric in British Columbia, 1884-1951," *Canadian Historical Review* 68, 2 (1992): 163. For other readings of this potlatch, see Helen Codere, "Dan Cranmer's Potlatch," in *Indians of the North Pacific Coast,* ed. Tom McFeat (Toronto: McClelland and Stewart, 1966), 116-18; Douglas Cole, "The History of the Kwakiutl Potlatch,"

in *Chiefly Feasts: The Enduring Kwakiutl Potlatch,* ed. Aldona Jonaitis (Seattle: University of Washington Press, 1991), 135-68; and Saunders, "From a Colonized Consciousness to Autonomous Identity," 137-58.

63 Loo, "Dan Cranmer's Potlatch," 163.

64 Ibid.

65 Robin Brownlie and Mary-Ellen Kelm, "Desperately Seeking Absolution: Native Agency as Colonialist Alibi?" *Canadian Historical Review* 75, 4 (1994): 554.

66 Ibid., 545. Their discussion of Jane Cook is set within a critical review of works by Tina Loo, Douglas Cole, and Ira Chaiken wherein they state that these authors "go beyond the argument for the recognition of Native agency to one that uses evidence of Native resilience and strength to soften, and at times to deny," the devastating impacts of colonial incursion.

67 Ibid.

68 Douglas Cole and J.R. Miller, "Desperately Seeking Absolution: Responses and a Reply," *Canadian Historical Review* 76, 4 (1995): 630.

69 See also Bronwen Douglas, "Provocative Readings in Intransigent Archives: Finding Aneityumese Women," *Oceania* 70, 2 (1999): 111-12.

70 Jennifer Brown, "Reading beyond the Missionaries, Dissecting Responses," *Ethnohistory* 43, 4 (1996): 717.

71 Robert Galois, *Kwakwaka'wakw Settlements, 1775-1920: A Geographical Analysis and Gazetteer* (Vancouver: UBC Press, 1994), 314.

72 Ibid., 19; see also Cole Harris, *Making Native Space: Colonialism, Resistance, and Reserves in British Columbia* (Vancouver: UBC Press, 2002).

73 Margaret Whitehead, "A Useful Christian Woman: First Nations' Women and Protestant Missionary Work in British Columbia," *Atlantis* 18, 1-2 (1992-93): 144-45.

74 Whitehead notes that Jane Cook was called "a great Chieftainess" by one missionary (ibid., 147) and wrongly assumes from her birth place in Seattle that she was of Salish heritage (ibid., 161n38).

75 Ibid., 145.

76 Comaroff and Comaroff, *Ethnograghy and the Historical Imagination,* 211.

77 See L.L. Langness and Gelya Frank, *Lives: An Anthropological Approach to Biography* (Novato, CA: Chandler and Sharp, 1981); David Mandelbaum, "The Study of Life History: Gandhi," *Current Anthropology* 14, 3 (1973): 177-96; James Freeman, *Untouchable: An Indian Life History* (Palo Alto, CA: Stanford University Press, 1979); Vincent Crapanzano, "Life Histories," *American Anthropologist* 86, 4 (1984): 953-60, and *Tuhami: Portrait of a Moroccan* (Chicago: University of Chicago Press, 1980); Julie Cruikshank, in collaboration with Angela Sidney, Kitty Smith, and Annie Ned, *Life Lived Like a Story: Life Stories of Three Yukon Elders* (Vancouver: UBC Press, 1990); Blanca Muratorio, *The Life and Times of Grandfather Alonso: Culture and History in the Upper Amazon* (New Brunswick, NJ: Rutgers University Press, 1991); and Caroline B. Brettell, "Gendered Lives: Transitions and Turning Points in Personal, Family, and Historical Time," *Current Anthropology* 43, 4 (2002): 45-61.

78 See, for examples, Personal Narratives Group, *Interpreting Women's Lives: Feminist Theory and Personal Narratives* (Bloomington: Indiana University Press, 1989); Ruth Behar, "Rage and Redemption: Reading the Life Story of a Mexican

Marketing Woman," *Feminist Studies* 16, 2 (1990): 223-58; Lila Abu-Lughod, *Writing Women's Worlds: Bedouin Stories* (Berkeley: University of California Press, 1993); Ruth Behar and Deborah Gordon, eds., *Women Writing Culture* (Berkeley: University of California Press, 1995); Caroline B. Brettell, "Blurred Genres and Blended Voices: Life History, Biography, Autobiography, and the Auto/Ethnography of Women's Lives," in *Auto/Ethnography: Rewriting the Self and the Social,* ed. Deborah Reed-Danahay (Oxford: Berg, 1997), 223-46; and Karen McCarthy-Brown, *Mama Lola: A Vodou Priestess in Brooklyn* (Berkeley: University of California Press, 2001).

79 See Wendy Wickwire and Harry Robinson, *Write It on Your Heart: The Epic World of an Okanagan Storyteller* (Vancouver: Talonbooks/Theytus, 1989); Cruikshank et al., *Life Lived Like a Story;* Cruikshank, *The Social Life of Stories* and *Do Glaciers Listen?;* Muratorio, *The Life and Times of Grandfather Alonso;* Margaret Blackman, *During My Time: Florence Edenshaw Davidson, a Haida Woman* (Seattle: University of Washington Press, 1982) and "The Individual and Beyond: Reflections on the Life History Process," *Anthropology and Humanism Quarterly* 16, 2 (1991): 56-62; Jonathan Friedman, "Myth, History and Political Identity," *Cultural Anthropology* 7, 2 (1992): 194-210; Richard Price, *Travels with Tooy: History, Memory, and African-American Imagination* (Chicago: University of Chicago Press, 2008); Jeremy MacClancy, "Nakomaha: A Counter-Colonial Life and Its Contexts – Anthropological Approaches to Biography," *Oceania* 77, 2 (2007): 191-214; and Didier Fassin, Frédéric Le Marcis, and Todd Lethata, "Life and Times of Magda A: Telling a Story of Violence in South Africa," *Current Anthropology* 49, 2 (2008): 225-46.

80 Charles Nowell, *Smoke from Their Fires: The Life of a Kwakiutl Chief,* ed. Clellan Ford (New Haven: Yale University Press, 1941), 1.

81 Harry Assu and Joy Inglis, *Assu of Cape Mudge: Recollections of a Coastal Indian Chief* (Vancouver: UBC Press, 1989), ix.

82 Nowell, *Smoke from Their Fires,* 214.

83 Reincarnation is recognized as a culturally relevant explanation for reckoning relatedness among families and is sometimes used by people with whom I work.

84 James Sewid, *Guests Never Leave Hungry: The Autobiography of James Sewid, a Kwakiutl Indian,* ed. James Spradley (New Haven: Yale University Press, 1969), 49.

85 Assu and Inglis, *Assu of Cape Mudge,* 12-13.

86 This work encompasses the spectrum of Kwakwa̲ka̲'wakw oratory, including several kinds of *'nuy'em* (myth), *'cek'alem* (genealogies), oral histories, chants and songs, and speeches and personal reminiscences. See Martine Reid, ed., *Paddling to Where I Stand: Agnes Alfred, Qwiqwasutinuxw Noblewoman,* trans. Daisy Sewid-Smith (Vancouver: UBC Press, 2004), xxiv.

87 Ibid., xxvii.

88 As Daisy Sewid-Smith writes: "Our ritual world is not a democracy, nor has it a consensus-building process in which the whole Clan participates. It has, however, a strict line of succession for most positions ... I do not need to use footnotes for this discussion, since I am a primary source and a trained specialist who has the lineage and authority to speak as I do": Daisy Sewid-Smith (My-yah-nelth), "The Continuing Reshaping of Our Ritual World by Academic Adjuncts," *Anthropology and Education Quarterly* 28, 4 (1997): 549, 594.

89 Reid, *Paddling to Where I Stand,* 69.
90 Ibid., 119.
91 Ibid., 180.
92 Ibid., 109. According to Helen Codere (see the introduction to *Kwakiutl Ethnology,* 95), *p̓a̱sa* means "to flatten" in Kwak̓wala. It refers to flattening "a rival under a pile of blankets," what is commonly understood as the potlatch. Irving Goldman (*Mouth of Heaven,* 133) interprets *p̓a̱sa* as "refer[ring] to the gradual flattening of a soft basket from which objects had been removed," the "emptying out in behalf of a name." The term *potlatch* is a Chinook jargon word that means "to give away." Its use became popular on the Coast in the early nineteenth century.
93 Reid, *Paddling to Where I Stand,* 177.
94 Ibid., 243n13.
95 Ibid., 195-206.
96 Daisy Sewid-Smith, *Prosecution or Persecution* (Cape Mudge: Nu-yum-baleess Society, 1979), 87.
97 Indian Agent William Halliday to the Secretary, 19 May 1922, Library and Archives Canada (LAC), Department of Indian Affairs, RG 10, vol. 3630, file 6244-4, pt. 2.
98 Sewid-Smith, *Prosecution or Persecution,* 2.
99 Forrest LaViolette, *The Struggle for Survival: Indian Cultures and the Protestant Ethic in British Columbia* (Toronto: University of Toronto Press, 1973), 97.
100 In the summer of 2006, I received a phone call from someone in the family who had contributed to the book. According to the caller, "potlatchers" were not supportive of writing a book to commemorate Jane Cook because the memory of their ancestors' suffering in prison was still too close. This was the only time I encountered this term.
101 A number of indigenous women have been singled out as cultural betrayers in the annals of history and in the tides of community judgment: La Malinche (ca. 1496-1529), among Mexican Mayans; Sacajawea (1790-1812) of the Shoshone; and Truganini (ca. 1803-76), a Tasmanian Aboriginal. In all instances, the women were involved with Europeans – intimately, or more often in the capacity of guides, translators, and advocates for their people.
102 The Black Elk family also contend with the question of spiritual authenticity. Esther DeSersa et al., *Black Elk Lives: Conversations with the Black Elk Family,* ed. Hilda Nierhardt and Lori Utrecht (Lincoln: University of Nebraska Press, 2000), xiv. See also Thomas Johnson, *Also Called Sacajawea: Chief Woman's Stolen Identity* (Long Grove, IL: Waveland Press, 2008).
103 Briggs and Bauman, "The Foundation of All Future Researches," 479; see also Goldman, *The Mouth of Heaven,* viii.
104 Briggs and Bauman, "The Foundation of All Future Researches," 479.
105 James Werbner, ed., *Postcolonial Subjectivities in Africa* (New York: Zed Books, 2002), 19. On the current questions riddling memory studies, see, for example, Michel-Rolph Trouillot, *Silencing the Past: Power and the Production of History* (Boston: Beacon, 1995); David Berliner, "The Abuses of Memory: Reflections on the Memory Boom in Anthropology," *Anthropological Quarterly* 78, 1 (2005): 197-211; and Katharine Hodgkin and Susannah Radstone, eds., *Contested Pasts: The Politics of Memory* (New York: Routledge 2003).

Part II: *Du̲k̲wa̲'esa̲la* (Looking Around on the Beach)

1 The title of this chapter was suggested by Wedłidi Speck. Other suggestions included "*Bak'way'thla* (Character of a Person)," "*Hutłilala* (Pay Attention)," and "*Awi'nak̓wa* (Rocky Place)." I use these titles for other sections.

2 Jane received the name G̲a'ax̲sta'las from her grandmother of the Munday family, who was a member of the *Ts!o'tsena 'na̲'mima* from Dzawadi (Knight Inlet). Within each 'na̲'mima, there are approximately fifty ranked names distributed among the children of chiefs. The names are part of a noble suite of positions that originate from first ancestors and designate their seats. Among the Kwakwa̲ka̲'wakw, according to Irving Goldman, in *The Mouth of Heaven: An Introduction to Kwakiutl Religious Thought* (New York: Wiley, 1975), 61, there are 658 ranked positions or names.

3 See Franz Boas, *Kwakiutl Ethnography,* ed. Helen Codere (Chicago: University of Chicago Press, 1966), 44, and Eric Wolf, *Envisioning Power: Ideologies of Dominance and Crisis* (Berkeley: University of California Press, 1999), 83-84.

4 By way of illustration, in the oft-cited list of twenty-two tribes that make up the Kwakwa̲ka̲'wakw confederacy, the Kwagu'ł (of Tsax̲is) occupy the highest rank, the Da̲'naxda'x̲w (of T'sadzis'nukwa̲ame) peoples are ranked fifth, and the G̲usgima̲xw (of X̲wa̲tis) tribes occupy the fifteenth position. See Robert Galois, *Kwakwa̲ka̲'wakw Settlements, 1775-1920: A Geographical Analysis and Gazetteer* (Vancouver: UBC Press, 1994), 7, 147, 207, 366.

5 According to William Wasden Jr., *'Nulis* translates as "Oldest in the World."

6 *Wadzedalaga* translates as "You're so important, I'm a slave to you." Several individuals from other clans have the name G̲a'ax̲sta'las. The name is not exclusive to Jane Constance Cook. In this book it is used interchangeably with her English name.

7 The origins of English names are intriguing. Missionaries invested in baptism named some people. The Reverend Alfred Hall baptized individuals in the name of his acquaintances in England (upon their request). See Charles Nowell, *Smoke from Their Fires: The Life of a Kwakiutl Chief,* ed. Clellan Ford (New Haven: Yale University Press, 1941). Some Kwakwa̲ka̲'wakw people assumed descriptive names composed by other members of their community. Others took names in reference to friendships with European traders or explorers.

8 *Numaym* is an earlier linguistic rendition of *'na̲'mima* used by Franz Boas and others until the introduction of the U'mista grammar. In quotes from other sources, I maintain the original spelling.

9 George Speck, "An Outline History of the Kwa̲kwa̲ka'wakw Struggle for the Recognition of Aboriginal Title and Self-Determination" (paper prepared for the Kwakiutl District Council, 1990), 2. See also Wayne Suttles, "Streams of Property, Armor of Wealth: The Traditional Kwakiutl Potlatch," in *Chiefly Feasts: The Enduring Kwakiutl Potlatch,* ed. Aldona Jonaitis (Vancouver: Douglas and McIntyre, 1991), 71-134.

10 Speck, "An Outline History of the Kwa̲kwa̲ka'wakw Struggle for the Recognition of Aboriginal Title and Self-Determination."

11 Ṫła̲kwa'ił was the daughter of Hiłdzakw (Bella Bella) Chief Ha̲mzid.

12 See Edward Curtis, *The North American Indian,* vol. 10, *The Kwakiutl* (Norwood, MA: Plimpton Press, 1915), 114, 220-26, 242. For a thorough discussion of

Hamat̓sa, see Aaron Glass, "Conspicuous Consumption: An Intercultural History of the Kwakwaka'wakw Ha'mat'sa" (PhD diss., New York University, 2006).

13 Julia Averkieva and Mary Hunt, Kwakiutl Autobiographies, September 1930, American Philosophical Society Library and Archives (APS), 491.3 B63c 20.

14 Inherited privileges may include the right to give property away and rights to particular feast dishes, songs, and coppers. See Franz Boas, *Ethnology of the Kwakiutl,* Thirty-Fifth Annual Report (Washington, DC: Bureau of American Ethnology, 1921), 83.

15 Quoted in Franz Boas, *Contributions to the Ethnology of the Kwakiutl,* Columbia University Contributions to Anthropology, Vol. 3, (New York: Columbia University Press, 1925), 52-53.

16 Franz Boas, 1895, Report of the US National Museum, 358.

17 Wilson Duff, field notes, U'mista Cultural Centre Archives (UCCA).

18 Family members say that Stephen was seven years old when he and his mother returned to Friendly Cove.

19 See Galois, *Kwakwaka'wakw Settlements,* 310. According to Wedłidi Speck, Agnes Alfred spoke about Gaga keeping a smokehouse at the Nimpkish village Udzalas. Other 'Namgis villages and important fishing sites included Nenelgas and Xwalkw (at the mouth of the Nimpkish River).

20 In 'Yalis, they say that Gaga was *wiwak'wa* ("brothers" or first cousins) with Gwi'molas (Dan Cranmer's father).

21 Philip Drucker, *Northern and Central Nootkan Tribes,* Bureau of American Ethnology Bulletin 144 (Washington, DC: Smithsonian Institution/Bureau of American Ethnology, 1951), 375.

22 Traditions Consulting Services, "Mowachaht Aboriginal Title," prepared for Mowachaht/Muchalaht First Nation by Richard Ingles, Kevin Neary, and Sheila Savey, 2005, 30, 40.

23 They also traded goat wool and button blankets used in ceremonials. Kwakwaka'wakw communities acquired status items such as dentalia shells or woven cedar-bark baskets. See ibid.

24 According to Bell, "Her father was Dr. Billy, and he was the fourth-ranked chief of Mowachaht."

25 Curtis, in *The North American Indian,* 114, wrote that muskets were called "makayu, [magical death-dealing instrument]."

26 Friendly Cove was the summer site for Chief Maquinna's village.

27 The nations are Gwitalla, Kwixa, 'Walas Kwagu'ł, and Qwemkutes.

28 Speck, "An Outline History of the Kwakwaka'wakw Struggle for the Recognition of Aboriginal Title and Self-Determination," 6-7. See also Galois, *Kwakwaka'wakw Settlements,* 201-2, and Cole Harris, *Making Native Space: Colonialism, Resistance, and Reserves in British Columbia* (Vancouver: UBC Press, 2002), 17-44.

29 Joseph Masco, "'It Is a Strict Law That Bids Us Dance': Cosmologies, Colonialism, and Ritual Authority in the Kwakwaka'wakw Potlatch, 1849-1922," *Comparative Studies in Society and History* 37, 1 (1995): 53.

30 Wilson Duff, field notes, "The Village of the Kwakiutl Indians," UCCA.

31 Boas, *Contributions to the Ethnology of the Kwakiutl,* 111.

32 Gloria Cranmer-Webster, "Contemporary Kwakwaka'wakw Potlatches," in *The Spirit Within: Northwest Coast Native Art from the John H. Hauberg Collection* (Seattle: Seattle Art Museum, 1995), 195.

33 Gloria Cranmer-Webster, "Consumers, Then and Now," in *Constructing Cultures Then and Now: The Legacy of Franz Boas and the Jesup North Pacific Expedition, 1897-1902,* ed. Laurel Kendall and Igor Krupnik (Washington, DC: Arctic Studies Centre, National Museum of Natural History, Smithsonian Institution, 2003), 1-10.
34 Cranmer-Webster, "Contemporary Kwakwaka'wakw Potlatches," 193.
35 Judith Berman, "George Hunt and the Kwak'wala Texts," *Anthropological Linguistics* 36, 4 (1994): 489. As Francis Pine makes clear, genealogical knowledge may be used to exclude as well as to include. See "Naming the House and Naming the Land: Kinship and Social Groups in Highland Poland," *Journal of the Royal Anthropological Institute* 2, 3 (1996): 443-59.
36 Helen Codere, "Kwakiutl," in *Perspectives in American Indian Culture Change,* ed. Edward Spicer (Chicago: University of Chicago Press, 1961), 451.
37 Boas, *Ethnology of the Kwakiutl,* 836-1269.
38 Codere, "Kwakiutl," 466.
39 See Ruth Benedict, *Patterns of Culture* (Boston: Houghton and Mifflin Company, 1934); Wolf, *Envisioning Power;* and Codere, "Kwakiutl," 468-70.
40 Codere, "Kwakiutl," 467.
41 Speck, "An Outline History," 4.
42 Codere, "Kwakiutl," 454-81. The period was preceded by the "sharp decline" of the Kwakwaka'wakw population, by "a similarly sharp increase in the numbers of white Europeans in the area and in the frequency and intensity of contacts with Whites; and, last, a marked increase in the material wealth of the Kwakiutl" (ibid., 454-55).
43 Julia Averkieva and Mary Hunt, Kwakiutl Autobiographies, APS.
44 Ellen Neel was the daughter of Jane Cook's brother, Charlie Newman. She is remembered as the first Kwakwaka'wakw woman to become a notable carver. She apprenticed under her maternal grandfather, Charlie James, a renowned pole carver from Tsaxis. In the 1940s, Neel moved to Vancouver, where she became famous for her miniature totem poles, a form that her grandfather had created in the 1920s for sale to Alaska-bound tourists passing through Alert Bay. Her design was later adopted for tourism promotions to represent the City of Vancouver. See Phil Nuytten, *The Totem Pole Carvers: Charlie James, Ellen Neel, Mungo Martin* (Vancouver: Panorama Publications, 1982), 43.
45 *Native Voice* 5, 9 (1951): 9.
46 Robin Fisher, *Contact and Conflict: Indian-European Relations in British Columbia, 1774-1890* (Vancouver: UBC Press, 1990), 50-51.
47 Christie Jefferson, *Conquest by Law* (Ottawa: Solicitor General of Canada, 1994), 126-27.
48 Fisher, *Contact and Conflict,* 50-51. According to Barry Gough, an observer noted in 1859 that the HBC had also participated in the "indigenous practice of paying a reward" to slave-taking chiefs for slaves who were then returned to their communities. See Barry Gough, "Send a Gunboat! Checking Slavery and Controlling Liquor Traffic among Coast Indians of British Columbia in the 1860s," *Pacific Northwest Quarterly* 69, 4 (1978): 161.
49 Fisher, *Contact and Conflict,* 52; see also Jefferson, *Conquest by Law,* 127.
50 "A slave is designated by the expression q!aku q!ak'o, the basis of which is the root q!ak', which means 'to cut off the head.'" See Julia P. Averkieva, "Slavery

among the Indians of North America," translated by G. Elliott in 1957 and revised in 1966 (master's thesis, USSR Academy of Sciences, 1941), 80.

51 Franz Boas, "Kwakiutl Ethnography," APS, Franz Boas Collection of American Indian Linguistics, 497.3 B63c, part 1, pp. 702, 29. It is difficult to say who might have edited this text and when. Corrections and supplementary notes provided by Dan Cranmer and his daughter Gloria Cranmer-Webster at later dates were also apparent.

52 We must include our own work in this observation, for we made little effort to contact people known to have strong negative opinions about Jane Cook or this work. In her examination of George Hunt's research methods, Judith Berman notes that he was aware of the discrepancy in accounts by rival chiefs and would often seek out second and third versions. "Some of his most fascinating accounts," she wrote, "are reports of arguments between Kwakwaka'wakw over various matters of custom, social organization, history, cosmology, and so forth." See Berman, "George Hunt and the Kwak'wala Texts," 489.

53 "Slaves were, in all respects, property. Their masters might kill them, sell them or set them free": Franz Boas, *Tenth Report on Northwestern Tribes of Canada* (London: British Association for the Advancement of Science, 1895), 36. In a Marxist-Leninist analysis of slavery on the Northwest Coast, Julia Averkieva worked from an evolutionary scheme that embraced stages of clan organization, private ownership, production, and commerce while noting gaps in the ethnographic literature on social class and slavery. She wrote that the commerce in slaves occurred along a coastal route between the northern tribes and a "regular market" known as "the Dalles" in Washington. See "Slavery among the Indians of North America," 92-96. Slaves were exchanged, purchased or, more often, acquired through raids (ibid., 82-92). They provided domestic labour in chiefly houses: fishing and food preparation and acting as messengers, bodyguards, childminders, and canoe paddlers (ibid., 69-77). Averkieva reported a chilling trade in female slaves that became more lucrative, particularly after the start of the gold rush, when large numbers of single, non-Aboriginal men populated Victoria (ibid., 93). See also Franz Boas, "Social Organization and Secret Societies," in *Report of the US National Museum for 1895* (Washington, DC: US Government Printing Office, 1897), 338; Gough, "Send a Gunboat!"; and William MacLeod, "Economic Aspects of Indigenous American Slavery," *American Anthropologist* 30, 4 (1928): 632-50.

54 Raids were launched to uphold tribal status; to enforce against territorial incursions; and to acquire slaves, new territory, or ceremonial and supernatural wealth. See Codere, "Kwakiutl," 440. In this oft-told story, the Kwakwaka'wakw acquired the most prestigious of dances – the Hamatsa or cannibal dance – from a neighbouring nation.

55 Cannibalism perhaps remains the most potent marker of so-called uncivilized being, brandished by colonial scholars and administrators to justify their projects of assimilation and progress. See Christon Archer, "Cannibalism in the Early History of the Northwest Coast: Enduring Myths and Neglected Realities," *Canadian Historical Review* 61, 4 (1980): 453-79, and Shirley Lindenbaum, "Thinking about Cannibalism," *Annual Review of Anthropology* 33 (2004): 475-98.

56 Small-scale killings of a retributive nature were said to "wipe away the sorrow" or "let someone else wail" for the death of a relative (by natural or deliberate

causes). To take a head in grief was also said to cause someone "to die with those who are dead" (see Codere, "Kwakiutl," 472). For a related discussion on headhunting and bereavement practices, see Renato Rosaldo's "Grief and a Headhunter's Rage: On the Cultural Force of Emotions," in *Text, Play, and Story: The Construction and Reconstruction of Self and Society,* ed. Edward Bruner (Washington, DC: American Ethnological Society, 1984), 178-95. I heard several stories about head-taking in situations of trespass through territorial waters without permission. The head was displayed on a stake to warn others. In some of the stories, trespassers are castrated.

57 John Gowlland, journal, 11 September 1862, quoted in Richard Wallace, "Charting the North West Coast 1857-62: A Case Study in the Use of Knowledge as Power in Britain's Imperial Ascendency," (master's thesis, University of British Columbia, 1993), 155.

58 George Dawson, *Notes and Observations on the Kwakiool,* Transactions of the Royal Society of Canada, vol. 5, sec. 2 (1888): 35.

59 Archibald Menzies, in *Menzies' Journal of Vancouver's Voyage April to October, 1792,* ed. Charles Newcombe (Victoria: William H. Cullen, 1923), 88.

60 Among the words recorded by George Dawson was this term for a trader, which means "keeping a place for trade." See Dawson, *Notes and Observations,* 36.

61 Codere, "Kwakiutl," 437.

62 HBC employees, for the most part, adhered to protocols of trade compatible with their First Nation counterparts. To settlers, however, the company traders were "crude, unrefined" men who displayed a certain air of superiority and thus earned the taunt that *HBC* stood for "Here before Christ." Traders outside the company were not compelled to work "within the context of Indigenous culture." See Fisher, *Contact and Conflict,* 59.

63 Cited in Codere, "Kwakiutl," 457.

64 Ibid., 455. During the fur trade, women's labour increased by virtue of their obligations to contribute to clan production. They were the primary preparers of skins and furs. See Marjorie Mitchell and Anna Franklin, "When You Don't Know the Language, Listen to the Silence," in *Not Just Pin Money,* ed. Barbara Latham and Roberta Pazdro (Victoria: Camosun College, 1984), 56.

65 Quoted in Chris Arnett, *The Terror of the Coast: Land Alienation and Colonial War on Vancouver Island and the Gulf Islands, 1849-1863* (Vancouver: Talonbooks, 1999), 50.

66 Ibid. See also Robert Campbell, "Making Sober Citizens: The Legacy of Indigenous Alcohol Regulation in Canada, 1777-1985," *Journal of Canadian Studies* 42, 1 (2008): 105-26.

67 Quoted in Galois, *Kwakwaka'wakw Settlements,* 71n93. Historian Barry Gough suggests that drinking "represented a means of self-validation ... a way of reducing boredom ... and a protest against the rising white tide of empire." See Gough, "Send a Gunboat!" 163.

68 Codere, "Kwakiutl," 460.

69 Gough, "Send a Gunboat!" 165.

70 Coppers were described by George Dawson (*Notes and Observations,* 14) as "the most valuable possession of the Kwakiool and other northern tribes ... A conventional face is often scraped out upon the surface of the 'copper.' The most valued coppers are very old." Coppers are said to have lives. They are named

and have a unique value that increases upon each transfer or sale to a new owner. Codere noted that the people with whom she worked compared coppers to cheques. They belong, however, only to high-ranking people or those who participate in the potlatch and feast system.

71 See Benedict, *Patterns of Culture.*

72 See Boas, *Contributions to the Ethnology of the Kwakiutl,* 93-95, for a history that includes details of the southern sex trade.

73 See Leslie Robertson and Dara Culhane's *In Plain Sight: Reflections on Life in Downtown Eastside Vancouver* (Vancouver: Talonbooks, 2005) for contemporary narratives about work in Vancouver's sex economy.

74 Codere, "Kwakiutl," 444-45. Helen Codere later surmised that during the Fort Rupert subperiod the significance of crests and treasures, as well as the supernatural experiences through which they were acquired, was overshadowed completely by the "distributions of property that validated them" (ibid., 467).

75 Goldman, *Mouth of Heaven,* 134.

76 In June 1857, when William Duncan (soon to be an infamous missionary at Metlakatla) arrived on Vancouver Island, he was met by Governor James Douglas, also the chief factor of the HBC's fort at Victoria. He learned that standard HBC pay for fifty marten furs was one coarse black blanket; for thirty furs, one white blanket; and for one marten, "a fore-finger's width of soap." Mink skins fetched one inch of copper (for bracelets), while a bear or land otter skin fetched a tin cup. Occasionally, muskets and, later, two-barrelled guns were offered for a chest-height pile of mink furs. See Peter Murray, *The Devil and Mr. Duncan: A History of the Two Metlakatlas* (Victoria: Sono Nis Press, 1985), 32. In 1859, there were eleven missionaries working on Vancouver Island. They represented Methodist and Anglican missionary societies and the Society for Propagation of the Gospel. See Forrest LaViolette, *The Struggle for Survival: Indian Cultures and the Protestant Ethic in British Columbia* (Toronto: University of Toronto Press, 1973), 21.

77 That intensity was conveyed by Governor James Douglas in a letter dated 19 July 1856. He wrote that Vancouver Island was like a "smouldering volcano, which may at any moment explode with the most destructive force." Quoted in Harris, *Making Native Space,* 22.

78 Codere, "Kwakiutl," 438.

79 Gough, "Send a Gunboat!" 160.

80 After 1850, legal power could be administered by Hudson's Bay Company employees. Their discretionary powers extended to conducting trials and ordering executions. See Jefferson, *Conquest by Law,* 126.

81 Hudson's Bay Company officials, of which James Douglas counted himself, were not enthusiastic about settlement. Early restrictions on European settlers made it difficult for them to establish themselves. In the 1850s, for example, settlers had to purchase land and locate five men or three families upon it to retain their stake (ibid., 124). In the late 1840s, there were only 450 Europeans on Vancouver Island. Everything changed abruptly in 1858, however, when gold was discovered. Fort Victoria's population exploded. That same year, Douglas dropped his dual role as head officer of the Hudson's Bay Company and became governor of the Crown Colony of Vancouver Island. His new role marked the end of company domination and the beginning of a conscious strategy to encourage settlement.

82 "Libel & order of Wm. Gilbert VS Schooner Reporter," Washington State Archives (WSA), Jefferson County Government-Territorial District Court Admiralty Records, 1862-89, vol 0.2 cf(2v), NW316 3-3.
83 Gough, "Send a Gunboat!" 159.
84 The article, titled "THE CRUISE OF THE CLIO; Highly Interesting Diary," was reprinted from the *Nanaimo Gazette* (no date was noted). See the *British Colonist,* 6 January 1866.
85 *British Colonist,* 6 January 1866.
86 "Statement of Lieutenant Carry," included in "Captain Turnour's Report to Arthur Birch, Administrator of the Government, New Westminster, BC," 29 December 1865, British Columbia Archives (BCA), Colonial Correspondence, 1857-72, GR 1372, file 1209a, (HMS *Clio*).
87 *British Colonist,* 6 January 1866.
88 "Statement of Lieutenant Carry."
89 Ibid.
90 *British Colonist,* 10 January 1886.
91 Boas, "Kwakiutl Ethnography," part 1, p. 702, 29.
92 In 1853, Douglas estimated there were three thousand people from northern tribes in Fort Victoria. See Robert Galois, "Colonial Encounters: The Worlds of Arthur Wellington Clah, 1855-1881," *BC Studies* 115-16 (1997-98): 114. The non-aboriginal population around this time was 774. By 1860, it had risen to 2,000 (ibid., 115).
93 Fisher, *Contact and Conflict,* 64-65. Barry Gough writes of the efforts of members of the Royal Navy to stem the flow of slaves and liquor on the Northwest Coast. In 1860, colonial authorities sent three warships to inform chiefs of the primary northern villages to stop raids during their yearly voyages south to Victoria. If the raids continued, the members of the northern villages would not be allowed into Victoria. English law would apply on their southerly excursions, and the captains promised that the northern villages would be visited regularly by gunboats. See Gough, "Send a Gunboat!" 161-63.
94 Robert McKechnie, *Strong Medicine: History of Healing on the Northwest Coast* (Victoria: Morris, 1972), 75.
95 Duncan arrived in Victoria almost a decade before Jane Cook's predecessors were arrested and brought there for trial. See Murray, *The Devil and Mr. Duncan,* 30.
96 Ibid., 32.
97 Mrs. William Murray Thain, "A Few Remarks on Fifty Years Ago," *Log of the Columbia* 5, 4 (1909): 4.
98 Galois, "Colonial Encounters," 116.
99 Jean Barman, "Aboriginal Women on the Streets of Victoria: Rethinking Transgressive Sexuality during the Colonial Encounter," in *Contact Zones: Aboriginal and Settler Women in Canada's Colonial Past,* ed. Katie Pickles and Myra Rutherdale (Vancouver: UBC Press, 2005), 207.
100 Ibid., 206. See also Jean Barman, "Taming Aboriginal Sexuality: Gender, Power, and Race in British Columbia, 1850-1900," *BC Studies* 115-16 (1997-98): 237-66.
101 Marjorie Mitchell and Anna Franklin note that many women found agricultural work in the United States in the late nineteenth century. They picked fruit and

berries, potatoes, and hops and often worked twelve to thirteen hours at a rate of one dollar per day. Some were hired as contractors to organize and recruit groups of pickers. All were dependent on the "grower's store, on the grower's food scrip or tokens." See "When You Don't Know the Language, Listen to the Silence," 61.

102 The story of Charlie James is one example. James was born in Port Townsend around 1870 to a Kwagu'ł mother and a European father. His mother died while away from Fort Rupert, whereupon his father looked after him. He was eventually brought back to Tsa<u>x</u>is and placed in the care of a grandparent. See Nuytten, *The Totem Pole Carvers.*

103 Mitchell and Franklin, "When You Don't Know the Language," 56.

104 See Boas, *Ethnology of the Kwakiutl,* 1112-16, and Goldman, *The Mouth of Heaven,* 217-19. Given the recursive power of what I call "the living text," the Boasian account of this transfer and the many incarnations of it that followed should be regarded as scholarly exercises to advance theoretical debates about rank and status. Regarding descriptions of Hyałkin as a slave or a commoner in the early anthropological record, I was told that these terms reveal the rhetoric of nineteenth-century chiefs in a society that favoured birth order, for Hyałkin had survived two older brothers who had drowned.

Part III: Stranger Than Fiction

1 Charles Nowell, *Smoke from Their Fires: The Life of a Kwakiutl Chief,* ed. Clellan Ford (New Haven, CT: Yale University Press, 1941), 105.

2 Norma Boutillier, "Socialization and Symbolic Interaction in an Indian-White Community" (master's thesis, Simon Fraser University, 1963), 172-73. In the late 1960s, according to Boutillier, even people she calls the fishing aristocracy (which included hereditary chiefs and active potlatchers, people who were band and village leaders and participating members of the Anglican Church) "look to traditional values in the Indian culture, and White values, both in business and in church, and are guided by the norms operative in both" (ibid., 194).

3 See Rosemary Keen, "General Introduction and Guide to the Archive," Church Mission Society Archives, http://www.ampltd.co.uk/digital_guides/church_missionary_society_archive_general/.

4 Bronwen Douglas critiques writing that depicts "the conversion of indigenous women as a simple lineal shift to the grip of the moral and practical hegemonies of missionaries and Christian men." See Bronwen Douglas, "Christian Citizens: Women and Negotiations of Modernity in Vanuatu," *Contemporary Pacific* 14, 1 (2002): 3.

5 See Marshall Sahlins, "Goodbye to Tristes Tropes: Ethnography in the Context of Modern World History," *Journal of Modern History* 65, 1 (1993): 1-25. See also Nicholas Thomas, *Colonialism's Culture: Anthropology, Travel and Government* (Princeton, NJ: Princeton University Press, 1994).

6 The term *imperial fallacy* refers to the idea that "Europe produced history and Natives submitted to it." See Brett Christophers, *Positioning the Missionary: John Booth Good and the Confluence of Cultures in Nineteenth-Century British Columbia*

(Vancouver: UBC Press, 1998), 9. On the erasure of aboriginal agency, see Ingo Shroder, "From Parkman to Postcolonial Theory: What's New in the Ethnohistory of Missions?" *Ethnohistory* 46, 4 (1999): 812, 810.

7 Bronwen Douglas, "Provocative Readings in Intransigent Archives: Finding Aneityumese Women," *Oceania* 70 (1999): 111. See also Margaret Whitehead, "A Useful Christian Woman: First Nations' Women and Protestant Missionary Work in British Columbia," *Atlantis* 18, 1-2 (1992-93): 142-66, and Michael Harkin and Sergei Kan eds., "Native Women's Responses to Christianity," special issue, *Ethnohistory* 43, 4 (1996).

8 On Hall's work in this period, see Barry Gough, "A Priest versus the Potlatch: Reverend Alfred James Hall and the Fort Rupert Kwakiutl, 1878-1880," *Journal of the Canadian Church Historical Society* 24, 2 (1982): 75-89. Gough's presentation of the chronology is thorough, but it differs from mine in focus and interpretation. In his review of scholarly representations of colonial missions, "From Parkman to Postcolonial Theory," Ingo Shroder suggests that the process involved "structural frameworks and local action that transform[ed] cultural imaginaries, then cultural praxis, and, finally, cultural and historical realities" (810).

9 All letters referred to in this chapter are located in the Church Mission Society Archives (CMSA), Alfred James Hall Papers, 1877-80, and Reverend Alfred Hall Original Papers, Metlakatla, Fort Rupert, 1878-80, 011/1-17, C C2/08/1-92, also available at Library and Archives Canada (LAC).

10 In *The Struggle for Survival,* historian Forrest LaViolette provides examples of this flow of information about inhabitants of the Northwest Coast, including John Meares's *Voyage from China to the Northwest Coast of America* (1791) and Commander R.C. Mayne's *Four Years in British Columbia and Vancouver Island* (1962). See Forrest LaViolette, *The Struggle for Survival: Indian Cultures and the Protestant Ethic in British Columbia* (Toronto: University of Toronto Press, 1973), 19-20.

11 According to Rosemary Keen, a former archivist of the CMS, these secretaries were men of great influence within the society. Often returned missionaries themselves, they offered spiritual and practical encouragement to men in the missionary field. Four or five secretaries worked for the CMS at any given time. Alfred Hall corresponded with the Reverend Henry Wright, who drowned in 1880, and his successor, Christopher Fenn. See Keen, "General Introduction and Guide to the Archive," "The Supporters."

12 The first hearing resulted in the establishment of the Select Committee on Aboriginal Tribes. See Sidney Harring, *White Man's Law: Native People in Nineteenth-Century Canadian Jurisprudence.* (Toronto: University of Toronto Press/Osgoode Society for Canadian Legal History, 1998), 24.

13 Jacob Gruber, "Ethnographic Salvage and the Shaping of Anthropology," *American Anthropologist* 72, 6 (1970): 1292.

14 The British Association for the Advancement of Science was one such initiative. It helped fund Franz Boas's research several years later.

15 See Jean Comaroff and John Comaroff, *Of Revelation and Revolution: Christianity, Colonialism, and Consciousness in South Africa,* vol. 1 (Chicago: University of Chicago Press, 1991), 121-22.

16 Alfred Hall to Henry Wright, 16 July 1877.

17 Published originally in 1849 as *The Life of Josiah Henson, Formerly a Slave, Now an Inhabitant of Canada, as Narrated by Himself.*
18 Through the man-on-the-spot observations included in their annual letters and calls for humanitarian support, missionaries participated fully in broadcasting "otherness." See LaViolette, *Struggle for Survival,* 19-26, for examples of these accounts written by William Duncan, J.A. McCullagh, and Thomas Crosby.
19 The Hudson's Bay Company proclaimed slavery illegal. In 1838, however, James Douglas wrote that a "forcible emancipation" was out of the question, owing to Native people's feelings. He believed the "immoral system" of slave traffic could be suppressed through "moral influence." See Barry Gough, "Send A Gunboat! Checking Slavery and Controlling Liquor Traffic among Coast Indians of British Columbia in the 1860s," *Pacific Northwest Quarterly* 69, 4 (1978): 160-61, quoting from James Douglas to Governor and Committee, 18 October 1838, in Derek Pethik, *James Douglas: Servant of Two Empires* (Vancouver: Mitchell Press, 1969), 31.
20 Gough, "Send a Gunboat!" 160-61. As many have noted, slavery was part of an integrated economy of wealth and prestige. In the 1980s, James Wallas contextualized a traditional narrative by stating: "In the old days, slavery was common. There was more slave-taking than killing between tribes that lived not too far from each other. Slaves were desirable not only for helping with the work, but also for bartering in trade. Sometimes a child slave would be given away at a potlatch and was considered a very valuable gift." See Pamela Whitaker and Chief James Wallas, *Kwakiutl Legends* (Blaine, WA: Hancock House 1989), 48.
21 Michael Harkin, "Engendering Discipline: Discourse and Counterdiscourse in the Methodist-Heiltsuk Dialogue," in "Native American Women's Responses to Christianity," ed. Michael Harkin and Sergei Kan, special issue, *Ethnohistory* 43, 4 (1996): 646.
22 Alfred Hall to Henry Wright, 30 September 1878.
23 Alfred Hall, annual letter, 1 March 1879. A series of Oblate priests had been at Fort Rupert since sometime in the early 1860s. Hall wrote: "they endeavoured to get a hold upon this people" for seven years but had left to establish a new mission on Harbledown Island in 1866. Roman Catholic missionaries withdrew from Kwakwa̲ka̲'wakw territories in 1874.
24 Ibid.
25 Alfred Hall to Mr. Wright, 20 March 1878. Ethnologist Marius Barbeau compiled narratives describing poles and carvings from the northern Coast in the late nineteenth century that included depictions of Europeans. The meanings of these carvings and poles are as varied as the internal social contexts of the communities within which they were erected. Barbeau discusses Tlingit poles of Abraham Lincoln and a pole said to represent Captain Cook but which is likely the wife of a trader. Haida poles included likenesses of a uniformed military official, a Russian missionary, a Russian saint, a Greek Orthodox Church certificate, and a Hudson's Bay Company trader. Chiefs raised some of them to either ridicule or honour particular traders, soldiers, or priests. One pole might have commemorated a chief's conversion to Christianity, while another was intended to ridicule priests and the "religion of the white man" for their "failure to convert

... people to their faith." See Marius Barbeau, *Totem Poles* (Ottawa: National Museum of Canada, 1950), 1:402-11.

26 Hall to Wright, 20 March 1878.

27 Ibid.

28 William Duncan to the Committee of the Church Mission Society London, 4 March 1878.

29 Ibid.

30 Ibid.

31 Alfred Hall to Committee of the Church Mission Society, 6 March 1878.

32 Ibid.

33 See LaViolette, *The Struggle for Survival,* and Peter Murray, *The Devil and Mr. Duncan: A History of the Two Metlakatlas* (Victoria: Sono Nis Press, 1985).

34 Hall to Wright, 20 March 1878.

35 Alfred Hall to Mr. Wright, 16 October 1878. Quote from the *Church Intelligencer,* a CMS publication, page 463, edition unknown.

36 Duncan to CMS Committee, 4 March 1878.

37 Hall to Wright, 30 September 1878.

38 Hall to Wright, 16 October 1878. In this letter, Hall describes his language regime: "I engaged a native to come to my house for one hour every evening – during the day I wrote down sentences used in ordinary conversation and in the evenings I had them translated, together with many important texts of scripture, parts of the Burial Baptism and Marriage services and nearly one half of the little book 'Peep of day.' And besides putting translations in my book, I mastered them by hard and continued study during the day. [B]y these translations I also learnt the idiom of the language." Hall refers to *The Peep of Day: A Series of the Earliest Religious Instruction the Infant Mind Is Capable of Receiving,* an anonymous text published in 1842 (62 pages) and 1879 (264 pages).

39 Alfred Hall to Mr. Fenn, 16 January 1878.

40 Robert Hunt purchased an Indian house near the centre of the village for Hall to live in, teach school, and give his "addresses." They hoped the house would provide a more familiar setting than a room in the fort or a newly built schoolhouse. Alfred Hall, annual letter, 1 March 1879. Hunt paid sixty blankets for the house. Ironically, in another letter, Hall criticizes a man who had sold his house for sixty blankets to further his standing in the custom. See Alfred Hall to Mr. Wright, 11 June 1878.

41 Hall to Wright, 30 September 1878.

42 Hall to Wright, 11 June 1878.

43 Hall, annual letter, 1 March 1879.

44 Hall to Wright, 11 June 1878.

45 Alfred Hall to Henry Wright, 13 January 1879.

46 Hall to Wright, 11 June 1878.

47 Franz Boas, *Kwakiutl Ethnography,* ed. Helen Codere (Chicago: University of Chicago Press, 1966), 305.

48 Ibid., 304-5. Boas writes, "The most valued stories of the Kwakiutl refer to the origin of the numayms, of the descent of the ancestor from the sky or his origins from the sea ... The typical form of the tales is that of the ancestor who lands on earth coming down from the sky in the form of a bird or in human form, out

of the sea as a sea-animal, brought up by a sea monster, or a ghost from underground. He takes off his animal garment, which returns to the sky, and creates his tribe from figures he carves, from people who are drifting about and whom he pulls ashore, from birds, eggs or shells. Then he shouts in order to ascertain whether anyone else lives in this world and is answered by the shout of another ancestor."

49 Hall to Wright, 20 March 1878.

50 Alfred Hall to Mr. Wright, 12 September 1879.

51 In her work on the colonial intersection of aboriginal and European medical knowledge, historian Mary-Ellen Kelm notes that in the face of devastating epidemics and new diseases, people on the Northwest Coast were open to the pharmaceutical and surgical interventions of Europeans. She suggests a kind of taxonomy of ailments in which aboriginal peoples "might select non-Native medicine to get treatment for a disease they considered to be a 'white' disease, to expand their range of treatment options, or to assert strategically their status in relation to Euro-Canadian society." See Mary-Ellen Kelm, *Colonizing Bodies: Aboriginal Health and Healing in British Columbia, 1900-50* (Vancouver: UBC Press, 1998), 154.

52 As Robert Galois makes clear, these figures are only estimates, given the frequent "silence" in visitors' accounts. See Robert Galois, *Kwakwa̱ka̱'wakw Settlements, 1775-1920: A Geographical Analysis and Gazetteer* (Vancouver: UBC Press, 1994), 39, 43.

53 Kelm cites a number of such statements in *Colonizing Bodies,* 104-5.

54 Hall to Wright, 30 September 1878.

55 Dara Culhane Speck, *An Error in Judgement: The Politics of Medical Care in an Indian/White Community* (Vancouver: Talonbooks, 1987), 69-70. See Agnes Alfred's narratives about male and female shamans. She asserts that witchcraft was "practiced by ordinary men." Martine Reid, ed., *Paddling to Where I Stand: Agnes Alfred, Qwiqwasutinuxw Noblewoman,* trans. Daisy Sewid-Smith (Vancouver: UBC Press, 2004), 166-68.

56 Culhane Speck, *An Error in Judgement,* 70.

57 Sadie Thompson scrapbook, Alert Bay Library and Museum (ABLM), 993-349-2, Book 1-2, p. 25.

58 After a cursory search for the "big medical book" she might have used in the 1880s, I found two main texts: *A System of Human Anatomy, General and Specific* (a.k.a. *Wilson's Human Anatomy, with Three Hundred and Ninety-Seven Illustrations*) by Erasmus Wilson, first published in 1859, and Calvin Cutter's 1871 edition of *First Book on Anatomy, and Hygiene, for Grammar Schools and Families (with Eighty-Four Engravings)*.

59 Report on the Conference on Indian Affairs, April 1948, British Columbia Archives (BCA), NW 970.5 B862r, pp. 22-23.

60 Douglas, "Christian Citizens," 3.

61 In Hall's letter to Wright dated 20 March 1878, he wrote about a Tsimshian woman "brought up by Mr. Duncan from her childhood" who had translated the gospel of St. Mark for the bishop. For accounts about several other women on the Northwest Coast who took up Christianity and vitally assisted missionaries in their work, see Margaret Whitehead, "A Useful Christian Woman: First Nations

Women and Protestant Missionary Work in British Columbia," *Atlantis* 18, 1-2 (1992-93): 142-66.

62 Hall to Wright, 20 March 1878.

63 Working with material from the Methodist mission among the Heiltsuk peoples, Michael Harkin suggests several possibilities for why the mission experience may have appealed: "moral guidance during rapid change," "compassion for bereaved, especially during a period of increased mortality," and "new ideas about sacredness, power, morality and gender." See Harkin, "Engendering Discipline," 657-58.

64 Alfred Hall to Henry Wright, 13 June 1879.

65 Hall, annual letter, 1 March 1879. In their history of southern Kwakwa̲ka̲'wakw villages, Philip Drucker and Robert Heizer assert that the people from these villages were the first to go continuously to Victoria to work for wages after the depletion of the fur trade economy. See Philip Drucker and Robert Heizer, *To Make My Name Good: A Reexamination of the Southern Kwakiutl Potlatch* (Berkeley: University of California Press, 1967), 16-18.

66 Hall noted that one woman had returned home with seven bales, a bale consisting of fifty blankets. See Hall to Wright, 11 June 1878. As Helen Codere notes in her extensive lists of "industries" and "Kwakiutl occupations," women's economic labour during this period of time was remarkably diverse. See Helen Codere, *Fighting with Property: A Study of Kwakiutl Potlatching and Warfare, 1792-1930,* Monographs of the American Ethnological Society 18 (New York: J.J. Augustin, 1950), 14-15, 31-32.

67 Harkin, "Engendering Discipline," 646-49.

68 Ibid., 647-48.

69 Hall, annual letter, 1 March 1879.

70 In his annual letter of 1 March 1879, Hall included a copy of *The Primary Manual of the Fort Rupert C.M.S. Mission,* printed in Victoria by British Colonist Stream Presses.

71 Hall, annual letter, 1 March 1879. Such practicalities are too often overlooked in considerations of Christianity. Instead, it is the exotic cosmological transformations of conversion and questions about political resistance and accommodation that are too often overexamined. See Harkin and Kan, "Native American Women's Responses to Christianity," special issue, *Ethnohistory,* for excellent examples of scholarly approaches to this subject that seek contextualized analyses.

72 Christophers, *Positioning the Missionary*. The Kwagu'ł had already entered into a treaty in 1851, one of the five agreements known as the Douglas Treaties.

73 Helen Codere notes this shift in the 1880s, a shift from an "aboriginal surplus-producing economy to a successful participation in the modern cash economy." See Codere, *Fighting with Property,* and "Kwakiutl," in *Perspectives in American Indian Culture Change,* ed. Edward Spicer (Chicago: University of Chicago Press, 1961), 431-516. See also Drucker and Heizer, *To Make My Name Good,* 13.

74 Hall to Wright, 13 January 1879.

75 Gough, "A Priest versus the Potlatch," 88n33.

76 Hall to Wright, 11 June 1878.

77 Judith Berman calls this *ćə w`ənx,* the time when "predatory spirits hunted for humans," the inverse of the secular summer season, the time when "humans

fished for salmon." See Judith Berman, "Red Salmon and Red Cedar Bark: Another Look at the Nineteenth-Century Kwakwaka'wakw Winter Ceremonial," *BC Studies* 125-26 (2000): 56, 59. See also Joseph Masco, "'It Is a Strict Law That Bids Us Dance': Cosmologies, Colonialism, and Ritual Authority in the Kwakwa̱ka̱'wakw Potlatch, 1849-1922," *Comparative Studies in Society and History* 37, 1 (1995): 46. Both authors draw upon Franz Boas's distinction between the summer season called *Baxus* or "profane" and the winter season called *Tsetsaeqa,* meaning "secrets." See Franz Boas, "Social Organization and Secret Societies of the Kwakiutl Indians," in *Report of the US National Museum for 1895* (Washington, DC: US Government Printing Office, 1897), 418. Berman describes the turn to the season of ceremonial activities as a time when "initiates and officials of the ceremonial" switched from their summer names to "a completely different set of winter ceremonial names," a time when "everyone wore his or her cedar-bark head and neck-rings until the winter ceremonial spirits had departed." Social organization also turned from status identities within 'ni'na̱'mima to divisions based on ceremonial procedure that included "secular uninitiated commoners [who] formed the audience"; high-ranking "initiates under the influence of the spirits," called Seals; and Sparrows, "the hereditary officials and the managers who conducted the proceedings." See Berman, "Red Salmon and Red Cedar Bark," 58.

78 Alfred Hall to Mr. Wright, 6 March 1880. His letter provides details about his journey to "Lou-wit-ti-anoo," Alert Bay, and to the villages of the "Mamalillakulla," the "Klowitches," and the "Malithby."

79 Hall, annual letter, 1 March 1879.

80 Hall to Wright, 30 September 1878.

81 Pronnounced "Gostoclay." These translations and names were provided by William Wasden Jr.

82 Brackets appear in the original text. Reid, *Paddling to Where I Stand,* 139.

83 Hall to Wright, 30 September 1878.

84 Ibid.

85 George Dawson, *Notes and Observations on the Kwakiool,* Transactions of the Royal Society of Canada, vol. 5, sec. 2 (Montreal: Dawson, 1888), 19-22. Dawson notes that Reverend Alfred Hall "writes the name "Kānīkēlāg" and that Franz Boas recorded it as "Kanikilak" (ibid., 19). Dawson appears to have collected several versions through his own acquaintance with individuals in many villages; for the "Nim-kish tribe" he included a rendition written by Hall (ibid., 22). In a paper published in 1887, Boas apparently agreed to some extent with Hall. Although, in Boas's analysis, Kanikilak was a son of the "supreme being": "The most important legends of the Kwakiutl are those referring to Kanikilak. They believe in a supreme being living in heaven, whom they call Kantsoump ('our father,' or, in some instances, 'our elder brother'). He sent down to the earth his two sons Kanikilak and Nomokois, who were born there." See Franz Boas, "The Coast Tribes of British Columbia," *Science* 9, 216 (1887): 288. The name Kantsoump, although spelled differently, was used by Hall and Hunt in their earlier translation of prayers and hymns.

86 Dawson, *Notes and Observations,* 25.

87 These tenets were established at a meeting March 1799 and still inform the society.

88 Alfred Hall to Mr. Wright, 6 March 1878.

89 *Charismatic Christianity* is a general term connoting belief in spiritual gifts and manifestations of the Holy Spirit.
90 Hall, annual letter, 1 March 1879.
91 Question marks or words in square brackets represent illegible markings on the letters. Hall to Wright, 20 March 1878.
92 Hall to Wright, annual letter, 1 March 1879.
93 Ibid.
94 Alfred Hall to Mr. Wright, 20 August 1880.
95 Their perspective must have been influenced by heated debates about ritualism in the church at that time, by which Anglicans tried to distance themselves from Roman Catholics.
96 "Popular accounts suggest that people of the Northwest Coast occupied a paradise where food-gathering was a simple and assured matter. A careful examination of native accounts indicates that this is not the case; every day of the year saw a good proportion of the population involved in some aspect of the food quest ... Stories of privation and even starvation are part of the histories of the Kwakwaka'wakw and other Northwest Coast peoples, and an easy life was not assured." See Peter MacNair, "From Kwakiutl to Kwakwaka'wakw," in *Native Peoples: The Canadian Experience,* ed. R. Bruce Morrison and C. Roderick Wilson (Toronto: McClelland and Stewart, 1986), 506-7.
97 Interview with Gilbert Cook Sr., 1973, Alert Bay Library and Museum (ABLM), Cook Family file.
98 Galois, *Kwakwaka'wakw Settlements,* 31-33.
99 Included were 108 men, 69 women, 17 male youth, 5 female youth, 22 male children, and 19 female children.
100 J.S. Dermis to Dept. of the Interior, 12 July 1875, Library and Archives Canada (LAC), Department of Indian Affairs, RG 10, vol. 36281, f. 6244-1.
101 Hall to Wright, 30 September 1878.
102 George Blenkinsop, "Kwahkewlth Agency Annual Report," 23 September 1881, "Canada, *Annual Report of the Department of Indian Affairs for the Year Ended June 30, 1900* (Ottawa: Queen's Printer, 1900), 167-68.
103 There are, Codere wrote, "over one hundred separately named and separately held sites at [the] great oulachen [sic] fishing spot" at Knight Inlet. See Codere, *Fighting with Property,* 26.
104 Dorothee Schreiber, "'A Liberal and Paternal Spirit': Indian Agents and Native Fisheries in Canada," *Ethnohistory* 55, 1 (2008): 88.
105 Ibid., 89.
106 Blenkinsop, "Kwahkewlth Agency Annual Report," 23 September 1881, 167-68.
107 Indian Claims Commission, *Inquiry into the Cormorant Island Claim of the 'Namgis First Nation,* March 1996, 1, available online; Galois, *Kwakwaka'wakw Settlements,* 310.
108 Galois, *Kwakwaka'wakw Settlements,* 311.
109 Ibid., 311.
110 Blenkinsop, "Kwahkewlth Agency Annual Report," 23 September 1881, 168.
111 Drucker and Heizer, *To Make My Name Good,* 15.
112 British Columbia's 1888 fishing regulations restricted aboriginal fishers to fishing "for the purpose of providing food for themselves." To sell their catch, they

required the same licence as non-aboriginal fishers. Regulation changes in 1894 stipulated that aboriginal fishers required permission from the federal Department of Marine and Fisheries to obtain food fish. Added to this was a crippling prohibition on the use of customary fishing technologies, "which tended to be locally adapted and highly effective in the place-based fisheries." See "Fishery Regulations for British Columbia," supplement, *Canada Gazette,* 31 August 1889; "Regulations Relating to Fishing in Manitoba and the North-West Territories," *Canada Gazette,* 19 May 1894; and "Fishery Regulations for the Province of British Columbia," *Canada Gazette,* 3 March 1894, in Schreiber, "A Liberal and Paternal Spirit," 89.

113 Randy Bell is referencing his relationship through the Hunt family. See Barbeau, *Totem Poles,* 2:654.

114 Blenkinsop, "Kwahkewlth Agency Annual Report," 30 June 1883, DIA Annual Reports 1880-1935, UBC Library Archives (UBCLA), AWI.R6622.

115 "Special Meeting Held at Alert Bay, June 1st, 1936," 4, ADBCA Archives.

116 Following the patrilineal bias of the government, members of the Hunt family with the exception of Mary Hunt and Lucy Hunt are likewise listed as English in origin.

117 Blenkinsop, "Kwahkewlth Agency Annual Report," 23 September 1881, 167-71.

118 Ibid, 171.

119 See Helen Codere's classic paper, "The Amiable Side of Kwakiutl Life: The Potlatch and the Play Potlatch," American Anthropologist 28 (1956): 334-51.

120 Nowell, *Smoke from Their Fires,* 78-79.

121 This CMS mission post became the centre of a great controversy that pitted the bishop and the CMS against William Duncan and "nine-tenths" of the residents at Metlakatla. See I.W. Powell, *Annual Report of the Department of Indian Affairs for the Year Ended December 31, 1883* (Ottawa: Queen's Printer, 1883), lx.

122 Nowell, *Smoke from Their Fires,* 103-4. These are accounts of camaraderie, as Stephen Cook and Charlie Nowell fought off a bully in the communal kitchen.

123 Ibid., 88.

124 Ibid., 90.

125 Ibid., 94. It must have been strange for a people with so rich a custom of naming to find themselves with monikers unrelated to their predecessors or to their own naming protocols. The practice of bestowing English names highlights the mission's connection with an overseas organization known as Friends of the Mission, which partly funded operations. It also makes visible the degree to which European naming enabled colonial agents to monitor, record, and incorporate aboriginal peoples within a massive administrative project or system of governance.

126 Ibid., 90-91.

127 Ibid., 105.

128 Blenkinsop, "Kwahkewlth Agency Annual Report," 30 June 1883, 47.

129 Blenkinsop wrote that "the majority of mothers objected to that operation [vaccination] last year," that there was a known case of a vaccinated child dying from the disease, and that "numbers who were vaccinated caught the disease." Ibid., 49.

130 Ibid., 47, 49.

131 DIA Annual Reports 1880-1935, 1883.
132 Dawson, *Notes and Observations,* 17.
133 Ibid.
134 Ibid.
135 Ibid., 25.
136 Ibid.
137 Ibid., 26.
138 Ibid., 36. Under "Persons," age and gender figure prominently in the vocabulary, but marital status (unless one is widowed) appears without a special name. Dawson lists Kwak̓wala terms for *great talker* and *silent person,* for *man of knowledge* and *half-breed,* and for *white man* and *"Negro."* There are terms for male and female orphans; for men afflicted with blindness, lameness, or deafness; and for the afflictions themselves. "New Words" includes terms for metal commodities, weapons, foodstuffs, clothing, stimulants, means of transportation, parts of houses, newspapers, and writing utensils.
139 Lori Speck, "Spirits Broken and Innocence Stolen," *U'mista News,* Spring 1999, 10, 11. Speck's story of the residential school system includes excerpts from Department of Indian Affairs officials, from early Anglican school principals, from the chief for the Assembly of First Nations, and from former residential school students.
140 The industrial school opened 1893 with five pupils. By the end of that year, eighteen boys lived in residence and were taught carpentry. See North Pacific Mission Annual Report, (1895-96), Anglican Diocese of British Columbia Archives (ADBCA), BV 2500 P7C3 (1895-96).
141 Speck, "Spirits Broken," 13.
142 Church documents are rather confusing regarding the establishment of girls' day schools. Their existence seemed to depend largely on extra funding and the availability of staff. ADBCA, Synod Office General Files, Alert Bay Mission, vol. 1, f. 10, 1910-15, text 63, box 12/23.
143 Steffen Nielsen, "Civilizing Kwakiutl: Contexts and Contests of Kwakiutl Personhood, 1880-1999" (PhD diss., University of Aarhus, 2001), 253.
144 Speck, "Spirits Broken," 18.
145 Ibid., 1.
146 Adele Perry, "Metropolitan Knowledge, Colonial Practice, and Indigenous Womanhood: Missions in Nineteenth-Century British Columbia," in *Contact Zones: Aboriginal and Settler Women in Canada's Colonial Past,* ed. Katie Pickles and Myra Rutherdale (Vancouver: UBC Press, 2005), 114-15.
147 *Sixties Scoop* refers to the extensive child welfare program conducted during the 1960s, '70s, and '80s, whereby aboriginal and Metis children were removed from their families and adopted or fostered out, often into white, middle-class homes. The program was discontinued in the mid-1980s when Ontario chiefs passed resolutions against it and a judicial inquiry in Manitoba condemned it. See Susan Fournier and Ernie Crey, *Stolen from Our Embrace: The Abduction of First Nations Children and the Restoration of Aboriginal Communities* (Vancouver: Douglas and McIntyre, 1997).
148 Speck, "Spirits Broken," 10.
149 Quoted in Nielsen, "Civilizing Kwakiutl," 253.

150 Alfred Hall, "Report on Missions," 1902, CMSA, sec. 5, part 4, British Columbia, 1856-1925.

151 William Halliday to William Sloan, MP, Ottawa, 7 November 1907, U'mista Cultural Centre Archives (UCCA), A96-021-70.11.

152 Ibid.

153 Culhane Speck, *An Error in Judgement,* 83.

154 In response to the 1996 Royal Commission on Aboriginal Peoples, Jane Stewart, Canada's minister of Indian Affairs and Northern Development, delivered a "Statement of Reconciliation" on 7 January 1998. The statement included an apology to residential school students and established the Aboriginal Healing Foundation. Three years later, Indian Residential Schools Resolution Canada (IRSRC) was created. The department introduced the National Resolution Framework, which included the Alternative Dispute Resolution Program. The government also pledged 3.5 million dollars toward a "healing fund" for counselling within aboriginal communities. Ovide Mercredi responded to the federal government's acknowledgment of the report: "The expression of sorrow is directed at those individuals who suffered abuse. It was not directed at all First Nations people, who have all lost something because of the residential schools, whether they experienced physical or sexual abuse or not." Quoted in *Windspeaker News,* March 1998. That same year, 1998, representing the United Church of Canada, Bill Phipps also issued an official apology to former students of Native residential schools. Students who had attended residential school in London, Ontario, launched a class action lawsuit against the federal government and the Anglican Church of Canada.

155 "On May 10, 2006, the Government of Canada announced the approval of a final Indian Residential Schools Settlement Agreement. The settlement provides for a Common Experience Payment. A lump sum payment will be available to former students who lived at one of the listed residential schools. Payments will be $10,000 for the first school year plus $3,000 for each school year after that. The Settlement Agreement also includes an Independent Assessment Process. A process which will allow those former students who suffered sexual or serious physical abuses, or other abuses that caused serious psychological effects, to apply for compensation. The Settlement Agreement also includes collective measures, including a Truth and Reconciliation Commission, a Commemoration initiative, and funding for the Aboriginal Healing Foundation and other health support programs." See Indian and Northern Affairs website, Resolution Sector, "Residential Schools" (accessed 27 January 2009).

156 "Apology to Former Students of Indian Residential Schools," Canada, *House of Commons Debates* (11 June 2008), p. 1515 (Stephen Harper, PM).

157 Prime Minister Harper concluded his apology with a statement on the initiatives put forth by the government: "In moving toward healing, reconciliation and resolution of the sad legacy of Indian residential schools, the implementation of the Indian residential schools settlement agreement began on September 19, 2007." Ibid.

158 Paulette Reagan, *Unsettling the Settler Within: Indian Residential Schools, Truth Telling, and Reconciliation in Canada* (Vancouver: UBC Press, 2010), 7.

Part IV: "Children of the Potlatch System," 1888-1912

1 In Franz Boas, *Kwakiutl Tales,* Columbia University Contributions to Anthropology, 2 (New York: Columbia University Press, 1910), 473.

2 Adele Perry, "Metropolitan Knowledge, Colonial Practice, and Indigenous Womanhood: Missions in Nineteenth-Century British Columbia," in *Contact Zones: Aboriginal and Settler Women in Canada's Colonial Past,* ed. Katie Pickles and Myra Rutherdale (Vancouver: UBC Press, 2005), 113.

3 Ibid., 115.

4 Ibid., 116.

5 Sarah Carter, "Creating 'Semi-Widows' and 'Supernumerary Wives': Prohibiting Polygamy in Prairie Canada's Aboriginal Communities to 1900," in *Contact Zones: Aboriginal and Settler Women in Canada's Colonial Past,* ed. Katie Pickles and Myra Rutherdale (Vancouver: UBC Press, 2005), 137.

6 Sarah Carter provides an interesting discussion of the gendered nature of this decision. Bishops resolved to baptize "wives of polygamists" but not their male counterparts. Carter traces church edicts and marriage law in Canada to the arrival, in 1890, of the first polygamous community of Latter-Day Saints in southern Alberta. The community was fleeing anti-polygamy laws in the United States.

7 "Special Meeting Held at Alert Bay, June 1st, 1936," p. 5, 7, Anglican Diocese of British Columbia Archives (ADBCA), 85-69-198-50.

8 Quoted in Perry, "Metropolitan Knowledge," 121.

9 Perry, "Metropolitan Knowledge," 119-20.

10 R.H. Pidcock to A.W. Vowell, Indian Superintendent, 19 March 1888, Library and Archives Canada (LAC), Department of Indian Affairs, RG 10, vol. 3628, file 6244-1.

11 See Aaron Glass, "The Thin Edge of the Wedge: Dancing around the Potlatch Ban, 1921-1951," in *Right to Dance: Dancing for Rights,* ed. Naomi Jackson (Banff: Banff Centre, 2004).

12 Pidcock to Vowell, 19 March 1888.

13 Wedłidi is referring to William Halliday's *Potlatch and Totem and the Recollections of an Indian Agent* (Toronto: J.M. Dent and Sons, 1935). Halliday, a former Indian Agent, wrote that he cites names "in common use" and describes events that "occurred to a greater or less extent at every big potlatch gathering" (11). His composite "sketch" includes a chapter titled "Outcasts," to which Wedłidi refers.

14 These were the petition of northern tribes from the Methodist and Anglican mission fields (1883), a petition from Salish people at Lytton adopting bylaws prohibiting the potlatch (1879), and a petition by Nass Christians for legal abolition of the potlatch (1883).

15 CMS Secretary Charles Fenn to Alfred Hall, 16 November 1888, Church Mission Society Archives (CMSA), Correspondence of the North Pacific Mission, Reel AW1 R4796, Reel A 1460.

16 This letter was offered from the personal collection of a family member. Given the nature of the topics it includes, we (myself and family members) were concerned to protect the anonymity of those who are mentioned. One person felt that we should keep the personal names in the text but remove the village names and references to fathers, as these provide the crucial proof for locating specific

individuals among many who were so named. Another suggestion was to insert the names of characters from Kwakwaka'wakw oral traditions, matching the reported actions of individuals to a storied counterpart. Perhaps erring on the side of caution, I omit personal names and village locations altogether, but retain initials to assist readers.

17 Colonial officials also called "Tamanawas" "Medicine Dances." They included the practices of so-called Indian doctors and were often distinguished from the potlatch by rituals that involved body piercing, scarification, sacrifices, or ritualized cannibalism. In the late 1870s, Reverend Hall wrote explicitly that he had not witnessed these practices among the people in Fort Rupert.

18 "Extracts from I.A. Powell's Annual Report," Victoria, November 22, 1882, LAC, RG 10, vol. 3628, f. 6244-1.

19 Quoted in Douglas Cole and Ira Chaikin, *An Iron Hand upon the People: The Law against the Potlatch on the Northwest Coast* (Vancouver: Douglas and McIntyre, 1990), 43.

20 *Daily Columbian,* 26 February 1896.

21 *R. v. He-ma-sak,* notes of chief justice on application of habeas corpus, LAC, RG 10, vol. 3628, file 6244-1. See also Forrest LaViolette, *The Struggle for Survival: Indian Cultures and the Protestant Ethic in British Columbia* (Toronto: University of Toronto Press, 1973), 60.

22 Mamalilacala, 10 August 1889, included in correspondence from R.H. Pidcock to Superintendent General of Indian Affairs, 2 October 1889, LAC, RG 10, vol. 3628, file 6244-1. See also LaViolette, *The Struggle for Survival,* 61.

23 R.H. Pidcock to Israel Powell, Superintendent General of Indian Affairs, 2 October 1889, LAC, RG 10, vol. 3628, file 6244-1.

24 A.W. Vowell to R.H. Pidcock, 4 September 1895, LAC, Department of Indian Affairs, RG 10, vol. 3628, file 6244-1.

25 A.W. Vowell to R.H. Pidcock, 13 May 1895, LAC, Department of Indian Affairs, RG 10, vol. 3628, file 6244-1.

26 A.W. Vowell to R.H. Pidcock, 4 February 1895, LAC, Department of Indian Affairs, RG 10, vol. 3628, file 6244-1.

27 Philip Drucker and Robert Heizer, *To Make My Name Good: A Reexamination of the Southern Kwakiutl Potlatch* (Berkeley: University of California Press, 1967), 24-25.

28 See Helen Codere, *Fighting with Property: A Study of Kwakiutl Potlatching and Warfare, 1792-1930,* Monographs of the American Ethnological Society 18 (New York: J.J. Augustin, 1950), 91. Included in his list for one potlatch was the distribution of 13,450 blankets; 200 silver bracelets; 7,000 brass bracelets; 240 basins; spoons, abalone shells, and kettles; and calico cloth for "women and children."

29 See Martine Reid, ed., *Paddling to Where I Stand: Agnes Alfred, Qwiqwasutinuxw Noblewoman,* trans. Daisy Sewid-Smith (Vancouver: UBC Press, 2004), 168-69, for a discussion of witchcraft and Agnes Alfred's father's death "because of the *pəsa* [potlatch] rankings."

30 Charles Nowell, *Smoke from Their Fires: The Life of a Kwakiutl Chief,* ed. Clellan Ford (New Haven, CT: Yale University Press, 1941), 96. At Nowell's request, Ford also included the narrative of a woman whose jilted fiancé had "witchcrafted" her. See 96-97. Archival records attest to the social actuality of sorcery

or witchcraft on the Northwest Coast from the late nineteenth century to as late as 1931. A cursory scan of incoming correspondence to the BC Attorney General's Office reveals a witchcraft case in 1895, an accusation against a northern "Indian doctor" in 1897 and his release one year later, and, between 1897 and 1901, an official charge of "murder by witchcraft" and a subsequent confession. The correspondence for the latter case includes a description of healing practices.

31 R.W. Large to the Attorney General, 1908, British Columbia Archives (BCA), BC Attorney General, GR-0429, reel B09 323, box 16, file 2. His reference to two justices of the peace might have been in response to an amendment of the Indian Act – section 117, c. 32.

32 Codere, *Fighting with Property,* 58.

33 Mrs. Lucy Brown, interviewed by Vicki Cook, 30 January 1976, Cook Family file, Alert Bay Library and Museum (ABLM). According to the work of George Hunt and Franz Boas, "It is believed that the spirits of the dead are always poor and hungry ... The souls of the dead can use only objects that have been burnt. Property of a person or objects made by him in his actual use at the time of his death are burnt ... otherwise they are deposited behind the grave. This is evidently not a sacrifice but a recognition of ownership." See Franz Boas, *Kwakiutl Ethnography,* ed. Helen Codere (Chicago: University of Chicago Press, 1966), 165.

34 See Franz Boas, "Current Beliefs of the Kwakiutl Indians," *Journal of American Folklore* 45, 176 (1932): 220, for a list of raven soundings and their interpretations.

35 A.W. Vowell to R.H. Pidcock, 2 April 1895, LAC, Department of Indian Affairs, RG 10, vol. 3628, file 6244-1.

36 CMS North Pacific Mission Annual Report, 1895, p. 320, ADBCA.

37 Quote from circular letter by Reverend M. Tate, in A.W. Vowell to R.H. Pidcock, 24 December 1895, LAC, Department of Indian Affairs, RG 10, vol. 3628, file 6244-1.

38 Letter by Amos Gosnell to Mr. H.D. Helmcken, MPP, 2 March 1896, in response to a letter by Reverend Tate published in the *Victoria Daily Colonist* on 29 February 1896.

39 *Victoria Daily Colonist,* 20 February 1896.

40 Quoted in LaViolette, *The Struggle for Survival,* 71.

41 Ibid., 71-72.

42 See Randy Bouchard and Dorothy Kennedy, eds., *Myths and Legends from the North Pacific Coast of America* (Vancouver: Talonbooks, 2006). During his fieldwork in 1886 in Victoria, Boas called on the assistance of "Dr. Tolmie ... the Indian Agent Dr. Powell, and the Catholic priest" (ibid., 22). Hall and Boas had established a brief correspondence prior to his field trip to Alert Bay in October 1886.

43 Translated and quoted in Codere in *Fighting with Property,* 53.

44 Ibid., 55.

45 Ibid., 54.

46 Robert McKechnie, *Strong Medicine: History of Healing on the Northwest Coast* (Victoria: Morris Printing, 1972), 138-39.

47 Drucker and Heizer, *To Make My Name Good,* 23.

48 Mary-Ellen Kelm, *Colonizing Bodies: Aboriginal Health and Healing in British Columbia, 1900-50* (Vancouver: UBC Press, 1998), 17.

49 If Ga'axsta'las's father, William Gilbert, was still the captain of the schooner *Winifred,* his sealing days might have been over. Consider a *New York Times* article from 24 August 1892:

> A British Sealer Captured Towed into Sitka and Delivered to the Collector
>
> Washington, Aug. 23. – Capt. Tanner. Commanding the Fish Commission steamer Albatross, reports to the Treasury Department ... that the Albatross arrived at that place [Sitka] with the British schooner Winifred in tow. The Winifred was captured by the revenue steamer Rush for illicit sealing and for violating the navigation laws of the United States in transferring her cargo to the British steamer Coquitlan without permission from the Customs authorities ... The Captain said that the boilers of his steamer were leaking badly ... As soon as the necessary repairs were made she would proceed to Port Townsend via Departure Bay."

We do not know how long William Gilbert lived, how he died, or where he spent his last years. Ilma Cook, Jane Cook's daughter-in-law, recalled that Ga'axsta'las came across his obituary in one of the newspapers that had made their way into the Cook family big house.

50 Helen Codere marks 1895 as the year this competition formally began. See Codere, *Fighting with Property,* 41.

51 Rolf Knight, *Indians at Work: An Informal History of Native Labour in British Columbia, 1858-1930* (Vancouver: New Star, 1996), 190.

52 The aboriginal food fishery (for subsistence purposes only) was created in the 1880s to regulate and limit aboriginal fishing in the context of an expanding commercial fishery. By 1894, aboriginal people had to acquire permission from the inspector of fisheries to fish for food. Non-aboriginal fishers were able to purchase a licence for one dollar and did not require permission. Since R. v. Sparrow (1990), the aboriginal right to fish for food and for social and ceremonial purposes has been upheld, unless it contravenes conservation measures. Commercial fishing rights are controversial because the commercial trading of fish has not been legally proven to have predated European incursions. Given the mechanisms of reciprocity engaged in through the feastings and the potlatching complex, such distinctions are nebulous to First Nations.

53 Pam Brown, "Cannery Days: A Chapter in the Lives of the Heiltsuk" (master's thesis, University of British Columbia, 1993), 5-6.

54 *Canada Gazette,* 19 May 1894, "Regulations Relating to Fishing in Manitoba and the North-West Territories," and 3 March 1894, "Fishery Regulations for the Province of British Columbia." Quoted in Dorothee Schreiber, "'A Liberal and Paternal Spirit': Indian Agents and Native Fisheries in Canada," *Ethnohistory* 55, 1 (2008): 89.

55 See Kelm, *Colonizing Bodies,* 50-55, for a discussion of living conditions and health risks at these labour sites. For information on aboriginal labour in the hop fields of Puget Sound, see Paige Raibmon, *Authentic Indians: Episodes of Encounter from the Late-Nineteenth-Century Northwest Coast* (Durham, NC: Duke University Press, 2005), 74-97.

56 Interview summary or excerpt, no date, courtesy of William Wasden Jr. Mrs. Sam Hunt (Elizabeth Kasalas) was married in 1899 at 'Yalis.

57 Also in the sphere of the church that year, Bishop Ridley was appointed the first Anglican bishop of Caledonia. Thirty-two boys and thirty girls attended one of the three schools run by the Church. There was one male "Native lay teacher," and fifteen adults and sixteen children were baptized. "Native contributions" amounted to $129.45. Reverend Hall reported that the "Native teacher George Kamano passed away in July." He was followed by William Brotchie, who eventually assisted Hall in translating the prayer book. Hall reported that he was using "scripture pictures" and that there was special interest in "the work of the Son and the Spirit." CMS North Pacific Mission Annual Report, 1895-1896, p. 318, p. 408, ADBCA, BV2500 P7C3.

58 Alfred Hall, North Pacific Mission, Annual Report, 1895, ibid., 408. Almost to the day, three years before the report above was penned, the first church service in English and Kwak̓wala had been performed at Christmas.

59 The headline of this article, "An Old-Time Potlatch; Three of the Indian Residents of Alert Bay Charged with Cannibalism," refers to the upcoming trial of George Hunt, Ahkow, and Igluk on charges of ritual cannibalism.

60 The archived record of an early grievance against the missionaries in Alert Bay offers a glimpse into how the sawmill operated. In 1919, an official list of complaints was lodged by representatives of a "committee sent to Ottawa to interview the Department of Indian Affairs." That committee – headed by Charlie Nowell – made several charges. Among them was charge 7: "The Missionaries have lost the respect and sympathy of the Indians and, therefore, their influence is not for good. This is due to the missionaries' own acts. To give an example: Some time ago a sawmill was erected and money collected from the Indians by the Missionaries for the purpose, also the sawmill was built solely with the labour of the Indians. The Missionary leased the sawmill to the British Columbia Packing Company. The latter now pay the rental to the Christian Missionary Society. The Indians get nothing whatever for it ... they cannot even get employment in the mill, preference being given to the Japanese and the Chinese." W.E. Ditchburn, Chief Inspector of Indian Agencies to Bishop Charles Schofield, 11 June 1919, ADBCA, Synod Office General Administrative Files, 1928-30, text 63, box 12/23. The charge was retracted in a full (and legalistic) written apology. Another complaint about substandard education was similarly dismissed.

61 Europeans perceived people of varied ancestry as a degraded class of not-quite-European persons or as a threatening class of something-more-than-Native persons. Among Kwakwa̲ka̲'wakw, so-called half-breeds were addressed as just half or "fifty cents" of a Kwakwa̲ka̲'wakw person. Figured through biological descent, members of the nobility maintained their high ranking.

62 Codere, *Fighting with Property,* 31-33.

63 Nellie Hamilton Cook, interview with Joan Skogan and Vicki Cook, August 1973, ABLM, Cook Family file.

64 For a contemporary memoir of big house life in 'Ya̲lis, see Diane Jacobson, *My Life in a Kwagu'ł Big House* (Penticton, BC: Theytus Books, 2005). Many people in the family commented on the placement of the Cook family big house on a hill above the church and administration buildings and commercial areas and fishing docks in 'Ya̲lis. In several people's descriptions, the size of the home was linked to a geography of rank. See Paige Raibmon's article on the differing

contexts of aboriginal domestic spaces as imagined, constructed, and inhabited by First Nation and non-aboriginal peoples on the nineteenth-century Coast: "Living on Display," *BC Studies* 140 (2003-4): 69-89, especially 85-87.

65 Reid, *Paddling to Where I Stand,* 98.

66 The two chiefs threatened to break coppers, an act that would have been directed at other chiefs, who would then have had to produce the equal value of the broken coppers to "make their name good" again. This was an accepted social sanction at that time. At present, there is an agreement that coppers will not be broken to settle disputes.

67 Mayria Kamano was Michael Kamano's sister or possibly his first cousin. Kinship terminology includes cousins as brothers and sisters. The reference is to the Goldthorpe Inquiry into the health care needs of First Nation residents in Alert Bay. See Dara Culhane Speck's book *An Error in Judgement: The Politics of Medical Care in an Indian/White Community* (Vancouver: Talonbooks, 1987).

68 Codere, *Fighting with Property,* 31-32. There is a prolific literature that documents the period of salvage ethnography on the Northwest Coast.

69 These included Israel Wood Powell, Indian Commissioner; Johan Jacobsen; Franz Boas; Harlan Smith; Charlie Newcombe; and Edward Curtis. See Ira Jacknis, "George Hunt, Collector of Indian Specimens," in *Chiefly Feasts: The Enduring Kwakiutl Potlatch,* ed. Aldona Jonaitis (Seattle: University of Washington Press, 1991), 177-224. See also Aldona Jonaitis, *From the Land of the Totem Poles: The Northwest Coast Indian Art Collection at the American Museum of Natural History* (New York/Vancouver: American Museum of Natural History/Douglas and McIntyre, 1988). According to Ira Jacknis, George Hunt's career as "collector of Indian specimens" actually began in 1879, when he worked with the Indian Reserve Commission survey as an interpreter for Israel Wood Powell. Powell enlisted Hunt's services to collect artifacts for the Museum of the Geological Survey of Canada (the Canadian Museum of Civilization). In 1881, Johan Adrian Jacobsen, of the Berlin Royal Ethnographic Museum, enlisted Hunt's services. He returned again in 1885 to collect more artifacts from Kwakwa̱ka̱'wakw villages. Boas began his famous acquaintance with Hunt in 1888. They met in Victoria, where Hunt was interpreting for the courts and where Boas was conducting field trips for the British Association for the Advancement of Science under Edward Burnett Tylor. See Jacknis, "George Hunt, Collector of Indian Specimens," 181.

70 In 1889, Boas searched for the services of a translator. He wrote to Reverend Hall, who recommended William Brotchie, the Native teacher at his mission. Two months later, Hall wrote that Henry Buler had failed to do translations for Boas because he had broken his leg and couldn't find the papers. Hall wrote again four months later, stating that Buler was back, on crutches, and that he had the papers "in hand" for Boas. "Was it too late for your book?" Hall inquired and offered to get other information if Boas needed it. Alfred Hall to Franz Boas, 16 August 1889, 23 October 1889, and 4 February 1890, UBC Library Archives, Professional Correspondence, Franz Boas.

71 In *Smoke from Their Fires,* Nowell told Ford that he had worked with Newcombe (who was also a psychiatrist) for thirty years as an interpreter and collector of "Indian curios" (167). Newcombe also collected for the University of Pennsylvania

Museum and the Peabody Museum at Harvard. Intellectually, he was close to George Mercer Dawson, with whom he criticized Boas for exporting cultural property to the United States.

72 George Horse Capture, "Edward Curtis, Shadow Catcher," *American Masters,* 23 April 2001, http://www.pbs.org/.

73 The first was *Edward Curtis Meets the Kwakwaka'wakw: In the Land of the Headhunters,* a touring performance of dance and film now "restored, re-evaluated and framed with a live orchestral arrangement of the original score and a performance by descendants of the original cast." See Aaron Glass, Brad Evans, and Andrea Sanborn, producers, http://www.curtisfilm.rutgers.edu. The second was *The Edward Curtis Project,* described by playwright Marie Clements as "a photographic and spirit-catching investigation between the life and controversial photographic legacy of Edward Curtis and the documentation and ultimate dialogue between his 'non-vanishing' subjects in *The North American Indian Project.*" The multidisciplinary theatre performance and photographic installation premiered in 2010 and was a collaboration between Clements and Rita Leistner. See *The Edward Curtis Project: A Modern Picture Story* (Vancouver: Talonbooks, 2010).

74 Mick Gidley, *Edward S. Curtis and the North American Indian, Incorporated* (New York: Cambridge University Press, 1998), 89. See this account for a list of duties and activities performed by George Hunt on behalf of the North American Indian Project (ibid., 88-91.)

75 Shamoon Zamir, "Native Agency and the Making of *The North American Indian,*" *American Indian Quarterly* 31, 4 (2007): 613.

76 Gidley, *Edward S. Curtis,* 139. Curtis himself notes in his Introduction, "The research for this volume was greatly simplified and made more effective by the very complete work of Dr. Franz Boas on "The Social Organization of the Kwakiutl Indians": Edward Curtis, *The North American Indian,* vol. 10, *The Kwakiutl* (Norwood, MA: Plimpton Press, 1915), xii.

77 Gidley, *Edward S. Curtis,* 193.

Part V: "We As the Suppressed People," 1913-18

1 Kwakwalla to the Bishop of Columbia, 11 January 1913, Anglican Diocese of British Columbia Archives (ADBCA), "Aboriginal – Alert Bay," box 1, text 277.

2 Paul Tennant, *Aboriginal Peoples and Politics: The Indian Land Question in British Columbia* (Vancouver: UBC Press, 1990), 84. Some missionaries offered members of their congregations what Brett Christophers calls "temporal advice." Being "Anglican English in a British colony" offered the advantage of a shared language with those "who oversaw land decisions." See Brett Christophers, *Positioning the Missionary: John Booth Good and the Confluence of Cultures in Nineteenth-Century British Columbia* (Vancouver: UBC Press, 1998), 17-18.

3 Robert Galois, *Kwakwaka'wakw Settlements, 1775-1920: A Geographical Analysis and Gazetteer* (Vancouver: UBC Press, 1994), 33.

4 In 1909, the Department of Indian Affairs (DIA) initiated a report on these questions. In the early 1900s, in the prairie provinces, "the Dominion actively negotiated reserve surrenders." See Cole Harris, *Making Native Space: Colonialism,*

Resistance, and Reserves in British Columbia (Vancouver: UBC Press, 2002), 216, 224.

5 For a detailed historical analysis of land policy and aboriginal organization during this period, see Harris, *Making Native Space,* 216-28. Much of the material that follows is from Union of BC Indian Chiefs, "Chronology," *Stolen Lands, Broken Promises:* Dispossession and Resistance in British Columbia, 13-26, http://ubcic.bc.ca.

6 Galois, *Kwakwaka'wakw Settlements,* 32-33.

7 In Ottawa, the prime minister, Wilfrid Laurier, sympathized with aboriginal peoples' articulate demands for a judicial reckoning on title. See Harris, *Making Native Space,* 216-28.

8 Philip Drucker, *Native Brotherhoods: Modern Intertribal Organizations on the Northwest Coast,* Bureau of American Ethnology Bulletin 168 (Washington, DC: Smithsonian Institute, 1958), 88.

9 Harris, *Making Native Space,* 228.

10 Ibid., 225-26. In 1909, Arthur O'Meara, a Methodist missionary and lawyer, drafted the Cowichan petition and presented it to the Privy Council in London on behalf of the Qa'watsa'n people. "The ten-page petition asserts Quw'utsun' possession and occupation of their land since 'time immemorial' and invokes the 1763 Royal Proclamation as a guarantee that these lands, not having been surrendered to the Crown, remain reserved for the Quw'utsun.'" See Union of BC Indian Chiefs, *Stolen Lands,* 22-23.

11 That statement was "unanimously adopted at a meeting of the Nisga'a Nation held at the village of Kincolith" on 22 January 1913. Speech of Chief Gosnell to the British Columbia Legislature, Victoria, 12 February, 1998, The Nisga'a Treaty, Speeches and Commentary, http://www.kermode.net/nisgaa/speeches/speeches.make.html.

12 See Harris, *Making Native Space.*

13 For example, in 1864, "thousands of Sto:lo and other Coast Salish travel[led] to New Westminster on Queen Victoria's birthday to protest the swell of European immigration and settlement in their territories ... Oral history among the Sto:lo records that Governor Seymour responded with a promise that one-third of the proceeds from land sales in the Fraser Valley would be taken by the colonial government, one-third would be given directly to the Sto:lo, and one-third would be set aside for the delivery of educational and social services for the Sto:lo people." See Union of BC Indian Chiefs, *Stolen Lands,* 18-19. In 1881, "Chief Mountain [led] a Nisga'a delegation to Victoria to protest increasing encroachment of farmers, fishermen and loggers in the Nass and Skeena valleys. The Nisga'a denounce[d] O'Reilly's reserve allocations" (ibid., 20). "In 1887, Tsimshian and Nisga'a chiefs [met] with ... [William] Smithe at his home to reject a reserve that had been set aside for them and to request a treaty" (ibid., 21). In 1885, "three Tsimshian chiefs travel[led] to Ottawa to express their concerns about land rights. They [were] the first Indigenous delegation from BC to take their protests to Ottawa" (ibid., 21). In 1908, "a delegation of 25 coastal chiefs travel[led] to Ottawa and present[ed] Prime Minister Laurier with two petitions, which he promise[d] to forward to King Edward VII" (ibid., 22). In 1906, "amid much media attention, a delegation of Squamish, Quw'utsun, Secwepemc, Okanagan, Nlaka'pamux and St'át'imc Chiefs travel[led] to London

and present[ed] King Edward VII with a petition protesting the lack of treaties and adequate reserves in BC" (ibid., 22).

14 In 1907, the Nisga'a Land Committee reformulated its objectives. Thereafter it functioned to "raise funds, solicit legal advice and enter into alliances with other indigenous peoples in order to assert territorial ownership and reject inadequate reserves" (ibid., 22). See also Drucker, *The Native Brotherhoods,* 91.

15 Formed by Secwepemc, Okanagan, Nlaka'pamux, and St'át'imc leaders. "James Teit, a local ethnographer, was recruited to translate their concerns and demands" (ibid., 23).

16 The Indian Rights Association raised money for legal expenses and included northern and southern coastal leaders. Appointed as secretary, missionary Charles Tate "drafted a legal position, *A Statement of Facts and Claims on Behalf of the Indians of British Columbia,* as a basis for a Privy Council hearing on Aboriginal Title" (ibid., 23).

17 Philip Drucker describes the group as "consisting principally of white members of congregations of one of the churches which was supporting considerable missionary work along the coast." They were likely Methodists who encouraged the settlement of land claims through petitions and financial aid. See Drucker *The Native Brotherhoods,* 92. See also Harry Hawthorn, Cyril Belshaw, and Stuart Jamieson, *The Indians of British Columbia: A Study of Contemporary Social Adjustment* (Berkeley/Toronto: University of California Press/University of Toronto Press, 1960), 54.

18 Forest LaViolette, *The Struggle for Survival: Indian Cultures and the Protestant Ethic in British Columbia* (Toronto: University of Toronto Press, 1973), 128-29.

19 Although there were others before 1873, the first petition included in the Union of BC Indian Chief's chronology was submitted by fifty-six Salish and Tsilhqot'in chiefs to the superintendent of Indian Affairs. In it, the chiefs demand compensation for lands given to settlers and reserve allotments of eighty acres per family. See Union of BC Indian Chiefs, *Stolen Lands,* 19. Other petitions listed are as follows: two petitions sent to Prime Minister Laurier from twenty-five coastal chiefs (1908); a petition to the Department of Indian Affairs from fourteen Secwepemc, Okanagan, Nlaka'pamux, and St'át'imc chiefs (1908); the Cowichan petition (1909); the "Petition of the Chiefs of Indian Bands of the Southern Interior at Spences Bridge" (1910); and the Nisga'a petition (1913).

20 Ravi de Costa, "Identity, Authority, and the Moral Worlds of Indigenous Petitions," *Comparative Studies in Society and History* 48, 3 (2006): 670.

21 See ibid., 675-77, for a similar analysis of a letter petition sent to Queen Victoria in 1846 from an aboriginal community in Tasmania.

22 Harris, *Making Native Space,* 153.

23 In 1904, for example, Chillihitza, an Okanagan chief, and Louie, a Secwepemc chief, travelled to Europe with Father LeJeune and met with Pope Leo XIII. It is not clear if there was an appeal at this time to recognize aboriginal title. Union of BC Indian Chiefs, *Stolen Lands,* 22. See also Galois, *Kwakwaka'wakw Settlements,* 30-31; Hawthorn, Belshaw, and Jamieson, *The Indians of British Columbia,* 53-54; and Drucker, *The Native Brotherhoods,* 90. Regarding the land question in BC, Hawthorn, Belshaw, and Jamieson and Drucker cite G.E. Shankel's PhD dissertation, "The Development of Indian Policy in British Columbia," as their primary source.

24 LaViolette, *Struggle for Survival,* 115.

25 Galois, *Kwakwaka'wakw Settlements,* and Harris, *Making Native Space,* 229.
26 Harris, *Making Native Space,* 228.
27 For an engaging collection of essays about aboriginal women's activism in Canadian and American cities, see Susan Applegate Krouse and Heather Howard, eds., *Keeping the Campfires Burning: Native Women's Activism in Urban Communities* (Lincoln: University of Nebraska Press, 2009).
28 Vestry Minutes, 1909-28, 19 April 1910, ADBCA, box 1, text 271.
29 ADBCA, "Aboriginal – Alert Bay," box 1, text 277.
30 Judith Okely, "Defiant Moments: Gender, Resistance and Individuals," *Man,* n.s., 26, 1 (1991): 8, 10.
31 Unsigned copy of letter, ADBCA, Alert Bay, Indians – General, 87-14, 277-2-27, 41-43.
32 "Intoxicants means and includes all spirits, strong waters, spirituous liquors, wines, or fermented or compounded liquors, or intoxicating drink of any kind whatsoever, and any intoxicating liquor or fluid, and opium, and any preparation there of, whether liquid or solid, and any other intoxicating drug or substance, and tobacco or tea mixed or compounded or impregnated with opium or with other intoxicating drugs, spirits or substances, and whether the same or any of them are liquid or solid." Indian Act, RSC 1906, c 43, s 1.
33 Ibid.
34 Renisa Mawani, in "In Between and Out of Place: Racial Hybridity, Liquor and the Law in Late 19th- and Early 20th-Century British Columbia," *Canadian Journal of Law and Society* 15, 2 (2000): 12, 25, suggests that the regulation of liquor was "among other things ... about space – who could drink, where, and with whom." Her list of those prohibited from drinking includes working-class whites, "half-breeds," and foreigners, who "blatantly disregarded the spatial restrictions ... imposed upon them and Indigenous populations." Her analysis suggests that liquor laws effectively restricted the "movements of mixed-race people" and sought to prevent their assimilation into both white and aboriginal worlds.
35 Union of BC Indian Chiefs, "McKenna-McBride Royal Commission, Kwawkewlth Agency Testimony," 1 June 1914, p. 109, Our Homes Are Bleeding, http://ubcic.bc.ca/Resources/ourhomesare/testimonies.htm.
36 Ibid., 2 June 1914, p. 132.
37 Bishop Roper to Mr. Chambers, no date, ADBCA, Indians – General, 87-14 277-2-27, 49.
38 Bishop Roper to Mrs. Cook, no date, ADBCA, Indians – General, 87-14 277-2-27, 50.
39 Jane Cook to Mr. Bowser, 15 December 1913, ADBCA, Indians – General, 87-14, 277-2-27, 41-43.
40 Archival evidence suggests that even at the turn of the century, among people residing at the Kwawkewlth Agency, there was a good deal of ambiguity about racialized identity and formal "Indian" status. People of mixed ancestry and noble ranking, whose families recognized them in the customary arena of the potlatch, were recorded on status lists for the agency. Stephen Cook, George Hunt, and his sons, Tom and Charlie Nowell, were included. In the 1890s, DIA officials compiled a "Half-Breed Census." Renisa Mawani suggests that there were attempts to have these people removed from reserved lands. As she writes, "Half-breeds" were the subject of particular attention in early colonial policy.

They threatened to obtain the rights and privileges of both settler and aboriginal groups. Most importantly, they could inhabit lands meant for settlers or stake claims for reserved lands. See Mawani, "In Between and Out of Place," 10-11.

41 DIA Circular on Marriage, 12 July 1906, Library and Archives Canada (LAC), Department of Indian Affairs, RG 10, vol. 3630, file 6244-41, part 2, Kwawkewlth Agency.

42 Ibid. See also Sarah Carter, "Creating 'Semi-Widows' and 'Supernumerary Wives': Prohibiting Polygamy in Prairie Canada's Aboriginal Communities to 1900," in *Contact Zones: Aboriginal and Settler Women in Canada's Colonial Past,* ed. Katie Pickles and Myra Rutherdale (Vancouver: UBC Press, 2005), 141.

43 In *Smoke from Their Fires,* Charlie Nowell describes in detail the marriage ceremony of his sixteen-year-old son Alfred to Ethel's sister Lucy, the daughter of Chief Iwakalas of Mamalilikala (Village Island):

> When all the tribes, except the Fort Ruperts, got through speaking, a thing was put up that was made like a mountain where the ancestor of the Mamaleleqala chief was living. They say that sometimes the road going up to his house was flat, when an enemy came to him, the road would slip back and be straight up and down, so the enemies couldn't get to where he was. This thing they had was an imitation to it – all made out of boards, about ten to fifteen feet high. Lucy, the chief's daughter, was sitting on top of this mountain with a mask of one of the wild women of the woods on her face, wearing a button blanket, and a man standing by her side is looking after the rope that pulls the board to make it steep ... All the different tribes had a young man that tried, and they couldn't make it. After that a Nimkis young man got up ... So he went while they beat the drums ... and there he stood by the chief's daughter ... This young man that went up there, received twenty-five pairs of blankets for getting up.

See Charles Nowell, *Smoke from Their Fires: The Life of a Kwakiutl Chief,* ed. Clellan Ford (New Haven: Yale University Press, 1941), 212.

44 Carter, "Creating 'Semi-Widows' and 'Supernumerary Wives,'" 141.

45 According to Sarah Carter, in 1894, every Indian Agent in western Canada was ordered to submit a list of polygamous families within their agencies. See Carter, "Creating 'Semi-Widows' and 'Supernumerary Wives,'" 147.

46 Ibid., 145.

47 ADBCA, 86-17, 63-12-10, 93-95.

48 Resolution 25, Lambeth Conference, 1888, Resolutions Archive, http://www.lambethconference.org.

49 From *Across the Rockies* 3, 11 (1912): 294.

50 Anglican Women's Auxiliary to Presbyterian Church of Canada, 30 November 1909, quoted in Margaret Whitehead, "A Useful Christian Woman: First Nations' Women and Protestant Missionary Work in British Columbia," *Atlantis* 18, 1-2 (1992-93): 155.

51 ADBCA, 86-17, 63-12-10, 93-95.

52 William Halliday to Bishop Roper, 2 March 1914, ADBCA, Indians – General, 87-14, 277-2-27-37.

53 In 1975, when the Department of Indian Affairs closed its office in Campbell River, some community members were invited to peruse and copy records from

the Kwawkewlth Agency. This letter, and a few others included in this book, are among materials that have made their way into personal archives.

54 Gilbert Cook Sr. states that this occurred in 1913. Interview with Gilbert Cook Sr., by Susan Day, August 1974, Alert Bay Library and Museum (ABLM), Cook Family file.

55 Douglas Cole and Ira Chaikin, *An Iron Hand upon the People: The Law against the Potlatch on the Northwest Coast* (Vancouver: Douglas and McIntyre, 1990), 97.

56 See Galois, *Kwakwa̱ka̱'wakw Settlements,* 148, 151.

57 Helen Codere calculated that the "Kwakiutl income" generated during 1913 was $138,260. Of that figure, $115,040 was earned in wages and through the fishing economy. See Codere, *Fighting with Property,* 45.

58 Courtesy of a family member, personal archive.

59 Drucker, *Native Brotherhoods,* 86-87.

60 Union of BC Indian Chiefs, "McKenna-McBride Royal Commission [MMRC], Kwawkewlth Agency Testimony." According to the transcripts, the following represented the tribes on the first day of hearings: "Chief Owahagaleese (Head Chief, Kwawkewlth Nation), Charles Nowell, Chief Lageuse (Nimkish Band), Sub-chief Cesaholis (Kingcombe Inlet Tribe), Willie Haris (Chief Nimkish Tribe), Chief Negai (Mahmalillikullah or Village Island), Chief Oats-ta-tollis, Johnnie Scow, Chief Lagis (Malilpi Band)."

61 I quote Douglas Harris, who paraphrases the opening address delivered at a hearing with Cowichan people in May 1913. See Douglas Harris, *Landing Native Fisheries: Indian Reserves and Fishing Rights in British Columbia, 1849-1925* (Vancouver: UBC Press, 2008), 167.

62 Two commissioners represented the provincial Government, two represented the federal government, and one was intended to be an impartial chairperson.

63 Drucker, *The Native Brotherhoods,* 93.

64 Tennant, *Aboriginal Peoples and Politics,* 88-89. Pre-emption is a process whereby an individual can claim provincial land for settlement or agriculture.

65 In part, given the diversity among First Nation societies, aboriginal rights are not clearly defined but are generally seen to encompass inherent collective rights that follow from precontact ways of life and include governance, land (title), resources, and all forms of cultural expression. Following a series of contemporary Supreme Court cases: "To define an aboriginal right, one must identify the practices, traditions and customs central to aboriginal societies that existed in North America prior to contact with Europeans ... the practice, tradition or custom must be an integral part of the distinctive culture of aboriginal peoples." Jane May Allain, Library of Parliament, Research Branch, *Aboriginal Fishing Rights: Supreme Court Decisions* (Ottawa: Supply and Services Canada, 1996).

66 Philip Drucker lists "the Skidegate Haida, several Gitksan villages and a few others" as those who rejected the commission. See Drucker, *Native Brotherhoods,* 94-95.

67 MMRC, "Kwawkewlth Agency testimony," Charlie Nowell, evidence and testimony, 1 June 1914, 93.

68 Among the speakers who testified in English were Charlie Nowell and Moses Alfred.

69 Brotchie translated for Alfred Hall and was the first "Native teacher" at the schools in 'Ya̱lis. He is listed as an interpreter at Royal Commission hearings on

board the *Tees,* where he worked with Koskimo, Quatsino, Nuhwitti, Quawshelch, Nahkwockte, and Fort Rupert speakers.

70 See Galois, *Kwakwaka'wakw Settlements,* 144-46, 149, 151-53, 313-14, and 316-18 for the list of land applications at the commission in which Jane Cook participated.

71 MMRC, "Kwawkewlth Agency testimony," 1 June 1914, 85.

72 Ibid.

73 MMRC, Progress Report 2, 21 April 1914.

74 MMRC, "Kwawkewlth Agency testimony," testimony of Chief Alf Lageuse, 2 June 1914.

75 See Harris, *Landing Native Fisheries,* 170-86, for an excellent discussion of fisheries and the McKenna-McBride Royal Commission.

76 MMRC, "Kwawkewlth Agency testimony," Nimpkish Band, 2 June 1914, 148.

77 Lagius told commissioners that, in 1913, for "the first time ever," eight 'Namgis fishers had stayed in 'Yalis to fish for the cannery. They earned $900 each for the five-week season. Women working at the cannery earned fifteen, thirty, or forty dollars "net." See MMRC,"Kwawkewlth Agency testimony," 2 June 1914, 142.

78 George Pokleetami, identified as a "Nahkwockte Band Chief," testified to the price of supplies purchased from cannery stores: tin of biscuits ($3.00), sack of flour ($2.50), eighteen pounds of sugar ($1.50), sack of potatoes ($3.00), and tea ($0.50/pound). Women working at the canneries cut fish and filled cans. They were paid three cents per tray (at twenty-five cans per tray) and generally made about twenty-five dollars over the course of five weeks. MMRC, 2 June 1914, 69.

79 Harris, *Landing Native Fisheries,* 112.

80 MMRC, "Kwawkewlth Agency testimony," 2 June 1914, 148.

81 Enfranchisement, or loss of Indian status, was among the mechanisms by which the province could claim reserve lands. See Drucker, *Native Brotherhoods,* 88-89, for a discussion of the history of the reversionary right to reserved land. Interestingly, William Duncan at Metlakatla sowed the seeds for this concept, which was eventually claimed by the province and is at the base of what Drucker calls the problem of dual ownership.

82 MMRC, "Kwawkewlth Agency testimony," 2 June 1914, 148.

83 Wedłidi referred me to Charles Nowell, *Smoke from Their Fires: The Life of a Kwakiutl Chief,* ed. Clellan Ford (New Haven, CT: Yale University Press, 1941), 51-52, in which Charlie Nowell states that women at Fort Rupert *owned* gardens. They marked the four corners of their property with sticks and guarded against trespass. Gardens were passed from mother to daughters. Nowell told Clellan Ford that clover-root gardens were eaten by cows brought in to the fort and that potatoes and other roots were also grown. At other hearings before the commission, several chiefs, when asked, remarked on the importance of gardens in their villages. They mentioned fruit trees, potatoes, turnips, garden vegetables, and traditional roots and grasses. When a commissioner asked Humseet, a Da'naxda'xw chief, to name the traditional foods grown and collected by his forefathers, he offered a list that included the following: "Toksus (clover root) Clicksum (Wild Lupin), Kwane, Kukum (wild rice) and Khutum, that is all the vegetables. Now the berries, high bush cranberries, wild crab apples, and then the salmon berries and the wild strawberries, huckleberries, blue huckleberries,

wild gooseberries, blackberries, salal berries, thimble berries." MMRC, Tenakteuk Band, 3 June 1914, 188.

84 Philip Drucker suggests that the fence was explicitly understood as such a symbol and refused by many aboriginal people "for fear of weakening ... title claims to unenclosed portions." He provides an example from 1865 among the Cowichan people. See Drucker, *Native Brotherhoods,* 87.

85 Thomas Biolsi discusses the colonial process of "empropertyment" as it played out in Lakota communities. See Thomas Biolsi, "The Birth of the Reservation: Making the Modern Individual among the Lakota," *American Ethnologist* 22, 1 (1995): 28-53.

86 MMRC, "Kwawkewlth Agency testimony," 2 June 1914, 149.

87 Ibid., 156-57.

88 Ibid., 157-59.

89 The Alert Bay Industrial School Reserve was initially intended for those who had given up the potlatch. By 1904, there were eight houses built on "the residential school site," which had been set aside for former industrial school students who chose to stay in 'Ya̱lis.

90 There was a good deal of talk about these lands. In response to McKenna's statements about dominion ownership, Ma̱malilika̱la chief Negai asked: "When did they buy it? Who did they buy it from, and why didn't they let me know about it?" MMRC,"Kwawkewlth Agency testimony," 2 June 1914, 194.

91 Harris, *Making Native Space,* 274, 275.

92 The letter stated: "Reverend Hall asserted that it was Mr. Huson who had proposed cancelling his (Huson's) lease in exchange for a free grant of 160 acres, and then making the balance an Indian reserve." Indian Claims Commission, *Inquiry into the Cormorant Island Claim of the 'Na̱mgis First Nation,* March 1996, 29, available online.

93 In *Kwakwa̱ka̱'wakw Settlements,* 139, Galois suggests the chief's name as "Ha̱mdxid." It appears with a question mark in his work.

94 MMRC, Tananteuk Band, 3 June 1914, 185.

95 On Franz Boas's 1934 map of Knight Inlet, he shows fourteen eulachon fishing sites owned by ten different tribes; see Galois, *Kwakwa̱ka̱'wakw Settlements,* 137. See also Franz Boas, *Kwakiutl Ethnography,* ed. Helen Codere (Chicago: University of Chicago Press, 1966), 24-28, for a map of 152 named sites on the Klinaklini River.

96 Applications no. 80 and 111, quoted in Galois, *Kwakwa̱ka̱'wakw Settlements,* 151, from MMRC evidence, Tananteuk Band, 3 June 1914, 184.

97 He was from the family of brothers that included Munday Seaweed, Johnson Seaweed, Bob Harris, Tom Duncan, and Mike Louie. As Wedłidi Speck explained, they chose the English names themselves, and although different, these men were brothers.

98 MMRC, Tananteuk Band, 3 June 1914.

99 See Harris, *Making Native Space,* 234-35, for a discussion of the clash between "local knowledges" and the commisssioners' "quantitative procedures," including maps.

100 Aboriginal title is a communal right: an individual cannot hold aboriginal title. The traditional territory of a First Nation is the land it occupied and used historically, including sites outside of the primary territorial range, where groups

had interests, where they held the right to access and use particular resources. Legally, property is considered a bundle of rights: the right to exclude, the right to use or enjoy, and the right to transfer. Property can be private, common, or shared, and it can include tangible and intangible things.

101 MMRC, Chief Tsukaite, 8 June 1914, 243.

102 MMRC, Chief Qua-wha-lagha-loose, 8 June 1914, 243.

103 MMRC, "Kwawkewlth Agency testimony," Chief Lageuse, 2 June 1914, 138.

104 Galois, *Kwakwaka'wakw Settlements,* 61.

105 Tennant, *Aboriginal Peoples and Politics,* 97-98.

106 ACDBCA, Indians – General, 87-14 277-2-27-38/39.

107 MMRC, "Kwawkewlth Agency testimony," Chief Lageuse, 2 June 1914, 147.

108 MMRC, "Kwawkewlth Agency testimony," Harry Mountain, 1 June 1914, 127.

109 Ibid.

110 MMRC, "Kwawkewlth Agency testimony," Charlie Nowell, 1 June 1914, 104.

111 In 1874, according to Renisa Mawani, Justice Matthew Baillie Begbie had drafted a bill for the BC government to provide "for Indian concubines and destitute half-breed children of persons dying intestate and leaving property in the province." The bill was never passed. See Mawani, "In Between and Out of Place," 23.

112 LAC, RG 10, vol. 3630, file 6244-4, pt. 2. These microfilm records are difficult to decipher.

113 William Halliday, Notice to Chiefs of all Bands, 1 September 1914, U'mista Cultural Centre Archives (UCCA), A96-021-70.11.

114 The Keatzie petition represented several Salish groups, people from Campbell River, Cape Mudge, and Salmon River, the One-ka tribes and the Keatzie tribes: "We want our old costume to stand by without no alteration whatever." See Keatzie petition, Port Hammond, BC, 7 September 1914, UCCA, A 96-021-0-11.

115 Charlie Nowell to A.S. Clements, MP, 28 January 1915, LAC, RG 10, vol. 3629, file 6244-3.

116 Fort Rupert, BC, to Secretary, Department for Indian Affairs, Ottawa, 2 March 1915, UCCA, A96-021-70.11.

117 Jane Cook to William Halliday, 13 June 1915, UCCA, A96-18-60-19a.

118 According to Brian Titley, Duncan Campbell Scott saw their service as an indication of their patriotism. Returning soldiers were given the federal franchise without having to enfranchise, or lose their status. Under the Soldier Settlement Act, veterans were eligible for land grants and could participate in a loan system. See E. Brian Titley, *A Narrow Vision: Duncan Campbell Scott and the Administration of Indian Affairs* (Vancouver: UBC Press, 1986), 101.

119 The other men who enlisted were Arthur Stanley, Benjamin Blenkinsop, William Roberts, and Carey Newman. William Halliday to Secretary, Department of Indian Affairs, 26 December 1918, LAC, RG 10, vol. 3630, file 6244-41, pt. 2, Kwawkewlth Agency.

120 "All shipping was ... directed that on passing the upper end of Vancouver Island they must proceed ... to the entrance of Blackney Passage, there to be given permission to enter Johnston[e] Straits. Broughton Strait was closed and mined across from the lighthouse on Malcolm Island to Vancouver Island at McNeill Point." Two small boats armed with torpedoes cruised the waters each night.

"Fish carriers" tied up at the sawmill docks were also equipped with torpedoes. See "Fred Wastell, Alert Bay," City of Vancouver Archives, S62-F-4, file 8.

121 Gilbert Cook Sr., interviewed by Susan Day, August 1974, ABLM, Cook Family file.

122 Nellie Hamilton Cook, interview with Joan Skogan and Vicki Cook, August 1973, ABLM, Cook Family file.

123 Petition from Kwagutl to Deputy Superintendent of Indian Affairs, 17 February 1919, UCCA, A96-021-70.11.

124 See Galois, *Kwakwaka'wakw Settlements,* 201, 312. According to Galois, the total population of all nine tribal groupings in 1914 was 1,183 persons.

Part VI: "We Are the Aboriginee, Which Is Not a Citizen," 1918-27

1 Letter from NWA to Chief and Council, 3 December 1987, courtesy of Pearl Alfred.

2 Dara Culhane Speck, *An Error in Judgement: The Politics of Medical Care in an Indian Community* (Vancouver: Talonbooks, 1987), 35, 225.

3 Culhane Speck, *An Error in Judgement,* 83.

4 See also Helen Codere, *Fighting with Property: A Study of Kwakiutl Potlatching and Warfare, 1792-1930,* Monographs of the American Ethnological Society 18 (New York: J.J. Augustin, 1950), 61.

5 Franz Boas, Kwakiutl Ethnographic Notes, 1918-31, American Philosophical Society Library and Archives (APS), 497.3c, p. 71.

6 Charlie Nowell told Drucker and Heizer that "although the missionaries vigorously denounced the Shaman's Society performances (aka the Winter Dances or Red Cedar Bark ceremonies), the potlatch ... was opposed not as 'heathenish' or non-Christian, but simply because participation was in violation of the law." See Philip Drucker and Robert Heizer, *To Make My Name Good: A Reexamination of the Southern Kwakiutl Potlatch* (Berkeley: University of California Press, 1967), 22.

7 Charlie Nowell and Moses Alfred spoke out against the quality of education in 'Yalis. The following charge is included in their complaint against the missionaries: "The school system is also insufficient. The teacher deliberately refuses to impart education beyond a certain limit, stating that the Indian must not be allowed to acquire too much knowledge." School officials also cited a residential school regulation – "pupils should only remain in class-rooms a half day and have the other half outside" – in defence of making the students perform manual labour. According to the DIA, the rule was, apparently, "for consideration of the health of the Indians, as it had been found that the Indian children could not stand the confinement of class-rooms for the full day's study the same as white children." Rather than dealing with the strains children endured under the new regimen of separation from families and the rhythms of their communities, the church responded with an explanation that medicalized and racialized the children's tolerance for "confinement." Anglican Diocese of British Columbia Archives (ADBCA), Synod Office General Administrative files, 1928-30, text 63, box 12/23.

8 William Halliday to Secretary, Department of Indian Affairs, 19 October 1918, family papers.
9 Titley, *A Narrow Vision,* 176-77.
10 "Memorandum of Prosecutions under Section 149 of the Indian Act," submitted to DIA by Andrew Paull, Allied Tribes, no date, 1922, Library and Archives Canada (LAC), Department of Indian Affairs, RG 10, vol. 3630, file 6244-4, pt. 2.
11 William Halliday to D.C. Scott, 13 February 1919, family papers.
12 F. Comley to Bishop of Columbia, 12 February 1919, ADBCA, text 55, box 2, file 1.
13 Handwritten letter Jane Cook to William Halliday, UCCA, Withheld Items, Potlatch Files, A96-18-60-19a.
14 Douglas Cole, "The History of the Kwakiutl Potlatch," in *Chiefly Feasts: The Enduring Kwakiutl Potlatch,* ed. Aldona Jonaitis (Seattle: University of Washington Press, 1991), 152.
15 U'mista Cultural Centre Archives (UCCA), Withheld Items, Potlatch Files, A96-18-60-19a; LAC, RG 10, vol. 8481, file 1/24-3, pt. 1.
16 LAC, RG 10, vol. 8481, file 1/24-3, pt. 1.
17 From their reading of Anglican records, Douglas Cole and Ira Chaikin estimate that between eight and eighteen couples had been married in the church after 1884. They do qualify this estimate by writing that it depends on "how one counts half bloods and names not readily identifiable." See Douglas Cole and Ira Chaikin, *An Iron Hand upon the People: The Law against the Potlatch on the Northwest Coast* (Vancouver: Douglas and McIntyre, 1990), 202n27.
18 Petition presented to D.C. Scott, Ottawa, on behalf of the Kwagutl Agency, 17 February 1919, UCCA, A96-021-70.11.
19 Ibid.
20 Ibid.
21 Response to petition, J.D. McLean, Assistant Deputy and Secretary DIA, 18 February 1919, UCCA, A96-021-70.11.
22 The response included the following points:

2nd Regarding "Entertainments" such as moving pictures, dancing and social gatherings, these were allowed; but it was against the law to "give away, pay or give back money, goods or articles of any sort at any Indian Festival or ceremony."

3rd The DIA agreed that the government allowance of $1.25 per month is too little, but they refused to amend Section 149, to allow people to look after their sick and poor. William Halliday was instructed that he may increase allowances where necessary.

4th In response to the request "for enfranchisement and political rights equal to the white man," along with the charge of "taxation without representation," the DIA replied that they do not control the $5.00 Provincial Head Tax, but the $1.00 Dog Tax is part of the Indian Act and will not change.

5th Regarding the demand for Indian representation in Parliament, the DIA stated that the request is beyond its scope but "will no doubt be duly considered should the Indians become enfranchised."

6th W.E. Ditchburn will investigate complaints that Indian Agent Halliday is "unreliable, inefficient and neglects the affairs of the Indian giving preference to his private interests." He did not go among the sick during the Spanish Flu epidemic, or obtain supplies; he refused firewood to a sick woman.

7th Ditchburn will also investigate complaints that the Missionaries have lost "the respect and sympathy of the Indians," that the Sawmill is exploitative, and the standard of education is inadequate.

23 William Halliday to Secretary, Department of Indian Affairs, 29 March 1919, family papers.

24 "An Act to Amend the Marriage Act," RSBC 1919, 29 March 1919. The amendment also included sec. 24a: "If parents of any child born out of lawful wedlock marry each other after the birth of the child, that child shall for all purposes be deemed the legitimate child of the parents from the time of birth." The amendment was retroactive, covering the period before "the enactment of this section."

25 Cole and Chaikin, *An Iron Hand,* 112.

26 Ibid.

27 Ibid., 115. In letters to lawyers seeking the report, the DIA referred to the so-called anthropological division of the National Museum, a nonexistent body. The archived copy of Barbeau's report cites the anthropological sector of the Department of Mines. Lawyers for the potlatchers saw hope in the elusive report. Having elicited the services of Vancouver law firm Dickie & DeBeck, Kwakwaka'wakw chiefs were advised that "any report against the Potlatch will kill it for all time. On the other hand, if we could get a report sufficiently strong in favor of the Potlatch, it would probably lead to either a change in the Law or to a change in the administration of Indian Affairs." Dickie & DeBeck to Johnny Scow, 15 December 1920, LAC, RG 10, vol. 3631, file 6244-5.

28 William Halliday to Secretary, Department of Indian Affairs, 19 April 1919, family papers.

29 Letter from A.W. Corker to Bishop Schofield, 22 April 1919, ADBCA, Bishop's Papers, 85-38, 55-2-1-94.

30 W.E. Ditchburn, Chief Inspector of Indian Agencies, Ottawa, to Bishop Schofield, Victoria, 11 June 1919, ADBCA, Synod Office General Administrative Files, text 63, box 12/23.

31 James Sewid, *Guests Never Leave Hungry: The Autobiography of James Sewid, a Kwakiutl Indian,* ed. James Spradley (New Haven: Yale University Press, 1969), 49.

32 Handwritten Oaths for Interpreters, BC Supreme Court, New Westminster, BC Archives (BCA), GR-3145, reel B14170.

33 William Halliday to Secretary, Department of Indian Affairs, Ottawa, 19 December 1922, LAC, RG 10, vol. 3630, file 6244-4, pt. 2.

34 William Halliday to Secretary, Department of Indian Affairs, Ottawa, 30 August 1922, LAC, RG 10, vol. 3630, file 6244-4, pt. 2.

35 See Tina Loo, "Dan Cranmer's Potlatch: Law as Coercion, Symbol, and Rhetoric in British Columbia, 1884-1951," *Canadian Historical Review* 68, 2 (1992): 125-65, for a discussion of possible motivations for testifying.

36 Cole and Chaikin, *An Iron Hand,* 116.

37 Ibid.

38 "This grease really belongs to all the people," Halliday wrote in 1918, "as each man knows to a pint how much he is entitled to and I have been asked to give

permission to have the people come together for this distribution." William Halliday to Duncan Scott, 27 December 1918, UCCA, DIA Correspondence, 1913-19, A96-021-70.11.

39 See Aaron Glass, "The Thin Edge of the Wedge: Dancing around the Potlatch Ban, 1921-1951," in *Right to Dance: Dancing for Rights,* ed. Naomi Jackson (Banff: Banff Centre, 2004), 6.

40 A.W. Corker, Alert Bay, to Duncan Scott, Ottawa, 6 March 1920, ADBCA, Synod Office General Administration, text 63, box 12/23.

41 Regarding marriage, the committee stated that neither groom nor bride had the option of consent. The southern sex trade, they wrote, still played a part in raising money for prestige marriages, and it was extremely rare for a girl to refuse the man chosen by her father. They used the term "mortgages" to describe the marriage contract. Financial hardship included the committee's description of the custom and role of "digita," "a continuous strain" on the father who often has to borrow money at "100% interest" to "give away [when] a child meets an accident of any description." Ibid.

42 This is Munday Siwiti.

43 Cole and Chaikin, *An Iron Hand,* 117.

44 Royal Canadian Mounted Police, "E" Division, Alert Bay Detachment, Crime Report, Mrs. MacDougall and Munday [Siwiti], 31 January 1921, LAC, RG 10, vol. 3630, file 6244-4, pt. 1.

45 Ibid. See also Agnes Alfred's account of the incident in Martine Reid, ed., *Paddling to Where I Stand: Agnes Alfred, Qwiqwasutinuxw Noblewoman,* trans. Daisy Sewid-Smith (Vancouver: UBC Press, 2004), 205.

46 "Jennie MacDougall was born in 1907, and Munday was born in 1860" (Wedłidi Speck).

47 The ellipses are in Nella Nelson's original text.

48 Alice Olney's daughter Dorothy had recently died from tuberculosis.

49 "Am I right in entering this conviction on the ground that the proceedings constituted a ceremony?" the judge wrote in his case notes. Unsigned, undated, "Form of Case Stated, In the High Court of Justice re: Code 7-61," LAC, RG 10, vol. 3630, file 6244-4, pt. 2.

50 There is a prolific literature about this potlatch, which has come to represent what Aaron Glass calls "the emblematic moment in twentieth-century Kwa̱kwa̱ka'wakw life." See the work of Tina Loo, Daisy Sewid-Smith, Forrest LaViolette, Douglas Cole and Ira Chaikin, and Barbara Saunders, and also see the film *Potlatch: A Strict Law Bids Us Dance.*

51 Gloria Cranmer-Webster, Foreword to *Kesu': The Art and Life of Doug Cranmer,* by Jennifer Kramer (Toronto: Douglas and McIntyre, 2012), 1.

52 Cole and Chaikin, *An Iron Hand,* 118.

53 See Daisy Sewid-Smith, *Prosecution or Persecution* (Cape Mudge: Nu-yum-baleess Society, 1979), 57, for Herbert Martin's account. The men were said to have been working for "Gah-uk-sta-lus."

54 Royal Canadian Mounted Police, "E" Division, Alert Bay Division, Crime Report, 1 March 1922, LAC, RG 10, vol. 3630, file 6244-4, pt. 2.

55 Reid, *Paddling to Where I Stand,* 46.

56 Halliday to Duncan Campbell Scott, 1 March 1922, LAC, RG 10, vol. 3630, file 6244-4, pt. 2.

57 In the report on the prosecutions that Halliday sent to Duncan Campbell Scott, he names Charlie Hunt as a "man of the Nimkish Band ... [who] refused to sign the agreement and ... turn in his paraphernalia." See William Halliday to Duncan Campbell Scott, 10 April 1922, LAC, RG 10, vol. 3630, file 6244-4, pt. 2.

58 Sewid-Smith, *Prosecution or Persecution,* 59. In the Kwawkewlth Agency Report of April 1922, Halliday writes: "Fifty eight informations had been laid which after being heard resulted in nine dismissals, twenty-three were given suspended sentence, twenty two were sentenced to two months' imprisonment and four to six months' imprisonment. In the case of three of the latter the stay on execution was suspended and an application made for parole." William Halliday, Report of the Kwawkewlth Agency, April 1922, LAC, RG 10, vol. 3630, file 6244-4, pt. 2.

59 Sewid-Smith, *Prosecution or Persecution,* 60.

60 William Halliday to Secretary, DIA, Ottawa, 19 May 1922, LAC, RG 10, vol. 3630, file 6244-4, pt. 2.

61 *Victoria Colonist,* 30 August 1922. Boas was then sixty-four. He travelled to the West Coast to do linguistic work with interior Salish groups. See Ronald Rohner, "The Boas Canon: A Posthumous Addition – Review of Kwakiutl Ethnography by Franz Boas, Helen Codere," *Science* 158, 3799 (1967): 362-64.

62 William Ditchburn to Duncan Campbell Scott, 1 September 1922, LAC, RG 10, vol. 3630, file 6244-4, pt. 2.

63 Duncan Campbell Scott to Edward Sapir, 9 October 1922, LAC, RG 10, vol. 3630, file 6244-4, pt. 2.

64 For a sum of $291. William Halliday to Secretary, DIA, 5 September 1922, LAC, RG 10, vol. 3630, file 6244-4, pt. 2.

65 Scott to Sapir, 9 October 1922.

66 Duncan Campbell Scott to Wm. Kearns, Assistant Auditor General, Ottawa, 26 January 1924, LAC, RG 10, vol. 3630, file 6244-4, pt. 2.

67 Barbeau concluded that "deny[ing] the Kwakiutl Indians the institution of the Potlatch would: 1) deprive them of their natural laws and customs which are calculated to bring peace and happiness to their minds. 2) Destroy initiative. 3) Force them to assimilate with the white race which is impossible. 4) Abolish the fundamental principles in their economic methods. 5) Destroy their methods and customs of trade and commerce[?]. 6) [Illegible] and death. All of which are a direct outcome and consolidated with the principles of the Potlatch. 7) Extinguish his vested rights and result in a material loss." C.M. Barbeau, "Report of the Anthropological Division of the Department of Mines regarding Potlatch," 1921, LAC, RG 10, vol. 3631, file 6244-X.

68 In April 1923, after convicting ten "Nakwato Band potlatchers living at Blunder Harbour," he was obviously vexed when convictions were dropped because of a clerical error. Public opinion, it seems, was beginning to turn. As Halliday wrote to the secretary of the Department of Indian Affairs, "Convictions for potlatching do not as a general rule meet with favorable comment by the general public. In fact I myself received a very insulting letter after the last conviction signed KKK." William Halliday to Secretary, DIA, 14 April 1923, LAC, RG 10, vol. 3630, file 6244-4, pt. 2.

69 This delegation included Billy Assu, Charles Nowell, Johnny Drabble, Harry Mountain, Bob Harris and five others. See Cole and Chaikin, *An Iron Hand,* 134-35.

70 Philip Drucker, *The Native Brotherhoods: Modern Intertribal Organizations on the Northwest Coast,* Bureau of American Ethnology Bulletin 168 (Washington, DC: Smithsonian Institute, 1958), 95, 98-99. More specifically, they sought an "increase of reserved lands to one hundred and sixty acres per person; rights to foreshores; 'beneficial ownership' in Tribal [language group] control; management of their own trust funds; a reimbursement of expenses to Allied Tribes for pursuing their claims; and, removal of restrictions in the Provincial Land Act regarding pre-emption of Crown lands by Indians."

71 Ibid., 96.

72 Ibid., 96, 97.

73 Allied Tribes, "Conference of Dr. Duncan Campbell Scott, Deputy Superintendent General of Indian Affairs, and W.E. Ditchburn, with the Executive Committee of the Allied Tribes of BC, Victoria, 7 August 1923," 116, BCA, ADD MSS 997.

74 James Teit to Andrew Paull, 10 May 1922, LAC, RG 10, vol. 3630, file 6244-4, pt. 2. He cited condition 19, page 14, of the Allied Tribes' "Statement to the Government of BC," 1919.

75 Edwin DeBeck was a good choice. He had lived in Alert Bay from 1902, when, upon the death of R.H. Pidcock, DeBeck's father, George, took over as Indian Agent of the Kwawkewlth Agency. He resigned in 1906.

76 Edwin DeBeck to D.C. Scott, 2 August 1922, LAC, RG 10, vol. 3630, file 6244-4, pt. 2.

77 Edwin DeBeck to Moses Alfred, 1 August 1922, LAC, RG 10, vol. 3630, file 6244-4, pt. 2.

78 U'mista Cultural Centre, *Box of Treasures,* Chuck Olin, director and producer (Watertown, MA: Documentary Educational Resources, 1983).

79 Pam Brown, "Cannery Days: A Chapter in the Lives of the Heiltsuk" (master's thesis, University of British Columbia, 1993), 5-6.

80 While jarring, this use of the Anglo-Canadian label for Japanese immigrants suggests aboriginal participation in the mainstream discourse of the 1920s. Just as the epithet *Indian* is deemed pejorative when used by particular speakers today, the term *Jap* had not yet accumulated the stigma associated with it during the Second World War. I retain it here in order to explicitly recognize the context of racialized identities on the Coast.

81 Allied Tribes, "Conference of Dr. Duncan Campbell Scott," 157-65.

82 The McKenna-McBride commissioners penned a twenty-eight-page confidential report denouncing the exclusion of aboriginal fishers from employment by canneries. By law they were obligated to hire these men first. See Douglas Harris, *Landing Native Fisheries: Indian Reserves and Fishing Rights in British Columbia, 1849-1925* (Vancouver: UBC Press, 2008), 179-80.

83 Ibid., 141-42, 156. Harris quotes from a chilling statement by BC Packers officials in 1913: "It is not deemed advisable to grant Indians 'Independent' licenses, as they are liable to mis-interpret the reason and become difficult to manage by the authorities" (141).

84 Ibid., 179.

85 Ibid., 163.

86 Ibid., 137n35, 163.

87 Ibid., 180.

88 Ibid., 149, 157.

89 Ibid., 113.
90 See Leslie Robertson, *Imagining Difference: Legend, Curse, and Spectacle in a Canadian Mining Town* (Vancouver: UBC Press, 2005).
91 Scott had been pushing for compulsory enfranchisement for some time. "It is neither just nor reasonable that the state should continue to bear expense and responsibility on behalf of those who are quite capable of conducting their own affairs." Duncan Campbell Scott, *Report of the Department of Indian Affairs for the year ended 31 March, 1917,* 20, quoted in Titley, *A Narrow Vision,* 48. Under Scott's insistence, section 122 of the Indian Act (1918) was later amended to allow "Indians ... who held no land on a reserve and did not follow 'the Indian way of life' to apply [for] enfranchisement" (ibid.) Titley notes that under the prior legislation for voluntary enfranchisement (1867-1918), only 65 families (102 persons) had opted for enfranchisement. "In the two years following the 1920 Bill 14, 97 families, 258 persons, underwent the process" (ibid.).
92 Ibid., 48-49.
93 Ibid., 49, 50.
94 Ibid., 51.
95 See Harris, *Landing Native Fisheries,* 184.
96 Forrest LaViolette, *The Struggle for Survival: Indian Cultures and the Protestant Ethic in British Columbia* (Toronto: University of Toronto Press, 1973), 138.
97 Gilbert Cook Jr., as told to Rob Morris, "The Cook Family of Alert Bay," *Western Mariner* 2, 10 (2004): 24.
98 Tennant, *Aboriginal People and Politics,* 73.
99 Nutrition was a prominent concern during the years of this research: nutrition and its relationship to diabetes; nutrition and its relationship to traditional food sources and cultural pride; and, as Pearl Alfred states above, nutrition and its relationship to the food fishery – and so, to climate change, economic downturns, and Department of Fisheries and Oceans regulations.
100 "Statement of the Allied Indian Tribes of British Columbia for the Government of British Columbia," 1919, 14.
101 Allied Tribes, "Conference of Dr. Duncan Campbell Scott," 209.
102 Ibid., 211.
103 Ibid., 212.
104 Ibid., 213-15.
105 Ibid., 215.
106 Chief Lageus, 2 June 1914, 140, Union of BC Indian Chiefs, "McKenna-McBride Royal Commission, Kwawkewlth Agency Testimony," Our Homes Are Bleeding, http://ubcic.bc.ca/Resources/ourhomesare/testimonies.htm.
107 DIA Annual Report, Kwawkewlth Agency, Expenditures 1881, declassified files, family papers.
108 A.W. Vowell to Richard Pidcock, 21 January 1895; A.W. Vowell to Richard Pidcock, 17 December 1895, declassified files, family papers.
109 A.W. Vowell to George DeBeck, 1 November 1902, declassified files, family papers.
110 A.W. Vowell to George DeBeck, 3 October 1902, declassified files, family papers.
111 George DeBeck to A.W. Vowell, 17 December 1904, declassified files, family papers.

112 Culhane Speck, *An Error in Judgement,* 83.
113 See Charles Briggs, "Communicability, Racial Discourse and Disease," *Annual Review of Anthropology* 34 (2005): 276.
114 Castor oil and epsom salts were among the common medicines distributed by missionaries, Indian Agents, and physicians.
115 Allied Tribes, "Conference of Dr. Duncan Campbell Scott," 217.
116 Ibid., 217-18.
117 Codere, *Fighting with Property,* 54.
118 The records of Christ Church indicate that between 1919 and 1923 thirty-six people were buried in its cemetery. The numbers represent Anglicans only, and only those buried at the Anglican cemetery. Fifteen people died from TB, eight from accidents, four by drowning, two each from cancer and pneumonia, and one each from heart disease, paralysis, poisoning, and bronchitis. Anglican Diocese Archival Records, Baptisms and Burials, 1881-1926, UCCA, A96-018-60.20.
119 See Culhane Speck, *An Error in Judgement,* 83, for a detailed account of the ceremony.
120 Cole and Chaikin, *An Iron Hand,* 137.
121 Memorandum for the Minister of the Interior, Statement Re the Potlatch by the Indians of the Kwawkewlth Agency, 20 September 1925, LAC, RG 10, vol. 3630, file 6244-4, pt. 2.
122 Edwin DeBeck to Moses Alfred, 1 August 1922, LAC, RG 10, vol. 3630, file 6244-4, pt. 2.
123 Andrew Paull to Duncan Campbell Scott, 30 August 1923, LAC, RG 10, vol. 3630, file 6244-4, pt. 2.
124 Jane Cook to D.C. Scott, 17 November 1923, LAC, RG 10, vol. 3630, file 6244-4, pt. 2.
125 William Halliday to W.E. Ditchburn, 26 January 1924, UCCA, Withheld Items, Potlatch files, A96-18-60-19a.
126 W.E. Ditchburn to William Halliday, 29 January 1924, LAC, RG 10, vol. 3630, file 6244-4, pt. 2.
127 William Halliday to Duncan Scott, 6 February 1924, LAC, RG 10, vol. 3630, file 6244-4, pt. 2.
128 William Halliday to D.C. Scott, 2 March 1924, LAC, RG 10, vol. 3630, file 6244-4, pt. 2.
129 D.C. Scott to William Halliday, 3 March 1924, LAC, RG 10, vol. 3630, file 6244-4, pt. 2.
130 Andrew Paull to D.C. Scott, 30 September 1925, LAC, RG 10, vol. 3630, file 6244-4, pt. 2.
131 Memorandum for the Minister of the Interior, 20 September 1925.
132 Drucker, *Native Brotherhoods,* 99.
133 Ibid., 101.
134 According to William Wasden Jr., the name translates as "Copper in the House."

Part VII: "With the Potlatch Custom in My Blood," 1930-39

1 See Fay Blaney, "Aboriginal Women's Action Network," in *Strong Women Stories: Native Vision and Community Survival,* ed. Kim Anderson and Bonita Lawrence

(Toronto: Sumach Press, 2003), 167; Jennifer Nez Denetdale, "Chairmen, Presidents, and Princesses: The Navajo Nation, Gender, and the Politics of Tradition," *Wicazo Sa Review* 21, 1 (2006): 9-28; Emma LaRoque, "Métis and Feminist: Ethical Reflections on Feminism, Human Rights and Decolonization," in *Making Space for Indigenous Feminism,* ed. Joyce Green (Blackpoint, NS: Fernwood, 2007), 62.

2 Joyce Green, "Taking Account of Aboriginal Feminism," in *Making Space for Indigenous Feminism,* ed. Joyce Green (Blackpoint, NS: Fernwood, 2007), 26-27.

3 In the scholarly works about the history of aboriginal rights activism on the Northwest Coast that I have consulted, Jane Cook is mentioned only in Robert Galois's *Kwakwaka'wakw Settlements, 1775-1920: A Geographical Analysis and Gazetteer* (Vancouver: UBC Press, 1994) and Douglas Harris's *Landing Native Fisheries: Indian Reserves and Fishing Rights in British Columbia, 1849-1925* (Vancouver: UBC Press, 2008).

4 C.K.K. Prosser to Anglican Bishop, 18 January 1931, Anglican Diocese of British Columbia Archives (ADBCA), box 1, text 203.

5 Ibid.

6 Ruth Benedict to Franz Boas, 21 November 1930, UBC Library Archives (UBCLA), Franz Boas Correspondence.

7 Acculturation "is neither a passive nor a colorless absorption. It is culture-producing as well as a culture-receiving process. Acculturation, particularly when not forced, is essentially creative." Margaret Blackman, "Creativity in Acculturation," *Ethnohistory* 23, 4 (1976): 388.

8 Ibid., 388, 391.

9 At the invitation of Finnish residents there, Averkieva also spent some time at the utopian community of Sointula on neighbouring Malcolm Island. Averkieva was born in a "small coastal village of Poduzhemyeh, located on the White Sea in Karelia, just east of Finland." Mark Sherman, Introduction to *Kwakiutl String Figures,* by Julia Averkieva (Vancouver: UBC Press, 1992), xvii.

10 William Halliday to Franz Boas, 18 December 1930, UBCLA. Weeks later, Boas wrote to his dean at Columbia University in New York. "On December 18th I had a sudden attack of weakness of the heart and I have been on my back ever since." He informed Dean McBain that it would be two weeks before he could return to the university. See Boas to Dean McBain, 4 January 1931, UBCLA.

11 Boas to Governor of British Columbia, 25 November 1930, UBCLA. Boas stated clearly that he had not witnessed these conditions himself but that he considered "it a humanitarian duty to try to help in remedying the situation." He wrote that there had been two deaths in as many months from dysentery, caused by drinking water running too close to latrines. "Syphilis," he wrote "was introduced through the women who lived as prostitutes in Victoria." Regarding the inoculations, Boas might have been referring to the "intravenous arsenical preparations" and injections of "silver compounds" used to treat syphilis after the turn of the century. See Robert McKechnie, *Strong Medicine: History of Healing on the Northwest Coast* (Victoria: Morris, 1972), 140.

12 Franz Boas to Ernst Boas, 5 January 1931, in Ronald Rohner, *The Ethnography of Franz Boas* (Chicago: University of Chicago Press, 1969), 299.

13 Franz Boas to Ernst Boas, 11 January 1931, American Philosophical Library and Archives (APS), Franz Boas Papers, 497.3 Am3.

14 Franz Boas to Ernst Boas, 11 January 1931, in Rohner, *The Ethnography of Franz Boas,* 301.

15 See Judith Berman, "George Hunt and the Kwak'wala Texts," *Anthropological Linguistics* 36, 4 (1994): 491, for a careful critique of George Hunt's linguistic skills and the correspondence between Hunt and Boas regarding them.

16 Franz Boas to Ruth Benedict, 13 November 1930, in Rohner, *The Ethnography of Franz Boas,* 291.

17 Franz Boas to Ruth Benedict, 26 November 1930, in Rohner, *The Ethnography of Franz Boas,* 293.

18 There were already several styles. Most were phonetic, developed by ear. Alfred Hall systematized Kwak̓wala in his "Grammar of the Kwagiutl Language," *Transactions of the Royal Society of Canada* (1889) 6, 2: 59-105. Indian Agents relied on more idiosyncratic styles, writing place names and personal names simply as they heard them with an English ear. According to Judith Berman, Boas revised his own orthography at least once, in 1900. Later, he adopted George Hunt's spelling. After having corrected it for years, he realized he had actually inserted some mistakes in the material.

19 Field notes of Franz Boas's linguistic work with Jane Cook are among his papers at the American Philosophical Society Archive. See "January 5, Alert Bay, Mrs. Cook," Franz Boas Papers, B.B61, Kwakiutl Field Notes, 1930-31.

20 Berman, "George Hunt," 483-514.

21 Helen Codere, introduction to *Kwakiutl Ethnography,* by Franz Boas, ed. Helen Codere (Chicago: University of Chicago Press, 1961), xxvii; Berman, "George Hunt," 502-3.

22 This is what linguists call a lexical suffix. Berman, "George Hunt," 503.

23 Franz Boas to George Hunt, 9 February 1931, APS, Franz Boas Papers, 497.3 Am3.

24 George Hunt to Franz Boas, 17 February 1931, APS, Franz Boas Papers, 497.3 Am3.

25 Berman, "George Hunt," 504.

26 He gave an example of a stream of words: "If the chiefs make a speech in a feast the first word he says is [?] or Now I will begin Now chiefs and there's lots of these changing words used." George Hunt to Franz Boas, 10 March 1931, APS, Franz Boas Papers, 497.3 Am3.

27 Franz Boas, "Notes on Some Recent Changes in the Kwakiutl Language," *International Journal of American Linguistics* 8 (1932): 90.

28 Berman, "George Hunt," 492.

29 Ibid., 505.

30 Ibid., 506.

31 In *An Iron Hand upon the People: The Law against the Potlatch on the Northwest Coast* (Vancouver: Douglas and McIntyre, 1990), 142, Douglas Cole and Ira Chaikin note that the term *disjointed potlatch* was coined by William Ditchburn, inspector of Indian agencies for the Department of Indian Affairs.

32 Douglas Cole, "Underground Potlatch: How the Kwakiutl Kept the Faith," *Natural History* 100, 10 (1991): 52.

33 Boas to [his sister?] Toni, 25 December 1930, in Rohner, *The Ethnography of Franz Boas,* 298.

34 Cole and Chaikin, *An Iron Hand,* 163, 164.

35 Franz Boas to Toni, 8 December 1930, in Rohner, *The Ethnography of Franz Boas,* 294.
36 Ibid., 295.
37 Ibid.
38 Franz Boas to Ernst Boas, 14 December 1930, ibid., 297.
39 Ibid.
40 Franz Boas to Ernst Boas, 11 January 1931, ibid., 301.
41 Ibid.
42 Franz Boas and W. Halliday to W. Ditchburn, 18 November 1930, UBCLA.
43 C.K.K. Prosser to Anglican Bishop, 18 January 1931, ADBCA, Indians – General, text 203, box 1.
44 Martine Reid, ed., *Paddling to Where I Stand: Agnes Alfred, Qwiqwasutinuxw Noblewoman,* trans. Daisy Sewid-Smith (Vancouver: UBC Press, 2004), 119. Mrs. Alfred identified the new preacher as Mr. Howard. The Apostolic Church was set up in a building previously used as a poolroom, cider store, and general store (ibid., 118).
45 Cole and Chaikin, *An Iron Hand,* 161-62.
46 "Report of the Committee Considering the Indian Potlatch," 1930, no author, ACDBCA, Indians – General, text 277, box 1.
47 The cited works were P.E. Goddard's *Indians of the Northwest Coast* (1924) and Charles Hill-Tout's *The Native Races of the British Empire – North America* (1907). Within the church, the committee consulted Reverend J.B. McCullagh's booklet *The Indian Potlatch.*
48 "Report of the Committee Considering the Indian Potlatch."
49 Ibid. There had been controversy for a number of years as women and men who had married previously in the potlatch approached clergy with new partners and requested church marriages. "Morally, I feel I am justified in refusing to perform the marriage, but am I legally?" the Reverend F. Comley asked the BC attorney general in 1928. See Reverend F. Comley to Mr. Manson, 29 February 1928, ADBCA, Synod Office General Administration files, 1928-30, text 63, box 12/23. He also wrote to Bishop Schofield to ask for his advice: "Ottawa says the 'Indian Ceremony' is binding, but according to the Potlatch Law illegal, what is a parson to do?" See Reverend F. Comley to Bishop of Columbia, 16 April 1928, ADBCA, Synod Office General Administration files, 1928-30, text 63, box 12/23. "I note that you feel as I do in connection with the matter," the attorney general replied. "And I have no hesitation in saying to you that there is no legal obligation whatever upon you." BC Attorney General Manson to F. Comley, 26 April 1928, ADBCA, Synod Office General Administration files, 1928-30, text 63, Box 12/23.
50 Bishop Charles Schofield to Reverend C.K.K. Prosser, 20 January 1931, ADBCA, Synod Office General Administration files, 1928-30, text 55, box 2, file 1.
51 "Indian Marriages, Memo of Statements by Rev. Corker; Antle and Comley, 1931," no author, ADBCA, Indians – General, 87-14, 277-2-27-14.
52 Prosser and John Antle saw the potlatch as a complex of ceremonies and meanings, both sacred and secular. They argued that, were the law to be modified, the potlatch could be appropriated for Christian teaching and would minimize the social effects of the ban that had criminalized potlatchers. Similarly, Reverend Comley suggested retaining the law against the giveaway but dropping the law

against other aspects of the potlatch ceremonial. His predecessor, Arthur Corker, made statements about what he saw as the "demoralization" of debt, and "destitution" caused by the potlatch, but like Prosser, he rejected the idea that a marriage contract meant the sale of women. Corker thought the term *mortgage* more apt. He connected marriage to the powerful authority of fathers who pressed young people to participate in the potlatch. See "Indian Marriages." Today, only Prosser is publicized as opposing the potlatch ban. These statements by church officials in Alert Bay offer more diverse opinions. Douglas Cole and Ira Chaikin write that the Reverends Hall, Corker, and Comley supported the potlatch ban and that C.K.K. Prosser was its only opponent among the clergy in 'Y̲alis. In Cole and Chaikin, *An Iron Hand,* 145.

53 "Indian Marriages, Memo of Statements."

54 Her fourth wedding took place in a church, and a sum of money was paid to the groom by the bride's daughter. "I did not want to marry him," Xe maxodayugwa said to Averkieva, "because he had been married too often; he had been married nine times." The bride's daughter held a "party" (feast) after the church ceremony, and they then returned to the groom's house, where marriage gifts and cash were presented to him. He distributed the gifts "among his tribe" at a potlatch and, in return, he was given the bride's father's song and a dance. See Julia Averkieva, "How She Became a Modzil," 116-19, APS, Kwakiutl Autobiographies, 497.3 B63C20.

55 Douglas Cole writes that multiple marriages "made [a woman] heavy" and honoured her children. Douglas Cole, "The History of the Kwakiutl Potlatch," in *Chiefly Feasts: The Enduring Kwakiutl Potlatch,* ed. Aldona Jonaitis (Seattle: University of Washington Press, 1991), 150.

56 A legal term referring to the nature of the marriage contract when the marital relation is begun immediately.

57 Letter and Opinion from Harold McGill, Deputy Superintendent General, DIA, 4 October 1933, Library and Archives Canada (LAC), RG 10, vol. 6426, file 875-1, pt. 3.

58 According to the circular, the lieutenant-governor appointed marriage commissioners and clergy; two or more witnesses were required, as was a licence, which cost one dollar; and the marriage could only take place eight days after filing an application. Ibid.

59 Ibid.

60 The onus of the prohibition was on poolhall owners to bar entrance to any "Indian" who, according to government opinion, was liable to "misspend or waste his time or means to the detriment of himself, his family, or household."

61 In this letter, Averkieva mentions "a letter of protest against execution of nine negro boys in Scottsboro" and notes that "no single anthropologist except [Boas] did rise his voice against this linching." Julia Averkieva to Franz Boas, 25 October 1931, APS, Boas Collection, Averkieva Correspondence with Franz Boas, 1931-34.

62 Bostonite writer Mabel F. Knight was known for her public lectures, often delivered in a white deerskin dress, and for her writings on diverse forms of aboriginal folklore. The name Ta-de-win was given to her by the Omaha Tribe.

63 Ta-de-win (a.k.a. Mabel F. Knight), "Totem Poles of Vancouver Are Insignia of Tribal Rank; Their Erection by Kwakiutl Indians of Island Depends on Whether

They Have Held a 'Potlatch' or Are Owners of a 'Copper,'" *Christian Science Monitor,* 12 November 1932.

64 Nellie Hamilton Cook, interview with Joan Skogan and Vicki Cook, August 1973, ABLM, Cook Family file.

65 Like other Euro-Canadian projects at that time, the intention was "to give to the present and succeeding generations an adequate conception of the work and social life of the aborigines before the advent of the whiteman." John Goodfellow, *Totem Poles of Stanley Park* (Vancouver: Art, Historical and Scientific Association 1931), 29.

66 Ibid., 29.

67 "Several individuals acted as 'agents' for the Association," Goodfellow writes. "The [Wakius] pole cost the AHS $700," a sum that was "raised by public subscription." Chief Sisa-kaulas's pole was "presented to the A.H.S. by Mr. W.C. Shelly," an associate of the Parks Board. See Goodfellow, *Totem Poles,* 29.

68 The narrative is too lengthy to include here, but it is available in Goodfellow's *Totem Poles of Stanley Park* and in Marius Barbeau's *Totem Poles* (Ottawa: National Museum of Canada, 1950), 2:681. In Volume 1, the Reverend G.H. Ralley is quoted for this narrative (256).

69 It is possible that these are the "Tsa-wee-noth Posts of Kingcome Inlet" mentioned a decade later by Marius Barbeau as being located in Stanley Park. At this time, according to Barbeau, the primary carvers among the Kwakwa̲ka̲'wakw were Charlie James, Willie Seaweed, Dick Price, Mungo Martin, and Albert Shaughnessy.

70 As early as 1930, William Halliday refused outside requests for "old tools, masks, rattles, headdresses etc." There were, in his words, no relics to be had except by "making personal canvass and spending considerable time." William Halliday to Axel Rasmuncen, Wrangell Public School, Alaska, 7 February 1930, declassified files, family papers.

71 John Tierney, "Tips from the Potlatch; Where Giving Knows No Slump," *New York Times,* 16 December 2008.

72 Ibid.

73 For an extensive study of the history of law and fishing in BC, see Dianne Newell, *Tangled Webs of History: Indians and the Law in Canada's Pacific Coast Fisheries* (Toronto: University of Toronto Press, 1993).

74 Philip Drucker, *Native Brotherhoods: Modern Intertribal Organizations on the Northwest Coast,* Bureau of American Ethnology Bulletin 168 (Washington, DC: Smithsonian Institute, 1958), 104. Expenses included "necessary repairs, readying the vessel for sea, insurance, fuel and the rest, and in addition the very expensive nets which can be expected to last but a season or two at best" (125).

75 Ibid., 124.

76 Cole and Chaikin, *An Iron Hand,* 164.

77 Rolf Knight, *Indians at Work: An Informal History of Native Labour in British Columbia, 1858-1930* (Vancouver: New Star, 1996 [1978]), 322.

78 E. Newnham to C. Perry, Assistant Commissioner for DIA, BC, 22 August 1933. All documents pertaining to *R v Stephen Cook et al.* are courtesy of a family member's personal collection.

79 See Douglas Harris for a detailed discussion of coastal and inland groups' struggle to maintain a food fishery. Tactics to limit fishing under food fish permits

included confiscating weirs, shifting regulations to fishing with rod and line only, prohibiting women from participating in the food fishery, imposing fines, and even imprisonment at Oakalla Prison Farm. In 1930, as Harris notes, there was a general sentiment that aboriginal communities should be turned off their dependence on salmon. He includes a story from the first issue of *BC Fisherman* (1930), in which the author concludes that "the Indian will have to change his diet. Salmon has become an extravagance for him." See Harris, *Landing Native Fisheries,* 111-26.

80 Testimony, *R v Stephen Cook et al.,* 6 September 1933. Unless stated otherwise, all direct quotes and descriptions of the case are from this file.

81 Deputy Attorney General of BC to E. Newnham, 13 September 1933.

82 Ibid. Newnham eventually urged the DIA to take action against the fishing company, because it had told Stephen Cook that the "BC Fisheries Act is 'ultra vires,' and these taxes need not be paid by Indians." Notice from R. Payne, Production Manager, Canadian Fishing Company, to Stephen Cook, quoted in E. Newnham to Deputy Attorney General of BC, 3 October 1933.

83 Stephen Cook to Dorman, 19 September 1933.

84 E. Newnham to Stephen Cook, 20 September 1933.

85 E. Newnham to Deputy Attorney General of BC, 22 September 1933. Newnham told Stephen that the company would not cover their overdue taxes. Stephen Cook paid the twenty-five-dollar tax for one drag-seine boat the next month. The Indian Agent recommended that the other tax be waived.

86 In "Native Indians and the Fishing Industry of British Columbia," *Canadian Journal of Economics and Political Science* 19, 1 (1953): 20-34, Percy Gladstone provides a concise chronology of the strikes and union activities that affected aboriginal fishers. The Fraser River Fishermen's Benevolent Society staged a strike in 1893 for a higher daily wage. Its members were abandoned by "white" fishermen, who broke the strike. At Skeena River, there were strikes in 1894, 1896, and 1897 over fish prices and cannery wages. Following the gold rush of the 1890s, Japanese fishers moved into the industry, and aboriginal fishers on the Fraser River went on strike but failed to "win the support of the Japanese" (ibid., 29). By 1901, canneries had begun to employ Japanese women workers, and another strike was unsuccessfully staged to push the Japanese fishery from the Fraser River. Four years later, on the Naas and Skeena rivers, aboriginal fishers went on strike for higher fish prices; "no agreement was reached ... and over 300 Indians left the northern area to fish in the Fraser River" (ibid., 30). Aboriginal women who demanded higher wages in the canneries won a victory in 1907 in the face of a labour shortage. According to Philip Drucker, the first Indian Union was formed in 1914 by W.H. Pierce, a "Tsimshian missionary at Port Essington on the Skeena River." The union was established to compete with Japanese fishers and by 1919 had branches on the Skeena and Naas rivers, at Haida Gwaii (Queen Charlotte Islands), and at Rivers Inlet. It was eventually known as the Nass River Fishermen's Association. See Drucker, *Native Brotherhoods,* 128.

87 Drucker, *Native Brotherhoods,* 127.

88 Gladstone, "Native Indians and the Fishing Industry of British Columbia," 30.

89 Ibid., 31. Several fishers' unions were active: in 1931, the Fishermen's Industrial Union was formed for those who worked in fishing and processing. It disbanded

in 1936 and split into two organizations: the Salmon Purse Seiners Union and the Pacific Coast Fish Union. Working from cannery statistics, Helen Lee notes that, by 1936, 5,200 people were employed at canneries. Nine hundred were "white," 1,600 were "Indians," and 2,700 were Asian. They laboured for as little as fifteen cents per hour. See Helen Lee, "Corporate Strategy in the BC Fish-Processing Sector" (master's thesis: Simon Fraser University, 1983), 65.

90 Drucker, *Native Brotherhoods,* 124.

91 Thomas Gosnell, Special Joint Committee of Parliament, 2 May 1947, in Forrest LaViolette, *The Struggle for Survival: Indian Cultures and the Protestant Ethic in British Columbia* (Toronto: University of Toronto Press, 1973), 149.

92 Percy Gladstone dates this as 1934. See "Native Indians and the Fishing Industry of British Columbia," 31. Philip Drucker dates the first meeting of the Native Brotherhood of British Columbia as December 1931. See *Native Brotherhoods,* 105.

93 Gladstone, "Native Indians and the Fishing Industry of British Columbia," 31.

94 Ibid.

95 Julia Averkieva to Franz Boas, 9 October 1933, APS, Boas Collection, Averkieva Correspondence with Franz Boas..

96 Marcel Mauss, "Essai sur le don: Forme et raison de l'échange dans les sociétés archaïques" [An essay on the gift: The form and reason for exchange in archaic societies], *Année Sociologique* 1 (1923-24): 30-186.

97 Marcel Mauss, *The Gift: The Form and Reason for Exchange in Archaic Societies* (New York: W.W. Norton, 1990), 33.

98 Norman Hacking, "Barbaric Potlatch Still Survives among Alert Bay Natives," *Vancouver Province,* 29 June 1935.

99 Ibid.

100 Ibid.

101 LaViolette, *The Struggle for Survival,* 143.

102 As Cole and Chaikin write, "not even the Christian Indians would cooperate," and "Christ Church parishioners ... were not prepared to supply evidence to the police." See *An Iron Hand,* 143-45.

103 Ibid., 144.

104 Monthly Report of M.S. Todd, Kwawkewlth Agency, November 1935, LAC, RG 10, vol. 8481, file 1/24/3, pt. 1.

105 G. Pragnell to H. McGill, 21 December 1935, LAC, RG 10, vol. 8481, file 1/24/3, pt. 1.

106 C.K.K. Prosser to Bishop Schofield, 29 February 1931, ADBCA, Bishop Schofield Correspondence, box 12/23, text 63.

107 A.F. MacKenzie to Bishop Charles Schofield, 13 June 1933, ADBCA, Bishop Schofield Correspondence, box 12/23, text 63.

108 "Indians Marry in Mass Ceremony," *Vancouver Herald,* 16 January 1934.

109 Reverend Anfield to the editor of the *Vancouver Sun,* 20 January 1934, ADBCA, Indians Alert Bay, box 1, text 203.

110 Bishop Charles Schofield to A.F. MacKenzie, 22 June 1933, ADBCA, Bishop Schofield Correspondence, text 63, box 12/23.

111 In attendance at the first meeting were the new bishop, Harold Sexton, and another representative of the church from Victoria; Indian Agent Todd; Miss K. O'Brian, a missionary from Village Island; Miss P. Arrowsmith and Miss. A.

Wakefield, missionaries from Kingcome Inlet; and members of the church committee of Christ Church. Joining them at the second meeting were the Reverend A. Green, superintendent of the Columbia Coast Mission; the Reverend B. Dance, chaplain of the missionary ship *Columbia;* and "various Indians who are definitely still connected with the Potlatch." Special Meeting Held at Alert Bay, 1 June 1936, ADBCA, 85-69-198-50.

112 Special Meeting Held at Alert Bay, 31 May 1936, Sadie Thompson scrapbooks, ABLM.

113 Special Meeting Held at Alert Bay, 1 June 1936.

114 Christopher Roth, *Becoming Tsimshian: The Social Life of Names* (Seattle: University of Washington Press, 2008), 102.

115 M.S. Todd to A.S. Williams, Secretary, Department of Mines and Resources, 11 February 1936, LAC, RG 10, vol. 8481, file 1/24-3, pt. 1.

116 Cole and Chaikin, *An Iron Hand,* 147.

117 Ibid., 147-50.

118 Special Meeting Held at Alert Bay, 30 May 1936.

119 Ibid.

120 Ibid.

121 Ibid. M. Todd stated, "This is what happens right now; the Church has come between the Department and the Indians as far as enforcement of the law is concerned."

122 Ibid.

123 Baxwbakwalanuksiwe' is the man-eater spirit who possesses the Hamat̓sa initiate. See Aaron Glass, "Conspicuous Consumption: An Intercultural History of the Kwa̱kwa̱ka'wakw Ha'mat'sa" (PhD diss., New York University, 2006).

124 Special Meeting Held at Alert Bay, 30 May 1936.

125 In 1931, C.K.K. Prosser estimated that 487 of the 511 people he called "Indians" in Alert Bay and Village Island were Anglicans. Just twelve were what he called "heathen." Among the "whites" were sixty-five Anglicans. C.K.K. Prosser to Bishop Schofield, 8 January 1931, ADBCA, text 203, box 1.

126 Special Meeting Held at Alert Bay, 30 May 1936.

127 When family members read the transcript, they identified chiefs from several villages who were present. Some were then active in the potlatch and others were not, as is indicated by the word *antipotlatch* in brackets by their names. Many of the men were frequent visitors to the Cook family big house.

128 Special Meeting Held at Alert Bay, 1 June 1936. Speaking with Mary Hunt in Tsax̱is, Julia Averkieva found that accusations of illegitimacy were a form of insult among women at the time: "bE'wigciiālayois the name given to a girl who has an illegitimate child. This name means that the mother was in her family before she was married legally. It is a derisive word when the women fight with each other they are always insult each other by using that name." See Julia Averkieva, Kwakiutl Autobiography, 1930, APS, Franz Boas Collection, 497.3 B63c 20.

129 His choice of words is interesting. "Status" did not enter into definitions of those classified as "Indians" until the "registry of Indians" was introduced in 1951. Special Meeting Held at Alert Bay, 1 June 1936.

130 According to Douglas Cole, this payment ensured "the right of membership in [the bride's] clan for future children of the couple." The repayment likely included

important names and privileges passed from the woman's father to his son-in-law and thus to their children. See Douglas Cole, "The History of the Kwakiutl Potlatch," 148. I was told during research that Kwakwaka'wakw people practise ambilineal descent – descent through both parents – but have a patrilineal bias through the father, who is sanctioned to give such names and privileges.

131 Since the 1876 Indian Act, the government, rather than aboriginal groups themselves, has defined the category "Indian." The original definition of an Indian was any male of Indian blood reputed to belong to a particular band, any child of an Indian, or any woman who was or had been married to an Indian. Compulsory enfranchisement (loss of Indian legal standing) was included in the 1876 act. It applied to any aboriginal person who received a university degree or who became a doctor, lawyer, or clergyman, regardless of his or her consent.

132 Regarding marriage, Irving Goldman wrote: "the rituals of marriage concern only the chiefs, for they alone have anything of value to transmit. Saying all others simply 'stick together like dogs,' Kwakiutl deny marriage to commoners, thus clearly defining marriage as a peculiarly spiritual relationship irrelevant for those who lack the spiritual qualities." See Irving Goldman, *The Mouth of Heaven: An Introduction to Kwakiutl Religious Thought* (New York: Wiley, 1975), 78. One may infer from Goldman's analysis of the Boas-Hunt materials that formal unions conducted without customary exchange would have been disregarded socially.

133 See Bruce Miller's discussion of the complex of apologies and exchanges that constitute performances of reconciliation between states and aboriginal nations. His central point – that it is necessary to understand the social relationships behind enduring "ritual practices" – is also relevant to the *internal* resolution of historical conflict *within* indigenous communities. See Bruce G. Miller, "Bringing Culture In: Community Responses to Apology, Reconciliation, and Reparations," *American Indian Culture and Research Journal* 30, 4 (2006): 1-17.

134 Special Meeting Held at Alert Bay, 1 June 1936.

135 Ibid.

136 The Native Women's Association of Canada was established in 1974 through the amalgamation of thirteen aboriginal women's organizations. The association's website states that its mandate includes "enhancing and promoting the social, economic, cultural and political well-being of First Nations and Métis women" in national and international arenas.

137 As a former Indian Agent of the West Coast Agency, Neill had tolerated dancing and potlatching. When he became a politician, he advised a delegation of Kwakwaka'wakw potlatchers that "there was no harm in [potlatching]" (Cole and Chaikin, *An Iron Hand,* 151). To Murray Todd's chagrin, a member of the delegation returned to Alert Bay and distributed goods (ibid., 149). Although Neill may be regarded as an advocate for aboriginal peoples (he warned of high mortality in the industrial schools), he strongly opposed Japanese and Doukhobor enfranchisement and was an avid nationalist.

138 Rev. O.T. Hodgson to M.S. Todd, 17 February 1937. LAC, RG 10, vol. 8481, file 1/24-3, pt. 1.

139 D.M. MacKay to Secretary of Indian Affairs Branch, Ottawa, 10 March 1937, LAC, RG 10, vol. 8481, file 1/24-3, pt. 1.

140 MacKay's letter to his Ottawa superiors thus recommended amending subsection 1 of section 140 of the Indian Act. Ibid.

141 Included in D.M. McKay to the Secretary of Indian Affairs Branch, Ottawa, 8 April 1937, LAC, RG 10, vol. 8481, file 1/24-3, pt. 1.

142 Stephen and Jane Cook to J.S. Taylor, MP, 15 April 1937, LAC, RG 10, vol. 8481, file 1/24-3, pt. 1.

143 Helen Codere, "Kwakiutl," in *Perspectives in American Indian Culture Change,* ed. Edward Spicer (Chicago: University of Chicago Press, 1961), 483. Dara Culhane Speck suggests that by the end of the 1930s upward mobility was linked with Christian conversion, missionary education, denunciation of the potlatch, mixed blood, and residence in the commercial village of Alert Bay rather than the more isolated villages. See Dara Culhane Speck, *An Error In Judgement: The Politics of Medical Care in an Indian/White Community* (Vancouver: Talonbooks, 1987), 85.

144 Codere, "Kwakiutl," 483.

145 *Journal of the Thirty-Sixth Session of the Synod of British Columbia, Victoria, Wednesday the 24th and 25th of February, 1937,* ADBCA, M221.

146 M.S. Todd, Agent's Report, Kwawkewlth Agency, January 1939, LAC, RG 10, vol. 8481, file 1/24-3, pt. 1.

147 "To Fight Coast Scourge, Preventorium Is Ready to Open," 18 February 1939, newspaper clipping in Sadie Thompson scrapbooks, ABLM, 993-349-2, p. 10

148 Ibid.

149 Ibid.

150 Ibid.

151 According to the newspaper article: "A pleasing feature of the opening of the preventorium will be the presentation of a modern quartz light machine, which has been purchased by gifts received from nearly 400 graduates and other Indian friends of the school." Ibid.

Part VIII: One Voice from Many

1 Percy Gladstone, "Native Indians and the Fishing Industry of British Columbia," *Canadian Journal of Economics and Political Science* 19, 1 (1953): 24.

2 The party included two missionaries, a teacher, a nurse, and the superintendent of the Columbia Coast Mission. The missionaries are listed only as "Mrs. Drabble" and "Alice." The teacher is listed as "Miss Arrowsmith," the nurse as "Miss Vivash." The Reverend Alan Greene was the superintendent of the Columbia Coast Mission. "Meeting at Indian Office on 5 April 1940 for Discussion of Certain Entertainments at Kingcome Reserve during Holy Week, 1939," U'mista Cultural Centre Archives (UCCA), Withheld Items, Potlatch Files, A-96-18-60-19a.

3 Todd asked who had been present, what dances had been shown, whether there had been a feast, who had exchanged money, and what had been given away. He was told that the dances had been held after church services during Holy Week. He was interested to hear that neither the superintendent of the Columbia Coast Mission nor any other Euro-Canadian guests wore blankets. As Mrs. Thomas King told Todd, "one of Tsawataineuk people ... explained to the white people

what the different masks and dances meant as they came out ... The masks came out from the secret place two by two until the house was full." F.E. Anfield, "Personal Report on Two Conferences Attended in Connection with the Indian Custom Known as the 'Potlatch' on April 7th-9th at Kingcome Indian Village, and on April 23rd at Alert Bay Indian Village," UCCA, Withheld Items, Potlatch Files, A-96-18-60-19a.

4 Ibid.

5 The delegation included the archbishop of New Westminster, the inspector of Indian Agencies in BC, Agent Todd, and Reverends Anfield and Greene.

6 Anfield, "Personal Report on Two Conferences."

7 Ibid.

8 Ibid.

9 Ibid.

10 Ibid.

11 Ibid.

12 Ibid.

13 Her views continued to be compatible with those of aboriginal rights activists of the day, even though they had experienced illegal land grabs, interference with political autonomy, and the extinguishment of their rights. See Ronald Neizen, "Recognizing Indigenism: Canadian Unity and the International Movement of Indigenous Peoples," *Comparative Study of Society and History* 42, 1 (2000): 141.

14 "Notes Taken at a Meeting of Indians at Alert Bay, April 23rd, 1940; Held in Christ Church Rectory, Alert Bay, Re Potlatch and Indian Custom," UCCA, Withheld Items, Potlatch Files, A-96-18-60-19a.

15 Ibid.

16 Ibid.

17 "Notes Taken at a Meeting of Indians at Alert Bay."

18 In the "Cook Calendar" (1992), members of the first Cormorant team of 1926 also included Harry Brown, Alfred Dawson, Gideon Whonnock, Robert Mountain, Peter Gonzales, and Stanley Hunt.

19 Rolf Knight, *Indians at Work: An Informal History of Native Labour in British Columbia, 1858-1930* (Vancouver: New Star, 1996 [1978]), 325. Citing Geoff Meggs and Duncan Stacey's work *Cork Line and Canning Lines* (1992, 159), Knight writes that the canneries acquired 660 of the 887 Japanese-Canadian vessels auctioned.

20 *Dog* and *chum* are used interchangeably. *Tzum* comes from Chinook jargon and means "spotted."

21 Gene Joseph, "A Brief History of the Native Brotherhood of British Columbia," report prepared for the Native Brotherhood of British Columbia, 1981, n.p. Courtesy of a family member.

22 Ibid.

23 Ibid.

24 Ibid. Alfred Adams of Masset is commemorated as their founder. His organizational model was based on the union structure of the Alaska Native Brotherhood and on the arguments for aboriginal rights and title waged earlier by the Allied Tribes.

25 Harry Assu and Joy Inglis, *Assu of Cape Mudge: Recollections of a Coastal Indian Chief* (Vancouver: UBC Press, 1989), 71.
26 Gladstone, "Native Indians and the Fishing Industry," 31.
27 Philip Drucker, *The Native Brotherhoods: Modern Intertribal Organizations on the Northwest Coast,* Bureau of American Ethnology Bulletin 168 (Washington, DC: Smithsonian Institute, 1958), 129.
28 Gill netting is a technique geared to catch salmon as they return to their spawning grounds. Ibid., 32, 23.
29 Harry Assu states that the organization of fishers happened earlier, after a strike on Rivers Inlet in 1916. Assu and Inglis, *Assu of Cape Mudge,* 72.
30 Drucker, *Native Brotherhoods,* 129-30.
31 Ibid., 128-29.
32 According to Harry Assu, "Alfred Adams, Douglas Edenshaw and Heber Clifton came down the coast from the Charlottes forming the Native Brotherhood." See Assu and Inglis, *Assu of Cape Mudge,* 72. A history written for the Native Brotherhood of British Columbia lists people from the Kwakwaka'wakw villages, Bella Coola, the Fraser Valley, North Vancouver, and Pemberton under new members for the "Southern Area" in 1938. Joseph, "A Brief History," n.p.
33 At the next Brotherhood convention, according to Philip Drucker, Paull was charged by northern delegates "with having exceeded his authority," but he was later "aggressively supported by the Kwakiutl," who threatened to leave the Brotherhood if his initiatives were not recognized. Drucker, *The Native Brotherhoods,* 109.
34 Gladstone, "Native Indians and the Fishing Industry," 1953.
35 In 1944, the vice-presidents of the Southern Coast and Alert Bay districts were William Scow, Frank Assu, and Tom Shewish. Stephen Cook, Harry Mountain, Alfred Scow, and James Sewid were elected vice-presidents in 1949. Joseph, "A Brief History," n.p.
36 Ronald Hawker, *Tales of Ghosts: First Nations Art in British Columbia, 1922-1961* (Vancouver: UBC Press, 2003), 111.
37 Drucker, *The Native Brotherhoods,* 109.
38 Another former member of the executive of the Allied Tribes, Peter Kelly was chairman of the Legislative Committee of the Brotherhood from 1946 until 1965.
39 Gladstone, "Native Indians and the Fishing Industry," 32.
40 Editorial, "The Indians Act," *Native Voice* 1, 1 (1946): 1.
41 The constitution was drafted at a meeting held in Port Simpson on 15 December 1931. The organization's primary goal was stated as follows: "To keep in closer communication with one another to co-operate with each other and with all the authorities, for the further interest of the Natives." See Joseph, "A Brief History," n.p.
42 Ibid.
43 Ibid.
44 Recommendations for family allowances were made in the postwar Marsh Report (1943) but had been debated in Parliament as early as 1929. Distinct from social welfare, the family allowance was intended to support large families regardless of employment status. What became known as the "baby bonus" was tax free and based on the age of children in each household: age five and under, parents

received five dollars a month; age six to nine, six dollars a month; age ten to twelve, seven dollars a month; and age thirteen to fifteen, eight dollars a month.

45 The Old Age Pension was available to British subjects aged seventy years or over who had lived in Canada for twenty years. Only those whose income was less than $365 per year were eligible. The maximum pension payment was $20 per month or $240 per year.

46 Gladstone, "Native Indians and the Fishing Industry," 26; Dara Culhane Speck, *An Error in Judgement: The Politics of Medical Care in an Indian/White Community* (Vancouver: Talonbooks, 1987), 85-86.

47 The Butedale cannery and reduction plant had been operated by the Canadian Fishing Company since 1923. Located on Princess Royal Island, the cannery shut down after an excessive snowfall collapsed the roof in 1950. See K. Mack Campbell, *Cannery Village, Company Town: A History of British Columbia's Outlying Salmon Canneries* (Victoria: Trafford, 2004), 77.

48 As Drucker notes, a share included the expenses (fuel, oil, and food) and the catch. A seiner crew of five to six people had eleven shares: 2.5 for the boat, 1.5 for the net, 2 for the captain, and 1 each for the crew members. If the boat was company-owned, the cannery paid the fuel and oil costs, and the crew split the food costs. The owner of the net paid for the labour at net lofts. Drucker, *The Native Brotherhoods,* 125.

49 Interview with George Cook conducted by his daughter Nella Nelson, Victoria, November 2009.

50 Each cannery also operated a net loft to store fishing gear. Labourers, mostly women, hung, mended, and dipped the nets.

51 Drucker, *The Native Brotherhoods,* 118.

52 Joseph, "A Brief History," n.p.

53 Ibid.

54 Kitty Carpenter was Lydia Whonnock's sister.

55 Joseph, "A Brief History," n.p.

56 In the 1953 amendment to sec. 101 of the Indian Act, police were given the authority to enter houses on reserves without a warrant. See Harry Hawthorn, Cyril Belshaw, and Stuart Jamieson, *The Indians of British Columbia: A Study of Contemporary Social Adjustment* (Berkeley/Toronto: University of California Press/University of Toronto Press, 1960), 433.

57 Murray Todd to Mrs. Cook, 24 October 1945. Courtesy of a family member.

58 Todd stated that the Government of Canada was then working through the United Nations Relief and Rehabilitation Administration to assist those in wartorn nations.

59 Todd reminded Jane Cook that "the Bonds may be sold for cash at any time" and that "this money is not going to be used for war ... but to assist mankind and help restore the fundamental principles of our Christian faith to society the world over." Murray Todd to Mrs. Cook, 24 October 1945.

60 Forrest LaViolette, *The Struggle for Survival: Indian Cultures and the Protestant Ethic in British Columbia* (Toronto: University of Toronto Press, 1973), 152.

61 Hawker, *Tales of Ghosts,* 92.

62 LaViolette, *The Struggle for Survival.* The Special Joint Committee on the Indian Act (1946-49) led eventually to the revised Indian Act of 1951. The Native

Brotherhood of British Columbia presented briefs before the committee in May 1947, acting as the sole representatives for aboriginal groups in BC. See Hawker, *Tales of Ghosts,* 113.

63 See LaViolette, *The Struggle for Survival,* for a detailed discussion of the *Native Voice,* 152-76.

64 Maizie Armytage-Moore was an associate life member of the Native Brotherhood and Sisterhood. She often visited reserves to record the "conditions and problems experienced by tribes." Her detailed reports were submitted to the organization's president William Scow at Alert Bay. See Constance Cox, "White Woman Honoured," *Native Voice* 3, 7 (1949): 5.

65 Maizie Armytage-Moore, "A Shining Quality," *Native Voice* 1, 12 (1947): 3.

66 Sebastien Grammond, *Identity Captured by Law: Membership in Canada's Indigenous Peoples and Linguistic Minorities* (Montreal and Kingston: McGill-Queen's University Press, 2009), 99.

67 LaViolette, *Struggle for Survival,* 174.

68 Grammond, *Identity Captured by Law,* 100. As Grammond notes, compulsory enfranchisement was attempted from 1869 to 1876, from 1920 to 1922, and from 1933 to 1951. Harry Hawthorn, Cyril Belshaw, and Stuart Jamieson include loss of taxation privileges, prevention of living on or owning property on the reserve, "or ever becoming an Indian again." See Hawthorn, Belshaw, and Jamieson, *The Indians of British Columbia,* 483.

69 *Native Voice,* January 1947, quoted in LaViolette, *The Struggle for Survival,* 169.

70 Testimony of Chief William Scow, minutes of the Joint Special Committee of the Senate and House of Commons regarding the Indian Act, 1 May 1947, quoted in Hawker, *Tales of Ghosts,* 112.

71 Grammond, *Identity Captured by Law,* 93. The legal standing of women vis-à-vis membership was not amended until 1976, when Sandra Lovelace entered a complaint before the United Nations Human Rights Committee. She argued that sec. 12(1)(b) of the Indian Act contravened her rights to choose residence, to marry, and to "enjoy [her] culture in common with other members of [her] group," as defined in art. 27 of the UN Covenant on Political and Civil Rights. Ibid., 96-97.

72 Hawker, *Tales of Ghosts,* 94-96.

73 Ibid., 99.

74 Ibid., 97.

75 See Aaron Glass, "From Cultural Salvage to Brokerage: The Mythologization of Mungo Martin and the Emergence of Northwest Coast Art," *Museum Anthropology* 29, 1 (2006): 20-43.

76 "Report of the Conference on Native Indian Affairs, BC Indian Arts and Welfare Society, 1-3 April 1948," BC Archives (BCA), NW 970.40-065r.

77 The exhibit included works by Emily Carr, Judith Morgan, George Clutesi, and Ellen Neel; children's art from the Inkameep, Port Alberni, and Christie residential schools; and literature, "antiques," and needlework. See Hawker, *Tales of Ghosts,* 94.

78 "Report of the Conference on Native Indian Affairs," "Foreword."

79 The North American Indian Brotherhood was a national lobby group that followed from the Canadian League of Indians. The organization "was established

in the late 1940's, but like its predecessor, the N.A.I.B.'s efforts were hindered by a lack of nation-wide support and suppressive government actions, especially in Saskatchewan, where the Cooperative Commonwealth Federation government actively worked against all First Nations initiatives. Internal administrative problems caused the organization to break into regional factions, causing the N.A.I.B. to be disbanded by the early 1950's." Assembly of First Nations, "Our Story," http://www.afn.ca/.

80 "Report of the Conference on Native Indian Affairs," 2 April 1948, 22.

81 Ibid., 26.

82 Just over four thousand children then attended Indian schools throughout the province. There were thirteen residential schools, fifty-five day schools, three hospital schools, and nine seasonal schools in operation. See "Presentation of R.F. Davey, Inspector of Indian Schools for BC, April 3, 1948," in "Report of the Conference on Native Indian Affairs," 40. He also noted that 311 pupils were then attending "white schools."

83 Ibid. Students who attended "white" high schools close to Indian schools boarded at the residential schools. Instruction in residential schools included home economics, industrial arts, and farming and gardening.

84 Ibid., 41. "The Department does not favour the establishment of Indian High Schools," Davey concluded (ibid., 44).

85 "Report of Rev. Father J.L. Bradley, Superintendent of Indian Missions, Diocese of Victoria, April 3, 1948," in "Report of the Conference on Native Indian Affairs," 45.

86 Ibid., 46.

87 "Report of Dr. R.G. Raley, Former Principal Coqualeetza Institute, April 3, 1948," in "Report of the Conference on Native Indian Affairs," 47.

88 Ibid., 50.

89 "Report of Chief William Scow, President, Native Brotherhood of B.C., April 3, 1948," in "Report of Conference on Native Indian Affairs," 51.

90 Ibid., 52.

91 Ibid.

92 Session on Education, 3 April 1948, in "Report of the Conference on Native Indian Affairs," 53-55. The session was held at Acadia Camp, University of British Columbia.

93 See Aldona Jonaitis and Aaron Glass, *The Totem Pole: An Intercultural History* (Seattle/Vancouver: University of Washington Press/Douglas and McIntyre, 2010).

Part IX: A Tower of Strength

1 Forrest LaViolette, *The Struggle for Survival: Indian Cultures and the Protestant Ethic in British Columbia* (Toronto: University of Toronto Press, 1973), 182-84. "Any Indian and his wife living on a reserve is entitled to vote if he has signed a waiver from tax exemption prior to the date of the writ for an election. Other Canadian Indians entitled to vote federally are Indians who have served in either or both of the last world wars, and their wives, or Indians who are not living

on the reserve and who are earning their livelihood outside the reserve." N.J. Castonguay, Chief Electoral Officer, Ottawa, quoted in the *Native Voice* 5, 1 (1951): 16.

2 Ibid., 5.

3 *Native Voice* 5, 5 (1951): 1, 3.

4 Ibid., 9.

5 Ibid., 15.

6 *Native Voice* 5, 6 (1951): 11, 15.

7 *Native Voice* 5, 7 (1951): 7; and *Native Voice* 5, 8 (1951): 8.

8 *Native Voice* 5, 9 (1951): 11.

9 Ellen Neel, "Beloved Native Lady Passes; Alert Bay Mourns Death of Mrs. Cook," *Native Voice* 5, 9 (1951): 9.

10 Harry Hawthorn, Cyril Belshaw, and Stuart Jamieson, *The Indians of British Columbia: A Study of Contemporary Social Adjustment* (Berkeley/Toronto: University of California Press/University of Toronto Press, 1960), 331-33. According to the authors, from March 1951 to March 1952, 401 men and women received sentences for liquor violations.

11 Hawthorn, Belshaw, and Jamieson, *The Indians of British Columbia,* 481. The authors note that in 1954 there were just 174 persons who chose voluntary enfranchisement in the province. This number excludes women who automatically lost their status upon marriage to a non-aboriginal man.

Part x: Dłax̱w'itsine' (For Your Standing), Feasting

1 Charles Nowell, *Smoke from Their Fires: The Life of a Kwakiutl Chief,* ed. Clellan Ford (New Haven, CT: Yale University Press, 1941), 244-48. This ancestor narrative, told by Charlie Nowell, represents the Gix̱sa̱m clan. At the time of writing, Chief Wedłidi Speck chose to replace the ancestor's name "Yakotlalaseme" with "Gix̱sa̱m."

2 What are called Sa̱ntła (washing of tears). Women paraded in and were seated. Their button blankets were inverted to express grief for twenty-six people who had recently passed away. Many songs later, the women's blankets were lifted from their shoulders and returned button-side out, an act that signalled the end of mourning and the start of a series of dances in the potlatch program.

3 I am inspired by Michael Harkin: "One constant theme of the encounter between Western and tribal cultures in North America and elsewhere is destruction: the destruction of persons, of cultures, of entire populations. These events are experienced and remembered with emotion; emotions are inserted into the acting out and the interpretation of events. We cannot hope to present rich accounts of events unless we take note of the emotional valence of those events, the emotional states of the actors, and above all, the specific cultural content of emotions and their positions in those cultures." See Michael Harkin, "Feeling and Thinking in Memory and Forgetting: Toward an Ethnohistory of the Emotions," *Ethnohistory* 50, 2 (2003): 262. In her chapter on the collaboration between George Hunt and Franz Boas, Judith Berman suggests that Boas, too, concentrated on the emotional life of "the Kwakiutl," even though he phrased it in terms of the "interests" and "passions of the people." Judith Berman, "The

Culture as It Appears to the Indian Himself: Boas, George Hunt, and the Methods of Ethnography," in *Volksgeist as Method and Ethic: Essays on Boasian Ethnography and the German Anthropological Tradition,* ed. George Stocking (Madison: University of Wisconsin Press, 1996), 220. See also Franz Boas, *Kwakiutl Ethnography,* ed. Helen Codere (Chicago: University of Chicago Press, 1966), 315. Franz Boas and George Hunt collected and compiled narratives of the nobility. In particular, they focussed on *nuqiləm,* a term translated by Hunt as the "history of chiefs" and referred to by Boas as "myths, legends and tales."

4 Such emotional veracity may be at the heart of the silence that oral historian Luisa Passerini attributes to a colonial politic of oblivion in North America. For many non-aboriginal Canadians and Euro-Canadians – no matter their grasp of historical context, their progressive politics, their ideological stance – their distant ancestors are simply not close enough to evoke a sense of intimate proximity to colonial history. Few Euro-Canadians look to the colonial actions of their predecessors as extensions of themselves, their social characters, or their future opportunities within a collective. If they know of the acts of a particularly notorious predecessor, they may feel some family shame. Others likely feel a more dissipated white guilt at the deeds perpetrated by white people, or they may be inspired to mobilize in solidarity with indigenous peoples. (Such expressions were apparent to me in classroom discussions about colonialism at UBC in the late 1990s. For many students, it was the first time they had been informed of the colonial realities of First Nation peoples in Canada.) Conversely, they may argue against responsibility for "the deeds of their grandfathers," against a perceived agenda of special rights based on so-called racial lines. Or they may agree with the inevitabilities of conquest or civilization. Discursively, the so-called white man's burden, Social Darwinism, and scientific race theory are resilient resources that Euro-Canadians draw upon. See Luisa Passerini, "Memories between Silence and Oblivion," in *Contested Pasts: The Politics of Memory,* ed. Katharine Hodgkin and Susannah Radstone (New York: Routledge, 2003), 238-54, and Leslie Robertson, *Imagining Difference: Legend, Curse, and Spectacle in a Canadian Mining Town* (Vancouver: UBC Press, 2005). For a discussion of the role of emotions in processes of reconciliation, see Sara Ahmed, "The Contingency of Pain," Chapter 1 in *The Cultural Politics of Emotion* (New York: Routledge, 2004), 20-41.

5 Anthropologist Christopher Roth works among Tsimshian peoples, but his work is relevant to this cultural context. Christopher Roth, *Becoming Tsimshian: The Social Life of Names* (Seattle: University of Washington Press, 2008), 7.

6 Marshall Sahlins, "What Kinship Is (Part One)," *Journal of the Royal Anthropological Institute,* n.s., 17 (2011): 2.

7 Also called the perpetual or kinship I. See Alan Rumsay, "Agency, Personhood and the 'I' of Discourse in the Pacific and Beyond," *Journal of the Royal Anthropological Institute* 6, 1 (2000): 104, and Anne Salmond, "Māori and Modernity: Ruatara's Dying," in *Signifying Identities,* ed. Anthony Cohen (New York: Routledge, 2000), 37-54. These concepts come from anthropological analyses of self and personhood in the South Pacific, where societies are also structured by hierarchical principles, by chieftainships and corporate descent groups. South Pacific ethnographer Marshall Sahlins suggests the provocative idea that within particular societies, "History is anthropomorphic in principle" – that is, it is

given a human face through the lives of preceding generations. History is the eternal link to ancestors in the present. See Marshall Sahlins, "Other Times, Other Customs: The Anthropology of History," *American Anthropologist* 85, 3 (1983): 35-36. Working with the narratives of chiefs, Sahlins employs the concept of the heroic *I* – contemporary chiefs' use of the first-person pronoun *I* while narrating events from many generations past.

8 Roth, *Becoming Tsimshian*, 4.

9 Irving Goldman, *The Mouth of Heaven: An Introduction to Kwakiutl Religious Thought* (New York: Wiley, 1975), 42. Wedłidi Speck told me that he believes Goldman to be the first anthropologist to really consider the influence of anthropology on Kwakwa̱ka̱'wakw peoples.

10 Ibid., 25-26.

11 There is a good deal of resonance here with the ethnographic work on other peoples who belong to descent groups. See Maurice Bloch, "Internal and External Memory: Different Ways of Being in History," in *Tense Past: Cultural Essays in Trauma and Memory*, ed. Paul Antze and Michael Lambek (New York: Routledge, 1996), 217.

12 Johannes Fabian, *Power and Performance: Ethnographic Explorations through Proverbial Wisdom and Theatre in Shaba, Zaïre* (Madison: University of Wisconsin Press, 1990), 13.

13 Ibid., 11.

14 Anthropologists Philip Drucker and Robert Heizer viewed the potlatch as a way "to make [a] name good" – that is, a way to identify "an individual as a member of a certain social unit" and define "[his or her] social position within that unit." See Philip Drucker and Robert Heizer, *To Make My Name Good: A Re-examination of the Southern Kwakiutl Potlatch* (Berkeley: University of California Press, 1967), 8.

15 Audra Simpson, "To the Reserve and Back Again: Kahnawake Mohawk Narratives of Self, Home and Nation" (PhD diss., McGill University, 2003), 249.

16 The photographer is Sharon Grainger.

17 What follows does not adhere to the original sequence and content of our discussion but has been edited for flow, to preserve privacy, and for clarity. I have removed my questions if they are irrelevant or unnecessary to the narrative. They are retained in places where they signal topical changes.

18 William Wasden Jr.'s aunt Mary is here referred to as "Granny" following the system of kinship nomenclature that is classified by anthropologists as the "Hawaiian" model. Among Kwakwa̱ka̱'wakw peoples, all relatives of the grandparents' generation may be called "grandparents."

19 William Wasden Jr. refers here to receiving names and dances and other privileges in the Big House.

20 At William Wasden Jr.'s potlatch, members of the Hamatsa Society wore grey blankets and sat together at the front of the Big House, the place more conventionally reserved for chiefs. During the ceremonies, they were called on to enforce respectable behaviour among the guests, both inside and in the parking lot of the Big House.

21 At this time, the Cook family had decided to host a feast, and George Speck refers to his brother, Wedłidi, who would soon assume the role of chief in the Gix̱sa̱m 'na̱'mima.

22 Bethany was first adopted by another 'na'mima before the marriage ceremony began.
23 See also Gloria Cranmer Webster, "The Contemporary Potlatch," in *Chiefly Feasts: The Enduring Kwakiutl Potlatch,* ed. Aldona Jonaitis (Vancouver: Douglas and McIntyre, 1991), 227-48.
24 See Stanley Walens, *Feasting with Cannibals: On Kwakiutl Cosmology* (Princeton, NJ: Princeton University Press, 1981) for a detailed interpretation of the role of orality in "Kwakiutl Cosmology."
25 See Aaron Glass, "Crests on Cotton: 'Souvenir' T-Shirts and the Materiality of Remembrance among the Kwakwaka'wakw of British Columbia," *Museum Anthropology* 31, 1 (2008): 1-18.
26 Maple Ridge is a district adjacent to Metro Vancouver.
27 *Gilakas'la* is used for greetings, thanks, and welcome.
28 I spoke briefly with Chief Robert Joseph the following morning and asked him about why he had used the term *reconciliation.* "This is an important one," he said, referring to the Gixsam Feast. "Colonialism affected us all differently, and we all reacted in different ways. We did what we had to do."
29 Names were bestowed in birth order, beginning with the eldest lineage of Grace Cook.
30 Chief Edwin Newman and Chief Wedłidi Speck were on either side of the box (a cross-section from a log) where family members stood to receive their names. William Wasden Jr. told the name to Chief Robert Joseph, who called each person forward, announced whose child or grandchild they were, and gave them their new name. Chief Joseph also often announced the name of a person who had carried the name in the past. Nella Nelson stood nearby and recorded new names in a book. The family sent the list of names to everyone on the email list so that they would, as members of the Gixsam 'na'mima, "have a record of lifting up people to add to," to use the words of Chris Cook.
31 Chiefs' speeches were translated by Chief Bill Cranmer.
32 The Musga'makw Tsawataineuk Tribal Council includes the Kwikwasutinexw (Gilford Island), Dzawada'enuxw (Kingcome), Haxwa'mis (Wakeman), and Gwawa'enuxw (Hopetown).

Bibliography

Published Sources

Abu-Lughod, Lila. "Writing against Culture." In *Recapturing Anthropology: Working in the Present,* edited by Richard G. Fox, 137-62. Santa Fe, NM: School of American Research, 1991.

–. *Writing Women's Worlds: Bedouin Stories.* Berkeley: University of California Press, 1993.

Ahmed, Sara. "The Contingency of Pain." Chapter 1 in *The Cultural Politics of Emotion,* 20-41. New York: Routledge, 2004.

Allain, Jane May, Library of Parliament, Research Branch. *Aboriginal Fishing Rights: Supreme Court Decisions.* Ottawa: Supply and Services Canada, 1996.

Allan, Anne E. Guernsey. "All the World's a Stage: The Nineteenth-Century Kwakwa̱ka̱'wakw (Kwakiutl) House as Theater." *American Indian Culture and Research Journal* 21, 4 (1997): 29-73.

Archer, Christon. "Cannibalism in the Early History of the Northwest Coast: Enduring Myths and Neglected Realities." *Canadian Historical Review* 61, 4 (1980): 453-79.

Armytage-Moore, Maizie. "A Shining Quality." *Native Voice: Official Organ of the Native Brotherhood of British Columbia* 1, 12 (1947): 3.

Arnett, Chris. *The Terror of the Coast: Land Alienation and Colonial War on Vancouver Island and the Gulf Islands, 1849-1863.* Vancouver: Talonbooks, 1999.

Assembly of First Nations. "Our Story." http://www.afn.ca/.

Assu, Harry, and Joy Inglis. *Assu of Cape Mudge: Recollections of a Coastal Indian Chief.* Vancouver: UBC Press, 1989.

Averkieva, Julia P. "Slavery among the Indians of North America." Translated by G. Elliott in 1957 and revised in 1966. Master's thesis, USSR Academy of Sciences, 1941.

Averkieva, Julia P., and Mark A. Sherman. "Introduction." *Kwakiutl String Figures,* xviii-xxxi. Vancouver: UBC Press, 1992.

Barbeau, Marius. *Totem Poles.* 2 vols. Ottawa: National Museum of Canada, 1950.

Barker, John. "Tangled Reconciliations: The Anglican Church and the Nisga'a of British Columbia." *American Ethnologist* 25, 3 (1998): 433-51.

Barman, Jean. "Aboriginal Women on the Streets of Victoria: Rethinking Transgressive Sexuality during the Colonial Encounter." In *Contact Zones: Aboriginal and Settler Women in Canada's Colonial Past,* edited by Katie Pickles and Myra Rutherdale, 205-27. Vancouver: UBC Press, 2005.

–. "Taming Aboriginal Sexuality: Gender, Power, and Race in British Columbia, 1850-1900." *BC Studies* 115-16 (1997-98): 237-66.

Barnett, Homer. "The Nature of the Potlatch." *American Anthropologist* 40, 3 (1938): 349-58.

Bear, Laura. "Ruins and Ghosts: The Domestic Uncanny and the Materialization of Anglo-Indian Genealogies in Karagpur." In *Ghosts of Memory: Essays on Remembrance and Relatedness,* edited by Janet Carsten, 36-57. Malden: Blackwell, 2007.

Behar, Ruth. "Rage and Redemption: Reading the Life Story of a Mexican Marketing Woman." *Feminist Studies* 16, 2 (1990): 223-58.

Behar, Ruth, and Deborah Gordon, eds. *Women Writing Culture.* Berkeley: University of California Press, 1995.

Benedict, Ruth. *Patterns of Culture.* Boston: Houghton and Mifflin Company, 1934.

Berkhofer, Robert. *The White Man's Indian.* New York: Vintage Books, 1979.

Berliner, David. "The Abuses of Memory: Reflections on the Memory Boom in Anthropology." *Anthropological Quarterly* 78, 1 (2005): 197-211.

Berman, Judith. "The Culture as It Appears to the Indian Himself: Boas, George Hunt, and the Methods of Ethnography." In *Volksgeist as Method and Ethic: Essays on Boasian Ethnography and the German Anthropological Tradition,* edited by George Stocking, 215-56. Madison: University of Wisconsin Press, 1996.

–. "George Hunt and the Kwak'wala Texts." *Anthropological Linguistics* 36, 4 (1994): 483-514.

–. "Red Salmon and Red Cedar Bark: Another Look at the Nineteenth-Century Kwakwaka'wakw Winter Ceremonial." *BC Studies* 125-26 (2000): 53-98.

Biolsi, Thomas. "The Birth of the Reservation: Making the Modern Individual among the Lakota." *American Ethnologist* 22, 1 (1995): 28-53.

Bishop, Russell. "Freeing Ourselves from Neo-colonial Domination in Research: A Kaupapa Maori Approach to Creating Knowledge." In *The Sage Handbook of Qualitative Research,* edited by Norman Denzin and Yvonna Lincoln, 109-38. Thousand Oaks, CA: Sage, 2005.

Blackman, Margaret. "Creativity in Acculturation." *Ethnohistory* 23, 4 (1976): 387-413.

–. *During My Time: Florence Edenshaw Davidson, a Haida Woman.* Seattle: University of Washington Press, 1982.

–. "The Individual and Beyond: Reflections on the Life History Process." *Anthropology and Humanism Quarterly* 16, 2 (1991): 56-62.

Blaney, Fay. "Aboriginal Women's Action Network." In *Strong Women Stories: Native Vision and Community Survival,* edited by Kim Anderson and Bonita Lawrence, 156-70. Toronto: Sumach Press, 2003.

Bloch, Maurice. "Internal and External Memory: Different Ways of Being in History. In *Tense Past: Cultural Essays in Trauma and Memory,* edited by Paul Antze and Michael Lambek, 215-33. New York: Routledge, 1996.

Boas, Franz. "The Coast Tribes of British Columbia." *Science* 9, 216 (1887): 288-89.

–. *Contributions to the Ethnology of the Kwakiutl.* Columbia University Contributions to Anthropology, Vol. 10. New York: Columbia University Press, 1925.

–. "Current Beliefs of the Kwakiutl Indians." *Journal of American Folklore* 45, 176 (1932): 177-260.

–. *Ethnology of the Kwakiutl.* Thirty-Fifth Annual Report. Washington, DC: Bureau of American Ethnology, 1921.

–. *Kwakiutl Ethnography.* Edited by Helen Codere. Chicago: University of Chicago Press, 1966.

–. *Kwakiutl Tales.* Columbia University Contributions to Anthropology, 2. New York: Columbia University Press, 1910.

–. "Notes on Some Recent Changes in the Kwakiutl Language." *International Journal of American Linguistics* 7, 1-2 (1932): 90-93.

–. "Social Organization and Secret Societies of the Kwakiutl Indians." In *Report of the US National Museum for 1895,* 311-738. Washington, DC: US Government Printing Office, 1897.

–. *Tenth Report on Northwestern Tribes of Canada.* London: British Association for the Advancement of Science, 1895.

Bölscher, Marianne. *The Potlatch in Anthropological Theory: A Re-evaluation of Certain Ethnographic Data and Theoretical Approaches.* Nortorf, Germany: Volkerkundliche Arbeitsgemeinschaft, 1982.

Bouchard, Randy, and Dorothy Kennedy, eds. *Myths and Legends from the North Pacific Coast of America.* Vancouver: Talonbooks, 2006.

Boutillier, Norma. "Socialization and Symbolic Interaction in an Indian-White Community." Master's thesis, Simon Fraser University, 1963.

Bracken, Christopher. *The Potlatch Papers: A Colonial Case History.* Chicago: University of Chicago Press, 1997.

Brettell, Caroline B. "Blurred Genres and Blended Voices: Life History, Biography, Autobiography, and the Auto/Ethnography of Women's Lives." In *Auto/Ethnography: Rewriting the Self and the Social,* edited by Deborah Reed-Danahay, 223-46. Oxford: Berg, 1997.

–. "Gendered Lives: Transitions and Turning Points in Personal, Family, and Historical Time." *Current Anthropology* 43, 4 (2002): 45-61.

Briggs, Charles. "Communicability, Racial Discourse and Disease." *Annual Review of Anthropology* 34 (2005): 269-91.

Briggs, Charles, and Richard Bauman. "'The Foundation of All Future Researches': Franz Boas, George Hunt, Native American Texts, and the Construction of Modernity." *American Quarterly* 51, 3 (1999): 479-528.

Brown, Jennifer. "Reading beyond the Missionaries, Dissecting Responses." *Ethnohistory* 43, 4 (1996): 713-19.

Brown, Michael. "On Resisting Resistance." *American Anthropologist* 98, 4 (1996): 729-35.

Brown, Pam. "Cannery Days: A Chapter in the Lives of the Heiltsuk." Master's thesis, University of British Columbia, 1993.

Brownlie, Robin, and Mary-Ellen Kelm. "Desperately Seeking Absolution: Native Agency as Colonialist Alibi?" *Canadian Historical Review* 75, 4 (1994): 543-56.

Bruner, M. Edward. "Ethnography as Narrative." In *The Anthropology of Experience,* edited by Victor W. Turner and Edward M. Bruner, 139-55. Urbana: University of Illinois Press, 1986.

–, ed. *Text, Play, and Story: The Construction and Reconstruction of Self and Society.* Washington, D.C.: American Ethnological Society, 1984.

Campbell, K. Mack. *Cannery Village, Company Town: A History of British Columbia's Outlying Salmon Canneries.* Victoria: Trafford, 2004.

Campbell, Robert. "Making Sober Citizens: The Legacy of Indigenous Alcohol Regulation in Canada, 1777-1985." *Journal of Canadian Studies* 42, 1 (2008): 105-26.

Cannizzo, Janine. "George Hunt and the Invention of Kwakiutl Culture." *Canadian Review of Sociology and Anthropology* 20, 1 (1982): 44-58.

Carter, Sarah. "Creating 'Semi-Widows' and 'Supernumerary Wives': Prohibiting Polygamy in Prairie Canada's Aboriginal Communities to 1900." In *Contact Zones: Aboriginal and Settler Women in Canada's Colonial Past,* edited by Katie Pickles and Myra Rutherdale, 131-59. Vancouver: UBC Press, 2005.

Christophers, Brett. *Positioning the Missionary: John Booth Good and the Confluence of Cultures in Nineteenth-Century British Columbia.* Vancouver: UBC Press, 1998.

Clements, Marie, and Rita Leistner. *The Edward Curtis Project: A Modern Picture Story.* Vancouver: Talonbooks, 2010.

Clifford, James, and George Marcus, eds. *Writing Culture: The Poetics and Politics of Ethnography.* Berkeley: University of California Press, 1986.

Codere, Helen. "The Amiable Side of Kwakiutl Life: The Potlatch and the Play Potlatch." *American Anthropologist* 28 (1956): 334-51.

–. "Dan Cranmer's Potlatch." In *Indians of the North Pacific Coast,* edited by Tom McFeat, 116-18. Toronto: McClelland and Stewart, 1966.

–. *Fighting with Property: A Study of Kwakiutl Potlatching and Warfare, 1792-1930.* Monographs of the American Ethnological Society 18. New York: J.J. Augustin, 1950.

–. Introduction to *Kwakiutl Ethnography,* by Franz Boas, edited by Helen Codere, xi-xxxii. Chicago: University of Chicago Press, 1966.

–. "Kwakiutl." In *Perspectives in American Indian Culture Change,* edited by Edward Spicer, 431-516. Chicago: University of Chicago Press, 1961.

Cole, Douglas. "The History of the Kwakiutl Potlatch." In *Chiefly Feasts: The Enduring Kwakiutl Potlatch,* edited by Aldona Jonaitis, 135-68. Seattle: University of Washington Press, 1991.

–. "Underground Potlatch: How the Kwakiutl Kept the Faith." *Natural History* 100, 10 (1991): 50-56.

Cole, Douglas, and Ira Chaikin. *An Iron Hand upon the People: The Law against the Potlatch on the Northwest Coast.* Vancouver: Douglas and McIntyre, 1990.

Cole, Douglas, and J.R. Miller. "Desperately Seeking Absolution: Responses and a Reply." *Canadian Historical Review* 76, 4 (1995): 628-40.

Comaroff, Jean, and John Comaroff. *Of Revelation and Revolution: Christianity, Colonialism, and Consciousness in South Africa.* Vol. 1. Chicago: University of Chicago Press, 1991.

Comaroff, John, and Jean Comaroff. *Ethnography and the Historical Imagination.* Boulder, CO: Westview Press, 1992.

Cranmer-Webster, Gloria. "Consumers, Then and Now." In *Constructing Cultures Then and Now: The Legacy of Franz Boas and the Jesup North Pacific Expedition, 1897-1902,* edited by Laurel Kendall and Igor Krupnik, 1-10. Washington, DC: Arctic Studies Centre, National Museum of Natural History, Smithsonian Institution, 2003.

–. "Contemporary Kwakwak'wakw Potlatches." In *The Spirit Within: Northwest Coast Native Art from the John H. Hauberg Collection.* Seattle: Seattle Art Museum, 1995.

–. "The Contemporary Potlatch." In *Chiefly Feasts: The Enduring Kwakiutl Potlatch,* edited by Aldona Jonaitis, 227-48. Vancouver: Douglas and McIntyre, 1991.

–. Foreword to *Kesu': The Art and Life of Doug Cranmer,* by Jennifer Kramer. Toronto: Douglas and McIntyre, 2012.

Cox, Constance. "White Woman Honoured." *Native Voice* 3, 7 (1949): 5.

Crapanzano, Vincent. "Life Histories." *American Anthropologist* 86, 4 (1984): 953-60.

–. *Tuhami: Portrait of a Moroccan.* Chicago: University of Chicago Press, 1980.

Crosby, Marcia. "Construction of the Imaginary Indian." In *Vancouver Anthology: The Institutional Politics of Art,* edited by Stan Douglas, 267-91. Vancouver: Talonbooks, 1991.

Cruikshank, Julie. *Do Glaciers Listen? Local Knowledge, Colonial Encounters, and Social Imagination.* Vancouver: UBC Press, 2005.

–. *The Social Life of Stories: Narrative and Knowledge in the Yukon Territory.* Lincoln: University of Nebraska, 1998.

Cruikshank, Julie, in collaboration with Angela Sidney, Kitty Smith, and Annie Ned. *Life Lived Like a Story: Life Stories of Three Yukon Elders.* Vancouver: UBC Press, 1990.

Culhane Speck, Dara. *An Error in Judgement: The Politics of Medical Care in an Indian/White Community.* Vancouver: Talonbooks, 1987.

Curtis, Edward. *The North American Indian.* Vol. 10, *The Kwakiutl.* Norwood, MA: Plimpton Press, 1915.

Damm, Kateri. "Says Who? Colonialism, Identity and Defining Indigenous Literature." In *Looking at the Words of Our People,* edited by Jeanette Armstrong, 9-26. Penticton: Theytus, 1993.

Dawson, George. *Notes and Observations on the Kwakiool People.* Transactions of the Royal Society of Canada, Vol. 5, Sec. 2. Montreal: Dawson, 1888.

De Costa, Ravi. "Identity, Authority, and the Moral Worlds of Indigenous Petitions." *Comparative Study in Society and History* 48, 3 (2006): 669-98.

Deloria, Vine, Jr. *Custer Died for Your Sins: An Indian Manifesto.* Norman: University of Oklahoma Press, 1973.

Denetdale, Jennifer Nez. "Chairmen, Presidents, and Princesses: The Navajo Nation, Gender, and the Politics of Tradition." *Wicazo Sa Review* 21, 1 (2006): 9-28.

–. *Reclaiming Diné History: The Legacies of Navajo Chief Manuelito and Juanita.* Tucson: University of Arizona Press, 2007.

DeSersa, Esther, Olivia Black Elk Pourier, Aaron DeSersa Jr., and Clifton DeSersa. *Black Elk Lives: Conversations with the Black Elk Family.* Edited by Hilda Nierhardt and Lori Utrecht. Lincoln: University of Nebraska Press, 2000.

Dominguez, Virginia. "For a Politics of Love and Rescue." *Cultural Anthropology* 15, 3 (2000): 361-93.

Douglas, Bronwen. "Christian Citizens: Women and Negotiations of Modernity in Vanuatu." *Contemporary Pacific* 14, 1 (2002): 1-38.

–. "Provocative Readings in Intransigent Archives: Finding Aneityumese Women." *Oceania* 70, 2 (1999): 111-29.

Drucker, Philip. *The Native Brotherhoods: Modern Intertribal Organizations on the Northwest Coast.* Bureau of American Ethnology Bulletin 168. Washington, DC: Smithsonian Institution, 1958.

–. *The Northern and Central Nootkan Tribes.* Bureau of American Ethnology Bulletin 144. Washington, DC: Smithsonian Institution/Bureau of American Ethnology, 1951.

Drucker, Philip, and Robert Heizer. *To Make My Name Good: A Reexamination of the Southern Kwakiutl Potlatch.* Berkeley: University of California Press, 1967.

Dundes, Alan. "Heads or Tails: A Psychoanalytic Study of Potlatch." *Journal of Psychological Anthropology* 2, 4 (1979): 395-424.

Fabian, Johannes. *Power and Performance: Ethnographic Explorations through Proverbial Wisdom and Theatre in Shaba, Zaïre.* Madison: University of Wisconsin Press, 1990.

Fassin, Didier, Frédéric Le Marcis, and Todd Lethata. "Life and Times of Magda A: Telling a Story of Violence in South Africa." *Current Anthropology* 49, 2 (2008): 225-46.

Fisher, Robin. *Contact and Conflict: Indian-European Relations in British Columbia, 1774-1890.* Vancouver: UBC Press, 1990.

Fleisher, Mark. "The Potlatch: A Symbolic and Psychoanalytic View." *Current Anthropology* 22, 1 (1981): 69-71.

Fournier, Suzanne, and Ernie Crey. *Stolen from Our Embrace: The Abduction of First Nations Children and the Restoration of Aboriginal Communities.* Vancouver: Douglas and McIntyre, 1997.

Francis, Daniel. *The Imaginary Indian: The Image of the Indian in Canadian Culture.* Vancouver: Arsenal Pulp Press, 1992.

Freeman, James. *Untouchable: An Indian Life History.* Palo Alto, CA: Stanford University Press, 1979.

Friedman, Jonathan. "From Roots to Routes: Tropes for Trippers." *Anthropological Theory* 2, 1 (2002): 21-36.

–. "Myth, History and Political Identity." *Cultural Anthropology* 7, 2 (1992): 194-210.

–. "The Past in the Future: History and the Politics of Identity." *American Anthropologist* 94 (1992): 837-59.

Galois, Robert. "Colonial Encounters: The Worlds of Arthur Wellington Clah, 1855-1881." *BC Studies* 115-16 (1997-98): 105-47.

–. *Kwakwa̱ka̱'wakw Settlements, 1775-1920: A Geographical Analysis and Gazetteer.* Vancouver: UBC Press, 1994.

Gidley, Mick. *Edward S. Curtis and the North American Indian, Incorporated.* New York: Cambridge University Press, 1998.

Gladstone, Percy. "Native Indians and the Fishing Industry of British Columbia." *Canadian Journal of Economics and Political Science* 19, 1 (1953): 20-34.

Glass, Aaron. "Conspicuous Consumption: An Intercultural History of the Kwa̲kwa̲ka'wakw Hamat'sa." PhD diss., New York University, 2006.

–. "Crests on Cotton: 'Souvenir' T-Shirts and the Materiality of Remembrance among the Kwakwaka'wakw of British Columbia." *Museum Anthropology* 31, 1 (2008): 1-18.

–. "From Cultural Salvage to Brokerage: The Mythologization of Mungo Martin and the Emergence of Northwest Coast Art," *Museum Anthropology* 29, 1 (2006): 20-43.

–. "The Thin Edge of the Wedge: Dancing around the Potlatch Ban, 1921-1951." In *Right to Dance: Dancing for Rights,* edited by Naomi Jackson, 51-82. Banff: Banff Centre, 2004.

Goldman, Irving. *The Mouth of Heaven: An Introduction to Kwakiutl Religious Thought.* New York: Wiley, 1975.

Goodfellow, John. *Totem Poles of Stanley Park*. Vancouver: Art, Historical and Scientific Association, 1931.

Gough, Barry. "A Priest versus the Potlatch: Reverend Alfred James Hall and the Fort Rupert Kwakiutl, 1878-1880." *Journal of the Canadian Church Historical Society* 24, 2 (1982): 75-89.

–. "Send a Gunboat! Checking Slavery and Controlling Liquor Traffic among Coast Indians of British Columbia in the 1860s." *Pacific Northwest Quarterly* 69, 4 (1978): 159-68.

Gough, Kathleen. "Anthropology and Imperialism." *Monthly Review* 19, 11 (1968): 403-35.

Gow, Peter. *An Amazonian Myth and Its History*. Oxford: Oxford University Press, 2001.

Grammond, Sebastien. *Identity Captured by Law: Membership in Canada's Indigenous Peoples and Linguistic Minorities.* Montreal and Kingston: McGill-Queen's University Press, 2009.

Green, Joyce. "Taking Account of Aboriginal Feminism." In *Making Space for Indigenous Feminism,* edited by Joyce Green, 20-32. Blackpoint, NS: Fernwood, 2007.

Gruber, Jacob. "Ethnographic Salvage and the Shaping of Anthropology." *American Anthropologist* 72, 6 (1970): 1289-99.

Hacking, Norman. "Barbaric Potlatch Still Survives among Alert Bay Natives." *Vancouver Province,* 29 June 1935.

Hall, Alfred. "Grammar of the Kwagiutl Language: Transactions of the Royal Society of Canada" 6, 2 (1889): 59-105.

Halliday, William. *Potlatch and Totem and the Recollections of an Indian Agent.* Toronto: J.M. Dent and Sons, 1935.

Hames, Raymond. "The Ecologically Noble Savage Debate." *Annual Review of Anthropology* 36 (2007): 177-90.

Harkin, Michael. "Engendering Discipline: Discourse and Counterdiscourse in the Methodist-Heiltsuk Dialogue." In "Native American Women's Responses to Christianity," ed. Michael Harkin and Sergei Kan, special issue, *Ethnohistory* 43, 4 (1996): 643-61.

–. "Ethnographic Deep Play: Boas, McIlwraith, and Fictive Adoption on the Northwest Coast." In *Strangers to Relatives,* edited by Sergei Kan, 57-79. Lincoln: University of Nebraska Press, 2001.

–. "Feeling and Thinking in Memory and Forgetting: Toward an Ethnohistory of the Emotions." *Ethnohistory* 50, 2 (2003): 261-84.

Harkin, Michael, and Sergei Kan, eds. "Native American Women's Responses to Christianity," special issue, *Ethnohistory* 43, 4 (1996).

Harring, Sidney. *White Man's Law: Native People in Nineteenth-Century Canadian Jurisprudence.* Toronto: University of Toronto Press/Osgoode Society for Canadian Legal History, 1998.

Harris, Cole. *Making Native Space: Colonialism, Resistance, and Reserves in British Columbia.* Vancouver: UBC Press, 2002.

Harris, Douglas. *Landing Native Fisheries: Indian Reserves and Fishing Rights in British Columbia, 1849-1925.* Vancouver: UBC Press, 2008.

Hawker, Ronald. *Tales of Ghosts: First Nations Art in British Columbia, 1922-1961.* Vancouver: UBC Press, 2003.

Hawthorn, Harry, Cyril Belshaw, and Stuart Jamieson. *The Indians of British Columbia: A Study of Contemporary Social Adjustment.* Berkeley/Toronto: University of California Press/University of Toronto Press, 1960.

Herskovits, Melville. *Economic Anthropology.* New York: Knopf, 1952.

Hilsdon, Anne Marie. "Reconsidering Agency: Feminist Anthropologies in Asia." *Australian Journal of Anthropology* 18, 2 (2007): 127-37.

Hodgkin, Katharine, and Susannah Radstone, eds. *Contested Pasts: The Politics of Memory.* New York: Routledge, 2003.

Horse Capture, George. "Edward Curtis, Shadow Catcher." *American Masters,* 23 April 2001. http://www.pbs.org/.

Ignace, Ron, George Speck, and Renee Taylor. "Some Native Perspectives on Anthropology and Public Policy." In *Anthropology, Public Policy and Native Peoples in Canada,* edited by Noel Dyck and James Waldram, 166-91. Montreal and Kingston: McGill-Queen's University Press, 1993.

Indian Claims Commission. *Inquiry into the Cormorant Island Claim of the 'Namgis First Nation.* March 1996. Available online, publications.gc.ca.

Irvin, Thomas. "The Northwest Coast Potlatch since Boas, 1897-1972." *Anthropology* 1, 1 (1977): 65-77.

Jacknis, Ira. "George Hunt, Collector of Indian Specimens." In *Chiefly Feasts: The Enduring Kwakiutl Potlatch,* edited by Aldona Jonaitis, 177-224. Seattle: University of Washington Press, 1991.

–. *The Storage Box of Tradition: Kwakiutl Art, Anthropologists, and Museums, 1881-1981.* Washington, DC: Smithsonian Institution, 2002.

Jacobson, Diane. *My Life in a Kwagu'ł Big House.* Penticton, BC: Theytus Books, 2005.

Jefferson, Christie. *Conquest by Law.* Ottawa: Solicitor General of Canada, 1994.

Johnsen, D.B. "The Formation and Protection of Property Rights among the Southern Kwakiutl Indians." *Journal of Legal Studies* 15, 1 (1986): 41-67.

Johnson, Thomas, with Helen Johnson. *Also Called Sacajawea: Chief Woman's Stolen Identity.* Long Grove, IL: Waveland Press, 2008.

Jonaitis, Aldona, ed. *Chiefly Feasts: The Enduring Kwakiutl Potlatch.* Seattle: University of Washington Press, 1991.

–. *From the Land of the Totem Poles: The Northwest Coast Indian Art Collection at the American Museum of Natural History.* New York/Vancouver: American Museum of Natural History/Douglas and McIntyre, 1988.

Jonaitis, Aldona, and Aaron Glass. *The Totem Pole: An Intercultural History*. Seattle/Vancouver: University of Washington Press/Douglas and McIntyre, 2010.

Joseph, Gene. "A Brief History of the Native Brotherhood of British Columbia." Report prepared for the Native Brotherhood of British Columbia, 1981. In possession of the author.

Keen, Rosemary. "General Introduction and Guide to the Archive," Church Mission Society Archives. http://www.ampltd.co.uk/digital_guides/church_missionary_society_archive_general/.

Kelm, Mary-Ellen. *Colonizing Bodies: Aboriginal Health and Healing in British Columbia, 1900-50.* Vancouver: UBC Press, 1998.

Knight, Rolf. *Indians at Work: An Informal History of Native Labour in British Columbia, 1858-1930.* Vancouver: New Star, 1996 [1978].

Kobrinsky, Vernon. "Dynamics of the Fort Rupert Class Struggle: Fighting with Property Vertically Revisited." In *Papers in Honour of Harry Hawthorn,* edited by Verne Serle and Herbert Taylor, 32-59. Bellingham, WA: Northwest Scientific Association, 1975.

Krouse, Susan Applegate, and Heather Howard, eds. *Keeping the Campfires Going: Native Women's Activism in Urban Communities.* Lincoln: University of Nebraska Press, 2009.

Kwakiutl Indian Band. "Our Land: In the Beginning." http://www.kwakiutl.bc.ca/land/beginning.htm.

Langness, L.L., and Gelya Frank. *Lives: An Anthropological Approach to Biography*. Novato, CA: Chandler and Sharp, 1981.

LaRoque, Emma. "Métis and Feminist: Ethical Reflections on Feminism, Human Rights and Decolonization." In *Making Space for Indigenous Feminism,* edited by Joyce Green, 53-71. Blackpoint, NS: Fernwood, 2007.

Lassiter, Luke. *The Chicago Guide to Collaborative Ethnography*. Chicago: University of Chicago Press, 2005.

–. "From 'Reading over the Shoulders of Natives' to 'Reading alongside Natives,' Literally: Toward a Collaborative and Reciprocal Ethnography." *Journal of Anthropological Research* 57, 2 (2001): 137-49.

LaViolette, Forrest. *The Struggle for Survival: Indian Cultures and the Protestant Ethic in British Columbia.* Toronto: University of Toronto Press, 1973.

Lawrence, Bonita. *"Real" Indians and Others: Mixed-Blood Urban Native Peoples and Indigenous Nationhood.* Vancouver: UBC Press, 2004.

Lee, Helen. "Corporate Strategy in the BC Fish-Processing Sector." Master's thesis, Simon Fraser University, 1983.

Lévi-Strauss, Claude. "The Sorcerer and His Magic." In *Structural Anthropology,* Vol. 1, 167-85. London: Peregrine, 1963.

Lindembaum, Shirley. "Thinking about Cannibalism." *Annual Review of Anthropology* 33 (2004): 475-98.

Loo, Tina. "Dan Cranmer's Potlatch: Law as Coercion, Symbol, and Rhetoric in British Columbia, 1884-1951." *Canadian Historical Review* 68, 2 (1992): 125-65.

MacClancy, Jeremy. "Nakomaha: A Counter-Colonial Life and Its Contexts – Anthropological Approaches to Biography." *Oceania* 77, 2 (2007): 191-214.

MacLeod, William. "Economic Aspects of Indigenous American Slavery." *American Anthropologist* 30, 4 (1928): 632-50.

Macnair, Peter. "From Kwakiutl to Kwakwaka'wakw." In *Native Peoples: The Canadian Experience,* edited by R. Bruce Morrison and C. Roderick Wilson, 586-605. Toronto: Oxford University Press, 1986.

Mandelbaum, David. "The Study of Life History: Gandhi." *Current Anthropology* 14, 3 (1973): 177-96.

Masco, Joseph. "Competitive Displays: Negotiating Genealogical Rights to the Potlatch at the American Museum of Natural History." *American Anthropologist* 98, 4 (1996): 837-52.

–. "'It Is a Strict Law That Bids Us Dance': Cosmologies, Colonialism, and Ritual Authority in the Kwakwa̱ka̱'wakw Potlatch, 1849-1922." *Comparative Studies in Society and History* 37, 1 (1995): 41-75.

Mauss, Marcel. "Essai sur le don: Forme et raison de l'échange dans les sociétés archaïques" [An essay on the gift: The form and reason for exchange in archaic societies]. *Année Sociologique* 1 (1923-24): 30-188.

–. *The Gift: The Form and Reason for Exchange in Archaic Societies.* New York: W.W. Norton, 1990.

Mawani, Renisa. "In Between and Out of Place: Racial Hybridity, Liquor and the Law in Late 19th- and Early 20th-Century British Columbia." *Canadian Journal of Law and Society* 15, 2 (2000): 9-38.

McCarthy Brown, Karen. *Mama Lola: A Vodou Priestess in Brooklyn.* Berkeley: University of California Press, 2001.

McFeat, Tom, ed. *Indians of the North Pacific Coast.* Toronto: McClelland and Stewart, 1966.

McKechnie, Robert. *Strong Medicine: History of Healing on the Northwest Coast.* Victoria: Morris, 1972.

Miller, Bruce G. "Bringing Culture In: Community Responses to Apology, Reconciliation, and Reparations." *American Indian Culture and Research Journal* 30, 4 (2006): 1-17.

–. Review of *Paddling to Where I Stand: Agnes Alfred, Qwiqwasutinuxw Noblewoman,* edited by Martine Reid and translated by Daisy Sewid-Smith. *American Indian Culture and Research Journal* 29, 2 (2005): 149-51.

Mitchell, Marjorie, and Anna Franklin. "When You Don't Know the Language, Listen to the Silence: An Historical Overview of Native Indian Women in BC." In *Not Just Pin Money,* edited by Barbara Latham and Roberta Pazdro, 49-68. Victoria: Camosun College, 1984.

Miyazaki, Hirokazu. *The Method of Hope: Anthropology, Philosophy, and Fijian Knowledge.* Palo Alto, CA: Stanford University Press, 2004.

Muratorio, Blanca. *The Life and Times of Grandfather Alonso: Culture and History in the Upper Amazon.* New Brunswick, NJ: Rutgers University Press, 1991.

Murray, Peter. *The Devil and Mr. Duncan: A History of the Two Metlakatlas.* Victoria: Sono Nis Press, 1985.

Napoleon, Val. "Who Gets to Say What Happened?" In *Reconciliation Issues for the Gitksan: Intercultural Dispute Resolution in Aboriginal Contexts,* edited by Catherine Bell and David Kahane, 176-95. Vancouver: UBC Press, 2004.

Nash, June. "Defying Deterritorialization: Autonomy Movements against Globalization." In *Social Movements: An Anthropological Reader,* edited by June Nash, 177-86. Malden, MA: John Wiley and Sons, 2004.

Newcombe, Charles, ed. *Menzies' Journal of Vancouver's Voyage, April to October 1792.* Archives of British Columbia, Memoir No. V, 171 pp. Victoria: William H. Cullen, 1923.

Newell, Dianne. *Tangled Webs of History: Indians and the Law in Canada's Pacific Coast Fisheries.* Toronto: University of Toronto Press, 1993.

Newell, Dianne, and Dorothee Schreiber. "Collaborations on the Periphery: The Wolcott-Sewid Potlatch Controversy." *BC Studies* 152 (2006): 7-34.

Nielsen, Steffen. "Civilizing Kwakiutl: Contexts and Contests of Kwakiutl Personhood, 1880-1999." PhD diss., University of Aarhus, 2001.

Niezen, Ronald. "Recognizing Indigenism: Canadian Unity and the International Movement of Indigenous Peoples." *Comparative Study of Society and History* 42, 1 (2000): 119-48.

Nowell, Charlie. *Smoke from Their Fires: The Life of a Kwakiutl Chief.* Edited by Clellan Ford. New Haven: Yale University Press, 1941.

Nuytten, Phil. *The Totem Pole Carvers: Charlie James, Ellen Neel, Mungo Martin.* Vancouver: Panorama Publications, 1982.

Okely, Judith. "Defiant Moments: Gender, Resistance and Individuals." *Man,* n.s., 26, 1 (1991): 3-22.

Ortner, Sherry. *Anthropology and Social Theory: Culture, Power, and the Acting Subject.* Durham, NC: Duke University Press, 2006.

Paine, Robert. "Aboriginality, Authenticity and the Settler World." In *Signifying Identities: Anthropological Perspectives on Boundaries and Contested Values,* edited by Anthony Cohen, 77-116. Routledge: New York, 2000.

Passerini, Luisa."Memories between Silence and Oblivion." In *Contested Pasts: The Politics of Memory,* edited by Katharine Hodgkin and Susannah Radstone, 238-54. New York: Routledge, 2003.

Pearce, Roy Harvey. *Savagism and Civilization: A Study of the Indian and the American Mind.* Berkeley: University of California Press, 1988.

Perry, Adele. "Metropolitan Knowledge, Colonial Practice, and Indigenous Womanhood: Missions in Nineteenth-Century British Columbia." In *Contact Zones: Aboriginal and Settler Women in Canada's Colonial Past,* edited by Katie Pickles and Myra Rutherdale, 109-30. Vancouver: UBC Press, 2005.

Personal Narratives Group. *Interpreting Women's Lives: Feminist Theory and Personal Narratives.* Bloomington: Indiana University Press, 1989.

Pethik, Derek. *James Douglas: Servant of Two Empires.* Vancouver: Mitchell Press, 1969.

Piddocke, Stuart. "The Potlatch System of the Southern Kwakiutl: A New Perspective." *Southwestern Journal of Anthropology* 21 (1965): 244-64.

Pine, Francis. "Naming the House and Naming the Land: Kinship and Social Groups in Highland Poland." *Journal of the Royal Anthropological Institute* 2, 3 (1996): 443-59.

Price, Richard. *Alabi's World.* Baltimore: Johns Hopkins University Press, 1990.

–. *Travels with Tooy: History, Memory, and African-American Imagination.* Chicago: University of Chicago Press, 2008.

Raibmon, Paige. *Authentic Indians: Episodes of Encounter from the Late-Nineteenth-Century Northwest Coast.* Durham, NC: Duke University Press, 2005.

–. "Living on Display." *BC Studies* 140 (2003-04): 69-89.

Reagan, Paulette. *Unsettling the Settler Within: Indian Residential Schools, Truth Telling, and Reconciliation in Canada.* Vancouver: UBC Press, 2010.

Reid, Martine, ed. *Paddling to Where I Stand: Agnes Alfred, Qwiqwasutinuxw Noblewoman.* Translated by Daisy Sewid-Smith. Vancouver: UBC Press, 2004.

Robertson, Leslie. *Imagining Difference: Legend, Curse, and Spectacle in a Canadian Mining Town.* Vancouver: UBC Press, 2005.

Robertson, Leslie, and Dara Culhane. *In Plain Sight: Reflections on Life in Downtown Eastside Vancouver.* Vancouver: Talonbooks, 2005.

Rohner, Ronald. "The Boas Canon: A Posthumous Addition – Review of Kwakiutl Ethnography by Franz Boas, Helen Codere." *Science* 158, 3799 (1967): 362-64.

–. *The Ethnography of Franz Boas.* Chicago: University of Chicago Press, 1969.

Rosaldo, Renato. "Grief and a Headhunter's Rage: On the Cultural Force of Emotions." In *Text, Play, and Story: The Construction and Reconstruction of Self and Society,* edited by Edward Bruner, 178-95. Washington, DC: American Ethnological Society, 1984.

–. "Imperialist Nostalgia." In "Memory and Counter-Memory," special issue, *Representations* 26 (1989): 107-22.

Roth, Christopher. *Becoming Tsimshian: The Social Life of Names.* Seattle: University of Washington Press, 2008.

Rumsey, Alan. "Agency, Personhood and the 'I' of Discourse in the Pacific and Beyond." *Journal of the Royal Anthropological Institute* 6, 1 (2000): 101-15.

Sahlins, Marshall. "Goodbye to Tristes Tropes: Ethnography in the Context of Modern World History." *Journal of Modern History* 65, 1 (1993): 1-25.

–. "Other Times, Other Customs: the Anthropology of History." *American Anthropologist* 85, 3 (1983): 517-44.

–. "What Kinship Is (Part One)." *Journal of the Royal Anthropological Institute,* n.s., 17 (2011): 2-19.

Salmond, Anne. "Māori and Modernity: Ruatara's Dying." In *Signifying Identities,* edited by Anthony Cohen, 37-54. New York: Routledge, 2000.

Saunders, Barbara. "From a Colonized Consciousness to Autonomous Identity: Shifting Relations between the Kwa̱kwa̱ka'wakw and Canadian Nations." *Dialectical Anthropology* 22, 2 (1997): 137-58.

Schreiber, Dorothee. "'A Liberal and Paternal Spirit': Indian Agents and Native Fisheries in Canada." *Ethnohistory* 55, 1 (2008): 87-118.

Schulte-Tenckhoff, Isabelle. "Misrepresenting the Potlatch." In *Expanding the Economic Concept of Exchange: Deception, Self-Deception, and Illusions,* edited by Caroline Gerschlager, 167-88. Boston: Kluwer Academic Publishers, 2001.

–. "Potlatch and Totem: The Attraction of America's Northwest Coast." In *Tourism: Manufacturing the Exotic,* edited by Pierre Rossel, 117-47. Copenhagen: International Working Group for International Affairs, 1988.

Schwartz, Joan, and Terry Cook. "Archives, Records and Power." *Archival Science* 2, 1-2 (2002): 1-19.

Seguin, Margaret Anderson, and Tammy Anderson Blumhagen. "Memories and Moments: Conversations and Recollections." *BC Studies* 104 (1995): 69-83.

Sewid, James. *Guests Never Leave Hungry: The Autobiography of James Sewid, a Kwakiutl Indian.* Edited by James Spradley. New Haven: Yale University Press, 1969.

Sewid-Smith, Daisy (My-yah-nelth). "The Continuing Reshaping of Our Ritual World by Academic Adjuncts." *Anthropology and Education Quarterly* 28, 4 (1997): 594-602.

–. *Prosecution or Persecution.* Cape Mudge: Nu-yum-baleess Society, 1979.

Sherman, Mark. Introduction to *Kwakiutl String Figures,* by Julia Averkieva, xvii-xxxi. Vancouver: UBC Press, 1992.

Shroder, Ingo. "From Parkman to Postcolonial Theory: What's New in the Ethnohistory of Missions?" *Ethnohistory* 46, 4 (1999): 809-15.

Simpson, Audra. "On Ethnographic Refusal: Indigeneity, 'Voice' and Colonial Citizenship." *Junctures* 9 (2007): 67-80.

–. "To the Reserve and Back Again: Kahnawake Mohawk Narratives of Self, Home and Nation." PhD diss., McGill University, 2003.

Sissons, Jeffrey. *First Peoples: Indigenous Cultures and Their Futures.* London: Reaktion Press, 2005.

Speck, George. "An Outline History of the Kwakwaka'wakw Struggle for the Recognition of Aboriginal Title and Self-Determination." Paper prepared for the Kwakiutl District Council, 1990.

Speck, Lori. "Spirits Broken and Innocence Stolen." *U'mista News,* Spring 1999, 10-18.

Stoler, Ann Laura. "Colonial Archives and the Arts of Governance: On the Content in the Form." In *Refiguring the Archive,* edited by C. Hamilton, V. Harris, J. Taylor, M. Pickover, G. Reid, and R. Saleh. London: Kluwer Academic Publishers, 2002.

–. "Imperial Debris: Reflections on Ruins and Ruination." *Cultural Anthropology* 23, 2 (2008): 191-219.

Suttles, Wayne. "Streams of Property, Armor of Wealth: The Traditional Kwakiutl Potlatch." in *Chiefly Feasts: The Enduring Kwakiutl Potlatch,* edited by Aldona Jonaitis, 71-134. Vancouver: Douglas and McIntyre, 1991.

Suttles, Wayne, and Aldona Jonaitis. "History of Research in Ethnology." In *Handbook of the North American Indian.* Vol. 7, *Northwest Coast,* edited by Wayne Suttles, 73-87. Washington, DC: Smithsonian Institution, 1990.

Ta-de-win (a.k.a. Mabel F. Knight). "Totem Poles of Vancouver Are Insignia of Tribal Rank; Their Erection by Kwakiutl Indians of Island Depends on Whether They Have Held a 'Potlatch' or Are Owners of a 'Copper.'" *Christian Science Monitor,* 12 November 1932.

Tennant, Paul. *Aboriginal Peoples and Politics: The Indian Land Question in British Columbia.* Vancouver: UBC Press, 1990.

Thain, Mrs. William Murray. "A Few Remarks on Fifty Years Ago." *Log of the Columbia* 5, 4 (1909).

Thomas, Nicholas. *Colonialism's Culture: Anthropology, Travel and Government.* Princeton, NJ: Princeton University Press, 1994.

Tierney, John. "Tips from the Potlatch; Where Giving Knows No Slump." *New York Times,* 16 December 2008.

Titley, E. Brian. *A Narrow Vision: Duncan Campbell Scott and the Administration of Indian Affairs.* Vancouver: UBC Press, 1986.

Traditions Consulting Services. "Mowachaht Aboriginal Title." Prepared for Mowachaht/Muchalaht First Nation by Richard Ingles, Kevin Neary, and Sheila Savey, 2005.

Trosper, Ronald. "Northwest Coast Indigenous Institutions That Supported Resilience and Sustainability." *Ecological Economics* 41, 2 (2002): 329-44.

Trouillot, Michel-Rolph. *Silencing the Past: Power and the Production of History*. Boston: Beacon, 1995.

Tsing, Anna. "Indigenous Voice." In *Indigenous Experience Today,* edited by Marisol de la Cadena and Orin Starn, 33-67. New York: Berg, 2007.

Tuhiwai Smith, Linda. *Decolonizing Methodologies: Research and Indigenous Peoples.* New York: Zed Books, 1999.

U'mista Cultural Centre. *Box of Treasures*. Chuck Olin, director and producer. Watertown, MA: Documentary Educational Resources, 1983.

Union of BC Indian Chiefs. "McKenna-McBride Royal Commission, Kwawkewlth Agency Testimony." Our Homes Are Bleeding. http://ubcic.bc.ca/Resources/ourhomesare/testimonies.htm.

–. *Stolen Lands, Broken Promises: Dispossession and Resistance in British Columbia.* http://ubcic.bc.ca.

Valaskakis, Gail. "Rights and Warriors, First Nations, Media and Identity." *ARIEL* 25, 1 (1994): 60-72.

Walens, Stanley. *Feasting with Cannibals: On Kwakiutl Cosmology*. Princeton, NJ: Princeton University Press, 1981.

Wallace, Richard. "Charting the North West Coast 1857-62: A Case Study in the Use of Knowledge as Power in Britain's Imperial Ascendency." Master's thesis, University of British Columbia, 1993.

Warren, Kay. "Perils and Promises." In *Engaged Observers: Anthropology, Advocacy and Activism,* edited by Victoria Stanford and Asale Angel-Anjani, 213-27. Newark, NJ: Rutgers University Press, 2008.

Werbner, James, ed. *Postcolonial Subjectivities in Africa.* New York: Zed Books, 2002.

Whitaker, Pamela, and Chief James Wallas. *Kwakiutl Legends.* Blaine, WA: Hancock House, 1989.

Whitehead, Harry. "The Hunt for Quesalid: Tracking Levi-Strauss' Shaman." *Anthropology and Medicine* 7, 2 (2000): 149-68.

Whitehead, Margaret. "A Useful Christian Woman: First Nations' Women and Protestant Missionary Work in British Columbia." *Atlantis* 18, 1-2 (1992-93): 142-66.

Wickwire, Wendy. "Stories from the Margins: Toward a More Inclusive British Columbia Historiography." *Journal of American Folklore* 118, 470 (2005): 453-74.

Wickwire, Wendy, and Harry Robinson. *Write It on Your Heart: The Epic World of an Okanagan Storyteller*. Vancouver: Talonbooks/Theytus, 1989.

Williams, Judith. *Two Wolves at the Dawn of Time (Kingcome Inlet Pictographs 1893-1998).* Vancouver: New Star Books, 2001.

Wilson, Shawn. 2008. *Research Is Ceremony: Indigenous Research Methods.* Winnipeg: Fernwood, 2008.

Wolf, Eric. *Envisioning Power: Ideologies of Dominance and Crisis.* Berkeley: University of California Press, 1999.

Zamir, Shamoon. "Native Agency and the Making of *The North American Indian.*" *American Indian Quarterly* 31, 4 (2007): 613-53.

Index

aboriginal rights, 6, 31, 32, 47, 52, 138, 213-26, 280, 292, 348, 351, 359, 361-62, 473n3, 511n65, 523n3, 533n13, 533n24. *See also* aboriginal title; Allied Indian Tribes of BC; fishing; G̲a'ax̲sta'las (Jane Cook); land rights; McKenna-McBride Royal Commission; Native Brotherhood of BC; timber rights and logging

aboriginal title, 54, 70, 118, 126, 133, 138, 163, 183, 193, 194-97, 213, 235, 351, 366, 379, 380, 431, 441, 507n5, 507n7, 507n10, 507n13, 508n14, 508n16, 508n17, 508n19, 508n23, 511n64, 511n65, 512n82, 513n84, 513n90, 520n70, 533n24; and Allied Indian Tribes of BC, 257-58, 268-69, 271, 280, 321; defined, 513n100; and McKenna-McBride Royal Commission, 6, 197, 213-27, 238, 512n70, 513n90. *See also aweetna-kul/oweetna-kula;* Native Brotherhood of BC; reserves

Alert Bay ('Ya̲lis). *See* 'Na̲mgis (Alert Bay) ("Nimpkish")

Alfred, Emma, 136, 151, 242, 343, 346, 354, 365, 367, 369-71, 392, 393, 394, 459

Alfred, Ethel, 23, 25, 56, 172-73, 175, 205-6, 223, 257, 391, 398

Alfred, Pearl, 10, 12, 14, 23, 26, 56, 84, 96, 98, 109, 136-37, 141, 148, 149, 153, 168, 173, 178, 180, 197, 205, 216, 232-36, 243, 270, 281, 287, 296, 324, 331, 345, 356, 392, 394, 395, 398, 437, 441, 459, 521n99

Allied Indian Tribes of BC, 6, 47, 256, 257-75; Executive Committee, 258-59, 262; and fishing, 260-71; and health, 271-75; and potlatching, 259, 277-80

ancestor narratives, 8, 9, 13, 17, 51-52, 56, 57, 74-75, 121, 185, 319, 407, 418, 419, 451, 475n16, 480n86, 487n74, 492n48, 538n1, 538n3; Gix̲sa̲m, 403-6; Kwa̲nu'sila, 154, 306; origins of, 60. *See also* feasting; naming; potlatch *and entries following;* rank; treasures

Anglican Church, 37, 157, 199, 208-9, 238, 289, 297-99, 489n2,

499n154, 504n57, 530n125; and the potlatch, 42, 251, 287, 297-99, 348-49; special meetings, 251-52, 320-30, 350-52; Synod, 297, 335, 339, 367-68. *See also* Christianity; Church Mission Society (CMS); Hall, Alfred; marriage (colonial)
Anglican Women's Auxiliary, 5, 37, 104, 108, 171-75, 198, 228, 326-27, 366, 367
anthropology (discipline of), 10-11, 13, 38, 44-45, 84-85, 113, 249, 256-57, 289, 302, 309, 388-89, 434, 475n20, 477n40, 478n49, 489n104, 517n27, 518n67, 526n61, 539n7, 540n18; and the "Kwakiutl," 13, 18-19, 29-40, 53-54, 75, 84, 185, 302, 407, 474n11, 474n13, 475n14-17, 476n23, 489n104, 540n9; and life history approaches, 11, 44-48, 479n77, 480n79. *See also* Averkieva, Julia; Barbeau, Marius; Boas, Franz; Codere, Helen; Hunt, George; memory; methodology; potlatch *and entries following*
archives, xvi-xvii, 12-13, 17, 18, 30, 40, 42, 44, 48, 55, 110-12, 142, 200, 476n31, 485n51; "cultural archive," 406. *See also* memory; methodology
authenticity, 30, 33-39, 42, 49-51, 380, 476n23, 476n24, 477n41, 481n102; missionary, 109-10, 113, 132; and representation (politics of), 325; scholarly, 54-55, 81-82
Averkieva, Julia, 61, 77, 290, 300, 301, 317-18, 485n53, 523n9, 526n54, 526n61, 530n128
A̲'wa̲'etła̲la, (Knight Inlet) Dzawadi, 6, 58, 188, 215, 223-25, 313, 349, 434, 437, 482n2, 496n103, 513n53
aweetna-kula/oweetna-kula, 19, 75, 213, 473n17. *See also* aboriginal title

Barbeau, Marius, 249, 256, 491n25, 517n27, 518n67, 519n67, 527n69
Barnes, Rita, 97-98, 100, 325-26, 368, 370, 374-77, 398
Bell, Diane, 439, 441
Bell, Randy, 27, 36, 53, 67-70, 108, 141-42, 398, 410, 437, 453
Bella Bella First Nation. *See* Hiłdzak̲w (Bella Bella First Nation)
bishops (Anglican), 347, 529n111; Hills, George, 157; Ridley, William, 46, 115, 144, 497n121, 504n57; Roper, John, 194-95, 197, 199, 203, 206-7, 209, 228, 230; de Veber Schofield, Charles, 240, 250, 294, 298-99, 334, 525n49
Boas, Franz, 13, 19, 31-32, 34, 54, 56, 63, 85, 86,120, 161, 317, 476n23, 476n31, 492n48, 495n85, 502n33, 523n11, 526n61, 538n3; Kwakwa̲ka̲'wakw views on, 31, 37, 80, 191, 237, 291, 415, 422, 489n104; on language,19, 36, 291-93, 482n8, 524n18; and memory culture, 19, 36, 74, 289; methodology and fieldwork of, 35-36, 51, 74-75, 77, 80, 169-70, 237, 288, 301-32, 485n52, 502n42, 505n69, 505n70, 505n71, 519n61, 523n10, 538n3; and the potlatch, 86, 164, 237, 256, 289, 293-94; work with Jane Cook, 35, 48-49, 185, 288-93, 302. *See also* anthropology (discipline of); Codere, Helen; Hunt, George; potlatch *and entries following*
box of treasures. *See* treasures

Cannibal Society. *See* Hamatsa (Cannibal Society)
cannibalism, 32, 61, 81, 113, 131, 134, 168, 169, 175, 323-25, 485n55, 501n17, 504n59; Dzunuk̲wa, 388
chiefs (Giga̲me'), 5, 15, 60, 62, 81, 87, 101, 125, 159, 165, 217, 237, 513n90; and Christianity, 127,

133; customary roles of, 83-84, 213, 305, 451-52, 459; and feasting and potlatching, 61, 83-84, 116, 128, 158, 211, 237, 413-35. *See also* Cook, Chris Jr.; feasting; McKenna-McBride Royal Commission; Newman, Edwin; 'Nulis, John; potlatch *and entries following;* Speck, George; Speck, Wedłidi; Wasden, William Jr.

Christianity, 29, 34, 37-38, 43, 50, 52, 107-10, 113, 118, 124, 138, 148, 150, 197, 204, 289, 297, 385-86, 434; and capitalism, 7, 118, 127, 135, 138, 142, 146-47, 160, 162, 168, 175, 330, 494n71; and conversion, 7, 38-39, 42-43, 108-9, 118-22, 126, 134, 157-58, 164, 205, 241- 242, 322, 333, 350-51, 383, 416, 439, 491n25, 494n63, 506n2. *See also* Anglican Church; Church Mission Society (CMS); colonialism; education; residential schools

Church Mission Society (CMS), 111-13, 118, 125-34, 142, 146, 148, 168, 273, 490n8, 490n11, 504n57, 525n52; Duncan, William (and Metlakatla), 91, 94-95, 115, 117-19, 125, 157-58, 487n76, 497n121, 512n82. *See also* Anglican Church; Christianity; Hall, Alfred

citizenship, 6, 238, 263, 265, 266, 268-69, 301, 333, 348-49, 350-51, 357, 365-66, 379-80, 386, 390, 472n10, 537n1

clan. *See* 'na̲'mima (clan)

Codere, Helen, 31, 35, 37, 41, 54, 75, 76, 165, 185, 339, 354, 481n92, 484n42, 485n56, 486n70, 494n66, 494n73, 501n28, 511n57

collaboration, 4, 11-15, 16, 17-20, 25, 44, 61, 110, 286, 179, 471n5, 472n15. *See also* anthropology (discipline of); Boas, Franz; Hunt, George; methodology

colonial memory. *See* memory

colonialism, 3, 8, 10-11, 29-31, 43-44, 52, 74, 102, 110, 113, 138, 149-50, 160, 286, 351, 407, 408, 411-12, 490n8, 498n147, 506n2, 539n4, 541n28; and assimilation (enfranchisement), 29, 74, 119, 148-52, 169, 183, 256-57, 269, 288, 353, 380, 408, 485n55, 509n34, 512n82, 514n118; imperialist nostalgia, 33, 131; and settlement, 33, 56, 87, 160, 169, 194, 195-96, 267, 274, 487n81, 507n13, 511n64; and social theories (civilization, racism, social evolution), 32, 34, 81, 109, 110, 113, 132, 286, 303, 317, 339, 373-74, 378, 380, 387, 509n40, 520n80, 539n4; and violence (military and physical), 77, 86-87, 90-94, 151, 487n77, 491n19. *See also* Christianity; education; epidemics (historical); Indian Act; Indian Agents; marriage (colonial); memory; reserves; residential schools

Cook, Bert, 73, 184, 240, 248, 357, 459

Cook big house (life in), xv, xvi, 5, 29, 107-8, 167-68, 173, 175-82, 238, 254, 280-84, 295-97, 306, 343-45, 347, 354-55, 358, 367-73, 394, 397-98, 402, 467, 504n64

Cook, Chris Jr., xxiii, 27, 36, 98, 107, 260-61, 377, 408-9, 435, 436, 438, 443, 446, 450, 452, 459, 468-69, 541n30

Cook fishing fleet, 135, 140, 269, 310-13, 360, 362-63

Cook, George, xxiii, 14, 43, 69, 107, 123, 175-77, 179, 223, 247, 355, 359, 362, 369, 370, 394, 413, 435, 440, 442, 450, 451

Cook, Gilbert Jr., xxiii, 99, 137, 231, 300, 310-13, 399

Cook, Gilbert Sr., xxiii, 137, 458, 511n54

Cook, Ilma, xxiii, 275-77, 294-96, 354, 392, 393, 399, 503n49

Cook, Jane. *See* G̲a'a̲xstalas (Jane Cook)
Cook, Kitty. *See* G̲aga (Kitty Cook)
Cook, Maureen, 180, 181, 365
Cook, Nellie, xxiii, 24, 25, 46, 87, 105-6, 179, 180-81, 198, 230-31, 239, 240, 276, 282, 296, 306, 331-32, 358, 364, 369, 373, 391, 395, 399
Cook, Reggie Jr., xxiii, 355
Cook, Reggie Sr. ("Daddy Cook"), xxiii, 179, 198, 230-31, 270, 288, 311, 312, 331, 332, 344, 354, 357, 359, 360, 362, 364, 369, 370, 390, 392, 458, 461
Cook, Ruth, xxiii, 253, 359, 363, 452, 454
Cook, Shelly, xxiii, 439
Cook, Stephen (Na̲ge) ("Papa Cook"), xxii, 4, 6, 24, 46, 56-57, 66-74, 96, 118, 130, 144-45, 148, 154-55, 158-59, 175-77, 179, 181, 219, 231, 240, 247-48, 249, 269-70, 281, 295, 300, 307, 311-13, 330, 333, 343-45, 355, 358, 360, 362, 367-69, 393-95, 397-98, 402, 408, 409, 412, 436, 449, 456-57, 467; and the Native Brotherhood, 346, 358-59, 534n35; *Rex v Cook et al.*, 313-17, 483n18, 528n85. *See also* Cook fishing fleet; Cook store; G̲aga (Kitty Cook); Pacific Coast Native Fishermen's Association (PCNFA)
Cook, Vivian, xxiii, 275-76, 295
Cook store, 5, 23, 25, 176-77, 179, 240, 247, 343, 369, 467
coppers *(Ṫłakwa)*, 58, 63, 83, 92, 116, 205-6, 252, 254, 294, 305-6, 309, 410, 425, 486n70. *See also* chiefs (Giga̲me'); potlatch *and entries following;* rank; treasures
Cormorants (soccer team), 145, 354, 391; and Flying Hens, 354
Cranmer, Dan, 67, 254-56, 361, 485n51
Cranmer-Webster, Gloria, 31, 38, 67, 74, 77, 90-91, 124, 125, 158, 166, 254-55, 255-56, 361, 367, 369, 485n51
crests. *See* treasures
Culhane, Dara, 10, 122, 236, 237, 441-42, 457, 471n1, 472n15, 505n67, 532n143
Curtis, Edward, 5, 60-61, 184-91, 506n73, 506n74, 506n76
custom (the). *See* ancestor narratives; feasting; marriage (colonial); marriage (customary, *K̲adzitła,* in potlatch); potlatch *and entries following;* rank; treasures

Da̲'naxda'x̲w (New Vancouver). *See* T'sadzis'nukwa̲ame, (New Vancouver) Da̲'naxda'x̲w
dances. *See* treasures
Dawson, George M., 82, 83, 131, 146-47, 486n60, 486n70, 495n85, 498n138, 505n71
Depression, the (Great), 288, 294, 302, 317, 331; and potlatching, 289, 293-94, 302-6, 308-9, 336, 339
Duncan, William. *See* Church Mission Society (CMS)
Dzawada̲'enux̲w, (Kingcome) Gwa'yi, 96, 180, 188-91 231, 254, 255, 266, 325-26, 334, 349-50, 354, 369, 374, 422, 452, 464, 466, 527n69, 529n111, 532n2, 532n3
Dzawadi (Knight Inlet). *See* A̲'wa̲'etła̲la, (Knight Inlet) Dzawadi

education, 5, 35, 49, 122, 123, 143-44, 215, 236, 253, 257, 259, 271, 300, 301, 346, 361-62, 373-75, 381-86, 532n143; Indian day school, 148, 149, 151, 172, 374, 377, 382; industrial school, 147-51, 172, 175, 200, 220, 222-23, 239, 289, 299, 498n140, 513n89, 531n137; missionary teaching, 109, 111, 114, 115, 117-22, 124, 126, 128-29, 132-34, 144-45, 150, 245, 298, 337, 389, 493n61, 504n60, 515n7, 532n2; Native teachers, 133, 148, 298, 303, 504n57, 505n70, 511n69. *See also* Christianity; Church Mission Society (CMS); colonialism; Indian Act; residential schools

enfranchisement. *See* colonialism; Indian Act; Indian Agents

epidemics (historical), 55, 67, 70, 74, 75-76, 94, 121, 290, 411, 412, 493n51; flu, 122, 170, 231, 294, 516n22; measles, 82, 121, 146, 169, 170; mortality, 55, 99, 121, 146, 160, 170, 199-200, 231, 237, 411, 412, 427, 484n42, 494n63, 496n96, 531n137; smallpox, 82, 84, 99, 121, 131-32, 146, 169, 170, 497n129; tuberculosis, xxiii, 6, 67, 82, 122, 143, 170, 179, 234, 252, 294, 341, 369, 375, 397. *See also* health

eulachon grease *(t'lina),* 5, 24, 54, 58, 61, 67, 137, 180, 231, 251, 282, 295, 442, 513n95, 517n38. *See also* A̲'wa̲'etła̲la, (Knight Inlet) Dzawadi; feasting; grease trail; potlatch *and entries following*

family allowance, 151, 346, 361-62, 366, 534n44

feasting, 9, 12, 20, 36, 57, 58, 59, 92, 119, 120, 144, 162, 228-29, 254, 293, 363; and food, 119, 163, 189, 251, 252, 261, 310, 430-31, 436-37, 441-42, 454, 483n14, 503n52; historical descriptions of, 36, 61, 72, 76, 93, 101, 128-30, 289, 294, 318, 524n26, 526n54; meanings of, 60, 76, 87, 159, 206, 261, 304-6, 352, 413, 419, 435-36. *See also* ancestor narratives; Kwaguł Gix̱sa̲m Feast; naming; potlatch *and entries following;* treasures

"fish as wealth" (Pam Brown), 171, 261

fishing, 137, 260-62; and Allied Indian Tribes of BC, 259-60, 262, 269; commercial, xvi, 74, 136, 140, 142, 170-71, 219, 262-70, 313-16, 331, 362, 503n52, 520n83; and ethnicity, 34, 170, 218, 267, 281, 316, 331, 346, 355-56, 503n52, 504n60, 528n86, 533n19; food fishery, 6, 135, 139-42, 171, 198, 215, 218, 236, 259-60, 261, 262-69, 270, 282, 310, 314, 331, 430-31, 496n96, 496n112, 503n52, 521n99, 527n79; and Jane Cook testimony, 262-67; and McKenna-McBride Royal Commission, 215, 218, 512n82; and racism, 362; and strikes, 331, 358, 359, 528n86, 534n29; and tax, 313-17, 359, 528n82; and women, 362- 64. *See also* aboriginal rights; Cook fishing fleet; Native Brotherhood of BC; Pacific Coast Native Fishermen's Association (PCNFA)

Fitch, Doreen, 96-97, 100, 308, 341-42, 421, 459-60

Fort Rupert. *See* Kwagu'ł, (Fort Rupert) Tsa̲x̲is

fur trade, 54-59, 69-71, 74, 81-83, 87, 94-95, 486n64, 487n76, 494n65

G̱a'ax̱sta'las (Jane Cook), xxi, xxiii; activism of, xvii, 5-6, 7, 8, 16-17, 25-26, 43, 50, 51, 54, 99, 107, 114, 183, 197, 200, 216, 236, 238, 243, 246-47, 261, 270, 280, 285-89, 298, 319-22, 329-30, 333-34, 351, 364, 398-401; and Anglican Women's Auxiliary (AWA), 5, 37, 47, 104, 107-8, 171-75, 208, 228, 326-27, 366-67; beliefs of, 3, 108, 136, 157, 166-68, 171-72, 177, 192, 322, 329-30, 333, 345, 347, 357, 365, 375-76, 383-88, 502n33, 502n34; childhood, 3, 4, 48-49, 97-102, 114, 116, 122-23, 143, 324, 384, 387; on colonialism, 8, 194-95, 384-85; on the custom, 6-7, 48, 84, 157-59, 165, 285-87, 303-6, 308, 319, 321-22, 323-24, 326-28, 333-38, 347-48, 350-53, 384, 470; death, 345, 347, 390-402, 502n33; education of, 5, 49, 122, 123, 259; and

Edward Curtis, 5, 184-91; and fishing (*see* Allied Indian Tribes of BC; fishing; McKenna-McBride Royal Commission); and food, 4-5, 108, 173, 180, 262, 282, 283, 295-96, 343, 370, 375, 397; and Franz Boas (1931), 5, 35, 185, 288-95; and garden, 24, 108, 123, 178, 180, 220-21, 281, 296, 343, 355, 357, 373, 392, 394, 467, 512n83; and Indian Arts and Welfare Conference (1948), 380, 383-89; and kinship ties (importance of), 5, 7, 193, 203-9, 216, 217, 252, 352, 368-69; and Kwak̓wala, 5-6, 35-37, 288, 290-95, 366-67 (*see also* Anglican Women's Auxiliary; Boas, Franz; Codere, Helen; Curtis, Edward; Hunt, Lorraine); and land, 138, 194-97, 209, 215, 219-21, 225-27, 258, 270, 351, 366, 387-88, 398, 467, 533n13; and liquor, 99, 199-202, 211-12, 364-65; and marriage (her own), 4, 57, 155-58, 327-30; marriage (potlatch), 6-7, 40, 54, 165, 203-12, 230, 240-43, 298, 327-29, 333, 337, 352-54; and Native Brotherhood of BC (1940s), 6, 270, 361-62, 364; as nurse-midwife, 104, 122, 172, 276, 282-83, 344, 347, 370, 382-83; and potlatch trials, xvi, 7, 49, 211, 240, 248-57; standing of (rank), xxi, 4, 6, 7, 8, 17, 42, 48, 49, 56-66, 78, 100, 101, 246, 303, 329, 378-79, 396-97, 401; and totem poles, 167, 303-7, 384-85, 388. *See also* marriage (colonial); marriage (customary, *K̲adzitła*, in potlatch); potlatch *and entries following*

G̲a'ax̲sta'las, and Allied Indian Tribes of BC, 6, 258-60, 270, 280, 293; potlatch petition, 6, 279-80; representing potlatchers, 277-79, 293; testimony, 262-67

G̲a'ax̲sta'las, letters of, 161-62, 194, 200-1, 203-4, 206-7, 208-9, 211-12, 222, 227-28, 241, 243-45, 277-78, 335

G̲a'ax̲sta'las, and McKenna-McBride Royal Commission (1914), 6, 24-25, 42, 214, 216; as translator, 193, 215-16, 223; as witness, 193, 211, 216, 218-23, 224-26

G̲a'ax̲sta'las, representations of, 26, 407; by anthropologists, xvi-xvii, 10-11, 15, 25, 26, 33-39, 50-51, 407-8; by historians, 39-42, 523n3; by journalists, 78, 122, 303-6, 318-19, 378, 390, 396-97; by Kwakwa̲ka̲'wakw writers or narrators, xvii, 17, 26-27, 38, 43-52, 246-47, 253-54, 398-401, 438, 457, 481n100, 481n105. *See also* Boas, Franz; Codere, Helen; living text; stigmatization (sense of)

G̲a'ax̲sta'las, testimonies of, 218-23, 224-26, 262-67, 272-73, 321, 331-33, 334, 352, 383-89

G̲a'ax̲sta'las, as translator-interpreter, xvi, 5-7, 25, 35, 48-49, 163, 171, 184-91, 193, 211, 213-19, 223-56, 258, 278-79, 288-306, 314, 321, 324, 333, 366-67, 379, 383, 387, 388-89, 395, 456-57. *See also* Hunt, George; living text; methodology; stigmatization (sense of)

G̲aga (Kitty Cook), xxii, 66-67, 71-74, 177, 181-84, 217, 282, 295, 483n19, 483n20

gender, 11, 16, 34, 39, 42, 44, 78, 84, 114, 119, 121, 124-25, 144, 149-50, 157, 199-200, 243, 287, 293, 299-300, 309, 329-30, 353-54, 494n63, 498n138. *See also* chiefs (Giga̲me'); Christianity; marriage (colonial); marriage (customary, *K̲adzitła,* in potlatch); women

genealogical knowledge, 9, 14, 46-47, 54, 56-73, 74-75, 89, 101, 120, 127, 410-11, 480n86. *See also* ancestor narratives; memory; methodology; treasures

Gilbert, William, xxi, 4, 29, 56, 77, 78-79, 89-90, 94, 97, 98, 102, 116, 397, 503n49
Gilford Island, Gwa'yasdams. *See* Kwikwasutinexw, (Gilford Island) Gway'yasdams
grease trail, 54, 67-72. *See also* eulachon grease *(t'lina);* Nuu-chah-nulth; potlatch *and entries following*
Gusgimaxw (Quatsino) Xwatis ("Koskimo"), 58, 66, 78, 127, 177, 379, 396, 482n4, 512n69
Gwayułalas (Emily Whonnock), xxi, 4, 58, 60, 63, 77-80, 94, 96-101, 225, 252, 397, 489n104

Hall, Alfred, 4, 102, 105-7, 109, 111-14, 148, 157, 197, 250, 299, 482n7, 495n85, 504n57, 525n52; language and, 35, 46, 104, 114-15, 118-22, 124, 288, 492n38, 505n70, 511n69, 524n18; letters of, 111-13, 114-34, 138, 169, 490n9, 490n11, 495n78; Metlakatla, 117-18, 125; Tsaxis, 114-22, 124-34, 143-44, 490n8, 491n23, 492n40, 501n17; 'Yalis, 133-35, 138, 142, 144-46, 155, 159-60,169, 172, 175, 218-19, 223, 513n92. *See also* Anglican Church; Christianity; Church Mission Society (CMS)
Hall, Elizabeth, 105-6, 111, 133, 143-45, 148, 172, 176
Hamatsa (Cannibal Society), 5, 28, 60, 61, 81, 128, 130, 144, 323, 325, 330, 388, 420, 421, 430, 432, 434, 485n54, 530n123, 540n20; representations of, 131, 168, 322-23, 324, 485n55. *See also* treasures
Harris, Roberta, xxiii, 439-40
Hawinalał (Warrior Society), 130-31, 467
health, 6, 121-22, 124, 170, 198, 232, 234, 252, 257, 261, 270-71, 282-83, 294-95, 362, 364, 370, 381, 427, 437, 493n51, 497n129, 499n155, 503n55, 515n7, 522n114; chicken pox, 373; diphtheria, 370; dysentery, xxiii, 5, 290, 294, 523n11; Goldthorpe Inquiry (1980), 183, 236, 443, 505n67; hospitals, 215, 274, 301, 273-74, 277, 282, 290, 294-95, 301, 318, 360; illnesses: 5, 290, 522n118; influenza, 231, 294; preventorium (TB), 275-76, 295, 339-42, 373, 532n151; syphilis, 94, 121, 143, 170, 290, 523n11; tuberculosis, 5, 6, 143, 234, 252, 254, 271-77, 281, 294, 295, 339, 361, 368, 370, 394, 397; typhoid, 371. *See also* epidemics (historical)
Hiłdzakw (Bella Bella First Nation), xxi, 58, 63, 67, 96, 114, 153, 273, 275, 362, 373, 420, 437, 448, 460, 482n11
Hunt, George, 34-38, 40, 51, 54, 60, 63, 72, 74-75, 80, 102, 117, 120, 143, 160-61, 185-86, 190-91, 237, 293, 306, 377, 388, 421, 485n52, 497n116, 502n33, 504n59, 505n69, 506n74, 509n40; and language, 115-16, 120, 191, 288, 291-93, 495n85, 524n15, 524n26, 538n3. *See also* anthropology (discipline of); Boas, Franz; Codere, Helen; Kwagu'ł, (Fort Rupert) Tsaxis
Hunt, Lorraine, xxiii, 291-92
Huson, David, xxiii, 95-96

Indian Act, 3, 249-50, 300-1, 315, 365, 379, 391, 397, 502n31, 516n22, 535n56, 535n62; and education, 150, 236-37; and enfranchisement, 379, 397, 512n82, 514n118, 521n91, 536n68; and health, 271-72; and land, 280, 319, 360, 365, 379-80, 509n40, 511n64, 512n82; and liquor, 201-2, 365, 391, 397, 509n32; and marriage, 248, 300, 531n131; and membership (status), 101, 148, 183, 230-31, 234, 269, 301, 328-29, 349, 362, 379-80, 397, 412, 509n40, 530n129; and the potlatch, 162, 169, 230, 240, 243-45, 251, 259, 277, 279-80, 321, 348, 349, 397;

and women, 168, 379-80, 536n71, 538n11. *See also* colonialism; potlatch *and entries following;* racism; women
Indian agents, 7, 50, 87, 90, 102, 122, 125, 139, 156, 163-64, 194, 196, 197, 204, 209, 210, 213, 293, 300, 301, 348, 522n114, 524n18, 531n137; George Blenkinsop, 79, 138-39, 140, 142-46, 219, 497n129; George DeBeck, 273, 277, 520n75; William Halliday, 41, 48, 150, 199-213, 220-24, 226, 230, 238-43, 249, 251, 256-57, 278-79, 283, 288, 290, 358, 500n13, 516n22, 517n38, 519n58, 519n68, 527n70; E.G. Newnham, 288, 314-17, 528n82, 528n85; Richard Pidcock, 158, 162-63, 168, 273, 520n75; Murray Todd, 288, 318, 321-22, 339, 349, 366, 531n137, 535n59. *See also* colonialism; Indian Act; potlatch, ban on; racism

Japanese people, 170, 218, 248, 267, 281, 289, 303, 316, 354-56, 504n60, 520n80, 528n86, 531n137, 533n19

Kamano, Annie, xxi, 4, 63, 79, 96-100, 325, 340, 341, 368, 370, 395, 438, 448, 458. *See also* Barnes, Rita; Fitch, Doreen
Kelly, Peter, 258, 259, 269, 274, 359, 397, 534n38
Kingcome, Gwa'yi. *See* Dzawada̠'enux̠w, (Kingcome) Gwa'yi
Knight Inlet, Dzawadi. *See* A̠'wa̠'etła̠la, (Knight Inlet) Dzawadi
Kwagu'ł, (Fort Rupert) Tsax̠is, 4, 8, 29-39, 49, 51, 58, 76, 86, 102, 115-16, 120-27, 143, 146, 176, 185-91, 231, 289-94, 409, 437, 446-47, 450-51, 461-471n4, 482n4, 492n40, 494n72, 497n116; bombardment of Tsax̠is, 77, 80, 90-94; coal, 70-71. *See also* Averkieva, Julia; Boas, Franz; Codere, Helen; feasting; Ga'ax̠sta'las (Jane Cook); Hall, Alfred; Hunt, George; rank
Kwaguł Gix̠sa̠m Feast, 1-3, 8-9, 108-9, 114, 116, 403, 413, 441, 444-70, 540n21, 541n28; preparation for, 408-9, 435-43. *See also* ancestor narratives; feasting; 'na̠'mima (clan); reconciliation; treasures
K̠wik̠wa̠sutinex̠w, (Gilford Island) Gwa'yasda̠ms, xxii, 47, 72-73, 289, 308, 340-41, 374, 541n32

land rights, 223, 225-26, 267, 431, 441, 473n3, 507n5, 507n13, 508n14, 508n17, 508n23; property, 183, 195, 219-21, 231, 379, 512n83, 513n85, 514n100, 514n111, 536n68; territory, 225-26, 431, 475n16, 496n103, 514n100; title, 195, 513n100, 514n100. *See also* Allied Indian Tribes of BC; McKenna-McBride Royal Commission; reserves
Ławits'is, (Turnour Island) K̠alugwis, 26, 61, 176, 188, 205, 237, 255, 277-78, 289, 293, 425-35, 437, 462-63
Lawrence, Jeane, xxiii, 173, 281-84, 355-56, 369, 370, 373, 399
living text , xvi, 15, 18-19, 23-29, 30-52, 53-54, 285-86, 293, 411, 456-57, 473n2, 489n104. *See also* anthropology (discipline of); memory; methodology; reconciliation; stigmatization (sense of)

Ma̠ma̠lilik̠ala (Village Island), 'Mi'mkwamlis, 28, 46, 47, 149, 167, 173, 198, 252-53, 255, 293, 232, 325, 326, 345-46, 367, 374, 416, 437, 510n43, 511n60, 529n111, 530n125
marriage (colonial), 77, 150, 156-58, 168, 208, 212, 238, 279, 298-99, 318, 335, 348-51, 525n52, 538n11; Christian marriage, 124-25, 133, 155, 172, 177, 200-4, 208, 298, 300, 318, 327, 492n38; divorce,

157, 206, 209, 229, 248; laws and policies on, 204-5, 206, 208, 238, 248-49, 286, 297-98, 300-1, 320, 500n6, 517n24, 525n49, 526n56, 526n58, 538n11. *See also* Anglican Church; bishops (Anglican); Christianity; Church Mission Society (CMS); G̲a'ax̲sta'las (Jane Cook); Hall, Alfred

marriage (customary, *K̲adzitła,* in potlatch), 6-7, 28, 57, 63, 77-78, 83, 84, 114, 101, 120, 125-26, 157, 202-6, 209, 215, 227-31, 240-48, 248, 252-53, 279, 286, 287, 298-300, 325, 327-29, 330, 336, 350-54, 425-26, 510n43, 518n41, 526n54, 531n132; bride price, 48, 61-62, 63, 327-29, 417, 419, 446; business contract, "sham marriage," 77-78, 114, 229, 388; divorce/repayment *(gwał),* 204-5, 228-29, 241-42, 248, 255, 329, 337, 518n41; dowry. *See also* G̲a'ax̲sta'las (Jane Cook); rank; treasures

masks. *See* treasures

Matilpe, Florrie, xxiii, 28, 149, 167-68, 242-43, 253, 367, 371-74, 399-400, 435, 459

McKenna-McBride Royal Commission, 213-30, 257, 271, 280, 387, 511n60, 520n82; and Da̲'naxda'x̲w, 224, 225; and fishing, 215-19, 267, 268; and interpreters, 215-16; and Kwagu'ł, 216-17, 226, 229, 513n90; and Mama̲lilik̲ala, 228-29; and marriage, 227-30; and 'Nak'waxda'xw, 226; and 'Na̲mgis, 217-18, 222, 226, 273; and potlatch, 215; and reserved land, 219-22; and timber access, 202, 213, 224, 226, 387. *See also* G̲a'ax̲sta'las (Jane Cook); McKenna-McBride Royal Commission

memory, 11, 15, 30, 44, 49, 51-52, 69, 74, 253, 289, 407, 472n12; "anthropology as memory" genre, 53-54, 74; colonial memory, 16, 37, 51-52, 54-55, 74, 286-87, 408, 411, 538n3, 539n4; intergenerational, 4, 9, 11, 20, 23-29, 47, 51-56, 69, 101-2, 149-50, 345, 408-11, 471n4, 539n4, 540n11, 484n35; and potlatch complex, 9, 20, 319, 406, 411. *See also* ancestor narratives; living text; methodology; treasures

methodology, 4, 9-21, 25, 40, 42, 44, 50-51, 53-56, 61, 76, 101, 127, 136, 155, 185, 232-33, 254, 325, 345, 357, 480n86, 485n52; anonymity, 16, 17, 200, 411, 500n16; ethnographic history, 15-16; family motivations, xvii, 23-29, 36, 50-52, 96, 411, 456-58; feasting and potlatching as, 403, 406, 410-11, 413. *See also* anthropology (discipline of); archives; collaboration; memory; reconciliation; stigmatization (sense of)

Musga̲makw Tsawataineuk, 464, 541n32

Nage. *See* Cook, Stephen (Na̲ge) ("Papa Cook")

'Na̲mgis (Alert Bay) ("Nimpkish"), 18, 24, 26, 28, 42, 47, 66-67, 69-74, 76-77, 82, 108, 134-35, 138, 144, 147-53, 154-55, 172-74, 188, 190-91, 200-2, 210-11, 231, 236, 251, 270-71, 273, 276-77, 288, 290, 294, 297-98, 316, 320, 326, 328, 331-33, 339, 348, 350-51, 354, 373-75, 377, 437, 444, 446-48, 471n5, 483n19, 504n64, 513n89, 515n7, 525n52; chiefs of, 27, 48, 74, 159, 177, 183, 211, 217-23, 228, 254-55, 273, 290, 306, 309, 333, 408-10, 413-25, 437, 449-50, 466-69; fishing, 137-42, 346, 354-55, 358-62, 512n77 (*see also* Allied Indian Tribes of BC; Cook fishing fleet; fishing); land, 6, 138-42, 215-16, 217-23, 513n92; Nimpkish Fishermen's Association, 358;

Nimpkish River, 263-69, 313-14, 355-56, 441; 'Yalis (descriptions of), 136-39, 175, 192, 232-33, 288-89, 302-3, 318, 348

'na'mima (clan), 7, 8-9, 11, 15, 19-20, 57, 59-62, 76, 87, 143, 155, 183, 185, 318, 352, 410-11, 412-13, 438, 445, 447, 450, 459, 475n16, 482n8. *See also* ancestor narratives; feasting; naming; potlatch *and entries following;* reconciliation; treasures

naming, 6, 8, 11, 13, 28, 46, 57-63, 69, 75-76, 78, 86, 111, 114-15, 120, 127, 147, 148, 164, 211, 237, 279, 321, 323, 352, 377, 407-15, 417-19, 422-23, 425, 426-28, 435-36, 437, 438, 442, 452, 458-59, 468, 476n23, 482n2, 482n7, 494n77, 497n125, 524n18, 531n130, 541n29, 541n30. *See also* ancestor narratives; feasting; potlatch *and entries following;* treasures

Native Brotherhood of BC, 104, 124, 198, 234, 270, 317, 331, 346, 358-64, 365-66, 377-78, 380, 382, 383, 385, 390, 520n70, 529n92, 533n24, 534n32, 534n33, 534n38, 535n62; *Native Voice,* 66-67, 78, 378-80, 390-91, 395-97

Native Sisterhood, 198, 363-64, 390, 536n64

Native Women's Alliance, 233-36

Native Women's Association of Canada, 334, 531n136

Neel, Ellen, 78-79, 376, 380-81, 391, 395-96, 484n44, 536n77

Nestman, John, xxiii, 164-65, 177-78, 349, 397-98

Nelson, Nella, xv-xvii, xxiii, 14, 35, 48, 49, 68, 85, 107, 175, 242, 247, 250-51, 253, 263, 373, 394-95, 400, 456-58, 459, 472n15, 541n30

Newman, Annie. *See* Kamano, Annie

Newman, Charlie, xxi, 4, 63, 79, 99-100, 116, 364, 375-76, 381, 438, 458, 484n44

Newman, Edwin, 63, 64, 364, 447-49, 459, 461, 469, 541n30

Newman, James, xxi, 4, 97, 98, 99-100

Nimpkish River. *See* Allied Indian Tribes of BC; ancestor narratives; McKenna-McBride Royal Commission; 'Namgis (Alert Bay) ("Nimpkish")

North American Indian Brotherhood, 381, 536n79

Nowell, Charlie, 30, 45-47, 49, 105, 130, 144-45, 164-65, 184, 185, 202, 205, 215, 217, 229-30, 248, 250, 252, 256, 290, 327-29, 361, 406, 501n30, 504n60, 505n71, 509n40, 510n43

'Nulis, John, xxi, 4, 8, 13, 46, 58-66, 77, 80-81, 94, 101, 127, 143, 188, 237, 397, 412, 448, 458, 460, 482n5. *See also* anthropology (discipline of); Boas, Franz; Gwayułalas (Emily Whonnock); Newman, Charlie; Newman, Edwin

Nuu-chah-nulth, 4, 56, 66-72, 159, 183, 358, 359, 409, 446, 449, 531n137

oral history. *See* memory; methodology; oral traditions; treasures

oral traditions, 18, 36, 44, 50, 54-55, 76, 89, 119-20, 137, 169, 185-86, 188, 290, 416, 447, 477n37, 480n86. *See also* ancestor narratives; memory; traditional narratives; treasures

Pacific Coast Native Fishermen's Association (PCNFA), 346, 358

Paull, Andrew, 124, 240, 258-59, 262, 271, 274, 277, 279, 358-59, 381, 534n33

pensions: old age, 346, 361-62, 381, 397, 535n45; widow's, 249, 280

petitions, xvii, 196, 209, 231, 257, 359, 386, 508n17, 508n21; land, 196-97, 217, 222, 257, 280, 507n10, 507n13, 508n19; potlatch,

6, 159, 162, 163, 169, 230, 248, 277, 279-80, 350, 500n14, 514n114; tuberculosis, 274-75
poles and posts (carved), 58, 83-85, 116, 147, 167, 252, 303-7, 318, 384, 388, 403-6, 484, 491n25, 527n67. *See also* ancestor narratives; Neel, Ellen; potlatch *and entries following;* treasures
potlatch, 9, 31-32, 50, 60, 63, 168, 256-57, 292, 297, 301-2, 320, 322-24, 352, 381, 408-9, 419, 436, 475n16, 481n92, 518n50; and the Allied Indian Tribes of BC, 259, 277-80; contemporary, 407, 408-10, 413-35, 459, 538n2, 540n20; economics and, 86, 92, 237, 247, 240, 247-48, 299, 304-6, 308-9, 337, 339, 347, 352-53, 423-24; marriage *(K̲adzitła),* 6-7, 63, 84, 125-26, 150, 203-12, 230, 238, 240-46, 289, 298-300, 327-28, 335, 337, 350-51, 525n49, 525n52, 526n54, 531n130; and the McKenna-McBride Royal Commission, 229-30; meanings of, 60, 83, 100, 215, 261, 302-6, 320-21; and witchcraft, 161-66, 501n29. *See also* anthropology (discipline of); ancestor narratives; chiefs (Gig̲ame'); Cook, Chris Jr.; feasting; Indian Act; marriage (colonial); marriage (customary, *K̲adzitła,* in potlatch); 'na̲'mima (clan); naming; Speck, George; Speck, Wedłidi; treasures; Wasden, William Jr.
potlatch, ban on, 3, 6, 16-17, 40-41, 50, 74, 124, 134, 148, 158, 162-64, 169, 230, 236, 238, 240, 248, 251, 257, 277, 279-80, 287, 293-94, 297-98, 319-20, 321, 334-35, 338, 348-49, 354, 515n6, 517n27, 519n67, 525n52; arrests, 47-48, 162-63, 210-12, 240, 248, 254, 381, 400, 519n68, 524n31. *See also* Indian Act; petitions; potlatch trials
potlatch, changes in, 16-17, 26, 29, 36, 51-52, 54, 75, 81, 84-86, 104, 110, 146, 164, 231, 237-38, 246-47, 286-87, 293-94, 298-300, 308, 325, 333-34, 339, 350, 353. *See also* G̲a'ax̲sta'las (Jane Cook)
potlatch, historical descriptions of, 46, 76-77, 81, 83-84, 93, 116, 124, 128-30, 143-44, 146, 243-45, 302-6, 308, 318-19, 322-23, 325-26, 335-37, 339, 495n77, 532n3
potlatch, identity and, 1-2, 8-9, 15, 26-28, 50, 52, 69, 143, 169, 247, 256-57, 260, 279-80, 301, 318, 328-29, 332-33, 352, 377, 408, 411, 519n67, 540n14. *See also* chiefs (Gig̲ame'); Cook, Chris Jr.; feasting; Kwaguł Gix̲sa̲m Feast; Speck, George; Speck, Wedłidi; standing up; treasures; Wasden, William Jr.
potlatch, and property (gifting, give-away), 76, 84, 86, 115-16, 146, 159, 164, 168, 240, 251, 278-79, 318, 319-21, 337, 491n20, 501n28
potlatch, reasons for leaving, 2, 8, 28, 157-61, 237, 246, 322, 327-29, 333, 350-51, 400, 411-13. *See also* colonialism; G̲a'ax̲sta'las (Jane Cook); Indian Act; marriage (colonial); marriage (customary, *K̲adzitła,* in potlatch); residential schools
potlatch trials, xvi, xvii, 7, 48-49, 162-63, 211, 238, 240, 248-57, 456
preventorium (TB). *See* health
prostitution, 84-86, 116-17, 125, 168, 170, 337-38, 485n53

racism, 6, 34, 109-10, 271-73, 286, 341, 362, 377, 378, 387, 439, 497n121. *See also* Christianity; colonialism; education; Indian Act; reconciliation; residential schools
rank, 15, 29, 32, 46, 47, 52, 59, 75, 84, 91, 100-1, 116, 127, 161, 164-65, 241-42, 247, 289, 300, 301-2,

304-5, 432, 480n88, 482n4, 489n104, 504n64; described, 57, 60, 76, 78; and fishing, 140. *See also* chiefs (Gigame'); feasting; Ga'axsta'las (Jane Cook); naming; potlatch *and entries following;* treasures
reconciliation, 55, 157, 387, 408, 499, 499n154, 499n155, 531n133, 539n4; internal, 1-2, 8, 9, 23-29, 51, 52, 108, 330, 411, 438, 444-69, 445-56, 473n19, 531n133, 541n28. *See also* colonialism; residential schools
relief, government, 136, 137, 278, 279-80, 317, 320, 339, 358, 381, 534n44
reserves, 3, 28, 94, 148, 168, 178-79, 200-2, 223, 230, 234, 273, 314-15, 351, 359, 387, 431, 441, 508n14, 508n19, 509n40, 512n82; commissions, 138, 139-40, 195-97, 263, 148, 223, 226-27, 263, 267, 288, 351, 505n69, 507n13; Cormorant Island, 138-40, 223, 513n92; industrial school, 178-79, 200, 220, 222-23, 513n89. *See also* aboriginal rights; aboriginal title; Allied Indian Tribes of BC; land rights; McKenna-McBride Royal Commission
residential schools, 23, 74, 124, 147-53, 362, 381-83, 408, 410-11, 413, 498n139, 499n154, 515n7, 536n77, 537n82, 537n83; and apology (Canadian government and churches), 150-52; and silence (of survivors), 149-51; St. Michael's Residential School, 46, 119, 124, 147-49, 151-53, 234, 242, 275-76, 287-89, 294-95, 302, 318, 337-38, 341-42, 367, 373-77, 387, 408, 513n89; Truth and Reconciliation Commission, 152, 408, 499n155. *See also* Christianity; colonialism; education; reconciliation
revitalization (cultural), 26-27, 36-37, 38, 49, 111, 183. *See also* feasting; memory; 'na̲'mima (clan); naming; potlatch *and entries following;* reconciliation

Scott, Duncan Campbell, 238, 239-40, 248, 258, 269, 279, 288, 514n118, 521n91
settlement. *See* colonialism
Sixties Scoop, 69, 149, 498n147
slavery, 47, 80-81, 90-91, 111-14, 162, 324, 434, 441, 484n48, 484n50, 485n53, 489n104, 491n19, 491n20
songs. *See* treasures
Speck, George, xxiii, 26, 54, 60, 70, 76, 78, 81-82, 83-84, 86, 109, 110, 134-36, 140-41, 164, 192, 209, 213, 225-26, 243, 270, 323, 324, 325, 330, 386, 387-88, 400, 413, 425-35, 462-63, 472n15, 540n21. *See also* chiefs (Gigame'); Ławits'is, (Turnour Island) K̲alugwis; treasures
Speck, Kelly-Anne, xxiii, 54, 55, 149-50, 246-47, 285-86, 296-97, 436-37, 439-40, 443, 445-46, 472n15
Speck, Lori, xxiii, 148-50, 164, 426, 498n139
Speck, Wedłidi, xxiii, 13, 19-20, 37, 52, 54, 55, 58-59, 61, 66, 68, 69, 75-76, 79, 80, 83, 87-88, 97, 103-4, 111, 115, 116, 118, 126, 127, 143, 155, 159, 165-66, 183, 188-89, 216, 217, 220, 223, 224, 225, 231, 237, 254, 292, 299-300, 323, 325, 329-30, 333, 334, 351, 365, 385, 386, 389, 400, 406, 410, 413, 428, 435, 436, 438, 439, 440, 449, 450, 451, 455, 459, 463, 464, 466, 467, 469, 472n15, 482n1, 483n19, 513n97, 518n46, 538n1, 540n9, 541n30. *See also* chiefs (Gigame'); Kwagu'ł, (Fort Rupert) Tsax̲is; Ławits'is, (Turnour Island) K̲alugwis; treasures
Speck-Culhane, Dara. *See* Culhane, Dara
standing up, 2, 52, 410, 440, 444-70. *See also* feasting; naming; potlatch *and entries following;* reconciliation

stigmatization (sense of), xvi, 8, 14, 23-30, 36, 43, 50, 51, 52, 98-99, 104, 108-9, 286, 328, 377, 411, 456-57
strikes, labour, 70, 316, 331, 358-59, 362, 390, 528n86, 534n29
Svanvik, Peggy, 165, 231, 364-65, 366, 368, 400-2

timber rights and logging, 136, 176, 192, 195, 202, 213, 215, 224, 231, 237, 257, 266, 276-77, 310, 333, 384, 387-88, 441. *See also* aboriginal rights
totem poles. *See* poles and posts (carved)
traditional narratives, 60, 75-76, 118, 131, 154, 188-90, 306, 319, 323, 386, 418-19, 480n86, 495n85, 403-6, 500n16. *See also* ancestor narratives; naming; potlatch *and entries following;* treasures
translation, 3, 35, 86, 160, 163-64, 215, 225, 255, 292, 328-30; missionaries and, 115-16, 117, 118-21, 324, 492n38, 493n61, 511n69; and scholarly work, 11, 19, 42, 44, 53-54, 290-92, 388, 477n37, 495n85, 505n69, 505n70, 505n71. *See also* Boas, Franz; G̲a'ax̲sta'las, as translator-interpreter; Hall, Alfred; methodology
treasures, 57, 120, 436, 481n92, 487n74; box of, 51, 81, 96, 189, 260, 418, 419, 425, 433, 459-60; crests, 9, 11, 24, 57, 72, 120, 155, 304-6, 319, 407, 437, 444, 487n74; dances, 27, 54, 81, 93, 128-30, 131, 230, 244, 319, 323, 330, 405-8, 417-19, 420-23, 428-30, 432-34, 437, 446-49, 452, 458, 460, 506n73, 526n54; masks, 51, 60, 63-66, 154, 189, 254, 255, 260, 280, 410, 423, 434, 448, 510n43, 527n70, 532n3; songs, 19-20, 28, 36, 63-66, 128, 130, 189, 261, 407, 409-10, 421, 436-38, 444, 446, 447, 450, 452, 454, 458, 463, 466, 468, 469, 526n54. *See also* ancestor narratives; feasting; Hamat̓sa (Cannibal Society); Hawinalał (Warrior Society); memory; naming; poles and posts (carved); potlatch *and entries following;* traditional narratives
treaties, 70-71, 126, 196, 213, 232, 280, 391, 408, 431, 494n72, 507n13; and social status, 201-2, 248, 379
T'sadzis'nukwa̲ame, (New Vancouver) Da̲'naxda'x̲w, xxi, 6, 58, 59, 215, 223-24, 253, 255, 289, 431, 446, 463, 464, 482n4, 512n83
tuberculosis. *See* epidemics (historical); health

U'mista Cultural Centre, 13, 19, 147-48, 260, 413-14
Union of BC Indian Chiefs, 365, 507n5

Village Island ('Mi'mkwa̲mlis). *See* Mama̲lilik̲ala, (Village Island) 'Mi'mkwa̲mlis

wanukw, xxi, 58-63, 101, 115, 412, 460
Wasden, Bill, xxiii, 49, 68, 412, 439, 457, 469
Wasden, William Jr., xxiii, 13, 29, 36, 46, 54, 58, 61-62, 66, 71-72, 78, 80-81, 85-86, 91-93, 100-1, 130, 147, 181, 189-91, 206, 211, 214, 217, 224-25, 229, 246, 261, 308, 323, 352-54, 388, 402, 407, 412, 413-25, 431, 435, 437-38, 442, 444, 448, 449, 453, 459, 469, 540n18, 540n20, 541n30. *See also* chiefs (Giga̲me'); 'Na̲mgis (Alert Bay) ("Nimpkish"); treasures
Whonnock, Emily. *See* G̲wa̲yuła̲las (Emily Whonnock)
Winter Ceremonial (T̓sek̲a). *See* potlatch *and entries following*
witchcraft, 103-4, 144, 161-68, 493n55, 501n29, 501n30. *See also* potlatch *and entries following*

women, 25, 77-78, 79, 101, 122, 128-29, 149, 197-98, 200, 202, 221, 233-36, 246, 247, 280, 286-87, 290, 380, 381, 397, 410, 481n101, 509n27; and Christianity, 39, 42-44, 119, 124-26, 351, 489n4, 493n61; and the custom, 7, 28, 84, 144, 160, 164, 169, 227-30, 241-43, 298, 299-300, 326-30, 348-49, 354, 407, 436-37, 442, 454, 463; and gardens, 512n83; and mobility, 95, 125, 155-57, 168-70. *See also* Anglican Women's Auxiliary; G̲a'ax̲sta'las (Jane Cook); gender; marriage (colonial); marriage (customary, *K̲adzitła,* in potlatch); Native Women's Alliance; Native Sisterhood

women, and work, 86, 95, 135, 140, 142, 146, 168-69, 171, 242, 267, 288, 313, 316, 346, 358, 361-64, 437, 486n64, 488n101, 494n66, 503n55, 512n77, 512n78, 528n86, 528n89

World War I, 5, 24, 47, 105, 179, 231, 239, 247, 249-50, 268-69, 289, 348, 370, 514n119

World War II, 346, 348, 354, 355-57, 378, 520n80, 537n1

Zurkowski, Christine, xxiii, 24-25, 43, 97-98, 105-7, 181, 365-66, 366-67, 368, 395, 402